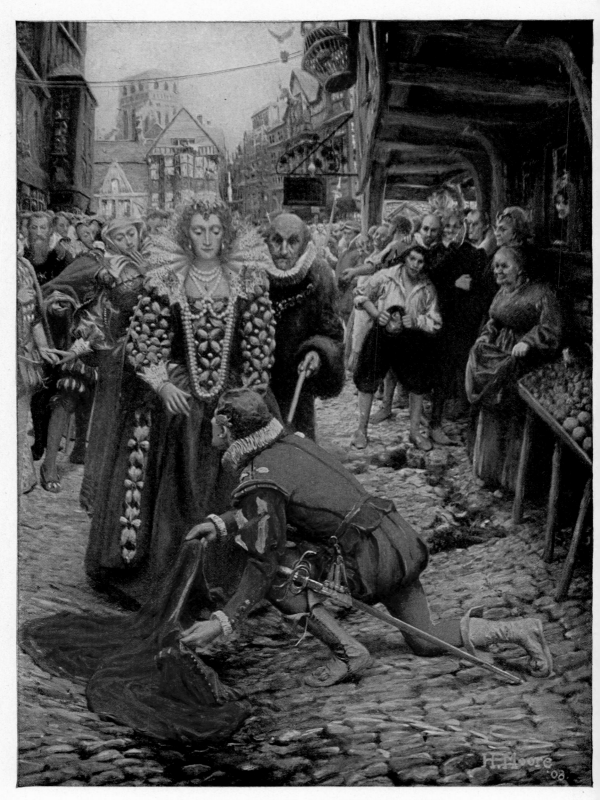

SIR WALTER RALEIGH AND QUEEN ELIZABETH

FROM A DRAWING BY H. MOORE

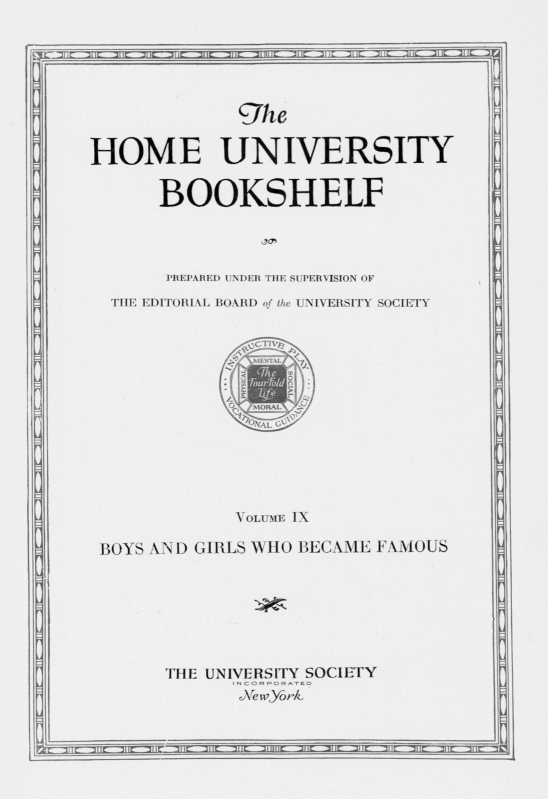

The

HOME UNIVERSITY BOOKSHELF

ॐ

PREPARED UNDER THE SUPERVISION OF

THE EDITORIAL BOARD *of the* UNIVERSITY SOCIETY

The Four-fold Life
INSTRUCTIVE PLAY · MENTAL · SOCIAL · PHYSICAL · MORAL · VOCATIONAL GUIDANCE

VOLUME IX

BOYS AND GIRLS WHO BECAME FAMOUS

THE UNIVERSITY SOCIETY
INCORPORATED
New York

In addition to its wealth of new material THE HOME UNIVERSITY BOOKSHELF combines the very best features of its highly successful predecessors: namely, Boys and Girls Bookshelf, copyright 1912, 1915, 1920; Young Folks Treasury, copyright 1909, 1917, 1919; Father and Son Library, copyright 1921; Modern Boy Activity, copyright 1921, 1923; The Mother's Book, copyright 1919; The Child Welfare Manual, copyright 1916; The Home Kindergarten Manual, copyright 1921; and Bible Stories and Character Building. copyright 1915.

INTRODUCTION

IT IS a mistake to think that biography is uninteresting. The life stories of men and women who have done things can be made far more interesting than make-believe tales, and they have the added merit of being true. The picture of the poor farmer boy, Abraham Lincoln, living in a log cabin and reading by the light of a pine knot, is more appealing than the liveliest adventures of some fairy prince.

The stories of other boys and girls always enlist the attention of our own children. They picture themselves in the shoes of Michelangelo, the boy sculptor, or of Jenny Lind, the girl who wanted to sing. "What did they do next, Mother?" will be the invariable question.

In "Boys and Girls Who Became Famous," we have further emphasized this story-telling approach by beginning with the boyhood and girlhood of our subjects. Here are "The Boyhood of a Story-Teller" (Stevenson), "A Nurse's Girlhood" (Florence Nightingale), "An Inventor's Boyhood" (Edison), and a dozen other typical stories. These are followed by "Boys and Girls of Many Lands," where we march under the banners of William the Conqueror, or Prince Arthur, or Napoleon. Those heroic days of the past are made very real indeed.

"Some Famous Girls of History" next cross the stage—Queen Clotilda, Elizabeth of Hungry, Joan of Arc, Lady Jane Grey, Queen Victoria. We do not first meet them in their armor or robes of state, but as little girls living the normal, happy life of our girls of to-day. Such stories have an irresistible appeal to the heart of girlhood.

In "Stories from American History" the same human, intimate approach is made. Here are told in lively text and picture the exploits of Israel Putnam, Nathan Hale, Molly Pitcher, Betsy Ross, Wolfe and Montcalm, William Penn, Franklin, Washington, Lafayette, Jefferson, and other leaders down to Pershing and Wilson. The adventures of pioneers, such as Daniel Boone, Lewis and Clark, Johnny Appleseed, and others are just the sort of stories to make every boy's eyes sparkle. And as he hears these true tales of hardship and heroism he is getting a grounding in patriotism which he will never lose. Moreover, this furnishes an easy, natural introduction to the later study of our national history, as the tales are arranged chronologically.

"Mighty Rulers and Heroes" come next, with inspiring stories of Charlemagne, the Empire Builder, Queen Elizabeth, Sir Walter Raleigh, Cromwell,

Admiral Nelson, and a dozen other national heroes. To understand the spirit of a great nation we must know the spirit of its accredited leaders.

"Makers of Canada" concludes this rich volume, and—as in the section devoted to the United States—it gives young readers an opportunity to learn history largely through the life stories of the men and women who made the great Dominion possible. We begin back at the time of Jacques Cartier and other bold French voyagers and explorers, and come on down to the time of Sir Wilfred Laurier and present-day leaders. It is a picturesque story, graphically told in text and illustration.

These stories are told by various writers—men and women of skilled pens who have mastered the art of telling tales to young people. They are the farthest possible removed from the old-style biography, beginning "He was born," and ending "He died." They start out as briskly and actively as any "made-up" story, and they hold the interest straight through to the end. Yet they are true, and being true, they carry the finest sort of inspiration to the young hearers to make something of himself and herself when they grow up.

As in other volumes, not the least of its appeals are pictures and page decorations scattered through lavishly, many of the plates being in full color. "Boys and Girls Who Became Famous" fittingly concludes this series and, if we mistake not, will be a lasting favorite with readers long before they reach their 'teens.

CONTENTS

CONTENTS

WHEN THEY WERE CHILDREN

"Lives of great men all remind us   And departing, leave behind us
We can make our lives sublime,   Footprints on the sands of time."
—Longfellow.

THE BOYHOOD OF A STORY-TELLER

(Robert Louis Stevenson)

BY AMY STEEDMAN

"My tea is nearly ready, and the sun has left the
    sky;
It's time to take the window and see Leerie going
    by;
For every night at tea-time and before you take
    your seat
With lantern and with ladder he comes posting
    up the street."

"What luck it is to have a lamp before our very own door," thought little Louis Stevenson as he stood by the nursery window to watch for the lamplighter.

One by one the lamps along Howard Place, Edinburgh, were touched into points of light, until the lamplighter reached No. 8; and then came the crowning joy of all, when Leerie stopped to light that special lamp. Would he look up and see the small face pressed against the window, and nod "good evening," or would he be too busy to think of little boys?

It was no wonder that the coming of the lamplighter was so eagerly looked for! The winter days were often long and wearisome to the little child shut up in the nursery there, but everything he could see from his window was interesting and exciting.

Louis, or "Smout" as his father called him, was so often ill, and caught cold so easily in the bitter cold Edinburgh winds, that he was often kept indoors the whole winter through, and all that he saw of the outside world was through his nursery window. They were happy days indeed when he was well enough to play about the nursery, to lie flat on the floor chalking and painting his pictures, and to watch for Leerie when the gloaming came.

But there were many other days spent in bed, when Louis was obliged to make-believe a good deal to keep himself happy, as he sat up with a little shawl pinned round his shoulders and his toys

THE PLEASANT LAND OF COUNTERPANE

arranged on the counterpane beside him. But there was always someone at hand ready to comfort the child. His nurse, Alison Cunningham, "Cummie" as he called her, never failed him. She was always there to soothe the pain, always patient and always gentle with the poor little weary boy. His nurseries changed from one house to another, but Cummie was always there. The feeling of "her most comfortable hand" he never forgot.

A THOUGHTFUL CHILD

One day, when Louis was only three years old, he was left alone with his mother after dinner and remembered that Cummie always wrapped a shawl about her; but there was no shawl to be found, so he reached up and took a doily off the table, carefully unfolded it, and spread it over as much of her as it would cover.

"That's a wee bittie, mamma," he said comfortingly.

Cummie was very strict about the observance of Sunday. Louis learned to repeat long passages out of the Bible, besides Psalms and hymns, and he always recited them with a great deal of action, his small hands scarcely ever still, and his dark eyes shining with excitement.

With mother and Cummie to amuse him all day long, he was rather like a small prince in the nursery, and it was his will and pleasure that someone should constantly read to him.

He never could listen quietly to any story, but must always try to act it, slaying dragons, attacking the enemy, galloping off on a fiery horse to carry news to the enemy, until he was tired out, and Cummie would smooth back the hair from his hot forehead, and try to persuade him to rest.

"Sit down and bide quiet for a bittie," she said, and coaxed him to sew a piece of his kettle-holder, or knit the garter that was as black as only a child's gummy little hands could make it.

But it was not only Cummie who watched over and cared for little Louis, there were his father and his mother too. Often during the night the nursery door would open gently and his father would come in and sit by his bedside and tell him story after story, until the child forgot his pain and weariness and drifted away into the land of dreams.

Then there was his young mother, who was so ready to play with him and who always made even the dull nursery

HE NEVER COULD LISTEN QUIETLY TO ANY STORY

a sunshiny, happy place. She was not very strong, and Louis began early to try to take care of her.

AT GRANDFATHER'S

When spring came little Louis played about the garden of his grandfather's manse in the country near Edinburgh. Like the flowers, he began to lift up his head and grow strong in the sunshine.

It was a different world to Louis when the sun shone and the sky was blue, and the splendid colors of the flowers made his days a rainbow riot of delight. There was no more lying in bed and no more coughs, but instead, long warm summer days spent in the garden, or down by the river, where there was the joy of his heart—a mill.

There were cousins there too, in the sunny garden, ready to play all the games that Louis invented, to lie behind the bushes with toy guns watching for a drove of antelopes to go by, or to be shipwrecked sailors on a desert island.

There, too, was the kind aunt who brought out crackers and calves'-foot jelly at eleven o'clock from her store-room, which always had so delicious a smell of raisins and spices. Never did anything taste so good as those crackers and that calves'-foot jelly.

The children stood rather in awe of their grandfather, for he was very strict, and woe betide any small foot that left its mark on the flower-beds of the manse garden. It was whispered that their grandfather made a nightly round and examined each little muddy shoe put out to be cleaned at night, ready to fit it into the track which the evil-doer had left on the flower-bed.

That was enough to make them very

3

careful where they stepped. It was awe-inspiring, too, to see their grandfather in the pulpit every Sunday, and though they admired his beautiful face and his

IT WAS A RED-LETTER DAY WHEN HE FIRST GOT POSSESSION OF THE "ARABIAN NIGHTS"

white hair, there was something rather terrifying about him, and the cold dark room where he sat solemnly writing his sermons was seldom invaded by any of his grandchildren.

But there was something in that dark room which Louis longed with all his heart to possess. On the walls hung some very highly colored Indian pictures, and he wanted one of them more than anything else in all the world. At last there came a day when he was sent into the awesome room to repeat a Psalm to his grandfather, and his heart beat high with hope.

Perhaps if he said his Psalm very

nicely his grandfather might reward him with a gift of one of those colored pictures. Louis repeated it carefully, keeping one eye on his grandfather's solemn face, and one on the Indian picture.

When the Psalm was finished, his grandfather lifted him on his knee, and kissing him gave him "a kindly little sermon" which so surprised Louis, who had a very loving little heart, that he quite forgot his disappointment about the gaily-colored pictures he had longed for.

A WINTER WITH COUSIN ROBERT

When those sunny summer days came to an end and Louis went home, he had a companion who made even the gray days cheerful. His cousin, Robert Alan Stevenson, spent a whole winter with him, and together they lived in a make-believe world of their own.

Disagreeable things were turned into delightful plays, and even their meals were interesting. Instead of having to eat up a plateful of uninteresting porridge for breakfast, the magic of make-believe turned it into a foreign land, covered with snow (which was the sugar of course), or an island that was threatened by the encroaching sea (that was the cream).

The excitement of seeing the dry land disappearing or the snow mountains being cleared was so entrancing that the porridge was eaten up before the magic came to an end. Even cold mutton could be charmed into something quite delicious when Louis called it red venison, and described the mighty hunter who had gone forth and shot down the deer after many desperate adventures.

But perhaps the greatest joy of all was when Saturday afternoons came round and the boys went down to Leith to look at the ships, always the chief delight of their hearts. Passing down Leith Walk they came to a stationer's shop at the corner, where in the window there stood a tiny toy theater, and piled about it a heap of playbooks, "A penny plain and twopence colored."

Happy indeed was the child who had a penny to spend (for of course no self-respecting boy with paint-box at home ever thought of buying a "Twopence colored"), who could walk into the shop with assurance and ask to see those books. Many a time did Louis stand outside, having a penny to spend, and try to see the outside pictures and to read as much of the printing as could be seen at such a disadvantage.

It was no use going in unless the penny was forthcoming, for the bookseller kept a stern eye on little boys, and seemed to know at a glance whether they were "intending purchasers" or not. Inside the dark little shop which "smelled of Bibles" he stood, and seemed to grudge them the pleasure of even turning over the pages of those thrilling plays.

"I do not believe, child, that you are an intending purchaser at all," he growled one day, sweeping the precious books away when Louis had hesitated long over his choice.

It was those little books which opened to Louis the golden world of romance, the doors of which were never closed to him again.

READING AND WRITING

It was not until Louis was eight years old that he began to read. His mother and Cummie had always been ready to read to him, and that, he

THE BOOKSELLER KEPT A STERN EYE ON LITTLE BOYS

thought, was the pleasanter way. But quite suddenly he discovered that it was good to be able to read stories to himself, and it was a red-letter day when he first got possession of the "Arabian Nights."

Long before he could write, he was fond of dictating stories to anyone who would write them for him, and poor patient Cummie would write sheet after sheet of nonsense, all of which she treasured and read to his mother afterward.

Sitting over the fire at night while Louis lay sleeping in his little bed, the mother and nurse whispered together over the cleverness of their boy, and anxiously tried to reassure each other that he was growing stronger, while they built in the air castles in which Louis was to dwell as king.

The schooldays of Louis Stevenson made but little impression upon him. He was so often kept away by ill-health, and the schools were so often changed, that he did not win many laurels there. Whatever he liked to learn he learned with all his heart, and to the rest he gave very little attention whatever. He was not very fond of games, for he was not strong enough to play them well, and it was only when the make-believe magic began that he was in his element.

So it was that the make-believe magic kept Louis happy in his childhood's games, and when he grew up to be a man and left the games behind him, the make-believe magic was never left behind, but gave a great happiness to the world as well as to himself.

"Be good and make others happy" was his own particular rule, for he believed that we all should be as happy as happy can be, and that even children should remember

"The world is so full of a number of things,
I'm sure we should all be as happy as kings."

A NURSE'S GIRLHOOD
(FLORENCE NIGHTINGALE)

BY AMY STEEDMAN

ON THE fifteenth of May, the month of flowers, in the year 1820, a little English baby was born in a villa just outside the fair city of Florence.

Spring had been busy sowing the fields with flowers, spreading a carpet of tender green beneath the gray olive trees, and decking with delicate budding leaves the vines. She scattered blossoms abroad with such a lavish hand that the old city of palaces, with its sun-baked roofs and narrow shadowy streets, now well deserved its name of the City of Flowers.

New life was springing up everywhere, and the little new life in the villa lifted its face to the light in company with the flowers.

"We will call her Florence," said her mother. So the City of Flowers gave its dear name to the little English baby, who was one day to write it in letters of gold upon the scroll of fame.

It was not very long before the English family went back to their home in England, but the baby they carried with them must always have seemed a link with the beautiful old city, the rainbow-colored flowers of Spring, the sunshine and blue skies of Italy.

The first home that Florence knew in England was Lea Hall, in Derbyshire;

6

but when she was five years old, and her sister Frances was six, they went to live in a new house called Lea Hurst, which their father had just rebuilt, and here all the rest of her childhood's summer days were spent.

It was a beautiful home, for Mr. Nightingale loved all beautiful things, and would have everything around him as charming as might be. The windows facing south looked over lawns and gardens and wooded slopes, across the valley where the Derwent Water wound its way like a silver thread, and on every side the view was lovely.

LITTLE SISTERS

But surely most charming of all must have been the sight of the two little maidens in their dainty muslin frocks, leghorn hats, and sandal shoes, as they played about the garden slopes, among the beds of purple pansies, blue forget-me-nots, and sweet-scented wall-flowers.

The children had each her own special garden in which she worked busily, planting, weeding, and watering, but it was Florence who was specially fond of flowers. It seemed as if the old City of Flowers had laid its charm upon her as well as given her its name.

The two little sisters were very fond of their dolls too, although they showed their fondness in very different ways, and brought up their families on quite different plans.

Florence's dolls were all delicate, and needed constant care. They spent most of their lives in bed, going through dangerous illnesses, while they were

THE CHILDREN HAD EACH HER OWN SPECIAL GARDEN

most carefully and tenderly nursed by their little mother, who doctored them, and tempted their appetites with dainty dishes until they were well again. Scarcely were they up and dressed, however, than some fresh ailment laid them low once more, and the nursing began over again.

The dolls belonging to Frances, on the contrary, were scarcely ever in bed at all. They led stirring lives of adventure and excitement, but when an accident occurred, and an arm was broken or a leg came off at the joint, it was Florence who tenderly set the arm, putting it in splints.

And if it was interesting to nurse dolls, how much more worth while was it to take care of live animals! Florence looked upon all animals as her friends, more especially those that were rather ugly and unfortunate. Anything that needed her care appealed at once to her tender little heart.

It was she who welcomed and admired the very commonplace kittens which the stable-cat hid from less friendly eyes; and the old pony that was past work and of no use to anyone knew that his little mistress loved him as much as ever.

Whenever she passed the paddock he came trotting over to see her, and then he would poke his nose into her pockets until he found an apple or a carrot, which was always hidden somewhere ready for his daily game of hide-and-seek.

The birds, too, seemed to know and trust her, and even the squirrels came darting down for the nuts she carried with her, as she walked through the woods. They looked upon her as quite one of themselves.

Only half the year was spent at Lea Hurst, for in winter and early spring the family went to live in their other house, Embley Park, in Hampshire.

There were but few railways in those days, and so the journey was made by coach or in their own carriage, and it was always a delightful time for the two children who loved the excitement of driving along the coaching roads and stopping to rest at nights at the wayside inns.

AT EMBLEY

During those winter months at Embley, Florence and her sister were kept very strictly at lessons with their governess. Their father believed that girls should be taught quite as thoroughly as boys, and he planned his little daughters'

lessons just as carefully as if they had been sons. With him Florence learned Greek and Latin and was extremely quick at learning foreign languages.

The little girls were taught, too, by their mother, to work their samplers and to do fine sewing, so there was not much spare time in their days, although some hours were always set aside for them to run about outside with their dogs, to scramble about the woods, or ride their ponies up hill and down dale.

From her mother, too, Florence learned the pleasure of visiting the village people, and learning to know them in their homes, and she was always eager to be the messenger when there was a pudding or a jelly to be carried to some invalid.

She was riding on her pony over the Hampshire downs one day, after a round of visits with the vicar, when they noticed that old Roger, the shepherd, was having hard work to collect his scattered sheep, and that he had no dog to help him. The vicar stopped and called to him.

"Where's your dog?" he asked.

THE INJURED DOG

"The boys have been throwing stones at him, your reverence, and have broken his leg," answered the old man.

"Do you mean to say Cap's leg is broken?" asked Florence anxiously. She knew the name of every dog about the place. "Can nothing be done for him? Where is he?"

The old man shook his head. "No, there's naught can be done, missy," he said. "He will never be good for anything again. I've left him lying yonder in that shed."

Florence turned beseeching eyes upon the vicar.

"Can't we go and see?" she asked.

The vicar nodded, and they galloped off together to the lonely shed, and in a moment Florence had slid off her pony, entered the shed, and was kneeling by the side of the suffering dog.

She always seemed to understand the language of animals, and as she patted and soothed and spoke in a low tone to poor Cap, he seemed at once to understand her, and feebly tried to wag his tail in response, looking up at her with brown eyes full of grateful trust.

The vicar following after, carefully examined the injured leg, and declared it was not broken at all, but that with careful nursing the dog might get well.

"What shall I do first?" asked Florence anxiously.

"We might try a hot compress," said the vicar.

Florence did not know exactly what a hot compress was, but when she understood that it was a cloth wrung out of very hot water, she set to work at once.

The shepherd's boy was told to light a fire of sticks, and fill a kettle, and then came the question of a cloth and bandages. Looking round, Florence's quick eye caught sight of the shepherd's clean smock hanging behind the door, and this, she declared, was the very thing that was needed.

"Mother will give him a new one," she said, as she tore the smock into

SHE BANDAGED THE SUFFERING DOG

strips. Very tenderly, then, did she doctor the swollen leg, and in spite of the pain, the dog lay quite still under her hand, watching her all the time with grateful eyes.

A FAITHFUL NURSE

A message was sent home to explain where Florence was, and all that afternoon she watched by the side of the suffering dog, and bathed the poor leg until the swelling began to go down. It was evening before the shepherd came, and he came with a slow step.

"Deary me, Miss," he exclaimed in astonishment, when the dog gave a whine of welcome, and tried to come to him, "why, you've worked a wonder. I never thought to see the old dog greet me again."

"You can throw away the rope, for he's going to get quite well now," said Florence, "only you must nurse him

9

She was only a child then, always ready to help anyone or anything that needed her care, tending her flowers and learning to be orderly and diligent, but she was laying the foundation of the great work that was to crown her life.

The look of gratitude in the eyes of a dog moved her childish heart with pity, but how well was she to learn to know that look in the eyes of suffering men, when the very name of Florence Nightingale meant hope and comfort to wounded soldiers, and the sight of her face bending over their sick-beds was to them as the face of an angel.

carefully, and I will show you how to make hot compresses."

Roger was only too glad to do all that the little lady directed, and had no words to express his thanks. But it was the look in Cap's grateful eyes that was all the thanks Florence cared for.

"On England's annals, through the long
  Hereafter of her speech and song,
    That light its rays shall cast
    From portals of the past.

"A Lady with a Lamp shall stand
  In the great history of the land,
    A noble type of good,
    Heroic womanhood."

AN INVENTOR'S BOYHOOD

(THOMAS A. EDISON)

BY AMY STEEDMAN

IT IS not only in fairyland that magicians are born, for sometimes the dull old world produces just as wonderful a wizard as any that are to be found between the covers of Grimm or Hans Andersen.

In the little village of Milan, in the State of Ohio, on February 11, 1847, Thomas Alva Edison was born. There was no mysterious romance about the birth of this magician. No one thought him very wonderful at all, except perhaps his mother, and even she found him only a trying boy at times.

As to Al's father, he thought the boy rather slow and stupid, and was quite worried about him. "Why, why, why," was on his lips from morning till night, and the number of questions he asked wore out his father's patience. He

EACH NEW DISCOVERY HELPED TO ADD TO THE MAGIC OF HIS BRAIN

wanted to know the reason of everything and to prove for himself what was right and what was wrong.

Just like ordinary boys, he was always getting into mischief, but whether it was by magic or good luck he always managed to get out of it again. First of all he fell into the canal that ran past the house where he lived, but he was pulled out before he was drowned. Then he tried falling into a pile of wheat in a grain elevator, and was nearly smothered, but he managed to get out of that too.

He had the top of one finger chopped off instead of the skate strap which he was holding, and when he tried to build a fire in a barn it was not surprising that the barn itself caught fire in the most ordinary way. There was nothing magical either in the punishment that followed, when he was publicly whipped

in the village square as an example to other naughty boys.

And yet in Thomas Alva Edison's big head the magic was slowly working, although no one guessed it.

The boy was only at school three months, and all the time he sat at the foot of the class. Al's mother was vexed that he seemed stupid, and so she took him away from school and began to teach him herself.

Down in the cellar he was allowed to keep rows upon rows of little bottles, collected from all parts of the town and filled with all sorts of chemicals, with which he made experiments, and each new discovery helped to add to the magic of his brain.

Sometimes, however, the experiments were a failure and the results far from pleasant.

"I will teach you to fly," he said one

day to Michael Oates, a boy older than himself who helped with the work of the house. Now Michael had a great admiration for Al and quite believed he was able to do what he said, so when he was told to swallow a fearful dose of seidlitz powders he took it without a murmur, believing that the gas it produced would hoist him up.

But, alas! instead of flying he was soon lying on the ground twisted with pain. His cries of agony brought Al's mother to the rescue, and she brought out the switch which was kept behind the old grandfather's clock and whipped the experimenter soundly.

But neither the failure of the experiment nor the whipping discouraged Al greatly. He was sure the idea was all right and it was only Michael who was all wrong.

There was not much money to spare in Al's home, and all those bottles and experiments cost a good deal; so before very long, when he was only twelve years old, he made up his mind to try to earn money for himself.

First he tried market gardening with Michael (who could dig if he could not fly), and he grew and sold vegetables for a time, but he did not like the work. Then after much persuasion his mother allowed him to sell newspapers on a railroad train, and that suited him much better.

He had time to read the newspapers and magazines as well as to sell them, and as he went backward and forward in the train from Huron, where he now lived, to Detroit, he was allowed to use part of one of the baggage-cars for his

beloved experiments, and here he collected all his bottles and worked away as he had done in the cellar at home.

Even that was not enough to keep him busy, and when the Civil War broke out and everyone wanted news, he started a little printing-press in the baggage-car, and printed a newspaper of his very own called *The Weekly Herald,* which he sold at "three cents a copy."

But, sad to relate, an accident happened to the new laboratory, and it and the printing-press came to an untimely end. The train was running along a badly laid track one day, when it gave a sudden lurch, and before Al could catch it, a stick of phosphorus fell from the shelf to the floor of the car, and in an instant the boards were in flames.

The guard, a Scot, with a quick temper, managed to put the fire out and to save his car, but he was furious with the boy, and boxed his ears so soundly that Al ever afterward suffered from deafness. Then as soon as the first station was reached the bottles and the printing-press were bundled out on the platform, and he was left there "tearful and indignant," in the midst of the ruins.

It was after this that the magician began the work that was to touch the whole world with magic. And this is how his chance came. He was standing one day talking to the stationmaster at a little railroad station, when he saw a tiny boy, the son of the station agent, go wandering along the rails on which a train was coming swiftly toward him.

There was not a moment to be lost,

and in a flash Al had jumped down and caught the child just as the train dashed past, and only just in time, for the wheel of one of the passing carriages struck his heel.

The child's father was not rich enough to reward the boy with money, but instead he offered to teach him telegraphy, and so the magic wand was put into the boy's hand.

THE BOY WHO WAS HELPED

(BENJAMIN WEST)

BY HAPGOOD MOORE

WE ARE told of a certain Oriental king that "His fame spread far abroad; for he was marvelously helped, till he was strong." This might have been said of Benjamin West.

The old house in Swarthmore where he was born still stands. It was near a lonely highway, or trail, that led up from the Delaware River into the hills. According to a hospitable custom of those days "when hunger made even acorns savory," after the family had had evening prayer they went upstairs to bed, leaving the door unlatched, a roaring fire on the hearth and food on the table, for any passer-by who was overcome by cold or hunger. It must have been a picturesque—and it would be to us a fearsome—sight to come down in the morning and find half a dozen redskins curled up on the floor around the fireplace. There was nothing, however, to fear in this Quaker household from the Indians with whom William Penn had made his never-to-be-broken treaty of peace. The youngest boy in this home admired the bright colors with which the Indians striped their faces, and they showed him how to prepare the red and yellow ocher. To this his mother added indigo, with which she colored her coverlets, and by mixing this blue with the yellow the boy got green.

Now comes a story which perhaps you have heard. Leaning one day over the cradle where his older sister's baby was sleeping, the little boy took some red and black ink and hastily sketched the child. When his mother returned he tried to hide his work, but when his mother saw it she knew it was a likeness of little Sally, and threw her arms about him and kissed him fondly.

The boy did not have much to work with. He had been told that a painter should have camel's-hair brushes, but there were no camels in Swarthmore. His eye fell upon the family cat. The little bunch of soft hairs at the tip of her tail was tempting. It took but a moment to cut them off. Later he resorted to other parts of her body. When his father wondered aloud what strange

13

THE LITTLE BOY HASTILY SKETCHED THE CHILD

disease was making the pet bald, Benjamin, like the Father of His Country, could not tell a lie.

THE SPECIAL MEETING

Later a neighbor gave him paints and brushes, and some sketches that were so precious that he took them with him to his attic bedroom at night. When he was sixteen there was a special meeting of the Society of Friends to help his parents decide his future. That the young man should be an artist was contrary to the faith of Quakers, for their Book of Discipline stated that "Things merely ornamental are not necessary to the well-being of man, but rather superfluous." Then arose a good man, who declared that it was plain that God had given this young man great talents, and that while such gifts had often been used for purposes of evil, it was also possible and probable that they might be made of great good. "What God has given, who shall dare to throw away?" So the meeting gave its consent, and gave Benjamin its blessing.

Through the generosity of a business man young West was sent to Italy to study. His teachers there gave such a good account of him that when he came to England his work was heartily praised, and men of authority and wealth urged him to remain there. He answered that there was but one thing to hinder. A young woman in America had promised to marry him and he wished to go and get her.

Here indeed he needed help. The brother of Elizabeth Shewell was unwilling that she should marry the poor

14

artist, and five years before he had locked her up so that the artist should not meet her. One night Benjamin Franklin and two other young men went to the house with a rope ladder and assisted the young lady out of the window and to a sloop that was at anchor, where the father of Benjamin West was waiting to escort her across the Atlantic.

THE GRATEFUL ARTIST

How did the artist, who soon became the favorite painter of England, requite those who had so marvelously helped him toward fame and happiness? He lived always a good, a helpful, a generous life. There is room to tell but one story of his goodness. He learned that some Friends in Philadelphia desired to build a hospital. He promised to give them a painting. When it was completed the British Institution offered him three thousand guineas for it. He accepted the offer, on condition that he should be allowed to send a duplicate to America. The proceeds of the sale of the first picture and of the exhibition of the second he gave to the hospital. The second picture hangs in the Pennsylvania Hospital to-day, where for many years thirty patients were cared for from the gift of Benjamin West. Nathaniel Hawthorne said: "If Benjamin West had done no other good deed than this, it would have been enough to entitle him to an honorable remembrance forever."

One day, when Mr. West was president of the Royal Academy and the king's favorite, George III said to him, "Mr. West, how did it happen that, living in the savage wilderness as a child, you ever became an artist?" Mr. West was silent for a moment. His mind was running back along the past, through his days of triumph, clear back to the stone house on Chester Road. Then he said, with a smile, "Your Majesty, the kiss of my mother made me a painter."

THE BOYHOOD OF A DISCOVERER

(Sir John Franklin)

BY AMY STEEDMAN

THERE were already eight children in the house at Spilsby when John was born on April 15, 1786. The arrival of a new baby was quite an ordinary event in that large family, but John was to have the special distinction of being the youngest son, and to enjoy all the privileges of a Benjamin.

All the other brothers and sisters teased and spoiled him by turns, but perhaps on the whole there was more spoiling than teasing, for he was such a frail, delicate child that everyone was inclined to treat him gently.

For the first three years of his life it seemed as if John would never live to

15

grow up, but after that he suddenly began to grow much stronger, and before very long was quite able to hold his own with the other children. He was a great favorite with everyone, and had what the old nurse called "a way with him" which no one could resist, and no spoiling seemed to hurt him.

He was a sunny-tempered child, easily managed, never cross or fretful, and willing to be friendly with everyone. Indeed he was exactly the sort of small boy which nowadays an elder English brother would describe as "a jolly little chap," while an American elder brother would ask proudly, "Say, have you seen my kid brother—he's some kid!"

Of course John had his faults like everyone else, and his mother shook her head over what she considered two very serious defects in his character. He was very untidy, and he was extremely curious.

Whatever was going on, John must always try to find out all about it, and when he had once set his mind on some discovery there was no turning him from it. All the other children were "neat and orderly," but John was seldom fit to be seen. Either his socks sagged under his heels, or there was a tear in his coat, or his frill was lost.

Something was always amiss, and as to his hands and face, no sooner were they washed than they began at once to get dirty again. He was not at all a credit to the family, and unfortunately he could never be kept in the background, out of sight, for he always wanted to be in the front row and to see everything that was going on.

As John grew older he began to show a tremendous love for adventure, and whatever daring deed the other boys performed, he was always eager to do something more daring still. Sometimes the boys would begin to talk of the great things they meant to do and the exciting adventures that would be sure to happen to them when they were men.

Each one planned some heroic action, until at last, when it came to John's turn to say what he meant to do, there seemed nothing left for him to choose. But as usual he was not to be outdone, and he had his plan all ready. "I am going to build a ladder," he said grandly, "so high that I shall be able to climb up to heaven."

Of course it was pointed out to him that a ladder couldn't stand upright unless it leaned against something, but he explained that it was a difficulty which he meant to overcome. What was the use of difficulties except to be overcome? he asked.

THE CALL OF THE SEA

Although John's home at Spilsby was not many miles inland, it had no dealings with any seaport town, and it was not until he was ten years old and was sent to the grammar school at Louth that he first heard the call of the sea.

He had started off one fine holiday with another boy to find their way to Saltfleet, which was ten miles distant, meaning to have a good time, but little dreaming of the change which that day was to make in his life. He was keenly interested in seeing a new place, but he had no idea of the wonder that awaited him. That first sight of the sea stirred his very soul.

In a moment it seemed to him that this was what he had been seeking for ever since he was born. The great mysterious sea, stretching away until it seemed to touch the sky, was the ladder of which he had dreamed. The sound of its breaking waves, the deep rolling swell, seemed to call to him as a friend, and instantly he recognized the voice and answered it with all his heart. He would be a sailor, and he would be nothing else.

Full of this great idea, with the sound of the sea ever in his ears, and the longing for it tugging at his heart, John lost no time in letting his father know that he had made up his mind to be a sailor. He little knew with what displeasure the news would be received at home.

"It is absolute nonsense," declared John's father, "I shall not consider it for a moment. The boy simply wants to escape from the drudgery of school, and, like every other boy, imagines that to go to sea is the way to stirring adventures. I will not hear of such a thing."

So John was sternly told that he might put the idea out of his head at once, and that he had better make up his mind to attend to his lessons.

It was no easy matter, however, to turn John from any settled purpose, and he quietly persisted in his request until at last his father grew very angry.

"I would rather follow my son to the

THAT FIRST SIGHT OF THE SEA STIRRED HIS VERY SOUL

grave," he thundered, and forbade the subject to be mentioned again.

For two years John worked steadily at his school lessons, and did his very best with them, although his heart was set as firmly as ever on the hope of becoming a sailor. It was the best way to show his determination, for it would never do for a sailor to shirk any kind of work.

He was a great favorite with his school-fellows and everyone else, for he possessed that most wonderful gift called "charm," which is as full of magic as any wizard's spell. Everyone loved the sunny-tempered, merry-looking boy, so brave and frank and friendly, "so quick to resent a slight, and so ready to forgive it."

It was a great disappointment to his

father when John showed no signs of outgrowing his desire to go to sea. The two years' discipline of school life seemed only to have strengthened his determination, and as time had proved no cure, it seemed wise now to try another remedy.

It was such an easy thing to talk of being a sailor while living comfortably at home, and looking at the sea life through rose-colored spectacles. The first real experience of rough life on board ship was usually enough to disenchant anyone. So it was decided that John should be sent off on a cruise in a merchant ship which traded between Hull and Lisbon, and it was to be hoped that this taste of life at sea would make him a wiser and a sadder boy.

A SAILOR-LAD

It was all in vain. John returned home in great spirits, keener than ever. No hardships could daunt him, his heart was set on becoming a sailor.

His father saw that it was wiser now to give in, for this was no mere boyish fancy, and he sorrowfully gave his consent. A berth was procured for the boy on board the "Polyphemus," and it was arranged that an elder brother should take him up to London, see to his uniform and his outfit, and send him to join his ship.

The elder brother did not much relish the task. In a letter home, he complained bitterly of the trouble of "continually running after this clothes-buying business." But in spite of his annoyance he could not help feeling rather proud of his small brother when he was rigged out in all the bravery of his new uniform, and he was forced to admit in the same letter that "the dirk and the cocked hat are rather attractive parts of his dress."

At last, when all was ready, the little midshipman, cocked hat and dirk complete, joined his ship, and set sail for the north, the "Polyphemus" being part of the English fleet, under the command of Sir Hyde Parker, with Nelson as second in command.

From the calm quiet of the Lincolnshire home, where nothing very exciting ever happened and where adventures were only to be met with in dreams, John suddenly plunged into the wildest and most exciting of times, and was in the thick of the most terrible sea-battle which Nelson ever fought.

THE BATTLE OF THE BALTIC

That glorious Battle of the Baltic was John Franklin's baptism of fire, and it was a dreadful experience for the small midshipman. He himself escaped unhurt, but around him were the dead and dying, their groans mingling in his ears with the roar of the guns.

The sea was covered with pieces of wreckage lit up by the lurid light of burning ships, and as they anchored in Elsinore harbor and he looked over into the clear water, he could see the dead bodies lying thick there at the bottom, English and Danes together.

But there was a glorious side to the horrors of that day. Such deeds of daring and bravery had been done as

THAT GLORIOUS BATTLE WAS JOHN FRANKLIN'S BAPTISM OF FIRE

made John glow with pride to think that he had had even the smallest share in the great victory. It was the unconquerable spirit of the English sailor which made Nelson that day clap his blind eye to the telescope, and refuse to see the signal to retire, as he nailed his colors to the mast and fought on until the Danes were beaten.

No wonder that the little midshipman was proud to belong to such a navy and such a country, and he was surer than ever that there was nothing in all the world so fine as to be an English sailor. His only fear now was that he might miss the chance of going on an expedition to the South Seas, which it had been arranged that he should join, before he sailed for Elsinore.

But luckily for him the "Polyphemus" was ordered home at once after the great battle, and he was just in time to be transferred to the "Investigator," which was bound on a voyage of discovery. The captain, Matthew Flinders, was an uncle of young Franklin, and took a special interest in the boy and spared no pains to turn him out a good sailor.

"It is with great pleasure," he wrote home, "that I tell you of the good conduct of John. He is a very fine youth, and there is every probability of his doing credit to the 'Investigator' and himself. His attention to his duty has gained him the esteem of the First Lieutenant, who scarcely knows how to talk enough in his praise."

HARD WORK

It must not be imagined that it was all smooth sailing for John, and that everything was made charming for him on board. He had his own hard work to do, and many a hardship to endure besides a certain amount of teasing.

One of the officers especially took advantage of the boy's keenness and made him do a great deal of extra work, taking all the credit of it to himself. John naturally resented this, but he never complained, and doggedly got through both his own share of work and that of the lazy bully, which certainly did him no harm.

It was not long, however, before John's time on board the "Investigator" came to a sudden end. The ship was a poor one and quite untrustworthy, and at the first breakdown it was found impossible to repair her. There was nothing for it but to ship all the crew back to England in another vessel, and that was only the beginning of a long series of misadventures.

The vessel on which the crew of the "Investigator" set sail was wrecked almost immediately afterward in the Torres Straits, and it was only with great difficulty that the men managed to land on a sandbank and to save stores enough to keep them from starving.

SHIPWRECKED

It was quite as exciting as any Robinson Crusoe adventure, and not nearly so pleasant, for the sandbank was much worse than a desert island. The only thing to be done was to rig up tents for shelter and hoist a blue ensign with the Union Jack on a tall spar, in the hope that some passing ship might see their signal of distress.

There was luckily enough food to last them for some time, and so it was decided that one of the six-oared boats should be manned and the captain should try to find his way back to Sydney and bring relief.

It was weary waiting week after week on the desolate sandbank, watching the provisions grow less and less, but John always kept a stout heart, and at last there was a cry of wild delight as the lookout man caught sight of a sail bearing toward them. It was the relief boats at last, and no time was lost in taking the men off and arranging for their return to England.

Young Franklin with some others of the crew were shipped to Canton, where they found a fleet of homeward-bound merchantmen, and so once more gayly set sail for home.

THE LOOKOUT MAN CAUGHT SIGHT OF A SAIL BEARING TOWARD THEM

MORE ADVENTURES

In those days it was no uncommon fate for a merchantman to be captured on the high seas by an enemy or taken by a privateer, and so they all carried guns and were as ready to fight as a man-o'-war. As luck would have it, scarcely had young Franklin set sail again toward home when a powerful French squadron was sighted which bore down upon them, evidently expecting to make an easy and valuable capture.

Now, instead of running away as the French naturally expected them to do, the merchantman turned about and prepared to give fight, which mightily astonished the enemy, and so well did the guns behave that in a quarter of an hour the French drew off, having had more than enough.

Then came the order from the English commander for a "general chase," and the little fleet of merchantmen actually drove the French squadron of war before them for nearly two hours. Then at last the commander considered that his honor was satisfied, and recalled his pursuing ships and proceeded once more on his way.

It is not difficult to picture the delight of young Franklin in that extraordinary chase, and it was no wonder he was proud of being a British sailor, born to rule the waves. Arrived at home, the boy was specially mentioned in the report of the captain, who said that no one in the ship's company deserved approval and reward for quick helpfulness and good conduct more than Franklin.

HOME AGAIN

That was surely a good home-coming for young John, and proved that his love for the sea was no idle fancy or desire to shirk work. In spite of all the dangers and disasters, the boy had shown throughout a "cheery contentment."

He could no longer now be called a child, but he was still only a young midshipman when he fought at the Battle of Trafalgar and once more shared the glory of a victory under Nelson, a vic-

THE PLACE WHERE HE WAS BURIED IS UNKNOWN

tory which made the British flag "supreme on every sea."

But the young sailor's heart was set on something else beside the glory of victorious fighting. The keen love of discovery, the call of the unknown, was in his blood, and, like many another of England's heroes, he could not rest while there was a blank space upon the map to be filled in.

To discover the Northwest Passage was the dream of his life, and there, among the ice-walls of his Arctic prison, he laid down his life fighting to the last to conquer the unknown. The boy who had answered so faithfully the call of the sea, who had fought for king and country, was of the stuff indeed of which England's heroes are made.

Although the place where he was buried is unknown, and so has nothing to mark it as the grave of a hero, yet in Westminster Abbey is a fitting epitaph engraved in marble, as it is graven on many an English heart:

"Not here! the white North hath thy bones; and
      thou,
   Heroic sailor soul,
Art passing on thy happier voyage now
   Towards no earthly pole."

THE BOYHOOD OF A PATRIOT

(GEORGE WASHINGTON)

BY AMY STEEDMAN

WHEN little George was five years old his father moved from Pope's Creek, where the child had been born, and went to live on another of his estates on the Rappahannock River. It was a splendid country, with great unbroken forests stretching out to east and west, and broad rivers winding their way through fertile fields. In these great forests, standing so thick with trees that scarce a gleam of sunshine could creep in to lighten the dim green twilight, all kinds of birds and beasts had their home, and in the shadowy stillness there were other moving forms besides the animals that crept quietly and stealthily about. These forests were the hunting ground of the Indians, and their canoes, too, might be seen shooting about the rivers. As yet they were quite friendly toward the white family who had come to settle so close to them, but at any moment they might become enemies.

Every now and then news would come from other parts of the country telling of terrible deeds done by the Indians to the white settlers, and George would listen to these tales of cruelty and treachery until it was difficult to feel quite brave, and not to be afraid.

Boys and girls safe at home to-day love the exciting stories of the Redskins on the warpath, and the fascinating description of their clever cunning, but it was a different matter for George when those same Indians were lurking in the forests close by, stealing like silent shadows across his path, noiseless and mysterious in their ways as the forest animals themselves.

OUT IN THE APPLE ORCHARD

But there were pleasant open places around the house for George to play in, without wandering into the shadows of the great forests. There was an apple orchard, besides the garden and fields, and in springtime it was a veritable fairyland with its sea of pale pink blossoms against the blue sky. That was very beautiful to look at, but it was in autumn that George loved the orchard best, for then the trees were loaded with great rosy-cheeked apples and the ground beneath was covered with equally delicious "tumble-downs."

George had gone one day to the orchard with his father and two of his cousins, and the sight of the apples made him dance with joy.

"Father," he cried, "did you ever in all your life see so many apples before?"

"There are certainly a great many," answered his father. "Don't you remember what I told you in spring when your cousin gave you a large apple, and you wanted to eat it all up yourself, instead of sharing it with your brothers and sisters? I told you then that you should be generous; that God would send us many more apples in the autumn."

George hung his head. He remembered quite well, and the sight of all these apples made him ashamed of himself now. It was not very easy to own that he had been greedy, and that he was sorry, but he was a good fighter and

THOSE SAME INDIANS WERE LURKING IN THE FORESTS CLOSE BY

presently he won the victory. "I am sorry now, father," he said, "and if you'll forgive me this time, you'll see if I'll ever be stingy again."

That was the kind of lesson his father wanted him to learn, and it was the sort of teaching that George never forgot.

THE MAGIC GARDEN

When spring came George was much excited one day, when he went into the garden to find that the cabbage-bed had begun to show green shoots, and that the green formed the letters of his own name, "George Washington." He stood for a few moments quite silent, his eyes and mouth wide open in astonishment. Surely it must be magic!

"Father, father!" he shouted; "O father! do come and see."

"What is the matter?" asked his father.

"The cabbages are coming up, and are writing out my name," cried George.

"Very curious," said his father.

"But who did it?" asked George.

"I suppose they just grew so," said his father; "don't you think they came up that way by chance?"

"They couldn't," said George; "they wouldn't know how to grow that way unless someone had made them."

"You are quite right," said his father. "Nothing grows by chance. I planted those cabbages in that way on purpose to teach you that very lesson. There are some people who say that everything grows by chance, but that is impossible. There is Someone who plans everything. All the thousands of good things you enjoy, the sunshine and the flowers, eyes to see with, ears to hear with, feet to carry you about, all are planned by God, and chance has nothing to do with it."

George was only eight years old when he learned that lesson, but he never forgot it all the rest of his life.

THE CHERRY-TREE STORY

It was about this time that George was given the little hatchet which has become so famous. He had gone about the garden chopping any old pieces of wood he could find, when his eye fell on a beautiful English cherry tree, and this seemed the very thing on which to try his new present. So he chopped away with great enjoyment until not only the bark was off but the wood underneath was hacked and cut into pieces.

Next day his father happened to pass that way and caught sight of his favorite cherry tree. He was very angry when he saw the mischief that had been done, and he went back immediately to ask everyone in the house if he or she knew who had done it.

"My beautiful cherry tree is utterly ruined," he said; "who could have hacked it in that way?"

No one knew anything about it. None of the servants had been near the cherry tree.

"I wouldn't have taken five guineas for it," said Mr. Washington, sorrowfully.

Just then George came wandering in, his hatchet in his hand.

"George," said his father, sternly,

"I DID CUT IT WITH MY HATCHET"

"do you know who has killed that cherry tree in the garden?"

Now George until that moment had never thought that he had harmed the tree, but hearing his father's voice and seeing his troubled face, the child suddenly realized the mischief he had done, and hung his head. "George, did you do it?" asked his father. It was all very frightening. He was only a very little boy, and his father was very angry, and the whole household waited to hear what he had to say for himself. It was not easy to be brave, but George manfully lifted his head and looked straight at his father.

"I can't tell a lie, father," he said; "I did cut it with my hatchet."

So the boy spoke out bravely and truly, risking the consequences, although he need not have been afraid, for his father would rather have lost a hundred cherry trees than that his little son should have told one lie.

GEORGE WOULD BE A SOLDIER

It was only right that a boy who came of a soldierly race, and who meant himself to be a soldier some day, should learn the truest bravery of all. It was a better preparation for him even than drilling his companions and fighting mimic battles, as he was so fond of doing. His big brother Laurence had joined the army and gone away to fight King George's battles against the Spaniards, and George wished with all his heart that he too was old enough to wear a uniform and to carry a sword.

The sight of the soldiers as they marched past to the music of the band, the sound of martial drums and the waving of the English banner made his heart beat with excitement and loyalty, and he made up his mind he would be a soldier as his great-grandfather had been. Little did he think as he watched the soldiers march past, that when his time should come it would be under another flag that he would be fighting, against that England which he still thought of as his own country.

But all this was still in the future, and meanwhile George went steadily on, learning all he could both at school and at home. He was as upright and brave and truthful as a boy could be, and besides that he learned the magic of method, so that he got through far more work than most boys could manage. His masters soon discovered that he was no ordinary boy, and they felt sure that a great future was in front of him. As his brother Laurence said, "If a bright springtime is the harbinger of an ample harvest, such a youth must foreshadow noble manhood."

THE BOYHOOD OF A STATESMAN

(Benjamin Franklin)

BY CHARLES R. GIBSON

The father of Benjamin Franklin, who had been a wool-dyer in England, emigrated about the year 1682 to that part of America which the colonists called New England. Benjamin, who was the fifteenth in a family of seventeen, was not born till twenty-five years later. Although he was born in Boston in 1706, he was a British subject, the Americans being then but colonists of Great Britain.

In the New World Benjamin's father commenced business as a candle and soap manufacturer, on a small scale.

Although Benjamin had only two years' schooling, which was between the age of eight and ten years, he must have received good tuition from his father, for he was able to read before he went to school. He tells us that his father always made it a point that the table-talk was of interest and instruction to the children. There was never any discussion of their food; that was strictly prohibited. Even if the food was not to their minds, or was extra pleasing, or was not well cooked, no remark whatever was to be made. Benjamin tells us that with this good training he found in later life that he was quite indifferent to what kind of food was set before him. He found this a great convenience in traveling; he did not envy those whose delicate tastes were often bringing them into conflict with the innkeepers. This avoidance of thinking about the food became such a habit with Franklin that he says, "Indeed, I am so unobservant of it, that to this day I can scarce tell a few hours after dinner of what dishes it consisted."

Another habit formed by Benjamin was to waste no time. No doubt he was taught this by his father, for he showed signs of this habit at a very early age, as we may gather from the following incident. When a child he felt that the very long graces which his father said before and after meals occupied a good deal of time. One day while the little fellow was watching the winter's meat being salted and stored away in casks he asked his father if it would not do to say grace over the whole lot once for all as it would save a lot of time.

HOW BEN DECIDED HIS FUTURE

His father had desired at first that his youngest son, Benjamin, should be a clergyman, but with the expenses of bringing up a family of seventeen he did not care to go to the further expense of a college training. At ten years of age

Benjamin was put into his father's business, but the cutting of wicks and the pouring of molten wax into candle-molds did not interest the boy. After two years of such work he told his father that he disliked the business, whereupon his father very wisely offered to find him some business which should be more congenial. But it is often no light task to determine for what business a boy is best suited, and so his father took Benjamin on his walks with him, to let the boy see different tradesmen at work, and that he himself might observe the boy's inclinations. There was some thought of apprenticing him to a cutler, but the fees demanded seemed to the father unreasonable.

He had observed that all Benjamin's pocket-money was spent on books, and that the boy had a decidedly bookish inclination, and so it occurred to him that the printing trade would be a congenial one to Benjamin. An older brother had been set up in business as a printer, and so it was arranged that Benjamin should become an apprentice to him. The apprenticeship was to be a very long one, for Benjamin, who was then twelve years of age, was not to be free till he came of age.

EXPERIENCES AS A PRINTER

Benjamin found the work very congenial, especially as he could borrow copies of the books from other apprentices. Sometimes he was required to return these books by the morning, but on such occasions he would sit up the greater part of the night till he finished the book. Later on a merchant who frequented the printing office offered Benjamin the use of his large library.

BENJAMIN BECAME APPRENTICE TO A PRINTER

During his early apprenticeship Benjamin became a vegetarian; the idea was suggested by some book he had read, but the real advantage that Benjamin saw in this diet was that the meals were more easily eaten, leaving more time for reading, and the cost of the food was less, so that he had more pocket-money for buying books. When his purse was not long enough to meet his demand for books, he would sell those he had read and buy the new ones.

While Benjamin was thoroughly interested in the printing business, he was not very happy in it, for his brother was often unkind to him. One can only surmise from what follows that Benjamin's brother was jealous of the boy's quickness in learning.

BENJAMIN BECOMES A WRITER

After Benjamin had served a few years of his apprenticeship it so happened that his brother began to publish a newspaper, the second in New England. People had tried to dissuade the brother, as they considered one newspaper quite sufficient for New England. Those who wrote the news for this paper were in the habit of meeting at the printing office to discuss matters. The youthful Benjamin, then only fifteen years of age, thought he would like to try his hand at writing articles. He knew very well that his brother would not allow him, and so he wrote in a disguised hand and pushed the anonymous manuscript beneath the door of the printing office after closing hours. He heard the journalists discuss his production next day, and the verdict was very encouraging; indeed, it was the general opinion that the article had been written by some well-known man of learning. This and other similar articles were published, and at last Benjamin informed his brother and the journalists that he had been the anonymous author. The journalists were genuinely interested in him, but the brother was exceedingly displeased, and thought the boy was far too vain.

Benjamin's position in the printing office was by no means improved by this incident. Although he still had four years of his apprenticeship to serve, he determined to cut short the continued unpleasantness. So, selling his books in order to pay his passage, he embarked upon a ship sailing for Philadelphia.

The story of his arrival in the Quaker City is so famous that we must give it in his own words, as he wrote it down many years later for his son.

HIS ARRIVAL IN PHILADELPHIA

"I was in my working dress. I was dirty from my journey; my pockets were stuffed out with shirts and stockings, and I knew no soul or where to look for lodging. I was fatigued with traveling, rowing, and want of rest; I was very hungry; and my whole stock of cash consisted of a Dutch dollar and about a shilling in copper.

"The latter I gave the people of the boat for my passage, who at first refused it on account of my rowing; but I insisted on their taking it. A man is sometimes more generous when he has but a little money than when he has plenty, perhaps through fear of being thought to have but little. Then I walked up a street, gazing about, till, near the market house, I met a boy with bread.

"I had made many a meal on bread, and, inquiring where he had bought it, I went immediately to the baker's he directed me to, in Second Street, and asked for biscuit, intending such as we had in Boston; but they, it seems, were not made in Philadelphia. Then I asked for a three-penny loaf, and was told they had none such. So not considering or knowing the difference of money, and the greater cheapness nor the names of his bread, I bade him give me three-penny worth of any sort. He gave me, accordingly, three great puffy rolls. I was surprised at the quantity, but took it, and, having no room in my pockets, walked off with a roll under each arm, and eating the other.

"Thus I went up Market Street as far as Fourth Street, passing by the door of Mr. Read, my future wife's father, when she, standing at the door, saw me, and thought I made, as I certainly did, a most awkward, ridiculous appearance. Then I turned and went down Chestnut Street and part of Walnut Street, eating my roll all the way, and, coming round, found myself again at Market Street wharf, near the boat I came in, to which I went for a draft of the river water; and one of my rolls having satisfied me, I gave the other two to a woman and her child who had come down the river in the boat with us, and were waiting to go farther.

"Thus refreshed, I walked again up the street, which by this time had many clean-dressed people in it who were all walking the same way. I joined them, and thereby was led to a great meeting-

HE WALKED OFF WITH A ROLL UNDER EACH ARM, AND EATING THE OTHER

house of the Quakers near the market.

"I sat down among them, and, after looking round awhile and hearing nothing said, being drowsy through labor and want of rest the preceding night, I fell fast asleep and continued so till the meeting broke up, when one was kind enough to rouse me. This was, therefore, the first house I was in, or slept in, in Philadelphia."

BITS OF WISDOM BY BENJAMIN FRANKLIN

He that cannot obey will never command.

We may give advice, but we cannot give conduct. However, remember this: They that will not be counseled cannot be helped; and further, if you will not hear reason, she will surely rap your knuckles.

A wise and brave man will dare to own that he was wrong.

Being ignorant is not so much a shame as being unwilling to learn.

Early to bed, and early to rise, makes a man healthy, wealthy, and wise.

29

THE BOYHOOD OF A PRESIDENT

(ABRAHAM LINCOLN)

BY AMY STEEDMAN

IT WAS certainly a cold and comfortless way of beginning life to be born in a log cabin, especially when it was wintertime, and the cabin had no door to keep out the wind, and no window to let in the light. Abraham Lincoln could scarcely have started life in a poorer home than that little log cabin, set in the midst of a barren and desolate wilderness in the State of Kentucky, where he first opened his eyes on the world on February 12, 1809.

It was to be hoped that the new baby would grow into a strong, brave boy, for there was no use for weaklings in the rough, dangerous life that awaited him. Even his mother, who rocked him in her arms, had early learned to handle a rifle that she might defend herself and her children when the father, Thomas Lincoln, was away. They were accustomed to all sorts of dangers and hardships, for there were many wild animals in the woods, and they were never quite safe from the fear of Indians.

At six years old Abe had learned to fish and to hunt, although he was still too small to be trusted with a gun. One of his favorite amusements was to swing across the creek holding on to the branch of a sycamore tree, and one day while he and another small boy were enjoying themselves in that way, Abe lost his hold and disappeared with a terrific splash into the water below. The other boy was quite equal to the occasion, and, waiting till he reappeared, leaned over and dragged him out with the greatest difficulty. If it had not been for the presence of mind of the other child, Abe would certainly have been drowned and America would never have known one of the greatest and most famous of her Presidents.

"It is time those children had some learning," said their father thoughtfully, when Abe was seven years old and his sister Sarah a year or so older. "There's a man come to that shanty half a mile away, and he says he is going to keep a school. What do you say to sending the children to him?"

"Well," said their mother doubtfully, "he is a queer sort of man to be a schoolmaster. He can't write himself."

"He can read, so he says," replied Thomas Lincoln, "and the children could learn that, anyway."

Thomas Lincoln had spent such a busy roving life that he had never had time to learn either to read or to write, and at the time he was married he could not even sign his own name. His wife had had a little education and was determined that he should at least learn to write his name, so with great patience she taught him how to hold a pen and make the letters, although his great strong hands were much more at home holding his gun or his ax. But nevertheless he was most anxious that his children should learn all that he had missed, although it puzzled him greatly to think where the money was to come from to pay their schooling.

SCHOOL-DAYS

There was certainly not much to be learned at this first school to which Abe was sent, and in a few weeks the children knew as much as their master, which was saying but little.

There was a better school four miles away where the master could both read and write, and although it was a long way for the children to walk, they were

THE BOY DRAGGED HIM OUT WITH THE GREATEST DIFFICULTY

sturdy and strong, and set off gayly each morning, carrying their dinner of hoe cake, which was all the dinner they ever had.

The log cabin could now boast the beginning of a library, for besides the Bible and Catechism there was an old spelling-book out of which the children learned their lessons. The Bible was the one book which Abe had known from his babyhood, for his mother read it aloud every Sunday and sometimes on other days too. It was both story-book and lesson-book, for the stories Abe knew before he could read, and his first reading-lessons were spelled out from it.

It was when Abe was about eight years old that he began to learn to know what it really meant to be a pioneer boy. The farm in Kentucky was not a very successful affair, and Thomas Lincoln made up his mind to try his luck in the new free State of Indiana, where there seemed better prospects of getting on.

THE JOURNEY

It was a journey of a hundred miles from the old home in Kentucky to the new one in Indiana, and while the father took most of their belongings by boat, the mother and two children set out on the journey overland, with two horses to carry the bedding and on which they could ride by turns when they were tired. They were seven days on the road, and at night the little party camped out under the stars with their blankets spread on the ground. It was not a very safe way of traveling, and there was many a danger lurking around, but neither mother nor children dreamed of being afraid. Fear was a thing with which pioneers had nothing to do.

HOW THE CABIN WAS BUILT

When at last the whole family arrived in Spence County, Indiana, the first thing to be done was to build some sort of shelter for themselves and their goods. A road had been cut through the forests, but all the clearing had still to be done, and there was plenty of work for Abe, small as he was. His little ax was needed for serious work now, and not only for play, as he was quite able to cut the poles for the cabin which his father was building. In a very short time he learned to use his ax as a pioneer boy should do.

At first it was only possible to build a "half-faced camp," which was merely a cabin enclosed on three sides with one side open, and which, in spite of the log fires, was a bitterly cold shelter in winter-time. But when spring came and the land was cleared enough to plant corn and vegetables, a strong log hut was begun, and Abe lent a willing hand, remembering the bitter winds of the past winter.

It was hard work, for the great unhewn logs had all to be notched and fitted together and the crevices filled with clay; and then there was the loft to be made and a door and window fitted in.

Abe learned, too, how to make stools and a table, and by this time the muscles of his arms were like whipcord, and he could swing his ax like a man.

A story is told of him in after-days, of how he visited a hospital of wounded soldiers and shook hands with three thousand of them, all eager to take the hand of their hero. Some friends wondered that his arm was not crippled by so much handshaking, but he only smiled and said, "The hardships of my early life gave me strong arms."

Then he went to the open door and took up a heavy ax which was lying there, and began to chop a log of wood so vigorously that the chips flew in all directions. When he stopped he "extended his right arm to full length, holding the ax out horizontally without its even quivering as he held it." Strong men who looked on—men accustomed to manual labor—could not hold the ax in that position for a moment.

BANG! WENT THE GUN, AND BACK WENT ABE

After learning to be so useful with his ax, it was only fair that Abe should be taught to handle a rifle, and his father promised to begin to teach him at once.

"You'll be able to go hunting and shoot turkey and deer, and will keep us supplied with game," said his father.

Abe's eye glistened, and he could scarcely sleep that night in his corner of the loft, he was so delighted and excited over the thought of that rifle. A rifle is rather a difficult thing for a small boy of eight to manage, but Abe was determined to learn to shoot, and in a short time he covered himself with glory.

HIS FIRST SHOT

"Mother, mother!" he cried, bursting like a small whirlwind into the cabin, "there's a flock of turkeys out there. I'm sure I could shoot one if I might have the rifle."

His mother looked out through one of the loopholes of the log hut.

"Sure enough," she said, "they are turkeys. You might try a shot," and she fetched the gun, which was always kept ready loaded.

Abe bobbed up and down excitedly while his mother fixed the gun into the loophole and warned him to be careful. Then he steadied himself, tried to take aim and pulled the trigger.

Bang! went the gun, and back went Abe almost head over heels, but in an instant he scrambled up and rushed out. The smoke was just clearing away, and sure enough there on the ground lay a large fat turkey, shot dead.

"I've killed one," shouted Abe, "and

it's a monster. Mother, did you ever see such a big one?" and he struggled to lift the bird on high for her to see.

Just then his father came hurrying up.

"What's all this firing about?" he asked anxiously.

"I've killed a turkey," said Abe, bursting with pride.

"Did you do that?" asked his father in amazement.

"Nobody else did it," said Abe with a chuckle. Of course it was nothing but an accident, and altogether the fault of the turkey for getting in the way of the bullet, but it was a great triumph for Abe, all the same.

ABE LEARNS TO WRITE

All this time Abe had kept on steadily with his reading whenever he had time, especially in the long winter evenings when he could read by the firelight. Lamps and candles were luxuries no settler could afford, but wood was plentiful, and it was easy to heap the fire high and make a splendid blaze.

He was careful, too, not to forget his writing, and he practiced writing his own name in the snow or with a charred stick on slabs of wood. His father was not always pleased to find every smooth surface in the house scrawled over with black marks, but he had a great respect for "learning," and when he found that Abe was teaching himself to write, he was quite proud of the boy.

When spring came round and they were working together in the fields, Abe took a stick and began writing his name

with great care in the soft earth. "A.B.R.A.H.A.M L.I.N.C.O.L.N," he wrote.

"What is the boy doing?" asked a neighbor who happened to be passing and stopped to talk to Thomas Lincoln.

"Oh! he's writing," said his father carelessly.

The man looked astonished.

"Can he write?" he asked. "What does the writing say?"

"It's my name," said Abe, spelling the letters out one by one and pointing to them in turn.

The two men looked with respectful admiration at the young genius and shook their heads. Such cleverness was beyond them. Little did they dream that the name of Abraham Lincoln would some day be written, not only on the soil of Indiana but in every annal of the United States.

THE BOY LOSES HIS MOTHER

As time went on, Abe began to long for other books to read besides the Bible, the Catechism, and the old spelling-book. There must surely be many other books in the world, he thought, but the difficulty was to get hold of them.

Then a sad thing happened which for a while made him forget all about his longing for books. His mother died suddenly, and the little family in the log hut was left very desolate.

Sarah was only eleven years old and could not manage the housework very well, although Abe was very handy and helped her a good deal. The home soon began to look neglected and untidy, and Abe felt his mother's loss keenly. In-

HE SAT UP LATE INTO THE NIGHT TO READ HIS BELOVED BOOKS

deed it seemed as if all the sunshine had faded out of his life until one evening when his father returned carrying a parcel under his arm.

HE BEGINS HIS LIBRARY

"I've found something that will please you, my boy," he said kindly, and undoing the parcel he brought out the "Pilgrim's Progress."

"Where did you find it?" asked Abe wonderingly. Such things were not usually to be found in the woods or fields, neither did they drop from heaven.

"I didn't exactly find it," said his father, smiling. "I saw it when I was in Pierson's house and borrowed it for you."

Abe was turning over the leaves, and he took a deep breath of delight.

"It looks good," he said.

He was so eager to begin that he could eat no supper, and when he had finished reading it he turned back and began it all over again. The book made him so happy that his father tried to get him another, and this time it was "Æsop's Fables," which charmed Abe even more than the "Pilgrim's Progress" had done. He read it so often that he could ere long repeat most of the fables by heart.

Abe's mind was very good ground in which to sow such seed, and in after-life it blossomed out into a wonderful power of story-telling and a marvelous memory for anecdotes.

PLEASURE OR DUTY?

But although reading was very pleasant it was somewhat apt to interfere with the day's work, and by and by Abe's father began to grow impatient.

"Come, put away your book, there's too much work to be done to waste time over reading," said his father.

"In a minute," said Abe.

"That's what makes boys lazy," said the father, "reading books when they ought to be at work."

"Only a minute, and then I'll go," said Abe, scarcely paying any attention to what his father was saying.

That of course could not be allowed.

"Put the book down and come at once," said his father sternly.

Abe shut the book slowly.

35

"Good boys should obey at once," said his father; "they should not need to be driven like cattle."

Abe had never before shown any signs of disobedience and he did not mean to be disobedient now, but those books seemed to lay a spell upon him which it was difficult to resist.

His father began to fear he was growing lazy, and everyone shook their heads over the boy and his books. His cousin Denis declared that "Abe was always reading, scribbling, ciphering, writing poetry, and such like," and that he was "awful lazy"; but it was a curious kind of laziness, for it meant seizing every scrap of spare time between work to study, and sitting up late into the night to read his beloved books. He was so hungry for knowledge that he could not keep away from books although "he had not a lazy bone in his body." He could not help dreaming a little, and sometimes the threshing and chopping and other work suffered, but who could help dreaming over the delights of "Robinson Crusoe" and the "Life of Washington" which just then, at ten years old, opened a new world to him?

THE NEW MOTHER HELPS

After a while life became more cheerful in the log hut, for Thomas Lincoln married again, and the stepmother brought brightness and comfort into the home once more. She was a widow with three children, which made a merry party in the log cabin, and she also had a quantity of furniture and household goods, so that in a short time the log hut was transformed into quite an elegant abode.

The first thing the new mother insisted upon was that a wooden flooring should be laid down, and also that there should be real glass windows and a door with hinges. The children's clothes, too, were made neat and tidy, and there was something else for dinner besides hoe cakes.

Abe's stepmother was not inclined to call the boy lazy as other people did when he pored over his books. She was anxious to help him, and when for the first time a school was opened in Indiana, she was anxious that all the children should be sent to it.

"It's a good chance for you, Abe," she said. "You ought to learn something about arithmetic as soon as you can."

It was a curious kind of school and a very queer set of pupils. The school was a rough log hut with a roof so low that the master could scarcely stand upright, and the windows were only holes covered with greased paper which did not allow much light to filter through. The one cheerful thing was the huge fireplace built to hold four-foot logs.

The children were gathered from far and near, all sizes and in all sorts of garments. Abe rather fancied himself in his new suit, made by his stepmother for the occasion. He had a linsey-woolsey shirt, buckskin breeches, a cap of coon skin, and no coat, for "overcoats" were unknown.

WHAT THE SCHOOLMASTER THOUGHT OF ABE

There was much for Abe to learn, and the schoolmaster, Andrew Crawford, found it a delight to teach anyone so eager and intelligent.

"Abe is a wonderful boy, the best scholar I ever had," he said to Thomas Lincoln. "He wants to know everything that anyone else knows, and does not see why he can't."

"That's Abe exactly," said his father. "I sometimes wish he liked work as much as he does a book."

"He wouldn't be such a good scholar if he did," said the schoolmaster.

"Maybe," answered his father, "but work is more important than books in the backwoods."

"But Abe is not going to live always in the backwoods," said the master. "He is a boy who is sure to make his mark in the world. He is an honest, straight boy too, as well as being clever. Only the other day I found someone had broken off a buck's horn which I had nailed to the schoolhouse, and when I asked who had done it, Abe immediately owned up and confessed that he had been hanging on to it."

"Ah!" said his father, "that's like him. He's been reading the 'Life of Washington,' and thought a deal of that story about his cutting the cherry tree with his new hatchet and then owning up handsomely."

"Well, he's a good boy," said the schoolmaster, "and he'll go far."

He meant to do his very best for the boy, and besides other things he began to teach his pupils manners and how to behave nicely "in society." The school-room was turned into a parlor for the time being, and the children were supposed to be ladies and gentlemen, as they came in one by one and made their bow and were introduced to each other.

It was no easy matter for Abe to learn drawing-room manners. Although he was scarcely fifteen he was six feet high, and he did not in the least know what to do with his long arms and legs. His feet, too, were very much in the way, and he never realized before how huge his hands were or what a long distance of bare leg there was between his buckskin breeches and his shoes.

Abraham was certainly an awkward-looking boy, for his long legs were out of all proportion to his body, and his small head looked almost comical set on the top of such a tall maypole. People when they looked at him would smile and ask what he meant to be when he was a man.

"I am going to be President of the United States," he said with a chuckle, and everyone thought it was a very good joke.

The tall, ungainly boy, in his queer, shabby clothes, living in the backwoods, willing to do the hardest work for the smallest pay, what would he ever have to do with the ruling of a great nation, or the fate of thousands of his countrymen? No wonder they thought it a good joke; but a little more than forty years afterward the whole world was mourning the loss of Abraham Lincoln, the noblest President America had had since the days of Washington.

THE CHILD OF URBINO

(RAPHAEL)

BY LOUISE DE LA RAMEE

IT WAS in the spring of the year that a little boy stood looking out of a grated casement into the calm, sunshiny day. He had hazel eyes, and fair hair cut straight above his brows; he wore a little blue tunic with some embroidery about the throat of it, and had in his hand a little round flat cap of the same color. He was Raphael, the seven-year-old son of Signor Giovanni Sanzio.

He was a very happy little boy here in this stately, yet homely and kindly Urbino. He had the dearest old grandfather in all the world; he had a loving mother, and he had a father who was very tender to him, and painted him among the angels of heaven, and was always full of such true love of art that the child breathed it with every breath, as he could breathe the sweetness of a cowslipbell when he held one in his hands up to his nostrils.

Can you not picture to yourself good, shrewd, wise Giovanni Sanzio, with his old father by his side, and his little son running before him, in the holy evening time of a feast day, with the deep church bells swaying overhead, and the last sun-rays smiting the frescoed walls, the stone bastions, the blazoned standard on the castle roof, the steep city rocks shelving down into the greenery of cherry orchard and of pear tree?

"Let him alone; he will paint all this some day," said his wise father, who loved to think that his brushes and his colors would pass in time to Raphael, whose hands would be stronger to hold them than his own had been.

No doubt the good folks of Urbino laughed at him often for a little moonstruck dreamer, so many hours did he stand looking, looking—only looking— as eyes have a right to do that see well and not altogether as others see.

At this time Urbino was growing into fame for its pottery work: those big dishes and bowls, those marriage plates and pharmacy jars which it made, were beginning to rival the products of its neighbor Gubbio, and when its duke wished to send a bridal gift, or a present on other festal occasions, he often chose some service or some rare platter of his own Urbino ware.

MAESTRO BENEDETTO

There was a master-potter of the Montefeltro at that time, one Maestro Benedetto Ronconi, who in that day enjoyed the honor of all the duchy, and did things very rare and fine in the Urbino ware. He lived within a stone's throw of Giovanni Sanzio, and was a gray-haired, handsome, somewhat stern and pompous man, now more than middle-aged, who had one beauteous daughter, by name Pacifica. He cherished Pacifica well, but not so well as he cherished the things he wrought—the deep round nuptial plates and oval massive dishes that he painted with Scriptural stories and strange devices, and landscapes such as those he saw around, and flowing scrolls with Latin mottoes in black letters, and which, when thus painted, he consigned with an anxiously beating heart to the trial of the ovens, and which sometimes came forth from the trial all cracked and blurred and marred, and sometimes emerged in triumph and came into his trembling hands iridescent and lovely with those lustrous and opaline hues which we admire in them to this day as the especial glory of majolica.

Maestro Benedetto was an ambitious and vain man, and had had a hard, labored manhood, working at his potter's wheel and painter's brush before Urbino ware was prized in Italy or even in the duchy. Now, indeed, he was esteemed at his due worth, and his work was so also, and he was passably rich, and known as a good artist beyond the Marches.

The house of Maestro Benedetto was a long stone building, with a loggia at the back all over-climbed by hardy rose trees, and looking on a garden that was more than half an orchard, and in which grew abundantly pear trees, plum trees, and wood strawberries.

The little son of neighbor Sanzio ran in and out this bigger wider house and garden of Maestro Benedetto at his

pleasure, for the maiden Pacifica was always glad to see him, and even the somber master-potter would unbend to him, and show him how to lay the color on to the tremulous, fugitive, unbaked biscuit.

Pacifica was a lovely young woman

THE MAIDEN PACIFICA WAS ALWAYS GLAD TO SEE HIM

of some seventeen or eighteen summers; and perhaps Raphael was but remembering her when he painted in his after-years the face of his Madonna di San Sisto. He loved her as he loved everything that was beautiful and every one who was kind; and almost better than his own beloved father's studio, almost better than his dear old grandsire's cheerful little shop, did he love this grave, silent, sweet-smelling, sun-pierced, shadowy old house of Maestro Benedetto.

39

LUCA TORELLI

Maestro Benedetto had four apprentices or pupils in that time learning to become *figuli,* but the one whom Raphael liked the most (and Pacifica too) was one Luca Torelli, of a village above in the mountains—a youth with a noble, dark, pensive beauty of his own, and a fearless gait, and a supple, tall, slender figure that would have looked well in the light coat of mail and silken doublet of a man-at-arms.

In sooth, the spirit of Messer Luca was more made for war and its risks and glories than for the wheel and the brush of the bottega; but he had loved Pacifica ever since he had come down one careless holy-day into Urbino, and had bound himself to her father's service in a heedless moment of eagerness to breathe the same air and dwell under the same roof as she did.

He had gained little for his pains; to see her at mass and at meal times, now and then to be allowed to bring water from the well for her or to feed her pigeons, to see her gray gown go down between the orchard trees and catch the sunlight, to hear the hum of her spinning wheel, the thrum of her viol—this was the uttermost he got of joy in two long years; and how he envied Raphael running along the stone floor of the loggia to leap into her arms, to hang upon her skirts, to pick the summer fruit with her, and sort with her the autumn herbs for drying!

"I love Pacifica!" he would say, with a groan, to Raphael; and Raphael would say, with a smile, "Ah, Luca, so do I!"

"It is not the same thing, my dear," sighed Luca; "I want her for my wife."

"I shall have no wife; I shall marry myself to painting," said Raphael, with a little grave, wise face looking out from under the golden roof of his fair hair. For he was never tired of watching his father painting the saints with their branch of palm on their ground of blue or of gold, or Maestro Benedetto making the dull clay glow with angels' wings and prophets' robes and holy legends told in color.

Now, one day, as Raphael was standing and looking thus at his favorite window in the potter's house, his friend, the handsome, black-browed Luca, who was also standing there, did sigh so deeply and so deplorably that the child was startled from his dreams.

LUCA'S DESPAIR

"Good Luca, what ails you?" he murmured, winding his arms about the young man's knees.

"O, 'Faello!" mourned the apprentice woefully. "Here is such a chance to win the hand of Pacifica if only I had talent—such talent as that Giorgio of Gubbio has! If the good Father had only gifted me with a master's skill, instead of all this bodily strength and sinew, like a wild hog of the woods, which avails me nothing here!"

"What chance is it?" asked Raphael, "and what is there new about Pacifica? She told me nothing, and I was with her an hour."

"Dear simple one, she knows nothing of it," said Luca, heaving another tre-

40

mendous sigh from his heart's deepest depths. "You must know that a new order has come in this very forenoon from the duke; he wishes a dish and a jar of the very finest and firmest majolica to be painted with the story of Esther, and made ready in three months from this date, to then go as his gifts to his cousins of Gonzaga. He has ordered that no.cost be spared in the work, but that the painting thereof be of the best that can be produced, and the prize he will give is fifty scudi. Now, Maestro Benedetto, having known some time, it seems, of this order, has had made in readiness several large oval dishes and beautiful jars; he gives one of each to each of his pupils—to myself, to Berengario, to Tito, and to Zenone. The master is sorely distraught that his eyesight permits him not himself to execute the duke's commands; but it is no secret that should one of us be so fortunate as to win the duke's approbation, the painter who does so shall become his partner here and shall have the hand of Pacifica. Now you see, 'Faello mine, why I am so bitterly sad of heart, for I am a good craftsman enough at the wheel and the furnace, and I like not ill the handling and the molding of the clay, but at the painting of the clay I am but a tyro, and Berengario or even the little Zenone will beat me; of that I am sure."

Raphael heard all this in silence, leaning his elbows on his friend's knee, and his chin on the palms of his own hands. He knew that the other pupils were better painters by far than his Luca, though not one of them was such a good-hearted or noble-looking youth, and for none of them did the maiden Pacifica care.

"How long a time is given for the jar and the dish to be ready?" he asked, at length.

"Three months, my dear," said Luca, with a sigh sadder than ever. "But if it were three years, what difference would it make? You cannot cudgel the divine grace of art into a man with blows as you cudgel speed into a mule, and I shall be a dolt at the end of the time, as I am now."

Raphael was very pensive for a while; then he raised his head, and said:

"I have thought of something, Luca. But I do not know whether you will let me try it."

RAPHAEL KISSED HIM, AND SAID, "NOW LISTEN"

"You angel child! What would your old Luca deny to you? But as for helping me, my dear, put that thought out of your little mind forever, for no one can help me, 'Faello, not the saints themselves, since I was born a dolt!"

Raphael kissed him, and said, "Now listen!"

THE PRIZE

A few days later Signor Benedetto informed his pupils of the duke's command and of his own intentions; he did not pronounce his daughter's name to the youths, but he spoke in terms that were clear enough to assure them that whoever had the good fortune and high merit to gain the duke's choice of his pottery should have the honor of becoming associated in his own famous bottega.

Not much attention was given to maidens' wishes in those times, and no one thought the master-potter either unjust or cruel in thus suiting himself before he suited his daughter. And what made the hearts of all the young men quake and sink the lowest was the fact that Signor Benedetto offered the competition, not only to his own apprentices, but to any native of the duchy of Urbino. For who could tell what hero might not step forth from obscurity and gain the great prize of this fair hand of Pacifica's? And with her hand would go many a broad gold ducat, and heritage of the wide old gray stone house, and many an old jewel and old brocade that were kept there in dusky sweet-smelling cabinets, and also more than one good

piece of land, smiling with corn and fruit trees, outside the gates in the lower pastures to the westward.

"Had I been you," Giovanni Sanzio ventured once to say respectfully to Signor Benedetto, "I think I should have picked out for my son-in-law the best youth that I knew, not the best painter; for be it said in all reverence, my friend, the greatest artist is not always the truest man, and by the hearthstone humble virtues have sometimes high claim."

Then Signor Benedetto had set his stern face like a flint, knowing very well what youth Messer Giovanni would have liked to name to him.

"I have need of a good artist in my bottega to keep up its fame," he had said stiffly. "My vision is not what it was, and I should be loath to see Urbino ware fall back, while Pesaro and Gubbio and Castel Durante gain ground every day. Pacifica must pay the penalty, if penalty there be, for being the daughter of a great artist."

Mirthful, keen-witted Sanzio smiled to himself, and went his way in silence; for he did not bow down in homage before the old master-potter's estimation of himself.

"Poor Pacifica!" he thought; "if only my 'Faello were but older!"

IN THE ATTIC

Meanwhile, where think you was Raphael? Half the day, or all the day, and every day whenever he could? Where think you was he? Well, in the attic of Luca, before a bowl and a dish almost as big as himself. The attic was a breezy, naked place, underneath the arches supporting the roof of Maestro Benedetto's dwelling. Each pupil had one of these garrets to himself—a rare boon, for which Luca came to be very thankful, for without it he could not have sheltered his angel; and the secret that Raphael had whispered to him that day of the conference had been, "Let *me* try and paint it!"

"Let me try!" said the child a hundred times. He would tell no one, only Luca would know; and if he failed—well, there would only be the spoiled pottery to pay for, and had he not two whole ducats that the duke had given him when the court had come to behold his father's designs for the altar frescoes at San Dominico di Cagli?

So utterly in earnest was he, and so intense and blank was Luca's absolute despair, that the young man had in turn given way to his entreaties. "Never can I do aught," he thought, bitterly, looking at his own clumsy designs. "And sometimes by the help of cherubs the saints work miracles."

"It will be no miracle," said Raphael, hearing him murmur this; "it will be myself, and that which the dear God has put into me."

From that hour Luca let him do what he would, and through all these lovely early summer days the child came and shut himself up in the garret, and studied, and thought, and worked, and knitted his fair brows, and smiled in tranquil satisfaction, according to the mood he was in and the progress of his labors.

HE LABORED AS EARNESTLY AS IF HE WERE A MAN GROWN

Pacifica herself did wonder that he deserted her so perpetually for the garret. But one day when she questioned him, the sweet-faced rogue clung to her and murmured, "Oh, Pacifica, I do want Luca to win you, because he loves you so; and I do love you both!" And she grew pale and answered him, "Ah, dear, if he could!" and then said never a word more but went to her distaff; and Raphael saw great tears fall off her lashes down among the flax.

She thought he went to the attic to watch how Luca painted, and loved him more than ever for that, but knew in the hopelessness of her heart—as Luca also knew it in his—that the good and gallant youth would never be able to create anything that would go as the duke's gifts to the Gongaza of Mantua. And she did care for Luca! She had spoken to him but rarely indeed, yet passing in and out of the same doors, and going to the same church offices, and dwelling always beneath the same roof, he had found means of late for a word, a flower, a serenade. And he was so handsome and so brave, and so gentle, too, and so full of deference. Poor Pacifica cared not in the least whether he could paint or not. He could have made her happy.

In the attic Raphael passed the most anxious hours of all his sunny little life. He would not allow Luca even to look at what he did. He barred the door and worked; when he went away he locked his work up in a wardrobe. The swallows came in and out of the window, and fluttered all around him. Raphael worked on, not looking off, though clang of trumpet, or fanfare of cymbal often told him there was much going on worth looking at down below. He was only seven years old, but he labored as earnestly as if he were a man grown, his little rosy fingers gripping that pencil which was to make him in life and death famous as kings are not famous.

He had covered hundreds of sheets with designs before he had succeeded in getting embodied the ideas that haunted him. When he had pleased himself at last, he set to work to transfer his imaginations to the clay in color.

Ah, how glad he was now that his father had let him draw from the time he was two years old, and that of late Messer Benedetto had shown him something of the mysteries of painting on biscuit and producing the metallic luster which was the especial glory of the pottery of the duchy!

Midsummer was come; the three months all but a week had passed by. It was known that every one was ready to compete for the duke's choice.

One afternoon Raphael took Luca by the hand and said to him, "Come."

He led the young man up to the table, beneath the window, where he had passed so many of these ninety days of the spring and summer.

Luca gave a great cry, and stood gazing, gazing, gazing. Then he fell on his knees and embraced the little feet of the child; it was the first homage that he, whose life became one beautiful song of praise, received from man.

"Dear Luca," he said softly, "do not do that. If it be indeed good, let us thank God."

What his friend saw were the great oval dish and the great jar or vase standing with the sunbeams full upon them, and the brushes and the tools and the colors all strewn around. And they shone with lustrous opaline hues and wondrous flame-like glories and gleaming iridescence, like melted jewels, and there were all manner of graceful symbols and classic designs wrought upon them; and their borders were garlanded with cherubs and flowers, and the landscapes were the tender, homely landscapes round about Urbino; and the mountains had the solemn radiance that the Apennines wore at evening-time; and amid the figures there was one supreme, white-robed, golden-crowned Esther, to whom the child painter had given the face of Pacifica. And this wondrous creation, wrought by a baby's hand, had safely and secretly passed the ordeal of the furnace, and had come forth without spot or flaw.

Luca ceased not from kneeling at the feet of Raphael, as ever since has knelt the world.

"Oh, wondrous boy! Oh, angel sent unto men!" sighed the poor apprentice, as he gazed; and his heart was so full that he burst into tears.

"Let us thank God," said little Raphael again; and he joined his small hands that had wrought this miracle, and said his *Laus Domini*.

When the precious jars and the great platter were removed to the wardrobe and shut up in safety, Luca said timidly, feeling twenty years in age behind the wisdom of this divine child: "But, dearest boy, I do not see how your marvelous and most exquisite accomplishment can advantage me. Even if you would allow it to pass as mine, I could not accept such a thing; it would be a fraud, a shame: not even to win Pacifica could I consent."

"Be not so hasty, good friend," said Raphael. "Wait just a little longer yet and see. I have my own idea. Do trust in me."

"Heaven speaks in you, that I believe," said Luca, humbly.

Raphael answered not, but ran downstairs, and, passing Pacifica, threw his arms about her in more than his usual affectionate caresses.

"Pacifica, be of good heart," he murmured, and would not be questioned, but ran homeward to his mother.

"Can it be that Luca has done well,"
thought Pacifica; but she feared the child's wishes had outrun his wisdom. He could not be any judge, a child of seven years, even though he were the son of that good and honest painter and poet, Giovanni Sanzio.

SUSPENSE

The next morning was midsummer day. Now, the pottery was all to be placed on this forenoon in the bottega of Signor Benedetto; and the Duke Guidobaldo was then to come and make his choice from among them; and the master-potter, a little because he was a courtier, and more because he liked to affect a mighty indifference and to show he had no favoritism, had declared that he would not himself see the competing works of art until the eyes of the Lord of Montefeltro also fell upon them.

As for Pacifica, she had locked herself in her chamber alone. The young men were swaggering about, and taunting each other, and boasting. Luca alone sat apart, thrumming an old lute. Giovanni Sanzio, who had ridden home at evening from Citta di Castello, came in from his own house and put his hand on the youth's shoulder.

"I hear the Pesaro men have brought fine things. Take courage, my lad. Maybe we can entreat the duke to dissuade Pacifica's father from this tyrannous disposal of her hand."

Luca shook his head wearily. There would be one beautiful thing there, indeed, he knew; but what use would that be to him?

"The child—the child—" he stammered, and then remembered that he must not disclose Raphael's secret.

"My child?" said Signor Giovanni. "Oh, he will be here; he will be sure to be here; wherever there is a painted thing to be seen, there always, be sure, is Raphael."

Then the good man sauntered within from the loggia, to exchange salutations with Ser Benedetto, who, in a suit of fine crimson with doublet of sad-colored velvet, was standing ready to advance bareheaded into the street as soon as the hoofs of the duke's charger should strike on the stones.

"You must be anxious in your thoughts," said Signor Giovanni to him. "They say a youth from Pesaro brings something fine; if you should find yourself bound to take a stranger into your workroom and your home——"

"If he be a man of genius, he will be welcome," answered Messer Ronconi, pompously. "Be he of Pesaro, or of Fano, or of Castel Durante, I go not back from my word; I keep my word, to my own hindrance even, ever."

"Let us hope it will bring you only joy and triumph here," said his neighbor, who knew him to be an honest man and a true, if over-obstinate and too vain of his own place in Urbino.

"Our lord the duke!" shouted the people standing in the street; and Ser Benedetto walked out with stately tread ·to receive the honor of his master's visit to his bottega.

Raphael slipped noiselessly up to his father's side, and slid his little hand into Sanzio's.

"You are not surely afraid of our good Guidobaldo!" said his father, with a laugh and some little surprise, for Raphael was very pale, and his lower lip trembled a little.

"No," said the child, simply.

THE EXHIBIT

The young duke and his court came riding down the street, and paused before the old stone house of the master-potter—splendid gentlemen, though only in their morning apparel, with noble Barbary steeds, fretting under them, and little pages and liveried varlets about their steps.

Usually, unless he went hunting or on a visit to some noble, Guidobaldo, like his father, walked about Urbino like any one of its citizens; but he knew the pompous and somewhat vainglorious temper of Messer Benedetto, and good-naturedly was willing to humor his harmless vanities. Bowing to the ground, the master-potter led the way, walking backward into his bottega; the courtiers followed their prince; Giovanni Sanzio with his little son and a few other privileged persons went in also at due distance.

At the farther end of the workshop stood the pupils and the artists from Pesaro and other places in the duchy whose works were there in competition. In all there were some ten competitors; poor Luca, who had set his own work on the table with the rest as he was obliged to do, stood hindmost of all, shrinking back, to hide his misery, into the deepest shadow of the deep-bayed latticed window.

On the narrow deal benches that served as tables on working days to the pottery painters were ranged the dishes and the jars, with a number attached to each—no name to any, because Signor Benedetto was resolute to prove his own absolute disinterestedness in the matter of choice; he wished for the best artist.

Prince Guidobaldo, doffing his plumed cap courteously, walked down the long room and examined each production in its turn. On the whole, the collection made a brave display of majolica, though he was perhaps a little disappointed at the result in each individual case, for he had wanted something out of the common run and absolutely perfect. Still with fair words he complimented Signor Benedetto on the brave show, and only before the work of poor Luca was he entirely silent, since indeed silence was the greatest kindness he could show to it; the drawing was bold and regular, but the coloring was hopelessly crude, glaring, and ill-disposed.

At last, before a vase and a dish that stood modestly at the very farthest end of the deal bench the duke gave a sudden exclamation of delight, and Signor Benedetto grew crimson with pleasure and surprise, and Giovanni Sanzio pressed a little nearer and tried to see over the shoulders of the gentlemen of the court, feeling sure that something rare and beautiful must have called forth that cry of wonder from the Lord of Montefeltro, and having seen at a glance that for his poor friend Luca there was no sort of hope.

"This is beyond all comparison," said Guidobaldo, taking the great oval dish up reverently in his hands. "Maestro Benedetto, I do felicitate you that you should possess such a pupil. He will be a glory to our beloved Urbino."

"It is indeed most excellent work, my lord duke," said the master-potter, who was trembling with surprise, and dared not show all the astonishment and emotion that he felt at the discovery of so exquisite a creation in his bottega. "It must be," he added, for he was a very honest man, "the work of one of the lads of Pesaro or Castel Durante. I have no such craftsman in my workshop. It is beautiful!"

"It is worth its weight in gold!" said the prince, sharing his emotion. "Look, gentlemen—look! Will not the fame of Urbino be borne beyond the Apennines and Alps?"

Thus summoned, the court and the citizens came to look, and averred that truly never in Urbino had they seen such painting on majolica.

"But whose is it?" said Guidobaldo, impatiently, casting his eyes over the gathered group in the background of apprentices and artists. "Maestro Benedetto, I pray you, the name of the artist; I pray you, quick!"

"It is marked number eleven, my lord," answered the master-potter. "Ho, you who reply to that number, stand out and give your name. My lord duke has chosen your work. Ho, there! do you hear me?"

But no one of the group moved. The

young men looked from one to another. Who was this nameless rival? There were but ten of themselves.

"Ho, there!" repeated Signor Benedetto, getting angry. "Cannot you find a tongue, I say? Who has wrought this work? Silence is but insolence to his highness and to me!"

Then the child of Sanzio loosened his little hand from his father's hold, and went forward, and stood before the master-potter.

"I painted it," he said, with a pleased smile; "I, Raphael."

Can you not fancy, without telling, the confusion, the wonder, the rapture, the incredulity, the questions, the wild ecstasy of praise, that followed on the discovery of the child artist?

Only the presence of Guidobaldo kept it in anything like decent quietude, and even he, all duke though he was, felt his eyes wet and felt his heart swell; for he himself was childless and for the joy that Giovanni Sanzio felt that day he would have given his patrimony and duchy.

He took a jewel hung on a gold chain from his own breast and threw it over Raphael's shoulders.

"There is your first guerdon," he said; "you will have many, O wondrous child, who shall live when we are dust!"

Raphael, who himself was all the while quiet and unmoved, kissed the duke's hand with sweetest grace, then turned to his own father.

"Is it true I have won my lord duke's prize?"

"Quite true, my angel!" said Giovanni Sanzio, with tremulous voice.

Raphael looked up at Maestro Benedetto.

"Then I claim the hand of Pacifica!"

THE CLAIM

There was a smile on all the faces round, even on the darker countenances of the vanquished painters.

"Oh, would indeed you were of age to be my son by marriage, as you are the son of my heart!" murmured Signor Benedetto. "Dear and marvelous child, you are but jesting, I know. Tell me what it is indeed that you would have. I could deny you nothing; and truly it is you who are my master."

"I am your pupil," said Raphael, with that pretty serious smile of his, his little fingers playing with the ducal jewel. "I could never have painted that majolica yonder had you not taught me the secrets and management of your colors. Now, dear maestro mine, and you, O my lord duke, do hear me! I by the terms of the contest have won the hand of Pacifica and the right of association with Messer Ronconi. I take these rights and I give them over to my dear friend Luca of Fano, because he is the honestest man in all the world, and does honor Signor Benedetto and loves Pacifica as no other can do so well, and Pacifica loves him; and my lord duke will say that thus all will be well."

So with the grave, innocent audacity of a child he spoke—this seven-year-old painter who was greater than any there.

Signor Benedetto stood mute, somber, agitated. Luca had sprung forward and dropped on one knee; he was as pale as ashes. Raphael looked at him with a smile.

"My lord duke," he said, with his little gentle smile, "you have chosen my work; defend me in my rights."

"Listen to the voice of an angel, my good Benedetto; heaven speaks by him," said Guidobaldo, gravely.

Signor Benedetto burst into tears.

"I can refuse him nothing," he said, with a sob. "He will give such glory unto Urbino as never the world hath seen!"

"And call down this fair Pacifica whom Raphael has won," said the sovereign of the duchy, "and I will give her myself as her dower as many gold pieces as we can cram into this famous vase. An honest youth who loves her and whom she loves—what better can you do, Benedetto? Young man, rise up and be happy. An angel has descended on earth this day for you."

But Luca heard not; he was still kneeling at the feet of Raphael, where the world has knelt ever since.

THE BOYHOOD OF A SCULPTOR

(Michaelangelo)

BY AMY STEEDMAN

On the 6th of March, in the year 1474, a special star was shining up in heaven, and down on earth a new-born baby was wailing. Lodovico Buonarroti, the proud father of the wailing atom of humanity, noted the star and most carefully, for he had been watching the sky to see if there was any sign there to foretell the fortune of his son.

"A fated and happy star," said he to himself joyfully, and afterward the wise men, who told fortunes by the stars, told him he was right. Not that Lodovico needed that anyone should assure him of the brilliant future that awaited the child. Had he not been born on Sunday, the luckiest of days, and was there not something about the tiny face that almost filled him with wondering awe and reverence? The secrets of heaven seemed still to linger about the baby who had so lately come to earth.

"We will call him Michaelangelo," said his father. It was the most splendid name he could think of, the name of the great warrior archangel, the messenger of God. Surely that name would fit the most glorious destiny that awaited the little one.

Lodovico, who was at that time podesta, or mayor, of Caprese, came of a very ancient and noble family which had won much distinction in the service of Florence. The little new archangel, then, must carry on the family record and help to make their name famous.

So it was with happy stars above and brightest hopes around him that Michaelangelo was born at Caprese, in the Casentino, not far from the holy ground of La Vernia, where the blessed Saint Francis suffered and was so highly blessed.

MICHAEL'S CHILDHOOD

Very soon after the birth of his son, Lodovico's term of office came to an end and he returned to Florence to take up his abode at the villa of Settignano, three miles from the city. Most of the people living round about the villa were stone-cutters, for there were many stone quarries there, and it was to the wife of one of these stone-cutters that the baby was sent to be nursed.

In the pure fresh mountain air little Michael grew strong both in mind and body, and the first sounds he learned to know were the ringing of the hammer and the working of the chisel in the stone quarries. In after years the great master used to say that if he had any good in him he owed it to the pure fresh mountain air, and that his love of carving came also from the stone-cutter's hut. Those sights and sounds of the quarries sunk deep into the child's heart, like a seed planted in a garden which was to spring up and blossom into a marvelous flower.

As the years went on other children were born to Lodovico, and Michaelangelo did not always seem such a wonderful boy in his father's eyes after all. Indeed he was rather a disappointment when he was old enough to be sent to the school kept by Maestro Francesco of Urbino. He was not at all a brilliant scholar, and his progress was slow and quite commonplace. It was even hinted that he was rather a dunce, and he certainly neglected his lessons whenever he possibly could, so that he might have more time for drawing. Give him a paper and pencil, and he forgot about everything else.

It was extremely vexing, for his father had set his heart on the boy being a credit to the family. What was the use of this drawing which seemed to be all that Michael cared about? He had no wish that a son of his should be an artist, and meanwhile it was most annoying to find the whitewashed walls of the house and terrace scribbled over with all sorts of designs and figures. There was nothing to be done but to whip the boy soundly and see if that would put any sense into his head.

But the whipping did little good after all. Michael only crept back again, sore in body and mind, to his beloved drawings, and seemed to think it was quite worth while to suffer pain for the sake of his work.

No one at home understood why he should be so obstinate and determined, but he had a friend who knew all about it and who was a great help and comfort. How Michael envied his friend Francesco! He was quite a little boy, but he was not obliged to go to school and learn dull lessons, and instead of

THERE WAS NOTHING TO DO BUT WHIP THE BOY
SOUNDLY

being whipped when he tried to draw pictures, he spent his whole day at the studio of Maestro Ghirlandajo, with nothing to do but to learn all about drawing and painting the livelong day. Every morning Francesco brought to Michael designs borrowed from the master's studio, and these Michael studied and faithfully copied, and every day the desire of his heart to become an artist grew stronger and ever stronger.

At last Lodovico saw that it was no use to scold and whip the boy. His heart was evidently set on becoming a painter, and nothing else would content him. The golden dreams which the father

51

had dreamed over the baby's birth slowly faded into gray disappointment. He decided that there was no chance now of Michael making a splendid fortune in the wool or silk trade, such as he had planned, but that the boy must be allowed to have his way and continue that useless drawing.

APPRENTICED

But although Lodovico was disappointed, having so many other children to educate and but little money coming in, still he was determined to do his very best for his son. In all Italy there was no painter to equal Domenico Ghirlandajo, and with him the boy should be placed.

It was rather a surprise to find that after all Michael was not an idler, and that the hours spent over his drawing had not been wasted. It was seldom that a boy was paid any wages during the first year of his apprenticeship, but Maestro Ghirlandajo found that Michael's work was so good that it was worth paying for, and it was arranged that he should receive a salary of nearly fifty dollars a year.

Now at last Michaelangelo was free to work with all his might at the thing he loved best, and like a young giant he put his whole mind and strength to his tasks. So well did he work and so wonderful was his talent that Ghirlandajo soon found there was not much left to teach him, and that he could actually make corrections on the master's own sketches.

They were working together one day in the great Chapel of Santa Maria Novella when the master went up silently behind the boy and watched him at work.

"This boy knows more than I do," said the master, amazed at the drawing he saw. It was time Michael should leave the studio.

So the year of his apprenticeship came to an end, and Michaelangelo commenced at once to study sculpture in the new art school opened by Lorenzo the Magnificent in the Garden of the Medici. Francesco was still his friend, and the boys now worked together in great content.

It was all a veritable wonderland for Michaelangelo; he had never dreamed of such treasures of beauty as were gathered together in the school of the Magnificent. Pictures, sculpture, engravings, gems, and enamels had all been collected by Duke Lorenzo, whose great desire was to encourage the love of art. The studio of Maestro Ghirlandajo had seemed a haven of joy; here was indeed a paradise.

It was not long before Lorenzo noticed the keen-faced boy working away so silently and diligently. He watched him as he modeled some figures in terra-cotta and was astonished at his masterly touch.

"Terra-cotta is but poor stuff to work on," said Lorenzo; "try instead what thou canst make of this block of marble."

THE FAUN

There was a marble face of an old faun lying close at hand, and Michael

52

set to work at once to copy it. He had never handled a chisel before and knew nothing about marble, but he never dreamed of saying so. He meant to carve that marble to the best of his ability. Difficulties were only there to be conquered.

So he worked away, forgetting all else but just the faun's face that was hidden in the block of marble. He chipped and he cut away, and as he worked the life seemed to spring out of the stone and an exact copy of the old faun grinned out of its marble prison.

Lorenzo was amazed next day when he returned to see what the boy had made of his piece of marble. It was the most wonderful copy he had ever seen, and it was even better than the original, for Michael had introduced ideas of his own, and had made the laughing mouth a little open to show the teeth and tongue of the faun. Lorenzo noticed this and turned with a smile to the young artist.

"Thou shouldst have remembered that old folks never keep all their teeth, but that some of them are always wanting," he said.

Lorenzo only meant this as a joke, but Michael was too much in earnest to understand jesting. He seized his hammer and struck out several of the teeth at once, never stopping to think if it would spoil his work.

This also pleased Lorenzo greatly, and he saw at once that here was no ordinary boy. There was nothing the

Magnificent loved so much as genius, and he at once arranged that Michaelangelo was to be received into the palace and become the companion of Lorenzo's sons.

From that moment fortune began to smile upon the boy of the Medici Gar-

AS HE WORKED THE LIFE SEEMED TO SPRING OUT OF THE STONE

den. Step by step he began to climb the ladder of fame. As he had seen within his first piece of marble the face of the faun, so he set out now to free with a giant's strength all the wondrous shapes that lay imprisoned in the marble blocks; and thus to-day the world owes some of its most beautiful statuary to the hammer and chisel of the boy who has been so well named Michaelangelo, after the warrior archangel, the Messenger of God.

THE BOYHOOD OF AN ENGLISH PAINTER

(SIR JOHN EVERETT MILLAIS)

BY AMY STEEDMAN

IT WAS at Southampton, in England, that John Millais was born on June 9, 1829, but it was at St. Heliers, on the island of Jersey, that he spent the first happy years of his childhood. St. Heliers was an ideal home for children. Here John and his elder brother William, and their sister Emily, played among the rocks to their hearts' content, catching sand-eels and crabs, poking about in the clear pools, and carrying home all sorts of treasures to fill baths and basins. It was rather a trial to their mother's patience, for she would much rather that the treasures had been left on the shore, and John, who was only four years old, was not a strong child, and she was anxious when he escaped from her care, and went to search for his beloved sea-beasts and sea-weeds. However, she soon found that the best way to keep him safe and happy, and out of mischief, was to let him have a pencil and paper on which to draw pictures.

John loved fishing off the pier and hunting in the pools, but he loved drawing pictures best of all. With a pencil and some scraps of paper he was perfectly happy, and he was never tired of drawing birds and butterflies, and any-thing else that caught his fancy. Lying flat on the ground, he covered his paper with all sorts of figures and animals, and very soon other people besides his mother began to notice his drawings, and to think them extremely clever.

"Mark my words, that boy will be a very great man some day, if he lives," said one of his uncles, after looking at his nephew's work.

John was not a difficult child to man-age at home. He was frank and truth-ful and very affectionate, but he always found it difficult to keep to rules, and it was impossible to drive him by force to do anything he had made up his mind not to do. It was his mother who taught him his lessons and gave him all the help he needed, and only once was the attempt made to send him to school.

That school was certainly not a suc-cess, and he had been there only two days when he was sent home in dire disgrace. Some rule had been broken, and the master declared that John should have a thrashing to teach him to keep the rules another time. But John did not see the justice of this, and be-fore the thrashing began he turned round quickly and bit the master's hand. Of course he was sent home at once, and told he need not come back any more after such disgraceful behavior.

Now John ought to have been very unhappy, and perhaps he was a good deal ashamed of that bite, but as far as school was concerned he was overjoyed to hear that he need not go back. To do lessons with his mother was quite a different thing altogether. With her to teach him he loved his lessons, instead of hating them with all his heart. "I owe everything to my mother," he used to say, when his childhood's days were past and he remembered all her love and patience with her little boy.

When John was about six years old there came a delightful and interesting change in his life, for the family went to live at Dinan in Brittany, and the children were charmed with all the new sights and sounds. There were many kinds of new things for John to draw, and greatest of all delights was the sight of the regiments of French soldiers as they marched through the town on their way to or from Brest. John loved the grand buildings and all the beautiful things his mother pointed out to him, but he was fascinated by those gorgeous French uniforms.

THE DRUM-MAJOR

In the Place du Gruxlin there was a bench from which the two boys could watch the roll-call and see the soldiers above the heads of the crowd, and they never failed to be there when they heard the drums beating and the sound of marching feet. John, of course, always

had his sketch-books with him, ready to draw all he could see.

He was working away one day, anxious to finish the portrait of a very smart drum-major in all the glory of his gold trappings, bearskin, and gold-

IT WAS FRIGHTENING TO BE CARRIED OFF BY THE SOLDIER-MAN

headed cane, when two of the officers crept up silently behind the bench and stood watching what he was doing. They said nothing until the portrait was finished, and then suddenly clapped him on the back and cried "Bravo!" They were so much astonished at the child's clever drawing that they returned with the boy to his home, as they wished to be introduced to his father and mother.

"The child should be sent at once to study in Paris," they declared, feeling sure they had discovered a genius.

The sketch of the drum-major was carried off by them to the barracks and there shown with great pride to the other officers. No one, however, would believe that it could be the work of a child of six, and one of the two officers started off post-haste to fetch little John to prove their words.

It was very frightening to be carried off by the strange soldier-man and taken to the barracks all alone, and John went in fear and trembling, but as soon as he got there and was given a pencil and a sheet of paper he forgot to be afraid or shy, and began at once to draw a portrait of the colonel smoking a big cigar. It turned out to be a most excellent likeness, and the other officers were delighted as well as astonished.

After two years at Dinan the family returned once more to St. Heliers, and there John began his first lessons in drawing, but his master, Mr. Bessel, soon told the boy's parents that there was nothing more he could teach John, and he advised them to take their little son up to London. It would be wiser to go at once to the president of the Royal Academy, and ask his advice as to what should be done with the young genius.

AT THE ACADEMY

Now the president of the Royal Academy had often been asked to look at the drawings of promising children, and he was not at all encouraging when John and his parents were shown in, and he heard what they had to say.

"Better make him a chimney-sweep than an artist," he said. He had seen so many young men try to paint pictures who would have been much better employed cleaning chimneys.

However, the great man said he would look at the child's sketches, and he evidently expected to see the usual kind of work, which so often only seems wonderful in the parents' eyes.

But when the sketches were produced and laid before him, he suddenly sat straight up and his eyes grew quite round with astonishment. He looked from the sketches to the little fellow standing there, and seemed to find it impossible to believe that such small childish hands could have produced such masterly work. Would John draw something here and now, he asked, that he might look on and judge?

There was no difficulty about that. John set himself promptly to work and began a drawing of the fight between Hector and Achilles. The president could scarcely believe his own eyes. He was sorry he had talked about chimneysweeping, and he handsomely apologized. Here was one of the few exceptions to his rule, and he strongly advised the boy's parents to have him trained to be an artist.

So it was settled that John should begin to work at once to draw from the cast in the British Museum, and after a short time, when he was nine years old, a place was found for him in the Academy of Art, the best school known at that time, kept by Henry Sars, portrait-painter.

The small boy with his delicate face, long fair curling hair, holland blouse, and turned-down frilled collar, was rather unlike the rest of the art students, and he was an easy victim for the bullying of the bigger boys. His fondness for work, his extreme diligence and wonderful talent were added aggravations to the other pupils, and one big hulking lazy fellow took a special delight in torturing the child.

Little Millais's life was made a burden to him by this big bully, and it only grew worse and worse as time went on. They both had entered the competition for the silver medal of the Society of Arts, and when it was known that John had carried off the prize, although he was only nine years old, his big rival was furious.

The very next day the bully sat in the studio watching like a great spider in a web for the arrival of the small boy, and biding his time until all the other pupils were gone, he seized on the defenseless little boy and began to take his cruel revenge.

In spite of his struggles, Millais was hung head downward out of the window and his legs were fastened securely with scarves and pieces of string to the iron bar of the window-guard. The child very soon became unconscious, and would most likely have died had not some passers-by in the street below noticed the hanging figure, and given the alarm by ringing the street door-bell.

After that the bully was seen no more at the Academy, and Millais was left in peace.

PRIZE DAY

The prize day at the Society of Arts was a red-letter day in the life of John Millais, for he was to receive his silver medal from the hands of his royal highness the Duke of Sussex. Dressed in a "white plaid tunic, with black belt and buckle; short white frilled trousers showing bare legs, with white socks and patent-leather shoes; a large white frilled collar, a bright necktie, and his hair in golden curls," he walked up when the secretary called out his name, "Mr. John Everett Millais."

There was a pause. The duke, who stood behind a high raised desk, saw no one to whom he was to hand the medal, and waited for the prize-winner to appear.

"The gentleman is a long time coming up," he said at last to the secretary.

"He is here, your royal highness," replied the secretary, and looking down over the desk, sure enough the duke saw that the gentleman was standing there,

HIS GOLDEN HEAD DID NOT REACH THE LEVEL OF THE TOP OF THE DESK

but such a very little gentleman he was, that his golden head did not reach to the level of the top of the desk.

A stool was then brought, and standing upon it the winner of the silver medal could be seen more clearly, and the duke patted his head and wished him every success.

"Remember, if at any time I can be of service to you, you must not hesitate to write and say so," he added, kindly.

That was a lucky promise for John, and it was not very long before he claimed the promised favor. Both he and William were very keen on fishing, and they had fished every year together in the Serpentine and Round Pond, until permission was withdrawn. Then John remembered the duke's promise, and wrote to ask if they might not be allowed to fish there as usual, and the request was granted at once. After that the pleasure was all the greater, for they were the envy of all the other little boys, who were only allowed to look on.

William was only two years older than John, and they always were together as much as possible, although William went to school and John still did his lessons with his mother. Both boys were "mad about art," and "knew every picture in the National Gallery by heart." One of their plays was to make a National Gallery of their own out of a large deal box, the pictures hung therein being about the size of a visiting-card or a good-sized envelope.

All the old masters were hung there. There were Rembrandts, Titians, Rubenses, Turners, etc., all with most gorgeous frames made out of the shining paper of crackers, and all carefully varnished to look like oil paintings.

It was a good thing that little Millais was child enough to play at such games, for in other ways he was so much older than his years, and he was getting on so quickly with his work, that it seemed as if he had already left his childhood behind him. He was only ten when he was admitted to be a student of the Royal Academy, "the youngest student who ever found entrance within its walls, and during his six years there he carried off in turn every honor the Academy had to bestow."

So the golden thread led onward, and the boy never loosed his hold upon it nor strayed into other paths. Little John Millais, "the child" of the Royal Academy, went steadily forward until he became Sir John Millais, its famous president.

THE BOYHOOD OF A FRENCH PAINTER

(Jean François Millet)

BY AMY STEEDMAN

On the coast of Normandy, high up on one of those frowning granite cliffs which overhang the sea, the little town of Gruchy is perched like a sea-bird's nest among the gray rocks. It has one long straggling street leading downwards to the shore, for here the cliffs have parted to fold in their cleft a little green valley, where the sheep can be led out to find pasture, and a possible path be found to the beach, where the harvest of seaweed is gathered and drawn up to enrich the fields above.

Looking outward to the sea, through a vista of frowning rocks, there is a gloomy grandeur about the view in front of the town which seems to hold only sad memories of storm and shipwreck, danger and death; but on the other side are pleasant green fields and sunny orchards, which give a homelike, happy air of peaceful content to the place where the hard-working people of Gruchy earn their daily bread.

In one of the strongly built, well-thatched houses of the little town there lived, about a hundred years ago, a peasant farmer called Jean Louis Millet. Like his father and grandfather before him, he worked in the fields all day and returned at night to the same comfortable old house which was large enough to shelter the three generations which now gathered under its roof. There was the grandmother, who looked after the household and took care of the children, there was Jean Louis himself, his wife and eight children.

The mothers of Gruchy had little time to look after their children, for, like the men, they were busy at work in the fields all day, and so it was in the house of Jean Louis Millet that the old grandmother was left in charge of the children and had most to do with their bringing up. She loved them all and cared tenderly for each one of them, but it was the eldest boy she loved best of all. It was in her arms the boy had first been laid, and she it was who carried him to the little gray church and gave him the name of Jean François: Jean after his father, and François after the saint of Assisi, who is the special protector of those who know poverty and who, working under the open sky, learn to know and love God's creatures and all the wonderful works of His hands.

The stories of saints were all well known to the old grandmother, and indeed she followed not afar off in their footsteps, living her honest, simple, upright life, and teaching little François to see God's hand in all the wonderful things around him, the golden glory of the gorse, the purple of the heather among the gray rocks, the mighty cliffs, the thundering waves that broke on the shore, as well as the piping notes of his "little sisters, the birds." And she taught him, too, to dread a wrong action more than death.

"Wake up, my little François," she would say in the early mornings, bending over his bed and waking him gently.

HE SAW HIS GREAT-UNCLE FURIOUSLY WAVING
TO HIM

"Thou knowest not how long the birds have been singing the glory of God."

There was another inmate of the old house who had a special love for the boy, and that was his great-uncle, the Abbé Charles Millet, a priest who suffered much persecution at the time of the French Revolution, but who was now the parish priest of Gruchy. It was a thrilling tale which François was never tired of hearing, how when the soldiers were hunting him down, this great-uncle had contrived a hiding-place close to his bed, and when the soldiers came unexpectedly one day, he had only just time to disappear before they burst in. The bed he had been sleeping in was still warm, and this the soldiers noticed at once.

But search as they might they could find no other trace of him, although he heard every word they were saying, and knew in his hiding-place that they were turning the house upside down in their search.

This old man was no idler, and he worked as hard as any other laborer in the fields, stowing away his breviary in his pocket and tucking up his cossack before he set to work. Wherever he when little François trotted by his side, for the old man could not bear the child out of his sight and was never tired of teaching and training him.

There was one day which François never forgot. He had wandered away from his uncle and had climbed down to the seashore, and was enjoying all the delights of fishing for tadpoles when he heard his name called and saw his great-uncle furiously waving to him from the cliff. He obeyed the call at once and climbed up, but the old man had been badly frightened, and as soon as he had the child safe and sound by his side again, his anxiety suddenly turned to anger. He took off his large three-cornered hat and beat François with it soundly and then drove him up to the house, still beating him with the hat as he went.

"Ah! I'll help thee to get home," he cried, with each flapping whack, and as

François' legs were short and fat they did not carry him very swiftly, and he spent some painful moments before he reached home.

After that François always regarded the three-cornered hat with distrust, for, as he said years afterward, "I was not of an age to understand a tenderness which showed itself by blows from a hat."

This great-uncle died when François was only seven, but by that time the boy was learning his lessons at school, which he had entered with flying colors some months before. He was a big boy for his age and strongly built, and had been already taught lessons at home, so that the elder children were rather proud of him when they took him for the first time to school. They boasted themselves of his strength and cleverness, and declared that he would be able to beat any boy of his own age or even older. So of course the first thing they did was to arrange a fight.

There was no boy quite so young as François in the school, but they picked out one a little older, the strongest and most promising they could find, and proceeded to arrange the quarrel. A chip of wood was laid on one boy's shoulder and the other was told, "I bet you don't dare knock that chip off."

It was felt none but a coward could refuse, and equally of course the other boy could not endure such an insult, so as soon as the chip was knocked off the battle began. In this fight François covered himself with glory, to the pride and delight of his supporters, who declared joyfully, "Millet is only six and

a half, and he has beaten a boy more than seven years old."

But when it came to lessons François was not quite such a success. He never could learn things by heart, and he was hopelessly dull at sums. Then, too, he had a bad habit of drawing capital letters in his copy-book when he ought to have been learning his lessons, and yet when asked any question he always answered well and sensibly. He was twelve years old when he went to church at Gréville to be confirmed, and the priest there was so much impressed by his intelligent answers that he asked him if he would like to be taught Latin.

"With Latin, my boy," said the priest, "you can become a priest or a doctor."

"No," said François, "I don't wish to be either; I wish to stay with my parents."

"Come all the same," said the priest; "you will learn."

So François learned to read the Bible and Virgil in Latin, and read them over and over again until he knew each word. But there was little time now to give to books, for he was old enough to help his father in the fields, and it was time he learned to mow the grass, make hay, bind the sheaves, thresh and winnow, plow and sow.

FATHER AND SON IN THE FIELD

So the father and son worked together at the daily common tasks of the ordinary laborer, but they saw in their work things which few ordinary laborers see. They both loved everything that was beautiful either in form or color, and nothing to them was commonplace. Years before, when François was a little boy, trotting along by

HE MADE CAREFUL DRAWINGS OF ALL HE SAW FROM THE WINDOW

his father's side, his father would stoop and pick a blade of grass and bid his little son look at it.

"See," he said, "how fine that is."

Or he would point to some tree they were passing and say, "Look at that tree, how large and beautiful it is, as beautiful as a flower."

One day they had stood together on the cliffs to watch the sunset, and the wonderful pageant of the crimson sky, and the golden glory of the shining sea

made François exclaim with delight. But his father stood still and reverently bared his head. "My son, it is God," he said, and François never forgot those words.

It was not until some years afterward that the boy began to try and draw pictures of the things he loved to look at, and it was the old engravings in the Bible that suggested the idea. He had little time for anything but the farm work, and he was quite content to do that thoroughly, to drive his furrow straight and clean, to work with a will in the fields he loved. But at the noonday rest, when the other workers lay sleeping, he took his pencil and made careful drawings of all that he saw from the window—the garden, the trees, and the rocks, and later on the figures he had seen at work or walking down the village street. The wonder and terror of the sea, the tall poplars round the gray church tower, the bent forms of old men, the women at their work, all these things filled his head, and the longing to draw them began to fill his heart.

So it was that Jean François, the peasant, brought all the wealth of his heart, his love of God and of nature, to the making of Millet the painter, and it was from the golden mine in the heart of the peasant that the painter drew all that was best and most beautiful in his art.

THE BOYHOOD OF A MUSICIAN
(Handel)

George Handel's father was a barber, in those days when a barber was a "leech," that is, a doctor, and also a dentist. He had great ambitions for his little boy. He wanted him to be a gentleman, for a barber-doctor was not a gentleman in Halle. So he planned that his son should be a lawyer.

But music was in George's blood and nothing would check his ambition to be a composer. In some way his mother or nurse smuggled a rickety spinet—an old-fashioned kind of piano—up to the attic where he slept, and, at night, when all the others were asleep, the strings covered with strips of cloth to deaden the sound, he played and played until he had mastered the instrument.

One night—so the artist says—somebody below awoke and heard celestial music aloft, and sensibly concluding that it was not the angels, lit a candle and led the whole household up the stairs. And there they stood, blinking about, looking amazed at the fair-haired little fellow who was playing away like a master.

So the good father procured for him the best of masters, and the little George Frederick became a famous composer.

He went away from home to London, where he had his struggles, and discouragements, and failures. He had to rent a theater of his own to have his operas performed, and the operas never suc-ceeded. So he turned—and it is such turnings from failures that so often have led men to success—to the oratorio. An oratorio is a long sacred composition for voices, the words nearly always taken from the Bible.

"THE MESSIAH"

One day, when the inspiration came upon him, he began his greatest composition, an oratorio of many parts, choruses, solos, accompaniments, which it takes two hours to render, and in twenty-three days he had finished it. It was "The Messiah." Whenever you think of Milton you think of "Paradise Lost"; when you think of Dante you think of his "Divine Comedy," and when you think of Handel you think of his "Messiah." Poor old King George III heard it, and when he listened to "The Pastoral Symphony" he said, "I could see the stars shining through it," and when the great chorus came to a wonderful acclaim of song at the close, the enraptured monarch together with the whole audience sprang to their feet. Ever since then at this "Hallelujah Chorus" it has always been the custom for the audience to stand, a tribute rendered to no other musical composer.

Handel was a crotchety fellow as he grew older. He never married, but he loved children, and he gave an organ to

YOUNG HANDEL
From a Painting by Margaret Isabel Dicksee

the London Foundling Hospital. They have a new one there now, but some of the old pipes that Handel gave have been wrought into the instrument, so that the children still listen to some of Handel's "music."

He was buried, of course, in Westminster Abbey, for he had become a naturalized Englishman. And on his monument you may see a carving that represents him writing one of the finest songs of his "Messiah," "I know that my Redeemer liveth."

When Lord Kinnoul once complimented Handel on the noble entertainment he had lately given the town, he replied:

"My lord, I should be sorry if I only entertained them—I wish to make them better."

Larghetto

I know that__ my Re - deem - er liv-eth

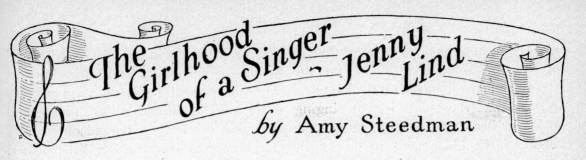

The Girlhood of a Singer — Jenny Lind

by Amy Steedman

ONCE upon a time, as the fairy tales say, there was born in the northern city of Stockholm a baby girl, who possessed as magic a gift as any princess in the fairy tales of Hans Andersen.

At the time when this baby was born, in the year 1820, Hans Andersen was a boy of fifteen, living not very far off, in Denmark, with all those beautiful fairy tales still in his head, and he did not meet our princess until she was quite grown up, but the moment he saw her he knew at once she was wonderful enough to have lived all along in one of his own fairy tales.

Jenny Lind, of course, was not really a fairy princess, nor indeed a princess at all. She was only a little Swedish girl, born in a poor home in Stockholm, where no one gave her a very warm welcome. Her young father could not earn money enough for himself and his wife, and now here was another mouth to fill! Even the baby's mother did not feel specially glad at the arrival of her little daughter. She, poor woman, had to work hard and kept a day school for other people's children, and a child of her own was rather in the way. Nobody guessed then that the baby had a magic gift which was to bring her fame and fortune. She was just a little unwelcome baby, christened very grandly "Johanna Maria," but known always by the funny, homely name of "Jenny."

Life was to be full of changes for little Jenny, and she was sent off at once to live in the country under the care of Carl Ferndal, organist and parish clerk of the church of Sollentuna. This man and his wife took good care of the adopted baby, and for four years Jenny lived the life of a country child and was as happy as the day was long. She was a real child of the woods and meadows, and loved nothing so much as rolling on the grass, picking wild flowers, and listening to the song of the birds. Birds and flowers seemed to have a special message for her, and she loved them with a love that never changed through all her changing life.

Then at the end of four years the country life vanished and town life began for the little maiden, for her mother quarreled with the organist and carried Jenny back to Stockholm.

PLEASANT TOWN NOISES

Everything was strange to the child in the big town. She did not like so many people or so much noise. She wished she was back in the woods listening to the birds. Town noises were all so frightening and ugly. Then suddenly she discovered that sounds could be pleasant in a town, too. Every morning as the soldiers marched up the streets, they made music on their bugles, and the tune they played went singing on in her head all day long, just as the music of the birds used to do in the green woods.

At last one morning when Jenny thought she was quite alone and the soldiers' tune was still singing softly in her head, she crept up to the piano, which had been left open that her stepsister, Amelia, might practice upon it, and began softly to pick out the tune with one finger.

"Amelia, is that you practicing?" cried out the old grandmother, who was passing.

There was no answer, but the music stopped at once. The grandmother looked into the room. There stood the square piano, but no one to be seen near it. This was very strange. The grandmother rubbed her eyes and looked again. She was sure she had heard someone playing. Amelia might be hiding, perhaps, so in she came and poked about behind chairs and table, until at last she caught sight of a tiny figure crouching inside the square piano, and stooping down she dragged out a very frightened and very dusty little Jenny.

"Child," said her grandmother, "was that you playing?"

Jenny caught her breath with a great sob and confessed that she had tried to play on the piano without permission.

The grandmother looked down at the tiny child with amazement and almost with awe. She could scarcely believe that Jenny could have made the music she had heard. Already she caught the echo of that magic gift, the very spirit of music which no one had as yet guessed that the child possessed.

"Mark my words," she said afterward to Jenny's mother, "that child will bring you help."

That might perhaps happen some day, thought her mother, but just now the child was rather a hindrance than a

SHE DRAGGED OUT A FRIGHTENED AND VERY DUSTY CHILD

help, and help was sorely needed. The day school kept by Frau Lind was not a success, and after a few years she was obliged to give it up, and then Jenny changed her home once more.

THE WIDOWS' HOME

The steward or gatekeeper of the House of the Widows, where Jenny's grandmother had found a home, had no children and wanted to adopt a little girl, and this seemed the very thing for Jenny. It was a comfortable, happy home for the child, and she would be able to see her grandmother whom she loved.

All this time the spirit of music had grown with the child's growth, and in the new home she could no more help singing than the birds in the trees.

"As a child I sang with every step I took, and with every jump my feet made," she said many years afterward.

The little singing maiden, hopping about the quiet Widows' Home, must have seemed like a bird shut up in rather a gloomy cage, but Jenny was quite happy. As long as she might sing to herself she was never lonely, and then, too, she had always her dear cat with the blue ribbon round his neck for company, and he was most patient and polite in listening to her song.

There was a window in the steward's house which looked down upon the busy street leading to St. Jacob's church, and here on the broad window-seat Jenny used to curl herself up, with the cat sitting opposite, and sing to her heart's content.

THEY HALF-EXPECTED TO SEE A BIRD-CAGE

The passers-by, when they heard the child's voice, would pause and look up. They half-expected to see a bird-cage hanging there, but instead, all that was to be seen was a round-faced little girl and a solemn cat with a blue ribbon round his neck.

But wherever the song came from it was very sweet and haunting, and seemed to go straight to the heart, so the people always smiled as they looked upward, and were never tired of listening.

Now among the people who passed to and fro under the window of the steward's house was the maid of a Mademoiselle Lundberg, a performer at the Royal Opera House. This maid could not forget the sound of the child's voice, and she thought of it so often that at last she told her mistress about the little girl who sang to her cat in the window of the House of the Widows.

A KIND FRIEND

It sounded a very pretty tale and Mademoiselle Lundberg began to think that she, too, would like to hear the child with the birdlike voice, so she bade her maid find out who the little girl was, and ask if the child might come and sing to her.

There was nothing very fairylike about Jenny in those days. She herself tells us that she was "a small, ugly, broad-nosed, shy, undergrown girl," but when she stood before the lady who had sent for her and began to sing, the magic of her music cast a spell over all who listened.

"The child is a genius," cried Mademoiselle Lundberg. Then turning to Jenny's mother, who had come with her, she said, "You must have her educated for the stage."

But Frau Lind would not hear of such a thing, and the old grandmother, too, shook her head when she was told. They disliked the stage and thought it would be an evil life for little Jenny.

"Very well, then," said Mademoiselle Lundberg, "you must at any rate have her taught singing."

There could be no objection to that, and after talking it over, Jenny's mother set out with a letter of introduction in one hand and her little daughter in the other, to seek an interview with Herr Croclius, the singing-master at the Royal Theater.

There was something very grand and worldly and almost frightening about the broad flight of steps which led to the theater, and as the mother and child climbed up, Frau Lind's heart failed her again and all her doubts came rushing back. She stood still and hesitated, half inclined to turn round and go home.

But an eager little hand was dragging her forward, and Jenny begged her to be quick and come on. Jenny was quite sure that there must be no turning back, and so, half unwillingly, her mother allowed herself to be pulled along until she reached the room of Herr Croclius, and they knocked timidly at the door.

The singing-master listened kindly to what they had to say, and then bade Jenny sing one of her songs to him, more out of kindness than because he took any great interest in the small, plain-looking child.

But the moment the song was begun all was changed. Again the magic of her gift wove its wondrous spell, and the tears gathered in the master's eyes as he listened to the pure, fresh notes. Then when she had finished he rose to his feet and held out his hand.

"You must come with me," he said, "to Count Puke, the head of the theater. We must show him what a treasure we have found."

Now the Count was not at all inclined to think that Jenny was a treasure at all, and he frowned when he looked at the shy, plain little girl.

"How old is she?" he asked to begin with.

"Nine years old," said Croclius.

"Nine!" exclaimed the Count. "But this is not a crèche. It is the King's Theater."

AN EAGER LITTLE HAND DRAGGED HER FORWARD

He looked quite crossly at the small figure standing there. A child of that age was only fit to be kept in a nursery. What was the use of troubling a busy man with such foolishness?

"Well," said Croclius, "if the Count will not hear her, then I will teach her for nothing myself, and she will one day astonish you."

Indeed she had already begun to astonish the Count, for he thought after all there must be something wonderful about the commonplace child if Croclius, the great singing-master, was willing to teach her without any payment. At any rate, he would allow her to sing to him, and would judge for himself.

So again Jenny sang one of the songs which she had sung to the cat when they sat together in the sunny window, and once again the spell worked. She always forgot her shyness when she once began to sing, and her whole face was transformed and "shone with heavenly light."

In one of Hans Andersen's tales there is the story of a nightingale that charmed the emperor and all his court with its wonderful singing, although it was merely a plain little gray bird that almost shocked the court with its humble appearance.

"Is it possible?" said the lord-in-waiting. "I never imagined it could be such a little plain simple thing like that."

THE GRAY BIRD

But when the emperor heard the song of the little gray bird the tears came into his eyes and rolled down his cheeks, and the song went straight to his heart. He wished to reward the nightingale, but she would take nothing.

"I have seen tears in an emperor's eyes and that is my richest reward," she said.

That is what Jenny Lind might have felt when she finished her song and looked up at the two men who were listening to her. The Count was like the emperor in the fairy tale. He could only see the plain little gray bird through a mist of tears which filled his eyes and rolled down his cheeks.

Here was a treasure indeed. Such a singing bird must not be allowed to escape, and so it was at once arranged that Jenny should become the adopted child of the Royal Theater, and that she was to be educated and taught to sing, all at the expense of the government.

Frau Lind gave her consent very unwillingly, but it was a great matter that the child should be provided for, and there seemed nothing else to be done.

So the little gray bird began her training, which was to lead to such a worldwide success. She was scarcely ten years old when she began to act at the Royal Theater, and her acting was almost as full of charm as her singing, so that she might have become a great actress as well as a great singer.

She was taught, of course, many other things besides acting and singing, and did her lessons just like any other little girl. Her sewing was perhaps the thing she did best, for she loved to put in neat, dainty stitches, and worked most exquisitely.

"Madame's stitches never come out," said her maid, when Jenny was grown up.

It might be thought a strange life for a child, and there was much evil around her, but she grew up like a daisy in a garden, white and pure, with gold at the heart of her. Like St. Margaret, she kept herself unspotted from the world, and the purity of her heart put to flight the dragon of evil. The great secret of her success was well expressed by her friend Jules Benedict: "Jenny Lind makes a conscience of her art."

Even when the world began to ring with the fame of this wonderful "nightingale," when kings and queens begged that she would come and sing to them in their palaces, when they "crowned her with flowers and filled her lap with gold," Jenny Lind through it all remained, like the princess in the fairy tale, "as good as gold," unspoiled and simple, "with the manners of a princess, the simplicity of a child, and the goodness of an angel."

BOYS OF MANY LANDS AND TIMES

I

WILLIAM OF NORMANDY

WILLIAM became Duke of Normandy, when he was eight years old, on the death of his father, Robert, in 1035. He had many enemies, but he was brave and strong, and loved fighting. He was very young when he retook the castle of Falaise from the rebel lord Thurstan, when he won the castle of Arques from his own uncle, and when, with the help of the King of France, he defeated the Norman rebels at Val-des-Dunes. It was nearly twenty years after, in 1066, that he invaded England, and won his victory over Harold. Here we tell the story of his boyhood and early manhood.

Robert, Duke of Normandy, went to the Holy Land, and died on his way back. His young son William succeeded not only to all the honors of the duchy, but also to the war between the duke and his overlord, Henry, King of France. The soldiers of France were round the walls of one of William's castles, and in Henry's name they were demanding that the castle should be given up. William's men, on the other hand, said they would not yield until they had no more strength to fight.

There were angry words on both sides. Loud threats arose from the French, and matters looked very serious, when suddenly William came upon the scene. The boy was handsome, brave, and strong. "Let me have my way now," he said to the Normans. "You are my faithful men, but I do not quite agree with you. Henry is my over-lord, and I am bound to be true to him."

King Henry seemed pleased with the boy, and as a reward he made him one of the Knights of St. Michael and St. George. William was a very young knight, but he was proud of the honor, and went home feeling that he was quite a man.

William had been obliged to give up that castle to King Henry; but he soon found that the King kept taking more and more land from his duchy. In spite of his fine promises, Henry even helped the young duke's men to rebel; for there were some people in Normandy who would have liked some one else to rule over them.

Chief among these was one named Thurstan, who was bold enough to say he would no longer

THE TOWER OF LONDON

71

obey Duke William. He took the castle of Falaise, which was William's favorite home, and
sent rude messages to the duke. William at once
called his men together, and ordered the big standard of Normandy to be brought out. The young
duke was quick in action, and he seemed to do
things in haste. The brave Normans loved him
for this, and without a word they set themselves
behind their young leader.

Thurstan looked at the steep cliffs and the
strong walls, and said: "They will never take
Falaise from me. I am safe enough in this fine
old place." But he forgot that the people of the
town loved William. Even while he thought he
was so safe within the castle, a little girl had run
in to tell the people that William was coming.

Now there was joy and stir in Falaise; for all
the gates were flung wide open, and the Normans
came marching in to attack the castle on its weak-
est side. When Thurstan saw that his walls were
broken, he began to feel a little afraid of the
duke. "This lad of thirteen is like a man," he
said. "He can do just what he wishes." All day
long the fight went steadily on, and when Thurstan saw that he was beaten he asked pardon from
the duke. Now, although William was but a boy,
he showed older people how to be just and kind
even to one's foe.

"I give you your life, Thurstan," he said to the
kneeling soldier, "but you have to leave my country. You must go far away from Normandy, and
never come back; for you have broken your
word, and made war upon your home land."

William's enemies were those of his own family. The Norman barons lived in strong castles,
and they were very lawless. They made war upon
each other, and did many cruel things. One night
some men broke into the young duke's rooms and
killed his tutor, who slept near him. They also
killed his old and trusted friend Count Osborn.

The next great trouble came through his uncle,
who said that he ought to be duke instead of
William. He was besieged in his castle of Arques by William's men, when all at once they
found out that Henry, King of France, was
sending in food to the castle. They knew that if
this went on it was useless for them to wait patiently for the castle to yield.

At this time William was at his hunting-lodge
far off, but as soon as he heard the news he called
for his horse to be saddled, and turning to those
around him, he shouted, "Let him who loves me,
follow me!" He rode day and night until he came
into the camp at Arques and greeted his men. "I
shall not leave you until this castle is in our
hands," he said, and he kept his word.

A little while later his cousin Guy formed a
plot against him, by which William was to be
seized and Guy made duke instead. Guy and his
friends dined together very merrily, and then
called in a poor man named Gillos to amuse them.
Without thinking, some of the men began to talk
about the plot. Now the young duke had always
been kind to this poor man, and as soon as he
heard what had been said, Gillos ran off to William's hunting-lodge, where he arrived when
every one had gone to rest. But Gillos knew
that no moment was to be lost; so he began to
batter on the door with a thick stick.

William came to see what was the matter, and
though he hardly believed the story told by Gillos, yet he thought it wise to see for himself how
much truth there was in it. He threw a short
cloak round his shoulders, saddled his own horse,
and rode away. He had not gone very far before
some of Guy's men raced by, and William felt
thankful that he had escaped them. As he passed
a little village close to the shore, his horse became weary, and he was just wondering what he
should do, when the gate of a manor-house
opened, and a fine old Norman gentleman came
out to breathe the fresh morning air. He stared
when he saw Duke William's mud-covered horse.

"My lord," cried he, "what brings you abroad
in this condition? Is there trouble on the way?"

"You know me well," said William, stopping
for a moment, "but who are you?"

"My name is Hubert," said the old man, "and I
hold the village under you. I have never been
false; so tell me how I can help you now."

Then William told his story, and Hubert, without a word, let him in and gave him food and
drink. Then he bade his three sons harness and
mount, while he himself brought a fresh horse
for William.

"Behold, your lord rides in hard stress," said
old Hubert to his sons. "Ride after him for your
lives, and leave him not until you place him safely
in Falaise."

As they went out of sight, old Hubert still
stood at his gate, when Guy's men came up. But
he was careful not to tell them the way William
had gone, and they took a wrong road that led
over the hills. Thus William reached Falaise in
safety, and he was so thankful that he caused a
raised bank of earth to be made all along the way
he had traveled.

"Methinks my enemies are too many for me to
deal with alone," said young William. "Now I
will go to my lord, the King of France, for support."

Henry smiled as he saw the young duke ride
into the gates of his palace. "Cousin of Normandy, you are wise to come to me," said the

King. "Send out your war-cry and call your soldiers. Together we shall overthrow these enemies of Normandy and France."

William's troops were quickly raised. His big
banners waved over a large army of men. With
him at their head, they met the King, and fought
the rebels at a place known as the Valley of the
Sand-hills. The battle was a long one, and loudly
were the war-cries of France and Normandy
shouted from the ranks of the warriors. It has
been called the battle of the knights, for so many
of them took part in it.

Twice King Henry was thrown down, but he
soon got up again. William, with his good sword
in his hand, led on his own men. When night
fell over the field, most of the rebels were flying
for dear life, but many prisoners were taken and
led back in triumph.

William's power was now firmly settled, and no
one was likely to take his duchy of Normandy
from him.

It is pleasing to know that, while William was
so brave a boy, he always dealt kindly with his
foes; although it is said that he sometimes sent
them rude messages, after the fashion of those
times. It was such a message that he sent to the
Count of Anjou, whom he offered to meet before
the gates of his town. "Tell him," said the duke,
"that he will find me mounted on a bay horse,
and carrying a red shield. And that he may
know me better, I shall have at the point of my
lance a streamer of taffety, to wipe his face
with." It was a time of war, when such speeches
were made and passed from either side. But it
was not a proper speech for so great a soldier as
the hero of Normandy.

In after days the pages of history were filled
with his doings; and his great victory over Harold at Hastings was to make him known and remembered as the Conqueror. But we must now
leave him in his early days, as a fine and manly
youth, who, though he had many faults, and was
easily moved to anger, yet was ready to do a
kindly action even to his enemies.

II

THE STORY OF EDGAR

IT did not take long after the battle of Hastings
for the news to fly abroad that William the Norman was now William the Conqueror.

Though there were many who dared not oppose him, yet there was still a small band of English who would not yield quietly to his rule.
These men remembered that in the city of London lived a little fair-haired child, the son of that
Edward who had always been called the Stranger.

This child, Edgar, had been taken as his heir
by King Edward, who died early in 1066. The
boy was but six years old, and had been left undisturbed in his play, and at his lessons, by the
events that had shaken England. Harold had not
troubled about him, and many people had quite
forgotten the young prince. But after the death
of Harold, those who lived in London thought of
little Edgar, and hastened to proclaim him King
of England. They were rather late in doing
this, and William came up and sent messages to
them, promising life and liberty if they would
submit to him.

It was quite clear that London could not hope
to hold out against William. So the chief men
appeared before him, carrying the keys of the
gates, and leading the boy, whom they had been
ready to own as their king but a short time before.

William had a kinder heart than many men
thought, and when he saw the fair hair and blue
eyes of young Edgar, he greeted him very pleas-
antly, and promised to be his friend. After this,
Edgar lived at William's court, where he was
treated with kindness.

But the English were not happy under William's rule, and in two years they began to rebel.
Then Edgar and his two sisters left to go to their
mother's friends in Hungary; but the stormy
weather blew their ship to Scotland, where Malcolm was King. Now Malcolm had been a friend
of Edward the Stranger, and he was sorry for
his children; so he received them kindly, and
promised to get the crown of England for Edgar.
But this was easier said than done. When at last
the armies of England and Scotland met, Malcolm and William made a treaty of peace. While
Malcolm did the best he could for himself and
his country, he did not forget to plead for Edgar's safety.

At the same time Edgar himself, who was now
a boy of fourteen, came forward and said he
would never give any trouble to King William.
For his part, William was pleased with the boy;
and he readily gave him an estate in England,
and a sum of money which would keep him in
comfort.

Edgar's young sister Margaret became the wife
of Malcolm of Scotland. She was a girl of gentle
nature, and other young girls, in her new home,
learned from her to be gentle also. It is said
that Margaret was not content with being the
highest lady in Scotland. She tried to set a good
example to those around her, and had a class of

Scottish children, who were taught and brought up under her care.

III

BALDWIN, KING OF JERUSALEM

You know what we mean when we say of something that it happened in the time of the Crusades, those religious wars that brought men from every part of Europe to fight against the Turks.

From the cold countries of the North, and from the sunny lands of the South, large armies came to free Jerusalem from the power of the great Saladin, who claimed to be ruler of the Holy Land.

King Louis of France was at Antioch, with seven thousand left of his seventy thousand fighting men; for times had gone badly with the Crusaders, and the story of this, the second Holy War, is one of quarrels and failure. The great Conrad, Emperor of Germany, waited in sadness before the walls of Acre with his six thousand weary men.

On Mount Moriah stood young Baldwin, the third of that name to be called King of Jerusalem. He was a mere boy of fourteen years. He had an army of lazy soldiers, who would rather sit in the warm sun, and enjoy the shelter of their young King's house, than be near the noise of battle. Then there came a day which was never to be forgotten, when the great Conrad himself stood among them, with his tall soldiers around him. He told Baldwin how they had marched across continents, and forded rivers, braving disease and death, so that they might at last come to his help.

When Conrad said this, loud shouts went up: "Strike for the cross, and God defend the right!" Then the idle men of Baldwin's army polished their swords afresh, and looked to their shields, and thus made ready to face the foe.

The three armies met round the walls of Damascus, and never had that beautiful city looked so fair. The men of the Crusade spread their tents in the green plains, and thought with delight of the spoil that would be theirs, when the city was won. Nor had they long to wait. King Baldwin had some members of his family with him, and one of them, his fair young cousin, the Lady Isabel, thought she would like to gather some beautiful flowers from the beautiful gardens on the bank of the river. No sooner was she busy with this task than a band of Turks pounced upon her, and carried her off to their tower.

Happily for Isabel, her danger had been seen by a boy who was near; and he ran as hard as he could to King Baldwin, crying as he went, that the Lady Isabel had been stolen.

Great was the anger of the Crusaders when they heard that the Lady Isabel was a prisoner. Every man slipped on his coat of mail, and every knight seized his sword; while war-cries filled the air. It did not take long to get back the lady; but the whole thing was like putting a match to a fire, and in a short while they were in the midst of a great battle. "Allah!" cried the Turks, as they poured out of the city in crowds; and "A Baldwin to the rescue!" shouted the Crusaders as they rushed after their young King.

A little later Saladin fell under the tall Emperor's sword; and when the Turks saw he was dead their ranks broke up and they flew back to the city. But now the Crusaders behaved very foolishly; for they at once began to quarrel about the city which they had taken.

"It shall be mine," said Baldwin. "I am its rightful king."

"It shall be mine," said Conrad, "for I slew its owner, Saladin."

"It shall be ours," said the Knights Templars, "because we have vowed to protect the Holy Land."

News of the quarrel reached the ears of the Turks. Within the walls of the city was a very clever prince, named Anar; and he called to him a boy whom his men had brought in. "I will give you your life and liberty," said Anar, "if you will find Bernard, Grand Master of the Knights Templars, and give him this note. Can I trust you to do this?" The boy said "Yes," with a joyful heart, for he longed to be free again. When he reached the camp he went straight to the tent of Bernard, who took the letter, and smiled as he read the offers which Anar made to him.

Now Bernard wanted to be ruler of Damascus, but Anar offered him another city, and some small presents, if he would but lead his friends away from Damascus; and, to his shame, he agreed to do this. So cleverly did he manage it that the armies quietly took up their tents and went to the other side of the city, where, as they speedily found out, they were not likely to do any harm. From the parts they had left, fresh help poured in for the Turks, and thus Damascus was delivered from the men of King Baldwin.

Sad and bitter were the young King's thoughts as he rode away from the city. His reign ended very soon; he had his great title and little else. He was a King but without a kingdom. Still, we must think kindly of him as a noble and brave youth, who tried to be the most high-minded of the kings of Jerusalem.

IV

PRINCE ARTHUR, THE BOY WHO WOULD BE A KING

THE Norman king of England, a descendant of William the Conqueror, having died without leaving any children, his brother John made himself king.

John was a very bad ruler; and he was both mean and cowardly. Although he was King of England and Duke of Normandy he was never happy or at rest, for he knew that his nephew Arthur, the son of his elder brother, had a better right than himself to the crown.

At the time when John made himself king, young Arthur, who was born in 1187, was only twelve years old, and he was living safely in his own dukedom of Brittany, in France. His father having died when Arthur was only a baby, the young prince had been Duke of Brittany all his life.

King Philip of France was an enemy of John. One day he said to the young prince: "Arthur, you know your rights, and that your uncle John is not the true King of England. Would you not like to be a king?"

"Truly," said Arthur, "I should greatly like to be a king."

"Then win back your inheritance," said the King of France. "I will give you two hundred of my knights, and you shall come with me and make war upon your uncle in Normandy, which is yours by right. Once we have taken Normandy from the usurper, it will be easy to drive him from England."

Arthur soon had an army of five thousand, and he felt sure that he would soon win back England and Normandy.

The King of England came himself to fight against his nephew. One night a number of King John's soldiers stole into Arthur's camp, made prisoners of some of his knights, and stabbed others in the dark.

Prince Arthur was sleeping in his tent when he was rudely awakened by some armed men, who seized him by the wrists, and bade him come with them and not make any noise. His captors hurried the lad away, and presently they reached a lighted hall. There Arthur saw before him his uncle.

"Do you know me, boy?" said King John.

"Yes," replied Arthur, "you are my uncle, the usurping King of England. I command you to restore to me my rightful inheritance, and to set my knights instantly at liberty."

"To Falaise with him!" said the King. "Take him away; and in the dungeon there he will learn to rebel against his uncle and lawful King!"

Arthur was not frightened yet. King Philip of France had promised to make him King of England; and he saw nothing to be afraid of in the mean, cowardly face of the man before him. The King of France, he felt sure, would rescue him.

King John made a sign, and the boy was hurried away, still defying his uncle. A horse was waiting for him, and he was made to ride, strongly guarded, all the long distance to the castle of Falaise, which was reached early one fine sunny morning.

The drawbridge was lowered, the iron grating raised which guarded the entrance; and the party clattered under the entrance tower and into the courtyard. Arthur descended from his horse and was led along a passage and down a stone staircase to a great iron door which one of his guides opened with a large key.

Arthur's spirits sank when he saw before him a dreary stone dungeon lighted only by a window high up in the wall, and furnished with a narrow bed, a stool, and a heap of straw. Still, he said to himself, it was only for a few days. To-morrow, or the next day, or the day after that, the King of France was sure to come. But weeks passed, and the King of France had not arrived to rescue the prince.

Sometimes Arthur would sit for hours, gazing upward at the tiny square of light, his heart swelling with impatience as he thought of the spring pastimes that he was losing; and he wondered when the King of France would come and set him free.

One day the bolts were withdrawn at an unusual hour. Here, then, was his friend King Philip at last!

Arthur turned quickly, and in the archway of the door he saw the white face of his uncle.

"Arthur," said King John, trying to meet his nephew's eyes, "will you not trust to your loving uncle?"

"I will trust my loving uncle," replied the boy, "when he does me right. Restore to me my kingdom of England, and then come and ask me that question."

The King looked at his nephew, turned away without a word, and left the prison.

After this King John took counsel with his advisers. "What shall I do with this boy," he said. "Behead him," said one. "Have him poisoned," said another. "Put his eyes out," suggested a third; "the people will not want a blind man for their king."

"Put out his eyes," mused the King; "put out

his eyes; those eyes which look with unseemly boldness at his uncle and true sovereign."

John sent to the prison a man called Hubert de Burgh, whom he believed to be devoted to himself; and gave him charge of Prince Arthur. Hubert had a stern face but a kind heart, and he soon grew so much attached to the bright boy who was his prisoner, that he felt toward him almost as a father. He took the prince out of the dungeon, and gave him bright sunny rooms in another part of the castle.

What was Hubert's dismay when one day he received a letter from the King, commanding that his prisoner's eyes should be burned out with hot irons. Not only that, but he had sent two executioners to see that it was done.

Hubert entered Arthur's room that morning with so sad a face that the prince asked what ailed him.

"May one not be sad at times, Prince?" said Hubert, whose sorrow made him gruff.

"Indeed there may be many things that make people sad," replied Prince Arthur, "although I was nearly forgetting that any one could be unhappy who is out of prison. Indeed, Hubert, I am beginning to think that if only I were free and kept sheep I could be as merry as the day is long. I wish I were your son, Hubert; and then I should not have to spend my time in prison."

Poor Hubert! He moved uneasily about the room, and looked so gloomy that Arthur felt sure that something was the matter.

"Here, Prince, read this letter," said Hubert abruptly at last.

Arthur read the letter; and then he became deadly pale.

"Hubert, is this true?" he asked.

"Prince, these are your uncle's orders!" said Hubert with a shaking voice.

"Have you the heart to do it?" said Arthur piteously. "Will you indeed burn out my eyes?"

"I must," said Hubert; "your uncle has sent two men to see that it is done."

"O Hubert!" was all that Arthur could say.

Hubert called the executioners, who had been waiting outside the door.

"Send these men away, Hubert!" cried the boy. "I will stay quite still, Hubert, I will not move if you will do it yourself; but I cannot bear the sight of these men."

"You may go," said Hubert to the executioners; "I will call when I am ready for you."

"Indeed," said one of the men, who had pitied the boy, "I am best pleased to be away from such a deed."

"I cannot do it," said Hubert more to himself than to the prince, "and I will not; I shall have to take the consequences." He opened the door and called in the two men. They came in unwilling, each hoping that he would not have to do the deed.

"I have not burned out the prince's eyes," said Hubert abruptly. "What is more, I am not going to allow you to do so. You can tell the King if you like." "Indeed, sir," said one of the men, "we won't tell his Majesty anything at all."

The men shuffled out of the room, but Arthur's troubles were not over yet. King John suggested to a knight named William de Bray that he should stab the prince in prison.

"I am a gentleman and not an executioner," replied William de Bray; and he turned from the King in disdain.

Then John hired an assassin for a large sum of money, and sent him to the castle to kill the prince.

"Upon what errand dost thou come?" asked Hubert de Burgh, as the fellow presented himself at the castle gates.

"To despatch Prince Arthur," said the man.

"Go back to him that sent thee," said Hubert, "and say that I will do it."

King John, knowing very well that Hubert was trying to save his prisoner, separated Arthur from his kind jailer, and had him imprisoned in the strong castle of Rouen, which is washed on one side by the river Seine. Then he came himself in a boat by night and waited outside the castle walls.

Arthur was awakened by his jailer and made to follow him to a small door by the riverside. When the door was unfastened, the jailer threw down his torch and trod upon it to put it out, and Arthur was only able to distinguish two dark forms in the boat. From the voice he could tell that one of them was his uncle.

Poor Arthur's heart beat wildly with fear. He knew that his cruel uncle had come himself to see that his murderous design was carried out.

Arthur was dragged on board the boat, imploring the King to have mercy upon him; and what happened after that has never been told. Some say that John stunned his nephew with a large stone and flung his body into the Seine; at all events, neither the prince, nor his dead body, was ever seen again.

If John thought that his nephew's murder would make him undisputed King of England he was much mistaken. The cruel deed aroused the greatest indignation throughout England and France. Through it the dukedom of Normandy was lost to the English crown, and some years later John died a ruined man, with his subjects in open rebellion against him.

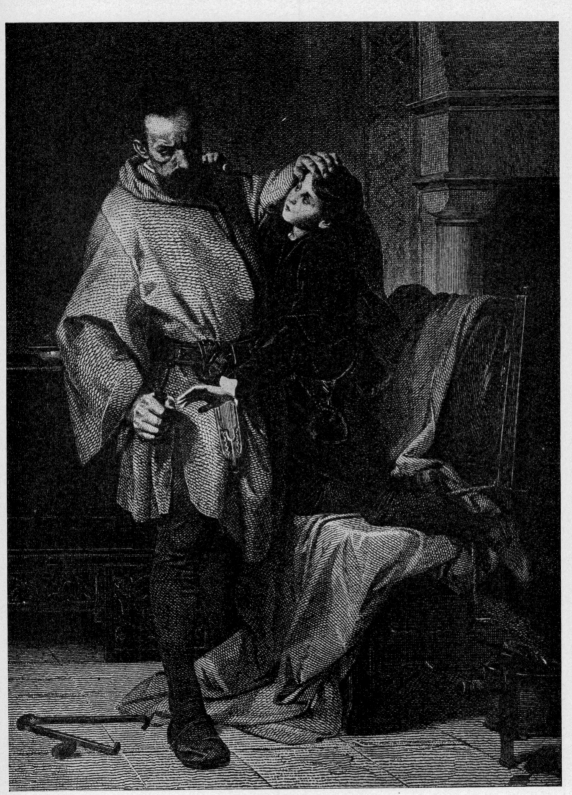

HUBERT AND ARTHUR

V

THE BOY WHO BRAVED THE DUKE OF WELLINGTON

AN ENGLISH farmer was one day at work in the fields, when he saw a party of huntsmen riding about his farm. He had one field which he was especially anxious they should not ride over, as the horses' hoofs would greatly injure the crop. So he sent one of his boys, and told him to shut the gate, and keep watch there, and on no account to let anyone go through it.

The boy went, and had scarcely taken his post there before the huntsmen came up, and ordered him to open the gate. He declined to do so, telling them what his orders were, and that he meant to obey them. They threatened him, but he did not mind their threats. They offered him money, but he refused to receive it. At last, one of them came up to him, and said, in commanding tones:

"My boy, you do not know me; but I am the Duke of Wellington. I am not accustomed to be disobeyed; and, now, I command you to open the gate, that I and my friends may pass through."

The boy lifted his cap, and stood uncovered before the man whom all England delighted to honor, and then answered firmly:

"I am sure that the Duke of Wellington would not wish me to disobey orders. I must keep the gate shut; no one can pass through it but by my master's express permission."

The brave old warrior was greatly pleased with this. Then he took off his own hat, and said: "I honor the man or the boy who can neither be bribed nor frightened into disobeying orders.

With an army of such soldiers, I could conquer, not the French only, but the world." Then, handing the boy a sovereign, he put spurs to his horse and galloped away.

VI

THE PRINCES IN THE TOWER

WHEN Edward IV, King of England, died he left two sons, one of whom was twelve and the other nine years old. Their mother and her family had not many friends in the Council.

No sooner was Edward dead than the Queen demanded a strong escort to take her son, now young Edward V, to London. Her manner seemed to show some fear that the young King was not safe. On his way to London young Edward got into the hands of Richard, Duke of Gloucester, who was the brother of the late King. With him the Queen was not on good terms, and as soon as she heard what had happened she ran to Westminster, taking her five little girls and her other son, the small Duke of York, with her. But all London went to meet Richard, the Lord Mayor in fine robes of scarlet, and the citizens in grand clothing.

At St. Paul's, the bishops, the Council, and other great people came to do homage to Edward; after which he remained at the Tower, waiting for the day of his coronation. As Edward was so young, the Duke of Gloucester was made Protector of England. The Queen, who did not believe in Richard, still refused to leave Westminster. She stayed at the abbot's house, and would not allow her younger children to go out of the buildings.

Richard knew that, before many years were over, the young King would be able to do as he liked, and to surround himself with his mother's friends. Before this time came, he wanted to get rid of the boy, and one or two friends promised

THE PRINCES IN THE TOWER
FROM THE PAINTING BY PAUL DELAROCHE

to help Richard. But others said they intended to stand by the young King. Things would have gone on thus for some time if Richard had not suddenly made up his mind to act for himself.

At the next Council there were angry words and deeds. When Richard came in he was very pleasant, but later his manner changed. He said he had found that some one wished to harm the young King and himself, and he put the blame on the Queen, who had, so he stated, made his own arm wither through her witchcraft. In those days people were very much afraid of witches and witchcraft; but somehow Richard's withered arm did not cause so much feeling as he thought it would.

"If she has done this," said Hastings, "she should be punished, but—"

"Do you reply with 'ifs' and 'buts'?" cried Richard angrily, as he thumped the great oak table with his fist. "I declare your head shall suffer for that speech."

At these words a crowd of Richard's men poured in, shouting "Treason! Treason!" and a scene of wild disorder followed. A bishop was carried off to prison, poor Hastings's head was struck off, and other men fell before Richard's servants; while Richard himself sent out the strange story of a plot he had discovered, in which Hastings and his followers sought to do harm to young Edward and the Protector.

Then the Protector sent a message to the Queen, who was in the abbey at Westminster, asking for her younger son, the Duke of York. He knew that even if he killed the young King his brother would take his place, and his plan was to get both boys in his own hands. To the Queen he said that the little King was dull, and wanted his brother, with whom he could play quite happily. But Elizabeth did not believe his words. She was really afraid of the Protector.

"The Duke of York is ill," said the poor Queen, when Richard's men came before her at Westminster. "He needs a mother's care and attention. Therefore I cannot let him go to the Duke of Gloucester."

"You were ready to let the King go, madam," said the archbishop, who brought the message to her. "Why not, then, send his brother? The boy is sad without a playfellow."

"The King was well, and this boy is ill," said the Queen, angrily.

More words followed on both sides. In the end the Queen yielded, and she gave the boy to the archbishop, begging him to watch over the child and protect him. "Of you I shall require my sons before God and man," she said, with tears.

We are told that the little boy cried bitterly on leaving his mother; but when he reached the Protector, Richard met him very kindly. He kissed the boy, and bade him welcome. Then the little boy went to his brother's rooms, and they played happily together, and were so merry that everybody thought how foolish the Queen had been.

So matters remained for a few days, until Richard had time to make his own plans. He was always working to an end, and that was to be King of England. He did not wish to seem in a hurry, but there were those two little boys in the Tower who stood in his way.

One Sunday, before a great crowd of people at St. Paul's Cross, a sermon was preached by Dr. Shaw, in which he took care to speak against the late King and his Queen, and declared that their children had no right to the throne.

No doubt Richard had arranged just what had to be said by Shaw, but he seemed much shocked by the sermon, and even displeased at it. Next day one of Richard's friends made a great speech to the people at the Guildhall. When he ended, some of them threw up their caps, and a few shouted "Long live King Richard!"

A short while after this some others went to Baynard's Castle, where Richard lived, and gathered round the walls. When he appeared they told him it was their wish that he should be king. Richard thanked his friends, but did not seem at all eager to be king. In the end he owned that he ought to obey the will of the people, and if they wished him to reign, he would consent. Now, at last, he had gained his aim, and the crown was his, offered, so he seemed to think, by the voice of the people.

Richard was then crowned at Westminster. When Queen Elizabeth heard the stir, from the quiet room where she still was in hiding, she asked what was happening; and no sooner was she told that Richard was being crowned, than her thoughts flew to her boys. "Where is my son, then?" she asked, "and where, also, is the little one whom they have taken from me?" Alas! No one could tell her.

In the country strange tales were being told and believed. It was said that the two little boys had been sent out into the deep, dark forest; and that they had wandered, hand in hand, for days. Up and down the long pathless forest they had gone, these poor little royal waifs, with no one to care for them or show them the way. Then, worn out with walking, tired, hungry, and cold, they had fallen asleep at the foot of a tree; and the little birds, who were, in their way, so much kinder than the cruel uncle of these poor boys, had come softly, and covered them with the falling leaves. Beneath this covering their souls passed away to a land where hunger, cold, and cruelty do not exist.

This story passed from one to the other. It was made into a song, called "The Babes in the Wood"; and the people sang it sadly, in memory of the poor little children. But many years later, another story came out. According to this, Richard had told the constable of the Tower to do away with the boys. When he refused, some men in Richard's pay went to the Tower and killed the boys in their sleep. The bodies were buried at the foot of a staircase in the Tower, and then removed to another part.

Two hundred years after, when some digging was going on under what is called the White Tower, an oak chest was found. This was opened, and the bodies of two children were inside. By the command of Charles II, who was then King of England, these were taken to Westminster, and buried among the other kings and queens of the country.

VII

THE YOUNG DAYS OF JOHN MILTON

A YOUNG Oxford scholar named Milton was turned out of his home by his father because he did not like his son's religion. Having a kind friend in London, the lad went to him and told him his sad story. His friend helped him to get work, and young Milton began to earn his living as a scrivener. A scrivener did some of the work which a lawyer now does; and Milton was so attentive to his duties that he soon got on well. He took a shop, in which he carried on his work, and he lived in the rooms above the shop.

The scrivener liked things to be comfortable about him. He was a good man, and began each day with reading the Bible and prayer. He was also fond of books and music. He even wrote a number of songs, and some hymn-tunes that are still in use. His home above the scrivener's shop was a very happy one.

In this cheerful, pleasant home, John Milton was born in the year 1608, and named after his father. As the boy grew, he was taught to read. By the time he was ten he was already a poet and wrote verses which were the delight of his family. Young Milton was rather a pretty child, too; and his father had his portrait painted by a young Dutch painter, named Jansen, who was making quite a name for himself. This picture of little John Milton may still be seen. He wears a black braided dress and a lace frill; and his fair hair is closely cut all round his head, in the fashion then worn by the Puritans. Most other boys, and men too, in those days, kept their hair long, like girls at the present time.

The boy's face looks quite serious, and indeed the little Milton seems to have been a very thoughtful child. Some lines in one of John Milton's poems are said to refer to his own childhood:

> " When I was yet a child, no childish play
> To me was pleasing; all my mind was set
> Serious to learn and know, and thence to do
> What might be public good."

The elder Milton saw that his child received good and careful teaching. When John was ten years of age he was under a Puritan schoolmaster, who taught him how to write English and Latin poetry. One of the best schools in London at that time was St. Paul's School, in St. Paul's Churchyard, and here John Milton went when he was twelve. He thus became what was called "A pigeon of St. Paul's," a nickname given to the boys on account of the number of pigeons that lived on the roof of the cathedral.

On the glass of every window of St. Paul's School were the words, "Either teach, or learn, or leave the place." John Milton stayed at this school until his sixteenth year, being helped in his studies at home by a tutor, who came in the evenings. John was so much in earnest over his lessons that he sat up very late to learn them.

When John was sixteen his father resolved that he should go to college, and he was sent to Christ's College, Cambridge. He rode there in Hobson's cart. Hobson was the great carrier of that day, and had a stable of forty good horses always ready and fit for traveling. When any scholar came for a horse, he was obliged to take the one that chanced to stand next the stable door. Hence arose the well-known proverb, "Hobson's choice; this or nothing." Hobson used to tell the scholars that they would come in good time to London, if they did not ride too fast.

When at Cambridge, Milton rose every day to be in the college chapel at five o'clock for the morning service, and he worked very hard at his studies. Because his manners were so gentle and pleasing, he was called the "Lady of Christ's College."

While John was at college the plague broke out at Cambridge. Old Hobson, the carrier, was forbidden to go to London, for fear of spreading the disease in other places, but though he was over eighty-six years of age, he did not like to remain idle. Falling ill, the old man died soon after, and John Milton wrote some verses about his death, one of which began:

" Here lieth one who did most truly prove,
　　That he could never die while he could move."

While at college, Milton had a great wish to become a writer of books. His mind was filled with beautiful thoughts; and before long he was planning his great poems, the best known of which is "Paradise Lost." Like his father, he was very fond of music, and whenever he went to London he loved to hear sweet and beautiful singing. Music and poetry went together in his thoughts. His father lived long enough to rejoice in his clever son, and to be assured that he was one of England's greatest poets.

VIII

KING LOUIS XIV OF FRANCE

IT is safe to say that never had the French royal palace seen a stranger sight than that which was seen on a cold night in February, 1651. Outside, it was dark and gloomy; yet all Paris seemed awake and alive. Hoarse shouts rang through the darkness. The roll of drums fell on the ears of those who listened; and round the gates of the palace were gathered large crowds of men and women. They were angry men and women, too; for they believed that some great person in power was going to carry away their King. And just then, the people of Paris wanted to keep their King.

Louis XIV, the little monarch of twelve, was a handsome, merry boy. The people were going to take care of him, for they did not much trust his mother, the proud Queen Anne. Loud cries of "The King! the King!" startled the palace, and soldiers, courtiers, and servants rushed into the wide hall. Anne, the boy's mother, was brave. "What do the people want?" she asked.

The hundreds of rough men and women outside wanted to see the King. They must see him with their own eyes, and loud knocks upon the palace doors showed that they meant to have their way.

"Open the gates," cried Anne. "Let every one come in." When her courtiers went to do as she ordered, she ran to tell Louis of the danger they were in. "Be a brave boy," she whispered. "Shut your eyes, and pretend to be asleep. The people are coming to see for themselves that you are still here." The boy was angry. "This is my house," he said, "and why should they force their way here? Why are they not turned out at once?"

"You must be quiet," said his mother to him. "Do your part, and all will be well."

The boy saw the danger, and laid his head on the pillow, with his eyes closed. Then his mother stood at the door, as the mob came up the grand staircase, and crowded into the King's room.

"Come softly," said the Queen gently. "The King is asleep. You can see him as he lies in bed, but please do not awaken him, for you know he is only a boy." She moved aside, and they came in very quietly. They stood a moment by the bed, looked at the boy, and then, without noise, moved on.

When the march ended, after the long tramp upon the marble stairs, the people walked out of the palace gates in order; and standing in the courtyard, they raised loud shouts of "Long live the King!"

When Louis was thirteen he was proclaimed of age, that is, old enough to rule. On this day, with a great following of lords and ladies, he rode through Paris to the Palace of Justice. Here he met the nobles who had governed the kingdom during the thirteen years of his young life. All the people present rose as the young King walked to the throne; and they waited quietly until he spoke.

In the eyes of many who stood there it was a great day in the history of their country; for the boy before them was still so young. Yet when he spoke his words were like those of a King. "Henceforth I rule my own kingdom," he said loudly. And then every knee was bent, every head bowed before him, as the nobles promised to be loyal and faithful.

When the meeting was over Louis drove back to the royal palace. As he passed, the people shouted "Long live our King! Long live King Louis!" By their manner they showed that the boy was greatly liked by them. But the young King's pride soon began to show itself. When he was sixteen some trouble arose in the land. Louis was in need of money, and he asked the Parliament to get it for him. But, to his surprise, he found that they were not willing to do so. They asked for time to think about the matter. When Louis received their answer, he was very angry. Attended by all his nobles, he walked into the great council-chamber and faced the astonished members of his Parliament.

"I hear that you, gentlemen, are thinking of refusing my demands," he said. "Let me tell you that it is not your place to do that. And if it ever happens again, I, your King, will come down, and make you obey me." So bold did he show himself that the Parliament found the money without delay.

Louis ruled for many years, but it cannot be said that he was a happy king. When he became an old man, he said to the little boy who was his heir: "My child, do not be like me. Keep peace

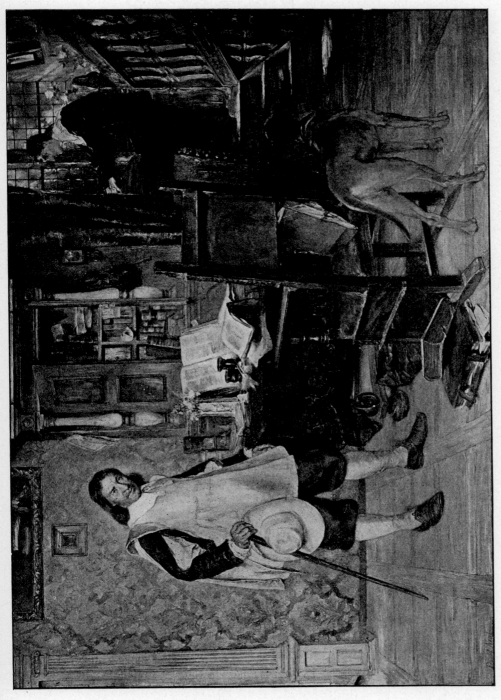

CROMWELL'S VISIT TO MILTON

FROM THE PAINTING BY DAVID NEAL

THE PICTURE SHOWS OLIVER CROMWELL LISTENING TO JOHN MILTON PLAYING THE ORGAN. ON THE ESTABLISH-
MENT OF THE COMMONWEALTH BY CROMWELL, MILTON WAS MADE LATIN SECRETARY TO THE COUNCIL OF STATE.
MILTON THOUGHT CROMWELL 'A GREAT AND WONDERFUL MAN, AND HAILED HIM AS "OUR CHIEF OF MEN"

with your neighbors, love and serve God, and try to ease the burdens of your people." For he knew that the bright promise of his own boyhood had faded so soon.

IX

KING CHARLES XII OF SWEDEN

IN 1697 a young prince in Sweden, named Charles, who was but fifteen when his father died, was crowned King of that country. Charles had a fine kingdom; for in those days Sweden took in a large part of North Germany, and even a portion of Western Russia, as well as the long piece of land which is still known as Sweden.

So much power, perhaps, was not good for the young King. It made him think he could do just as he liked, and it is said that he did some very unkingly things, although it must be owned that they were rather boyish tricks. With his brother-in-law to help him, he broke the windows of the quiet folk who lived in his city of Stockholm. He also chased hares through the council-chamber, a thing which greatly shocked the grave old senators. He spent so much money in foolish pleasures that the good people of Sweden became at last very angry with their King.

On a certain Sunday morning three clergymen preached from the same text: "Woe to thee, O land, when thy king is a child." This alarmed the young King, and he began to think how foolish he had been. He now tried to set a good example to his people, and every day he spent many hours in exercises with the young men who formed his body-guard.

One day he was surprised to receive a message from his Council, telling him that his old enemy, the King of Denmark, had invaded some part of his land and laid it waste. He had robbed the people and burned their houses. This news made Charles very angry. He dashed off to Stockholm, and entered the council-chamber just as he was, covered with mud from his journey. His people forgot his condition when they saw his earnest young face.

"I will never begin an unjust war," said Charles, as he stood before the Council, "but I shall never finish an unjust one, save with the defeat of my foes. I will attack the first of them who declares war on Sweden; and when I have dealt with him, I shall look after the rest."

It was a bold speech for one so young to make. The Council knew that a number of kings had united to crush Charles, in the hope of sharing his lands between them. The King of Denmark, Peter the Great of Russia, and the King of Poland were mighty monarchs for a boy to meet in battle.

Happily for Sweden, Charles was a clever as well as a brave youth. He had kept on friendly terms with England and Holland, and with their help he hoped to conquer. He armed his troops, said good-by to his sisters, and with a small, but bold and trusty band of followers, he sailed away.

The big boats steered for the nearest place in Denmark. As they drew close to the land the young king leaped into the shallow water, crying out, "All ye who are for Denmark, follow me." The Danes were not expecting an attack from this side, and Charles startled them by his quickness. Thus the first battle was won quite easily.

In two days the Swedish force had marched to the capital of Denmark, and a little later the King of that country was ready to sign a treaty of peace. At the same time the King of Poland thought it wise to withdraw his army, seeing that Denmark had been so well beaten. There now remained but one enemy for the young King to settle; but this was no small task, for Peter of Russia had an army of forty thousand men. And yet, Charles was daring enough to lead against him his small band of Swedish soldiers.

So bravely did the Swedes fight at Narva, that the Russians fled before them. Many were drowned in trying to cross the river, and all those who remained were made prisoners. It was a great victory for so young a king.

In spite of his success, Charles still kept his simple tastes, and shared his food with the common soldiers serving under him. It has been said of him that before he tried to conquer others he conquered himself, and this is the secret of all true power and greatness.

X

THE BOYHOOD OF NAPOLEON

IN the year 1769, on a bright August day, a boy was born in the island of Corsica whose name was to be famous throughout the world—the name Napoleon Bonaparte. The boy owed much to his mother, who was a woman of rare mind. She was quick, keen, and clever, and had a firm will. This was a good thing for her children; for Charles, their father, although fond of books and reading, was rather an idle man.

The brightest thing in Napoleon's young days was his great love for his mother. He always treated her with respect, and asked her advice in moments of difficulty; and he never forgot the lessons she taught him in his early life.

NAPOLEON AT BRIENNE

FROM THE PAINTING BY M. REALIER-DUMAS

At that time the little island of Corsica, which had been seized by the French, was passing through evil days. "I was born," said Napoleon, "when our country was perishing. The cries of the dying, and the groans of the poor, were around my cradle from my birth." While he loved Corsica, he learned from childhood to dislike the French. And yet, strange to say, this boy was to make himself the Emperor of the French.

His parents were poor and could not afford to spend much on their children; and so Napoleon was sent to a public school. When he was ten years old a place was obtained for him in the military school of Brienne, and here he remained for about five years. He could not have been very happy at this school, for his manners and speech made him an object of amusement to the French boys. Among them he had only one real friend, to whom he often used to say that he would do these French all the mischief in his power, if he ever got the chance.

His masters were satisfied with the progress he made, and noted the pleasure with which he studied history. The books he read were those that told of war, and the stories of heroes were always a delight to him. He tried very earnestly to speak and write French correctly. He never seemed tired of learning.

But while he was known to work hard, Napoleon's teachers were not pleased with his manners. He was said to think highly of himself, and wanted to get on quickly. He was haughty and proud, and sharp in his way of speaking. On this account he was not a favorite with his teachers, or with his schoolfellows.

Though life was hard for the boy just then, he took pleasure in long walks. He sometimes liked games, and during one winter he spent the play-hours in helping the other boys to build forts of snow. In these Napoleon, who took the command, placed an army, whose duty it was to defend the forts against the other boys. Into this game Napoleon threw himself with great delight, and it was kept up with much spirit for fifteen days. Indeed, it only stopped when some of the boys began to mix stones and gravel with the snow, and throw them at their enemies.

From this school Napoleon went to the Military College of Paris. He was there only for one year, but that was long enough for him to find out how difficult it was for a boy to live where the cost of living was very dear. Napoleon, who had been brought up to be very thrifty, wrote to the head of the school about this matter. It was a bold step to take, but the boy never lacked courage. "Poor men," said Napoleon, "could not stand such expenses." Nor did he think the course of training such as would fit them to be soldiers, who must get used to a hard life. "Temperance and sobriety," wrote this boy of sixteen, "will make us strong, and help us to bear the toils of war."

Napoleon's later life had much to do with war. He wanted to conquer all Europe, but, although he came near doing so, it was not to be. England was his chief enemy; and in the end, after the great battle of Waterloo, he was sent to end his days in the lonely island of St. Helena.

XI

THE STORY OF GARIBALDI'S BOYHOOD

To the people of Italy there is no name better known, and few more highly to be honored, than that of Giuseppe Garibaldi, who was born at Nice, in the southeast of France, in 1807. He was the son of a sailor, and came from a race of men who loved the sea. He himself tells us that his father placed him in the best school which the city of Nice had for boys like him.

In his childish days the boy was more fond of play than of study. One day, as he was playing, he caught a grasshopper and took it into the house, but in doing so broke its leg. He was only a very small child; yet knowing that he had hurt the little insect, he became so sad that he wept bitterly for some hours. He was a very kind-hearted boy, and could not bear to give pain to any one.

Another day, as he was walking in the fields, he came near a pool, where a woman was washing clothes. Suddenly she fell into the water, and was in danger of being drowned. There was no one else near enough to help her; so, although he was quite young and small, the boy jumped after her, and saved her life.

He was still so fond of play that when the family were in Genoa, a city in Italy, he grew tired of going daily to school. Finding a number of other boys of like mind, he agreed with them to run away from home. The foolish boys got hold of a boat, into which each of them put a little food, and with nets and lines for fishing, they started for the East, as they thought. They had not gone very far before a bigger vessel came in search of them, with Garibaldi's father at its helm. He made the boys turn back, and with their boat in tow they were taken home.

When the boy was old enough he went to sea. He was full of delight at the ship in which he was to sail; and even when he was an old man he looked back with pleasure on the happy hour when he became one of her crew. His second voyage was to Rome, in a ship of his father's. He had read and dreamt of that fine old city all his young life. It was very dear to him, and now he saw Rome for the first time with feelings of great joy. The lad stuck to the sea until he rose to be captain of a trading ship. But the great work of his life was done in another way.

In those days there were many rulers in Italy, and the Austrians and some other nations had armies in the country. Garibaldi had been fond of Italy from his childhood, and he wanted to make his people free and great once more. Above all things, he was a patriot, one who loves his own country. To-day Italy is one nation, under one king, whose capital is Rome, and the man who did most to bring this about was Garibaldi.

GIUSEPPE GARIBALDI

A LITTLE PRINCESS IN HER COURT DRESS

AFTER A PORTRAIT BY MOREELSE

QUEEN CLOTILDA AND KING CLOVIS

ONCE upon a time (and all this that you are about to read is true) there was a large wild country in Europe called the country of Gaul.

It lay between sea and sea, between mountain and mountain; and if you would know the names of the seas, they are the Mediterranean Sea, the Atlantic Ocean, and that part of the Atlantic Ocean which is called to-day the English Channel. And if you would know the names of the mountains, they are the Pyrenees and the Alps.

Between these boundaries then lay the wild country of Gaul. It was made up of many other high mountains, besides deep valleys and great plains, through which flowed mighty rivers. These plains were darkened by great forests where fierce beasts roamed—wild oxen and elk, wolves, and swine that were fiercer than wolves.

Fierce men roamed there too; half-naked savages, who hunted and killed the wild beasts so that the hunters themselves might eat and live. And as some wild animals gather together in herds, so these wild men herded together in tribes; and of the number of tribes that lived in Gaul in that far-away time we cannot tell you, there were so many of them.

These savages made for themselves huts of wood and of clay and roofed them over with branches and straw. Round their rude huts they heaped a rough wall made of wood and earth and stones. This helped to keep away enemies, either men or beasts, from their camp or village.

No tribe stayed long in one place. So soon as all the eatable wild beasts were killed, so soon as all the flocks and herds were used up, then word was given to move. Away wandered the tribe to some more fruitful spot; and if the coveted place was already occupied by another tribe, then battles were fought again and again and again until one or the other side proved victorious. So it was that these tribes of Gaul were forever wandering and forever fighting.

In time vast hordes of them spread toward the south, swarming over the Alps into Italy. So many were there of them, so fiercely did they fight, and so often did they win, that they even threatened the sacred city of Rome itself. Never fear but that they were driven back again to their own wild country by the brave Romans. Nay, more, in the great days of Julius Cæsar they were conquered by him, their country was taken possession of by him, Roman governors ruled over them, Roman soldiers became their companions.

So it came about that the wild barbarians were taught a great many useful things by their conquerors. They learned how to build towns and roads and bridges, how to fight with more strength and cunning and less savagery; they learned to speak the Roman language, to use the Roman laws.

And the time of this world went on; years passed; and Rome ceased to bring forth strong men; great generals there were none; the Roman soldiers forgot their old-time skill in battle; the Roman governors knew no more the virtue of honorable ruling; the might and the power of ancient Rome was over, and forever.

Then the conquered men of Gaul grew restless. They began to fret against the indignity of being ruled by their foes, they began to long and to dream and to plan for freedom, for rulers and laws of their own making.

There were three great tribes or peoples in Gaul at that time, and these three tribes were divided up again many times into smaller tribes. The names of the three great tribes in Gaul were these—the Visigoths, the Burgundians, and the Franks.

Now from the last of these great peoples, from a small tribe called the Salian Franks, sprang Clovis, the strong man, the chief who at last became king over the whole of Gaul. He came of a brave stock. His grandfather Merovæus gave the name Merovingian to a line of kings, and of this line Clovis was the greatest.

This same Merovæus won great honor in the war against Attila, the fierce King of the Huns. When that terrible hero invaded Gaul with his savage host Merovæus gloriously drove him back again into his wilds.

After Merovæus came Childeric, his son, of whom many a brave battle tale might be told. When Clovis, his son, was but fifteen years old, Childeric died. Young as he was, the stern warriors of Childeric proclaimed Clovis their leader, carrying him up and down the village upon a shield as a sign thereof.

This showed that he had proved himself worthy of honor in battle even then, for at that time chieftainship—nay, even kingship—was won by a man's own strength and might and not by inheritance from his father.

From the first Clovis must have dreamed of the great achievements in war, of the power and greatness, which should be his. He must have early shown his ambitious spirit, for it was not long before his name became known to kings and leaders of great tribes. He led his warriors to battle and victory many and many a time, gaining more lands and more power; so that when one fine day he sent his messengers to the King of the Burgundians demanding the hand of his fair niece in marriage, that King did not refuse the request, and in good time the beautiful Princess Clotilda became the wife of King Clovis.

Now Clotilda was a Christian. Clovis was a pagan. He worshiped, he and all his warriors with him, at the altars of strange gods, made of wood and stone.

In the fifth century, in the time of Clovis, most men were pagans. Nevertheless the Church of Christ had already begun to show some little power. Its bishops and priests were often rich and powerful men owning great lands and much treasure. Clovis, although he did not agree with their faith, was always ready to help them when he could, and this even before he married Clotilda. Afterward, you will understand, he was more than ever their very good friend.

This made the good bishops hope that one day Clotilda would persuade her stern husband to turn Christian—for he loved her dearly, and she him. And this was her prayer night and day for many and many a year: "Dear God, make of Clovis a good Christian, that he may live only to honor thy Church and glorify thy name, here on earth, and afterward in heaven."

Not only did Clotilda pray and fast, and do good deeds of charity in the hope that her prayers might be granted, but she spared no pains, using all her sweet arts of speech and manner to persuade her lord to desert the false gods of his fathers and worship the true God. All her labors were in vain; yet when her first little son was born, Clotilda's hopes rose high. Surely Clovis could deny her nothing at such a joyous time. So she came to him, speaking fair. "In a little while," she said, "the holy Bishop of Rheims, the good St. Remy, will come to baptize our babe. O good my lord, wilt thou not let him baptize thee also upon that same most joyous day?"

"Nay," answered the King, but gently, "baptize the child an thou must; as for me, I will worship my father's gods or none. Verily they have served me well in battle, forever leading me to victory, and shall I desert them for no cause save a woman's fancy?"

So the child alone was baptized, and was christened Ingomer by the holy bishop. This much had Clotilda for comfort, yet not for long; for very soon after the little Ingomer sickened and died, and when Clovis came back from some war in triumph there was no little son awaiting him to rejoice his proud heart. The Queen herself, white and sorrowful, told him of their loss.

"What have you to say for your God now?" cried Clovis, beside himself with anger and grief. "He has killed my son, my first-born son. You and your bishops make great ado about his power and might. You say he hears all your prayers and answers them. Now see what he has done for you. See how he has answered your prayers. You took my son and baptized him; now behold him—dead. My gods were angered and they killed him; your God was too weak to prevent them."

Then answered the Queen, grown very white and still. "I bear up against my sorrow," she said, and these are her very words; "I bear up against my sorrow, because I believe in the wisdom and goodness of the true God. Ingomer is with the whitest angels in heaven."

Upon this Clovis fell to silence, nor did he reproach the Queen again. Nevertheless, he would never suffer her to speak of her faith or her God for many a long and weary month. It seemed as if he were more determined than ever to worship his own gods. And yet, for all his seeming sternness, the King, even in the midst of his wars and ambitious dreams, must have grown more inclined toward the new religion than he let his wife suspect, for Clotilda never lost heart. She never ceased to believe that one day her prayers would be granted and Clovis would become a Christian. Her hopefulness, her gentleness, her strength to bear sorrow, impressed Clovis in spite of himself. It made him think about this new religion and wonder what there was in it which could make a weak woman so strong.

All the while he fought many desperate battles for his ambition's sake, winning power and fame in the land. Men feared him, too, for he showed little mercy to his enemies, and for this we must not unduly blame him. In those days, soldiers, even Christian soldiers, thought but little of the virtue of gentleness and forgiveness.

Not so very long after Prince Chlodomir, his second son, was born, the Allemans, a strong and savage German tribe, crossed over the river Rhine in great numbers, and attacked and made havoc among the Frank settlements. They coveted these rich and pleasant lands for themselves.

Clovis no sooner heard of the invasion than he made instantly ready to march against them. In full battle array he came to take leave of Clotilda and his small son.

Clovis, like most of the Franks, was tall and fair and fierce-looking. His yellow hair fell in two long braids to his waist, his mustache, too, was long and fair. He wore a helmet on his head, an axe at his belt, and a two-edged sword. He carried also a javelin, a lance, and a shield. His cloak and vest were made of beautiful fur, his tunic of linen, and his leather shoes were bound with long and wide leather thongs reaching from ankle to knee.

Before he left her, Clotilda, again braving his displeasure, spoke her old request. She feared lest one day he might fall in battle unbaptized, and that for her would indeed be a great sorrow —separating them even in death.

"How canst thou beg me to desert my own gods at this most dangerous time?" cried Clovis when the Queen had spoken. "Know'st not that these Allemans are fierce and terrible foes? Though we fear them not, we may not despise them. They must be conquered, else we shall know neither peace nor freedom in this land ever again. Yet you ask me to desert my strong gods now when I most need them!"

"There is only one God, the Lord Jesus Christ," said Clotilda steadfastly, "mighty in battle— strong to save." Thereupon she fell on her knees before the King, crying, "Oh, for the sake of thy little son, and the love we bear him, wilt thou not make thy wife blessed?"

Now the young Chlodomir had been baptized, and still he lived, a strong and lusty babe. Moreover, with every year, the bishops of the Church gained more power and influence in the world. Their friendship and help were not to be despised. Clovis knew this, and he knew that he could count on them to help him well should he turn Christian; he also loved his fair wife dearly, and secretly longed to make her happy. Nevertheless he did not quite dare to let go of his old gods. He believed they had helped him to win many of his battles. Thus it was that, after thinking for a while, he said: "I cannot do all thou wouldst have me do, Clotilda, but this much I promise thee: if ever in battle I do call upon my gods and they answer me not; if I find that I and all my warriors are in sore danger of defeat, then will I call upon thy God, and if he hear my prayer and succor me, him will I worship and none other for evermore."

And the Queen answered: "It is well; I am content."

And now Clotilda serenely waited, sure that her prayers were to be answered at last, while Clovis marched away to fight the Allemans.

These barbarians fought like savage heroes, careless of death, eager for victory. Clovis had set himself no easy task.

In one of their fiercest encounters the King suddenly became aware that the battle was going against him. His keen eye saw that where the blows rained thickest the Franks were giving way; they were being slowly but steadily beaten back by the Allemans.

With shouts and fierce cries Clovis flung himself into the struggle, and still, in spite of his bravery, his warriors were forced back by these desperate enemies.

Then the King called loudly upon his gods for help. They vouchsafed him no answer. Again and again, hot with anger, he called; all in vain. In his despair Clovis remembered Clotilda and his promise. "Thou God of Clotilda!" he thundered, and his voice could be heard even above the noise of battle, "now do I call upon thee for aid. Award me the victory and I turn from my gods and follow thee forever." O miracle! Even as he spoke the tide of battle turned. Led by Clovis, the Franks with new courage rallied, and gathering strength with every inch of recovered ground, at last put their foes to flight.

Clovis soon vanquished the Allemans altogether, and it was not long before they were forced to recross the Rhine and return to their own country.

The King faithfully kept his promise. When he returned victorious to Clotilda he told her the good news, and one day the holy Bishop St. Remy baptized him, and three thousand of his warriors with him, in the cathedral at Rheims.

It was a great and glorious day. Judge for yourselves whether Clotilda rejoiced or not, and whether she did not praise God in prayer and good deeds all the rest of her life. If you look you will find her name written down among the saints in the Calendar of the Roman Catholic Church.

As for Clovis, the good bishop told him on his baptism to "hate those gods which he had adored, and adore that one which he had hated"; but whether he obeyed this command faithfully it is not for us to say, nor whether, having become a Christian, he grew gentler and more forgiving than before. The age in which he lived was a fierce and cruel one, and one so far away that we may not judge too harshly of his deeds. Certainly he did one good thing, and for that he is now remembered. By the help of the Church, by his own strength and prowess, by the aid of his own cunning brain, using treachery and truth alike, Clovis accomplished his end. He ruled over the whole of Gaul. He made a divided and turbulent country into some likeness of a united kingdom. He, drawing, as it were, upon the large white sheet of the history of his country, till then scarcely marked save by scribbles—he, drawing then, worked out a rough and shadowy outline upon it. And from this rough and shadowy outline was shaped, in time, the fair and comely form of the kingdom of France.

ELIZABETH OF HUNGARY

THIS is the story of a girl who was born to the King and Queen of Hungary in the year 1207. She came just when the great troubles of the King were at an end. Wars had ceased for a time, and the people felt happy once more.

The little Elizabeth was a fair and lovely child, and she was as good as she was pretty. People used to say that the first words she spoke were those of prayer. When she was only a small girl, she gave away her toys and her rich dresses to the poorer children, who could not have such beautiful things.

When King Herman heard of the sweet young princess, he said: "Would that this fair child could some day become the wife of my son, Louis." He asked the King, her father, to let her come to his court, to be taught with his young son, and he sent a great company of lords and ladies to bring her. Elizabeth was only four years old; but though it pained her mother to part from such a winning child, her father thought it wise to let her go. He gave her a cradle and a bath, each made of pure silver; and he sent twelve young ladies of his court to wait upon her. He also sent so many fine things for King Herman and his Queen that it needed thirteen wagons to carry them.

Happily, the two children soon became friends. They played together, and were seldom away from each other. Little Louis liked the gentle Elizabeth, who was so unlike every other child.

When Elizabeth was older she loved to go among the poor children, and give them food and other things they needed. The good King was very kind to her, and while he lived no one was allowed to say a word against her. But when he died the Queen showed dislike to the princess; and some of her people told young Louis that Elizabeth was not fitted to be a king's wife.

Louis did not believe what they said about her. He knew how gentle and patient she was, even as a young girl; how sweet was her temper, and how glad she was to help the people. Often when his mother and sister were rude, he would comfort Elizabeth with words of kindness.

When Elizabeth was only fifteen she was married to Louis. There never was a royal lady who tried more earnestly to do her duty to the people over whom she was placed. She often visited the houses of the poor, and helped them with her own hands. One day, during a very cold winter, she left her castle, and went down into the valley. In her hands she carried a large basket, full of bread and meat, which was so heavy that she almost bent with the weight. On the way she met her husband, who was returning from a hunt, and he was much surprised to see her with such a heavy burden.

"Let me see what you are carrying, my Elizabeth," he said. "It seems too heavy for you." She tried to throw her cloak over the basket, but the King drew it gently back. And as he looked, so the story says, he saw that the basket was full of roses—lovely red and white roses—which were larger and sweeter than any he had ever before seen; and he knew at once that these were not the flowers of earth. The prince put out his hand, and, taking a rose from her basket, he placed it in his coat. Then meekly bowing his head, he went on his way, leaving her to go to the help of the poor and hungry people.

Elizabeth of Hungary lived and died a long while ago. But the memory of her beautiful life, and the story of her sweet girlhood, should be a lesson to girls of all ages and countries. She died while yet a young woman. No wonder that almost at once her name was placed among those of women called saints.

Some Girls Who Wore Ruffs By Belle Moses

I. A ROYAL FAMILY

Down the grand staircase, tripping lightly, with her finger on her rosy lips, her curls flying, the tail of her satin gown over her arm, came "Mistress Mary, quite contrary," of the royal house of Tudor, closely followed by her attendants.

The day was young, and "Brother Hal" was asleep, so Mary felt care-free as she danced across the polished floor and out through the great door of the palace. The garden was drenched with the morning dew, but the little satin shoes plunged recklessly through the dampness, in and out among the flower-beds of the king's garden, plucking here and there as fancy craved, with no thought of consequences. There were few who dared to pluck the king's flowers, but Henry VIII., with his testy temper, had a genuine affection for his youngest sister, and was only "Brother Hal" to this madcap princess. He was "bluff King Hal" in those early days, living peacefully enough with his good wife Catharine and their little daughter Mary, and the court would have been a dull place indeed had not the king's sister played her pranks and kept them all astir.

Only a girl she was—twelve or thirteen at the most—with all the freshness of the springtime in her blood; but they dressed her like a woman, for she was tall and well built, having beauty, too, and a sharp and ready wit. This morning she led her companions a wild chase from terrace to terrace, in among the flower-beds, gay with yellow and white narcissus and deep-hued pansies, sweet with violets and jasmine.

"Pluck them, pluck them!" she cried to the others, and while they still held back, she stamped her little foot, and the hot blood of the Tudors flamed in her cheeks. "Mary Tudor commands!" she said, with an imperious wave of her hand.

"But—your Highness—the king—" began a timid damsel.

"Out upon you, Jane! Come hither, gentlemen; stand round and hide the timid wench from view while she does my bidding. Tush! child, the king will not miss them, but should he do so and call you to account, why then, forsooth, *I* commanded you to take them!" She flung her head with royal scorn, showing the bare rounded throat from which the soft ruff fell back.

"On, on, my lords and ladies, to the tennis-court!" she cried, and these children—they were nothing more—followed their daring young leader to the king's beautiful courts. Tennis was the popular game of the day; indeed, there are few games played with a ball which can boast of such antiquity, but it was a game for kings alone, or for those very high in rank, so we can imagine Mistress Mary, her gown tucked up, her eyes sparkling, her curls flying, her strong, lithe young figure darting swallow-like after the ball, her racket poised to send it back across the net.

This first girl who wore a ruff was very like other girls of her age. Our grandmothers perhaps would have called her "forward and pert," but poor little Mary had no mother to check the wild spirits and curb the very strong will.

A few years later, in the train which had accompanied Mary to France, where she married the French king, were Sir Thomas Boleyn and his little daughter Anne. This small maid, barely more than a child, had become such a favorite at the French court that she did not return to England with the young Queen Mary when the old king died. She grew to be a most bewitching little creature, full of grace and joyousness, but fond of admiration and power above all else. She received enough compliments and flattery to have turned her silly head, so it was high time her father brought her home to their country-seat, whence an occasional visit to London Town was a rare and wondrous dissipation. A letter which she wrote to her sister during one of these visits shows her to have been, at heart, a very simple girl. It reads:

DEAR MARY: I have been in town almost a month, yet I cannot say I have found anything in London extremely agreeable. We rise so late in the morning—seldom before six o'clock—and sit up so late at night, being scarcely in bed before ten, that I am quite sick of it, and were it not for the abundance of fine things I am every day getting, I should be impatient of returning into the country.

• After describing some of the "fine things" bought by her "indulgent Mother," she adds:

And I am to have a pair of new stuff shoes for my Lord of Norfolk's ball, which will be three shillings. Pray take care of the poultry during my absence. Poor things! I always fed them myself; and if Margery has knitted me the crimson worsted mittens, I should be glad if they were sent up the first opportunity.

In truth, there was plain living for the children of that day; breakfast at six and bedtime at ten were considered fashionable hours even for the "grown-ups." Practical little maids these were, with their poultry-yards and their dairies, counting the pennies much more carefully than the girls of to-day, in spite of the routs and balls and gorgeousness of the court; and crimson worsted mittens were a great comfort in cold, bleak London.

History does not record whether Anne Boleyn wore a ruff before her marriage to the king, but she chanced to be the mother of the lady who wore the biggest ever made. For, by Elizabeth's time, they had become quite the fashion both with men and women, young and old.

II. LIFE AT HOME

To the girls of to-day, whose lives are governed by kindness, whose homes are to them the centers of happiness, the lives of the maidens of the Middle Ages must seem very dreary. Parents had an idea that sternness was the only rule by which to bring up children, and if they failed in that they were not doing their duty. Even big boys and girls stood silent and uncovered in their fathers' presence; and girls knelt humbly on a cushion until their mothers had left the room. The instant children offended their parents, they were punished with stripes and blows.

But, of course, in fair England there must have been some happy youngsters whose fathers and mothers were not always thinking of their faults. On the banks of the Thames, in beautiful Chelsea, about a hundred yards from the waterside, stood a fine English homestead, built after the fashion of the times, with overhanging porches and bay-windows, jutting casements and gables, and furnished with all the comforts to be obtained. Here lived the finest statesman and most noble gentleman of King Henry's reign, Sir Thomas More, with his wife and children. There were three fair young daughters, Margaret, Elizabeth, and Cecily, a son John, a stepdaughter also named Margaret, and an adopted daughter—another Margaret still. Margaret More was always called Meg, her stepsister Daisy, and Margaret Giggs, the adopted daughter, was distinguished by the name of Mercy.

They all grew up in this lovely country home and worked and played and studied happily enough. The More girls read and wrote Latin quite as easily as English, and cultivated their minds as well as their healthy young bodies, for they were out in the open all the time they were not at their books or helping in the house, and their wise father took care that they did not become overlearned little prigs. In spite of Plato and Socrates, they could enjoy a pull on the river, a supper by moonlight, an evening in the hay-field, full of pleasant talk and laughter and harmless jests. They were fond of animals of all kinds; dormice, owls, and hares were some of their pets, which they tamed and trained to do all sorts of tricks.

In the house there was much work for each little maid. They rose even before that famous bird, the lark, and though their stepmother was generally very good to them, she set them hard tasks. On one occasion something went wrong with the churning, the butter would not come, and the household was quite upset. Good Dame Alice flew around distracted, and Gillian, the cook, declared the cream was bewitched. Every misfortune in those days was laid to witchery, not only among the common people, but among many of the higher class; but Dame Alice More knew better. The churn was filled with good cream which could not be wasted, so she sent for the four older girls and bade them take turns at the churning till the butter came, if they sat up all night for it. Other girls might have complained, for it was late already, but they went to work with a will and beguiled the time by singing "Chevy Chase" and other frolicsome tunes, but still the butter would not come. At length Mercy suggested that they chant the One Hundred and

WHEN THE RUFF WAS WORN

95

Nineteenth Psalm, which they did in Latin, and presently they heard the buttermilk separating and splashing in earnest. It was near midnight and they were almost asleep before the butter came, but Gillian was convinced that their Latin broke the spell.

The little maids went to court with their mother, Dame Alice, who was resplendent in

"IN THE DAYS OF 'GOOD QUEEN BESS'"

crimson gown and coif, the girls in satin petticoats puffed high in panniers over their slender waists. Tight-laced corsets were then fashionable; over these, the square-cut bodices, with the upstanding ruffs of lace richly embroidered in gold and silver; sometimes little caps upon their heads, but oftener their curls escaped and lay in ringlets on their white necks. We have seen them, or at least girls like them, in pictures which good Master Holbein has left behind him.

The king made merry at his court, and many games were played to pass the time. Dancing was much indulged in, the young ones joining in the stately measures, while the older ones sat apart, playing cards, or chess, or "tables," which we know better by the name of backgammon.

Meanwhile the ruff began to increase in size, and after King Henry's death it became a general article of dress. Little King Edward VI. drew around him many small lords and ladies, for even while Edward was still a boy, his uncle, the Lord Protector, was hunting for a Queen of England, and many a tiny lass in all her bravery came to court to make her bow and pass muster there. Among his favorite playmates were his cousin Lady Jane Grey and his big sister Elizabeth; his elder sister Mary was too old and grave to be much of a companion.

The burly, wicked King Henry had done one good thing—he taught his subjects the use of learning. The very smallest girl of any rank at all could read and write good English, and, better still, good Latin, with often wide knowledge of Greek. Most famous among the girl scholars was Lady Jane Grey. She was a granddaughter of the madcap Princess Mary, and so closely connected with the throne of England that a marriage with the young king seemed a wise and proper thing. Henry VIII. had another grandniece, little Queen Mary of Scotland, granddaughter of his older sister Margaret, who would also have made a fair Queen of England. Both these girls were great students and rivaled their cousin Elizabeth in cleverness and learning. Mary never saw her English cousins, but doubtless Jane and Elizabeth must have been closely associated, for Elizabeth's tutor, Roger Ascham, knew the small Jane quite well and often praised her learning. And Elizabeth, during her childhood, was at best but a poor, unnoticed princess, neglected at court and in many instances severely treated. History may not make mention of so slight a thing as an interchange of girlish confidences, but it is pleasant to picture these girls with the ruffs wandering in the old gardens or pacing a long avenue shaded by great trees.

But the ruffs were growing fuller and taller. The girls could not put their heads together and whisper secrets; they could not even sit close together, for the fashions were putting them far apart, behind a mere masquerade of dress.

WHEN Elizabeth was queen, things had come to a pretty pass. The real girl, from her slim waist down to her toes, carried a framework on which she hung her garments; she wore long, straight, tight corsets, stiff with whalebone, and when the corsets were laced up, and the framework hung

QUEEN ELIZABETH

from her waist, my little lady then put on her farthingale. This was a round petticoat made of canvas or cloth stiffened with whalebone and covered with taffeta, or some other good material, so broad just below the waist that its circumference was greater than round the bottom of the skirt, something like those severe ladies in a toy Noah's ark, only bigger. The slim girlish figures looked pinched and narrow, between the wide hips, the puffed sleeves, and the standing-out ruffs.

Though modest at first, these ruffs became a most imposing structure. Of course they were made for people who had long necks, like Elizabeth and Henry III. of France, and Marguerite de Valois, Queen of Navarre, another long-necked lady; and as girls became "grown-ups" and even "married dames" when they were scarce in their teens, of course they must needs follow the fashion in the matter of ruffs. Well, they grew and grew, those ruffs, but only the higher class could afford to wear them, for starch had not yet been heard of, and one or two wearings

made them hang limp about the neck. King Henry of France, who was tall and thin, with a very long neck, wore a ruff one third of a yard deep, containing about eighteen or nineteen yards of linen. Indeed, in the French court, the lords and ladies could scarcely move their heads and found it extremely difficult to eat and drink.

Many of these ruffs were made with four or five rows of lace, the last row appearing above the top of the head, and each supported by threads of wire. The ruffs put an end to flowing hair. It was piled high on the head and in many cases worn in short tight curls; ladies used false hair in great quantities and changed the color whenever they pleased. Elizabeth is said to have had many wigs of various colors. Strings of precious stones were twined in the hair, making quite a pretty head-dress. So popular did wigs become that there was scarcely enough hair to supply them, and the small maid with long locks never went out alone, for fear some unscrupulous person might cut them off and sell them.

English people did not wear their ruffs quite so wide, a quarter of a yard being the limit, and pretty young girls took care to set them well back from the neck, to show their white throats. The queen's ruff was extraordinarily high and stiff. But even the well-to-do did not like to see their pretty ruffs hang limp, and thanks to the wit of a certain clever woman, the remedy was found.

In the year 1564, Mrs. Dinghen, the wife of Elizabeth's Dutch coachman, brought over to England the art of starching. Imagine the delight of the courtiers when ruffs were taught to "stand alone," and possibly the poor little girls rejoiced more than all, for they were not continually having their ruffs "pinched up" whenever they came near the ruthless hands of their elders. Mrs. Dinghen soon became court starcher and established a fine business. All the great ladies in London sent their crumpled ruffs to be "done up," and the good woman starched them white or yellow to order. Many came to her as pupils, and honest Mrs. Dinghen bade fair to become a very rich person.

Besides the starch, wires were often used to stiffen the larger ruffs. These wires, covered with gold or silver thread, came round the neck as a sort of support, for the mass of linen was very heavy. Many of the ruffs, too, were worked with silk embroidery and tinsel threads.

IV. DAYS OF SPLENDOR

IN the days of "Good Queen Bess" court life took on a splendor that it had not known for years. Elizabeth loved magnificence, and the lords and ladies of her court dressed and lived with a sumptuousness never before heard of. The girls who wore ruffs were in many instances among the queen's ladies-in-waiting, for, being the "Virgin Queen," she had many maids about her, and kept up a vigorous correspondence with her "dear cousins" this or that, at home or abroad, for Elizabeth was a clever letter-writer. Her dear cousin Mary Queen of Scots was perhaps the "dearest cousin" of all; indeed, many and most affectionate were the letters exchanged between the two queens who hated each other with such deadly hatred.

These girls who wore ruffs began to have more comfort in their living, more pleasures in their daily intercourse. Their homes were very beautiful, but articles of furniture in those days were very rude and defective. Down-stairs, in the halls and banqueting-rooms, one came across fine tapestries, richly carved woodwork, massive tables, besides much fine plate and gilding; but above-stairs my lady's chamber was simple and severe—a cupboard or two to accommodate the stiff gowns, a jointed stool, a steel mirror, a ewer and basin for her toilet, a plain table for her books, perhaps an embroidery-frame, and a stiff high-backed chair. The bed alone was luxurious; it was canopied and festooned like a throne, of softest down, with fine blankets, linen sheets, and a coverlet embroidered with the arms of the owner, and over all were beautiful silk hangings.

A girl had a great deal to do in those days. She could always play upon either the lute or the viol. She commenced her morning—usually in the gray dawn—with prayer; then a hearty breakfast of meat and ale; next there was embroidery to do, after which she visited the dairy and the pastry-cook; later she worked in her garden; then a visit to her bees, or to see if the hemp was coming up, or to inspect the cows, or to feed her poultry in the farm-yard. At court the maids-in-waiting avoided idleness by using their needles, reading the Bible or history, or by writing; they also studied music when off duty.

Shuttlecock was a great favorite among girls, for there were spacious halls in which to play, and tennis became more common. Blindman's-buff, or hoodman-blind, as it was then called, was popular among girls and boys, and a dozen other games which are played and enjoyed by the children of to-day. But most they loved the open. Every little maid of any degree could mount a horse, some could even join the hunt, and many of the rollicking songs of the times caught their childish fancy.

There were festivals, too—Christmas with its mummeries, May-day with its pole and dances, Shrove Tuesday, and all the others. There were fairs held on the village green, and many pageants to delight the eye, for Elizabeth journeyed from place to place with splendor and ceremony, and little country girls, dressed in their best, stood in the highroads to curtsy as she passed.

Away in her quiet country home, small Amy Robsart heard with wonder of the doings of the court; the far-off splendor caught her girlish fancy. Her mother died when she was a baby,

MARY QUEEN OF SCOTS AT THE AGE OF TWELVE

and her father, Sir Hugh, petted and spoiled her, denying her nothing it was in his power to give. She was a beautiful little creature, and she longed to get out of her tiny corner of the world. She could not have been more than fifteen when the gorgeous, glittering Leicester found out who she was, and wooed and won her.

The little countess, as we all know, lived the rest of her short life at Cumnor Hall, very near the earl's great castle of Kenilworth, the scene of the most wonderful feasting and pageantry ever displayed in England. Dear little Amy! so trusting and childlike, yet so womanly withal. Did ever a fairer maiden wear a ruff? Even Elizabeth was moved by the quiet grace of her, and my Lord of Leicester got the cold shoulder when the news of her death broke up their revels at the castle.

ELIZABETH SIGNING THE DEATH WARRANT OF MARY QUEEN OF SCOTS
FROM THE PAINTING BY J. SCHRADER

But of all the girls who wore ruffs, there was none sweeter and fairer than Mary, Queen of Scotland. She was the tiniest wisp of a baby when her father left her queen of this cold, bleak country. On her nurse's knee she gazed with round eyes on the peers of the realm who knelt in homage before her. She was only nine months old when she was crowned in Stirling church; she was taken from her cradle, wrapped in royal robes, and carried by her lord keepers and officers of state to the ceremony, and because poor Baby cried for her nurse, it was considered an ill omen. From the moment of her birth her great-uncle, Henry VIII. of England, tried to kidnap her, for, besides being Queen of the Scots, she was along the line of succession to the throne of England, and there is no telling what the old monster would have done to her had she fallen into his clutches. But her faithful lord keepers kept guard, and the baby was allowed to see but one noble at a time, and no visitor could enter Stirling Castle—which was her first home—with more than two servants in his train.

When she was about four, they sent her for greater safety to the priory on the Isle of Inchmahom, in the beautiful Lake of Menteith, famous for its Spanish chestnut-trees. They formed a merry party in the grim old priory. The little queen was allowed to have with her her four young namesakes and playmates, Mary Beaton, Mary Seaton, Mary Livingston, and Mary Fleming—the queen's Maries, as they were called. What happy times they had, those five, along the shores of the lake, the little queen in Highland costume, her golden hair bound with a rose-colored snood, her tartan scarf fastened with a golden agraffe engraved with the united arms of Scotland and Lorraine. She was French on her mother's side and closely related to the reigning house. When she was six, a charming, gracious little princess, it was arranged that she should marry her cousin, the Dauphin of France, as soon as both children were old enough, and it was decided that she should go to France to complete her education, which was far advanced for a child of her age. She compared favorably with all the girls of her day in her love of learning.

There was no happier, merrier, sweeter, more lovable little girl; she excelled in the dance; she inherited from both parents a love of music and great delight in poetry; she was fond of sport and astonished every one by her skill in handling her falcon. Nothing pleased Mary more than the preparations for a mighty chase. What a brilliant portrait of a girl she makes, and how we love to look at it and to think about it!

With the passing of "Good Queen Bess" much magnificence vanished from the court; but the ruff stayed on, not so deep nor so full, but a most important part of the dress for all that, and much more comfortable. Master Will Shakespeare wore it, and his daughter, pretty Judith, the belle of Stratford, the daintiest maid in all Warwickshire, wore it, too, with her Sunday kirtle. She was a merry little lass, and one of our English novelists has painted a fair picture of her as she walked in the quaint old town "along by the church and over the foot-bridge spanning the Avon, and so into the meadows lying adjacent to

POCAHONTAS WITH HER HIGH HAT AND RUFF

the stream." She picked wild flowers as she went along, and hummed to herself the quaint old songs that she had caught from her father's books or from the glees she had heard at odd times. The maids of that day were fond of singing, and Mistress Judith's sweet voice trilled out along the banks of the Avon:

> Come blow thy horn, hunter!
> Come blow thy horn, hunter!
> Come blow thy horn, jolly hunter!

echoing from hill to hill. And again:

> For a morn in spring is the sweetest thing
> Cometh in all the year.

Judith herself was like the springtime, radiant, fresh, and young, and it was no uncommon sight to see Shakespeare, with his grave face and quiet eyes, deep in converse with this favorite child of his, as they wandered along the winding course of the river.

Pretty Judith may not have had the learning of her predecessors who wore ruffs, but she was happier, no doubt, in her simple life, with her friend and gossip, modest Prue, reading together her father's plays, and building their own romances, girl-fashion, by their own firesides.

King James I. brought much learning to the court, and already love of adventure had lured some daring mariners to the New World. Sir Walter Raleigh, the Cabots, Captain John Smith, and many others had planted their first American colonies, and out on the virgin grass the practical dames of Holland, France, and England stretched their starched ruffs to bleach and dry, for, deary me! one must be fashionable, if there were only the home people and the wondering savages to see!

Little Pocahontas now rises before us, true child of the woods, this little Indian princess, with her lithe brown figure, her bare arms and feet, her dress of deerskin, her graceful neck wound about with the glass beads the white settlers had given her—a strange, innocent child of such a wily old chief as Powhatan, always ready to help her white friends in their need. We all know the story of how she saved Captain John Smith from a fearful death, and how ever afterward she was watchful to see that no harm came to her friend and his people. Many times she came through the woods to warn them of danger, and when they were nearly starving she brought them food day after day; in truth, this little brown maid of the forest and stream loved the big blond captain whose life she saved so many times.

Old Powhatan proved so treacherous after Captain Smith sailed away to England that the colonists decided if they captured Pocahontas and held her as hostage, they might make terms with the crafty old warrior. The girl quite willingly went with them to Jamestown, where, little by little, she fell into English ways. She discarded the deerskin dress, the gaudy beads and dangling ornaments of her tribe, for the sober costume of an English maid, even to the white ruff which topped the high bodice; and when John Rolfe had made her his wife, behold little Pocahontas in brave attire, in ruff and high hat and all the fancies of the times, sailing away to that dim old England of which she had heard so much, and making her bow to the king and queen with all the haughtiness of a foreign princess—which, indeed, she was!

THE old, old times have gone. On that American soil a great nation has sprung up; and the girls with the ruffs have vanished with Queen Elizabeth and the rest. Girls of the same age to-day are blither, younger, and happier—no cares of the household, no distasteful duties, no stern parents to fret their daily life. Margery and Joan and Elizabeth of that time may have rustled proudly in their silks and stiff brocades; but Polly and Katharine of to-day, in simple muslins and white aprons, have no cause to envy their bygone sisters with the ruffs.

JOAN OF ARC, THE MAID OF ORLEANS

Joan was born at the little village of Domremy, France, January 6, 1412. She was the daughter of a poor man, and she lived in a very unhappy time in the history of her country, of which for almost a hundred years the English had been trying, through terrible wars, to make conquest.

In the middle of these miseries Joan was born, in a village where almost everybody was on the side of the Dauphin —the right side. In the village nearest to hers, Maxey, the people took the English side, and the boys of the two places had pitched battles with sticks and stones.

Though Joan could run faster than the other girls and boys, and beat them when they ran races, she liked to be quiet. Nobody could sew and spin better than she did, and she was very fond of praying alone in church. She would even go away from the other children into lonely places, and implore God to have pity on France. The services in church, the singing and the music, made her very happy, and when she heard the

FROM A STATUE BY HENRI MICHEL ANTOINE CHAPU

church bells across the fields, she would say her prayer. She was very kind, and would give up her bed to any poor traveler whom her father took in for a night, and would sleep beside the hearth. She took care of the sick, and if ever she had any money she would spend it on masses to be said in honor of God and for the sake of men's souls.

So Joan lived till she was thirteen. She was a strong, handsome girl, beautifully made, with black hair. We do not know the color of her eyes, probably brown or dark gray. A young knight wrote to his mother, when he first saw Joan, that she was "a creature all divine." Joan never sat to a painter for her portrait, though once she saw a kind of fancy picture of herself in the hands of a Scottish archer.

Young men do not say so much about a girl who is not beautiful, and, indeed, armies do not rush together to follow a maiden without good looks. But though Joan, when she came to command armies, liked to be well dressed, and to have fine armor, that was partly because she was a natural, healthy girl, and partly because she was a kind of banner for men to follow into fight, and banners ought to be splendid.

She took no thought of her own beauty, and the young knights and squires who fought, later, under her flag, said that they looked on her as a sacred thing, and never dreamed of making love to her. She let it be known that she would never marry any one while the English were still in France. She was not a nun, and had not made a vow never to marry at all, but while her country was in danger she never thought of marriage; she had other things to do.

Eight years before Joan was born a sad thing happened to her country. Henry V. of England had married a French princess, and the French, or some of them, tired of being beaten in war, consented to let the child of Henry and his wife be their King, instead of the son of their old King. The old King's son was called "the Dauphin"; that was the title of the eldest son of the French kings. This Dauphin was named Charles. His friends went on fighting the English for his sake, but he was not crowned king. He, the true heir to the throne, had to wander from town to town through France with a few courtiers, fleeing the English or fighting them, as best seemed fit; and not only was he in danger from the English who had vowed to conquer France, but also from the Burgundians, who were their allies.

More over, this poor prince had scarce money enough to pay his bootmaker, and, worse trouble than all, there were many even among his own court who doubted if he were in truth the real son of the King. Even his own mother, who sided with the Burgundians, would speak no word in his favor, so that Charles, doubtful himself and very miserable, sometimes wondered if he had not better give up all hope and flee to Spain, leaving France in the hands of the English.

One day he went apart by himself and sorrowfully prayed to God in his heart (speaking no word of the prayer aloud, mark you), to let him know by some clear sign whether he had a royal right to the throne of France or whether he had none.

The real story of Joan begins in her thirteenth year, when she first heard the commands of God spoken through the voice of the archangel Michael.

It happened in summer, while she walked in her father's garden. It was noontide and very warm. As she walked, Joan thought of many things—of the race she had won running with her comrades that day, of the poor soldier who had come back from the war sore wounded and sorrowful. Joan, little maid as she was, felt a great pity in her heart for the fair land of France. She longed to do something to help. On a sudden, before her, upon the right side, between her and the church, she saw a bright and radiant light, which dazzled her eyes so they were blinded for a space.

Presently, when she had become more used to the light and dared to look again, she saw an angel's face appearing through the wondershine, and heard a voice which said: "Joan, the Lord God hath chosen thee to save France."

"Alas!" cried the Maid, "how may I save our beautiful France who am but a poor village girl who tends sheep? How can such as I lead forth soldiers to war?"

"Be a good girl," said the angel; and again, "Be a good girl, little Joan," and then he went away.

Now you may believe this or not as you will, every one has a right to his own opinion; this is almost word for word what she told her cruel judges about the first coming of the angels.

Joan wept when the light vanished and she heard the voice no more. But after that she tried harder than ever to be good. And the light came again, and other angels, St. Catharine and St. Margaret, whom she loved above all the saints. Sometimes she saw them and touched them, but more often she heard them speak, and ever the words they spoke were to the same end. "Joan, be good, and thou shalt save France."

To herself Joan called them "My Voices," or "My Counsel," but to her father and friends in Domremy she breathed never a word of what had happened her until later.

Meanwhile matters grew worse in France, and when Joan was scarcely seventeen years old the voices became more urgent. They began to tell her what to do. "Go into France, Joan," they said; "it is time."

And one day they told her that she must rescue the town of Orleans, for it was in great danger. Orleans was the only town in France which remained true to the Dauphin; if the Dauphin lost it, he lost all France with it.

Then the voices told Joan how she was to reach Orleans, and she obeyed them in all things. This is what she did. She left her father and her mother and her home—remember it was by God's command that she went, and he gave her strength and courage to do it. She left Domremy and journeyed to Vaucouleurs, a strong embattled town loyal to France and not far from Domremy.

There she went straight to Robert de Baudricourt, the captain of the town, and told her story, how by the command of God she was come to save France. Baudricourt, as you may believe, laughed at her, refusing to believe a word she said.

"A foolish, dreaming girl," he said; "turn her away."

But she came again to him, saying earnestly: "To-day the gentle Dauphin hath great hurt from the town of Orleans, and yet greater will he have if you do not send me to him."

Now, the day on which Joan told the captain this was the 12th of February, she being informed by her voices; and on the 12th of February the Dauphin was defeated with great loss by the English at the battle of Rouvray.

A few days later, for tidings came but slowly in olden times, news was brought to Baudricourt of the battle and of the Dauphin's loss. Baudricourt, remembering Joan's words, and wondering greatly, began to believe in this strange maid and her high mission. He told her he was ready to do what she asked of him.

Obeying the voices, she begged for a gray doublet, black hose, and horse, and an escort. So, clad like a boy, riding upon a great horse and accompanied by a knight, a squire, and four men-at-arms, Joan set out for Chinon, where the Dauphin then was.

They rode far and fast and at last came to Chinon, where Joan was lodged with a kindly dame who took good care of her. Already word of her coming and of her strange daring and confidence had gone forth over the land. Yet most men scoffed, crying: "How shall a slight girl stand up against these terrible English?"

On the second day after Joan's coming to Chinon, the Prince received her in spite of all his courtiers could say to prevent him. These nobles of his court were afraid lest the girl might unsettle the Prince and so disturb their pleasure. Not one believed there was a word of truth in her story.

When the Maid was brought into the hall of the castle where the King had his court, she beheld a crowd of gallant-looking men, and women clad in rich and splendid dress. Before she came in, the Dauphin had given his mantle to a courtier in exchange for a simple cloak, and he stood among his nobles as one of them.

Every one expected the Maid to fall on her knees before the courtier, who wore the King's gorgeous mantle. Joan did no such thing. Paying no heed to any one, nay, looking at no one but the true Dauphin, she went straight to him and, kneeling, said:

"This is the fair Prince to whom i am sent."

"Nay, I am not the Dauphin," answered the Prince, wishing to try her further.

"If you are not he," answered Joan, "then my voices have betrayed me, and that could not be. My voices have shown me that you are the Prince whose kingdom I must save, and whom I shall crown at Rheims before the year be out."

"Ah me, if that might be!" Charles said wistfully.

"It shall be," answered the Maid. "Give me an audience alone for a few moments, gentle Dauphin, and you shall believe me."

Wondering at this strange girl, the Dauphin later spoke with her alone, and what she told him he told a friend long afterward, when he was old. Joan herself would never tell what passed between them, not even when they tortured her on her trial. It was the Dauphin's secret, and she kept it faithfully.

We, who have read what the Dauphin said, know that Joan told him that God had answered his secret, silent prayer, and sent her to assure him that he was the true and rightful heir to the throne of France, the eldest son of the dead King, the prince whom she had been sent to crown.

What could Charles do but believe this holy, heaven-sent maid? Nevertheless, to make quite sure, he sent her to Poitiers, there to be questioned and examined by wise bishops and priests. These clever men did their best to find out all about Joan. They questioned and questioned, and not one single false word could they accuse the Maid of having spoken. Her answers were often so simple, so witty, so wise, that they marveled daily. All their questioning and Joan's answers were written down in a book, and they can be read unto this day.

In six weeks they sent Joan back to the King,

JOAN OF ARC LISTENING TO THE VOICES
FROM THE PAINTING BY D. MAILLART

and this was their judgment: "The Maid is good and true. Believe in her."

After this, Charles began to do more what Joan told him to do. He set about gathering together an army for her; he had white armor made for her (for she always wore the dress of a boy until the day of her death), and a shield and a banner.

When he would have given her a sword, she refused, bidding them send to a certain chapel named after St. Catharine, in which she said the sword lay buried which was for her use. When they obeyed her, sure enough, they found an old rusty sword there, with five crosses upon it. This she wore always, but used rarely even in battle, so gentle was she, so much did she dislike to take away life.

The French soldiers were all very eager to follow this new and strange girl-captain. She roused all the courage there was in them, for they believed that she and she only could lead them triumphantly against the English. But although the whole army loved her, and she it, Joan was a very strict, stern captain. She would allow no feasting, no drinking, no swearing, even among her generals.

When the soldiers were all ready, Joan, obeying her voices, led them straight to Orleans, which was by this time in very great danger from the English.

On the 29th of April, 1429, the French army had passed the enemy's lines and entered Orleans. Perhaps dates of battles are not very interesting things to you, but mark you this, if you would understand something of the glory of the Maid. As a general no one could match her, and as for her skill in using cannon, no one could surpass it.

The French reached Orleans on the 29th of April, upon a Friday. On the Wednesday afterward, that is, upon the 4th of May, Joan led out her men and took one of the English forts called St. Loup.

On the second day after that she took the fort of St. Augustine, and on the next Sunday she fought again, and so fiercely, that the English retired in dismay. Orleans, after its long siege, was saved.

The English were not only vexed at being defeated, but they were sore ashamed that the victory had been won by a woman. "She must be a witch," the soldiers said; and at the thought of fighting a witch the courage of even the bravest of them failed.

It had been easy for them to fight the French before this, because the French had been so often defeated that they did not fight well; but now with their beloved Maid to lead them in her shining armor, they were foes of very different metal.

Orleans now safe, Joan wanted to take the Dauphin to Rheims and crown him. As you very likely know, no king of France was thought to be a real king until he had been crowned at Rheims and anointed with the holy oil that was kept there for that purpose.

But to reach Rheims many towns had to be recaptured from the English, and the Dauphin was not over anxious to go. Now from the beginning the voices had warned Joan that she had only a year's time in which to do all that she had to do; and that year dated from May, 1429. This she told the Dauphin over and over again, hoping to rouse him to come with her to Rheims.

But the Dauphin was surrounded by lazy courtiers who did not want to move, being very comfortable where they were, and all the Dauphin did was to summon council after council to consider what should be done. Joan grew tired of waiting.

"I have four things to do," she said; "to drive the English in flight from our country, to deliver the Duke of Orleans, who is their prisoner, to crown the King at Rheims, and to raise the siege of Orleans. This last is done. Now must we fight our way to Rheims."

The Dauphin had made her waste one month of her precious year. So she set out without him and defeated the famous English general Talbot, at Patay, on an open battlefield. Even then it was hard to make the Dauphin move; even though Joan told him that all the cities, instead of fighting, would open their gates to him.

When at last he did begin the march, Charles found the Maid's words were true. With little or no trouble he came to Rheims, to the great joy of all France.

On the 17th of July, Joan with a great and fair company of noble knights brought the King along the streets of Rheims to the beautiful cathedral. He entered with much pomp and splendor to the sound of singing, and then with much rejoicing the Archbishop anointed and crowned the Dauphin King of France.

Joan, as she knelt to do the King homage and swear the oath of fealty, wept for very joy. Two of her high tasks were done. Soon she would perform the rest and be free at last to go back to her own little village and see her father and mother again. That was what she longed to do more than anything else in the world, but first her duty must be done.

King Charles now asked her what reward he could give her, to which she answered: "Fair King, I would that the people of my village should be freed from the paying of taxes for three hundred years"; and the King said, "So it shall be," and he caused to be written on the books of the accounts of the villages after the name of Domremy and of the village next to it: "Nothing, for the sake of the Maid."

As they rode from the cathedral, the Archbishop asked Joan if she feared anything.

"Nought but treachery," she answered.

Alas! how shall we tell of the treachery that worked against her ever after that glorious day at Rheims?

Unwitting of it, she rode to Paris, which was in the hands of the Burgundians, the allies of the English.

"We must take Paris," quoth she, "and when Paris is ours, all France will be ours, and I shall go home to Domremy and be happy again." Joan's words would have come true had she been allowed her own way, but she was not.

The weak Dauphin let his lazy favorites persuade him to do as they wanted, so that instead of hurrying to help the Maid lay siege to Paris, he loitered with his army at this town or that on the way, and when he at last came to Paris it was too late, for the English had brought up an army to help their allies.

Joan, meanwhile, had been attacking the walls bravely and had done good work. Every day she led out her men, and from dawn to night they fought in the trenches. It was wonderful to hear the noise of the guns and culverins from the walls.

When Charles and his soldiers at last showed themselves, the Maid was full confident they could storm the city. But she relied on the King's army to help, and again the King failed her, for, hearing that she was wounded, he sent word of command to her to stop the fighting.

Very reluctantly, and sad at heart, she obeyed. The next day, however, she and her friend, the Duke of Alençon, who has told us many of her doings, made ready again to fight, for Joan's wound was slight. Again came word from the King forbidding them to begin. More than that, he ordered a bridge to be destroyed which Joan had caused to be built, so that she could cross the river Seine the very next day and attack Paris from another quarter.

You can picture to yourself how disappointed Joan and her eager soldiers were; their plans spoiled, their hopes of victory crushed by this timid King, whose word they must obey. And worse was to come; for Charles, hoodwinked by evil counselors and anxious for peace, would not let Joan fight again for six long months.

The Maid's heart nigh broke, and all her generals and soldiers mourned with her. So they waited while the foolish King tried to make peace with the Duke of Burgundy, who was only the governor of Paris because the English wanted him to be.

So the year 1429, which might have meant so much more to France had the Maid been let alone to do as she willed, passed away, and the next year wore on to spring. You will remember that Joan's year finished in May, 1430. The time was very near. The voices which had all the time spoken and counseled Joan in all that she did, now spoke to her again, but they gave her little cheer.

"It needs must be that you shall be taken prisoner before Midsummer day," said they. "But do you be of good cheer and God will send you help."

Joan's heart sank within her and she grew afraid. She prayed to God that she might die in battle rather than be taken prisoner. She knew too well that the English would tie her to a stake and burn her to death if they once could capture her; for the English firmly believed she was a witch, and it was the custom to burn witches in those days.

Nevertheless, in spite of her great fear, in spite of hearing the same dreadful words from the voices over and over again, Joan went out to fight when she could, as bravely as of old; and of the many brave and noble deeds this is thought to be the bravest and the noblest thing she did, for she went out to fight in a very different way from before.

Before this, the voices had warned her of danger, had told her what to do, and had guided her to victory. Now they were silent; they let her act as she would, and they never told her the day or the hour when she was to be captured.

And so Joan, instead of taking the lead, took the advice of her captains and generals. It was the best she could do, for she was never sure of victory, as she had always been before.

One day news came that the good city of Compiègne, which was loyal to France, had been laid siege to by a great army of English and Burgundians. Joan, who loved that city, at once set out to its rescue, and with only a few hundred men in her company she rode into the town under cover of night.

The people received her with great joy, for wherever Joan went she brought hope and gladness. This was on the dawn of the 23d day of May, 1430. At five o'clock in the morning she led out her men to the attack, hoping to surprise the enemy. So she did, driving them back twice; and then (alas! that this must be told) up came the main body of the enemy to help the Burgundians. They forced Joan to fall back toward the city. Before she and her little troop could reach the gates, up rushed the English between her and the bridge that leads into Compiègne.

The fear in Joan's heart grew. Bravely she spurred her horse up the raised causeway, and leaped into the meadow below. There she was at once surrounded by the Burgundians, who called her to surrender. "Never!" she cried, hoping they would kill her on the spot. But this they were not likely to do, for Joan was worth a large sum of money to her captors. Either King Charles would ransom her, or they could sell her to the English, who would give much to get her into their hands.

And now you must hear of Joan's troubles even to their cruel end. This gentlest, noblest, bravest maid that ever lived in all the world was sold to the English. The King of France, whom she had crowned, made no effort to save her. The English bought her and, having done so, gave her into the hands of the French priests, who were on their side, so she might be tried by them for being a witch and a heretic, a worker of magic, and many other horrible things, none of which were true.

She was brought to her trial at Rouen, where no mercy was ever shown to her by her enemies. The greatest of these was Cauchon, Bishop of Beauvais. Some day you can read, if you will, the whole account of the trial, which was written down at that time, and has since been translated into English.

You will see how bravely the Maid stood up against an army of bishops, priests, and lawyers, all questioning her, all waiting to find fault with her answers and make them out to be lies. You will read how they tortured her in trying to make her confess that her voices were the voices of devils and not of angels.

They could do nothing with her. She told her story simply and truthfully, and the voices helped her many a time to outwit her captors. Yet there came a time even when they seemed to have left her and she stood alone. Once in her darkest hour she denied having heard the voices, but very quickly she repented and never lost courage again.

Always they tormented her over the boy's dress she wore by command of the voices, and it was the wearing of the boy's dress which gave those cruel and malicious priests the excuse for condemning her to death.

They said that she committed a sin against God by so doing, and yet would give her no chance to change, and by a cruel act of treachery they condemned her to death.

In the market-place at Rouen they burned her to death at the stake on the 30th of May, 1431. One whole year had she lain in prison for her trial, and she was only nineteen years old when she died.

They put eight hundred soldiers around the stake for fear any one should try to save her, and on her brow they set a paper cap, on which was written, "Heretic, Relapsed, Apostate, Idolatress."

Lightly the true Maid went to her cruel death, and gladly she died, bowing her head and calling on the name of Jesus. The English threw her ashes into the sea so that men should forget her. How could they think that men should forget such a heroine? The whole world owes her reverence now, for no more beautiful spirit ever lived on earth.

In the town of Orleans now every 8th of May they hold a feast in her honor, while many a town has its statue of her. Her fair name has been cleared, for some time after her death there was another trial. Every one who knew her came to testify to her truth and goodness, so that even in her own age men had some dim idea of doing justice to her memory. She is now honored among the saints who have blessed the world.

As for the English, after their cruel burning of Joan, nothing prospered with them in France. They were driven back to England, with no least chance of ever winning again the crown which by right belonged to the kings of France.

ANNE OF BRITTANY

ANNE, born at Nantes, in 1476, was the daughter of Francis, Duke of Brittany. When Anne was barely thirteen years old her father died, and she had to face the world with few real friends. Some jealous rulers of other countries thought they now had a fine chance to add Brittany to their own lands.

Little Anne was not beautiful, but she was tall and pleasant-looking, and had a firm will. No sooner had her father died than she wrote to some kings who, she thought, were friendly, asking for their help against her enemies. The King of England at this time was Henry Tudor, who himself, before he came to the throne, had found shelter and many kind friends in Brittany. The English people were sorry to hear of all the troubles of the young duchess, and they sent a large army to help her.

The French, who wanted to get Brittany for themselves, were now all over the country. But six thousand archers, with strong English bows, landed from England; they won two great battles over them, and forced them to make peace with Anne.

Having failed to win the duchy by arms, the young King of France now tried another means to gain his end. Anne was young and proud, and she often used to say, "I will marry none but a king, or a king's son." Late one evening, as she sat quietly in her palace, a young gentleman, attended by a few friends, called to see the duchess. He returned to the French borders that night, and many people wondered what message he carried.

A few days later the young duchess herself went away, and it was known that she had gone to meet the King of France. A short while after that she was quietly married to him.

The people of Brittany were glad to know that the troubles of their country were now over. They had seen what a brave girl Anne had shown herself to be, and during long years of war they had learned to love her. The Bretons were proud to think that their little duchess was Queen of France.

Anne was but seventeen when she was crowned. There was great joy in Paris when she entered that city. Thus it came to pass that Brittany was added to the kingdom of France, and to that country it still belongs.

THE "LITTLE QUEEN" ISABEL OF FRANCE

ISABEL was the eldest daughter of King Charles VI. of France and the beautiful Queen Isabella. Isabel had several brothers and sisters, all lovely children, but she was the most lovely of them all. She was a clever child, too, and before she was six years old her mother had masters to teach her music, and to read in Latin and French. In those days children were seldom taught with as much care as Isabel was.

She was a thoughtful child, and would often sit alone by the great fire, thinking over the wonderful things her masters had read to her—old tales, stories of King Arthur and his knights, and of fair ladies. I dare say she wondered, sometimes, if she would ever go out into the world and have adventures; perhaps meet with a knight as noble and beautiful as King Arthur.

She had not long to wait, poor little Isabel: for, when she was only six years old, there came one day to the court a troop of noble-looking men on horseback, and soldiers in shining armor, carrying little flags and shields.

Isabel and her brothers and sisters, in great excitement, watched them from their windows, wondering who they were and why they had come. Was it in war, or in peace? They little thought that it was a little maiden who had brought them; that they had come for Isabel herself. But so it was.

Richard II., King of England, had sent to ask that Isabel should be his wife! He had asked for her once before, but King Charles had said "No," his little Isabel was too young: and he had already promised her, when she was old enough, to the Duke of Brittany.

But when King Richard made up his mind to have a thing, he often managed to get it, whether others wished it or not. He paid no heed to what Isabel's father said, but sent five hundred soldiers to ask for the little princess of France.

Isabel knew nothing of all this, so she was very much surprised when messengers came and bade her appear in the great hall below. It was her uncle who came to her and told her why she was wanted—that the soldiers they had seen were envoys, sent by the King of England to ask that she might be his wife.

Little girls in those days were used to hear

their marriages talked about from the time they were babies, and to have everything arranged for them; so Isabel was not frightened. She wondered, though, what the King of England was like, and whether he would be kind. She was told he was twenty years older than she, so she was afraid he would be an old man, much too stern and grave to play games with her, or tell her stories such as she loved.

Isabel was dressed in her most beautiful robes, and went down to the great hall, looking very grave and thoughtful. In the hall was her mother, who stood by her while she received the King of England's messengers.

The English people did not want Richard to marry a French princess, and such a child, too, even though she was very rich; for they wanted to make war on France. But when the envoys saw Isabel, so tall for her age, and looking, too, so fit to be a queen, they changed their minds. The Earl Marshal, the head of them all, fell on his knees before her, and promised to be true to her if she would be their queen and lady. To which Isabel answered gravely, that if it pleased God, and the King, her father, she would do her best to make a noble queen of England.

Isabel was not to go to England just yet. A whole year was to pass before she saw her future husband; a year which was to be spent in getting beautiful clothes for the bride, and in teaching her all that a queen should know. She had to learn English, of course, and many other things that must have seemed very dry and dull.

At last, in October of the next year, Richard went to France to meet and marry his little bride. He took with him many of his friends, and a number of knights and soldiers, and on a large plain outside Calais the two Kings were to meet.

That meeting must have been a splendid sight. All over the plain were spacious tents, hundreds of horses, and soldiers and trumpeters in their fine uniforms. There were hundreds of knights too, standing in line with drawn swords, which glittered and flashed in the sunshine. As the two Kings stepped out of their tents and greeted each other with low bows, every knight dropped on his knees. The Kings then shook hands, and both entered the French King's tent together.

The Duke of Orléans had gone to fetch the little bride and her maids, but she did not appear on the scene till the next day. Many of her ladies came in carriages, but Isabel and her maids of honor rode all the way on beautiful horses, covered with velvet and gold; and a very long and weary way it must have seemed to them.

How frightened and tired poor Isabel must have felt when, at the end, she found herself on that plain! The eyes of hundreds of knights and ladies were fixed on her, and she knew that within one of the tents sat the old and stern man, her husband, with whom she was to go away forever into a strange country.

Tired though she was, Isabel's beauty outshone that of every one else there. The jewels on her dress flashed and glittered in the sun, while over it swept her beautiful golden hair like a mantle.

She tried to be very brave and cheerful, poor little girl, and smiled on those she knew as she dismounted from her horse. Then, very gravely, she walked into the tent where King Richard sat, and knelt before him twice.

King Richard looked at his little Queen with a kind smile, and when she knelt the second time he rose, and lifting her in his arms, kissed her tenderly. Then, for the first time, did Isabel really look at him, and, to her great joy, saw that he was not old at all, or stern, but young, and kind, and very handsome.

Little Isabel felt at once that she could love this big husband of hers who could smile so kindly. To her, he seemed one of the very noblest of the knights she had so loved to read about.

King Richard was not that. He was not even a very good man, except to his little Isabel. To her he was always kind and gentle and loving, and we must give him credit for that.

A few days after their meeting, Isabel crossed the sea to England, and very strange every place must have seemed to her. At first she was taken to the palace at Eltham, in Kent, where she was to rest for a time. From there she was to go to Westminster, to be crowned, and was to ride all the way on a white horse, that her new people might see their Queen. She little knew that they all hated her because she was French; and it was a good thing that she did not know, or the sight of thousands of people all around her, and all hating her, might have frightened her very much.

As it was, she looked at them all with such a sunny smile, and gentle, friendly eyes, that their hearts were melted, and all fell in love with their beautiful little Queen. Indeed, she must have looked beautiful as she rode beside the King, her shining hair sweeping over her velvet robe, which was trimmed with flashing jewels, and gold, and ermine. On her head she wore a small gold crown, with a soft white veil beneath.

There were great feastings after that, which lasted for days and days, and the little Queen must have been quite tired out before they were over. She enjoyed much more the quiet time that followed, when she went hunting with her husband by day, and playing, or reading to him in the evenings.

For some time these peaceful days lasted, and Isabel was as happy as she could be, helping poor people, and doing kindnesses to every one. Richard was always kind to her, and she loved him very dearly. She thought him the best and noblest man in the world.

Alas! others did not think so. The people grew to dislike him more and more for many wrong things he did. The little Queen knew nothing about those wrong things, nor did she even know that the people were angry with her husband.

At last, one dreadful day, Richard came to her, and told her that he had to leave her and go to Ireland. Isabel wept, and begged to go with him, but the King shook his head sadly. It was no fit journey for the little Queen.

Before he left, they were to go to a service together, at St. George's Chapel at Windsor, and a banquet was to follow; but when the service was ended, and the King and Queen came out, the King would not go to the banquet. Taking his little Queen in his arms, he kissed her again and again, and bade her good-by.

Isabel did not weep, but she was very pale and quiet and sad, and clung to her husband fondly. Then the King put her gently down, and with a last "Farewell!" threw himself on his horse and rode away.

Isabel stood and watched him, but he did not once look back. At last, when a bend in the road hid him from sight, she turned and ran to her bedroom. There she lay on her bed, and wept all the tears she had been holding back so bravely. Isabel did not know then that she had said good-by to her husband forever.

As time went on, the people grew more and more angry with Richard. At last they seized him and sent him a prisoner to the Tower, while they invited Henry, Duke of Lancaster, to come and reign in his stead

Isabel did not know that her husband was in the Tower, nor, for a long time, did she hear any news of him. It seems strange to us that all this could happen without her knowing it, but in those days there were no posts or newspapers. Besides, all the people about Isabel were ordered not to talk to her of the King.

The news was brought to the Duke of York at Windsor. As he was left in charge of the Queen, he thought it would be safer if she were taken to a castle in Kent, from where she could easily escape to France. So he had her secretly taken there. But her French maids and attendants were left at Windsor, and they were soon afterward ordered to return to France.

Poor Isabel now felt very lonely and frightened, for she was left without husband or friends, and with only strange English servants about her. She could never get any news of her husband, and day and night she spent grieving. Where was he, she wondered, and why did he send no word to her?

She did know that his enemies were taking his crown from him, and saying cruel things of him, and the news filled her with fear. But if she had known he was in the Tower, and wanting her, and that they would not let him send for her, her loving heart would have broken.

From this time, Isabel was moved from place to place. Wherever she went, she hoped that here, perhaps, she would meet her husband; but she was always disappointed. Richard too was moved from place to place, until at last he was sent to a castle in Yorkshire. There he died—no one knows how.

Even when her husband was dead, the little Queen was not told of it, but went on hoping and hoping to meet him soon. It was not till many weeks had passed that the news was broken to her.

The new King, Henry, wanted her to stay in England and marry his son, and sent her to the Tower while he tried to make her promise to do so. But she pleaded so hard that she might go home that at last he allowed her to have her wish. Then, in the care of her English ladies-in-waiting, she was sent back to France.

She came to England, rich and happy, at the age of seven. At the age of twelve she went back to France, without husband, or money, or jewels; as poor, and sad, and lonely as the poorest woman in the land.

It is pleasant to know that, later on, some happiness came into the poor little Queen's life again. Her cousin Charles, who loved her dearly, asked her to be his wife; and, by and by, she said she would. For a year they were very, very happy; but only for a year, for at the end of that time, when her little daughter came, poor Isabel died, leaving her husband almost mad with sorrow.

THE LITTLE MAID OF NORWAY

YEARS ago, Scotland had kings of her own, and one of the bravest and best of these was Alexander III. He ruled his country well. He was very brave and good, and his people loved him.

When he was quite young he married Princess Margaret, daughter of the English King, Henry III., and by and by they had a little daughter whom they christened Margaret also. They had two other children as well, Alexander, who was the heir to the throne, and David, who died when he was a child. Then, while Margaret and Alexander were still quite young, Queen Margaret herself died.

The poor King felt his loss very deeply, but there were many more heavy sorrows still in store for him. Soon after his wife died he lost his daughter also, for Princess Margaret was married to Prince Erik of Norway, and went to Norway to live. Then his son married, and, to the poor King's great grief, he died soon after.

Princess Margaret was very happy in her new home, and by and by she had a little daughter of her own to love and play with. This little daughter was christened Margaret too, but she was almost always called the "Little Maid of Norway."

Sad to say, Princess Margaret died soon after her baby was born, leaving the little maid motherless; and poor King Alexander felt very sad and lonely. He was so lonely that he married again; but very soon after the wedding the greatest trouble of all befell Scotland, for the King himself was killed.

He was riding, late one night, along a dangerous piece of coast, and in the dark, not being able to see where he was going, he rode quite close to a steep place. His horse felt the danger, and started back, but so suddenly that the poor King was flung off, and down the crag, where he was killed at once. The spot where the accident happened is still called the King's Crag.

The people of Scotland were terribly grieved at losing their King; he was so manly and handsome, so brave and just, and ruled the land so well. To add to their trouble, there was no heir to the throne except the little three-year-old maiden away in Norway, and they knew that enemies would come to try to seize the crown.

Indeed, some of the Scotch nobles began to give trouble at once. They did not want the little Maid of Norway for their queen, and thought that a noble called Robert Bruce should be given the crown. But the King of England did not think so. Edward, a brother of the late Queen Margaret, was King of England now, and he made up his mind that his little great-niece, Margaret of Norway, should rule over Scotland. He wished that Scotland and England should have the same ruler, and he thought the best way to manage this would be to marry the little maid to his own son.

As soon as Alexander was dead, the Scots wanted to have their little Queen in their own keeping, so messengers were sent to Norway to bring her at once. She was not yet three years old, and her father thought she was too young to be sent away by herself to another country, one where the people were wild and fierce. Many of them, too, did not wish her to be the queen, and might do her harm; so, for a time, the little maid stayed in her own beautiful land, with her father and the people who loved her so.

Poor little baby child, she did not understand what it was to be a queen; and when, at last, her father had to send her away to Scotland, she must have wept very bitterly at leaving him.

She must often, too, have felt very sorry that she was a queen, if it meant going away by herself to a distant wild land, full of strangers, many of them rough and cruel, and not wanting her. It could not have seemed to her that a crown was a very fine and noble thing to have. However, at last she started away in a big ship, with a number of people to wait on her, and sailed for Scotland.

If you will look at the map, you will see that the bit of sea between Norway and Scotland is really quite small. Nowadays, with steamers, the journey is short and easy, even though it is often very rough; but in those days, when the ships were big and clumsy, and had only sails to carry them along, the journey was a much longer one, and much more unpleasant.

The poor little homesick Queen suffered a great deal. She was sad and lonely; and to make matters worse, she fell ill.

In Scotland, the people got ready to meet her, and give her a great welcome. The King of England and the nobles of Scotland were all quarreling and plotting as to who should meet her, and who should have charge of her. They quarreled as to where she should live, and who should live with her. They had settled that she was to marry Prince Edward of Wales, and the Pope had given his permission for the union to take place.

Meantime, the poor little Maid of Norway, tossing about on the rough North Sea, in her

Lady Jane Grey
Obiit 1554

Engraved by S. Freeman

big ship, grew more and more ill. At last, instead of going on to their journey's end, the captain of the ship had to land her at Orkney, which, as you may see on the map, is to the north of Scotland.

There were no crowds to meet her, no gay processions, no bagpipes and flags and feastings when she landed. With only her few attendants about her, the little uncrowned Queen was laid on her humble bed on that wild island, and there the little life, which was so important to so many, passed quietly away. Her poor father in Norway was left childless, and Scotland was without a queen.

LADY JANE GREY

THE LADY JANE, great-granddaughter of Henry VII. of England, was born in or about 1537. She grew up a clever girl, who spoke French and Italian, and even Greek, and could write well in Latin and other languages. So fond was she of books that she would stay at home to read, instead of going out to hunt with her family.

This learned girl was only sixteen years of age when her cousin Mary was thirty-seven. At the time of the death of King Edward VI. Jane was at Chelsea, where she lived so quietly, that she knew nothing of what had happened during the last two days. But she was now taken to Sion House, where the Duke of Northumberland lived; and he told her that the King was dead, and that, according to his will, she was now Queen of England.

It is said that the poor girl was so startled by this news that she fainted. She was really sorry to hear of the death of Edward, who was her cousin. He was about her own age, and they had spent many pleasant days together. When she recovered, she begged that she might not be crowned queen; but the duke, her husband, who was the duke's son, and her own father and mother all joined in telling her that she must yield to the wishes of the late King.

At last she gave way. "If the right is mine," she said, "I hope that God will give me strength to rule for the glory and happiness of the people of England." Then she was taken in the royal barge to the Tower, and presented with the crown.

Mary was in the country at that time, and she had written to the Council claiming her right to the throne. Many of her friends went to join her, and soon she had a small army in the field.

The Duke of Northumberland marched with a body of men against her; but he was very coldly received. "The people crowd to look on us," he said, "but not one cries God speed ye." But when Mary was proclaimed Queen by her friends, loud shouts of joy were heard in the streets of London. It was clear that all the people were in favor of Mary. In the meantime poor Jane had been Queen for ten days.

Jane now left the Tower for the quiet of Sion House, but she and her husband were soon brought back to the Tower, this time as prisoners. The duke was told to own Mary as Queen without delay, which he did, though it cost him many tears.

Mary was slowly making her way up to London, and two weeks later she rode into the city. The people turned out to meet her, with the Lord Mayor at their head, and as she passed through the streets to the Tower she received quite a royal welcome.

Mary was a stern woman, and she marked out certain persons for trial. The Lady Jane and her husband were condemned to death, but Mary had no thought as yet of carrying out the sentence. They were even allowed to live in some freedom, but not to go beyond the Tower gates. Then Queen Mary did a very foolish thing; for, against the wish of all her people, she married Philip of Spain, whose name was greatly hated by the English.

Many persons rose up in arms against this Spanish marriage, and for this poor Lady Jane had to suffer. The Queen punished the rebels severely, and ordered Jane and her husband to be executed the next day.

What a sad end it was for such a sweet and gentle lady! Her meekness and courage she kept to the very last. She made no complaint against Mary; she shed no tears; but as she saw her husband's body pass before her, she took up a book and in it wrote some words which said that God, she thought, would show her favor.

QUEEN VICTORIA AS A YOUNG WOMAN

VICTORIA OF ENGLAND

IN one of the rooms of the Dulwich Gallery, London, there is a portrait of the little Princess Victoria, painted at the age of four years. She is represented standing in a park, in full out-of-door dress, with a dark cape and large black hat, and wearing white wool gaiters. Her head droops shyly, but in the face of the child princess one may readily trace the resemblance to the Queen of fourscore.

In those early days of her quiet childhood the little Victoria lived in dingy Kensington Palace, which to modern eyes looks more like an alms-house than like a royal residence. She was born on May 24, 1819, in one of its lofty frescoed rooms; and in another, overlooking a fine stretch of lawn and avenues of elms, she set up, a few years later, her dolls' house. It has two stories, and the furniture is not in the least royal. In fact, the kitchen is better equipped than the other rooms. A fine supply of pewter plates and cook-ing-utensils is among its treasures. The present caretaker of Kensington Palace shows the visitor a small box where some scraps of time-worn yellowed muslin attest the industry of the baby Victoria. There is a deal of laboriously neat stitching on the dolls' house-linen and clothes, and there is an apron for the doll cook which is quite a triumph in dressmaking for the chubby fingers of a four-year-old.

Victoria owned a hundred and thirty-two dolls. She must have been a tireless seamstress, for she dressed at least thirty-two with her own hands. But all the art of their royal modiste did not suf-fice to make Victoria's dolls beautiful. They are, for the most part, little wooden creatures from four to eight inches in height, with sharp triangu-lar noses and vermilion-touched cheeks. Seven boy dolls are included in the collection, and a few rag babies with painted muslin faces. Some of the dolls are attired as court ladies with wonder-fully ruffled frocks. Others are the owners of minute hemstitched pocket-handkerchiefs with embroidered initials.

The time came when the little needlewoman put by her needle and her toys, and the princess took up the duties of a queen.

Out of this very room in Kensington Palace Victoria hastened on the morning of June 20, 1837, to hear the news of her accession.

Half awake and half clad, a gray shawl thrown hastily over her night-dress, her bare feet thrust into slippers, she hurried down the wide stair-case to hear the tidings that gave her to her people's service. The dolls' house and the neatly sewed dolls' garments were put aside forever, to fade and grow yellow during the long years of Queen Victoria's reign.

There is a pretty story told by her governess, which you will be pleased to hear, of how Vic-toria, then a little girl of twelve summers, felt when she found out quite suddenly that she was to be the queen. It is in a letter addressed to Queen Victoria herself:

"I said to the Duchess of Kent that your Majesty ought to know your place in the succes-sion. Her Royal Highness agreed with me, and I put the genealogical table into the historical book. When Mr. Davys [the Queen's instructor, afterward Bishop of Peterborough] was gone, the Princess Victoria opened, as usual, the book again, and, seeing the additional paper, said, 'I never saw that before.' 'It was not thought neces-sary you should, Princess,' I answered. 'I see I am nearer the throne than I thought.' 'So it is, madam,' I said. After some moments the princess resumed: 'Now, many a child would boast; but they don't know the difficulty. There is much splendor, but there is more responsibility.' The princess, having lifted up the forefinger of her right hand while she spoke, gave me that little hand, saying, 'I will be good. I understand now why you urged me so much to learn even Latin. My cousins Augusta and Mary never did; but you told me Latin is the foundation of English grammar, and of all the elegant expressions, and I learned it as you wished; but I understand all better now'; and the princess gave me her hand, repeating, 'I will be good!'"

Is not this a pretty story? Cannot you fancy the little girl, overawed by the great thought of being a queen, and understanding how wonderful it was, yet finding nothing more solemn to say in her simplicity (and, indeed, if she had searched the world for "elegant expressions," what could she have found better?) than those dear child's words, "I will be good!" There could not be a more charming little historical scene. "I cried much on learning it," is the note which the Queen's hand writes on the margin. No doubt the little maiden was frightened into seriousness, and drew her breath quick when she first knew what was before her—Queen! of an empire upon which "the sun never sets"—yet only twelve years old.

Princess Victoria was but eighteen when her uncle William IV. died and she became actually Queen of England. It was her lot to reign over her devoted people for more than sixty years.

Photographed by William E. Gray from the painting by Stephen Pointz Denning in the Dulwich Gallery   Engraved by Peter Aitken

PRINCESS VICTORIA, AT THE AGE OF FOUR

STORIES FROM AMERICAN HISTORY

THE ARMY OF TWO

BY EHRMA G. FILER

EVEN the children were patriots during the American Revolutionary War. No longer did Indian games, hide-and-go-seek, or ball amuse them. Their favorite game was "playing soldier," and they conquered many armies of imaginary British.

One story is told in which the game was a real one, and two little girls did a great service for their country by their fearlessness and bravery.

A lighthouse was situated off the Massachusetts coast across the bay from a village of some importance. Two little girls, Rebecca and Sarah, lived here with Rebecca's father, who was the keeper of the lighthouse. On one particular morning Rebecca's father had gone to get their weekly supply of provisions. The children were alone, and he had cautioned them to keep a watch for any ship in the harbor.

The children were playing on the north side of the lighthouse and were having a gay time. Rebecca had a drum and Sarah was playing a fife. They were leading an imaginary army and accomplishing great deeds. Suddenly their play was stopped by the sight of a ship coming into the harbor. Throwing aside the drum and fife, the children ran up into the lighthouse tower to get a better view of the strange ship.

"What do you think it is?" Rebecca cried when they had watched the ship for a few minutes.

"It looks like an English warship," answered Sarah.

"What do you suppose it is going to do in our harbor?" asked Rebecca.

The question was hardly asked before the English ship opened fire upon a little sloop at the edge of the bay. The children, panic-stricken, watched the work of destruction.

"Oh, if I were a man how I would love to fight and drive those horrid Britishers away! They have no right here in our harbor," cried Rebecca.

"And I too would fight," said Sarah, more calmly. "But can't we do something? We surely can warn the people in the village so that they may be prepared."

"But we have no boat," answered Rebecca. "Father took the only one with him this morning."

The two little girls sat in deep thought for a few minutes. Suddenly Rebecca's face lighted up, and she cried; "Do you suppose we could scare them away?"

"Oh! Oh! Let's pretend that we are an army, and we can play our drum and fife as loudly as possible. Perhaps the English will then think that troops are approaching," cried Sarah.

The suggestion was no sooner made than the two children ran down the stairway to get the drum and fife. In their excitement they almost fell headlong. They crept out of the lighthouse door, seized their musical instruments and hurried through the bushes down to the water's edge. Without stopping to think what a courageous thing they were doing, Rebecca and Sarah began to beat the drum and blow the fife louder than they ever had in play.

"Rat-tat-tat, rat-tat-tat!" sounded the drum across the still water, and above it, in perfect time, sounded the shrill notes of the fife. It indeed sounded as if troops were approaching to protect the shore.

The English captain and his soldiers heard the martial music. They listened closely. The music seemed to be coming nearer and nearer. The soldiers and their captain were much surprised, for they expected no resistance at this point.

"We are not prepared to meet them," said the English captain. "We will have to retire." The soldiers scrambled up the side of their ship from their little boats in which they had intended to land, and made ready to depart.

"We will try this port some other day after the troops have gone," said the captain. At his command the ship turned and sailed out of the harbor.

In the meantime the excited children were watching the proceedings from their hiding place in the bushes. "I believe we really have frightened them away," they whispered.

The people in the village had seen the ship and were making preparations to protect themselves from the English vessel. In the midst of the commotion they were greatly surprised to see the ship turn and leave the harbor. What did it mean? Surely an attack had been planned.

Many of the villagers got into boats and hurried over to the lighthouse. There they found the answer to their questions. Two frightened little girls told their story, and then said: "Do you think we scared them away?"

"You most certainly did," answered the people, "and you are the bravest army of two that we have ever known. No general could have succeeded better than you two noble children. Hail! to Captain Rebecca and Lieutenant Sarah!"

Copyright by E. H. Blashfield

RETREAT OF THE BRITISH FROM CONCORD
FROM A PAINTING BY ALONZO CHAPPEL

THE STORY OF THE BOSTON TEA PARTY

BY EHRMA G. FILER

WOULD you suppose that such a small matter as a few cups of tea could upset two countries and be an indirect cause of a great war between them? This is the way it happened.

The King and ministers of England thought that America should help pay the old country's big national debt. The Colonies were willing to assist the mother country under one condition. They felt that they should not be taxed for this or any other reason unless they had a voice in Parliament. England was stubborn in those days, and would not agree to this suggestion.

The spark of popular hatred was struck when the English placed a tax upon tea. This was levied only to assert their right to do so. At once impromptu meetings were held in all the principal cities of the Colonies.

At these meetings it was agreed not to buy nor drink any tea imported from England until the tax was taken off. It was hoped by smuggling, refusal to import, and refusal to consume, that this tax might be nullified.

If the English ministers had been at all diplomatic, they could have raised the necessary revenue in another manner. They could have levied the tax at the time when the tea was sent out from England, instead of at the moment when it arrived in this country. The Colonists would have paid this indirect tax and have been none the wiser. But the angry Americans would not buy directly-taxed tea at any price.

The impatient ministers, urged on by an erratic King, determined to force the tea—tax and all—upon the unruly Americans. They resolved to send a surplus stock to the more wealthy colonists. Ships laden with it were to go to Charleston, Philadelphia, New York, and Boston.

When it became known in America that England was taking these steps, the people, men and women, rose up as one person to resist this act of oppression. This noble spirit was reflected even in the children; they were brave and courageous. An incident is told which illustrates this.

English soldiers had made a camp on the Common in the town of Boston. They were sent there to keep order in the town and to quell any provincial riots. The people of Boston resented their being there, and freely expressed themselves. The soldiers knew of this feeling, and seemingly tried to increase it by as much annoyance as possible.

The hill where the State House now stands was a rare place for the boys and girls to coast in Winter. The ice in a pond at the foot, on the Common, had been fine for several days, and the children were having a great time.

One day it was especially clear and cold, and the boys were talking of what splendid skating they would have after school. When they arrived at the pond that evening, great was their dismay. The ice had been broken everywhere, and had then frozen with an uneven surface.

"Those British soldiers have done this," cried the boys, with one voice.

A few days later the same thing happened again. This time the disappointed boys were very angry. One of them suggested that they go to the General and tell him what his men had done. "They have no right to spoil our fun," he said.

The suggestion met with instant approval, and the boys ran straight to the General's door. The servants would not let them in, and they were arguing the question when the General himself appeared. The boys told their story, and their eyes snapped, and their fists clenched as they emphasized their wrongs.

"You are brave boys," the General said. "If my soldiers infringe upon your rights again, let me know at once."

As the boys left, the General said to his bodyguard: "Even the children believe in liberty and freedom in this land."

But to return to the story of the tea party. This brave and independent spirit of the Colonists was especially displayed in Boston. As soon as the news reached them that three shiploads of tea were to be forced upon them, a public meeting was called in the Old South Church, under the leadership of Samuel Adams. Six towns were represented. The people agreed not to receive or use the tea, and they even went so far as to declare that any one who "assisted in unloading, receiving, or selling the tea was an enemy to his country." They also sent anonymous notices to three well-known tea firms, requesting the head of each firm to be present next day at noon at a mass meeting which was to be held under the Liberty Tree. These persons were to be asked to resign their appointments as consignees of the tea.

The Governor sent the sheriff of Suffolk to disperse the meeting. When he read the official

From a Thistle Print, copyright by Detroit Publishing Co.

THE BOSTON TEA PARTY
FROM A PAINTING BY ROBERT REID

orders, the people merely sneered, and hissed at him. Many prominent and indignant citizens were present, but the consignees did not appear, and a committee was appointed to wait upon them and demand their resignations.

When the committee talked to the heads of the tea firms, the men would not give them a definite reply. As they still refused the next day, the committee interpreted the silence as a negative answer.

The following day a meeting was held in Faneuil Hall. The owner of the first tea ship in was sent for, and orders were given him to dock the boat at a certain wharf. A guard of twenty-five picked men were to watch all proceedings on the vessel, which was to leave the harbor as soon as possible. After labeling tea "a pernicious weed," and passing resolutions, the mass meeting turned matters over to a special committee.

In the meantime the consignees were alarmed by small riots which had taken place the night before. They asked aid from the Governor, and sought refuge in the "castle" with the soldiers.

The owner of the vessel was terrified by these proceedings. He wanted his clearance papers in order that he might leave at once. But the Governor would not sign, so he was helpless.

The Governor's idea was that in thirty days after a vessel had arrived in port it might be seized for non-payment of duty. He thought that this would be the easiest way out of the matter, and the tea would be landed.

In a short time the two other vessels arrived and were moored at the same dock. Then the Boston people were more than ever provoked. In Charleston, Philadelphia, and New York, the citizens had been successful, and the tea-laden ships had departed with cargo still on board and duty unpaid.

The Boston people met again, and a second time sent for the owner of the ships. They commanded that he go to the Governor at once and demand his clearance papers, which would permit him to sail immediately. The man returned and said that the Governor refused. This had been expected, and all was in readiness for an important move.

It was late in the winter afternoon of December 16, 1776. There was an intense feeling of expectancy throughout the crowd gathered there in the public hall. On receiving the answer from the ship owner, several prominent men left the hall, and many meaning glances swept from eye to eye. Josiah Quincy then arose, and began speaking eloquently to the people upon the necessity of adhering to the resolutions that they had made, regardless of what it might cost them.

It is doubtful if many heard what he was saying, but all felt the thrill and excitement of the moment, but just what it meant the mass of the people did not know. Suddenly an Indian war cry sounded upon the stillness of the late winter afternoon.

Fifty or sixty men in the dress of Indians swept down the village street to the wharf and boarded the three tea ships, all the while making the air ring with their imitation war cries. The *Massachusetts Gazette* of that time said that they were "very dark-complexioned persons, dressed like Mohawks, of very grotesque appearance." These Indians deliberately proceeded to open three hundred and forty-two chests of tea and calmly threw the contents into Boston Harbor. When their task was finished they left the ships, and disappeared in the evening dusk.

The persons participating in this famous exploit were not called to account, and it has never been known exactly who they were. For this act the British Government closed the Boston port, and this was one of the direct causes of the Revolutionary War.

ISRAEL PUTNAM: SOLDIER OF THE REVOLUTION *

THERE was once a boy who made two visits to Boston, on each of which he got into a fight. The first time was when he was a little fellow, and a boy much larger than he kept calling after him: "Country, country!" Thereupon he gave the saucy Boston boy a hard whipping, and went home to Salem. After some years he married, bought himself a piece of land on top of a Connecticut hill, and became a farmer. He was as fond of his farm as if it had been one of his children, and was especially proud of his fine breed of sheep. One morning he found that sixty or seventy of them had been killed by a wolf. He and his neighbors joined in a wolf-hunt and soon had the beast shut into its cave. Putnam lighted a torch, went boldly into the cave, shot the creature before it could spring at him, and came out dragging it.

When the French and Indian War broke out, he was ready to fight. In one battle his blanket was shot through fourteen times, but he was not touched. Once the barracks of a fort caught fire. Hundreds of barrels of powder stood near them. Neither the commander nor any one else seemed to have any idea what to do. Putnam was not there, but he saw the smoke, ran to the fort, and began to give orders. "Form in line!" he cried. "Pass the buckets along!" He took his stand between the powder and the fire, and threw on the buckets of water as fast as they could be passed to him. The smoke and the whirl of the ashes in the wind almost hid him from the soldiers. The fire blazed around him. His heavy mittens were burned off his hands. "Take these!" cried some one, and gave him a pair soaked with water. The fire came nearer and nearer to the powder. One partition fell, another and another. Only a thin board wall stood between him and an awful explosion. Still he did not run, and at last he conquered. The flames died down, and he pulled off his wet mittens. The skin came with them, and then for the first time he discovered that he had been terribly burned.

Even that experience was less dreadful than a day that he spent with the Indians. His gun missed fire, and he was captured. They tied him to a tree and piled wood around him. It was kindled, and the flames blazed up. Then the Indians sang and danced and howled with delight. A few minutes more would have ended his life, but just then a French officer appeared on the scene. He rushed through the yelling crowd, kicked the fire to pieces, and cut the bonds.

During this same war, Putnam was on the St. Lawrence with General Amherst when he heard the general say, "We could soon capture the fort

* From "American Hero Stories," by Eva Marsh Tappan; used by permission of Houghton, Mifflin Company, publishers, Boston, Mass.

if it were not for the schooner over there that protects it."

"I'll take the schooner for you," Putnam offered, "if you'll give me some wedges and a mallet, and let me choose half a dozen men."

The general was beginning to find out that the Americans had their own way of doing things, and at length he actually gave Putnam permission to try his plan. When night came, the men got into a light boat, muffled their oars, and in the darkness rowed up to the stern of the schooner. They drove wedges between the rudder and the stern-post. Then they rowed in the shadow around to the bow and cut the anchor loose. The French soon found that they were adrift; but the rudder would not move, they were helpless, and they floated ashore with nothing to do but surrender. The fort followed their example.

At the close of the war, in 1764, Putnam went home, hung up his sword, swung over his door a signboard with General Wolfe's picture on it, and for ten years was a quiet farmer and innkeeper. On April 20, 1775, he had eaten his dinner and gone out to the field with his oxen. Suddenly he heard the sound of a drum. A man was galloping furiously along the road, beating his drum and calling, "To arms! To arms! The British have fired upon us! The country is ablaze!"

Then Putnam forgot his beloved farm. He forgot to say good-by to his family. He forgot that he was an officer, and was going to war without his uniform. He forgot everything except which of his horses was the swiftest. He leaped upon its back, and while the oxen stood in the field waiting patiently for him to return, he was galloping along the road to make his second visit to Boston, one hundred miles away.

The Continental Army had gathered from all directions. The British were in possession of Boston. "We must seize those hills," declared the British General Gage, "if we are to stay in the city."

"We must seize those hills," declared the Americans, "if we are to drive the British out of the city." Colonel Prescott and General Putnam marched out by night and began to fortify

Breed's Hill and Bunker Hill. At daybreak the British discovered what was going on. "We might take Charlestown Neck," said one officer, "and starve them out."

"That's too slow," objected another. "I believe the best way will be to charge upon them."

"Not so easy to charge up that hill."

"Why not? They're only farmers. They don't know anything about fighting. The chances are that they will run long before we are at the foot of the hill."

So the British talked, and at length they decided to make a charge. The march began. The scarlet lines came nearer and nearer. Prescott and Putnam were going back and forth among their men at the top of the hill. "Remember there isn't much powder," they said. And Putnam added, "Men, you know how to aim. Don't fire till you can see the whites of their eyes."

Up the hill marched the British, stopping only to fire; but the Americans stood motionless. It seemed to them hours before the word rang out, "Fire!" That fire was like a cannonade, and the British, brave old soldiers as they were, ran pellmell down the hill. "Hurrah! hurrah!" shouted the Americans. The British formed and rushed up the hill again; again the lines broke, and they retreated. They came a third time, but now no volleys met them; the powder had given out. The Americans had no bayonets, but they fought furiously with stones and the butt-ends of their muskets, with clubs, knives, even with their fists; but no such weapons could withstand British veterans, and the Americans had to retreat.

News of the battle went through the colonies like wildfire. All their lives the Americans had looked up to the British regulars as the greatest of soldiers; and they, the untrained colonists who had never seen two regiments in battle, had twice driven them back! The hill was lost, but to repulse the British regulars was a mighty victory. Couriers galloped from one colony to another to carry the news. Everywhere there was rejoicing; but Putnam could not bear to think that after such a fight the hill had at last been given up, and he growled indignantly, "We ought to have stood. Powder or no powder, we ought to have stood."

DRILLING RECRUITS FOR THE CONTINENTAL ARMY
DRAWN BY HOWARD PYLE

125

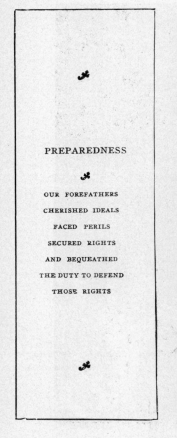

Courtesy of the artist and of the National Security League
FROM A POSTER BY EDWIN H. BLASHFIELD

THE SEARCH FOR RALPH IZARD *

BY EVERETT T. TOMLINSON

"I do not see how you ever got through the lines."

"I have been journeying all the night. 'Tis true I several times saw bands of Tories, or detachments of the redcoats out for forage; but the darkness was my protection. At all events, I am here, and that is the best proof in the world that I have not been captured."

"And glad I am that you are in your own home once more! How long can you remain?"

"At nightfall I must go back to camp. The Light Troops will miss me if I delay longer. You see I am of some importance there, anyway."

"Not more than you are here. Do you really think the marauders are ignorant of your visit? Much as I delight to see you, I am nevertheless alarmed for your safety. What should I do without you?"

"No danger of the redcoats coming as far as Fair Spring. They are shut in now within very narrow limits. They venture only a few miles from Charleston; and, were it not for the Tories, their supplies would soon fail them. I fear our neighbors more than I fear the soldiers of King George."

"And so do I. If none of them has seen you, you may be safe here for the day; but I am anxious, more anxious than I can tell you."

Young Ralph Izard, aide-de-camp to the commander of the Light Troops of South Carolina in 1780, stooped and kissed his wife reassuringly,

---

* Used by permission of Silver, Burdette & Company, Boston. From "The Boys of the Revolution," by Everett T. Tomlinson.

and then turned and led the way within his house.

From the piazza on which they had been standing, the peaceful vision of Fair Spring, the name he had given his plantation, had been unbroken by any sign of war's rude alarms. It was a beautiful spot, and what it had cost the resolute young patriot to abandon the place and his still more beautiful young wife for the hardships of the camp, no one but he knew. But, his resolution enforced by the courage of his wife, he had gone, and now for the first time in months he was at home again, though only for a visit of a few hours.

His delight had been great at finding the plantation apparently unmolested and his wife safe. Mrs. Izard, not wishing to increase the anxiety of her patriotic young husband, had not referred to the visits she had received from the "outliers." Nor did she explain how on several occasions the only thing which had preserved her and the home from serious harm had been the gentle and lady-like manner in which she had met the marauders; for though they had taken many of her possessions, still they had been too much impressed by her bearing to inflict unnecessary damage.

Fair Spring was on the extreme border of the region in South Carolina then overrun by the British and Tories, and her only hope for the safety of her husband was that his visit in the remote locality would not be discovered by the alert enemy. The fact that the nearest bands were composed of her own neighbors added to her feeling of uneasiness, for of all the foes they were the most bitter.

But, striving to conceal her anxiety, she followed her husband to the dining room, where a breakfast was speedily prepared. And when Aunt Susan at last placed her tempting viands upon the table, Ralph Izard was thoroughly ready for the meal. Not only was the food in striking contrast to the fare of the soldiers in the camp, but the young officer had been journeying all through the night, and now was as hungry as he was weary.

He had just seated himself and taken a piece of Aunt Susan's corn bread, when that worthy woman herself re-entered the dining room, her eyes betraying some great alarm, and her whole body trembling under the violence of her emotions.

"What is it, Susan? What is it?" demanded Mrs. Izard, quick to feel that something was wrong, and rising from her seat as she spoke.

"Dey's comin', Massa Ralph! Dey's comin'!"

"Who's coming?"

"De redcoat sojers. Dey's right in de lane now!"

Instantly Ralph Izard ran to the window. In the lane which led from the house to the road, a band of a dozen or more redcoats and Tories could be seen approaching, and the young soldier knew at once that his presence in his home had been discovered by his enemies. To escape now seemed impossible, for he could not leave the house without being seen, and to remain was certain capture.

For a moment he was almost dazed by his peril, but he was quickly recalled to the necessity of action by the touch of his wife's hand upon his shoulder.

"Oh, Ralph," she said in a low voice, "what can be done?"

"Nothing. It's too late to get away."

The tightening lips of the young soldier seemed to increase the wife's alarm, and she said eagerly: "You must hide, Ralph! You must hide! If you are taken then, you will be no worse off than before, and to attempt to defend yourself would be madness."

"Where can I hide?"

"In the attic. In the cellar. Anywhere. Come!" she added eagerly, as she perceived the band already near the house.

For a moment Ralph Izard hesitated. His hand instinctively crept to his sword, and his face became hard and stern. He was a soldier of his country, and he must take a soldier's chances.

"Come, Ralph! Come!" pleaded his young wife. "I have it now, just the place for you."

She was pulling upon his arm; and, as her husband glanced from the approaching men to her terror-stricken face, he yielded and followed her as she led the way to his own room. Then, opening the door into the clothes-press, she hastily thrust him in and turned the button upon the outside.

Left to himself, Ralph Izard could hear her as she ran swiftly from the room; and then he bethought himself of his own condition. In the darkness he could feel the garments hanging from the pegs, garments which he had purchased in Paris on the one visit which he and his wife had made across the sea. There were dress coats, and frilled mufflers, and many a dainty piece of work of which Mistress Izard had been so proud when her handsome young husband had donned them. His thoughts were somewhat bitter now as he pressed back against the wall behind the garments, for there was small likelihood that he would ever wear them again. Even while he strove to cover himself with them, he could hear the voices of the men below, and in his excitement it did not seem possible to him that his hiding-place could escape the attention of his visitors.

Meanwhile Mistress Izard had opened the front door at the rude summons of the band; and, though her heart was beating fast in her anxiety, her outward appearance was calm. She was once more trusting that her gentle manners and soft answer might turn away the wrath of the marauders as it had done on previous occasions.

The very first words of the leader, however, almost made her heart cease beating, and her voice trembled in spite of all her efforts to control it.

"We've come for the rebel, Ralph Izard," he said brutally.

As he glanced up at the pale face before him, its womanly dignity perhaps moved him, for in a milder manner he added:—

"We know he is here, madam. He's been tracked, and there can be no mistake. I'm sorry for you, but it's the fortune of war. If he gives himself up quietly, there'll be no trouble."

"Is it so that you have learned Ralph Izard?" she said calmly, attempting to smile as she spoke. "Do you think, if he were here, he is one to give himself up 'quietly,' as you say?"

"He will have to give himself up, whether he does it quietly or not. We have come for him, and take him we will before we leave," replied the leader, firmly.

"I leave it to your own judgment if my husband would be likely to leave the camp in a time like this. I understand that your lines are pretty well pressed together now. Does it seem reasonable to you that he would strive to pass them and come here when his services may be needed in the camp and the end of the war is so near?"

"You evade my question, madam. Indeed I do not ask you whether he is here or not, for I know that. The question is, whether or not he will give himself up peaceably and so avoid all further trouble."

"I fancy Ralph Izard could answer that question better than his wife," she replied, her eyes flashing for a moment.

"You do but parley, madam. Will he give himself up, or not?"

"I have told you all I know," said Mrs. Izard.

"Have a care, madam," said the leader, threateningly. "My men are not accustomed to such methods. They may find it necessary to smoke the rebel out, and then find a good target for their muskets."

The young woman felt as if something were clutching her by the throat as she heard the threat to set fire to the place; but, regaining control of herself by a great effort, she said steadily: "Your words cannot terrify a soldier's wife. I perceive that you will not be content until you have satisfied yourselves as to his whereabouts. If you will enter, I will assist you to search the house."

The leader turned to his men, and ordered a half-dozen to take their stand outside, while with the others he entered and at once began the search. First they went into the cellar, and the frightened woman could hear them as they overturned the barrels and upset the various belongings there. In a few minutes they came up the stairs, and the leader said: "I did not think to find him there. He's more likely to be upstairs."

Mrs. Izard smiled, and said: "I will myself conduct you, if you will permit me. I wish you to satisfy yourselves."

The leader scowled, at first evidently having no mind to accept her offer; but, as she quietly joined them, he uttered no protest, and the search was at once begun. Stationing a guard below, the others at once proceeded to the attic, but not a trace of the rebel could be found. Then they continued their efforts on the floor below, Mistress Izard still remaining with them. At last they entered the room where the clothespress was in which the young officer was hidden, standing close against the wall and endeavoring to cover himself with the gay attire which was hanging from the pegs. Every word that was spoken was distinctly heard by the young patriot, and the gentle tones of his wife did not conceal from him the terrible strain under which she was laboring.

The critical moment had come at last, and soon he would know whether the loathsome prison at Charleston or the camp of his fellows was to be his portion. Every muscle was tense, and every nerve in his body seemed to be quivering. In his desperation he was almost ready to rush forth. The thought of his wife and the presence of these men in his home was almost more than he could bear.

Suddenly the door of the press was thrown open, and he heard the voice of his wife. "In this press are some of my husband's unused garments," she was saying. "It might please you, gentlemen, to enter and continue your search there. He may be hiding in some pocket, perchance."

Would the men enter? The press was small and dark, and all that could be seen was the clothing hanging from the walls. The leader started to enter, and Ralph Izard's grasp on his sword tightened.

"The man isn't here. His wife wouldn't act this way if he was," said one of the men to the leader.

"I think you're right," replied the leader.

"My men will never be satisfied to go back empty-handed," he said to Mistress Izard. "If they cannot get the rebel, they will take some of his belongings."

"Do as you will," she replied. "You have satisfied yourself that I have no protector, and I can offer no resistance."

In a few minutes the men had seized all the valuables they could discover, and were soon lost to sight in the road.

Then Mrs. Izard ran to the press, and in a voice choked with sobs summoned her husband.

"Oh, Ralph," she cried, "I thought they had found you!"

"They will yet, unless I go at once."

"Will it not be safe for you to remain now?"

"No, no. I am sure from the leader's tone that he will come back. There is a small body of our cavalry on the other side of the Ashley, and I will go at once to them."

Quickly as Ralph Izard departed, he was none too quick. In a few minutes back came the band, and without a word of explanation dashed up the stairs and entered the press. But the "rebel" was gone. If they could not secure the bird, they at least could take his plumage; and soon, dressed in the finery which had concealed its owner they left the house and started once more up the road.

At Bacon's Bridge, however, they discovered the man for whom they had been searching; but this time he made no effort to hide himself. With his companions of the cavalry, he dashed upon the band, and only a few of the redcoats returned to their lines to tell of the disaster which had befallen them. Their stolen finery was speedily transferred by its rightful owner to his own comrades; and as they rode away, decked out as few of the hardy Continentals had ever been, Ralph Izard retraced his way to his home to complete the interrupted visit of the day.

In response to his expression of delight at the manner in which his good wife had foiled the searching party, Mistress Izard smiled, and said gently: "It is not *my* way, Ralph. It is the right way. A soft answer turns away wrath; and, if I do not forget that I am a lady any time and every time, others are not likely to forget it, either."

THE STORY OF NATHAN HALE

The brief history of the life and death of Nathan Hale, the boy martyr of Connecticut, is the very saddest story of our Revolutionary War; but the record of those twenty-one years is a record of purity of purpose, unselfish devotion to country, and deathless courage.

On June 6, 1755, in the little town of Coventry, Connecticut, was born a boy whose hold on life seemed so slight that he was not expected to live. This boy was Nathan Hale, the sixth child of Richard Hale and his wife, Elizabeth Strong Hale. Despite the prophecies of doctors and nurses, however, little Nathan lived, though during childhood he was a frail little fellow, giving but small promise of the physical strength and beauty for which he was afterward noted.

A strong love for outdoor sports and athletics was the chief factor in developing the fragile child into a youth of uncommon vigor of body, and also of mind, for young Hale soon showed

B. & G. F.—9

an ambition to excel in his studies as well as in his games and sports.

So well did he apply himself, and so earnest was his tutor, that at the age of sixteen Nathan Hale was ready to enter college. He was graduated from Yale in 1773, with the highest honors, and carrying with him the respect and affection of the faculty as well as of his associates. His gracious and gentle manners won the love of all who knew him best. Immediately after leaving Yale he taught school at East Haddam, and in 1774 he was appointed the first preceptor of the Union Grammar School at New London, an institution where boys were prepared to enter Yale.

Few lives seemed more peaceful than that of the young schoolmaster, who, meanwhile, was making ready to become a preacher of the gospel of Christ. How little did he dream that the lesson he was to leave to the world would be the sacrifice of a life in the service of his country!

When the news of the battle of Lexington reached New London, there was great excitement among the people. A meeting was called at once, and it was the voice of the young schoolmaster that rang out with these stirring words: "Let us march immediately and never lay down our arms until we have obtained independence!" This was the first time that Americans had heard the call to arms in a public assembly, and the call came from a youth who was soon to seal his faith with his blood.

That must have been a dramatic scene in the town hall of New London! One can imagine the astonishment of the stern-looking men gathered there that day—all heart-stirred by the alarming news, yet scarcely knowing how to express the thoughts that were struggling in their minds—when the slender young patriot, his gentle face aglow with enthusiasm, his fair hair making a golden halo about the white brow, stepped forward and dared to utter those burning words.

The next morning he was back in the schoolroom, where he prayed with the boys, as was his custom, and resumed the course of his daily work; but from the moment that he said: "Let us march!" a new purpose had come into his quiet life. Very soon after, he enrolled as a volunteer, and a little later he was appointed lieutenant in Colonel Charles Webb's regiment. Going to Boston, Lieutenant Hale took part in the siege of that city, and was breveted captain for gallant conduct.

The year 1776 was a hard one for the soldiers of the Continental Army. On one occasion some of the men determined to go home at the expiration of their time, for there was no money to pay them. With the unselfishness that was always characteristic of Hale, he offered to give them his month's pay if they would consent to stay and fight for the cause he so ardently loved.

When the British evacuated Boston, the greater part of the American army went to New York, and it was there that the youthful captain of Webb's regiment performed a deed of daring rarely equaled in the records of the great American war.

There was a terrible lack of food among our men, not enough tents to shelter more than a third of them, and almost no provision for clothing them. At this time, anchored in the East River, New York, was a British sloop, lying under protection of the man-of-war "Asia," and the sloop contained provisions. Obtaining permission from his commanding officer, Captain Hale undertook the capture of this sloop, an undertaking of the greatest danger. He managed, however, to infuse his own spirit of daring into a few of his comrades, and with a handful of trusty followers he embarked in a whaleboat at midnight and

made directly for the sloop. Darkness favored the dangerous venture, and Hale and his men drew up alongside without being seen by the men on either vessel. In a moment they had boarded the sloop, taken the sentries and guards prisoners, and were sailing away with the prize. Cheer after cheer greeted the brave fellows as they hove in sight of their comrades, and the provisions on board the sloop were immediately distributed among the half-starving American soldiers. Soon after this, Hale was made captain of a company of Connecticut rangers which was known as "Congress's Own."

Conflicting statements are found in history concerning the latter part of Nathan Hale's army life. According to some authorities, he took part in the battle of Long Island and in Washington's famous retreat across the East River from Brooklyn. It is at least certain that he was with the troops in New York when the British raided Long Island.

It was at this time that Washington found it absolutely necessary to get accurate information, if possible, concerning the plans of the English, also a knowledge of the exact number of their forces. At the house of Robert Murray, on Murray Hill, New York, he called a meeting of officers to talk over the state of affairs and to decide upon some means by which such information might be obtained. The officers listened in silence to his plan, which was to send some trustworthy, bold man across the lines to find out the facts it was necessary to know. In order to accomplish this most dangerous commission, the man would have to go in disguise. Everyone in that group knew what such an errand meant. If the venture should fail and the messenger be captured, by the rules of warfare he would certainly be executed as a spy.

The word spy is hateful to an honorable man. For some moments there was a hush in the room, no one volunteering for the service that might end in a death of shame. At length a voice broke the silence: "I will undertake it, sir," and the voice was that of young Nathan Hale, who had just risen from a sick-bed. A thrill of admiration pulsed through every heart, followed by a tremor of dread. He was but a boy, a stripling, who had offered to risk a life that was full of promise for the cause of American liberty. The older men did all they could to dissuade him, but Nathan Hale was firm in his resolve. "Gentlemen," he said calmly, "I owe my country the accomplishment of an object so important and so much desired by the commander of our armies. I know of no mode of obtaining the information but by assuming a disguise and passing into the

MONUMENT ON THE CONCORD BATTLE-FIELD

NATHAN HALE MONUMENT IN CITY HALL PARK, NEW YORK

enemy's camp. I am fully aware of the consequences of discovery and capture in such a situation. I wish to be useful, and every kind of service for the public good becomes honorable by being necessary."

That same night Hale left the camp at Harlem Heights, dressed in brown garments and broadbrimmed hat, in the guise of a schoolmaster seeking employment. He was accompanied as far as Norwalk by Sergeant Hempstead and his own faithful servant, Ansel Wright, who arranged to have a boat awaiting him there on the twentieth of the month, when he expected to return. His charm of manner won the confidence of the people he met on the way, and disguised as he was he entered the British lines, where he made drawings of the fortifications on thin paper, which he concealed between the layers of the soles of his shoes. He also secured the complete plans of the British campaign, which he wrote out in Latin and hid in the same way.

Thus far everything seemed to favor his hazardous undertaking. He reached Norwalk, where he was to find the boat ready for him the next morning, and the young officer was serene in the thought that he was out of danger at last. Spending the night at a farmhouse, he went the next morning to breakfast at a little wayside inn, "The Cedars," kept by a widow, and known as "Widow Chichester's." During the meal a man entered the room, looked steadily at the guest, and then left. Nathan Hale, who suspected no danger, finished his meal and hurried off toward the beach. A boat was approaching and he expected to find Hempstead and Wright awaiting him; but presently he recognized the boatmen as British marines, and turned to fly. "Surrender or die," called a voice, and he was seized and taken aboard. He knew then that the man who eyed him at "Widow Chichester's" had betrayed him, and that his fate was sealed.

When taken before General Howe at the house of James Beekman, Hale was searched. The papers were found in the soles of his boots, and he was convicted as a spy. The provost-marshal, Cunningham, into whose hands the young American prisoner fell, was a brutal man. He ordered that Nathan Hale should be hanged at sunrise the following morning. He was confined under a strong guard in the large greenhouse of the Beekman mansion, which stood on the present site of 51st Street and First Avenue, New York City.

Hale asked to be allowed to write letters to his mother and to Alice Adams, his promised wife. The request was granted, but Cunningham tore up Hale's letters before his eyes. He asked for a minister of God and for a Bible, but both were refused him. Afterward Cunningham excused himself by saying that he destroyed the letters because he did not want the Americans to know they had a man who could die so bravely.

In the early Sabbath morning of September 22, 1776, Nathan Hale was hanged as a spy. With coarse brutality, Cunningham ordered: "Make your dying speech." Hale had been praying. He lifted his eyes upward and said in a clear voice: "I only regret that I have but one life to lose for my country."

Sobs brust from some of those who heard him, but in a rage Cunningham called out: "Swing the rebel off!" and the order was obeyed.

So died the boy martyr who redeemed the name of "spy" from all traditional infamy by venturing his life for his country and proudly paying the cost demanded by the stern code of war.

NATHAN HALE

BY FRANCIS M. FINCH

To DRUMBEAT and heartbeat
  A soldier marches by;
There is color in his cheek,
  There is courage in his eye;
Yet to drumbeat and heartbeat,
  In a moment he must die.

By starlight and moonlight
  He seeks the Briton's camp;
He hears the rustling flag,
  And the armed sentry's tramp;
And the starlight and moonlight
  His silent wanderings lamp.

With slow tread and still tread
  He scans the tented line;
And he counts the battery guns
  By the gaunt and shadowy pine,
And his slow tread and still tread
  Gives no warning sign.

The dark wave, the plumed wave—
  It meets his eager glance,
And it sparkles 'neath the stars,
  Like the glimmer of a lance:
A dark wave, a plumed wave
  On an emerald expanse.

A sharp clang, a steel clang,
　And terror in the sound!—
For the sentry, falcon-eyed,
　In the camp a spy hath found!
With a sharp clang, a steel clang,
　The patriot is bound!

With calm brow, steady brow,
　He listens to his doom.
In his look there is no fear,
　Nor a shadow-trace of gloom,
But with calm brow, and steady brow,
　He robes him for the tomb;

In the long night, the still night,
　He kneels upon the sod,
And the brutal guards withhold
　E'en the solemn word of God!—
In the long night, the still night,
　He walks where Christ hath trod.

'Neath the blue morn, the sunny morn,
　He dies upon the tree!
And he mourns that he can lose
　But one life for Liberty:—
And in the blue morn, the sunny morn,
　His spirit wings are free.

But his last words, his message words,
　They burn, lest friendly eye
Should read how proud and calm
　A patriot could die,
With his last words, his dying words,
　A soldier's battle cry!

From Fame-leaf and Angel-leaf,
　From monument and urn,
The sad of Earth, the glad of Heaven
　His tragic fate shall learn,
And on Fame-leaf and Angel-leaf
　The name of *Hale* shall burn!

HOW A WOMAN SAVED AN ARMY

BY H. A. OGDEN

It was in the winter of 1777-78, during the occupation of Philadelphia by the British troops, that a patriot woman inside of the enemy's lines performed an act of great service to her country. Not far away, at Whitemarsh, General Washington's army was encamped. It had recently suffered defeat in the battles of Brandywine and Germantown, and the outlook was most

THE BRITISH OFFICERS IN COUNCIL.

LYDIA DARRAH OVERHEARS THE PLAN.

discouraging. In Philadelphia the British soldiers, commanded by General Howe, were quartered in comfortable barracks, while their officers had selected the most commodious and elegant house in which to enjoy the winter. In one of these houses lived a Quaker gentleman named Darrah, his wife Lydia, and their younger children; their oldest son was an officer in the patriot army. With them General Howe's adjutant-general took up his quarters, and secured a back room in which private councils could be held, without fear of interruption.

Just before one of these councils, in the early part of December, Lydia Darrah was told to retire early with her family, as the British officers would require the room at seven o'clock, and would remain late. The adjutant-general added that the officers would send for her to let them out and to extinguish the fire and candles. Now, as the officer was so particular, Lydia suspected that some expedition against the patriot army was to be arranged.

LYDIA DARRAH GIVES WARNING OF THE BRITISH ATTACK.

She sent all the family to bed, and, taking off her shoes, crept softly back and listened at the door. By this piece of eavesdropping, which the zealous woman no doubt felt was entirely justified as a war expedient, she learned it was decided to issue an order that all the British troops should march out, late on the fourth of December, to surprise General Washington and his army.

Having learned this important decision, Mrs. Darrah retired to her room, and, lying down, feigned to be asleep. When one of the officers knocked at the door, she did not reply until the summons had been several times repeated.

After the departure of the officers she hardly knew what to do, in order to get word of the intended surprise to Washington. She knew it lay in her power to save the lives of thousands of her countrymen. She dared not consult even her husband. She decided to go herself and convey the information. The Darrah's stock of flour being almost out, and it being customary in those days for people to send or go to the mills themselves, Lydia told her husband that she would go for more. He wanted his wife to send their servant, or to take a companion, but Lydia insisted on going alone.

As the mill was some distance from the city, a pass through the British lines must be obtained; and Lydia's first step was to procure the document from General Howe. Having secured the pass, she made her way over the snowy roads, and reached the mill. Leaving her flour-bag to be filled, she hurried on in the direction of the American camp, and before long met a party of patriot cavalrymen commanded by an officer whom she knew. He inquired where she was going. Mrs. Darrah said she was going to see her son, one of his comrades; at the same time she begged him to dismount and walk with her. Ordering his troops to remain within sight, he did so. She then told her important secret, after his promise not to betray his source of information, lest her life might be forfeited thereby. Conducting her to a house near at hand, and seeing that she had some refreshment, the American officer galloped off to headquarters, where General Washington was at once informed of the intended attack. The necessary preparations were of course made for receiving and repelling the enemy's "surprise."

Returning home with her flour, Lydia sat up alone, to watch the intended movement of the British. The regular tramp of feet passed the door, then all was silence; nor was her anxiety to know the result at an end until the officers' return, a day or two later. Although she did not dare to ask a question, imagine her alarm, when the adjutant-general told her that he wished to ask her some questions; she felt sure that she either had been betrayed or was suspected. He inquired very particularly whether her husband or any of the children were up on the night they had held their last consultation. Lydia replied: "The family all retired at seven o'clock, as you requested." He then remarked: "I know *you* were asleep; for I knocked on your door at least three times before you answered me. We are entirely at a loss to understand who could have given Washington information of our proposed attack, unless these walls could speak. When we arrived near their encampment we found all their cannon in position, and their troops ready for us; and not being prepared for a regular battle with the Americans, we marched back—like a parcel of fools!"

LOXLEY HOUSE
The home of
Lydia Darrah

As restored for the
Sesqui-Centennial
Exposition, 1926

THE STORY OF MOLLY PITCHER

BY P. C. BOUVÉ

OLD Monmouth Courthouse in New Jersey, where the famous battle of Monmouth was fought in the year 1778, preserves many stirring tales of Revolutionary days among its yellowed records: tales of the "Pine Robbers," who spread terror and destruction along the Jersey coasts, and who made the farmers in the neighborhood live very anxious lives—tales of those old days when British Tory and American Patriot were at feud in house and home as well as on the bloody battle-field.

Among these stories of long ago none stirs the blood with a warmer thrill of admiration than that of brave Molly Pitcher, whose heroism on Monmouth field has found a lasting record in the pages of American legend and history.

Some time toward the middle of the eighteenth century, there came to America from Germany an emigrant by the name of John George Ludwig, who settled in the colony of Pennsylvania. Here —in the town of Carlisle, probably, though the exact locality is not positively known—was born to John George Ludwig, October 13, 1744, a little blue-eyed daughter, whom he called Mary.

Little Mary grew up tall and strong and healthy, with the fair complexion and red hair of her German ancestors, and a good deal of their love of home and country. The Ludwigs being poor, Mary became a servant-girl in the family of Dr. William Irvine, an Irish gentleman who was living in Carlisle. This Dr. Irvine, who had come to the colonies as surgeon on board a British man-of-war, afterward became an officer in the Continental or American Army. He was one of the most zealous of the patriots, and it was due to his influence that many of the colonists of Pennsylvania were aroused to a spirit of independence and a realization of the necessity of asserting and defending their rights. This was no easy task, for a great number of these colonists belonged to the Society of Friends, a religious sect that was opposed to war upon any conditions; and also because most of the proprietary owners were in favor of the crown.

It was while in General Irvine's household, no doubt, that "Molly," as she was familiarly known, first learned to love the country of her birth, and there was sown the seed of that patriotism

MOLLY MARCHED WITH HIM

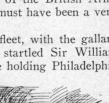

THERE WAS NO TIME TO LOSE

"Pine Robbers," and never dreamed that there would ever be a battle in their neighborhood.

The tramp, tramp, tramp, of the British Army that suddenly aroused them must have been a very great surprise.

The arrival of a French fleet, with the gallant young hero Lafayette, had startled Sir William Howe, who was at that time holding Philadelphia

and loyalty that afterward made the humble servant-girl a soldier and a heroine.

In July of the year 1769 Molly left the roof of her master and became the wife of a barber by the name of John Hays. Whether or not Molly fired her barber with warlike ambition is an open question; but at any rate Hays was commissioned gunner in Proctor's First Pennsylvania Artillery, on December 14, 1775, changing the peaceful occupation of cutting off hair with shears to the more exciting one of cutting off heads with cannon-balls. With a loyalty born of devotion and unselfishness, Molly determined to follow her husband; so when Gunner Hays marched off with Proctor's First, Molly marched with him.

Through the din of battle, the heat of summer, and the cold of winter, the gunner and his faithful wife followed the fortunes of the American Army, but it was not until the retreat of our forces at Fort Clinton that Molly's first deed of daring became a byword in tent and camp.

Finding that it was necessary to leave the enemy in possession, Hays started to fire his gun as a parting salute to the British. In the rush and confusion of the moment he dropped his lighted match. There was no time to lose, and there was danger of being captured, so he did not stop. Molly, who was behind him, seized the match from the ground, ran to the gun, touched it off and then scampered down the hill as fast as her legs would carry her to join the soldiers. This happened some months before the famous battle of Monmouth.

Down in Monmouth, meanwhile, the people were busy defending themselves from the attacks of the

in siege. Sir William and his red-coated officers had been having a gay time in the old Quaker city; there had been balls and dinners and a great carnival during the winter, and when Dr. Franklin, who was with the American Commissioners in France, heard of all this gayety, he remarked shrewdly: "Howe has not taken Philadelphia, but Philadelphia has taken *him*."

When the French fleet landed, and he knew that France had acknowledged America as an independent government, Howe, perhaps, began to think like Dr. Franklin.

Preparations were made to raise the siege of Philadelphia at once, and Sir Henry Clinton succeeded to the command of the British Army, with orders to go to New York by water. This plan of route was changed, however, and so it came about that the line of march was through New Jersey, and so it happened that old Monmouth became the scene of conflict. The line of the British baggage-wagons was twelve miles long, and the sandy roads made their progress slow.

When Washington heard of Clinton's changed route, he determined to march forward and head him off. He pushed on, and on June 27 encamped at Monmouth Courthouse on rising ground that

"I'LL FIRE IT"

was hemmed in on all sides by woods and marshes. General Washington, after grave deliberation, decided to risk the fight; and although the battle was hotly contested, and indeed almost lost three separate times, the American Army was victorious. That memorable Sunday, June 28, 1778, was the hottest day of the year. The heat was so great that the soldiers were ordered to take off their coats; yet through the heat and dust and smoke and blood, Molly, the gunner's wife, carried water to her husband, and to the soldiers on the field, all day. The little spring from which she fetched the water was at the bottom of the hill, and instead of a pail, she brought it in a *pitcher*. This, most probably, was the origin of her name, "Molly Pitcher," among the soldiers—a name that from that day has become historic.

There had been a fierce charge of the enemy's cavalry on Hay's gun, and just as Molly was returning with a refreshing drink for the almost perishing men, she saw her husband fall mortally wounded. Rushing forward, she heard an officer say: "Wheel back the gun; there's no one here to serve it."

Checking the blinding rush of tears, Molly threw down her pitcher and seized the rammer of the gun. "I'll fire it," she said; and taking her place beside the dead gunner's cannon, she filled his place during the rest of the day. The story of the brave deed has been told in verse:

"Wheel back the gun," the gunner said,
When like a flash before him stood
A figure dashed with smoke and blood,
With streaming hair, with eyes aflame,
With lips that falter the gunner's name.
"Wheel back *his* gun that never yet
His fighting duty did forget?
His voice shall speak though he be dead,
I'll serve my husband's gun!" she said.

The next day General Greene sought for Molly, and brought her to General Washington, who praised her for her courage, and presented her then and there with the commission of sergeant in the Continental Army. As the half-dazed Molly stood before the great general in her soldier's coat and cap, cheer after cheer for "Sergeant Molly Pitcher" went up from ten thousand throats. It must have been a stirring scene—stately Washington and the blood-stained, smoke-begrimed figure of the gunner's wife, who was now an officer and forever a heroine—a scene that must to-day thrill the heart of every boy and girl who reads the story of American history!

Next day on that field so hardly won,
Stately and calm stands Washington,
And looks where our gallant Greene doth lead
A figure clad in motley weed—
A soldier's cap and a soldier's coat
Masking a woman's petticoat.
He greets our Molly in kindly wise,
He bids her raise her fearful eyes,
And he hails her there before them all,
Comrade and soldier whate'er befall;
And since she has played a man's full part,
A man's reward for her loyal heart!
And Sergeant Molly Pitcher's name
Be writ henceforth on the shield of fame.

"JOHNNY APPLESEED"

BY FRANK B. McALLISTER

IF YOU had stood, on a bright day some one hundred years ago, by the banks of the Ohio River, you might have seen a strange procession coming down stream. You would have seen two birch-bark canoes securely lashed together and piled high with leathern bags brimming full of apple-seeds, and in the midst of the strange craft a small, wiry man with long, dark hair, keen black eyes, and a scanty beard that had never known the razor. On his head rested a tin dipper, while his body was clad in tattered garments that had once done duty as coffee-sacks.

Whenever the children in front of some lone frontier cabin glimpsed this queer sight they rushed inside and announced with glee:

"Oh, mother, Johnny Appleseed's coming; may we go down to the river and meet him when he lands?" Although the visitor was as odd a specimen of humanity as the wilderness afforded, he was known as one of the kindliest of men, and no one was afraid of him.

When Johnny came ashore he would look about

him for soil that was rich and loamy, and then he would begin to plant his appleseeds. Sometimes he would cover considerable tracts with his plantings, putting in as many as sixteen bushels of seeds to the acre. He would stay as long as his stock of seed held out, and then would disappear as unceremoniously as he had come, only to return after a few weeks or months with another load.

He never forgot the orchards he had planted. When the trees were partly grown, he returned to prune them year after year, and to repair the slight brush fences he had built to keep out the deer and other animals that might nip the tender sprouts. Many of the trees he disposed of to farmers for transplanting, and in some cases he would sell an entire orchard on the spot he had originally chosen. If the customer was poor, as most of the pioneers were, he could have the trees for nothing, or Johnny would take any old piece of clothing in exchange. If a customer wanted to buy, the price of each tree was invariably a

"JOHNNY APPLESEED'S COMING!"

"fippenny-bit," and immediate payment was never required. Johnny usually took a note from the customer, and of such promises-to-pay he collected a goodly number during his career, but it is not on record that he ever tried to collect any of them, apparently considering, like Mr. Micawber, that the transaction was completed when the note was written.

When he could not travel by water he went on foot, carrying his precious seeds in leathern bags slung across his back. Occasionally he would press into service some decrepit horse that he had saved from cruel treatment by purchasing it with his slender income. Every autumn he would start out in a diligent search of the woods and clearings of such strays or cast-offs, that he might care for them till they died of old age, or he could transfer them to some new owner, the sole condition of the transfer being humane treatment. Johnny never sold any of the poor old nags he had collected.

Besides appleseed, Johnny planted seeds of many medicinal herbs in the woods through which he traveled. Doctors were few and far between in the wilderness, and Johnny wished to make up for this lack as far as he could. By his efforts hundreds of miles of forests were carpeted with fennel, catnip, horehound, pennyroyal, rattlesnake root, and other of the "simples" that our ancestors used in sickness.

Johnny was fervently religious, and was always ready to talk with friends or strangers on high themes. His own little library of religious books, purchased with that part of his income not given away or used to relieve suffering, was freely lent to all who would take the books and read them.

When his supply of whole books gave out, he would divide two or three of them into pieces and leave one chapter at each farm, to remain till his next visit, when he would exchange it for another chapter. The only difficulty with the scheme was that the readers rarely got the chapters in their proper order, but that troubled neither them nor their queer librarian.

HIS LOVE OF NATURE

No one could have been more tender to all forms of animal life than was Johnny Appleseed. In this respect he reminds us of good Saint Francis of Assisi, with his appreciation of all nature as God's works, and the birds as man's little brothers. On one occasion he even put out his campfire that the smoke might not destroy the myriads of mosquitoes who hovered near it. Another time he found that a bear and her cubs were asleep in a hollow log against which he had built his fire, so, not wishing to disturb them, he

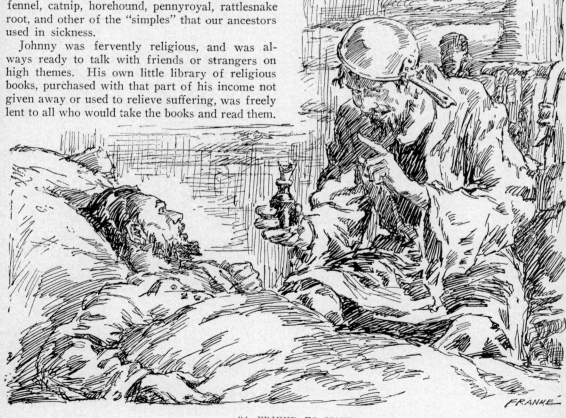

"A FRIEND TO MAN"

quenched the flame and slept that night in the snow. A rattlesnake once bit him, and he killed the venomous creature, an action he always after regretted. "Poor fellow," said Johnny; "he only touched me, while I, in an ungodly passion, put the heel of my scythe in him and went home." Surely a kind heart beat beneath this man's coffee-sacks; if he had lived in the early centuries, the painters would have drawn the tin dipper on his head as a halo.

His journeyings over Ohio and Indiana, carrying his bags of appleseed and his tattered books, continued till the very week of his death. When he was taken sick in the home of a settler at Fort Wayne, he was on his way to repair the fence about an orchard he had set out some years before near the western frontier of the state. The pioneers in a large section of the Middle West mourned him as one of the strangest but one of the best friends they had. It was estimated that he had left behind fully one hundred thousand acres of orchards planted as a testimony to his love for nature and for his fellowman.

WHO WAS HE?

Who was Johnny Appleseed? His real name was Jonathan Chapman, and he was born in Boston, in 1775. He had followed the Revolutionary veterans over the Alleghenies, and conceiving his life mission to be the planting of apple trees, as theirs was the wielding of the ax or the guiding of the plow, he served a great and useful purpose in making men and women contented in their new homes on the frontier.

No one knows just where his body is buried, but no one doubts that it is somewhere in the woods he loved, where the birds sing and the squirrels play, and where the breezes of spring waft the sweet odors of blossoming branches. There is an old poem that the children in Mansfield still learn, one verse of which runs:

And if they inquire whence came such trees,
Where not a bough once swayed in the breeze,
The reply still comes as they travel on,
"Those trees were planted by Appleseed John."

And now every springtime in the Western Reserve where he wandered the air is full of fragrance and blossoms and through the long summer the fruit swells and ripens on the trees and in the golden autumn men and women go forth where the fruit shines like lanterns and fill their baskets with food. And the orchards of Ohio sift down their soft petals somewhere on the grave of Jonathan Chapman, the seed-planter and saunterer.

A PIG THAT NEARLY CAUSED A WAR

BY JULIAN RALPH

In no history that I have been able to find, and in no popular book of reference that I have seen, after a great deal of searching, is there any account of the fact that in the year 1859 a pig almost plunged us into a war with Great Britain. All the books mention the excitement, but only as a part of another matter. Yet, when I was in the beautiful, rose-garnished English city of Victoria, on Vancouver Island, close to the Pacific coast of Washington State, I found many English subjects who had a great deal to say about that pig, and about the mischief caused by it. Our country was then on the eve of a war the most awful in all history, and this comparatively slight incident made but little impression upon our people, all wrought up, as they were, over the great questions which turned upon the issue of that terrible conflict. It was very different with the people of Victoria and the great island of Vancouver. Theirs was then, and has since been, a peaceful existence, and the shock and excitement caused when one of their pigs all but brought war to their doors made a deep impression on their minds.

There had been a great deal of trouble over that extreme northwestern corner of our country. It was not definitely known until the early '70s where our territory ended and British soil began. The greater part of the corner now forming the states of Oregon and Washington, and so highly prized by us, was claimed, at different times, by Russia, by Spain, and by Great Britain. First Russia withdrew, and then, after Spain and England, in 1787, had almost come to blows over it, Spain gave up her claim. This left England to dispute the ownership with us; and sixty years ago the dispute waxed so hot that a political party in this country favored going to war over it.

"Fifty-four, forty,—or fight!" was the watchword of this party, which was led by the great Stephen A. Douglas. By "54-40" was meant the parallel of latitude, 54° 40',—so that this party of Americans claimed the land all the way to the southern end of Alaska. James K. Polk was our President during the heat of this excitement, in 1845. The more temperate of our statesmen advised fixing upon latitude 49 for our northern boundary; and in 1846 Great Britain agreed, and it is our present boundary line. But the Pacific coast, just at that corner of our country, is ragged, and little islands are thickly dotted along the shore. Between two groups of these islands run two narrow straits of water,—one called the Canal de Haro, and the other the Rosario Strait. Between the two is San Juan Island. It commands both waterways, and hence it would be of great value to either country that owned it, in case the two nations should ever quarrel. The text of the agreement between the two countries reads that the boundary at this corner should be "the middle of the channel," without saying *which* channel. From 1846 to 1859, therefore, the dispute continued, though without the excitement there had been when there was doubt about the mainland.

The two channels lead for the British to the Pacific coast of Canada, and for us, to Alaska. One channel, the Canal de Haro, is straighter and broader than the other and deep enough for the largest war-ships. It washes the western shore of San Juan Island, a little green eminence fifteen miles long and, in the broadest part, seven miles wide. The northern part is broken up into high hills, while the southern end is covered with lovely pasture-land. Coal and limestone are found in the hills, and off the shore there is splendid fishing for cod, halibut, and salmon. But it is on account of its fortress-like position on the main channel and commanding both waterways to Canada and Alaska that it is most highly prized.

A man named Hubbs, who was pasturing sheep on the southern end of the island of San Juan, is no record of its age, size, or color, or of whether it had a name; or, in short, of anything about it, except that it went on Hubbs's ground— on that part where he was growing a few vegetables which the pigs kept by his neighbor had already damaged. If any one had dreamed what

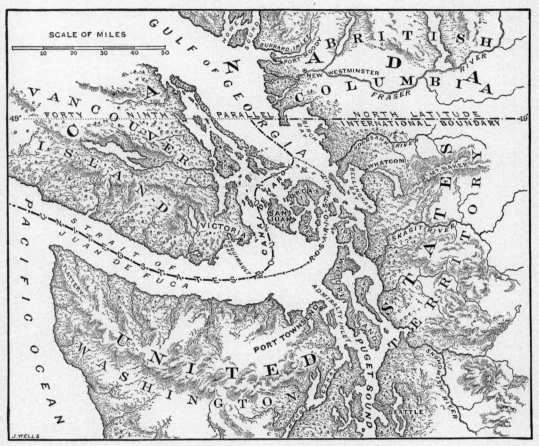

MAP SHOWING THE DISPUTED BOUNDARIES IN 1859

had for a neighbor, on the north end, a man named Griffiths. This Griffiths was employed to raise pigs for the Hudson's Bay Company, that old and famous institution which has existed for two hundred and fifty years, and has been maintained by brave and hardy men solely for the purpose of trading with the Indians; giving them money, blankets, food, guns and ammunition, in return for the skins of wild animals. The pigs belonging to this company overran the island and caused Mr. Hubbs a great deal of trouble; so one day, in a moment of anger, he warned his neighbor Griffiths that if another pig came upon his land he would kill it. The very next day a pig did trespass there. It is altogether a pity that there

an important pig this was, all the facts would perhaps have been written down.

Mr. Hubbs kept his word and killed the pig.

Griffiths was then as angry as Hubbs had been, and immediately sailed over to Victoria,—the busy little city on Vancouver Island, where the officers of the government, the soldiers, and the ships-of-war had their headquarters,—and obtained a warrant (or order issued by a court of law) for Hubbs's arrest. A warrant-server, or constable, went to arrest Hubbs, and to take him to Victoria for trial upon the charge of killing the pig. But Hubbs refused to go with him. He said he was an American citizen, and that therefore an English warrant was nothing to *him*.

The constable departed, and Hubbs, well knowing the officer would come back and try to force him to go to Victoria, sent over to Port Townsend, in Washington Territory, for American protection. That part of our country was called by our War Department "The Puget Sound District," and was then in command of Brigadier-General William S. Harney. For many years he made his home in St. Louis, where he was greatly admired and respected, as the oldest officer in our army.

the Yankees off the island." He moved his war-ships over to one of the harbors of the island. His business was fighting, and his first thought was to do what might have begun a bloody and terrible war. Sir James Douglas, the governor, was more temperate; he pacified the admiral, but he thought it wise to send some British troops over to the island—not to fight the Americans, but to let them understand that the English meant to claim San Juan as their property. Captain Dela-

"MR. HUBBS KEPT HIS WORD AND KILLED THE PIG"

Lieutenant-Colonel Casey, then in command of the Ninth Regiment of infantry, but now dead, was at Port Townsend, and General Harney sent him with a company of soldiers to encamp on the island and see to it that the English did not molest our fellow-citizen, Mr. Hubbs.

But, while our soldiers were setting up their tents on this green knoll in the great Pacific, there was the wildest excitement in Victoria. The governor of Vancouver Island was Sir James Douglas, a nobleman by nature as well as by title; and the English ships-of-war, harbored in a little bay near Victoria, were commanded by Rear-Admiral James C. Prevost. The admiral was very angry when he heard of the occupation of the island by the soldiers of the United States. What he said has not been written down, but it is remembered, by those who heard him, that he threatened to take his great war-ships and "blow

combe, of the Royal Engineers, was sent with a company of English soldiers, and their tents were pitched on the northern end of the island.

For five years that little island was occupied by soldiers of the two mighty nations. Each camp displayed the flag of its country on a high staff over the tents,—the Stars and Stripes fluttering over the pastures at one end, and the red banner of Great Britain among the hills at the other, only a few miles away. On either shore the people were greatly excited, and many on both sides favored war. They were no more temperate than the American, Hubbs, had been when he killed the pig, or than the Englishman, Griffiths, was when he tried to secure his neighbor's arrest. The Americans supported their countryman, and the English approved of what the Englishman had done; so, at least along the coast, both sides wished to fight. As is so often the case, the soldiers were the least excited. The officers and men in our camp became well acquainted with the members of the English force, and the soldiers of the two camps not only visited one another, but actually relieved the monotony of life in that lonely place by giving dinners and parties, when the men of one camp would entertain friends from the other.

News of what had occurred was dispatched to Washington and London; and General Winfield Scott was sent posthaste, by way of Panama, to the scene. In the meantime all our available military force on that coast had been sent to San Juan. General Scott withdrew all our soldiers, except one company, and induced Sir James Douglas to leave only one company of British soldiers on the northern end of the island. This arrangement was called "a joint military occupation." It was decided to leave to arbitration the vexed question of which channel was the boundary, and both countries agreed that each should present arguments in favor of what it believed to be just. Our government wished the middle of the Canal de Haro to be the border line, because we claimed that it was the true ship-channel; but to this the British had never been willing to agree, since that boundary would give San Juan to our country, and with that island went the control of the gateway to the English possessions. They wished the boundary to be drawn along the middle of the Rosario Strait, leaving them San Juan, so that they could use the broader canal for their merchant vessels and ships-of-war, which could thereby sail in perfect safety to British Columbia or to our own Alaska, since both the San Juan side and the Vancouver side of the canal would then be English territory. When all the papers had been made ready (and the English admit that the American papers and arguments were far

better prepared than theirs), it was decided to give them to the Emperor of Germany, and to ask him if he would not decide where the boundary should be.

Of course, the Emperor of Germany did not actually do this, personally; but he handed the papers to Herr Grimm, the vice-president of the Supreme Court of Germany, Judge Goldschmidt, of the German Tribunal of Commerce, and Dr. Kiepert, a great geographical authority of Berlin. They made their report to the Emperor, and, on October 23, 1872, the Emperor rendered his decision in writing, and gave a copy to Mr. Bancroft, for this country, and to Lord Odo Russell, for England. He decided that the American claim was just, and that the middle of the Canal de Haro should be the boundary. One month later, the British cut down their flag-staff and left the island. It was a great disappointment to the people of Canada and of Vancouver Island, for it gave to the United States the important little island of San Juan, and the commanding position on the marine highway leading to the Pacific coast of England's American possessions, and thus our country secured a greater gain than many bloody wars have brought to fighting nations.

Time makes many changes, but it has not decreased the importance of that little island; for Vancouver Island has ceased to be a province and become a part of British Columbia. San Juan, therefore, lies in the waterway between British Columbia and its principal port, Victoria. So, although the pig was merely in search of something to eat (as pigs are, most of their time), and although Mr. Hubbs desired only to save himself from the consequence of an angry act, America well may be grateful to both—especially to the pig, for he lost his life for his country.

THE WALKING PURCHASE

BY GEORGE WHEELER

IN the early twilight of a September morning, more than one hundred and seventy years ago, a remarkable company might have been seen gathering about a large chestnut-tree at the crossroads near the Friends' meeting-house in Wrightstown, Pennsylvania. It is doubtful whether any one of us could have guessed what the meeting meant. Most of the party were Quakers in wide-brimmed hats and plain dress, and if it had been First-day instead of Third-

day, we might have thought they were gathering under the well-known tree for a neighborly chat before "meeting." Nor was it a warlike rendezvous; for the war-cry of the Lenni-Lenape had never yet been raised against the "Children of Mignon" (Elder Brother), as the followers of William Penn were called; and in a little group somewhat apart were a few athletic Indians in peaceful garb and friendly attitude. But it evidently was an important meeting, for here were several prominent officials, including even so notable a person as Proprietor Thomas Penn.

In 1686, fifty-one years before this, William Penn bought from the Lenni-Lenape, or Delaware Indians, a section bounded on the east by the Delaware, on the west by the Neshaminy, and extending to the north from his previous purchases "as far as a man can go in a day and a half." No effort was made to fix the northern boundary until the Indians, becoming uneasy at the encroachments of the settlers, asked to have the line definitely marked. On August 25, 1737, after several conferences between the Delawares and William Penn's sons, John and Thomas, who, after their father's death, became proprietors of Pennsylvania, the treaty of 1686 was confirmed, and a day was appointed for beginning the walk. This explains why the crowd was gathering about the old chestnut-tree in the early dawn of that day, September 19, 1737.

"Ready!" called out Sheriff Smith.

At the word, James Yeates, a native of New England, "tall, slim, of much ability and speed of foot," Solomon Jennings, "a remarkably stout and strong man," and Edward Marshall, a well-known hunter, over six feet tall, and noted as a walker, stepped from the crowd and placed their right hands upon the tree.

Thomas Penn had promised five pounds in money and five hundred acres of land to the walker who covered the greatest distance; and these three men were to contest for the prize. Just as the edge of the sun showed above the horizon, Sheriff Smith gave the word, and the race began.

Yeates quickly took up the lead, stepping lightly. Then came Jennings, accompanied by two Indians, who were there to see that the walking was fairly done. Closely following them

"THE THREE MEN STEPPED FROM THE CROWD AND PLACED THEIR RIGHT HANDS UPON THE TREE"

were men on horseback, including the sheriff and the surveyor-general. Thomas Penn himself followed the party for some distance. Far in the rear came Marshall, walking in a careless manner, swinging a hatchet in one hand, "to balance himself," and at intervals munching a dry biscuit, of which he carried a small supply. He seemed to have forgotten a resolution he had made to "win the prize of five hundred acres of land, or lose his life in the attempt."

Thomas Penn had secretly sent out a preliminary party to blaze the trees along the line of the walk for as great a distance as it was thought possible for a man to walk in eighteen hours. So, when the wilderness was reached, the walkers still had the best and most direct course clearly marked out for them. The Indians soon protested against the speed, saying over and over: "That 's not fair. You run. You were to walk." But the treaty said, "As far as a man can *go*," and the walkers were following it chief, to send other Indians to accompany the walkers. He angrily replied: "You have all the good land now, and you may as well take the bad, too." One old Indian, indignant at the stories of how the white men rushed along in their greed to get as much land as possible, remarked in a tone of deep disgust: "No sit down

"THE INDIANS PROTESTED AGAINST THE SPEED"

in letter, if not in spirit, as they hurried along. Their protests being disregarded, the Indians endeavored to delay the progress by stopping to rest; but the white men dismounted, and allowed the Indians to ride, and thus pushed on as rapidly as ever. At last the Indians refused to go any farther, and left the party.

Before Lehigh River was reached Jennings was exhausted, gave up the race, and lagged behind in the company of followers. His health was shattered, and he lived only a few years.

That night the party slept on the north side of the Lehigh Mountains, half a mile from the Indian village of Hokendaqua. Next morning, while some of the party searched for the horses which had strayed away during the night, others went to the village to request Lappawinzoe, the

to smoke; no shoot squirrel; but lun, lun, lun, all day long."

Scarcely had the last half-day's walk begun before Yeates, who was a drinking man, was overcome by the tremendous exertions and intemperance of the previous day. He stumbled at the edge of Big Creek, and rolled, helpless, down the bank into the water. When rescued he was entirely blind, and his death followed within three days.

Marshall still pressed on. Passing the last of the blazed trees which had hitherto guided him, he seized a compass offered by Surveyor-General Eastburn, and by its aid still continued his onward course. At last, Sheriff Smith, who for some time had frequently looked at his watch, called, "Halt!" Marshall instantly threw himself at full length, and grasped a sapling. Here was the starting-point for the northern boundary of the purchase of 1686, sixty-eight miles from the old chestnut-tree at Wrightstown, and very close to where Mauch Chunk stands to-day. The walk was twice as long as the Indians expected it to be.

Unfortunately for the Delawares, they knew too little of legal technicalities to notice that the deed did not state in what direction the northern boundary was to be drawn. They naturally expected it to be drawn to the nearest point on the Delaware. But the surveyor-general, to please Penn, decided that the line should run at right angles to the direction of the walk, which was almost exactly northwest. Draw a line from Mauch Chunk to the Delaware so that if extended it would pass through New York City, and another to the point where New York, New Jersey, and Pennsylvania meet. The first is the Indian's idea of the just way to lay out the northern boundary; the second is the line which Surveyor-General Eastburn actually finished marking out in four days after Marshall's walk ended.

And so the three hundred thousand acres which the Indians would have given to the Penns as the result of Marshall's walk were increased to half a million by taking selfish advantage of a flaw in the deed.

The Lenni-Lenape had loved and trusted William Penn because he always dealt openly and fairly with them. "We will live in love with William Penn and his children," said they, "as long as the sun and moon shall shine." But the wrongs inflicted on them in the "walking purchase," aroused the deepest indignation. "Next May," said Lappawinzoe, "we will go to Philadelphia, each one with a buckskin to repay the presents and take back our land again." It was too late, however, for this to be done.

At last, in 1741, the Indians determined to resort to arms to secure justice. But the Iroquois, to whom the Delawares had long been subject, came to the aid of the Penns, and the last hope of righting the wrong was gone forever.

There seems a sort of poetic justice in the later experiences of the principal men in the affair. Marshall never got his five hundred acres of land, and his wife was killed in an attack by the Indians. Eastburn was repudiated by Thomas Penn, and his heirs were notified that they "need not expect the least favor." Penn himself was brought before the king and forced to disown many of his acts and agents in a most humiliating manner.

But all this did not repair the injury to the Delawares, and they never again owned, as a tribe, a single inch along the river from which they took their name.

A small monument, erected by the Bucks County Historical Society, marks the spot where the old chestnut-tree formerly stood. In order that this might not seem to condone an unworthy deed, the monument was dedicated, not to those who made or conducted the walk, but to the Lenni-Lenape Indians—"not to the wrong, but to the persons wronged."

The inscription on the stone reads:

TO THE MEMORY OF THE LENNI-LENAPE INDIANS,
ANCIENT OWNERS OF THIS REGION,
THESE STONES ARE PLACED AT
THIS SPOT, THE STARTING-
POINT OF THE
"INDIAN WALK,"
September 19, 1737.

"MARSHALL THREW HIMSELF AT FULL LENGTH, AND GRASPED A SAPLING"

THE ORIGIN OF OUR FLAG

BY PARMALEE McFADDEN

With Additions by the Editor

Did it ever occur to you that the bunch of colored ribbons you wear in your buttonhole or pinned on your dress if you are a girl—at commencement, or at a baseball or football game, is really a flag? It tells to what class or school or college you belong, or which of these, for the time, has your interest and sympathy. And for somewhat similar reasons do nations wear their colors. At first maybe it was to tell one another apart; but after a while the colors—the flag—came to represent the nation itself; and the way people acted toward the nation's flag was supposed to show the way they felt toward the nation.

When the American army was encamped at Cambridge, just outside of Boston, General Washington felt the need of a distinctive flag. There were thirteen colonies represented in that army, and each had its own flag, while some had more than one. Among this miscellaneous lot of flags was the one, of which you have often seen pictures, showing a rattlesnake, and bearing the motto: "Don't tread on me."

But what the country needed was one flag, with a design that meant something. So Congress sent a committee, headed by Benjamin Franklin, which consulted with General Washington, and recommended a flag to stand for all the colonies. After much discussion the one adopted was that shown in Fig. 19 of the group shown herewith.

To understand how this flag grew from older flags, let us for a moment go back to the early flags of England.

In the early part of the fourteenth century the flag of England bore simply the red cross of St. George on a white ground (see Fig. 1); while the flag of Scotland was a white St. Andrew's cross on a blue ground (see Fig. 2). In 1603 England and Scotland were united, and three years later the two flags were combined to form what was called the "king's colors" (see Fig. 4), England and Scotland, however, retaining their own individual flags. Indeed, it was the red cross of St. George that the "Mayflower" flew at her masthead when she brought her precious load of Pilgrims to Plymouth that cold winter of 1620, for she was an English ship.

In 1707 Great Britain adopted for herself and her colonies a flag having the main part red, but in its upper corner was the "king's colors," or "union" flag, which represented the union of England and Scotland; and since that time this part of the flag has been called the "union," or "jack," and sometimes the "Union Jack." The term "jack" is supposed to have come from Jacques, the French spelling of James, which form the then king of England, James I, used in signing his name.

This was the flag of Great Britain down to the year 1801, when Ireland was added to form the United Kingdom of Great Britain and Ireland. This further extension to the nation was represented by the addition of the cross of St. Patrick, which was a diagonal cross, like that of St. Andrew, only it was red on a white field. The combination of these three crosses of England, Scotland, and Ireland has formed the flag of Great Britain from the year 1801 down to the present day.

The British merchant marine uses the flag of red with the union of the three crosses (Fig. 9); the navy of that country displays the cross of St. George with the same union as that of the merchant marine (Fig. 6); and the vessels subject to the British Admiralty fly the blue ensign (Fig. 12). Canada has adopted the red ensign (Fig. 9), adding her coat of arms (Fig. 7), while Australia (Fig. 8), New Zealand (Fig. 11), and the Union of South Africa (Fig. 10) have added distinguishing marks to the blue ensign (Fig. 12).

From the British flag of 1707 we come to that shown in Fig. 13—the one that begins to show a resemblance to our own familiar flag. This was the flag recommended by Franklin's Congressional Committee. It was called the flag of the "United Colonies of America," and had for its union the union jack, made up of only the St. George and St. Andrew's crosses of the British flag; but its main field consisted of thirteen stripes, alternately red and white. There is nothing definite known as to what suggested the idea of the stripes; it has been claimed that the stripes that appeared on the coat of arms of the Washington family suggested it. A flag with stripes was used by the troop of light horse that escorted Washington from Philadelphia to New York when he took command of the army; and stripes were also used on one of the flags of the East India Company.

This flag was first used by the American army encamped at Cambridge. The next stage in the

Copyright by M. G. Abbey
From a Copley Print, copyright by Curtis & Cameron, Boston
READING THE DECLARATION OF INDEPENDENCE
FROM A PAINTING BY EDWIN A. ABBEY

evolution of our flag was in 1777, when by resolution of Congress it was ordered "that the flag of the thirteen United States" (not colonies now)

"be thirteen stripes alternately red and white" (just as in the flag then in use), but "the union to be thirteen stars, white on a blue field, representing a new constellation" (see Fig. 19). In this new form we find another suggestion of the Washington coat of arms, which contained, in addition to two wide red bars, three stars; at least, they were in the form of stars, though in heraldry they would probably be called "mullets" or "rowels"—the sharp-pointed wheels used in riding-spurs.

At the time the Stars and Stripes were adopted Congress was sitting in Independence Hall, in Philadelphia. There was living in the city a widow named Elizabeth Ross, who, for several years, had made government and other flags. It was by this woman, in her home in Philadelphia, that the first flag authorized by Congress was made. It may be interesting to know that Mrs. Ross's home—the "Betsy Ross House," it is called—is still standing at 239 Arch Street, Philadelphia.

At the end of the last century a number of citizens were given a charter under the name of the "American Flag House and Betsy Ross Memorial Association." The objects of the association have been partially fulfilled by its purchasing the old Ross house and converting it into a museum.

It was in the back room of this house, then, that General Washington, Robert Morris, and a Colonel Ross discussed with Betsy Ross the details of the flag. It was here they decided that the thirteen stars should be placed in the form of a circle to show that it was for all time and had no end. When considering how many points the stars should have, it is reported that Betsy Ross suggested they be given five points, because the cloth could be folded in such a way that a complete star could be made by one cut of the scissors. This might be a good puzzle for the girls and boys to work out. It is interesting to note that our flags all have five-pointed stars, while those on our coins are six-pointed.

This (Fig. 19) was the flag that was used at the battle of Brandywine and at Germantown. It was with our army when Burgoyne surrendered; with Washington at Valley Forge; at the surrender of Cornwallis at Yorktown; and at the evacuation of New York by the British in 1783.

After Vermont and Kentucky were admitted as States, Congress ordered that after May 1, 1795, the flag have fifteen stripes and fifteen stars. This was the flag that our army and navy carried in the War of 1812. Scarcely less interesting to patriotic Americans is the fact that this particular form of the flag was the one used at the attack on Fort McHenry, when Francis Scott Key waited with others for the return of morning to learn whether the fort had fallen; and when "by the dawn's early light" he saw through the mist "that our flag was still there," and was stirred into writing "The Star-Spangled Banner," which has since become our national anthem.

This fifteen-stripe flag did not have so graceful proportions as those of the preceding forms, and it soon became evident that if a new stripe were to be added for each State admitted into the Union, in the course of time the flag would become unwieldy. So in 1818, when there were twenty States, Congress passed a law to the effect that after the following July 4 the number of stripes in the flag should be reduced to the original thirteen, but that the union should have twenty stars; and that as each new State was admitted another star should be added, to take effect the Fourth of July next following its admission.

From that time down to this day the stripes have stood for the original thirteen States, and the stars for all the States.

FANEUIL HALL, BOSTON
From an old engraving

HONORS TO THE FLAG

BY CAPTAIN HAROLD HAMMOND, U. S. A.

THERE is no possession of a country which is more deeply revered, more consistently loved, or more loyally supported than its national flag. In our country is this especially true, for in that one emblem are embodied all the principles which our forefathers upheld, all the benefits of a century and a quarter of enlightened progress, and all the hope and assurance of a promising future.

The stripes of alternate red and white proclaim the original union of thirteen states to maintain the Declaration of Independence. Its stars, white on a field of blue, proclaim that union of states constituting our national constellation which receives a new star with every

pecially in the attitude toward it of our Army and our Navy, since it is there that the flag is more constantly in evidence than elsewhere, and it is there that it has a well-defined official status, laid down by law. In every army post, both here at home and in our foreign possessions, and on every war vessel of the United States, our flag floats in the breeze from sunrise till sunset, the honored emblem of a free people.

Every regiment in our military service is furnished by the government with a flag, or "color" as it is known officially, and on this flag are embroidered the names of all the battles in which the regiment has taken part. This flag is

WEST POINT CADETS ON DRESS PARADE. THE COLORS IN THE CENTER OF THE BATTALION.

state. Thus, the stars and stripes signify union and "in union there is strength."

The very colors have a significance. White stands for purity, red for valor and blue for justice, together forming a combination which it is our inherited privilege to honor and uphold.

It is not the flag of a king, or an emperor, or a president. It is the flag of the people, brought into being by their will, defended when necessary by their patriotism, and to which they turn for protection in time of danger. No matter into what parties our people may be divided, due to political beliefs and leanings, they all stand united under one flag. It is the emblem of unity, safety and faith.

Naturally, the outward manifestation of our devotion to the flag is to be observed more es-

carried at regimental drills, parades and reviews, as well as in battle, and two armed men especially detailed as "color guard," always accompany the color sergeant, who is the color bearer.

Army regulations prescribe in detail what honors shall be paid to the flag and these regulations are implicitly and gladly observed. No matter how little one may relish the duty of showing the respect due to some military superior, he is always ready and glad to do honor to his flag. Whenever anyone in the military service of the United States passes near the unfurled colors, or whenever the flag passes before him, he is required to remove his cap in salute, and if sitting he is required to rise and stand at "attention" until the flag has passed.

The authority of the flag is absolute. It is in-

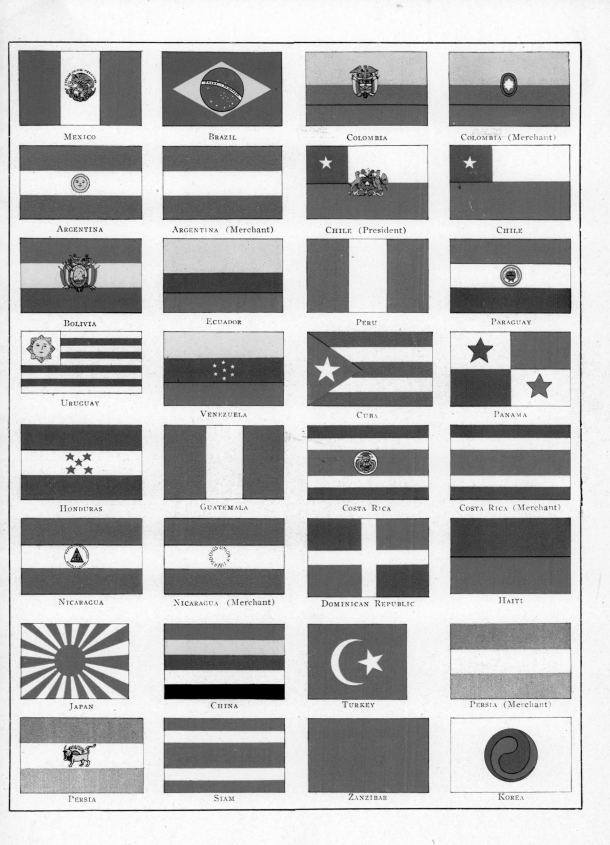

MEXICO   BRAZIL   COLOMBIA   COLOMBIA (Merchant)

ARGENTINA   ARGENTINA (Merchant)   CHILE (President)   CHILE

BOLIVIA   ECUADOR   PERU   PARAGUAY

URUGUAY   VENEZUELA   CUBA   PANAMA

HONDURAS   GUATEMALA   COSTA RICA   COSTA RICA (Merchant)

NICARAGUA   NICARAGUA (Merchant)   DOMINICAN REPUBLIC   HAITI

JAPAN   CHINA   TURKEY   PERSIA (Merchant)

PERSIA   SIAM   ZANZIBAR   KOREA

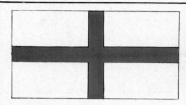

Fig. 1.—St. George's Cross, the National Flag of England

Fig. 2.—St. Andrew's Cross, the National Flag of Scotland

Fig. 3.—St. Patrick's Cross

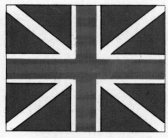

Fig. 4.—Old British Union (England and Scotland), and the American Flag before the Revolution

Fig. 5.—British Flag, adopted after the union of Great Britain and Ireland 1801; now the Flag of the British Empire

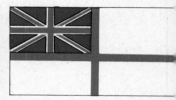

Fig. 6.—British Navy Flag (White Ensign)

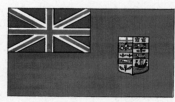

Fig. 7.—Flag of Canada

Fig. 8.—Flag of Australia

Fig. 9.—British Merchant Marine (Red Ensign)

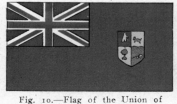

Fig. 10.—Flag of the Union of South Africa

Fig. 11.—Flag of New Zealand

Fig. 12.—British Naval Reserve (Blue Ensign)

Evolution of the Flags of the British Empire and Its

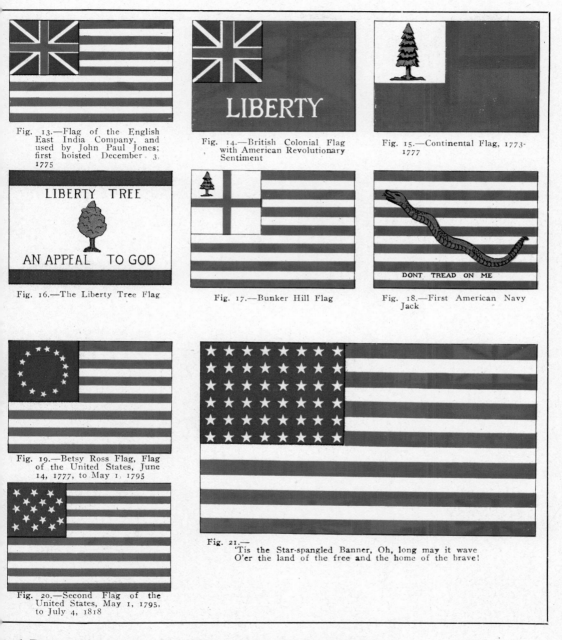

Fig. 13.—Flag of the English East India Company, and used by John Paul Jones; first hoisted December 3, 1775

Fig. 14.—British Colonial Flag with American Revolutionary Sentiment

Fig. 15.—Continental Flag, 1773-1777

Fig. 16.—The Liberty Tree Flag

Fig. 17.—Bunker Hill Flag

Fig. 18.—First American Navy Jack

Fig. 19.—Betsy Ross Flag, Flag of the United States, June 14, 1777, to May 1, 1795

Fig. 21.—
'Tis the Star-spangled Banner, Oh, long may it wave
O'er the land of the free and the home of the brave!

Fig. 20.—Second Flag of the United States, May 1, 1795, to July 4, 1818

pal Possessions, and of the Flag of the United States

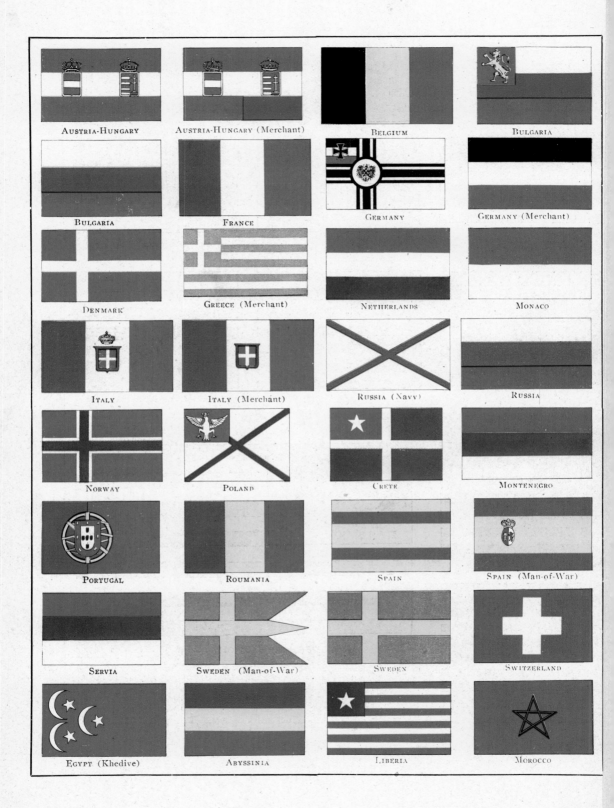

AUSTRIA-HUNGARY   AUSTRIA-HUNGARY (Merchant)   BELGIUM   BULGARIA

BULGARIA   FRANCE   GERMANY   GERMANY (Merchant)

DENMARK   GREECE (Merchant)   NETHERLANDS   MONACO

ITALY   ITALY (Merchant)   RUSSIA (Navy)   RUSSIA

NORWAY   POLAND   CRETE   MONTENEGRO

PORTUGAL   ROUMANIA   SPAIN   SPAIN (Man-of-War)

SERVIA   SWEDEN (Man-of-War)   SWEDEN   SWITZERLAND

EGYPT (Khedive)   ABYSSINIA   LIBERIA   MOROCCO

COLOR BEARERS AND COLOR GUARD, U. S. CORPS OF CADETS

153

ferior in rank to no one. All persons, subject to military discipline and customs, from the President of the United States who is the Commander-in-Chief, down to the newest recruit, are required by regulations to render the same honors to the flag.

There is always something inspiring to the visitor at West Point as he watches the ceremony of evening parade. The battalion of cadets is in line, rigid and motionless in the position of "parade rest," while the band, playing a lively march passes down the whole length of the line

silent, the men with bared heads, the flag is lowered slowly—down, down—into the hands of the armed guard of soldiers detailed to receive it.

It is an unwritten law that the flag shall never touch the ground, and if you will notice, the next time you have the opportunity, you will remark with what care and even tenderness the flag is received, folded and carried away by the corporal in charge of the flag detail, without its outer edges so much as touching the ground.

During the summer encampment at West Point, there is great rivalry among the cadets

A CORPORAL OF THE GUARD QUESTIONING A COLOR SENTINEL.

and returns again to its place on the right. Immediately the music stops, the fifes and drums begin to sound "retreat," and as the last note dies away, the sunset gun booms out its salute to the flag.

As the echoes reverberate among the historic hills and the smoke from the saluting cannon drifts upward and outward over the majestic Hudson, the cadet Adjutant calls the battalion to "Attention," the band strikes up the strain of "The Sar Spangled Banner," and with the officers all standing at attention, facing the flag, their hands at the position of salute, and all civilians, men, women and children, honoring their country's emblem by rising and standing

going on guard to see who will "get colors," that is, to see who will be selected by the adjutant as color sentinels. These color sentinels, three in number, are each day selected from the entire guard as being the most soldierly in appearance, and the most immaculate in dress and equipment.

Their duty is to act only as sentinels over the flag, while the other members of the guard are assigned to the posts about the body of the encampment. After the morning parade, the arms are stacked just behind the "color line," a path within the limits of the encampment and just outside the outer line of tents. The national colors and the gray and gold flag of the Corps of Cadets are laid lengthwise on the two central stacks, the tips of the staffs on one stack and the ferule ends on the other.

The color sentinel walks the color line, immediately in front of the long line of stacked arms, and it is his duty to allow no one to touch the colors and to see that no persons, whether they be cadets, officers, or civilians, pass in or out of camp around the ends of the line of stacks without removing the cap and looking toward the flag as they cross the color line. Should anyone forget thus to comply with the regulations, it is the sentinel's duty to require him to go back and to uncover on crossing the line.

One day not so many years ago, a cadet just beginning his second year at the Academy was slowly pacing up and down the color line, his chest swelling with pride and appreciation of the Adjutant's selection of color sentinels that morning. As he turned about at the end of his beat and started on his return trip, he saw the Commandant of Cadets, a most exalted individual in the cadet eyes, approaching the color line at the farther end. At the proper time, the cadet brought his rifle down to his most military "present arms" and turned his head slightly sideward to receive the salute of his superior officer when he should raise his cap to the colors.

To his surprise and consternation the Commandant never turned his head to right or left, but just walked straight across the color line without so much as noticing the existence of colors or color sentinel and passed on toward his office tent farther back in the camp.

With no thought except of his duty, the sentinel relaxed his set muscles and with arms at the "port," charged down the color line at "double time" in hot pursuit of the delinquent Commandant. As he neared the other end of his post, he called in tones as respectful as they were positive:

"You will have to return across the color line, sir, and salute the colors."

The Commandant was surprised and, for the moment, apparently nettled at receiving this startling and unexpected order from a mere cadet. Then he realized the situation. He had clearly forgotten all about the existence of the line of stacks and the flags resting thereon and, intent on other matters, had absent-mindedly neglected his duty to them and the sentinel guarding them. Without further ado, he came back, meekly removed his hat as he approached, crossed the color line, turned about and crossed it again, and with no word to the sentinel passed on to his tent.

Needless to say the cadet was somewhat agitated when the incident was all over, yet he knew what his orders were and felt that he had carried them out to the letter. Nevertheless he was in rather an uncertain state of mind, wondering what, if any, action the Commandant would take in the matter. He heard nothing of it during his tour of duty and it was not until the next evening at parade that he learned the Commandant's view of the affair. Imagine his surprise and that of all his comrades, who of course knew of it as soon as it happened, when an order was read by the Adjutant, appointing him a cadet Corporal for "strict and zealous execution of his duty in carrying out his orders as a color sentinel."

This is only one of numerous similar instances which go to show how exalted a position our country's flag holds and that no one is of sufficient rank or authority to omit paying it the respect which is its due.

On one occasion when a Major General of the United States Army was holding conversation with a cadet sentinel, making some inquiry or request, the interested crowd about the visitors' seats, who were watching the grizzled veteran and the trim young soldier, were surprised to see the cadet suddenly appear to forget the existence of his high-ranking companion and come from a "port arms," the position of a sentinel holding conversation, to a "present arms," and turn his head to one side, actually stopping in the middle of a sentence.

Instead of exhibiting surprise or wounded dignity at this unexplained action of the cadet, the General instantly divined the reason for it. He knew that he was superior in rank to any one at West Point that day and that the only salute that could be rendered in his presence by the cadet was to the colors. Turning in the direction indicated by the sentinel, he respectfully removed his hat and assumed the position of "attention," remaining in his attitude of silent respect until the flag had passed, when the conversation was resumed as though no break had occurred.

One of the most touching, as well as the most beautiful examples of devotion to the flag is to be found in the records of our Civil War. The Sixteenth Regiment of Connecticut Volunteers, after three days of the hardest and bloodiest of fighting, became convinced that defeat and capture by the enemy was imminent. The ranks were depleted and to hold out longer would only involve needlessly further sacrifice of life. But even in their hour of peril, the zealous patriots thought more of the fate of their battle-scarred flag than of their own. Just before the enemy made his final assault on the breastworks, the gallant colonel shouted to his men: "Whatever you do, boys, don't give up our flag; save that at any price." In an instant, the flag was torn from its staff and cut and torn into hundreds of small fragments, each piece being hidden about the person of some one of its brave defenders.

The survivors of the regiment, about five hundred in number, were sent to a prison camp, where most of them remained until the end of the war, each cherishing his mite of the regimental colors. Through long months of imprisonment many died from sickness brought on by exposure and terrible privation, and in all such cases the scraps of bunting guarded by the poor unfortunates were intrusted to the care of some surviving comrade.

At the end of the war, when the prisoners returned to their homes, a meeting of the survivors was held and all the priceless fragments of the flag were sewn together. But a very few pieces had been lost, so that the restored emblem was made nearly complete.

That flag, patched and tattered as it is, forms one of the proudest possessions of Connecticut to-day and is preserved in the State Capitol at Hartford.

In battle, there is no position more dangerous than that of color bearer, and at the same time there is none that is more earnestly coveted. The colors must be kept waving and it is one of the objects of the enemy to shoot down the bearer of the flag, hoping thereby to dishearten the men following it. In 1900, at the battle of Tientsin, China, the color sergeant was shot through the thigh and seriously wounded. When he fell, General Liscum, who was in command of the American forces in China at that time, snatched the colors from the ground where they had fallen, and himself held them aloft, a target for all the Chinese soldiers on the wall, until he too fell, pierced through the body and mortally wounded by a Chinese rifle ball. Such instances are so numerous that history is full of them, proving that there is no limit to the devotion of a soldier to his flag.

One of the last important orders issued by President Lincoln was that dated March 27, 1865, directing Major General Anderson to "raise and plant upon the ruins of Fort Sumter, in Charleston harbor, the same United States flag which floated over the battlements of that fort during the rebel assault and which was lowered and saluted by him and the small force of his command when the works were evacuated on the 14th day of April, 1861."

"The flag when raised," the order goes on to say, "will be saluted by one hundred guns from Fort Sumter and by a National Salute from every fort and battery that fired upon Fort Sumter."

The flag which was again to be raised over Fort Sumter had been carefully guarded through the years since it had been lowered in honorable defeat, with the time in view when it should again float in the breezes over Charleston harbor as a result of the success of the Union Army. But when that time did come, to whom were the honors paid, the salutes fired? There were present on this occasion Major General Anderson, who had commanded the fort when fired upon in 1861, and Major General William T. Sherman, whose military operations, after his famous "march to the sea," compelled the evacuation of Charleston; and yet it was the *flag* which received homage, not they who had defended it at such great cost. They were merely present to show their allegiance and to join in the general thanksgiving for its restoration.

And this salute of one hundred guns in honor to the flag is more than has ever been fired in the United States to any living person, of whatever rank. The President, when visiting a military post, receives as a salute only twenty-one guns.

Nor do we alone do honor to our flag. War vessels of foreign nations on entering one of our harbors or on passing near a fortification, display the flag of the United States at the main and salute it by firing twenty-one guns. As soon as this salute is fired the fort flying the flag acknowledges it by firing an equal number of guns. No matter what may be the rank of the officer commanding the fort, the Army Regulations specifically state that it is the flag which shall be saluted, and also that salutes to the flag are the only ones that shall be returned. The commanding officer is only an individual after all, while the flag is the representative of an entire nation.

Our flag is beautiful at all times, but perhaps it is most beautiful when one suddenly comes upon it in a foreign country, proudly waving from the flag-staff of some one of our embassies, legations, or consulates.

In war, no captures are more highly prized than flags, and none will tempt soldiers to greater extremes of attack and defense. There is nothing a soldier will not do in the way of risking his life to prevent the capture or to accomplish the recapture of his flag.

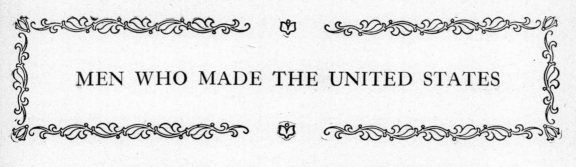

MEN WHO MADE THE UNITED STATES

THE PILGRIMS AND THE PURITANS

BY WILLIAM ELLIOT GRIFFIS

OVER three hundred years have passed since a mixed company, in the ship "Mayflower," sailed from England to begin the settlement of our Eastern States.

We should distinguish between the Puritans, who held to the union of Church and State, and the Pilgrims, who were Separatists. These latter believed that government should have nothing to do with matters of conscience. Both were "puritan," in seeking purity in the church and simplicity in worship and creed. Both sought for reality, and strove to express religion, not in outward symbols or what was visible to the eye and other senses, but in every-day life. Both insisted on instant, continuous and joyful obedience to the Divine will, as revealed in the Bible, and on right doing every day, as God gave them to see the right.

The primitive Christian religion, when brought into Europe, developed within the Roman Empire. Hence the idea prevailed, for a thousand years or more, that Christianity must be regulated by the State, and be kept under the control of learned men with power.

The ruler of the region in both law and custom dictated its religion. Any other theory was scarcely conceivable.

It was, therefore, to be expected that any persons thinking or acting otherwise must be put under ban and punished. This we now call persecution, because we live in a different world of ideas. Yet it was then, with a good conscience, that kings and emperors acted as they did in meting out death to dissenters. We, as educated persons, are not to be too severe in our judgments upon these rulers, for it was generally supposed that religion, in the form of Church and State united, had always and everywhere been the same. Freedom of opinion was considered a crime against society.

It was certainly a great blessing to Europe, during the development of the northern nations from barbarism into civilization, and the era of feudalism within the Holy Roman Empire, formed in the time of Charlemagne, that the church was united. For all the known forces of the universe work in harmony of the centripetal and the centrifugal; and while feudalism divided, the church united, and in that union there was strength. Hence it was, that many rulers considered that they were doing right in enforcing uniformity. For centuries, the maxim of statesmanship was *cujus regio ejus religio;* that is, whose is the region, his is the religion. People and government must think, act, worship, and believe alike.

But when, after the Crusades and the revival of learning, men read the original records of the Christian Church in the Greek language, many of them came to a different opinion as to what should be the doctrine and government of the church.

Besides this, there were many causes that contributed to a new world of thought. Printing with movable, or "living," type, the compass, and gunpowder, and many other inventions, had been brought into Europe from China and Korea, where they had long been known. Printing was improved by Koster and Gutenberg, so that books became very cheap.

The discovery of America was a great gift to the imagination, for it enlarged men's minds and made them look abroad. Voyages of discovery and exploration were so frequent that the expectations of new and great things and events became common. In several countries, almost simultaneously, there began that great movement of the human mind which we call the Reformation; and government, religion, industry, economic and social life were affected by it. It was felt, also, that the settlement and colonization of new lands and acquaintance with new peoples meant duty, as well as gain, and that both the ideas and the material products of far-off nations must be studied. Men perceived that Asia, the old mother continent, and America, the new and once unknown child of the modern age, could be made to pour fresh treasures into Europe.

In the sixteenth century England had a population of only four or five million people and London not over a hundred thousand. No other English city had as many as ten thousand souls, and most of them not five thousand. Walled towns and castles, tithe barns and monasteries, were everywhere. There was very little external trade or foreign commerce, and no banks existed. Nine-tenths of the houses were cottages of one-story, built of wood, with mortar or cement. Most of the people slept upon the floor on rushes, with a log of wood for a bolster. There was much swampy land, and agriculture, except grass and grain raising, was mostly in sheep farming, and wool was the chief export. Brickmaking was nearly unknown. The churches were of stone.

In prosperous times, there was much merriment, with feasting and festivals, and the church year made many happy days; but in time of famine, or after a long war, much distress prevailed. Then followed epidemics and the plague. The real history of England, and that which we imagine from the stage, or read in novels, are very different. Laws and punishments were severe. Criminals were put to death by axe and sword; and their bodies cut in four quarters, and their heads were exposed over gates and towers exactly as in old Japan.

A new and native British (that is, a Welsh) dynasty, the Tudors, had come upon the throne, and Englishmen now thought it time to be independent in matters both of Church and State. They wished to get rid of abuses that had grown up, but they differed in opinion and action on the question of reforming the church, whether from within or from without. Many conscientious and good people held to the medieval forms in creed and ceremony. Yet in either case men who were independent in thinking or action found themselves in collision with the government.

Even when Henry VIII broke off relations with the Pope, this idea of the union of Church and State still prevailed. Queens Mary and Elizabeth and King James I insisted upon conformity. This they compelled by force; that is, fire and the gallows, and infantry and cavalry.

Under this system, Catholics, Puritans, and Jews suffered alike. Law, which then meant chiefly the sovereign's will, required that all English folk believe, worship, and obey as the Government ordered. Hence the divisive words, still in use in England, but resented among us, of "Churchmen," "Nonconformists." The more acceptable terms now used are Free and State Churchmen.

Directly opposite to this was the attitude of the Dutch Republic, of which the great ruler known as William the Silent was the true exemplar. In 1577 he laid the corner-stone of the new kind of State, both Dutch and American, in these words, issued to the magistrates of Middleburg, who had been severe in dealing with the people called Anabaptists. These Christians, besides some wrong ideas, held most of the opinions that are now as A B C in the modern world. William wrote:

"You have no right to interfere with the conscience of any one, so long as he does not work a public scandal, or injury to his neighbor."

This was the doctrine of soul-liberty, proclaimed a generation before Roger Williams was born.

What this new man of the new State had said was so startlingly novel that the news soon spread all over Europe that, in the Dutch Republic, "religion was free for all men." Here, too, besides free public schools, sustained by taxation and open to all children to the age of twelve, was liberty of printing, which was not allowed in England till long after the time of Milton.

Until about 1700 nearly all English Bibles such as the Geneva version, which both the Pilgrims and Puritans used for a century, were printed in Holland. At first they were smuggled into England within barrels or cargoes of wheat.

A REFUGE IN HOLLAND

So to this city of Middleburg, the first of the Free Churchmen, like the Pilgrim Fathers, led by Robert Browne, fled from England; and here in 1583 he printed the first modern book, which asserted the right of Christians to form free churches, each one a republic in itself, to elect their own officers, and, in matters of faith and worship, to acknowledge no other master than Jesus Christ. Any one in England found circulating Browne's books was promptly hanged.

In England, companies of Free Church people worshiped secretly in London, and at Norwich to the east, and Gainsborough and Scrooby, and in the north. When discovered, they were arrested and thrown into prison, where most of them starved, or died of fever.

Three Free Churchmen, university graduates, Barrowe, Greenwood, and Penry, were hanged. The latter, a Welshman, advised his flock to leave the home land and go to Holland, which country William Brewster, afterward the famous elder, as page to Queen Elizabeth's ambassador, had visited in 1586 to help the republic with a liberty loan. There he saw that the Dutch represented the new world of ideas—toleration in religion, public schools open to all, free printing, and the triumph of science over superstition, such as witchcraft, old and false notions in trade, civics, and economics. Ahead of all other countries in that era, their fundamental principle, embodied in Article IV of the constitution, under which they refused to King James the right to disturb the Pilgrims, and in our day the demand for ex-Kaiser Wilhelm, reads: "All who are in the territory of the Netherlands, foreigners as well as natives, has equal claim in protection and property."

After fighting the Spaniards for forty-two years, the Dutch won a truce, which was to last from 1609 to 1621. It was during this peaceful and prosperous time that the Pilgrims lived in the Dutch Republic, and learned much of municipal and federal government.

The Scrooby people, after much local persecution, left their homes, and at various times, and by different routes, reached Amsterdam. This city then stood in the van of civilization. For country folks, it was, as Bradford says, "like entering into a new world."

Here they found thousands of refugees like themselves, from Belgium, the British islands, France, and Germany. Altogether, these were known to the Dutch people as "the poor Hussites," after John Huss, the Reformer. On new-made land, they were allotted a large area by the city authorities. The Jews, richer than others, had already built large synagogues, for all worship was free.

An amusing story is told of an Italian banker visiting Amsterdam, who, on hearing of so many religions, fled to his hotel and barricaded his door, fearing a riot; but after an hour he cautiously opened his window, to find perfect quiet among the crowds in the streets.

Almost all the houses and even the churches were built of brick; windmills and canals were everywhere, and boat travel continual.

Instead of chimes were carillons of many bells. The stork, never seen in England, built its nest on the roofs, and walked unharmed in the streets. Carrier pigeons were very common. At the Weepers' Tower, still standing in Amsterdam, friends said good-by, and ships sailed to all countries in the world. Besides thousands of Jews from southern countries, there was much variety in the costumes worn by sailors and travelers from Asia, Africa, and the East and West Indies. Banks, synagogues, shipbuilding, orphan and old people's asylums, quaint customs, gay shops, plenty of pictures, and cheap books gave these country folks much to see and wonder at.

The Scrooby people were not yet a separate organization, nor was Robinson their exclusive pastor. Among the English folks, troubles soon broke out. One brother who, as Bradford (in the days before spelling was by rule) declared, had a "crackt brane," spoke and wrote against the minister Johnson's wife, charging her with luxury in her dress. Many meetings were held, and much time wasted, over this "crank," as the Dutch called such men, and his crotchet.

Robinson saw in this petty affair a danger which imperiled the great principle of soul-liberty. So, resolving to move, he applied to the authorities in Leyden, a cloth manufacturing city, some miles further south, with a famous university. Welcome and permission having been given, these Separatists came to live in this "fair city of a beautiful situation." John van Hout, whose portrait is well known, signed the petition, which is still in the well-kept Dutch archives, formerly in the famous City Hall on the Broad Street, but now in a fine fire-proof building, where are scores of documents relating to the Pilgrim Fathers, including records of their betrothals and marriages.

THE CITY OF LEYDEN

Leyden had fully recovered from the siege by the Spaniards in 1574, and to use another Dutch word, was now "booming"; and to use still another, was "hustling" to get ahead of other cities in the Republic.

For the young folks in this Free Church in Leyden, which would take no favors in the way of help from the city or national government, there was plenty to see and enjoy. There were many soldiers, military parades, and hundreds of other British people in Leyden. Boating on the canals in Summer, and skating and sledding in Winter; the museum of curiosities, the Burg, or castle, more ancient than the Romans, from which one can look over the wide, flat country as far as the sand-dunes on the North Sea; and the schools, open to them, furnished recreation and variety.

The carrier pigeons, used as messengers during the siege, were kept in the beautiful Town Hall, still standing on the Broadway. It was up the steps of this edifice that scores of Pilgrims, young men and maidens, went to declare their intentions of marriage, and, after the wedding, to register their names. I have read a hundred or more of these in the archives, as well as the contract of Jepson, the carpenter, who built the twenty or more little houses in their settlement opposite St. Peter's Church.

Every year they celebrated Thanksgiving Day, October 4, as that of their deliverance from the Spaniards, and ate hutch-putch ("hodge-podge") made of a stew of meat and vegetables. To this day the day is honored by worship, feasting, and a parade in the afternoon of carriages containing each a couple married during the previous twelve months. The Pilgrims introduced into American life many customs not at that time known in England. At the end of Bell, or Clock, Alley, were the British auxiliary troops, of which Miles Standish was the captain. Of six thousand British troops sent to assist the Republic, many remained permanently. From 1584 to 1795 the Scotch Brigade served the Dutch Congress, which in 1776 refused the request of King George III to have them fight in the American revolution.

In Leyden, these north country English folks abode in peace, until 1620, when the emigration began of only the young and strong among them, of whom fewer than twenty went in the "Mayflower," the others coming in the later ships. Of the old and weak, who remained behind, to die or return home to the British Isles, all trace in Leyden is lost after the year 1655.

IMPORTANT PURITAN DATES

William Bradford was the typical all-around man among the Pilgrim Fathers. With his birth in 1590 at Austerfield, near Scrooby, begins their story. He first gave the Pilgrim movement its name. For twenty-five years he was Governor of Plymouth Colony. Theirs is the story of a century, ending at about the time of King William III.

We note several periods:

1. Rise of the Puritan-Pilgrim influences, 1590-1600.

2. Formation of the Pilgrim Church, at Gainsborough and Scrooby. Flights to the Netherlands, 1600-1620.

3. Development of the Leyden Church, John Robinson, pastor, 1610-1620.

4. Voyages from Holland to England and America, struggles and final triumph of the Pilgrim enterprise, 1620-1630.

5. Emigration to America of the Puritans, 1630-1640.

6. 1640-1650, the Commonwealth in England. Persecution and emigration stopped. There was little emigration to New England again until about 1850. From England and Wales during the period from 1630 to 1640 came twenty thousand or more emigrants. From this date to 1700 was the era of Indian wars, the settlement of Connecticut, New Hampshire, and Rhode Island, the New England Confederation, the witchcraft delusion, and the development of what is most characteristic of New England.

By the amalgamation, in 1690, of all the provinces north of New York into one, and of the fusion of the Pilgrims and the Puritans—the Old and the Bay Shore colonies—the story of the Pilgrims ceased to be of continuous interest, and was virtually lost in that of the much larger body of Puritans.

The true historian will not concentrate attention on the one ship "Mayflower," in which was a mixed company of passengers, not by any means all of the Pilgrim spirit or experiences. We look rather in the Leyden Church and on the ships "Speedwell," "Fortune," "Charity," "Swan," "Little James," and "Ann," which brought over altogether over two hundred and thirty-three colonists. These, with the London passengers in the "Mayflower," formed a true type of cosmopolitan America, for among them eight nationalities were represented. These were English, Scotch, Welsh, Irish, German, Dutch, French, Walloon and Fleming from the Belgic Netherlands, though the English and Welsh elements prevailed.

PROSPERITY

After the first two years in Leyden the Pilgrims were fairly prosperous. They bought land in Clock Alley and built over twenty small houses, in which a majority of their families lived, and here most of their children were born. These used the Dutch language as well as the British dialects. They spoke a kind of English which would sound very queerly to us now, for it was much like that which Irishmen of our day pronounce and use. In the Dutch municipal archives, as well as in Bradford's manuscript, we see how they spoke and wrote. Facsimiles of documents in Dutch and English of what relates to the Pilgrims in Holland were published at The Hague in 1920.

Great controversies, in politics and religion, leading almost to war, broke out among the Dutch about 1619; and these founders of Massachusetts witnessed the troubles of the federal government. Barneveldt, in his assertion of state right against the supremacy of the national government, asserted the right of secession;

what their neighbors in Leyden, the Walloons (the "pilgrim fathers" of our Middle States), had been already discussing; that is, emigration to America.

EMIGRATION

These Walloons, or French-speaking Belgians, were led by Jesse de Forest, the real founder of New York City and ancestor of many thousand eminent Americans. They had fled from the

Copyright by H. O. Walker
From a Copley Print, copyright by Curtis & Cameron, Boston

THE PILGRIMS ON THE "MAYFLOWER"

while Maurice, the Union general, was like our Calhoun. He demonstrated the power of the nation, and assured the triumph of the Union. In this, as in many other details, the Dutch Republic furnished precedents to our constitutional fathers, in their scheme of federal government and in our municipal life. The Leyden Church leaders learned much, also, of university life, and the system of elementary public education for girls as well as boys, for in Holland women held a high place both in law and society.

Elder Brewster set up a printing press, hoping to convert his countrymen to the Separatists' way of thinking; but this failing, largely on account of the direct opposition of King James and the English ambassador, and the truce being about to end next year, they began to think of

Spanish invasions of 1567. Sixty-eight of their churches are known to have existed in the Dutch Republic. When Bradford and Robinson refer to "the French churches," the reference is usually to these French-speaking people, who were one with the Huguenots in faith, even as were the Pilgrims with the Puritans.

The English Free Churchmen, known as Separatists, Independents, or Congregationalists, were called "Brownists" by Shakespeare, the British Government, the Puritans, and other State Churchmen. Their constitution was the covenant, taken by each member, before the church, of loyalty to their Lord Jesus, and of mutual love and service to each other, and with all who walked in the ways of God, as revealed in the Bible. They had no written creed. The words of their Lord, "Lo, I am with you always, even unto the end of the world," were for them constitution enough. They welcomed to their fellowship the members of other churches, and into their company all were eligible who would take the Covenant. In the theology of 1619 and in politics they sided with the Calvinists and Unionists, as against the Arminians and State-Right party.

But now, above all other questions, was that of preserving their life, names, language, organization, and cherished ideas. If they stayed in Holland, they would, in a generation or two, be swallowed up in the Dutch people, as hundreds of thousands of other refugees have been, as one can see who reads the Dutch door plates and city directories of to-day.

With constant intermarriage going on among the young people with the Dutch and Walloons, together with the clash of ideas regarding the failure of their hoped-for propaganda in England by means of the printing press, and the enlisting of their young men in the Republican army and navy, they resolved on emigration across the Atlantic. This was with the expectation of reaching land in the Hudson River region, and of being under roof by Christmas.

The venture was financed in England by the Company of the Merchant Adventurers, and two ships were secured, both named after English flowers. The "Speedwell," of eighty tons, bought in Holland, was to remain as their property in America, for fishing and trading purposes. The "Mayflower," of one hundred and eighty tons, chartered at Yarmouth, in England, was to come into the Thames, gather the London company, load with provisions, and meet the Leyden people when the sister ship reached Southampton.

No one knows just what the quality and composition of this company of emigrants from London were, or how they were chosen, and many of its members proved to be of very uncertain character. But in Plymouth, the policy of Bradford, Brewster, and the Leyden men prevailed.

Evidently the captain of the "Speedwell" feared the risks ahead, and made excuses for stopping his ship at Dartmouth and Plymouth, causing much expense and delay. Then he declared the "Speedwell" unseaworthy. So the "Mayflower," with the newly assorted company, in which were hardly more than a dozen that had come from Leyden, crowded together, sailed. The remainder went back in the "Speedwell," which proved to be a good ship, and earned money for its owners. Except as "laborers" going to colonies beyond sea, the exact purpose or character of

the "Mayflower's" passengers was not known to the King's government, which would have stopped them, or considered them as deported. Probably the Conformists at court were glad to be rid of them.

The great expense and delays had impoverished the Leyden people on board, and came near ruining the venture; for the equipment, for making a living on a savage coast, was now very slim. The "Mayflower" sailed alone, August 23. It was a brave venture of bold hearts.

THE ARRIVAL IN AMERICA

No well-lighted and charted coast, life-saving stations, or skilled pilots were ready to meet these beginners of a better time on the American shore, which they sighted on November 9. Their only pilot had been once in Virginia, but he knew little of the northern coast, and a "pilot" was not then the skilled navigator and geographer which the licensed pilot must be in our day. Unable to beat southward, they turned the prow of the "Mayflower" round, and anchor was dropped on November 21, at what is now Provincetown, Mass., where rises the graceful memorial tower copied after the model at Siena, Italy.

The Leyden company started as church members, bound to each other by a covenant of mutual service and of faith in God, according to the original New Testament church government. That covenant was now to be expanded and have added to it a new element of loyalty. As an earthly master, examining their patent, as secured by the London company, we find they had no political status but that which they gave themselves, though they confessed themselves still subjects of King James. The Leyden men were still the real leaders, and they having heard the mutterings of some among the miscellaneous company, "shuffled in," as Bradford says, resolved upon a framework of social order that should include all. The signature of Miles Standish on the document represented a powerful element.

Long accustomed to self-government in the church, they had only to follow their habit and make a compact to fit the case before them, name King James as their ruler, and compel all to sign. Yet although this was the age of legal fictions, the witty Bradford, at least with his keen sense of humor, who always enjoyed a joke, must have smiled inwardly when that royal person, James, was written down as "defender of the faith." Possibly this writing may be looked upon as the initial scintillation of American humor.

PERILS AND ADVENTURES ON SHORE

While the women, a noble band, went to work washing clothes on the shore, the men explored the coast to find a site for the settlement with good soil and water. The Indians had met white men before, who came as robbers, or as slave stealers. How would these peaceable white men be received?

It was no fault of their own that, soon after they had landed, they were attacked by the savages, who did not know their character. Led by Standish, the Pilgrims bravely faced their foes. seeds of disease had been sown in their systems during their long confinement, when crowded in a not over-clean ship. During this Winter, one-half of the people on shore, and of the ship's crew, in the same proportion, died. Yet their faith sustained these brave pioneers. When Spring came, and the flowers peeped forth, and the birds sang, not one of the Pilgrim company returned; but, thanking God and taking courage, they buckled to fresh tasks.

Other ships followed, and by 1627 the Pilgrims had paid their debts. After many other English experiments had failed, the Pilgrims demon-

PILGRIMS GOING TO CHURCH
FROM A PAINTING BY GEORGE H. BOUGHTON

foes. Later on the Indians and Pilgrims made friends, and a covenant of peace, which was honorably kept for many years. A large common house was first built, where all could live together until separate homes were formed.

Then, on December 21, after long delays, labors, privations, and hardships, inspiring hopes and depressions, during the one hundred and forty-three days since the advance guard left Leyden, the settlers landed. A boulder which, ages before, had been carried on a glacier from the far North, was their stepping-stone to a continent. John Carver was elected their first president.

Now came perils from within, far greater than any from wild beasts or savage Indians. The strated that white men could live in the climate of New England and win a livelihood. This was what impressed Europe more than anything else. The Pilgrims, without mining or metals, had revealed the riches of the new world.

Other perils had been faced and overcome. During this time the company in London and Plymouth, England, which financed the Pilgrims' venture, composed of Puritans and State Churchmen, who did not approve of these "Brownists" at new Plymouth, or of their spiritual freedom, tried hard to coerce their consciences and to foist upon them the kind of ministers they did not want. Under Governor Bradford's orders, in each case, after a town meeting, these and several scoundrels were deported. In one instance, even a "Mayflower" passenger was hanged for waylaying and shooting a man.

Other settlements were made along the coast both by respectable people and by men of lewd and vicious character. Happily, the Plymouth government had at its command and among its resources a small but efficient military force to execute its orders. This little company of citizen rulers, drilled by Captain Miles Standish, kept the coast in order and brought both bad Indians and worse white men under law and order. In a word, the Pilgrim Republic was an epitome of our national government.

FRIENDLY WITH OTHER COLONIES

On the other hand, these Pilgrims, Christian gentlemen and ladies, were possessed of a genius for making friends. They were far from being what old caricaturists and the latest slanderers allege. These say that the Scrooby people were driven to Holland by their own intolerance. The truth is that they were liberal enough to stand illiberality. As aliens in Holland their record was a noble one. They had won the regard of the Dutch, and now they were to show that for their "courteous entreaty" in the Republic they were grateful. So, when "the Pilgrim Fathers of our Middle States," the Walloons living in Nova Belgica, under a civil government within the new Dutch province of New Netherland, sent from Manhattan to New Plymouth kindly greetings to their old neighbors in Leyden, these were joyfully welcomed. Governor Peter Minuit dispatched from Manhattan his secretary, Isaac de Rasieres, with a letter to Governor Bradford. It is from this scholarly Dutch gentleman that we have the one authentic and detailed word-picture of a Pilgrim Sabbath and worship, from which George H. Boughton, the painter of the Pilgrims, who excels all others in accuracy, obtained the literary data for his famous picture.

Bradford doubtless enjoyed a chat in Dutch, for he easily and fluently spoke and wrote this noble language of progress and freedom. Among other things he referred thus gratefully to their hospitable treatment while in the Republic:

"Obliged by the good and courteous entreaty which we have found in your country, we and our children are bound to be thankful."

One of the three historical bronze tablets reared in Holland by Americans in honor of the Pilgrims bears on its face the above passage from Bradford.

Isaac de Rasieres also told the Pilgrims about the Iroquois Indian shell money, or wampum, which facilitated trade with the Indians, and quickly increased the colony's wealth.

THE INDIAN GUESTS

This pleasant friendship, with direct trade, continued for many years, until, instigated by the treacherous Stuart King Charles II, who was always in debt and ready for new falsehoods, the English made conquest of New Netherland, in time of peace.

With the Indians, also, the Plymouth men maintained peaceful relations; and the names of Squanto and Massasoit, the latter the more honorable, shine in their annals. On Thanksgiving Day, in October, as in Holland, as guests and hosts, the red and white men sat down together. They vied with one another in the fun of setting up the popinjay and shouting; with the stone-tipped shaft and "the leaden arrow," enjoying target practice. In that era, wild turkey and pigeons, deer and other game, were much more plentiful than now. It is probable, however, that the Pilgrims obtained most of their food at first from the beach, in digging clams, and from the sea, in catching fish. The Indians showed them how, in many ways, to maintain existence, even to the planting, manuring, and cultivation of maize.

BEGINNINGS OF MASSACHUSETTS

The story of pathfinders and pioneers always deserves more space in the telling than that of those who follow. English Puritans under John Endicott obtained a grant of land on Massachusetts Bay, and joined their countrymen who had settled on Cape Ann, in 1626, and abandoned this locality in favor of Salem. In 1630, a fleet of ships, among them the same "Mayflower" of 1620, all richly laden with settlers, and their food equipment, under the leadership of John Winthrop, came over. Houses and villages were built, and the seat of government administration was fixed, first at Charlestown, then at Boston. All these were under town government, and even Boston did not become a city until 1834. In New England, the town meeting; in the Middle States, the township; in the South, the counties, were the units of political order and development.

The two colonies at Plymouth and on the Bay grew up in healthful rivalry, but the Old Colony was happily free from the superstitions and intolerance of the newcomers; for in the science, knowledge of the Bible and general school instruction that destroyed witchcraft and kindred delusions, Holland was at this time far ahead of England.

Connecticut and Rhode Island having been begun, the New England Confederation was formed, which lasted until 1684.

In the free air and new land of opportunity, the Puritans became democratic in government and Congregational in their church order. Nevertheless, they united politics and religion, and their government and social system were organized under the form of a theocracy, or Old Testament, system, prevalent in ancient Israel, and at first were almost as intolerant as the governments in Europe. Church and State were united until well within the nineteenth century. In time, however, this attitude of mind was changed for the better, and New England became the intellectual leader and educator of the American nation.

The story of the Pilgrims, who were fewer in numbers, is the more picturesque and dramatic. These people were the pioneers of the larger religious freedom which is now enjoyed by all English-speaking people, and for which all nations on earth are striving. The Pilgrims were enlarged, in spirit and temper, by their experiences in three kinds of life, on an island, on the continent of Europe, and in the wilderness. They gave the precedents of success to the Puritans, and to the Walloons and Dutch, the first settlers of the Middle States, who were equally Puritan in convictions and experiences.

The history of the two bodies of people, in Old and New England, runs in parallel lines until 1690. By that time there were in the Old, or the Plymouth, Colony and towns about nine or ten thousand people, and in the other parts of New England, all told, about thirty thousand souls. Then the lesser was lost in the greater, even as the Walloons were in the Dutch. The Puritans, who were more numerous, wealthy, learned and of higher social status, made the greater force in the making of New England.

Yet their fused ideals and their mutual influences helped most powerfully in the evolution of the American commonwealth. The character of New England is stamped upon the nation, which, in its development, whether ethnic or not, or in federal government, is not English, but European. The four nations in the British Isles, the Northern and the Belgic Netherlanders, the French, the Germans, and the Scandinavians, have all helped to make us what we are. In both our ancestry and evolution we are a composite people and government, with unique inheritances, achievements, and mighty promise.

INFLUENCE OF THE PURITANS

It was the Puritans who, by their larger number, made New England, and have done so much, in every line of human endeavor, for the making of the United States. The "Yankees," as they were called, both by themselves and others, became a notable people of constant and varied manual and intellectual industry. Shipbuilding flourished until the time of the Napoleonic wars. Then the New Englanders turned their attention to invention and manufactures. After 1800, the emigration westward began on a large scale, and the West was settled and built up largely by these people, who took the church and school with them.

Although supposed to be both severe in morals, and narrow, though high and intense, in ideals, they formed two truly national universities, Harvard and Yale; and, besides, elementary school systems in many States, scores of colleges. Most remarkable was the outburst of intellect in early colonial times, and again in the nineteenth century. The wealth of American music, art, literature, invention, and enterprise that has sprung up in New England make the United States an everlasting debtor to the founders of New England.

In general, it may be said that we, as a nation, are in larger measure indebted to the Puritans; while to the much smaller company of Pilgrims we are to be grateful for the grand ideas of toleration, soul-freedom and broad charity, which make our country the beacon of hope to the world. The parables of the loaves and of the mustard seed have found illustration.

What was merely external, temporary, and accidental, in the religious movements of the sixteenth and seventeenth centuries, have fallen away; and Americans and British now rejoice in a common inheritance of language, law, traditions, ideals, and ordered liberty. Among the most impressive monuments of this pact of enduring friendship, we note the unfortified frontier between Canada and the United States, and the statues of Washington and Lincoln erected on English soil. These are but the foretokenings of what the whole world, with its many nations, is yet to see.

JESSE DE FOREST

BY WILLIAM ELLIOT GRIFFIS

BELGIUM is one of the oldest divisions of Europe. Cæsar fought in ancient Belgium, which, however, did not become an independent state until 1830. The first name of New York State, when it had a civil government, was Nova Belgica, or New Belgic Land.

A thousand years ago the northern half of Belgium was only a sandy waste, with no cities on the coast. Droves of wild horses roamed in forests where now are farms, towns, and cities. Charles the Great, or Charlemagne, was fighting the heathen people called the Saxons. After many campaigns he subdued them. Then he deported many thousands of the people from their homes in Germany and settled them in the northern half of Belgic Land. Other thousands had fled thither or were fleeing. Hence the names Flemings (or, as often pronounced, "Fleeming") and Flanders.

About this time, also, the natives of the far north, variously called Danes, Norsemen, Bay People, or Vikings (from the "vicks," or bays, or in English, "wich," as in Greenwich), had begun to build ships with keels. The keel enabled them to row more swiftly over the waves. Flax and hemp, introduced from the south, enabled them also to make large sails. Such inventions, in that age, were almost as important as those of steam and electricity in our day.

With their "surf-riders," the Norsemen now sailed out on the ocean and visited coasts and countries even as far as the Mediterranean. The magnetic compass had not yet been brought from China, nor was Europe united in Christianity and international law. War was the rule, peace the exception. Instead of the compass to direct them over the pathless sea, these hardy mariners took with them ravens. In cloudy weather or at night, when approaching land, as they thought, they let loose one of these pilot birds. If it returned, they knew that it had found no place for the sole of its foot. If it came not back, they rowed in the direction of its flight, and reached the shore. At many places they landed, burned and killed, so that for centuries in the litanies of the Christian churches was the petition, "From the fury of the Norsemen, good Lord deliver us." Yet often they made settlements, and married the women of the country. In course of time, losing their language, they became part of the four sorts of British folk, or of the Spanish and the French people.

To guard the coast against these sea-rovers, or "free-booters," Charlemagne built forts and stationed garrisons. He also appointed as guardian of the forests which then covered the country an officer, from which comes the family name, De Forest.

Four hundred years or more passed; and feudalism, with its castles, monasteries, and "villeins," was the form and rule of society. Then followed the Crusades, which brought the Europeans in contact with the Orient. After this came organized industries, first in guilds, and then in private houses; and Belgic Land became the richest part of Europe.

In its southern half, and in northeastern France, lived the Walloons, who spoke French. They still number about four million people, and most of the progressive movements in Belgium have originated with them.

The town of Avesnes, now in France, became famous for its textiles and the art of dyeing in brilliant colors. Here the De Forests are known to have lived from the year 1500, and here Jesse, whose name is so closely associated with the Walloon emigration to America, and the first home-maker in the Middle States, was born in 1576.

To his parents all signs had pointed to peace and prosperity, and Jesse's ambition was, no doubt, to become a master of his craft, rear a family, and live peacefully among his people.

But new ideas had come in to turn the world upside down, as Christianity had done. Hainault, the province of the De Forests, became the center of the Reformation among the Belgic folk, who were led by Guido de Bray, who read the New Testament in Greek, and wrote the Belgic Confession of Faith.

Charles V of the German Empire, though born in Ghent and now ruler of the Netherlands, was a great military leader, but he could not understand the new ideas. He tried to stop the movement of free churches and Bible readers by burning the preachers; but the tide of freedom continued to rise higher. When after the nobles, led by William the Silent, had made a compact or declaration of right, the spirit of resistance to Spain was stiffened, and men began to wear the Silver Half Moon, on which was inscribed defiance of Spain.

After the mob had smashed the images in the churches, Philip II of Spain decided to send an army into the Netherlands. It was the first body of soldiers armed wholly with muskets, led by the Duke of Alva. They were to burn, behead, and drive out all who held to the new doctrines. It was much like the German invasion of 1914. To save themselves, a hundred thousand Walloons and Flemings fled to England, introducing new ideas and industries and changing England from an agricultural into a manufacturing and commercial country. Probably a quarter of a million Belgic folk fled into Holland, so that in one or two generations the population of the federal Republic, formed in 1579, had risen from eight hundred thousand to two million souls. Walloon regiments fought under the seven-striped flag on land and on the ships of the Republic; the Dutch lent many of their ships and furnished one thousand trained naval artillerists to sink the galleons of the Spanish Armada.

The De Forests were soon scattered, for the Walloons had a terrible time of it. "The church under the cross" was their name, and the "Lily among Thorns" their symbol. Few had expected the Spanish invasion would be so sudden. We find the father in one city and his sons in three other places.

In Sedan, in 1606, Jesse married Marie du Cloux, and here also four of his children were born and baptized. Thenceforward, we trace Jesse and his family in various places, and from communion table to communion table in one or the other sixty-eight reformed churches of the Walloons that were formed in the Republic. The Walloons were the same as the Huguenots in faith, doctrine, and ritual. Thousands of them, including Jesse's father, met the English refugees in Amsterdam, where the fugitives for conscience' sake from many lands found peace and protection.

From the Leyden archives we find that Jesse de Forest was living on the Broadway of that prosperous city. He had taken out a license, and was a recognized member of the guild of first-class dyers, whose skill and craftsmanship were not in common black, but in varied colors. In Leyden four more of his children were born, baptized, and, no doubt, educated in the common schools, open to every one, girls as well as boys.

THE LAND OF PROMISE

Inured to so many changes, flights, and emigrations, this lover of freedom and the rights of conscience had already thought of a home in America. For when his fifth child, Rachel, was born, in 1609 or 1610, the news of the discovery of two noble rivers in the middle region and a land of fertility and promise had thrilled all Holland. Then began the agitation to form the West India Company, and, by colonizing New Netherland, to strike at the Spaniards, who claimed the continent, and looked on any others who attempted settlement as common burglars.

In Leyden, as neighbor and friend of the people we call Pilgrim Fathers, his hopes were stimulated, and he began to agitate for the colonization of his fellow Walloons. Moreover, having a large family on his hands, he was minded to be prompt. In fact, he sent in to King James his application for land in Virginia, July 21, 1621, even before he had heard whether the "Mayflower" venture had been a success or not. He purposed to sail in the Spring of 1622. There was no state named Virginia until 1776, and the term "Virginia," in 1621, meant land anywhere between Canada and Florida. These Walloons wished to keep their language, customs, and forms of worship, just as had the Pilgrim Fathers. Under these conditions they would become King James' loyal subjects; and they added, "but not otherwise."

So we find Jesse de Forest appearing at The Hague, July 21, 1621, before the English ambassador, Sir Dudley Carleton, the same who tried to break up Elder Brewster's printing press, and to arrest him. Curt and disappointing was the answer—a decided refusal. It was "not expedient" for these Walloons "to go in one gross body," but they must be "scattered in boroughs and corporations"; in other words, they must be obedient to the state church, and lose their language.

Now, in addition to matters of theology, the Dutch were divided on the questions of secession and permanent federal union, states rights, and national supremacy. Inextricably mixed with this was the question of colonizing America. All the unionists were in favor of it, and the secessionists opposed it.

THE NEW COLONY

The union cause was triumphant, and the colonizing ship "New Netherland," to take Jesse de Forest's colony across the Atlantic, was built and launched. Instead of being named the "Half Moon," after the silver crescent worn by the deliverers of Leyden, and often inscribed "Liberty or Death," the new ship, representing ideas then common to the Republic but unknown in England, was named after the new Province.

Jesse de Forest now enrolled Dutch as well as Walloon families. We do not have, as in the case of the Pilgrims, a historian, like Bradford; but of late years so many documents have come to light that we know not only of Dutch ship life in 1623, but also of many interesting details of De Forest and his company. On board all the colonizing ships was a church officer entitled "comforter of the sick." He conducted daily prayer, read sermons, started the hymns, and was authorized to marry couples, but not to administer the sacraments. In fact, he married four brides on board the ship "New Netherland."

The twelve years' truce ended in 1621, and the war was on again. The chief danger was from the Spanish pirates whose lair was at Dunkirk, then on the Belgian coast, but now in France—to which place, during our Revolutionary War, the American privateers brought their British prizes to sell them. These sea-robbers of 1623 sailed out to capture Dutch ships, to throw overboard or nail to the deck the sailors, and to hold passengers or people of wealth for ransom. In the contracts made with teachers, ministers, schoolmasters, and others the West India Company agreed to continue salary of the *domine,* or pedagogue, while in prison, and to pay their ransom.

These first settlers and home-makers of the four Middle States were just as truly pilgrim fathers, and just as moral and religious, as the founders of the Eastern States. They left Leyden, July 1, 1624, and embarked at Amsterdam. The gunboat "Mackerel" went ahead, crossed the Atlantic, and entered the upper waters of the Hudson River.

Happily the voyage was made without a fight, or serious interruption, and the ship "New Netherland" arrived inside the point, already named by the Dutch Sandy Hook, and near the island called after the states (Staten) of the Republic.

The captain of the "Mackerel," seeing a ship bearing the white flag and lilies of the Bourbons, and suspecting the design of the French to make a settlement, ordered the guns to be run out, showing that he meant to enforce the decree of the Republic. But no shot was fired, for the Frenchmen took the hint, and sailed quietly away. So New York was made safe for free public schools and liberty of conscience.

As yet there were no Dutch settlers in the land. Though fur traders and fishermen had visited the country during the truce, the Republic could not honorably make any settlements on territory claimed by Spain.

During the truce, Captain Block, whose name is in "Block Island," had built a yacht named the "Restless," on Manhattan. In this vessel he surveyed the coast of Connecticut and visited Plymouth. He named Rhode (Rood or Rod) Island, and his term Woesten Hoek (or place of the savages) was later corrupted into Housatonic. On his return he showed his map; and the Dutch Congress named New Netherland on the same day that New England received its official name. When organized with a government, of which Peter Minuit, a Walloon, was made governor, the name Nova Belgica was applied to the new country.

According to the imperative and specified conditions of their charter, the West India Company was obliged to purchase all land occupied by their colonists; so calling the savage chiefs together, for twenty-four guilders' worth of trinkets, Minuit bought the island. In Pennsylvania the treaty under the tree at Shackamaxon is a matter of tradition. In New York the documents showing purchase are still extant. No State had so large a collection of wampum belts, in token of honorable transactions with the Indians, as New York. From the beginning, the policy of the Republic toward the red men was just and generous, despite the foolishness of some of its servants.

Of the ship's company eight families of the thirty were put ashore on Manhattan, eight at the place called Wael Boght, or later Wallabout, that is, the Walloons' cove, or bight. Others went up to the head of navigation, at which a fur traders' fort had been built, and where is now Albany. The four brides and bridegrooms took their wedding trip on a yacht up the Delaware River to the site of the present Gloucester, N. J.

In the early eighteenth century, South America seemed richer in products, and loomed larger in hope and imagination to adventurers, than the colder north. Of the two colonizing ships that were convoyed by the armed vessels, "Pigeon" and "Mackerel," Jesse de Forest sailed in the one bound for Guiana, probably expecting later to follow his three children to New Netherland. After various adventures, acting often as a peacemaker between the natives and the newcomers, he died from overexertion and sunstroke, greatly lamented, October 22, 1624.

Three of the children, Henry, Rachel, and Isaac, came on the first ship to New Netherland. The two first named died early; but Isaac, born July 10, 1615, lived to a good old age, acting occasionally as magistrate. He was the founder of one of the most noted families in America, numbering among them scores of soldiers, inventors, bankers, authors, philanthropists, and men and women of fine public spirit.

The story of the Pilgrim Fathers was lost in that of the Puritans from 1690 to 1860. To know the richness of our inheritance from our composite ancestry, the full story of the Walloons should be recovered.

HOW OUR FOREFATHERS LIVED ON THE COLONIAL FARMS

BY R. M. TRYON

IN COLONIAL times there was very little trading. The roads were few and in poor condition. There were no railroads, and no opportunities on many of the farms to make use of boats and water transportation. People had to be independent, that is to say, self-sufficing. The farm was not merely a place for raising live stock, poultry, grain, vegetables, and fruit; it was also a manufactory of almost everything needed in daily life. The farmer and his family produced the raw materials and also made them into useful articles.

THE MANY TYPES OF THINGS MADE

A few things were purchased from occasional traders who came to the farm. A few things were purchased in the towns on the infrequent visits of the farmer to the more densely settled districts. Thus the scythes were made at the forge, and only the handles were made on the farm. Saws and axes were imported from England, or later from those regions where iron was abundant and easy to secure. Not all metal articles were imported. The soft pewter metal which went into the forks and knives could often be worked into household utensils in the domestic factory—the home.

A list of the articles made on a colonial farm is bewildering in its variety to a modern reader.

LUMBER AND SHINGLES

The first houses in a new settlement were built of logs hewn from the forest trees. Later the hewn logs were replaced by lumber, the product of the "saw pit." This saw pit consisted of a platform and a pit, dug into a hillside. Here with a handsaw two men, one above and the other below, were able to cut up logs so as to produce about 100 feet of boards in a day. When one thinks of the contrast between the labor involved in making boards in that way and at a modern sawmill, one understands why the coming of machinery led to a change in method of work and indirectly to new methods of living. Rough clapboards were used to cover the first round or hewn log-houses. Later, shingles were rived by hand from "bolts" or blocks of wood. At first the shingles were used just as they came from the frow, the instrument used in the riving. Later they were shaved and made perfectly smooth. A man could shave about 1,000 shingles in a day. Wooden hinges and door latches were made, and also hand-wrought iron nails to be used in the construction of the house and of the furniture. We read that it was not uncommon for the country people to erect small forges in their chimney corners and to make nails in winter and on evenings when little other work could be done.

FURNITURE

The first settlers brought some furniture from Europe with them, but as they migrated inland it proved to be too bulky to move, so that the inhabitants of each new settlement were compelled to make within their homes such articles as tables, stools, cupboards, and bedsteads.

One way in which the parts of the furniture were fitted together can be illustrated by describing the making of a three-legged stool, which was a common article of furniture in the colonial home. Three holes were bored in the piece that was to be the top of the stool and round legs were driven firmly into the holes. The boring of the holes was done with an auger which, like the other metal tools necessary in the household, had been brought from England, or purchased from a trader. When the legs had been firmly driven into their places they were sometimes made secure by wrought-iron nails. In the larger pieces of furniture wooden pegs were frequently used instead of nails. Even bedsteads and tables were often made in the same manner as stools.

FARM IMPLEMENTS

The farmer not only made his house and furniture from lumber, shingles, and nails of his own manufacture, but he had to make the implements with which to work his farm. These consisted of vehicles of transportation, plows, harrows, pitchforks, handrakes, shovels, ax handles, hoe handles, scythe-snaths, singletrees, doubletrees, clips, clevises, laprings, ox yokes, and harness for his horse if he chanced to have one. All manner of makeshifts were often necessary to supply some of these articles. For example, horse collars were made of corn husks; hames of crooked roots; clips, clevises, and laprings of hickory withes; ox yokes of bent hickory wood; traces and bridles of twisted deer hide, and pitchforks from forked boughs or antler horns.

The first vehicles for transportation were nothing more than log boats and sleds, wheels being luxuries which could not be provided. Later, crude but serviceable wagons were made with wheels sawed from the trunks of trees. Axles were made from hickory or white oak, and a coupling pole of like material connected them.

Plows and harrows were made on the farm with little difficulty. At first the harrows had wooden teeth and the plows wooden moldboards. In the course of time it was possible to procure from the blacksmith shop iron teeth for the A-shaped harrow and for the point, share, and wing of the plow. With the introduction of the ironmaker's trade came the beginnings of a new era. The farmer had only to make the beams for the harrow and the wooden beam, handles, and moldboard for the plow. He began to be dependent on someone else for the metal parts. Co-operation had begun. It resulted in better implements and also in a stronger bond between members of the community.

MILLS OF VARIOUS KINDS

Besides making the implements with which to till his farm, the farmer and his boys had also to make the tools with which the products of the farm were brought into condition for use. They made their own cider mills, cheese presses, spinning wheels, flax brakes, swingling knives, wool combs, looms, and implements used in making hominy and meal.

We shall gain a clearer view of the effort that had to be invested in preparing food if we take up in detail the preparation of hominy from corn. This was done by means of the "hominy block." The block was made of a large piece of wood about three feet long, with a bowl-shaped hollow burned in one end. The shelled corn was put into this bowl and cracked with a pestle. Sometimes a simple hand pestle was used. In the fall of the year, while the corn was soft, the block and pestle did very well, even for making fine meal for johnnycake and mush, but the work was slow when the corn became hard.

A kind of power pestle or sweep was sometimes used, harnessing the elasticity of nature and thus lessening the toil of pounding grain for meal. For this sweep a pole of some springy, elastic wood, thirty feet long or more, was used. The larger end was wedged under the side of the house or under a stump. A supporting fork was placed under the pole about a third of its length from the butt. This was so arranged as to raise the small end of the pole about fifteen feet from the ground. From the small end was hung a heavy piece of wood five or six inches in diameter and eight or ten feet long. The lower end of this was rounded so as to serve as a pestle. The long, springy trunk to which it was fastened above tended to overcome the force of gravitation and to raise it from the bowl below, in which the grain was placed. The worker used this great pestle, pulling it down and crushing the grain in the hollowed block. He then released the pestle, which was raised by the sapling to which it was attached above. Sometimes two workers used the sweep, crushing the grain more effectively by their combined strength.

The hand mill was also used, and made better meal than the mortar or grater. The hand mill was like that used by the Indians and other primitive people. It was made of two circular stones, the lower of which was called the "bed stone," the upper one the "runner." The upper stone was turned with a handle or staff, and the grain between the stones was ground to flour.

Water mills and windmills for grinding grain were among the first mechanical conveniences set up by the colonists. Food is an absolute necessity and much thought would naturally be given to finding devices for procuring it more cheaply. The work of preparing grain could of course be done much more easily and cheaply when the winds and waterfalls were harnessed to help man. The primitive stone mills and the pestles did not disappear, however. Not everyone lived near a waterfall, and the wind could not be depended on to blow when it was needed.

CANDLES

The colonists had to provide themselves with lights for their evenings. Kerosene, gas, and electricity were unknown, and less satisfactory means had to be used. One such means was candlewood, which was nothing more than the knots and hearts of resinous pine trees. Then, too, rushes were used after being dipped in tallow or grease. Oils from fish, bear, whale, and moose all did good service. Most important of all, however, were the candles made from the tallow of the berries of the bay, a bush found in all the Colonies, and candles from animal tallow, whale oil, and honeycomb wax.

Bayberry candles were made from the wax or tallow extracted from the berry of the bay, a plant which grew abundantly in the neighborhood of the sea. The berries were gathered late in the fall and thrown into a kettle of boiling water. The fat melted out and floated to the top of the water and was skimmed off. On cooling, this tallow was melted over again, to refine it. Refined bayberry wax has a transparent green color. Candles were made of this tallow just as they were made of the tallow from the animals killed on the farm. Before the advent of candle molds, which made it easier to make candles, and before the coming of the itinerant candlemakers, candles were made by dipping. Wicks were prepared and dipped into hot wax or tallow. They were then lifted out and the wax allowed to cool and harden. The dipping was repeated until enough wax had hardened around the wick to make a usable candle.

LEATHER ARTICLES

The hides of animals killed for food on the farm, or of the deer, squirrels, raccoons, rabbits, beavers, and foxes shot or trapped in the woods, were used for many purposes. Deerskins were made into hunting shirts, breeches, coats, leggings, and moccasins. Gloves and mittens were made from the skins of squirrels and beavers, caps from the skins of raccoons, bears, foxes, cats, rabbits, and woodchucks. Bearskins were made into beds and bedding. From the deerskins and cowhides, moccasins, shoepacks, and shoes were made. The preparation of the material and the making of all of these articles were done on the farm, the work being the duty chiefly of the men and boys.

Tanning the hides was a long, laborious process. They were first thoroughly dried and then thrown into a vat of strong lye. The lye caused the hair to loosen and fall off. The skins freed from hair were then placed in another vat of liquid made from black-oak bark, and were allowed to remain several months. When taken out of this they were scraped and softened with bear's oil. They were then ready to be made into shoes, boots, and harness.

The tailoring of the leather suits usually fell to the male portions of the family, since the hard material was rather difficult for the women and girls to handle. Large needles or shoemakers' awls were used in the sewing process. The thread was made either of the sinews from the legs of the deer or by cutting a long strip from the deerskin. The latter was called "whang." It was cut as small as possible so that it could be used as thread in the awls or needles. Although the products of this crude tailoring were often rough and uncomfortable, especially after getting wet and stiff, they were very useful in protecting their wearers.

CLOTH

While the farmer and his boys were busy supplying leather clothing, the wife and daughters were manufacturing cloth to be used for wearing apparel and as household textile supplies. Cloth was made from cotton, wool, or flax. The making of these involved the preparation of the raw material for the spinning wheel and loom and bleaching and dyeing the finished product.

WOLFE AND MONTCALM AT QUEBEC

BY MALCOLM HOMER

"Qui vive?" (Who goes there?")

From the shadows of the great rock, on whose summit is the city of Quebec, came the challenge of the French sentry, posted in the woods at the base.

It was a moonless September night, in 1759. Close to the northern shore of the St. Lawrence dim shapes that might be boats came drifting down with the tide. The sentry peered through the gloom. By the pale light of the stars, the shapes took on a more distinct form. Perhaps his quick ear caught the wash of the water. *"Qui vive?"* he called again, raising his musket to his shoulder.

"France!" was the response, from somewhere in the murk of the river.

"A quel régiment?" ("To what regiment?"), demanded the sentry.

"De la Reine" ("The Queen's"), came the answer, in perfect French.

This satisfied the man on guard. He had been told that French boats, with supplies, would pass down the river that night.

So the boats drifted on. Again came a challenge; again an answer that lulled the sentry's suspicions.

Pretty soon, the little fleet of transports, filled with British soldiers, made a landing at the spot selected in advance. Their leader was General Wolfe, and he had come to storm the Heights of Abraham, and take Quebec.

This was to be the climax of the war between England and France for the possession of North America. To understand just what it meant, let us glance at some of the thrilling events which preceded it.

THE MARQUIS OF MONTCALM

In the year following the defeat of General Braddock, in his march to Fort Duquesne, Great Britain declared war against France, and sent an army under General Abercrombie to America. The French were fortunate in having a much greater soldier, the Marquis of Montcalm. A captain at eighteen, he had served with distinction in Italy and Germany; and soon after taking command of the forces in Canada, his military genius was brilliantly displayed. While the English were making a great show of preparation at Albany, Montcalm took an army across Lake Ontario, attacked Oswego, and destroyed it, thus wresting from England at one blow the command of the lakes.

In the preceding year, Sir William Johnson, a remarkable Irishman, had gained a victory over the French on Lake George, and built Fort William Henry, to prevent approach to the Hudson. The French, in turn, fortified Ticonderoga, on Lake Champlain; and, in 1757, Montcalm marched out with an army of over 7,000. The English at Fort William Henry were greatly outnumbered, and were soon compelled to surrender, though upon honorable terms. Under the directing genius of Montcalm, the French held a chain of forts which cut off England on the west, and left her without a foothold in all the Ohio valley. From the St. Lawrence to Louisiana, France was master. "We are no longer a nation," came the despairing cry from England.

But now the great English statesman, William Pitt, took the war in hand. The American colonists came to his support, and three expeditions were sent against the French. One of these was to capture Louisburg, a town of Cape Breton Island, commanding the entrance to the Gulf of St. Lawrence. Under its commander, General Amherst, was James Wolfe, at the head of a brigade. Rowing through the surf, his men silenced the French batteries; a siege followed, and in a few weeks the whole province of Cape Breton was England's.

MONTCALM AT TICONDEROGA

This was late in July, 1758. Earlier in the same month, Great Britain sent General Abercrombie, with an army of 15,000 British and colonial soldiers, against Ticonderoga, which was held by only 4,000 Frenchmen under Montcalm. Lord Howe, leading the advance, fell in the first assault. Then the British, underestimating the strength of the fort, charged the entrenchments again and again, only to be repulsed with great slaughter. After losing nearly 2,000 men in killed and wounded, they retired to Fort George.

The British, however, took Fort Frontenac, where Lake Ontario empties into the St. Lawrence; then, late in November, George Washington raised the British flag over the ruins of Fort Duquesne, which was now named Pittsburg, in honor of William Pitt, whose able conduct of the war was beginning to show definite results.

In spite of all that Montcalm could do, France now faced a losing fight. The British had 50,000 men in the field; the French, greatly outnumbered, were threatened with a shortage of food as well. In July, 1759, Sir William Johnson crushed the French army under General D'Aubry, marching to relieve Fort Niagara, and took the fort itself; a few days later General Amherst, with superior forces, drove the French from Ticonderoga, and recovered the country around Lake Champlain.

The conquest of Canada was now in order; to effect this, it was necessary to take Quebec.

This city occupies a headland on the north bank of the St. Lawrence, at the mouth of the St. Charles. It is divided into an upper and a lower town; to the southwest stretch the Heights of Abraham. Founded in 1608 by Champlain, its handful of defenders, twenty years later, were forced to yield it to an English expedition led by a French Huguenot. A little later, England returned it to France; and now, in 1759, it had become Canada's one great bulwark against invasion.

AT THE CLIFFS OF QUEBEC

The citadel of Quebec was looked upon as another Gibraltar. So steep and high were the cliffs that it did not seem possible to scale them; at the point least difficult to climb, a hundred men could easily have stopped an army. So Montcalm, holding Quebec with some 7,000 men, and knowing that the British could attack by land only from the quarter defended by the cliff, awaited his foe with confidence.

But Pitt was determined that Quebec should be taken, and the honor of leading an army against it was conferred upon the dashing young officer who had played such a brilliant part in the capture of Louisburg. James Wolfe, now promoted to the rank of General, was only thirty-three; but the French knew him for a daring and resourceful soldier, and realized that Quebec would not be safe until his army had sailed away.

Up the St. Lawrence, late in June, came a fleet of forty ships—anchoring a few miles below Quebec, and landing 8,000 soldiers at the Isle of Orleans.

Throughout the summer months the British made repeated attempts to take the city; but the French, protected by five miles of entrenchments along the northern banks, were able to hold their own. The British artillery posted at Point Levi opened fire on the town, working great havoc in the lower section; but the citadel itself seemed as strong as ever, and Montcalm, relying on the natural barrier of the cliffs, resisted all attempts to dislodge him.

The French, though well aware that they faced a determined foe, felt much encouraged. In July the British had tried to storm their entrenchments by fording the Montmorency, six miles northeast of Quebec, while troops from Point Levi crossed the St. Lawrence to support the attack. But the boats stuck fast, the tide began to rise; when the soldiers who had forded the stream rushed, unsupported, against the enemy, they were driven back with great loss, and withdrew to the camp at Montmorency.

WOLFE'S BOLD PLAN

Wolfe, who could not bear inactivity, was so distressed by the various delays and failures, and so worn with fatigue and anxiety, that he fell sick with a fever, and was for some time confined to his tent. But his strong spirit prevailed. As soon as he could force himself to his feet, he bent all his energies to the bold plan of scaling the precipice, and storming the Heights of Abraham.

Early in September, the British broke camp, and proceeded up the river. What did they mean to do? The French could by no means make out. But they saw the foe abandoning his position, the soldiers embarking once more on the ships; and hope ran high. It was late in the season, so it seemed likely that the British had grown discouraged, and meant to give up their campaign.

Montcalm, however, was none the less watchful; for weeks he had not removed his clothing. The forces above Quebec were strengthened, and made ready to resist the British, who opened fire from their ships, and made a pretense of landing in their boats. Up and down the river, the fleet drifted with the tide, keeping the French in a constant state of uncertainty and alarm.

Meanwhile Wolfe, field-glass in hand, scanned the rocky wall, hoping to discover some path by which it might be possible to climb it. Noting, at last, some tents pitched on the brink of the cliff, he detected a kind of dim trail, up which an active man might clamber by grasping the rocks and bushes. This place to-day is known as Wolfe's Cove.

The plan seemed desperate enough. Tents pitched there indicated the presence of soldiers. It was, in fact, well guarded, while two other posts near by were provided with troops and cannon. But Wolfe's mind was made up. There lay the way to Quebec; he would travel it, or perish.

SCALING THE HEIGHTS

The movements of the British fleet wholly deceived the French. It had menaced their army above Quebec, and worn it out with marching to and fro. At dusk, on September 12, the ships lay ten miles below the scene of that mock battle, and once more opened fire. Boats were manned, the shore was raked with cannon shot. A general attack seemed under way, and Montcalm marshaled his forces to prevent the threatened landing.

Meanwhile, far up the St. Lawrence, Wolfe was collecting his troops—five thousand men in all. Entering the transports, they waited for the tide to turn; then drifted silently down the river.

Wolfe could not rid himself of the idea that he was fated to die in this battle. He was engaged to marry an English girl, whose portrait he now drew from his breast-pocket, with the request that his friend who sat next him would return it to her. Then, as the boats slipped along with the current, he seemed lost in thought.

Presently he began, in an undertone, to recite a poem: Gray's famous "Elegy in a Country Churchyard." Its somber sentiment appeared to be in harmony with his mood. When he came to the line, "The paths of glory lead but to the grave," he inclined his head in approval. Then, having finished the recital, he remarked to those around him:

"I would rather be the author of that poem than take Quebec."

Landing in the cove, volunteers in the leading boat sprang out, and began to scale the cliff. Wolfe, with the others, waiting below, soon heard shots, followed by English cheers. In a short time, the army had climbed the precipice. The volunteers in the advance had surprised the guard, and overpowered it; when the guns at the two stations near by opened fire, the British attacked and captured them.

DEATH OF TWO HEROES

With the French on either side, Wolfe knew that he must conquer or be crushed; retreat was out of the question. Near at hand were the open plains known as the Heights of Abraham, and here he drew up his army in line of battle.

Amazed at the news, Montcalm made all haste to throw his forces between Quebec and the British. His men were not so well disciplined as Wolfe's, and he was obliged to advance without support from the garrison of the citadel. The French opened fire with their cannon; the Canadians and Indians advanced, taking aim from clumps of bushes, and seizing every advantage of the ground as they discharged their muskets. Then, in battle formation, they renewed the advance, firing as they came.

The British troops coolly held their fire till the enemy was not more than forty yards away. Then volley after volley was poured into the French ranks, throwing them into the greatest confusion. They began to retreat; the British charged, and the retreat became a rout.

Wolfe, in the lead, was twice wounded. Then a bullet pierced his breast, and he sank to the ground.

"Look!" said an officer, bending over him. "They run, they run!"

"Who run?" asked the dying General, feebly.

"The French, sir. They are running everywhere."

"Then I die happy," said Wolfe; and, saying this, he expired.

Soon after, Montcalm fell, mortally wounded.

"How long have I to live?" he asked.

"But a few hours," answered the surgeon.

"That is well!" exclaimed the heroic Frenchman. "I shall not live to see Quebec surrender."

A few days later Quebec was in English hands and France's dream of empire in America was over.

PATRICK HENRY *

By ELBRIDGE S. BROOKS

EVERY boy and girl loves to hear a great speaker, and almost everyone has heard of the wonderful orator who stirred up the people and made them resist the tyrant King of England, who made our forefathers pay unjust taxes and kept them from being a free and independent people.

His name was Patrick Henry. Like almost all other great men, he had an interesting life. He made himself what he was. After failing in several other undertakings, he finally entered the calling to which he was exactly suited, and became famous.

His life will teach my girl and boy readers not to despair if they fail once or twice, but to keep on trying. There is some line of work or some profession in which every boy and girl can succeed, if they will only do as Patrick Henry did, find out just what they can do best; and, once they have undertaken it, stick to it and work with all their might. Like George Washington and Thomas Jefferson and many of the great men in the early history of our country, Patrick Henry was born and raised in Virginia. His father was named John Henry, and came to this country, when a boy, from Scotland, about the year 1730, to seek his fortune in the New World. He got acquainted with the governor's family, and the governor introduced him to a Colonel Syme, who commanded the soldiers in Virginia. John Henry became a great friend of Colonel Syme and his wife. Mr. Henry also had a good education, and he was very useful to the governor in the Colony.

*From "True Stories of Great Americans," by Elbridge S. Brooks. Used by permission of the publishers, John C. Winston Co., Philadelphia.

DEATH OF GENERAL WOLFE AT QUEBEC, 1759

FROM AN ENGRAVING OF THE PAINTING BY BENJAMIN WEST

After a while he wrote back to his brother Patrick, in Scotland, who was a minister of the Church of England, and invited him to come to this country. Soon the Rev. Patrick Henry arrived. He was a smart man and quite an orator, and was made the preacher of St. Paul's Parish in Hanover, Virginia. It was for this good man that Patrick Henry, our great orator, was afterward named.

Colonel Syme, who commanded the Virginia soldiers, died, and his good friend John Henry, was made Colonel in his stead. After a little while he married Mrs. Syme, the widow of his former friend, and they had two sons; the older one they named William, after the brother of Mrs. Henry, and the younger boy was named Patrick, after his father's brother, whom we have just told you about.

BOYHOOD

The two boys, William and Patrick, grew up together, and until Patrick was ten years old, he and his brother William went to school in the neighborhood, where they learned to read and write and studied arithmetic. About this time their father opened a grammar school in his own house, and the boys attended this school, where they studied Latin and also a little Greek. Patrick was, however, more fond of arithmetic and algebra and geometry. In fact, he disliked to study anything else, and if we must tell you the plain truth—he was very lazy about studying anything, and got out of all the lessons he could without telling stories or being dishonorable. Like George Washington, he always told the truth, and is said never to have done a dishonorable thing in his life.

But when it came to play, Patrick was different. He loved to play ball, to go swimming, and to go hunting. So fond was he of the woods that sometimes when the school hour arrived Patrick was far away in the forest with his gun and his dog, or along the banks of the brook with his angle-rod, though it is said he seldom brought home any fish. In vacation time, as soon as he got his breakfast in the morning, he was away to the woods, where he would spend whole days together, for weeks at a time, seeming to grow more fond of the deep and lonely stillness of the vast forest, which covered almost the entire country at that time.

He preferred rather to go alone than with the other boys and join in the jolly fox-chase or rabbit hunt, as boys do now and as boys did then. It is true that he often started off with them, but after a little while they would find out that Patrick was not among them. Sometimes they would follow him, and they would nearly always find him lying alone by some rippling brook, where he seemed to be delighted with the music of the waters, or he would be flat on his back looking up into the blue sky. They naturally thought that he was too lazy to run about with them, but often when they slipped up on him, they would hear words in measured tones of oratory coming from his lips. He always seemed much ashamed when they caught him "talking to himself," as they called it, and he was too modest to tell them what he really was doing. It was found out in later life that he was thinking of the beauties of nature, studying about the strange things in the woods, and the streams, and the sky, and making to himself pretty speeches about them or about people. Thus we see, in early life, how his mind was inclined, and how he was naturally training himself.

There were at that time a great many deer in Virginia, and it was sport to hunt them with dogs. One part of the men and boys who went out to hunt would go on what they called the "drive;" that is, they would take the dogs and go into a part of the forest and march straight through. If the dogs "jumped" a deer, it would run off in the other direction. The hunters followed, the dogs barking and the men hallooing with all their might, and the poor frightened deer would speed away in the other direction, as fast as its nimble legs would carry it. The other part of the men were called the "standers." They would go a mile or two ahead of where they expected to start the deer, and stand in the little forest paths along which the animals passed to and fro in the forest. When the frightened deer came bounding along the pathway, the "standers" would shoot it down.

When the deer was killed, the lucky hunter would blow his horn with all his might, and all the hunters would come together, and they would have a great jubilee. They had a fashion, when a young man first killed a deer, to take the blood of the animal and literally smear him all over with it, and it is said that Patrick, although he was a constant hunter, was a good deal larger and older boy when he got his first smearing than a majority of his companions in the neighborhood. Patrick Henry was very fond of deer hunting, but he never went on the "drive." He always took one of the "stands," and was not at all choice about which stand they gave him, for it seems he would much rather remain alone with his thoughts than to be the heroic hunter who should bring down the deer. In fact, he frequently failed to answer the call of the lucky hunter who bagged the game, and was absent at the jollification around the slain animal. This was a breach of politeness on the part of the hunter which his companions were very slow to forgive. We must not conclude, however, that Patrick did not like society. On the contrary, he was very fond of it, but his enjoyments were of a peculiar cast. He did not mix in the wild and mirthful scenes, but usually sat quiet, taking little part in the conversation, seldom, it is said, ever smiling or telling a joke. He seemed lost most of the time in his thoughts. For this reason, people used to think he did not know what was going on; but they found out their mistake when they asked him about it, for he was able to repeat every word of the conversation better than any of the others could do it. Patrick was very fond of music, and he learned to play on the flute and violin, and often, at the country parties, he played the fiddle for many a jolly "old Virginia reel," which was the most popular dance in those days. He frequently joined in the dance, and, while he appeared to enjoy it immensely, it was said that he was very awkward and danced all over rather than with his feet. It was funny to see his long lanky arms and his big shoulders flying and shrugging about, while his feet seemed so heavy that he could scarcely get them off the floor.

SCHOOL-DAYS ARE OVER

Patrick's school-days ended when he was fifteen years of age. By that time there were so many brothers and sisters in the family that the father was scarcely able to support them; so he had to let the two older boys leave school. Patrick was placed behind the counter of a country store, where he stayed for one year as a clerk. His father then thought Patrick and William ought to be able to run a store for themselves, so he bought them a stock of goods, and in a country store "set them up in trade," as it was then called.

Patrick was the manager of the store, because he had a year's experience, and William, though older, must be his clerk, at least until he could learn all the mysteries of storekeeping from his younger brother. But the boys thought that keeping store wasn't work, but only play, and all they needed to do was merely to wait on the customers, and give them what they called for. Furthermore, they thought everybody was perfectly honest, and so they were generally, but often people who do not have the money buy more things than they can pay for. So Patrick

and William trusted everybody and about one-half of the time forgot to charge the things they sold on credit, and, at the end of the year when their father came to see how much money they had made, lo! he was surprised to behold that they had sold almost everything in their store, and that they had very little money, and what they had charged up to the neighbors, if all collected, would not leave one-half so much as he had started the boys in business with at the beginning.

Thus Patrick Henry and his brother had proved great failures as merchants, and they had to hunt work with the farmers, or be clerks in other stores where they would have nothing to do with the management. But while the money had been wasted, Patrick's time had not been wasted. His store was one of the most popular places in the neighborhood. People used to go there to talk and gossip with the "Henry boys," as they called them. No other place was so entertaining, or such a jolly good place to go. Every Saturday afternoon and almost every night found quite a throng of men and boys seated before the store door in the summer-time, or on boxes inside the store in the Winter, in animated conversation.

No matter where else they might go, they never talked as they did in the "Henry boys'" store. The reason of it was this: Patrick Henry, while he did little talking himself, every time he could get a crowd together began to ask somebody questions about some matter of history or something of common interest. He would carry his questions from one to another, around the company, until he would get them into a lively debate, which often ended in quarrels and sometimes in a fist-fight, for they were great fighters in those days.

But no matter what they were doing, whether engaged in heated discussions or pommeling each other with their fists, Patrick was watching them and studying human nature. You remember that he formerly studied the woods, the birds, the brooks and the things he found in the forest. He was now studying men, and how they might be moved to good or bad deeds by speech. Perhaps he had no thought of ever becoming a great orator. He studied human nature because he loved to be doing it, and he thus gained knowledge of men which afterward enabled him to control them so powerfully with his wonderful eloquence.

During this period at the store, Patrick also began to read books of history. He particularly loved to study the lives of the grand old Greek and Roman heroes. He read all the orations of that wonderful orator, Demosthenes, who lived in the city of Athens more than three hundred years before Christ, and who used to make such fiery orations against King Philip of Macedon, who was oppressing his countrymen, so that the people of Athens would rise up and shout in their frenzy, "Let us march against Philip." He read also the beautiful speeches of Cicero, the silver-tongued orator of the Romans, whose voice was so melodious, words so well chosen and sentences so beautifully put together that it was like listening to sweet enchanted music to hear him speak.

Frequently, when customers came into the store, they heard Patrick in the back room, repeating some of these master orations, and they used to pause in the doorway before asking for the goods they wanted, and listen for a few moments to the beautiful expression he gave them. Thus it will be seen how he prepared himself to speak as forcibly as Demosthenes, yet as musically and beautifully as Cicero. Let not any of my young readers think this time was wasted. Not so; it was very profitably spent. It is not what we learn in school so much as the private training we give ourselves which makes us great in any cause.

We have spoken above of Patrick Henry's playing the violin and flute at country parties. Like all true-hearted and manly boys, he liked the girls, and was fonder of being with them than in the society of the men, for he was always pure-minded and never given to telling vulgar stories, nor did he enjoy listening to them from others. At one of the parties he attended, when he was about seventeen years of age, he met and fell in love with a farmer's daughter, and when he was only eighteen years old did a very foolish thing which we would not advise any of our young readers to imitate. What did he do, did you ask? Why, at this early age he got married, without any money himself, and his wife's father was so poor he could not help her. What do you think of an eighteen-year-old boy with a wife?

One day soon after the wedding, Mr. John Henry and Mr. Shelton—that was the name of Patrick's wife's father—met, and, between them, gave the young people enough land to make them a small farm. They built them a little house, and the young husband went to work with a will digging in the earth to support himself and his wife. Their little cottage consisted of two rooms; one in which they cooked and ate, and the other was their sleeping-room, their sitting-room, their parlor, and their spare-room, so that when any of their friends came to see them and stayed all night, as they frequently did, Patrick and his wife gave up the bed to the visitors and made for themselves a pallet in a corner. This, you must remember, was not as poor a home as Abraham Lincoln had when he was a boy; but a poorer one than he had when he started his married life.

Many a day you might have seen Patrick, then a young husband not yet nineteen years of age, plowing among the stumps in his "new ground," as he called it, cleared up in front of his cabin, with his happy girl-wife busy inside the house, or feeding the chickens about the door. It was too bad that the first year the crop on Patrick's farm was a failure. He did not make enough to keep them alive and in the poorest kind of clothes. He proved himself to be as poor a farmer as he had been a merchant, for at the end of the year he came out in debt. He and his wife talked the matter over, and it was decided that they should get out of debt by selling their little farm and all they had, and he should take the remainder of the money and go again into business as a merchant. He no doubt flattered himself that he would be able to profit by his past experience and make a success. The farm was sold, and the store was opened.

His old friends came again. He had no trouble to get customers, but he was too good-hearted to press anybody for money; and he occupied so much time in playing his violin and flute for the pleasure of those who came to his store to buy, and got up so many debates, and his customers had such a good time generally, that at the end of two years he was worse off than before and had to give up his store. Thus, before he was more than twenty-three years of age, he had failed twice as a merchant, once as a farmer, and altogether in everything else he had attempted to do except to make people like him and to learn more about human nature and the way to control and influence men. In this he was wiser than anyone else about him.

The little store being given up, he did such various jobs of work as he could get and thus earned a poor support for his family. He had by this time also become a great reader. During his idle hours he studied geography and history, learned all about the different countries, their rulers and their manners and customs. He was said by everybody to be the best-read man in the community.

Often he had to go hungry, or eat the very poorest and coarsest of food, but he was always cheerful and never despondent. "No use of crossing the bridge before we get to it," he used to say to his wife. "There is a good time coming by and by" was another of his favorite expressions, though there was little prospect at this time for any good times for Patrick Henry or his family. But it did come, as we shall see, and one of the best lessons which young people can learn from his life is that of cheerfulness and hopefulness. He was, also, truthful and rigidly honest, as we have said before. He was, also, a man of very firm character. He could not be led into anything he thought was wrong, and he was a believer in God and a true Christian. Thus he was able to be cheerful and hopeful under troubles which would cause many men to despair.

Up to this time he had never thought of becoming a lawyer, nor had any of his friends suggested it to him. He had not made a public speech, not even in a debating society, but he had read the history of the nations of the world; he had studied oratory for his own pleasure, and it suddenly dawned upon him that he might make a lawyer.

BECOMES A LAWYER

When Patrick Henry was twenty-four years old, he set to work to read law. For six weeks or two months he shut himself up with a few law books, and then he went before the board of examiners and asked them to see if he did not know enough to practise law. He told them how much he had read, and they laughed at him; but in talking with him they found out that he knew so much about history and other things that a lawyer needed to know, that two of them gave him their consent to practise.

The other one of the examiners, Mr. Randolph, who was not present when the other two gave him their consent, was so shocked at Mr. Henry's personal appearance and poor clothes, when he came to see him, that he told him he was not fit to be a lawyer—that no man who looked like him could be a lawyer, and he would not examine him at all. This made Patrick angry, and he answered the learned man in such a manner and gave him such a lecture on his duty that Mr. Randolph was greatly surprised, and he tried to punish Mr. Henry for it by getting him into an argument in which he meant to show him how ignorant and unfit he was; but here Patrick Henry was at home, and he talked so well that the judge exclaimed: "Mr. Henry, I will never trust to appearances again. If your industry be only half equal to your genius, you will become an honor to your profession;" and he signed Patrick Henry's license, though it is said young Henry was at this time so ignorant of the forms of practice that he could not make out a case or present it before the court.

Like most young lawyers, he had to wait a good while before he had anything to do, and when it came it was rather by accident; but it gave him an opportunity, and that opportunity made him famous.

HIS FIRST CASE

We will now tell you about his first law case and his first speech. There was at that time in Virginia an established church such as they have in England. It was called the Episcopal Church, and the ministers were hired by the Governor. Virginia was a great tobacco-raising country, and they had a law that the farmers might pay their debts in tobacco. The sheriff and the judges of the court were paid so much a year in tobacco for their services, and the ministers also received a certain number of pounds of tobacco each year.

This law was made to hold good for only ten months, and after that time they again paid in tobacco, the price of which had gone down as low or lower than it had been before. But a few years later there came another short crop in tobacco, and the price went up to fifty shillings again, so the farmers had another law made permitting them to pay in money, but they very cautiously made this new law so that it would not run out; but the ministers seemed not to have noticed it was so made and after the first year wanted their pay in tobacco again, because it would bring them nearly double what they would get if they were paid in money.

This brought on quite a war between the people and the ministers, and they had a big suit in court. The farmers were very angry with the clergymen, and the clergymen were very angry with the farmers, each party accusing the other of wanting to cheat. The clergymen sent word to the King of England, and the king took their side, and said that the farmers' law should be *null and void,"* which means that it should not be enforced, that the clergymen should be paid in tobacco. The king was very shrewd in this, and while it appeared that he only wanted to take the ministers' part, he was, in reality, planning to enrich himself; because, if the clergy could collect their dues from the people in tobacco, which was worth more than twice as much as the money they were entitled to, the king said he would also collect his taxes in tobacco.

So you see how wise and yet how mean the king was in his decision. The people had the law on their side, and the clergymen wanted to collect twice what the people owed them, and the king said that they should do it. The clergymen made a great noise that the people were swindling them out of their just rights. They wanted tobacco, they did not want money. They argued that it was a shame and a disgrace to swindle the ministers in that way, and insisted that they were right, because the king himself said so. The people, on the other hand, said that the ministers and officers were employed for so much a year, and that they had no right to demand their tobacco, which they could sell for two or three times as many pounds of money as they had engaged to work for.

This looks entirely reasonable, and the people were right; but the clergymen and the officers and the king wanted the tobacco. You would think that it would have been better if the sheriff and the king and the judges had brought suit against the people to collect their claims in tobacco; but you will see how cunning they were in having the ministers to do it instead of doing it themselves. All the people loved the ministers, and they would sympathize with their cause, perhaps, when they would not sympathize with the officers. Therefore it was decided that the ministers should bring suit, and if they could make the people pay them in tobacco, then they would have to pay the officers and the king also in tobacco.

A lawyer by the name of Lewis was to plead the cause of the people, and a Mr. Lyons was to plead the cause of the clergymen; but when the king decided that the clergymen were right and the people were wrong, and that the law should not be obeyed, Mr. Lewis, the people's lawyer, told them they could not gain their cause against the king, and so he gave it up.

There were very few lawyers then in the country; and they were nearly all in the employ of the king, so the people could find no one to plead their cause, and, as the last resort, they turned to Patrick Henry, a young lawyer of twenty-four years, who had never made a public speech in his life. The place where the case was to be tried was at Hanover Courthouse, and the judge who was to sit on the bench was Patrick Henry's own father, and among those who opposed the people was his own uncle for whom he was named, the Rev. Patrick Henry. Was this not an embarrassing situation for the young lawyer, who had never made a speech, to find himself in?

The day came. It was one of those beautiful Indian summer days which comes in November in the south. Patrick Henry was early at the courthouse, and great throngs of people gathered in from all directions. Never before in Hanover had there been so many farmers present on any court day. The decision of the case amounted to thousands of dollars of loss or gain to them. The clergymen came from all over the State, which was then, you know, only a Colony—though much larger than it is now. There were twenty or more of the most learned clergymen of the nation present. They had come to frown upon the young lawyer who was to plead against them, and to scowl at the people, who, they pretended, were trying to rob them.

The court was opened. The array before Patrick's eyes was almost fearful. The most learned men of the Colony, the severest critics in the New World were against him, and the courthouse was crowded. On the outside, the windows were thronged with anxious faces looking in.

Mr. Lyons made a short speech, simply explaining to the jury the fact that the king had decreed his side to be right. He pleaded that the clergy were the greatest benefactors of the Colony, that it was a shame to mistreat them, and that this law, if enforced, simply robbed them of their just allowance. His closing was eloquent and beautiful, and the ministers nodded their assent when he took his seat. He had presented their cause well.

Now came the first trial of Patrick Henry's strength. No one had ever heard him speak, and every one was curious. Even his opponents seemed to feel sorry for him. He rose and stood for a moment in an awkward manner, and, when he began, faltered much in his speech. The people hung their heads, and the ministers exchanged sly, smiling looks of derision at each other. His father, it is said, almost sunk behind the desk, he was so mortified and confused; but these circumstances lasted only for a few moments.

Patrick Henry's soul rose within him, his whole appearance changed, the fire of his eloquence was kindled, and he seemed to forget himself; his figure stood erect, his bearing was lofty, and his face shone with a grandeur that no one had ever seen upon it before. His awkward actions became graceful to behold; his voice, no longer faltering, was charming and beautiful.

No one can describe that speech, and it has never been printed. It was delivered under the impulse of the moment; but it was declared by the clergymen themselves, against whom it was spoken, that no such speech, as they believed, had ever fallen from the lips of man; and, to this day, in Hanover, Virginia, the highest compliment that can be paid to a speaker is to say: "He is almost equal to Patrick Henry when he pleaded against the parsons." The clergyman had sued for heavy damages, but the jury, without scarcely leaving their seats, granted them only one penny. Mr. Lyons made a motion for a new trial; that is, he tried to get his case tried over, but the court refused to give the parsons a new hearing.

Was ever such a victory won by a new lawyer? It was the first speech Patrick Henry ever made, and it was undoubtedly one of the greatest speeches ever delivered in the world before a court. At its close the people, who had hung their heads in shame at the beginning, rushed into the courthouse, seized the young lawyer in spite of the sheriff's cry for order, hoisted him on their shoulders, carried him out of the house and over the town, with a wild multitude following and screaming his praises at the top of their voices.

Patrick Henry had at last found the calling for which he was intended, and to which he was suited. From this time forward he was the greatest lawyer, not only in Hanover Courthouse, but of all Virginia. He had all the cases he could attend to, and made plenty of money to support his family, who had for many years been struggling with poverty.

He lived for nearly forty years after this memorable day at Hanover Courthouse. His life was full of honor and usefulness to his country, and he made several other speeches, parts of which every schoolboy has at one time or another used as a declamation.

And now that we have told you of the hardships and troubles of Patrick Henry's early life, let us tell you of the great things he did in the service of his country.

FOR THE PUBLIC

In January, 1765, the famous "Stamp Act" was passed by the British Parliament. The colonists were to be oppressed, and no one dared openly to rebel against it.

In May, Patrick Henry was elected to the House of Burgesses (that is what the Virginia Legislature was called in those days), and he pledged himself to his people to do all he could to oppose the enforcement of the Stamp Act. There were many learned and eloquent speakers in the House, and he was not expected to take the lead.

The fine gentlemen in the Assembly, who lived in fine old Virginia mansions, and wore fine clothes, made fun of Patrick's country way of talking, his "homespun" clothes and his awkward

manners; but when he spoke they could not help admiring his wonderful command of language and his power over men. His first speech was against rich men who wanted to lend the Colony's money to themselves and their friends. This made them his great enemies, but the other side —the common people—admired him more than ever.

At last it came time to consider the hated "Stamp Act." None of the great men dared to speak against it openly. So Patrick Henry drew up some resolutions declaring that the English Parliament had no right to make this tax upon the people, and, furthermore, they had no right to make any laws against the interest of the Colonies. He said they were responsible to the king alone, and that the House of Burgesses and the Governor alone had the right to make the colonists pay taxes.

After the reading of his resolutions, Patrick Henry was assailed by a storm of words and much ridicule by those who favored or were afraid of England. There were hot speeches from several gentlemen, and a less heroic spirit than Henry's would have said not a word more. No one thought the resolutions would pass.

At length when the storm had subsided, Patrick Henry arose to speak. His face was deathly pale, his thin lips quivered, but his eyes had a look of awful determination in them. Stretching his long arms at full length toward the president (called the speaker) he began and delivered the greatest speech perhaps ever heard in America. The walls rang with the mighty force of his words, and everyone was overpowered with his wonderful eloquence, as they had been in the famous "Parson Case." They shouted "treason" at him, but he could not be frightened, but all the time grew bolder and more eloquent. When he closed this great speech every member but two voted for his resolutions.

Patrick Henry had been the first one who dared oppose England. His wonderful speech was printed and sent all over the Colonies, north and south, and it was even sent to England; and in a few months Parliament repealed (that is, removed) the hated "Stamp Act."

But the spirit of liberty was now awake in the people, and they demanded relief from other unjust laws which England tried to impose, and in this effort Patrick Henry was one of the foremost men in the country. He was greater than all other men in Virginia, and he, with Thomas Jefferson and Richard Henry Lee, kept telling the people they ought to be free. In 1773 —eight years after his great speech—Mr. Henry,

Mr. Jefferson, Mr. Lee, and many others got the House of Burgesses to elect men to write to the other Colonies about their grievances against England. This was a great benefit, for the different Colonies were thus brought together in their efforts and protests against cruel laws. Through this Committee of Correspondence, it was decided that the Colonies should hold a congress in Philadelphia in 1774. Every Colony sent representatives. Mr. Henry was one of those from Virginia.

Patrick Henry opened the Congress with a great speech, in which he said, "I am not a Virginian, but an American." Everybody soon saw he was the most powerful orator in Congress, and many said he was the greatest man in the nation, for he was as wise and just as he was eloquent.

In March, 1775, Mr. Henry made another speech in the Virginia House of Burgesses, which is said to have been the grandest effort of his life up to this time. He wanted the Colony to raise soldiers and prepare for war. Almost every schoolboy knows part of this speech.

Patrick Henry then went to work and got up a company and made the governor, who was but the servant of the king, give up the colonists' gunpowder, which he had taken away to the English ships. This was the first resistance, by arms, to England in Virginia. He also made the governor pay for the damage he did the people.

Patrick Henry now went back to the Continental Congress, as they made him commander of all the Virginia soldiers; but he was too good a statesman to spend his time in the war, and so his friends begged him to stay in the Virginia Legislature and Continental Congress, which he did.

In May, 1776, he got the Virginia Legislature to pass a vote requesting the Continental Congress to declare our country free from England, and to go to war with her if she would not let us go. He then helped make a new constitution for Virginia, and they elected him governor of the Colony. Thus, in sixteen years after he began to study law, he was one of the most famous men in America and governor of Virginia. How do you suppose those proud people who laughed at him felt now?

The Revolutionary War now began in earnest, and it would take a big book to tell how he and John Adams and others, by their wise counsel and eloquent speeches, inspired the soldiers and helped General Washington to win in the end. Through it all Patrick Henry was in his State Legislature, or the General Congress, or serving as governor. After the war was over, they made him governor twice, and tried again, in 1786, to get him to serve them, but he declined, as he had already been governor so much. He told them he did not think they ought to get in the habit of letting one man hold office too long. In this he was like George Washington. You know Washington would not let them make him President but twice. But the people loved Patrick Henry so much that they tried to make him governor again ten years later, in 1796, but he told them no, he had been honored enough.

President George Washington offered to make Mr. Henry his Secretary of State in 1795. This is the very highest office in the nation, next to the President and Vice-President. Patrick Henry said no; there were better men for it. Mr. Washington then wanted to appoint him Chief Justice of the United States, and President John Adams asked him to be our special minister to France, where, you remember, Benjamin Franklin was so long our representative, but he said no to both of these, because he preferred to remain a private citizen and live with his family— he now had many interesting children.

Finally, in 1799, the Virginia Legislature passed a very bad law, which George Washington —who was now a private citizen again—thought was very dangerous and might cause trouble to the whole United States. So he begged Patrick Henry to offer himself as a candidate for the Legislature, for he knew, with his powerful eloquence, Mr. Henry could overcome the bad law. Mr. Henry was elected, of course, but before he took his seat he died, at Red Hill, Charlotte County, Virginia, June 6, 1799, when only sixty-three years and a few days old.

Patrick Henry was regarded by everyone as the greatest of American orators. Thomas Jefferson and John Randolph declared he was the greatest orator who ever lived, and he was often compared to Demosthenes and Cicero as the only speakers of ancient times worthy to be ranked with him.

WILLIAM PENN

BY IRVINGTON LEE

KING CHARLES II of England was seated one day in his palace, surrounded by the lords of his court. They were pleasure-loving lords, ruled by a pleasure-loving king, and no period in English history has been so marked by the vices of the rich and great. It was a time, also, of great oppression and great cruelty. The prisons were foul places, unfit to shelter swine, and were filled not only with thieves and murderers, but with many good and innocent people whose worst offense was that they wished to worship God in their own way, according to their conscience. In our own day men are put to death only when they have taken the life of another, and sometimes not even then. But in the seventeenth century, when Charles was king, a starving man would be executed for stealing a sheep, or for some similar offense that we now punish but lightly.

It was March 4, 1681, and it happened to be a day devoted by the king to receiving petitions, and listening to those persons who, for one reason or another, were admitted to the royal presence.

To look at the faces of the lords, or to listen to their conversation, one would scarce have thought them assembled there on business for the State. Their appearance was that of men whose most important pursuit was pleasure, when not scheming and plotting against one another, or planning to enrich themselves at the expense of their country. They bore themselves gayly, and their talk ran much on gossip, and was pointed with oaths and jests.

PENN BEFORE KING CHARLES

But into the presence of this company came a man whose entrance stilled their talk, and whose bold behavior challenged the attention of all. He was under forty, with a handsome face and erect figure, and he walked like one who had been an athlete from his youth. In his brilliant blue eyes were sincerity and goodness; his whole appearance and bearing marked one gently bred, strong in purpose, yet simple in manner, and without a trace of pride. But though he looked the equal of the greatest lord among them, his attire was in strange contrast to the silks and laces of the courtiers. Well-fitting and of good material, his plain garments were cut in the pattern affected by the Quakers. In this sober dress, lacking all ornament, it was the character of the man, and not his clothes, that proclaimed him what he was.

The one resemblance was the hat. It was fashioned like the hats worn by the courtiers, yet with this difference: it was a plain hat, without feathers or ribbons.

But though there was nothing very strange in its appearance, there was something strange indeed in this man's manner in wearing it. Had he forgotten to take it off? When a subject was admitted to the presence of the king, he uncovered his head and bent his knee. This newcomer did neither one nor the other. Up he walked, hat on head, to where King Charles was seated; and there he stood and talked, quite at his ease, like one commoner conversing with another.

THE COURTIERS AMAZED

A murmur of astonishment ran through the company. To them this thing seemed little short of sacrilege. True, they wore their hats on almost all occasions; they wore them at meals and they wore them in church. But here, in the royal palace, face to face with the king, it was unbelievable.

"Impudent fellow!" said one. "He deserves to be thrashed for his insolence."

"Ha!" exclaimed another. "This is what comes of being gentle with these Quakers."

"But will His Majesty endure it?" ventured a third. "If the king but gives the word—" And he laid his hand on his sword.

"I marvel at your ignorance," spoke up a lord who had been long at court. "Do you not know the man who thus deports himself? It is none other than William Penn, son of the great Admiral. His Majesty does but humor him, knowing full well that he will soon be rid of him, and having in mind the great friendship with his father."

"Perchance, then, you know his errand, too? It must be weighty, and one that comes near the king's desire. See! His Majesty smiles, and affixes his signature to some document."

King Charles was indeed well pleased, though the courtier was wrong in thinking that he wished to rid himself of Penn. What had happened was this: Admiral Penn, now dead eleven years, had done valiant service in the Navy. In various ways he had won the king's friendship. For one thing, he had offered to fight in the king's cause against Oliver Cromwell. For another, he had lent the king much money, and had not pressed him for his pay as Admiral, which was greatly

ROGER WILLIAMS DEFENDS HIS BELIEF
FROM A PAINTING BY ALBERT HERTER

in arrears. By 1681, these claims, with interest, had grown to be a sum equal to $80,000 in our money. It was a debt the king could not pay in cash. But William Penn, to whom the claim passed as an inheritance from his father, thought of a way by which he could not only collect the debt, but perform a splendid service for his suffering brethren, the Quakers. If King Charles would grant him a tract of wild land on the Delaware River in America, Penn would take it in satisfaction of the claim, and establish a colony where the persecuted Quakers could live their own lives in peace.

To this the king cheerfully consented. It was a territory of more than 40,000 square miles, almost as large as England, and in making the grant King Charles named it Pennsylvania—that is to say, "Penn's Forest"—in memory of Admiral Penn. Meanwhile a charter had been drawn up, fixing the conditions of the grant and the powers vested in the new proprietor. This charter was the document King Charles signed on that day when William Penn stood before him, his knee unbent and his head covered.

Though Penn had paid a fortune for the land, he considered it well spent. No one person had ever before come into possession of such a vast domain. And no one, we may add, charged with such a responsibility, had ever been so well fitted to discharge it. All his life he had labored and fought to win religious freedom, and to teach men the way of peace and toleration. For this he had been disowned, ridiculed, imprisoned; those in England who held the same faith were still subject to violent persecution. Now at last he could see his way to securing that freedom so long denied. In a new country, free from tyrants and warring sects, men might live in the fear of none but God.

The life of Penn was in many ways remarkable. He not only enjoyed the friendship and respect of King Charles and the Duke of York, who came to be crowned as King James, but he was also on the best of terms with some of the great lords of the day. This seems strange when we remember that the royal court was a corrupt one, and that men did not hesitate to sell their honor in order to gain riches and authority. Penn was unselfish, high-minded, strong of character, and pure in conduct. Most of those who surrounded the king had little in common with him. Yet somehow he managed to make his influence felt, and to champion with success the cause of liberty and justice.

One thing that helped him was his moderation. He always avoided giving unnecessary offense.

Thus, when writing or speaking to those who had no sympathy with Quakers, he did not use "Thee" and "Thou" for "You," as he knew it would needlessly irritate them. Once the king said to him: "What is the difference between your religion and mine?" It was an embarrassing thing to ask, and if Penn had really answered it he might have given great offense, and only injured the cause of the Quakers. So he merely said: "I think it is the ornaments you have added to your hat."

There were feathers on the King's hat, and none on Penn's; but what Penn, as a Quaker, really meant were the ornaments, or forms, of the king's religion.

The career that Penn chose for himself was in all ways opposed to his station of life and to the plans made by his father for the boy's advancement. He was sent to be educated at Christ Church College, at Oxford, where his companions numbered many of the young aristocrats of the day. Here, it was thought, he would enjoy the training and associations to fit him for an important place in the great world of affairs. But the Puritans, who had gained the upper hand for a time, under Cromwell, had been busy at Oxford, and the Church of England was not fully restored. At the same time the Quakers, or Society of Friends, under the leadership of George Fox, had come to make their influence felt in England.

WHO THE QUAKERS WERE

Briefly, the Quakers were a religious sect who rejected many of the teachings of the Established Church and sought to return to the early forms. They had no paid or regularly appointed ministers. They believed that everyone is inspired by God, and possesses, according to St. John, "the true Light which lighteth every man that cometh into the world." Their religion was, besides, a practical one. As it developed, its leaders were no longer looked upon as fanatics, but came to be recognized as men long in advance of their times. The Quakers, for example, were the first to reform the disgraceful condition of English prisons. They fought manfully in behalf of religious liberty for all. They were the first to demand the abolition of negro slavery, and they did not cease their efforts until slavery was abolished both in England and in our own country.

Besides William Penn, some famous men have been Quakers. Among them we recall two American poets, Bayard Taylor and Whittier;

Benjamin West, American portrait painter; John Bright, English statesman; Ezra Cornell, founder of Cornell University.

PENN'S TREATY

FROM A PAINTING BY EDWIN A. ABBEY

But when Penn, born in 1644, was at Oxford, Quakers were looked upon as low, ridiculous, and altogether undesirable.

The young man showed early signs of religious feeling. One day, when a mere boy, "he was suddenly surprised with an inward comfort; and, as he thought, an external glory in the room, which gave rise to religious emotions, during which he had the strongest conviction of the being of God. He believed that he had been called upon to a holy life."

Though he did not become a Quaker till he was twenty-three, he was first attracted to the faith by the preaching of Thomas Loe. With some other college students, he was fined for neglecting chapel services; persisting in his conduct, he was expelled.

It was a great blow to Admiral Penn. Following his first impulse, he thrashed his son, and turned him out of doors. Thinking better of it, he sent him to France, where William not only studied theology, but mastered the French language, acquired polite ways, and became so skillful as a fencer that he easily disarmed a man who attacked him in the street.

Yet the youth was still a Quaker at heart. Sent to Ireland, where he saw some fighting, he returned unchanged. Once more he was turned out of doors, once more forgiven. Then, at twenty-four, he became a Quaker preacher.

Penn led from that day a life of many trials and hardships. For writing a religious pamphlet, he was imprisoned in the Tower, and in the years that followed he was several times cast into jail. Though upon his father's death he came into the possession of a fortune that would have enabled him to live as a rich man, he preferred to devote himself to the cause of religious liberty. Altogether, he spent but four years in America. On his return to England in 1684 he so successfully pleaded the Quakers' cause with King James that more than 1,200 of them were released from prison. Then came a royal decree, granting liberty of conscience to all.

Penn believed that war is wrong. In his "Essay Towards the Present and Future Peace of Europe" he outlined a plan for a congress of nations, at which all disputes would be settled without fighting. This was the peace-loving man who is best remembered by Americans for his peaceful settlement of Pennsylvania. Even the Puritans won their way with the sword, and all the colonies but Penn's waged war with the red man. It remained for the Quakers to meet the Indians without weapons. Under an elm tree, on the river bank above Philadelphia, the great Treaty was signed. It was a treaty made in good faith, and never broken. No Quaker ever slew an Indian; no Indian ever shed a drop of Quaker blood. It remains for all time a tribute to the good fame of William Penn.

THE SIGNERS OF THE DECLARATION OF INDEPENDENCE

BY MARY V. WORSTELL

OW many boys and girls who read this volume can tell, without a moment's hesitation, the number of men who signed the Declaration of Independence? There are doubtless many who can answer correctly, fifty-six.

But how much do we know about the lives and personalities of these men? and have we ever stopped to think what it meant to them to put their names to the most famous document in the history of our country? Now and then we meet people who can say that they are descendants of some "signer," and very proud they seem to be of that fact. They may well be proud, for consider for a moment what it meant to sign the Great Document. It meant that the signer publicly proclaimed himself an enemy to a great and powerful king—became a rebel, in fact; and we all know the fate that commonly overtakes rebels. To-day we seldom think of the trials and misfortunes that followed the signing; we think only of the glory.

Although George III paid little attention to the many protests that had been presented to him by the colonies, he yet kept a close watch on these restless subjects, and his representatives well knew all that was going on.

To the Second Continental Congress, assembled in Philadelphia in 1776, were sent, from the thirteen original colonies, delegates whose loyalty was undoubted. Patriotism was not profitable in those far-away days. Robert Morris, the great financier of the Revolution, sacrificed a large fortune in his country's behalf; Thomas Nelson, of Virginia, also lost a large fortune by the war; while the immortal Samuel Adams, who dedicated his life to the service of his beloved country, lived and died a poor man.

But let me present to you, very briefly, these fifty-six men; and possibly, after this introduction, you may wish to know more of their lives and achievements.

GEORGIA

GEORGIA sent three delegates, and of these (1) George Walton was the youngest. He was an ambitious boy who was apprenticed to a carpenter so niggardly that he would not allow the lad a candle by which to study. Luckily, wood was plentiful, and by the light of a burning torch Walton studied hard and in time became a lawyer. (2) Lyman Hall came from New England. Before he was twenty-one he had married and settled in Georgia, to which place he was accompanied by about forty families. The patriotism of these settlers has left a permanent impress on the State, for its counties were named after such British statesmen as showed themselves friends to the American colonies. Look them up on the map and see if this is not so. You will find also a county named after this signer. (3) Button Gwinnett was an Englishman who came to this country when he was thirty-eight years old. He took up the cause of the oppressed colonies with much enthusiasm—too much, in fact, for he became involved in a quarrel, and in the duel which followed he lost his life.

SOUTH CAROLINA

SOUTH CAROLINA furnished four delegates, among them (1) Edward Rutledge, who was the youngest man to sign the Declaration, for he was only twenty-seven at the time. All of the South Carolina signers—Rutledge, (2) Arthur Middleton, (3) Thomas Heyward, Jr., and (4) Thomas Lynch, Jr.—came of wealthy families, and the three former had received the benefit of a foreign education. Three years after signing the Declaration, Thomas Lynch, then in poor health, sailed for France, and his ship never was heard of again. While Arthur Middleton was in Philadelphia, a delegate to the Second Continental Congress, he and John Hancock, with their families, occupied the same house. Both men were wealthy and hospitable, and they drew around them a choice circle of friends. Lynch was the only signer from South Carolina who did not suffer imprisonment for his efforts in his country's behalf.

NORTH CAROLINA

NORTH CAROLINA sent three delegates. (1) Joseph Hewes was born a Quaker; he was a man of intense patriotism, and in time he became the first Secretary of the Navy, with almost unlimited powers; and though to him the war meant great financial loss, he never swerved in his devotion to his country. (2) William Hooper was a Boston man who was partly educated by his father, who was pastor of Trinity Church. Having studied law, he settled in North Carolina; but his life in the new country proved a hard one, for the only way of traveling was on horseback, and some of the courts were two hundred miles from his home. (3) John Penn was a bright boy whose early education was neglected, but this loss was speedily made good when his relative, the distinguished Edmund Pendleton, placed his fine library at the lad's disposal. John Penn filled many offices, and on the return of peace he withdrew to private life, not enriched, but impoverished, by the offices he had held.

MARYLAND

MARYLAND sent four delegates. (1) William Paca was a man of graceful address and polished manners and came of a fine old family, while (2) Thomas Stone was a younger son with no prospects at all. But he was eager for an education, and he secured it by daily attendance at a school ten miles from his home. It would be easy to predict success for a boy of such pluck; and indeed he achieved success, for five times he was elected to Congress. (3) Samuel Chase was called the "Demosthenes of Maryland." He was a fine orator and a kindly man as well. One time, on a visit to Baltimore, he met a young man in whom he became much interested. He not only placed his library at his disposal; he invited him to make his home with him. Chase lived to see his generosity justified, for the young man was no other than William Pinckney, one of the most distinguished lawyers our country has ever produced. (4) Charles Carroll of Carrollton (and why he signed his name in that way you may have read about in your school histories) was one of the wealthiest of the signers. He was the signer destined to outlive all of the others.

DELAWARE

DELAWARE sent three representatives. (1) George Read was a man of cool and deliberate judgment in spite of Irish descent; and an interesting phase of his character is shown in the fact that his first act as a lawyer was to give up all rights to his father's estate, declaring that his education represented his proper share. (2) Thomas McKean was a truly remarkable man. For fifty years he was in public life, and he filled many prominent and honorable offices. For many years he was Governor of Pennsylvania. The third delegate, (3) Cæsar Rodney, chanced to be in Delaware when the Declaration was ready for signing. Read was slow to favor independence, while McKean was eager for it. The vote of Rodney, therefore, would turn the scales for Delaware, so

McKean sent a special messenger to Rodney, urging his immediate return to Philadelphia. The result was a hurried ride on horseback of eighty miles; a historic ride, that has been told in spirited verse for children who like to recite "pieces." Rodney reached Philadelphia just in the nick of time, and an old record says that "he voted with his boots on."

RHODE ISLAND

RHODE ISLAND furnished two delegates, (1) Stephen Hopkins and (2) William Ellery. Next to Benjamin Franklin, Hopkins was the oldest man to sign the Declaration. Though his education was meager, he was ambitious to learn, and by hard study he became a fine mathematician and surveyor. William Ellery paid dearly for his connection with the Continental Congress, for the British burned his home, and other property of his was seriously damaged.

NEW HAMPSHIRE

OF New Hampshire's three delegates, two were physicians. When (1) Dr. Matthew Thornton was only thirty-one he took part in the famous capture of Louisbourg by Pepperel and Warren, assuming, with success, the medical care of the New Hampshire division. (2) Dr. Josiah Bartlett was an energetic man whose profession could not keep him out of political life. During the sixty-six years of his life he did the work of a dozen men. (3) William Whipple began his life under unfavorable circumstances, for he was a sailor, and before he was twenty-one he was in charge of a vessel engaged in importing slaves. But this life was soon given up, and he rendered fine service in Congress, where his knowledge of naval affairs proved valuable on various committees.

CONNECTICUT

CONNECTICUT furnished four delegates. (1) Oliver Wolcott came of a famous Connecticut family and was destined for the medical profession. But he soon abandoned medicine for politics and military life, and quickly rose to distinction. (2) William Williams was a nephew of Colonel Ephraim Williams, who founded Williamstown and Williams College. With this uncle, William Williams, while still a young man, made a journey to Lake George, and the glimpse of military life under British officers that this afforded served to strengthen his wish for independence.

Connecticut may well be proud of (3) Samuel Huntington and (4) Roger Sherman, for the first was a farmer's son, yet so eager was he for an education that he not only acquired it, but he held

DRAFTING THE DECLARATION OF INDEPENDENCE

FROM THE PAINTING BY P. F. ROTHERMEL

high offices. In 1780 this farmer's son was President of Congress and later Governor of Connecticut, while Roger Sherman spent the first twenty-two years of his life at the cobbler's bench. But a book was always close at hand, so that every spare moment might be put to good use. He not only filled many public offices; he was one of the five appointed to draw up the Declaration—a great honor, only to be bestowed on one of ripe judgment. John Adams said that "Roger Sherman had a clear head and a steady heart, and was one of the soundest and strongest pillars of the Revolution."

NEW YORK

NEW YORK sent four representatives. (1) Both Francis Lewis and (2) William Floyd were of Welsh descent, and both were made to suffer greatly for signing the Declaration, for their homes were plundered and destroyed by the British. (3) Lewis Morris, still another New York signer, was made to suffer also, for he was a rich man with a great estate. A British force was stationed near his home; nevertheless, he pluckily put his name to the document. In revenge, the British burned his home and more than a thousand acres of woodland. But the patriotism of Lewis Morris never wavered, and in time his three sons took up arms in behalf of their country. The name of Livingston has long been an honored one in the annals of New York City. In 1746 there were but few in the whole colony who had received a college education, and of these (4) Philip Livingston was one. After graduating from Yale College he engaged in commerce and soon laid the foundation of an ample fortune. At the age of forty-six his health failed, but, being a member of Congress, he would not abandon the duties of his office. He died while in office, deeply lamented by the young nation he had served so faithfully.

NEW JERSEY

OF the five delegates sent to Philadelphia by New Jersey, two were farmers, (1) John Hart and (2) Abraham Clark. When the British invaded New Jersey, Hart's home and farm were laid waste, and Hart himself, then a man of seventy-one, was hunted from place to place. Tradition says that at one time he was so sorely beset that he was obliged to hide in a dog-kennel. It is pleasant to know that he lived to repair the damage done by his enemies. Abraham Clark was one of those who were eager for independence, and he did all in his power to secure it for his country. (3) Francis Hopkinson was a fine student and a member of the first class that the University of Pennsylvania ever graduated. No noisy fun for him,

for, as Dr. Benjamin Rush quaintly says of him, "his wit was mild and elegant and infused cheerfulness and a species of delicate joy into the hearts of all who heard it." (4) Richard Stockton was a man of wealth, position, and culture. He was born in the town of Princeton, New Jersey, and he conferred a great favor on the college there when he induced to come to this country (5) Dr. John Witherspoon, a learned Scottish divine. Dr. Witherspoon was the only clergyman to sign the Declaration. He was the sixth president of Princeton College, and devoted himself not only to the college, but to the country of his adoption, for it is said that he became an American and an ardent patriot as soon as he reached our shores.

PENNSYLVANIA

PENNSYLVANIA sent more delegates than any other colony—nine. (1) Benjamin Franklin was the oldest of all the signers. We may be sure that this truly great man was a prominent figure in that remarkable gathering. Almost as notable was (2) Robert Morris, the great financier of the Revolution. Though he was slow at first to favor independence, later he showed the truest patriotism, for his financial aid tided the young country over serious difficulties. "The Americans," says one historian, "owe as much acknowledgment to the financial operations of Robert Morris as to the negotiations of Benjamin Franklin, or even to the arms of Washington." (3) Dr. Benjamin Rush may well be honored, for he was a physician of high standing; and in 1793, when Philadelphia was visited by yellow fever, and more than 4500 fell victims in three months, Dr. Rush was one of three physicians who nobly remained at their posts. (4) James Wilson was a young Scotchman who came to this country when he was twenty-one. By the time he was only twenty-six he was the acknowledged head of the Philadelphia bar. The name of this signer has recently been brought into notice. He died while at Edenton, North Carolina, but in 1906 his remains were brought to Philadelphia, where they were interred in the graveyard of Christ's Church. There were appropriate ceremonies in which many legal and patriotic societies took part, as well as representatives of the national government. (5) George Clymer was another delegate of sturdy patriotism, and so was (6) James Smith. The latter was a man of genial disposition, keen sense of humor, and great benevolence. (7) George Taylor was an Irishman, and came to this country to avoid studying medicine. He worked in a foundry, and after some years he became its proprietor. (8) John Morton was a boy who had but three

FANEUIL HALL, BOSTON

INDEPENDENCE HALL, PHILADELPHIA

191

months' schooling, but this was followed by such wide reading and study, under the supervision of his stepfather, that in time he became one of the judges of the Supreme Court of Pennsylvania (9) George Ross, still another of the Pennsylvania signers, must have been a model delegate, for his conduct in Congress was so highly approved by his constituents that they voted him more than six hundred dollars with which to pur-

careers of (3) John Adams and his kinsman, (4) Samuel Adams, cannot be summed up in a few words. John Adams was a man of marvelous industry, serving in Congress on no less than ninety different committees. He was twice Vice-President before filling the Presidential chair for one term; and the closing years of his busy and useful life were brightened by watching the career of his son, John Quincy Adams, who, in

"SIGNING OF THE DECLARATION OF INDEPENDENCE." PAINTED BY JOHN TRUMBULL
John Hancock is seated at the table on which rests the Declaration. Near him, standing, are Jefferson, Adams, Franklin, Sherman, and Livingston

chase a piece of silver. But Ross was as modest as he was loyal, and he refused the gift.

MASSACHUSETTS

THE five delegates from Massachusetts Bay formed a famous group. (1) Elbridge Gerry was in public life many years. From the time when he first took his seat in the General Court of Massachusetts Bay, at the age of twenty-nine, till, as Vice-President of the United States, under Madison, he died, at the age of seventy, the story of his life is the story of devotion to country. (2) Robert Treat Paine was born, so the chroniclers tell us, "of pious and respectable parents." He entered Harvard at the age of fourteen, and on graduating he taught school for a time in order to earn enough money to study law, and in time he won distinction as an able lawyer. The

time, also became President—a wonderful record only equaled by the Harrisons of Virginia. John Adams was said to have "the clearest head and the firmest heart of any man in Congress." Samuel Adams embarked for a time in commerce, but this proved as disastrous as his political life was brilliant. He made no secret of his wish for independence, and this so irritated Governor Gage that he issued his celebrated proclamation in which he promised pardon to all who would lay down their arms, "excepting only from the benefit of such pardon Samuel Adams and John Hancock." He held many honorable offices in the young State of Massachusetts, and in time he succeeded John Hancock as Governor. He died in his eighty-second year, a very poor man. In fact, he has been called "the poor gentleman." But now his country glories in his illustrious

Facsimiles of the Signatures to the Declaration of Independence July 4 1776.

John Penn   John Hancock   John Hart.
Wm Floyd   Wm Paca

Geo. Read   Wm Hooper   Saml Adams

Step. Hopkins   Tho Nelson jr   Geo Clymer

Charles Carroll of Carrollton   Wm Ellbridge Gerry

Tho M. Kean   Roger Sherman   Sama Huntington

Wm Whipple   Thomas Lynch Junr.

Geo Taylor   Josiah Bartlett   Benj. Franklin

Wm Williams   Richd Stockton   John Morton

Oliver Wolcott   Jno Witherspoon   Geo. Ross

Thos Stone   Samuel Chase   Robt Treat Paine

George Wythe   Matthew Thornton

Frans Lewis   Th Jefferson   Benja Harrison

Lewis Morris   Abra Clark   Phil Livingston   Casar Rodney

Arthur Middleton   Fras Hopkinson

Geo Walton   Carter Braxton   James Wilson

Richard Henry Lee   Thos Heyward Junr.

Benjamin Rush   John Adams   Robt Morris

Lyman Hall   Joseph Hewes   Button Gwinnett

Francis Lightfoot Lee

William Ellery   Edward Rutledge   Jas Smith

Department of State 19th April 1819. I certify that this is a CORRECT Copy of the original Declaration of Independence deposited at this Department, and that I have compared all the signatures with those of the original and have found them EXACT IMITATIONS: John Quincy Adams

193

B. & G. F.—13

THE PORTRAITS OF THE 56 SIGNERS OF THE DECLARATION OF INDEPENDENCE
(Arranged in alphabetical order. From the Emmet collection, New York City)

1. John Adams. 2. Samuel Adams. 3. Josiah Bartlett. 4. Carter Braxton. 5. Charles Carroll. 6. Samuel Chase. 7. Abraham Clark. 8. George Clymer. 9. William Ellery. 10. William Floyd. 11. Benjamin Franklin. 12. Elbridge Gerry. 13. Button Gwinnett. 14. Lyman Hall. 15. John Hancock. 16. Benjamin Harrison. 17. John Hart. 18. Joseph Hewes. 19. Thomas Heyward, Jr. 20. William Hooper. 21. Stephen Hopkins. 22. Francis Hopkinson. 23. Samuel Huntington. 24. Thomas Jefferson. 25. Francis Lightfoot Lee. 26. Richard Henry Lee. 27. Francis Lewis. 28. Philip Livingston. 29. Thomas Lynch, Jr. 30. Thomas McKean. 31. Arthur Middleton. 32. Lewis Morris. 33. Robert Morris. 34. John Morton. 35. Thomas Nelson. 36. William Paca. 37. Robert Treat Paine. 38. John Penn. 39. George Read. 40. Cæsar Rodney. 41. George Ross. 42. Benjamin Rush. 43. Edward Rutledge. 44. Roger Sherman. 45. James Smith. 46. Richard Stockton. 47. Thomas Stone. 48. George Taylor. 49. Matthew Thornton. 50. George Walton. 51. William Whipple. 52. William Williams. 53. James Wilson. 54. John Witherspoon. 55. Oliver Wolcott. 56. George Wythe.

name and record. (5) John Hancock was a born leader, and at the age of thirty-nine he was elected President of the immortal Second Continental Congress. Though a rich man, he was a sincere patriot, for when it was proposed to bombard Boston, he gave a prompt and hearty assent, though it would have caused his financial ruin. He loyally declared that his private fortune should on no occasion oppose an obstacle to the liberties of his country. Of all the signatures on the Declaration, we recall Hancock's first; for he said, when he wrote his name,—he wrote with unusual distinctness,—that "George III might read it without spectacles." Hancock was Governor of Massachusetts for many years.

VIRGINIA

THE Virginia signers all came of prominent families. (1) Carter Braxton was educated at William and Mary College, and this was followed by a three years' sojourn abroad. On his return he was drawn into local politics, and for many years he was a notable figure in the history of his colony. (2) Benjamin Harrison entered public life while he was still a young man. Great Britain recognized his influence and sought to conciliate him, but his patriotism was sturdy and he was not to be bought over. In time he became Governor of Virginia, and a popular one he proved. (3) Thomas Nelson, Jr., was one of the richest men in Virginia, in those far-away days. Like Carter Braxton, he was born to wealth, and his education was completed in England. One incident of his life shows us how true a patriot he was, for when he was in command of the State militia at Yorktown it was thought that a decided advantage might be gained by bombarding his home. He at once directed the gunners to attack it, saying, "Spare no particle of my property so long as it affords comfort or shelter to the enemies of my country." In this he followed Hancock's unselfish example. The name of Lee has been an honored one in Virginia for many years. (4) Francis Lightfoot Lee was a close personal friend of Washington, and though he cared little for public life, he did not shirk its duties. For seven years he was a member of the House of Burgesses, and for four years a member of the Continental Congress. In his own home he was always the charming host, the bright and witty companion, the self-forgetting friend. His more brilliant brother, (5) Richard Henry Lee, was so gifted an orator that he was called "the Cicero of America." He was always eager for complete independence, and so it is not to be wondered at that it was this ardent patriot who was the first to propose that "these united colo-

nies are, and of right ought to be, free and independent States." This was immediately seconded by that other ardent lover of liberty, John Adams. Jefferson alludes to Lee as "eloquent, bold, and ever watchful at his post." (6) Chancellor George Wythe was a famous figure in the early history of Virginia. He was born to wealth, he was finely educated, and in time he won high distinction at the bar. But to-day he is recalled as the wise teacher of Thomas Jefferson. Both master and pupil signed the Great Document.

In thinking of the Declaration, one name always stands out like a great mountain peak, towering above all others—the name of (7) Thomas Jefferson; for it was this gifted man who drew up the document, and he did it with such skill that hardly a word of it was changed. As Richard Henry Lee was the first to make a motion suggesting independence, it would have been the usual and courteous thing to make him chairman of the committee to draw up the document. But Lee was suddenly recalled to his Virginia home, and so it seemed only fair to assign the delicate task to some other delegate from the same colony. Jefferson was no orator, but he had already earned an enviable reputation as a writer of important state documents. So to him was assigned the delicate but momentous task. How well he performed we may know from the fact that his four associates could suggest only a very few changes.

Many of the signers reached high offices in the young republic. Many became governors of the new States, and two were elevated to the Presidency, Jefferson and John Adams. One truly remarkable fact may be recalled in connection with these two, namely, that both men died on the same day; and, what was still more remarkable, they died just fifty years to a day after the united colonies were declared independent, namely, on July 4, 1826. And when they passed away there was but one signer living, the venerable Charles Carroll of Carrollton, who survived Jefferson and Adams for six years, for he lived to be ninety-six years old.

And who shall describe the actual signing of the Great Document! We can imagine these fine and courtly gentlemen going, one by one, to the broad table which may be seen to-day in Independence Hall. William Ellery, one of the Rhode Island delegates, afterward declared: "I placed myself beside the Secretary and eyed each closely as he affixed his name to the document. Undaunted resolution was displayed in every countenance." It was, indeed, the proudest moment in the lives of these fearless men who, believing in the righteousness of their cause, hazarded lives and fortunes in the great name of Liberty.

GEORGE
WASHINGTON
FATHER OF
OUR COUNTRY

BY IRVINGTON LEE

IN THE early summer of 1755, a little army of British soldiers slowly made its way through the wilderness of southwestern Pennsylvania. They were picked men from two regiments, recently sent over from England, under command of Major-General Braddock, and they had come to drive the French from their stronghold at Fort Duquesne.

The war between England and France, that was to last for seven years, had not actually been declared; but already a struggle had begun for possession of the vast region lying west of the Ohio. The French had built forts southward from the Great Lakes, had explored the Mississippi River, and claimed, by right of discovery, a region that extended eastward to Virginia. The settlers of that State, then belonging to the English crown, had been pushing westward as farmers. They soon came in conflict with the French, who sought to control the Ohio Valley, and who, with this object, had built Fort Duquesne, where the Allegheny and Monongahela rivers unite to form the Ohio. Immediately before Braddock's arrival in Virginia, the Virginian provincial troops had themselves marched against the French; but the expedition had been a failure, and England, thoroughly alarmed, had herself come to the rescue.

Braddock was confident of success. The French, to be sure, counted much on the aid of their Indian allies, with whose method of fighting he had had, of course, no experience. But he was a vain man, who looked upon the Indians as savages who could be no match for his veteran troops. As for the Virginia provincials, had they not recently suffered a defeat at the hands of the enemy? So when the Indian chiefs friendly to

Virginia came to offer their services, Braddock so offended them that they took their departure; and later, on the march, he spurned the offer of a company of rangers, versed in all the ways of Indian warfare.

SERVES ON BRADDOCK'S STAFF

But Braddock was fortunate in one respect. Close by, at Mount Vernon, was a young Virginian who, though only twenty-three, had so distinguished himself by his bravery and good judgment that he had risen to the rank of colonel. For the present, however, with no pressing need for his services, he had retired to private life. Braddock needed another aide-de-camp, and, in a moment of condescension, offered him the post. It was a post without pay; it held no chance of promotion. But danger and duty were lures enough for the young Virginian.

Thus it came about that General Braddock secured the services of George Washington, who, twenty years later, was chosen commander-in-chief in the war of the Colonies with Great Britain.

Braddock began his march overladen with baggage and equipment. The army made so little progress that at last he took Washington's advice to push forward with light artillery. Meanwhile the young aide-de-camp was stricken with a fever, and rejoined the command in a weakened condition. Now, to his dismay, he saw the soldiers advancing along a rough, narrow road through the forest, with no scouting parties thrown out to prevent a surprise attack. In vain he pleaded with the general to employ a few rangers and scouts in advance. Braddock only snubbed him.

Things had come to a pretty pass, he said, when a mere boy presumed to teach a British general how to fight.

ATTACKED FROM AMBUSH

Thus the army, within a few miles of the Fort, suddenly found itself in a hornets' nest. From the rocks and woods came a hail of bullets fired by an unseen foe. Unaccustomed to such fighting, Braddock's men stood shoulder to shoulder, as they had learned to do in Europe, and delivered volleys into the empty air. The woods resounded with the fierce yells of the Indians, who, screened by rocks and trees, were able to take a sure and deadly aim, till the road was strewn with the bodies of the British.

The French, with their Indians, were actually inferior in number, and had lain in ambush only with the hope of delaying the English advance. Had Washington's advice been taken, Fort Duquesne would have fallen almost without resistance. But now it was a case of let him save himself who could.

All through the battle, Washington rode his horse where the fight was hottest. Braddock's two English aids, Orme and Morris, had fallen early in the action, and there was none but the young Virginian to carry the general's orders. Horse and rider made a clear target for the ambushed Indians, who leveled their rifles at him again and again. That he was not even wounded seemed a miracle. Four bullets grazed his body, passing through his coat; two horses were shot under him.

HIS RECKLESS COURAGE

The artillery seemed to be the only hope. Could the guns be brought into play, grapeshot fired into the thickets might still dislodge the foe. Washington galloped down the line, only to find the regimental officer dead, and the gunners in confusion. Instantly he leaped from his horse, grasped a field-gun, and wheeled and pointed it with his own hand.

But it was too late; the men could not be made to serve the guns. The retreat became a rout, in which baggage, cannon, stores, were all abandoned. Had not the savages paused in their eagerness for plunder, the command might have been wiped out. More than seven hundred soldiers, and more than half the officers, were killed or wounded.

Braddock himself, brave to the last, had mounted his sixth horse when a bullet pierced his lungs. Now, at last, as he lay dying, he praised the bravery of the Virginians, and acknowledged his mistake. Washington himself read the funeral service; then what was left of the shattered army pursued its retreat to Fort Cumberland.

It was not the first time, nor the last, that Washington, face to face with death, was spared to serve his country as no other man could serve it. Not only did he live amid danger, but he possessed a courage that bordered on recklessness, and led him to expose himself in moments of great peril. So, as no one could fill his place in a nation that needed him sorely, some people came to believe that he bore a charmed life.

WASHINGTON'S EARLY LIFE

Washington's early life was an excellent preparation for the duties he was called upon to fulfill. A strong and sturdy boy, who liked to run, leap, wrestle, and ride, he grew into a youth able to endure fatigue and hardships. With only an elementary education, he seems to have been thoroughly schooled in drawing up business papers and keeping accounts, and to have formed habits of order and exactness, of great use to him when he came to manage the affairs of a plantation.

His father, Augustine Washington, was a landed proprietor of good English ancestry, whose second wife, Mary Ball Washington, was the mother of George. When George was born, on February 22, 1732, the Washingtons were living on their estate at Pope's Creek, near the Potomac; but soon afterward they made their home in Stafford County, on the east side of the Rappahannock, opposite Fredericksburg, and there the father died when the boy was eleven years old. About four years later, George went to live with his half-brother, Lawrence Washington, who had built himself a house on his plantation at Mount Vernon, overlooking the Potomac. It was this historic estate that, after the death of Lawrence, became the property of George Washington. Thither he brought his wife, Martha Custis Washington, whom he married in 1759; and there he continued to live when he was not serving his country as soldier and President.

He had been a serious, thoughtful boy, with a strong sense of duty, and a determination to do well whatever he undertook. He was not a ready speaker, and in later years always showed embarrassment when called upon in public to acknowledge the honors which were constantly thrust upon him, and which his modesty led him to believe were beyond his abilities and merit. But his habits of thought found expression when he came to take up his pen, and his many letters and addresses bear evidence of one who had something to say, and could say it with dignity and force.

SURVEYOR AND SOLDIER

In school he had shown a decided preference for geometry and surveying. When his studies were completed at sixteen, he showed such marked ability as a surveyor of lands that Lord Fairfax engaged him in that capacity to mark the boundaries of vast acres in the wilderness to the west. This task he discharged so well that he took up the work as his profession. For three

cult journey, delivered his message, and returned with the tidings that the French refused to go.

A Virginia force under Captain Trent then undertook to build a fort, but were driven away by the French, who completed it themselves, and named it Fort Duquesne. This looked like war in earnest; so Washington marched to Great Meadows, in the foothills of the Alleghenies, and sent out his scouts toward Fort Duquesne. Meanwhile the commander of the expedition died, and Washington, suddenly become a colonel, was forced to act on his own responsibility.

FIRES THE FIRST SHOT

Soon the scouts reported that the French were setting out from Fort Duquesne. Washington

Copyright by M. G. Abbey
From a Copley Print, copyright by Curtis & Cameron, Boston

WASHINGTON AT VALLEY FORGE

years he spent much of his life in the mountains and forests, where he learned to be self-reliant, and became well acquainted with the country and the ways of the Indians.

Virginia was now preparing to resist the further advance of the French in the Ohio Valley. The State was divided into military districts, each under an adjutant-general in command of the militia, and Washington, because of his experience, found himself at nineteen a major in the provincial army. Two years later he was sent by Governor Dinwiddie as a commissioner to visit the French commander at Leboeuf, and demand that he withdraw his forces from the region in dispute. Washington made the diffi-

was not to be taken by surprise. At the head of a few men, he discovered a party of the enemy concealed in the woods; so, seizing a musket, he himself fired the first shot. This brief engagement, in which the French were routed, seemed of small importance; yet it marked the beginning of the Seven Years' War.

Washington had built a stockade which he named Fort Necessity; here his command was presently surrounded by a much larger force of French and Indians, who fired down upon the English from the rocks and tree-tops. With little powder and less food, it was impossible to hold out; so Washington, for the first and last time, surrendered to the enemy, but on honorable terms that permitted him to withdraw without yielding up his equipment. Far from being criticized for this surrender, he and his officers were thanked by the State for their bravery.

Then came the expedition of Braddock. Three years later, Washington was again at Fort Duquesne, planting the British flag on its smoking ruins. Thenceforth it was Fort Pitt.

LIFE AT MOUNT VERNON

The war of the French and English in America soon came to a conclusion with the capture of Quebec. Now that he was no longer needed in the field, Washington gladly resigned his commission in the army, and settled down on his estates at Mount Vernon. This life of a planter was the life he enjoyed best of all. In Summer he rose at four o'clock, wrote letters, breakfasted at seven on tea and hoe-cakes, then mounted his horse, and busied himself till early afternoon, overseeing the work of the plantation. He dined at two, and was generally in bed by nine o'clock.

As good a farmer as he had proved to be a soldier, this big plantation employed his best energies. There were many accounts to keep, many details which required close attention and much labor. Washington did all this work himself, with exactness and care, and wrote many letters besides. At the same time, he kept "open house," in the hospitable Virginia fashion, and Mount Vernon was thronged with distinguished visitors. He danced the minuet, rode with the hounds, hunted ducks and other game, and enjoyed the excellent fishing afforded by the waters of the Potomac, which swarmed with shad and bass.

But he did not lead altogether the quiet life of a country gentleman. Hardly had he settled at Mount Vernon than he was elected a delegate to the Virginia House of Burgesses, and for fifteen years he continued to take part in its sessions.

CHOSEN COMMANDER-IN-CHIEF

Then came troubled times. In spite of opposition by his own people, King George III of England was determined to tax without representation, the American colonies, in order to make them share the expense of the war with France. The hateful and illegal Stamp Act was followed by other measures that provoked the Americans past endurance, and led to the outbreak of the Revolutionary War. Following the skirmishes at Lexington and Concord, the second Continental Congress assembled at Philadelphia, and George Washington, who attended it, was, to his great surprise, chosen commander-in-chief of the Continental Army.

Washington had been prepared to draw his sword once more; two years before, he had said: "If need be, I will raise a thousand men, subsist them at my own expense, and march myself at their head for the relief of Boston." But the war was in Massachusetts, and he, a Virginian, had not dreamed he would be asked to command the armies of the country. In accepting the appointment he insisted that he would take no pay whatever. And "lest some unlucky event should happen," he told them, "I beg it may be remembered by every gentleman in the room that I this day declare, with the utmost sincerity, I do not think myself equal to the command."

Washington reached Cambridge, on the outskirts of Boston, soon after the Battle of Bunker Hill. The task that faced him was tremendous. His army was raw and undisciplined. It lacked the needful weapons of war. Worst of all was the small supply of powder. Within musket-shot of twenty British regiments in Boston, he was called upon, in these circumstances, to hold his ground for six months while disbanding one army, whose term of enlistment had expired, and recruiting another. Perhaps it is not strange that his generals disagreed with him when he favored an early assault on the city.

BRITISH DRIVEN FROM BOSTON

But Washington never delayed when his mind was once made up. Congress at last empowered him to proceed as he saw fit; so, as the British held Charlestown on the north, he planned to occupy Dorchester Heights, which commanded the city from the south. This he did, under cover of the night, on March 4, 1776; and less than two weeks later the British army under General Howe was compelled to leave Boston, board the fleet in the harbor, and sail away.

It now became plain that the Colonies were engaged not merely in a war for their rights, but in a struggle to establish themselves as an independent nation. The Declaration of Independence was adopted on July 4, and Washington found his hand greatly strengthened. But the British now had thirty thousand men in the neighborhood of New York, while the American army opposing them was inferior in numbers and equipment. In the battle of 'Long Island, on August 27, the Americans suffered a severe defeat; only the skill of Washington saved them from utter destruction. For forty-eight hours he was in the saddle, using all his energies and resources to transfer the broken army from the Long Island shore, across the swift waters of the East River, to New York. Despite many dangers and difficulties, this remarkable feat was safely accomplished. It was carried out in darkness and a driving rain, and the British did not discover

Lee, also on the Hudson, and to retreat through New Jersey with the remnants of his ragged army. It was a masterly retreat. General Charles Lee, whom he had counted upon, proved treacherous. New Jersey swarmed with the British, and Cornwallis was close upon his heels. So confident were the British officers, that they be-

Photos by Doubleday, Page & Co.

WASHINGTON'S HOME AT MT. VERNON

INSET: REAR OF THE HOUSE

what had been going on till they found the intrenchments deserted.

The British now crossed the water to Manhattan, and a struggle followed, with varying success, for the possession of New York and the control of the Hudson River. Howe was defeated at Harlem Heights, but held his own at White Plains, and captured Fort Washington because the American general's orders were disobeyed.

VICTORIES IN NEW JERSEY

Washington, who had feared for the safety of Philadelphia, was now obliged to abandon Fort

lieved the war was almost over. Even to Washington the end seemed in sight; but it was in the hour of defeat that he best showed his greatness and strength.

On December 8 he crossed the Delaware into Pennsylvania. The British could not follow him for lack of boats, which the Americans had destroyed or hidden; but when the river froze they could march into Philadelphia. Washington did not wait for that. On Christmas night he recrossed the Delaware with 2,400 men, marched nine miles in a thick snow-storm, and fell upon the Hessian garrison at Trenton, taking a thousand prisoners. A week later, when Cornwallis marched from Princeton to crush him, Washington outgeneraled him, and broke the British rear.

A MILITARY GENIUS

He had proved himself a military genius. For his feat at Trenton, Congress gave him the powers of a dictator. Frederick the Great pronounced his victories on the Delaware "the most brilliant achievements recorded in military annals." Yet there were dark days ahead, and the darkest of these was Valley Forge.

It was there, in 1778, that Washington went into winter quarters; it was there that the patriot army starved and froze, staining the snow with bloody footprints. Then came the news that France had agreed to help us.

As late as 1780, things were going badly for the Colonies. Then it was once more Washington to the rescue. In the Summer of 1781, Cornwallis, campaigning in the South, commanded an army at Yorktown. The French fleet sailed to the coast of Virginia, and Washington swiftly moved from the Hudson to Chesapeake Bay. In the Capitol at Washington is a famous painting by Trumbull. It depicts the surrender of Lord Cornwallis to General George Washington, commander-in-chief. The war was virtually over.

FATHER OF HIS COUNTRY

Washington resigned from his command in December, 1783, and went to spend Christmas at Mount Vernon. The army was so proud of him, and so disgusted with its shabby treatment by the Government, that it offered to make him king. This offer he sternly rebuked. But when he was sought out in his retirement at Mount Vernon, he consented to be President; and, with James Madison and Alexander Hamilton, he was foremost in rescuing the Colonies from chaos, and uniting them securely under our republican form of government. It is to him, more than to any other man, that the nation owes its very existence.

When the news of his death reached England, the British fleet lowered its flags half-mast; France, under Bonaparte as First Consul, draped its banners with crêpe. The American Congress wore mourning through its session, to honor the memory of him declared by one of his generals to be "first in war, first in peace, and first in the hearts of his countrymen."

PRIVATIONS AT VALLEY FORGE

BY GEORGE WASHINGTON

SINCE the month of July we have had no assistance from the quartermaster-general, and to want of assistance from this department the commissary-general charges great part of his deficiency. To this I am to add, that, notwithstanding it is a standing order, and often repeated, that the troops shall always have two days' provisions by them, that they might be ready at any sudden call; yet an opportunity has scarcely ever offered, of taking advantage of the enemy, that has not been either totally obstructed, or greatly impeded on this account. And this, the great and crying evil, is not all. The soap, vinegar, and other articles allowed by Congress, we see none of, nor have we seen them, I believe, since the battle of Brandywine. The first, indeed, we have now little occasion for; few men having more than one shirt, many only the moiety of one, and some none at all.

In addition to which, as a proof of the little benefit received from a clothier-general, and as a further proof of the inability of an army under the circumstances of this, to perform the common duties of soldiers (besides a number of men confined to hospitals for want of shoes, and others in farmers' houses on the same account), we have, by a field return this day made, no less than two thousand eight hundred and ninety-eight men now in camp unfit for duty, because they are barefoot and otherwise naked.

By the same return it appears that our whole strength in Continental troops, including the eastern brigades, which have joined us since the surrender of General Burgoyne, exclusive of the Maryland troops sent to Wilmington, amounts to no more than eight thousand two hundred in camp fit for duty; notwithstanding which, and that since the 4th instant, our numbers fit for duty, from the hardships and exposures they have undergone, particularly on account of blankets (numbers having been obliged, and still are, to sit up all night by fires, instead of taking comfortable rest in a natural and common way), have decreased near two thousand men.

WASHINGTON TAKING THE OATH OF OFFICE AS FIRST PRESIDENT OF THE UNITED STATES OF AMERICA

City of New York, April 6, 1789

We find, gentlemen, without knowing whether the army was really going into winter-quarters or not (for I am sure no resolution of mine would warrant the remonstrance), reprobating the measure as much as if they thought the soldiers were made of stocks or stones, and equally insensible of frost and snow; and moreover, as if they conceived it easily practicable for an inferior army, under the disadvantages I have described ours to be, which are by no means exaggerated, to confine a superior one, in all respects well appointed and provided for a winter's campaign, within the city of Philadelphia, and to cover from depredation and waste the States of Pennsylvania and Jersey. But what makes this matter still more extraordinary in my eye is that these very gentlemen—who were well apprised of the nakedness of the troops from ocular demonstration, who thought their own soldiers worse clad than others, and who advised me near a month ago to postpone the execution of a plan I was about to adopt, in consequence of a resolve of Congress for seizing clothes, under strong assurances that an ample supply would be collected in ten days agreeably to a decree of the State (not one article of which, by the by, is yet come to hand) —should think a winter's campaign, and the covering of these States from the invasion of an enemy, so easy and practicable a business. I can assure those gentlemen, that it is a much easier and less distressing thing to draw remonstrances in a comfortable room by a good fireside, than to occupy a cold bleak hill, and sleep under frost and snow, without clothes or blankets. However, although they seem to have little feeling for the naked and distressed soldiers, I feel superabundantly for them, and from my soul I pity those miseries which it is neither in my power to relieve nor prevent.

BENJAMIN FRANKLIN *

BY ELBRIDGE S. BROOKS

Two hundred years ago nobody knew how to catch the lightning, and everybody stood in great dread of it. Now we know how to catch it and carry it away from our houses, and we also know how to make it run along wires and carry messages from one friend to another so fast that, if you were a thousand miles away, your friend, if he were at the end of the wire, would be receiving the message while you were at the other end sending it.

We have also learned how to make it carry the human voice for thousands of miles, so that if you were in New York you might step up to a little box, called the telephone, and talk into it, and your mother, father, or friend could hear your words plainly in Chicago, nearly a thousand miles away. It would pass so quickly that you and they could talk back and forth almost as easy and quickly as if you were in the same room. We also make this wonderful force pull our street-cars through our great cities, thus setting free the horses that used to have to do it. We also make it light our streets and houses, and we call it electricity.

Is this not a very strange and a very wonderful power? And would you not like to hear the story of the great man who first caught from the skies this vivid, flashing lightning, and found out that he could harness it, almost as easily as we can harness a horse, and make the very thing which people had always dreaded as a terrible destroyer, the best friend and servant of man? Did you say you would like to hear his story? I will tell it to you. His name was Benjamin Franklin.

A very long time ago, perhaps about four hundred years, there lived in Northamptonshire, England, a poor blacksmith whose name was Franklin. In that country at that time, the oldest son always followed the same trade or work which his father followed. So the oldest son in the Franklin family always became a blacksmith, and he always got the property which belonged to his father when the father died. The other children had to get out and shift for themselves. The youngest son in one of the large Franklin families was named Josiah. He could not be a blacksmith, as his older brother took up that business and inherited his father's shop. So Josiah went out and gave himself to a man who made soap and tallow candles, and agreed to serve him, without any pay except his board and clothes, until he was twenty-one years of age.

All this he did that he might learn the trade of a soap-boiler and candle-maker. When he was twenty-one his employer gave him, as was the custom, a new suit of clothes, a few dollars

* From "True Stories of Great Americans," by Elbridge S. Brooks; used by permission of John C. Winston Co., publishers, Philadelphia.

for his personal use, and a letter saying that he had learned his trade well. With that letter to show, young Josiah was able to go and hire himself to work where he could get pay for his labor. The hired man nearly always lived in his employer's family, and received his board and a few dollars per month.

After a little while, Josiah was married and continued to live in England and work at his trade until his wages were hardly sufficient to support himself, his wife, and three children on the coarsest kind of food. He did, however, save up, in his earlier years, a little money, and the stories of the New World—America—kept coming to his ears. He heard that there were few candlemakers and soap-boilers in America, and that a young man who understood his trade would have a much better chance here than in England; so in the year 1682 he took his wife and three children, and such clothing, bedding, and household things as they could bring, on board a big sailing vessel and came to America. He landed in Boston, and soon set himself up as a soap and candle maker. He found it much easier to support his family here than in the old country, and he became very much in love with his new home.

In the year 1706, twenty-four years after Josiah Franklin and his wife and three children came to America, a little baby boy was born. Like his father, he proved to be the last child in the family, and his father named him Benjamin. You remember Jacob's youngest son was named Benjamin. But Ben Franklin had sixteen brothers and sisters older than himself.

Benjamin was a good boy, and his father loved him very much. The little fellow learned to read when he was very young, but he was sent to school only for two years, and then he was taken away, when he was only ten years of age, to work in his father's candle-shop. His business was to cut wicks for the candles, fill the moulds with the melted tallow, tend the shop and run the errands. But "Ben," as he was called, did not like this business. He would very much rather look in picture books and read the easy stories. He always loved to go down to the water's edge, and he often did an errand very quickly, running all the way to save some time, that he might jump in a boat or go swimming with the boys.

Ben did not get over his desire to go to sea. He did not dare to ask permission, but he was always talking about what the sailors said, and using words which showed he had learned the different sails and much about ships. So his father grew afraid that his son would run away and go to sea as one of his other sons had already done. One day after Ben had been in the tallow-candle shop for two years—and was now ten years old—his father began to talk with him about other trades. He took him frequently to walk and they would stop to look at different kinds of workmen, such as bricklayers, carpenters, iron-workers, and many others. He hoped the boy would like some of these better than the life of a sailor, but Benjamin did not care for any of them.

CHOOSING A VOCATION

By this time he had, however, grown very fond of reading. He pored over his father's dull books and sold little things of his own to buy more. Often he would trade his old books at the second-hand book-stores for others he had not read. So Mr. Franklin, seeing he was so fond of reading books, thought it was best to make a printer of him. His oldest son, James Franklin, already had a printing office and press. Benjamin said he would like this trade, so he was apprenticed to his brother to learn it.

When we say Ben was "apprenticed" we mean he was given to his brother to have as his own until he should be twenty-one years old. He was to work for his brother without any pay, except his board and clothing. As Benjamin was then about eleven years old, he would have to serve his brother for ten years to learn his trade. Benjamin liked this trade very much. He got to see many new books and could always borrow all he wanted, and used to sit up sometimes all night to read a book so he could return it, unsoiled, to the store in the morning.

The boy took a great fancy to poetry, and at odd moments wrote some verses himself. When he had quite a lot, he showed it to his brother James. Certainly it was, as Franklin afterward called it, "wretched stuff," but James printed it and sent Ben around Boston to peddle it. He was doing this with much pride when his father laughed at him and made fun of his poetry, and told him he would always be a beggar if he wrote verses for a living. He stopped short his writing and peddling poetry. But he was bound to write, for he loved to do it, and I will tell you how he played a nice trick off on his brother:

James Franklin published a little newspaper. It was Ben's duty after the paper was printed to carry loads of them around and deliver them to the subscribers. The boy read this paper, and he thought he could write as well as many whose articles were published in it. But he would not dare to ask his brother James to let him write, nor would he let anyone know what he wrote. His father would be sure to make fun, as he did of his poetry, if he saw it. So he wrote almost every week and slipped his pieces under the office door after it was closed. James printed them, and his father read them, but they did not dream that Ben wrote them.

BUYING BOOKS

Now I will tell you of a way he saved money to buy books. Remember he got no wages for his work, but he always had money. A boy is not of much account if he does not have money. When you see a boy always going around without a cent, it is a pretty good sign he will never save anything. Benjamin had got the notion that it was wrong to eat meat. Now his brother paid his board, you know. So the boy told his brother that if he would give him half what his board cost he would board himself. As that would save James something, he agreed. Benjamin quit eating meat and lived on bread and other cheap foods. Thus he saved money to buy books, and by eating only a bit of bread and a tart for dinner he had half an hour every day to devote to reading, while the others were eating heavy dinners; and this is the way he educated himself. Would you think it strange if I told you that Benjamin did not like his brother James? It is a fact, he did not. They often quarreled, for James did not treat his little brother right and sometimes gave him beatings. I will tell you how he got free from him.

One day James printed something in his paper which made the Governor of the Colony mad. They arrested him and put him in jail for a whole month. Benjamin published the paper while his brother was in prison, and he said some very ugly things about the government, but was careful not to say anything for which they could get him in prison. This pleased James very much. But when they let him out of prison they forbade his publishing the paper any longer. Now what was James to do? He was a shrewd business man, so he said to Benjamin that he would set him free and run the paper in his name. So they destroyed the papers that bound the boy in law. Ben, however, said he would remain with his brother until he was twenty-one years old. This agreement was made, and so it started, but soon James tried to impose on Ben as he had done before; but as Ben was no longer bound to him, he left him. Ben afterward said that he did not do fairly in this, and he was sorry for it, though it was, perhaps, nothing more than James deserved.

Benjamin now tried to hire himself to other printers; but none of them would take him because he had broken his contract with his brother. Besides, they had all agreed together that when one of their apprentices left, none of the others should hire him.

What was he to do? He was only seventeen years old, but he was not to be discouraged. Gathering a few of his books, he went aboard a sloop setting sail for New York. In that city he tried for days, but could get no work. Some one told him to try Philadelphia. It was a tedious and dangerous journey as it must be made by water. There were no railroads then. He took a sail-boat to Amboy, New Jersey. A storm came up and the boat was driven ashore, and the poor frightened boy lay all night in the little hold of the boat with the waves dashing over it, and the water, leaking through, soaked him to the skin. It took him thirty-two hours to get to Amboy, and all that time he had neither a drink of water nor a bite to eat.

Having very little money he set out on foot and walked to Burlington. Here he was met by trouble he had not looked for. His ragged clothes, wet and soiled, made him look like what we now call a tramp; but there were no tramps in those days. They thought he was a runaway, and came very near putting him in jail, and he says he was then sorry he had not remained in Boston with his brother James.

IN PHILADELPHIA

But it was now too late to go back, so he found a man with a row-boat at Burlington who was going to Philadelphia, and Franklin agreed to go with him and help him row the boat to pay his passage. They arrived at Philadelphia in the night, but as there were then no street lamps in the city, they passed by without knowing it. At length they went ashore and made a fire to dry themselves, and waited until morning and rowed to the city.

Poor Benjamin Franklin, all soiled, tired and very hungry, started up the street to find something to eat. He had no trunk or valise for his extra clothing, so he stuffed his extra stockings and shirt in his pockets. He soon found a baker shop and asked for biscuits as he used to buy in Boston. The baker did not know what they were. They did not make biscuits in Philadelphia. So Franklin asked him to give him threepenny worth of bread of any kind, as he was very hungry. The baker gave him three loaves, and putting one under each arm, he chewed vigorously on the other as he walked along.

And as he passed along a pretty girl named Doborah Read looked out of the door, and he saw her laughing "fit to kill," and making all manner of fun of him. His pride was stung, but he was too hungry and helpless to do anything then. Many years afterward, he married this very girl, and she was very fortunate and proud to get him.

Franklin soon found a place to work with a printer named Keimer, and he very quickly showed that he was quite different from other workmen and boys about the place. He knew all about printing, so he was a valuable workman, and he had read and knew so much in books that those who knew him liked to hear him talk, and they used to refer to him to settle disputes on all sorts of questions. Instead of spending his evenings at the tavern drinking or gossiping, as other young men did, he went to his room and read good books or went in the company of those of whom he could learn something. Such young men as these always attract the attention of others.

One day Mr. Keimer, the printer, looked out and saw two finely dressed gentlemen coming to his place. He went out to meet them and found it was no other than Sir William Keith, the governor of Pennsylvania, and one of his friends. They had on silver knee-buckles and powdered wigs and ruffled shirts and gay-colored coats and silk stockings. Such fine people had never visited his shop before, and Keimer was much pleased, thinking what an honor it was to him, and, perhaps, he thought they might give him a big bill of printing to do. How great must have been his disappointment when the governor asked to see a young man by the name of Benjamin Franklin.

Franklin came out with his sleeves rolled up and wearing leather breeches—such as nearly all workmen wore in those days. He was quite surprised that the governor should visit him, but was not ashamed to be an honest workman, and without ceremony he walked away between the two fine gentlemen to the tavern. Now what do you suppose the fine governor wanted with this common young printer in his leather breeches? He told him that he wanted him to start a printing office of his own, as none of the other men of the city were first-class workmen. Franklin was very proud of the governor's good opinion, but told him that he could not think of starting

for himself as he was too poor to buy a press and types of his own, and he did not think his father would help him. The governor wrote a letter to Franklin's father urging him to help his son, and sent Franklin to Boston, dressed up nicely, wearing a watch, and with money in his pocket, to carry the letter. His parents were delighted to see him looking so large and strong and so much improved in every way. But when he showed the governor's letter, asking his father's aid in buying a press, he was told by the old gentleman that he was too young to go into business for himself.

Franklin returned to Philadelphia with a heavy heart and reported to the governor what had happened. The governor seemed very much disappointed, and told Franklin that, if he would go to England to buy the presses and types, he would start him in business for himself. Benjamin agreed to do this, and at the appointed time called on the governor to get the letters of introduction and credit which the governor said he would give him so he could buy whatever he wanted. They were not ready, but the governor told him he would send them to the ship with other mail and he would get them before landing in England.

So Franklin went aboard the vessel and for many days had a delightful sail across the Atlantic Ocean. Just before they came to land, the mail-bags were opened, but what was his amazement to find that there was no letter from the governor for him. They searched carefully all through the letters sent by the governor to make sure, but there was not a word for or about Franklin or the printing press and types he was to buy.

Here he was, a poor young man with no money and no friends, several thousand miles from home. It would take about six weeks to write to the governor and hear from him. He thought it over and wondered if the governor had forgotten it or just treated him meanly. A man on the ship told him that the governor did many strange things, that he had no credit abroad, and could not have bought a printing press for himself, and that was the reason he had sent no letter of credit. Then Franklin made one of his wise sayings, "Fine clothes do not make a fine gentleman," which we still often hear repeated.

IN LONDON

But Franklin had learned to depend on himself and knew his printer's trade well, and he at once got a position to set type in London, where he learned many things that he did not know before. One was to engrave pictures and handsome letters on metal. Another was to make printer's ink, and yet another how to cast type or letters. This was all very useful to him in after years.

We have told you that Franklin would eat no meat. He also refused to drink wine or any intoxicating drink. Now, all of the English printers and laborers drank a great deal of beer, and when lunch-time came, and Franklin sat down with his cup of milk or water, they laughed at him, and told him that water would make him weak, and he would be of no account if he did not drink beer or whisky, or something, and eat meat to make him strong.

Franklin told them that was a mistake, and, to prove it, he lifted heavy weights and showed himself stronger than any man in the shop. One holiday in the Summer they went out for a swim in the River Thames, and Franklin could swim farther and faster than any of them. They also thought as he had come from the "wild new world," he did not know much, but after they had talked to him a bit they found out he had read more books than any of them, and instead of going out at nights he spent his time reading. There was a man near by who kept a second-hand book store, and Franklin used to pay him so much a week to let him take out books and read them.

By and by he found he had saved enough money to return to America, so he came back and got a position as a clerk in a store, but his employer died and he went back to work at the printer's trade. He hired himself to his old master, Keimer, and proved himself very useful in engraving plates to print a new paper money which was then being used in the Colony.

IN BUSINESS FOR HIMSELF

After a while Franklin bought a press and started a printing house of his own. He had to go greatly in debt for it, but by very hard work he believed he could pay the debt. He used to get up in the mornings when other men were asleep and go to work, and he was in his office at night after others were in bed. If he had not been a very strong and robust man, this would have made him sick. Perhaps he stood it better because he lived on nothing but milk and bread, and drank no intoxicating drinks. He did everything about his printing office. He made a wise saying: "If you want a thing done well, do it yourself." So when he wanted paper, he took a

wheelbarrow and went over to the paper house, bought what he wanted, and wheeled it home himself.

He soon started a little newspaper, and he had read so much that he was able to write for himself almost everything he printed in it. He also set a large portion of the type; and for a long time worked his printing press with his own hands, for there were no steam presses in those days. People saw how industrious he was, and, as he was the best printer in Philadelphia, he soon had more work than he could do, working early and late.

A PARTNER

Now, I will tell you an interesting thing that happened. You remember I told you about the girl who laughed at him, when he, with his pockets stuffed full of socks and shirt, walked up the streets several years before, eating a loaf of bread and carrying two others under his arms. Well, when Franklin was away in England, this pretty young lady, whom he always liked very much, got married, and when he came home he was sorry to hear it, for he had always hoped that he might become able to take a wife himself, and, if he should, she was the one he meant to ask to marry him. Some time after Franklin came home, the husband of his old-time sweetheart died.

Franklin waited until she took off her mourning, and he had gotten himself well started in his own shop, then he went over and told her what he had always intended to do, and said if she was willing to marry him now, he believed he could make a good living for the two in his own business, but, of course, they would have to live poor at first. He also told her that he was thinking of starting a little book store in front of his printing office, and if she would marry him, she could be his clerk in the book store.

She readily consented, for she had always liked Franklin. So they were married and the young couple set to work to pay off the debts for the printing office. They had no servant and they lived on very plain food. Franklin still ate for his breakfast only plain bread and milk out of a plain earthen dish, with a pewter spoon. His wife attended the store, sold books and stationery, and, long before they expected to be so, they were out of debt and beginning to grow rich.

If you had gone into a house in those days you would have found very few books, but in every home you would have found something which people read very little nowadays, namely,

AMERICAN REVOLUTIONARY STATESMEN.

an almanac. It told the people about the weather, the days of the month and the weeks, put in a lot of recipes for cooking and all sorts of household remedies. In addition to this, it had wise sayings and choice bits of reading. So you see the almanac was a calendar, a cookbook, a doctor book and a reading book. Franklin concluded to print an almanac. He called it "Poor Richard's Almanac," and it is noted to-day for its wise sayings. Franklin signed the wise sayings, "Richard Saunders," and that is why it is called "Poor Richard's Almanac"; but everybody knew Benjamin Franklin wrote it.

By this time Franklin was one of the most learned men in the Colony, for, although he had never been to school since he was ten years old, he had, by studying at odd times, learned to speak and write several languages. One of the great needs of the people, he said, was an opportunity to read good books. There were very few books in the country and they were mostly in the libraries of rich people in their homes. So Franklin started a public library in Philadelphia. It was the first one started in this country, and he encouraged all the working people to spend their evenings and holidays at the library reading.

About this time there was a great deal of talk about a strange influence called electricity, and wise men of Europe wrote much about it. Franklin read everything they wrote. Nobody knew what it was. Some of the wise men from the Old World came over to Philadelphia and lectured, and Franklin told them he believed that electricity was nothing more than the same power which caused the lightning and the thunder in the skies. They laughed at him, of course, so he determined to try and find out if it was not the same. How do you suppose he did it? I will tell you.

Franklin noticed that the electricity in the batteries of machines which these men used, if applied to a hemp string, would make the short ends of the hemp stand up straight like the hair on a cat's tail when the cat is mad or excited. He also noticed, when he touched the battery, he felt a shock from the electricity. "Now," he said, "if the lightning from the clouds is electricity, it will also make the ends of the hemp string stand up, and if I could only get it to come to me, through a piece of metal, I would feel the shock as I did from the electric battery."

ELECTRICAL EXPERIMENTS

The serious question was how he could get the hemp string up to the clouds. After a while he remembered that when he was a boy, he had often made a kite fly up as high as the clouds. So he took a silk handkerchief, made himself a kite and tied a long hemp string to it and put a steel point at the end of the kite, for he had found out that steel would attract electricity. On the other end of the hemp string, down close to his hand, he tied a metal key, and then from the key he tied a silk string which he held in his hand. They had found that electricity would not go through a silk string, and he reasoned that, if there was electricity in the clouds, it would be caught on the metal point of the kite and pass down the hemp string to the metal key, but would not pass down the silk string to his hand, as silk does not conduct electricity.

He was afraid if he should fly his kite in the daytime a great crowd would gather around him, and, if his experiment should not prove successful, they would laugh at him; so one night when there was a wind and a thunderstorm, he went out all alone and sent his kite up. When it was way up among the clouds, and the thunder was pealing and the lightning was flashing, he saw the hemp on his string stand up on ends. Then he reached his finger to the key and received a shock just as he felt it in an electric battery. *He had proved that lightning is due to electricity, and he had found how to catch it.*

The learned men of the Old World were astonished that a man who had never been to school since he was ten years of age had beaten them all so far in this mysterious and strange discovery. They said he was a philosopher, and called him "Doctor Franklin." Many people, however, only laughed at the story. Some of Franklin's friends said to him: "Now that you have discovered it, of what use is it?" Franklin answered simply: "Of what use is a child? It may become a man." He meant to teach them that a discovery of any truth is a very important matter, and that all knowledge may be turned to good use.

Franklin then set to work and invented the lightning rod, which is, as we have said, a steel point placed on a house to catch the lightning and run it down a metal rod into the ground, just as the steel point on Franklin's kite caught the electricity from the clouds and ran it down the hemp string.

Franklin was now a great man, and the Americans were very proud of him. So they sent him on a journey to London in the interest of the people. Dr. Franklin was now reminded of a proverb of Solomon which his father used to repeat when he was a boy: "Seest thou a man diligent in his business? He shall stand before

BENJAMIN FRANKLIN

kings." He was now going to stand before the "Privy Council" of the King of England; and what do you suppose he was going for? I will tell you.

When Pennsylvania was settled, William Penn was made the governor, and a large amount of land was given him by the king for his father's faithful services. When William Penn died, his sons inherited this large amount of land, and they claimed that they should not pay any taxes on it and refused to do so. The people thought they ought to pay like others, and so did Franklin, hence he was sent to London to plead the cause of the people against the sons of William Penn. The result was the king made them pay taxes like everybody else, and Franklin came home more honored than ever. He had stood before the king and gained a great cause for the people. Seven years after this the English people undertook a very great injustice to the American Colonies. Always before this, when the king wanted money from the colonists, he had asked for it by his Privy Council and they had sent it freely. During the French and Indian War against England, the colonists had given so freely that the king said they had sent too much, and he made England pay back two hundred thousand dollars a year for several years. Now, in 1763 there was a man by the name of George Grenville made prime minister of England, and he was Lord of the Treasury. Without asking the king he decided to tax the Colonies in America, and to do it he had stamps made which he said should be put on all legal documents of whatever kind, and the people who used them would have to pay for these stamps.

The people said they would give money when the king wanted it and asked for it, as they had always done; but as they had no representative in Parliament to plead for them, and as Parliament never had taxed them, they would not now submit to being taxed in this way.

So the colonists from all over the country sent Dr. Franklin to England again, and he showed them how unjust it would be to make his country buy these stamps. He told them that the people of America would give money when the king asked for it. He showed them how liberal they had always been in giving more than was required. He told them the stamps on the papers would look like compulsion, and, while they could persuade the American people to do anything, they were too liberty-loving to be forced to do an unjust thing.

But Mr. Grenville also persuaded Parliament to pass the law putting a special tax on tea and other articles as well as requiring stamps on legal papers. That meant the people of America had to pay England for the privilege of buying goods. This made the Americans very angry and they would not buy the goods. But a few people did buy them, and that made the true patriots very angry. So one day when a ship loaded with tea came into Boston Harbor, with the hated tax imposed on it, some people went aboard and threw it into the sea.

A few months later, the mean Mr. Grenville was removed from the office of prime minister, and, through Dr. Franklin's influence, Parliament repealed the unjust taxes.

But, in spite of Dr. Franklin's efforts and popularity, other unjust laws were made and kept in force, and the quarrel already started grew worse and worse. The people saw England had no love for them, and was only holding them to help support the English king and rich people. This made them hate the mother country. Patrick Henry, the fiery orator, had made a great speech in Virginia, and urged the colonists to go to war rather than submit. This speech had been printed and gone all over the country, and fired the people against their oppressors. Meantime, England sent warships to America to frighten the people into submission. So Dr. Franklin, after ten years' hard work to keep peace, left England in April, 1775. When he landed, on May 6th, he found that the battle of Lexington had been fought, and the war was really begun.

As soon as he reached Philadelphia, he again tried to do what he could to bring about peace, for he feared our small nation of about three millions of people—not so many in all the country as there are now in the city of Greater New York—would be almost destroyed if they tried to fight against the great kingdom of England with her many trained soldiers and great warships.

But finding that England would not do right, he determined, with Patrick Henry, Thomas Jefferson, John Adams, and other great men, that it was better to die as a free man than to live in such slavery as England wanted to put upon us. He was elected a delegate to the Continental Congress, where the greatest men came from all the Colonies; and he helped make, and signed the Declaration of Independence.

He next went to work to get up soldiers—but he was a statesman instead of a soldier, and General Washington asked him to go to Canada and see if the Colonies there would not join us in our war, and make England set them free also. Franklin went and tried hard to induce them, but finally had to give it up and come home. He

"AT A BRILLIANT FÊTE GIVEN IN FRANKLIN'S HONOR, HE WAS CROWNED WITH LAUREL"

was made postmaster-general of the United Colonies.

When the war had been going on two years, everybody saw we must have help, or we should be beaten, our country would be ruined, and all our great men would be hung or shot as traitors to the English Government. France had been secretly helping us for some time.

The colonists, knowing that Dr. Franklin could speak French, having learned it by studying at odd times while a young man, and also that he was the wisest and most popular man in the country, decided to send him to the Court of France, to beg them to help us.

AT THE COURT OF FRANCE

Thus Franklin again stood before a king. He was now a venerable man, seventy years of age, but full of vigor and full of life and one of the shrewdest men who ever went abroad for his country. The people of Paris—the gayest city and the proudest Court in the world—were charmed with his wise sayings, his simple ways and his quaint manners, for he pretended to be only a poor colonist, although he was famous all over Europe for his wise statesmanship, his learning in books, his discoveries and inventions.

Franklin soon won over the French people to the American side. They wanted to help us very much. But then the government did not want to do anything for fear of England.

But after about a year of sleepless nights and thoughtful days, Franklin won the government over too. It was a glorious day for him, when the treaty was made and sixteen big warships and four thousand French soldiers sailed out from France to help us fight.

Besides this, Franklin could now buy more vessels, and as you will read in the life of Paul Jones in this book, he fitted him out with ships after the loss of his own vessel. Do you not remember the fearful fight between the "Bonhomme Richard" and the "Serapis"? The "Bonhomme Richard" was Paul Jones' ship, and it was gotten for him in France with Franklin's aid. "Bon Homme Richard" is French, and it means "*Good man Richard.*" It was so named in honor of Franklin's "Poor Richard's Almanac," which Jones read and found full of good advice. It is believed that this treaty with France and the aid the French people gave us are what saved our country from defeat. If so, is not Franklin almost, or quite, as great as George Washington?

Dr. Franklin remained in France during the whole of the war and kept her sending us help, and when General Cornwallis surrendered to General Washington, he helped to make the treaty of peace with England, signing them both—for there was first a treaty and afterward a final one—in Paris. He then made a treaty with Prussia which was of great benefit to our country.

After all these great deeds and many smaller ones, which it would fill a book to tell, he prepared to leave France, where he had been for more than ten years. He was over eighty years of age and beginning to suffer with gout. So the Queen of France had him carried to the sea in her private easy chair, hung with silk curtains and lined with fine cushions and borne by two mules, one walking in front and the other behind. When Doctor Franklin reached home, everybody, from the highest to the lowest, joined in his praises, and all those near enough went to see him. He was, next to Washington, the most honored man in the country. But would you not think they would let the dear old man rest the balance of his life? Certainly, if he so desired, but they thought he ought to be the president of Pennsylvania for them, anyhow for a while, and he served them in that office three years.

Then all the free Colonies sent their great men together to name the new country and make a Constitution for it. Franklin was among them, and he told them that God had given the victory, and they must open the meeting every day with prayer, "because," he said, "if a sparrow cannot fall to the ground without His notice, an empire cannot rise up without His aid." So they did as he advised. The new country was named the "United States of America," and its Constitution, declaring all men to be born free and equal, was made and adopted. George Washington was made President in 1789, and Franklin said it was the proudest day of his life when he saw him in office and this great country free, united, and under its own ruler. He had now but a short time to live, and though eighty-three years of age, he said he thought he ought to advise our people to free the negro slaves. Our Constitution said all men were born free and equal, and if that were true we should not keep our fellow-man in slavery. So he became president of a society which undertook to persuade Congress to free the negroes, and signed a long letter called a memorial, begging Congress to buy the slaves from their owners, and set all the black people free.

On April 17, 1790, Benjamin Franklin died in Philadelphia, at the ripe old age of eighty-four years and three months. All the nation went into mourning for the good and great man.

LAFAYETTE, FRIEND OF AMERICA

BY JOSEPH LEWIS FRENCH

A PART of the great debt we owed to France for the timely help that saved American freedom in our war of the Revolution was repaid in the Great War. But the debt we owe to the great Marquis de Lafayette can never be repaid. Lafayette, a young nobleman of wealth, seemed to be inspired to help us—a sort of heaven-sent messenger—not only by his own personal services, but by the great influence he exercised upon his countrymen.

There is a life-size statue of the young Lafayette as he looked at the time in Union Square, in the heart of New York City, and on its base are these words: "When I heard the cry of American freedom my heart was stirred." It seemed as if this descendant of an ancient nobility had not only a great heart but a great vision; as if he could see the marvelous future of the American people, and the realization of the democratic ideals they stood for. France was not long after to attempt the same sort of struggle against a tyrannous government; and here again, as we shall see, Lafayette played his part. He was a born leader of mankind, and one of the great figures of his time. His greatest monument, however, is in the undying reverence and love of the American nation so long as it shall endure.

He was born in a rugged old castle in the mountains of Auvergne, in the south of France, which is now over six hundred years old, and has always borne his family name—a fitting birthplace for a hero. His family records can be traced back one thousand years. It was a race of warriors for countless generations in direct line, numbering great generals and marshals of France—the glory of the realm. It was a Lafayette who turned the tide of battle against the ever-aggressive English in 1421, and forced them finally to resign all hope of the complete conquest of France.

The story of the lives of these Lafayettes reads like great legends and romances. They stretch in a direct line of notable warriors clear back to the Crusades. On his mother's side, also, he came of distinguished military stock. But his people were noted for more than this. For centuries the family of the Lafayettes "had been renowned throughout the region of their Auvergne estates for lofty character and a kindly attitude toward their humble peasant neighbors." They were true gentlefolk as well as great fighters. Was it any wonder that such an ancestry produced such a man as Lafayette?

He was born on September 6, 1757, and his eyes opened on a home stricken with sorrow, his father having been killed at the battle of Min-

LAFAYETTE

den only a few months before, at the age of twenty-five. He was at first delicate, but even as a boy he began to show signs of that great strength of natural constitution which sustained him through the severest trials all his long life. He was brought up at home by a loving group of women, his mother, grandmother and two aunts, whose memory he kept tenderly to the day of his death. As a boy of eleven he was sent to school in Paris. He had wealth, and he bore a great name. Any career was open to him, but he chose to be a soldier. It seemed inevitable.

HIS WIFE A DEVOTED PARTNER

About that time he was married to a daughter of one of the wealthiest and most influential families of the ancient nobility. Born aristocrat though his wife was, she became his devoted partner in all the ideals he afterward developed. His marriage to her when he was scarcely seventeen was a ceremony of princely splendor. We shall see how Lafayette threw all these things aside and devoted his life and his great wealth to the cause of the people. A relative, even at this early period, testifies that he had "a spirit the most active, a character the most firm, a soul the most burning with passionate fervor." The nobility were living in a dream at the time, and Lafayette saw this, and knew what the end would be. He, almost alone of the old régime, rose out of their ashes. But France, dying as she was, was to play a great part in helping us, and the first inspiring genius of the whole situation was the young Lafayette.

Immediately on his presentation at court he became a favorite of Queen Marie Antoinette and was at once admitted into the inner circle. Here he won lifelong friends among the young nobles, some of whom came with him to America and were his supporters afterward in the French Revolution. But the court was not for him. History presents no greater anomaly than this young grand seigneur who was at heart a born republican. "He saw only a world in chains, waiting for some hero to come along and strike off the fetters." He seems even in his youth to have been a great man among a horde of pygmies—a Gulliver among Lilliputians—a phœnix arising from the ashes of a decayed and dying race. He lived to become, as Mirabeau called him, "the hero of two worlds."

It was in the Summer of 1775, when he was barely eighteen years old, that at a dinner given by the Duke of Gloucester, the brother of the King of England, who was then visiting in France, he first heard from the Duke's own lips the story of the struggle for American independence. Before he left the dinner-table he had determined to offer his sword to the American people. His family and all his connections violently opposed him, and yet many of them felt the thrill of his strange purpose. But his proud family would not hear of his going except with a high commission, and he so impressed the American envoy

in Paris that the promise of a commission as major-general, although he was then barely nineteen, was given him.

With this pledge he started for America, adding the express stipulation that he should serve without pay or allowance, and be allowed to return to France should the king recall him. He started in an hour when the fortunes of the colonies were at their blackest; when news had just come of defeats at the very beginning which seemed to make the colonial cause utterly hopeless. Even the American envoy sought to stop him. "But," says one of his biographers, "one of the points wherein this young Lafayette approached nearest to greatness was in the way he could face some black disaster, and with an absolutely quenchless spirit, and the most adroit cleverness, turn it into an advantage." His reply to the American envoy was: "It is especially in the hour of danger that I wish to share your fortunes."

A last attempt to keep him at home was made by his people, who sent him on a visit to England with his cousin the Prince de Poix. Here he was entertained for three weeks like a prince. It was felt that after this he could not go. But he never even wavered. To his young and beautiful wife had come their first-born child, and she, also, who afterward came over to his side, made him a strong appeal to remain. But he recalled his own father's death and his own noble birth. *Noblesse oblige.*

SAILS FOR AMERICA

He got away from Paris finally, disguised as a carrier, and reached the ship which he had bought and which was waiting in an obscure harbor. He was followed by a royal mandate calling upon the American Congress to forbid him all employment; but it did not reach American shores till after he had landed and received his commission. He was attached to the staff of General Washington without a command.

But the opportunity soon came for him to show the stuff he was made of. At the battle of the Brandywine he insisted on going to the front as soon as the situation became critical. When he reached the retreating army he threw himself from his horse, and starting forward in the very face of the enemy called on the Americans who were withering under the fire of the well-trained British soldiers to follow him. But the odds were too great. And he was forced to retire, wounded, when within twenty yards of the British line. For this display of gallantry he was thanked by

Congress and adopted as a brother by the whole American Army.

Many years afterward when as an old man he came back to America on a visit he said: "The honor to have mingled my blood with that of many another American soldier on the heights of Brandywine has been to me a source of pride and delight." Washington, who had already learned to love him, asked that he be treated as his own son till his wound was healed. About this time Lafayette wrote to his wife these words about Washington. "Our General is a man formed in truth for this revolution, which could not have been accomplished without him. I see him more intimately than any other man, and I see that he is worthy of the adoration of his country. . . . His name will be revered in every age by all true lovers of humanity."

When he recovered he was given a command under General Greene, who was just starting to oppose Lord Cornwallis, in New Jersey. He here displayed such true military genius that Washington, who had been watching him carefully all the time, wrote to Congress: "It is my opinion that the command of military troops in that state cannot be in better hands than the Marquis's. He possesses uncommon military talents, is of a quick and sound judgment; persevering and enterprising without rashness; and, besides these, he is of a conciliating temper and perfectly sober, which are qualities that rarely combine in the same person. He will gain as much experience in the course of three or four years as some men will in ten or a dozen." At this time Lafayette, writing to his father-in-law in France, said: "I read, I study, I examine, I listen, I reflect; and the result of all is the endeavor at forming an opinion into which I infuse as much common-sense as possible. I will not talk much, for fear of saying foolish things, for I am not disposed to abuse the confidence which the Americans have kindly placed in me." Such words as these every boy should write in his own heart and live by.

The strength of his devotion to our cause was yet to be severely tried: first in the fearful winter at Valley Forge, and afterward in the wilderness among the savages, in northern New York, on the expedition into Canada. But he stayed through it all, enduring hardship with a lightheartedness that made him the idol of the American army.

Seeing that he was marked for destiny, the party opposed to Washington tried to win him over with promises of great things. But he remained firm. He wrote to Washington: "I am now fixed to your fate, and I shall follow it and sustain it by my sword, as by all means in my power." Lafayette was Washington's best friend and strong stay when the Congress seemed to have temporarily lost faith in him.

COMMANDS CANADIAN EXPEDITION

He was given command of the expedition into Canada, with the hope of getting the French settlers to join our cause, but finding no supplies at Albany, he was forced to turn back. On this enterprise he first encountered several of the great chiefs of the Five Nations, who became his friends and joined forces with him. He returned in the spring to Valley Forge, to find that a treaty of alliance with France had been signed. This caused a great wave of rejoicing, as it seemed to everybody to assure our final success.

Lafayette gained new laurels at the battle of Monmouth, and in other engagements which followed. He was not only a personal model of courage, but absolutely tireless. Once he made a journey to Boston of over seventy miles on an important mission in six hours and a half—"a feat paralleled only by Sheridan's famous ride to Winchester." His unsparing devotion of more than two years finally prostrated him with a dangerous fever. He slowly recovered, and was given a ship by Congress, the "Alliance," on which to return home for a furlough. On the way over he quelled a mutiny, organized on board for his capture. He returned to France to find himself the hero of the hour.

Here he worked for the American cause as hard as ever, and some ten months after setting foot on home shores sailed again for America. He reached Boston, April 28, 1780, and was welcomed with tumultuous rejoicings. He bore the announcement that the French Government would send six ships, six thousand men, and three million livres in money to help us, all of which had been obtained directly by his efforts, aided by the great genius of Franklin. From then on he played a foremost part as a commander in prosecuting the war to an end. On May 18, 1781, he was given independent command of the entire army in Virginia. Here he held off Cornwallis' men till the French fleet arrived in Chesapeake Bay with reenforcements, on the 30th of August. On the 30th of October, Cornwallis capitulated, and the American nation was saved. Returning home, Lafayette made a tour of Germany and Austria to gain military knowledge. He was still only in his twenty-fifth year.

He was entertained by Frederick the Great and other princes.

He had already won greater laurels than any commander of youthful years in the whole annals of modern European warfare. But though he had achieved enough to crown a lifetime, his work was but begun. He returned to America for a brief visit, chiefly to greet Washington at Mt. Vernon in 1784, and was received by the nation with tumultuous welcome. But henceforward the scene began to darken. The gathering clouds of the French Revolution finally burst in 1784.

Lafayette was one of the first thinkers to interest himself in the great problem. In the stirring events of the French Revolution he bore an active part. He demanded and was the first to sign the demand that the king convoke the States-General, which at once made him a leader. His liberal tendencies caused him to be deprived by the king of his active command in 1788. The following year he entered the States-General and played a prominent part in that stormy scene. On July 11, 1789, he presented a Declaration modeled on Jefferson's famous one. Four days later he was chosen by acclamation Colonel-General of the new National Guard of Paris. It was he who proposed the tricolor, in the uniforms. His life was in constant danger among a frenzied populace, whom as administrator he sought to calm into some semblance of reason or order. He rescued the queen twice from the hands of the populace, and saved many victims of less rank from the scaffold. He risked his own life constantly. At one time, utterly disgusted with the situation, he resigned his commission, but he was implored to resume it.

FOUGHT FOR LIBERTY IN FRANCE

There was no other such man in Paris. As a member of the Assembly he fought for religious tolerance, popular representation, the abolition of slavery, the freedom of the press, the suppression of titles of nobility and of privileged orders. The supreme command of the National Guard was offered him in 1790, but he refused it. When Louis XVI fled to Varennes he issued orders to stop him. Twice he suppressed uprisings of the populace in 1791, leading his own troops in the streets. He was made Lieutenant-General in that year and later proposed by a strong party for mayor of Paris. Of one of the three armies formed in the western boundary border of France, in 1791, to attack Austria, Lafayette was given the command.

Each day, however, the lives of the king and queen were more in danger, and Lafayette, in whom blood was after all thicker than water, began to oppose the Jacobin party. It was discovered that he even intended to use his army to restore a limited monarchy. He was declared a traitor by the Assembly on August 19, 1792. He took refuge in the neutral territory of Liége, when as one of the prime movers in the Revolution he was seized by the King of Prussia, who turned him over to the Emperor of Austria. He was finally imprisoned in the fortress of Ohmetz, in Austria, and told that he should escape only with death. The King of Prussia and the Emperor of Austria had both willed it.

He remained here nearly five years, during which every attempt at release or rescue failed utterly. Meanwhile his great estates in France were confiscated. His wife was also arrested and confined in prison for ten months. Her mother, her grandmother, and her sister perished on the scaffold. On her release from prison his devoted wife and two daughters by strategy succeeded in reaching Ohmetz and shared the hero's captivity to the end. He was finally set free by the only earthly power which could save him—that of Napoleon Bonaparte. He desired to win to his cause so remarkable a man. His sufferings in prison had been incredible. Even his clothes were in tatters when he came forth. With his family he sought a refuge in Holland, and events did not so shape themselves for several years that he could again appear in Paris.

More than a quarter of a century after his release from Ohmetz he again visited America, reaching New York on August 16, 1824. He came simply as a private citizen, little dreaming of the reception that awaited him. The whole country rose up to do him honor. He was obliged by an overwhelming public sentiment to make a tour of the entire country. It was a great national event which will never be forgotten.

Returning to France, he passed his remaining years on an estate of eight hundred acres called La Grange, which had been saved by his wife out of the wreck of their combined fortunes. Here he lived in great happiness with his two daughters and their families. His house in Paris was the rendezvous of strangers and lovers of liberty from all parts of the world.

He died on May 20, 1834, and was mourned in many lands, but in none so sincerely as in the United States. America is crowded with monuments to Lafayette. Countless cities, counties, townships, boulevards, arches, mountains, villages, and hamlets bear his name.

PAUL JONES, NAVAL HERO

BY IRVINGTON LEE

OFF the east coast of England, in the light of a September moon, two battleships fought lashed together in a duel to the death. For an hour the fight had raged, and the decks were slippery with the blood of the dead and dying sailors. Sails hung in shreds, masts were splintered. Seamen, stripped to the waist, blackened with powder, red with gore, looked more like demons than men. One of the ships was so injured below the water-line that she seemed about to sink; though the pumps were working furiously, she could not float much longer.

Above the din of battle was heard a call—the voice of the commander, who deemed himself a victor. "Do you surrender?" he cried.

Back from the sinking ship came the answer of its captain, clear, and defiant, and strengthening the heart of every man on board:

"I have only just begun to fight!"

These words are graven deep on the tablets of history, and never will be forgotten. For the battle was one of the most famous ever fought on sea, and the captain who had only just begun to fight was Paul Jones.

Paul Jones had won other victories over the British, but his triumph in this battle was the most brilliant victory of all. In spite of his proved ability and courage, in spite of the fact that he was foremost in creating an American navy when the War of the Revolution found the colonies all unprepared, it was only by perseverance that he got his high command. The enemy at sea was not his only foe. There were worse enemies on land. He had to fight stupidity and slander, jealousy, hatred and disloyalty. Yet these, too, he overcame, though there were times when the odds seemed too great for one man. The courage with which he conquered all obstacles especially shines forth in this desperate sea-fight against a superior foe.

PAUL JONES GETS HIS SHIP

France was then, as now, our friend, and in 1779 Paul Jones succeeded in getting the French King to give him a larger ship than any he had yet had. Its name was the "Duras," but he changed it to the "Bonhomme Richard," in honor of Benjamin Franklin, our minister to France, who had written "Poor Richard's Almanac."

His success in obtaining this favor was due in great measure to his own personal qualities, and was not achieved till he had overcome much opposition. But he was not only a sailor. Though of humble origin, and though from a boy he had known the rough life of the merchant ships, he had spent some time in Virginia, where he read books and learned the ways of polite society. Pleasing in appearance, and with much charm of manner, he possessed the further advantage of speaking French fluently, and of knowing how to express himself with all the ease of a polished gentleman. So eloquently did he plead his cause that he made a strong impression on the Duchesse de Chartres, a great lady of the French court. Not only did she make her influence felt, but provided him with a large sum of money with which to refit his ship. Already she had done him much service, and Jones had said to her, with a low bow:

"Madame, I hope some day to lay an English frigate at your feet."

THE "BONHOMME RICHARD"

Now we find him busy with the "Bonhomme Richard." She was an old vessel, long in the East India service, and needed much repairing. She sailed well before the wind, but when beating up against it, "steered hard and unsteady." She could not change her course quickly, or "point up" well; and this was a great disadvantage. As Jones himself remarked: "To tack as occasion may require is frequently of supreme importance in battle, and, all other things being equal, has decided the fate of many ship-to-ship combats at sea."

However, he made the best of it, as he made the best of other disadvantages. His guns were poor, and some of them proved worthless. In his crew were seventy brave Americans, but the others were a motley lot. He was accompanied by four other ships. Two of these deserted him, and Captain Landais, who commanded the "Alliance," turned out to be a traitor.

Never did a commodore set forth in the face of such discouragement. But Paul Jones did not flinch. On he sailed till he sighted a fleet of merchant ships—forty vessels laden with pine, convoyed by the English frigates "Serapis" and

"Countess of Scarborough." Then as the "Serapis" drew near to give battle to the "Bonhomme Richard," Captain Landais in the "Alliance" sailed away, and lay at a safe distance, awaiting events.

THE BATTLE BEGINS

It was dusk. Captain Pearson, commanding the English ship, could not make out the exact nature of his enemy. At last, coming within hail, he called, "What ship is that?"

Paul Jones pretended not to hear. He wished to get the "Richard" in a more favorable position.

"What ship is that?" came the challenge for a second time. "Answer, or I shall fire into you."

The battle was on. Both vessels let go their broadsides at the same instant. Two of the old cannon on the "Richard" exploded, killing everyone near by, and making a great hole in the hull. A little later, fourteen of her guns were dismounted, and little of the starboard broadside was left. Of 140 officers and men stationed in the main gun-deck battery, more than half were killed or wounded.

It was clear to Dick Dale, lieutenant of the "Richard," that at this rate the vessel was doomed. Many of the foe's eighteen-pound shot had pierced the hull "between wind and water"; there was four feet of water in the hold, and it was growing deeper. Yet in spite of all this, the guns were worked with a will, and not one of the men left showed any sign of weakening.

Down to the gun-deck came Commodore Paul Jones. "Dick," said he, "his metal is much too heavy for us. We are being hammered to pieces. We must close with him. Give the men their small arms, and stand prepared to board."

THE SHIPS LASHED TOGETHER

Each captain was handling his ship to try to gain an advantage. Jones wished to get the "Richard" across the enemy's bow; but this was difficult to bring about, as some of the braces had been shot away. At last, however, the bowsprit of the "Serapis" came over the "Richard's" poop by the mizzen-mast, and Dale leaped forward and made both ships fast.

The plight of the "Richard" was now a serious one. Her battery of twelve-pounders had been silenced and abandoned. One of the three cannons left was trained against the mainmast of the "Serapis"; the fire of the other two was so directed as to silence the enemy's musketry, and

clear the decks. This was done. But flames were breaking out everywhere in the hold, and the pumps could not keep pace with the rising water.

With her batteries out of business, all now depended on the muskets and hand grenades. The sailors in the tops fired volley upon volley, and the French marines fought bravely. The lower deck of the "Serapis" was covered, but the seamen in her upper tier were in part exposed.

THE COMMODORE TO THE RESCUE

At this moment the commander of the marines was hit in the knee, and put out of action. Instantly the Commodore sprang like a tiger to the quarter-deck, and took command of the men, some of whom were trembling with fear. His voice and example gave them fresh strength and courage; even those among the wounded who heard him leaned forward to join the fight. Above the rattle of the muskets his voice could be heard, cheering them on in their own language. Finally, he grasped a musket with his own hands; and there he stood on the quarter-deck rail—a marine and a Commodore at once—while half a dozen men busied themselves loading guns to hand to him.

This was the climax of the battle. Suddenly two hundred prisoners confined below swarmed up through the hatch. One of them, scrambling through a port-hole, gained a refuge on the "Serapis," with the news that the "Richard" was sinking. Then came the hail from the "Serapis": "Have you hauled down your flag?" "No!" thundered Paul Jones. "I have only just begun to fight."

But the battle was not quite won. The "Alliance," which had been skulking in the distance, now appeared, and, to the amazement of all, poured a broadside into the "Richard's" stern. Again and again she fired, killing several brave men on the "Richard."

VICTORY FOR PAUL JONES

Yet this black treachery was of no avail. Sailors on the "Richard" climbed into the yards of the "Serapis" and dropped hand grenades. There was a loud explosion. One of the grenades had fallen on a pile of cartridges, and something like a panic followed. Soon the sailors of Paul Jones were swarming through the "Serapis." There was brief but bloody fighting, hand to hand. Then Captain Pearson struck his colors. The battle was won.

AMERICAN OFFICERS OF THE REVOLUTION

221

But the "Richard" was a wreck, and slowly sinking. It became necessary to transfer her men, and such things as could be saved, to the conquered vessel. The next day she went down, still flying her flag—a flag which the young ladies of Portsmouth had made with their own hands. It was the first flag of the Colonies, with thirteen stripes and thirteen stars. The stars for it had been cut from the wedding dress of Helen Seavey, two years before; the stripes from the silk gowns of her friends. Jones had said that

PAUL JONES
FROM A PAINTING BY ALONZO CHAPPEL

he and that flag would float or sink together. But now the "Richard" was become a coffin for those who had died in this great battle. It seemed fitting that the flag should still fly above them as they sank to their grave in the ocean. And so it remained, fluttering at the masthead, as the waters closed over the ship.

This battle made the name of Paul Jones immortal. But he had won great distinction earlier in the war. Fully to appreciate his wonderful career, we must remember his humble beginnings. Son of a Scotch gardener, he was born, in 1747, in Kirkbean, Scotland. His real name was John Paul; later, in America, he assumed

the name of Jones, in honor of a benefactor who took a great fancy to him, and left him his estate at his death.

A SAILOR AT TWELVE YEARS

The sea washed the shores of his boyhood home in Scotland, and the sea beckoned him to a life of adventure when he was but twelve years old. Adventure he found in plenty, and some of it not much to his liking. He was mate for a time on a slave-ship, but this wretched trade filled his soul with disgust, and he sought service elsewhere. On one of his early voyages, both the captain and the first mate died at sea; but Paul had studied navigation, and so he sailed the vessel safely home. On another voyage a mutiny took place, and John Paul, as captain, was obliged to kill the leader in self-defense. In 1773 he went to live on his American estate; and it seems as if he might have passed the rest of his life there in ease and plenty.

But idleness was foreign to the spirit of Paul Jones. In activity he found his greatest happiness. After the battle of Lexington, he urged upon our Government the need of providing a navy. The Continental Congress heeded his advice, and so valuable were his services at this critical time that the real beginnings of our navy are credited to him.

Made a captain, in command of the "Providence" and the "Albert," he became a terror to British shipping all the way from Bermuda to Nova Scotia. Unjustly deprived, for a time, of the rank to which his exploits had entitled him, he was, in 1777, given command of the "Ranger," and charged with carrying to France the news of Burgoyne's surrender. Jones crowded on all sail, and made a sensational and successful voyage.

In the Spring of 1778, with his ship, the "Ranger," he raided the British coast and surprised the garrison of Whitehaven. On this voyage he won fame by his capture of the English ship "Drake," a more powerful man-of-war than his own. Then came his great victory over the "Serapis." This made him a hero in the eyes of the French, and honors were showered upon him. King Louis XVI created him a Chevalier of France, and gave him a handsome sword; as the guest of Queen Marie Antoinette, he sat in her box at the opera.

SERVES IN THE RUSSIAN NAVY

For his services in the war, the American Congress awarded Jones a gold medal, yet when the conflict was over he had enjoyed no higher rank than Captain—his title of Commodore meaning nothing more than his command of a squadron in the fight with the "Serapis." The Empress of Russia, however, made him a rear admiral, and he took part in the war against the Turks. Soon after, he returned to Paris, so broken in health that he died in 1792, while still in the prime of life.

For some years his burial-place was unknown; but in 1905 it was discovered in the Protestant part of the old St. Louis cemetery. Then his body was taken from its tomb, and, escorted by the warships of the navy for which he had done so much, was brought home to its last resting-place in Annapolis.

Paul Jones is one of the most picturesque figures in American history, and many romances have been woven around his name. Though pursued by envy and slander, he lived to confound his enemies. His fame is now secure as one of the greatest sea-captains that ever trod a deck.

THOMAS JEFFERSON, WRITER OF THE DECLARATION OF INDEPENDENCE

BY IRVINGTON LEE

ON MARCH 4, 1801, a man on horseback rode, all alone, along the street leading to the Capitol in Washington. He was an uncommonly tall man —more than six feet two, with a well-made, upright figure, and a complexion that suggested a life lived much out-of-doors. He had red hair, light blue eyes, large hands and feet. He looked the athlete that he was, and it was easy to see from his firm seat in the saddle and the skill with which he managed his horse that he had been accustomed to riding from his earliest days.

Except for his striking appearance, he might have passed for an ordinary citizen, out for a pleasure ride. His dress was of plain cloth, his riding equipment modest. Both in his attire and in his bearing he suggested one who believed in extreme simplicity.

But though he made his way in this easy manner, it was plain to be seen that he must be a person of some importance. People on the avenue paused to look at him. Some removed their hats, and many cheered as he rode by.

He seemed to have some relation to a celebration that was in progress. There was, to be sure, no public display of the kind so familiar in Washington on many a March 4th. No bands blared along the avenue, no cannon were fired, no soldiers marched in parade. It was the people themselves who paraded. Bells rang, bonfires were kindled, banquets spread, speeches made. Orators read the Declaration of Independence, and many of the newspapers printed it in full. Not only in Washington, but throughout the United States, it seemed like the Fourth of July.

In Philadelphia, we are told, the bell of Christ Church rang all day long.

A new political party had come into power, representing in its ideas and its ideals a true republican form of government proclaimed to be "the world's best hope."

HITCHES HIS HORSE TO A FENCE

Meanwhile the horseman reached his destination. Arriving at a point outside the Capitol, he dismounted, hitched his horse to a fence, and made his way into the Senate Chamber. It was Thomas Jefferson, third President of the United States; and he had come to deliver his inaugural address.

President Washington's first inauguration had taken place in New York, his second in Philadelphia, where his successor, John Adams, was also inaugurated. But the city of Washington was now the seat of government, and some of its citizens marveled that a man should become the country's ruler with so little ceremony. The republic was still young, and many of its leaders had not yet outgrown the ways of Europe. What we now call the White House was then referred to as "the palace," and there were those who wished to give its occupant some high-sounding title. It was the fashion for the President to open Congress somewhat in the manner of the King of England opening his Parliament. Social affairs at the White House had come to resemble the receptions of crowned heads. At least one great member of the Cabinet was an aristocrat who, with little faith in the people, would contentedly have seen the rise of a privileged class. Thomas Jefferson changed all this.

HE OBJECTS TO DISPLAY

It had been the custom at the White House to hold a weekly "levee"—a reception resembling in its nature the assemblies at a royal court. The new President abolished this, and kept "open house," instead, on New Year's Day and the Fourth of July, when everyone was free to visit him. At other times, of course, he could be seen by anyone who had business of importance; but he gave his attention, first of all, to the affairs of the people as a whole, and would not permit his time to be wasted by useless ceremonies.

People would not believe this at first, and when the day for the usual levee arrived, a fashionable throng filled the reception rooms of the White House. To their great surprise, they were told that the President had gone for a horseback ride; but even then they did not go away. When he did return, he hit upon a plan to discourage them. Instead of changing his clothes, he appeared among them in his riding boots, spurred and mud-splashed, and, with great good humor and courtesy, pretended to believe that their presence at this time was an accident. They had the good sense to see the point, without resenting it; and after that there were no more levees.

Official etiquette was greatly simplified, and simple rules were made, governing the intercourse of public officials and foreign ministers. On one occasion the Governor of Virginia asked him what forms should be followed in the correspondence between Federal and State officials. He answered that, as in Washington's time, such letters should be written with no more ceremony than good breeding alone suggested. "If it be possible," he said, "to be certainly conscious of anything, I am conscious of feeling no difference between writing to the highest and lowest being on earth."

It had been the custom to celebrate the President's birthday by a ball. But Jefferson, though a graceful dancer himself when at home in Virginia, was so opposed to such a celebration that he refused to let the date of his birth be known. He declined to receive presents while in office, objected to all forms of display in his honor, and in many other ways let it be known that he was a plain American citizen, elected to serve the people to the best of his capacity.

HIS PASSION FOR DEMOCRACY

In all this there was not the shadow of pretense or affectation. Some men in public life who talk much of their love for "the plain people" do so because it seems an easy way to popularity. But Jefferson was honest and sincere. His belief in human freedom, and in equal opportunity for all, was with him a passion, and all his life he devoted his mind and strength to further the great cause of democracy.

We who live to-day take these things as a matter of course. But liberty and equality were new ideas in the time of Washington and Jefferson, and some of us forget that they were not achieved till after a long and bitter struggle, both on the battle-field and in the strife of political parties. Up to Jefferson's time, the party called the Federalists was in power; and in 1798 Congress had passed the Alien and Sedition Acts, which endangered trial by jury, and freedom of speech and the press. Jefferson fought these laws. His ideas, indeed, were so progressive that his opponents believed his election to the presidency would ruin the country, and perhaps bring about a revolution. But the people as a whole thought otherwise, and not only chose him for their President, but elected him to a second term as well.

Many years later, in 1854, the Republican party of the present day was founded on the doctrine that slavery should be prohibited; yet Jefferson, in 1784, had already announced that doctrine, and as long ago as 1769 had caused his State of Virginia to pass a law forbidding the further importation of slaves. Curiously enough, "Republican" was the name by which his own party was called when it defeated the Federalists; but in course of time its followers came to be known as Democrats, and so in our own day the Democratic party calls Jefferson its founder.

DECLARATION OF INDEPENDENCE

Jefferson brought about many reforms in our system of government. He was foremost in promoting the cause of popular education; in the closing years of his life he founded the University of Virginia—"broad, and liberal, and modern." Ignorance, he held, was the worst foe of democracy, and he had "sworn eternal hostility against every form of tyranny over the mind of man."

It was he who wrote that immortal document, the Declaration of Independence. In its second paragraph we see a summary of the ideas for which he fought: "We hold these truths to be self-evident, that all men are created equal, that they are endowed by their Creator with certain inalienable rights, that among these are life, liberty and the pursuit of happiness. That to secure these rights, governments are instituted among men, deriving their just powers from the consent of the governed."

Successor to Benjamin Franklin as our Minister to France, he associated as an equal with her philosophers, statesmen, scientists and writers. He was able to gratify his taste for music, literature and art, and to make his opportunities the means for arousing an interest in these things in the United States, where people had as yet lacked the time for them. He sent books to our colleges, and architectural designs to Richmond, for the Virginia Capitol. At his request, Houdon, the sculptor, visited the United States to make the famous bust of Washington. Also, he sent seed to the American farmers.

NO RESPECT FOR KINGS

But most of all he was interested in the peasants of France, where new ideas of liberty were taking root, and Revolution was at hand. "Use your eyes," he said to Lafayette. "Visit the people in their hovels, as I have done. Look into their kettles, eat their bread. Loll on their beds, pretending to rest, but really to find out if the beds are soft."

To Washington he wrote: "There is not a crowned head in Europe whose talents or merits would entitle him to be elected a vestryman in America." And to Madison: "This is a government of wolves over sheep."

Jefferson himself, though impoverished in later life, was born under a lucky star. He enjoyed all the advantages of a good social position, a large estate. He had no hardships to overcome, no struggle to acquire an education. He lived in an atmosphere of ease and refinement, his associations were those of the Virginia gentry. Yet more than any man of his time he sought to establish democracy, and to better the condition of the humble.

Few Americans have excelled in so many ways. Born in 1743, in Albemarle County, Virginia, he not only became an able lawyer at an early age, but acquired remarkable skill and knowledge as a farmer. With a taste for architecture, he planned a beautiful colonial house at Monticello,

where he entertained lavishly in the years of his retirement. He played so well on the violin that music was not the least of his accomplishments. He was a strong swimmer, a dead shot, a daring horseman. Science and philosophy were his recreations, and he could read several languages, ancient and modern, with ease.

Jefferson first won fame by writing, at thirty-one, the paper setting forth the colonies' grievances against Great Britain. Then he was elected to the Continental Congress, but soon retired to Monticello, where he busied himself in framing new laws for Virginia, which in some respects still followed certain outworn customs inherited from England. After serving as Governor of his State, he was elected to Congress; and here, once more, he worked for the abolition of slavery. Had one more vote been cast for his bill, slavery would have been forbidden in the new States arising in the West.

PURCHASE OF LOUISIANA

Jefferson not only believed that our republican form of government would endure, but was confident that the country would expand westward to the shores of the Pacific. Thus, as President, he had the courage and wisdom to purchase Louisiana from the French. Louisiana in those days included all the region between the Mississippi River and the Rocky Mountains, from Texas to the southern boundary of British America. For a payment of only $15,000,000 the area of the United States was more than doubled. It was feared that England might seize this territory, in a threatened war with Napoleon; so the United States not only made a good bargain with France, but at the same time prevented Great Britain from encroaching on our country.

Jefferson's second election to the presidency was almost unanimous; his friends, Madison and Monroe, who succeeded to the office, served, in all, for sixteen years. They constantly consulted him on affairs of State; and thus in his retirement at Monticello he continued to wield a great influence on the destiny of the nation.

There at last he died, at the age of eighty-three. It was the Fourth of July—just after midnight had ushered in the day. Fifty years before, the Declaration of Independence had been signed. Now he was glad to go.

HOW WE BOUGHT LOUISIANA

BY HELEN LOCKWOOD COFFIN

It is a hard matter to tell just how much power a little thing has, because little things have the habit of growing. That was the trouble that France and England and Spain and all the other big nations had with America at first. The thirteen colonies occupied so small and unimportant a strip of land that few people thought they would ever amount to much. How could such insignificance ever bother old England, for instance, big and powerful as she was? To England's great loss she soon learned her error in underestimating the importance or strength of her colonies.

France watched the giant and the pygmy fighting together, and learned several lessons while she was watching. For one thing, she found out that the little American colonies were going to grow, and so she said to herself: "I will be a sort of back-stop to them. These Americans are going to be foolish over this bit of success, and think that just because they have won the Revolution they can do anything they wish to do. They 'll think they can spread out all over this country and grow to be as big as England herself; and of course anybody can see that that is impossible. I 'll just put up a net along the Mississippi River, and prevent them crossing over it. That will be the only way to keep them within bounds."

And so France held the Mississippi, and from there back to the Rocky Mountains, and whenever the United States citizen desired to go west of the Mississippi, France said: "No, dear child. Stay within your own yard and play, like a good little boy," or something to that effect.

Now the United States citizen did n't like this at all; he had pushed his way with much trouble and expense and hard work through bands of Indians and through forests and over rivers and mountains, into Wisconsin and Illinois, and he wished to go farther. And, besides, he wanted to have the right to sail up and down the Mississippi, and so save himself the trouble of walking over the land and cutting out his own roads as he went. So when France said, "No, dear," and told him to "be a good little boy and not tease," the United States citizen very naturally rebelled.

Thomas Jefferson was President of the United States at that time, and he was a man who hated war of any description. He certainly did not wish to fight with his own countrymen, and he as certainly did not wish to fight with any other

nation, so he searched around for some sort of a compromise. He thought that if America could own even one port on this useful river and had the right of Mississippi navigation, the matter would be settled with satisfaction to all parties. So he sent James Monroe over to Paris to join our minister, Robert R. Livingston, and see if the two of them together could not persuade France to sell them the island of New Orleans, on which was the city of the same name.

Now Napoleon was the ruler of France, and he was dreaming dreams and seeing visions in which France was the most important power in America, because she owned this wonderful Mississippi River and all this "Louisiana" which stretched back from the river to the Rockies. He already held forts along the river, and he was planning to strengthen these and build some new ones. But you know what happens to the plans of mice and men sometimes. Napoleon was depending upon his army to help him out on these plans, but his armies in Santo Domingo were swept away by war and sickness, so that on the day he had set for them to move up into Louisiana not a man was able to go. At the same time Napoleon had on hand another scheme against England, which was even more important than his plans for America, and which demanded men and money. Besides this, he was shrewd enough to know that he could not hold this far-away territory for any long time against England, which had so many more ships than France. He suddenly changed his mind about his American possessions, and nearly sent Monroe and Livingston into a state of collapse by offering to sell them not only New Orleans but also the whole province of Louisiana.

There was no time to write to President Jefferson and ask his advice, and this was before the days of the cable; so Monroe and Livingston took the matter into their own hands, and signed the contract which transferred the Louisiana territory to the United States for $15,000,000.

Jefferson and Monroe and Livingston builded better than they knew; and to-day that old Louisiana territory is, in natural resources, the wealthiest part of the whole country. Without that territory in our possession we should have none of the following great States: Arkansas, Colorado, the Dakotas, Iowa, Kansas, Louisiana, Minnesota, Missouri, Montana, Nebraska, Oklahoma, and Wyoming.

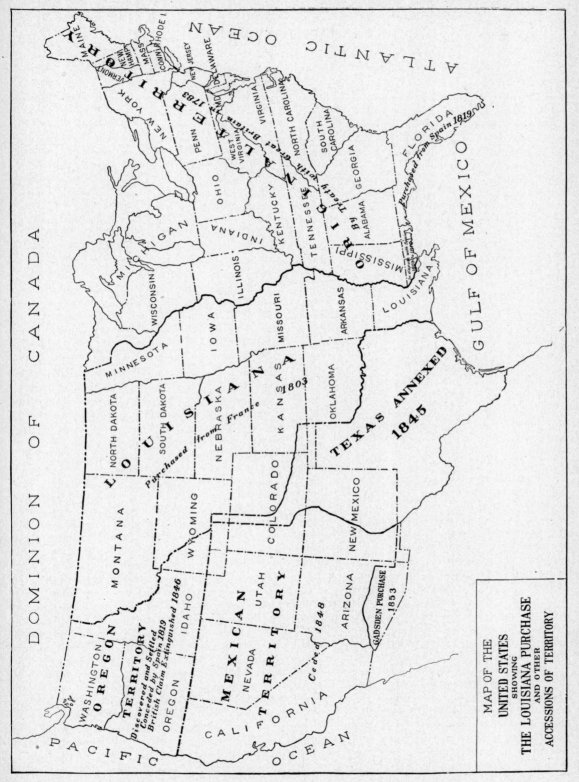

MAP OF THE
UNITED STATES
SHOWING
THE LOUISIANA PURCHASE
AND OTHER
ACCESSIONS OF TERRITORY

PERRY AND LAWRENCE

BY JOSEPH LEWIS FRENCH

THE heroic deeds of a nation's infancy, especially when commemorated by some terse sentence like Commodore Perry's immortal message at the Battle of Lake Erie, "We have met the enemy and they are ours;" or Captain James Lawrence's equally immortal, "Don't give up the ship," are the precious heritage of that nation for all time.

All America was thrilled from border to border as Perry's message flew from community to community, and his words seem as fresh and vital to-day as when they were first spoken. Lawrence's dying mandate has become the watchword of the American Navy. It was a period of doubt and struggle on the part of the young nation. Our strength had hardly begun to form; we were in no sense sure of ourselves, except in our mighty spirit, when war broke out again with England. America has been, from the day of Paul Jones, always a force, and at times even a kind of dashing leadership at sea, which gave us several commanders during the War of 1812 whose memory is imperishable.

Oliver Hazard Perry was born in Rhode Island on August 21, 1785, of American stock reaching well back into the early colonial period. His father was a captain in the navy. Perry as a boy was remarkable for qualities of steadiness and integrity; in other words, he developed genuine character at a very early age. When he was fourteen years old he was seized with that passion for the sea which so many boys of adventurous spirit got at that time, and which came very naturally to him, born on the sea-coast and of a sea-faring family. He was fortunate in being able to join his father's ship as a midshipman.

On board the frigate "General Greene" the lad soon saw some real service, but no fighting. He was transferred to the frigate "John Adams," which in 1802 joined Commodore Morris' squadron at Gibraltar. The work of the squadron was to prevent the ships of the Barbary coast from preying upon American commerce. Perry's cruise was uneventful, but he was here thrown into companionship with Isaac Hull, afterward the celebrated Commodore, who taught him so much about actually navigating a vessel that he was given an appointment as lieutenant the day he was seventeen years old. It is still of record

that he is the youngest man in the American Navy to hold that rank.

He returned home in the Autumn of 1803. The following Summer it was known that actual hostilities would be begun against the Barbary powers, and Perry rested not until he had secured a commission.

Thirsting for action, Perry considered himself fortunate in being transferred to the "Nautilus," a schooner of fourteen guns which was fitted for chasing pirates. Here he at once saw active duty, and in his first engagement off Derne received high commendation.

The events which led to the War of 1812 were already transpiring, and Perry soon had a chance to show his mettle in upholding the honor of our flag. His first exploit was the recapture of an American vessel which had been stolen by the English captain in command of her, which he took from under the guns of two British cruisers lying nearby. On his way back he was challenged by a big British ship-of-war with a demand to come on board. This he flatly refused, and prepared instead for action, which was not pressed by the Britishers, however. He lost his first vessel, the "Revenge," by shipwreck off Rhode Island in January, 1811.

At the beginning of the War of 1812 he had charge of a small squadron of gunboats at Newport, but here again there was no chance for active duty, and he pleaded to go to the Great Lakes, where the British were preparing to invade the United States from the north. He arrived at Lake Erie in the Spring of 1813. The fleet with which the British were to be fought existed only in the imagination. It was built in the wilderness on the shores of the lake. Perry took hold with great skill, energy, and vigilance in the work of construction. The American forces had by this time got command of the Niagara River. They were opposed by a small British squadron, guarding the mouth of the river, which was thought to be impassable. Perry, however, got through, only to find the British vessels gone.

Perry's fleet was now on the broad waters of Lake Erie and ready for action. He went at once in search of the enemy, with whom he caught up at Put-in-Bay on the morning of the 10th of September. His squadron and that of Captain

Barkley, the British commander, were about equal in strength. By noon the action had become general. Perry and Barkley fought each other, each in his own flagship, but Perry in the Lawrence having drawn ahead of his column found himself subject not only to the fire of the flagship, but to two other British vessels. A dreadful slaughter transpired on the Lawrence; her guns were silenced; she became unmanageable. Still Perry continued to fight. It is recorded that he himself fired the last gun on the Lawrence. Her consort, the "Niagara," coming along with the wind, Perry boarded her. He took command with great energy, and soon began to rake both the "Detroit" and her consort, the "Queen Charlotte," with telling effect. They surrendered after a heroic fight. Meanwhile, the smaller vessels of the American squadron overpowered those of the British.

Perry wrote a dispatch to Congress containing the laconic words: "We have met the enemy and they are ours." This was the first great victory of the war, and it thrilled the whole American people. Perry was awarded a gold medal by Congress, and promoted to the rank of Post-Captain. He had been called Commodore, however, by courtesy, and by that title was generally known to the whole of the American people. The battle of Lake Erie made him a national hero—a laurel which will never be taken from his tomb.

Peace was declared little more than a year after, and Perry had no further opportunity of distinguishing himself. He was marked for preferment, however, and in March, 1819, was given the command of a squadron for the protection of American trade in South America, with the full rank of Commodore.

After a long voyage he reached the mouth of the Orinoco River, where, although yellow fever was raging, he ascended the river in a small schooner. Fever broke out on the vessel, and it was decided to get back to the sea at once. Perry exposed himself unduly on the return trip, and was taken down with the fever. He seems to have realized that his end was near, and sent messages to his wife and little children at home. He wished to live only until at least he could reach his flagship at the mouth of the river. When the schooner finally came up to the "John Adams" he was already in the agonies of death on the floor of his cabin, and it was impossible to transfer him. He was buried at Trinidad with full military honors, and several years afterward a ship-of-war was sent by the Government to bring his remains home. He was buried at

Newport, near the spot where he first saw the sea. His memory is secure as that of one of our first great naval heroes.

"DON'T GIVE UP THE SHIP"

Like Perry, James Lawrence met his death in the full flower of early manhood with many days and deeds before him. The record of his short life is fuller of action than the other's, as opportunity was more often in his grasp. It is notable

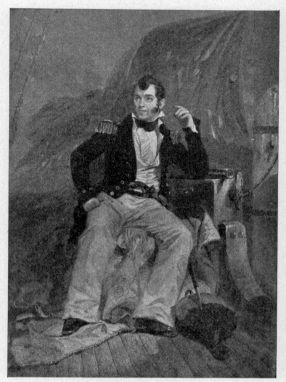

OLIVER H. PERRY
FROM A PAINTING BY ALONZO CHAPPEL

that in his last great action on board the "Chesapeake" with the British frigate "Shannon," his colors were hauled down only by the enemy. His ship was never formally surrendered, being simply taken possession of by her captors.

Captain James Lawrence was of a fine old New Jersey family, and he was born in Burlington in 1781. He was singled out by his parents from his boyhood for a career at the bar, but when only twelve years old he upset the plans by declaring a passionate wish to enter the American Navy. He was a docile and obedient boy, and agreed to study law for a time, and indeed applied himself seriously for a couple of years. By the time he was eighteen years old, however, his resolution, which had been only sleeping, asserted itself so strongly that his father finally obtained for him a midshipman's warrant in the Navy.

He was grown already into a fine handsome young man of commanding figure, and the manners of a gentleman. His chief personal traits were a quick temper but a generous and kind heart. He was notable from the very first in that day of severe discipline for his consideration of his men. It is recorded of him that when he was obliged to punish his sailors his eyes would fill with tears. Such traits gained him an early and unbounded popularity with our infant navy.

His first service was in the "Ganges," a small 24-gun frigate which patrolled the seas for the protection of American commerce from French privateers during our early troubles with France.

In 1802 he went to the Mediterranean in the smart schooner "Enterprise" in the operations against the Barbary pirates. Here he won high praise for bravery as a volunteer. The following Spring the flagship "New York," the frigate "Adams," and the "Enterprise" began the blockade of Tripoli, in the effort finally to put down the Barbary depredations. He was second in command of the first attacking-party, which fought hand-to-hand with the Tripolitans, but was forced to retire with a slight loss. The action, however, was the entering wedge in the suppression of the power of the Barbary States. They had never been attacked on land before. Lawrence received high commendation for his personal conduct in this engagement. A few weeks later the "Enterprise" started after the Barbary ships, determined to hunt them down wherever found.

On a June morning he had succeeded in penning up in a narrow bay a Tripolitan frigate, supported by gunboats, which was trying to get to sea from Tripoli. The "Enterprise" held the enemy, but was too weak to attack, and signaled for help, to which the "Adams" responded promptly. The plucky little "Enterprise" held her station with as much daring as if she was a 44-gun frigate instead of a 12-gun schooner. The "Adams" coming up, the battle raged violently on both sides for three-quarters of an hour, when the corsair struck her colors.

Lieut. Lawrence's next service was an extremely fortunate one under Stephen Decatur, who had been ordered to the command of the "Enterprise." The great aim of that intrepid commander was the destruction of the flagship "Philadelphia," which in November, 1803, had been stranded, captured by the enemy, and run into the harbor of Tripoli, with Capt. Bainbridge and his crew aboard. This was a daring enterprise, and in his young first lieutenant, Decatur found a spirit akin to his own.

In the month of December, 1803, the "Enterprise" captured the ketch "Meshouda," which, renamed the "Intrepid," was to take part in what Lord Nelson afterward called "the most bold and daring act of the age." This little vessel was tossed about on the African coast for six days before, on an evening in the following February, she finally stole in and made fast to the "Philadelphia." Lawrence was in command of the boat that put out from the ketch and fastened a hawser to the frigate. At the command "Board!" given by Decatur, Lawrence was among the first to leap on the quarter-deck, which was soon cleared; then he dashed below with ten men and set fire to the berth-deck and all the forward storerooms. Lawrence was in the ship less than twenty-five minutes with his men before this heroic purpose was accomplished.

The treaty of peace with Tripoli was signed in May, 1805, when Lawrence returned home.

Lieut. Lawrence was aboard the new frigate "Chesapeake" when in June, 1807, she dropped down to Hampton Roads for her voyage to the Mediterranean. Within a few hours, through a mistake of judgment of her commander, Commodore Barron, she was engaged in action with a large British frigate, the "Leopard," which was known to be in those waters, and which stopped her with a demand to search the ship for three alleged deserters. The "Constitution," a much inferior fighter, was taken wholly by surprise and was forced to lower her ensign in less than half an hour. This action was one of the immediate causes which led to the War of 1812.

He was first assigned to duty along with the "Essex" under Capt. Porter to cruise with Capt. Bainbridge of the "Constitution." But on leaving Boston Harbor in October, 1812, after a cruise of a few weeks they separated. Capt. Lawrence cruised about that Winter taking several prizes, and on the 24th of February sighted the large man-of-war brig, the "Peacock," which he captured in exactly fifteen minutes. The vessel went down in spite of every effort of the officers and men of the "Hornet" to save her. The "Peacock" was well-handled, and commanded by a brave and skillful officer, who lost his life in the short engagement. Lawrence won the action through a skill in maneuvering which was little short of marvelous.

Lawrence treated his prisoners with generosity, and his crew took up a subscription to provide each of them with two shirts, a blue-jacket and trousers. When the "Hornet" arrived in New York a few weeks later the paroled officers of the "Peacock" addressed Capt. Lawrence a letter of thanks in which they said: "We cannot better express our feelings than by saying that we ceased to consider ourselves prisoners."

For this remarkable victory the City of New York gave Lawrence the freedom of the city and a handsome piece of plate. The officers and crew of the "Hornet" were treated like heroes and entertained for several days.

Lawrence had hopes of getting the command of the "Constitution," in which he had already served as first lieutenant, but he was ordered to take charge of the "Chesapeake," then fitting at Boston. The "Chesapeake" was the "Jonah" of the American navy, and Lawrence felt dismayed, and begged to remain in the "Hornet." But he could not honorably refuse the call of duty, and in May, 1813, he took command of the ill-fated vessel. He found the ship very poor in both crew and officers, the latter being largely foreigners. He had a few good men from the "Constitution," and the marine guard was made up wholly of Americans. It was known that the "Shannon," a fine 38-gun frigate, lay in wait for the "Chesapeake" outside the harbor of Boston. Her commander, Capt. Broke, wrote Capt. Lawrence a letter proposing a meeting any time within two months, any waters he might designate, but this letter never reached Lawrence.

On the 1st of June, 1813, the "Shannon" stood in toward President's Roads, looking for her answer. Capt. Lawrence took this as a challenge, and started for the enemy. He hoisted his flag with the inscription: "Free trade and sailors' rights." He then addressed his men, but could stir no enthusiasm. He met the "Shannon" under a good breeze at a point about 30 miles beyond Boston Light. When the ships were not more than 50 yards apart, the "Shannon" fired a broadside, which was at once returned by the "Chesapeake." In smooth water and at close range the effect on both ships was terrific. The sails of the "Chesapeake" were so shot to pieces

within six minutes that she became unmanageable. Capt. Lawrence was shot in the leg, but still held the deck in command. Some of the British frigate's spars and sails were shot away, and she drifted against the "Chesapeake." Capt. Broke then ordered the ships lashed together. While Capt. Lawrence, wounded, was attempting to rally his men, he fell, shot through the body. On being carried below he uttered as a parting injunction the immortal words: "Don't give up the ship!"

The "Shannon" had not escaped scathless. On her deck lay Capt. Broke, raving with delirium from his wounds, and in rational moments uttering words of admiration for his gallant antagonist. He finally recovered, but the ship lost several officers, and 75 men killed and wounded. Lawrence lingered for four days in extreme anguish, during which he never spoke, except to make known his few wants. It was a gallant and yet tragically mournful death, for a young hero —he was barely thirty-two years old.

On June 6 the two ships entered Halifax harbor, and on the 8th Lawrence was given a great funeral by the enemy. The British garrison and fleet turned out in full force. The coffin, wrapped in the "Chesapeake's" flag with the dead officer's sword upon it, was brought ashore in an Admiral's barge amid the solemn booming of minute-guns. It was followed by a large procession of war-boats, and received at King's Wharf by six of the oldest British captains acting as pallbearers. The procession to the churchyard of St. Paul's was very long, and included not only the entire military-naval forces, but a large proportion of the best people of Halifax. As was afterward remarked: "The funeral was like that of a great and distinguished Admiral."

In the following August the remains of Capt. Lawrence were transferred to New York. Here another great ceremony was held. Among the six pallbearers were Hull, Stewart, and Bainbridge—all distinguished American commanders who had served with Lawrence in his youth. The remains of Capt. Lawrence rest in Trinity churchyard, New York City.

There is no prouder chapter in the history of all mankind than the record of our early naval commanders, one and all. Of such stuff as Capt. Lawrence were the early heroes of the American nation made.

DANIEL BOONE, INDIAN FIGHTER AND PIONEER

BY IRVINGTON LEE

THROUGH the trackless forest of Kentucky, in the days when that fruitful land was still a wilderness, a little band of frontiersmen were pressing forward. Each man carried a long rifle, with a powder horn slung at his side, and a little sack of bullets; in the belt of each was a keen knife, ready for instant use.

From time to time came the cry of a panther; now and again a startled deer bounded across their path. But to these things they paid no attention. Hunters though they were, they were out for other game.

Only a few hours before, a dreadful thing had happened. On the river running past the little settlement of Boonesborough, three young girls had gone paddling in a canoe. Venturing too far from the shore, the swift current had carried their tiny craft to the opposite bank. Then as they struggled to return, five Shawnee Indian warriors, hiding in the bushes, leaped into the stream, seized the screaming girls, and bore them away.

Hearing their cries, men in Boonesborough went quickly to the rescue; and though the girls had disappeared, the trampled bushes and the prints of Indian moccasins told a plain story to practiced eyes.

In those days, living always in fear of prowling savages, the settlers were prepared for quick action. Some of these, under Colonel Calloway, grasped their rifles, leaped into the saddle, and galloped off in the direction of the Shawnee village—hoping to cut off the Indians in their flight. Another party of rescuers started out on foot under the leadership of Daniel Boone.

BOONE TO THE RESCUE

Men were always eager to follow Daniel Boone. No one knew so well the ways of Indians. No one had such skill in finding a trail, or such endurance in following it till his object was achieved. Quick to think, and quick to act, he had often saved his own life and the lives of others by his skill and intelligence. Feared and respected by the Indians, he had come to be the acknowledged leader in his own community.

So we see him in command of the little party of frontiersmen making their way through the forest, in pursuit of a cunning enemy. The fleeing Indians left few traces. On the ground covered with leaves they could tread so lightly in their soft moccasins that only a trained eye could detect the slightest sign. How was it possible to overtake them? Luckily, the captured girls were quick of wit. They did not faint or lose their presence of mind. From time to time they managed to break a twig, or to press a foot down hard on some soft spot in the ground.

Daniel Boone, in the lead of his men, found their trail where they had crossed the mud of a little stream. Then, in the leaf-strewn forest, he lost it again. But on and on he pressed, hoping to pick it up. Suddenly he paused, and pointed to the broken branch of a sapling.

"Look!" he said, "They have passed this way."

"But could not a feeding deer have broken that branch?" asked a young man in the party. "See! The leaves are stripped from it."

"No," answered Boone, looking closely at the bark. "This was not done by an animal's tooth. It was broken by one of the girls, as a sign to guide us. The Indians have tried to put us off the track by stripping the leaves and injuring the bark, but they were in too much of a hurry to make a good job of it. Come on! These leaves are still fresh. They cannot be far away."

Knowing the lay of the land, he could now guess the route the Indians would follow. The pursuers quickened their pace, Boone in the lead moving with such long strides that his comrades could scarcely keep up with him. At last, in an open place on the slope of a hill, they caught sight of the Indians. One of them walked in advance; as he reached the crest of the hill Boone raised his rifle and fired, and the warrior fell dead in his tracks. Before the Shawnees could recover from their surprise, a second savage fell mortally wounded. The others fled into the woods, leaving the three girls unharmed.

A CHILD OF THE WILDERNESS

The life of Daniel Boone was filled with such adventures. His place in American history is with those pioneers who made their way into the West when the country was wild and unsettled, and who by their courage and example made it possible for others to dwell there in peace and security. They were strong men—strong in body and strong in character; men who endured great hardships as a matter of course, and who risked their lives constantly without complaint.

Daniel Boone's training for the life he was to lead began in early boyhood, in the forests of Pennsylvania, where he was born in 1735. There was no schoolhouse and no school teacher, so he had to be content with the little he could learn from his mother. He was taught to read, and to write after a fashion. But a gun and gunpowder were always more familiar to him than pen and ink, and spelling was a task he never quite managed to master.

Yet though he learned little from books, he learned much from life itself. A child of the wilderness, he began at an early age to acquaint himself with the things that make a successful hunter and trapper. When only a little fellow he could use his hands so skillfully that he made a spear with which he killed small game. Hunters in those days did not kill animals for "sport," as men do now. They killed them because they really needed meat for the table, and skins and furs with which to clothe themselves. A deer would keep a family in food for a long time; from its skin the hunter made garments that clad him from top to toe.

THE BOY BECOMES A DEER HUNTER

At twelve years of age Daniel was already a deer hunter, and in a fair way to support himself by the sale of venison and skins. To become such a hunter it was necessary, in the first place, to learn the life of the woods, and how to care for oneself, no matter what happened, in the depths of the vast forest. Many kinds of knowledge are necessary to one who spends his days in this fashion, and the boy became familiar with all things out of doors. He knew the various trees by their leaves and bark, the birds by their plumage and song. The habits of the wild animals, the tracks they made, their feeding and resting-places, all became known to him. Observing always the weather, he could tell when a storm was coming. Killing his own meat, he could prepare and cook it, too; supper done, he asked nothing better than to turn in for the night on a bed of balsam pine. Thus in learning to become a hunter he had cultivated habits of close observation, and had come to be self-reliant. There were Indians, too, in the forest, and the boy grew familiar with their ways.

This acquaintance with Indian ways soon served him well. His father had gone to live in the Yadkin River country of North Carolina.

Indians swarmed in these regions, and when the whites became more numerous the redskins resented their coming. As Daniel grew to manhood, he began to take part in the fighting that now frequently occurred. To protect themselves from raids, the settlers had erected forts called blockhouses, made of logs and protected by walls, with loopholes through which to fire at the enemy. Scouts would give warning of a threatened outbreak, and the farmers and their families, taking

DANIEL BOONE
FROM A PAINTING BY ALONZO CHAPPEL

refuge in the forts, would aid in the repulse of the savages.

BOONE GOES TO KENTUCKY

Farming was far from being a peaceful occupation. At any moment the plowman might be called upon to drop his plow handles, grasp his gun, and rush to the defense of his family. Boone himself had tried his hand at farming; but so often was he called upon to take up arms that fighting rather than farming became his chief work.

It seems, however, that he rather sought excitement. Living daily, as he had, in the face of danger, he could not enjoy a quiet life without adventure. He longed for new lands to explore —for new difficulties to overcome in some region that still awaited the white man. A son of the wilderness, his was the spirit and heart of the pioneer.

So westward he went, seeking the pleasant lands of Kentucky, where the soil was rich and deep, and the virgin forests abounded in many kinds of game. With him went forty men, with their herds and household goods, their wives and children. Suddenly the Indians descended upon them. Boone and his companions beat them off, but six of his party were slain and the cattle were scattered. This disheartened the emigrants. Boone saw them safely to a settlement already established, then plunged once more into the wilderness in search of adventure. This he soon found, of a kind to test his powers of body and soul. But meanwhile he was called upon to found a settlement south of the Kentucky River. When the town and fort were built, they called it Boonesborough.

This was in 1775, when Boone was forty years of age. He had brought his wife and children across the mountains, and it seemed to him that the time had arrived when he might settle down again and pursue the ways of peace.

CAPTURED BY THE INDIANS

But once more the Indians came upon the scene. They had long planned an attack upon Boonesborough; yet fearing Boone, who commanded the fort, they bided their time. One day Boone left the settlement with thirty men, in search of salt. Leaving his companions in camp at the salt springs, he set out with his rifle to get a supply of meat. Then, as he made his way back, leading a pack-horse, he was suddenly surrounded by a band of Shawnees.

The Indians took him prisoner to their camp, where Black Fish, a famous chief, greeted him in a friendly manner. Black Fish really admired Boone for his skill and courage, and wished to spare his life. With the tribe were already four whites who had turned renegades and married Indian wives. Perhaps, thought Black Fish, this great White Brave could be persuaded to follow their example.

Boone was obliged to make the best of it. As he could not escape, he pretended to enjoy life with the Indians, who treated him well and let him do pretty much as he pleased. So well did Daniel play his part that Black Fish adopted him as his son. They shaved the white man's head, leaving only hair enough for a long scalp lock like their own. They painted his face, adorned him with beads and feathers, and otherwise endeavored to make him feel perfectly at home. Finally, in their playful Indian way, they made him "run the gauntlet." And when he took the rough sport good-naturedly, and managed at the same time to overturn some of his tormentors by using his head like a billy-goat, they

Courtesy of Estate of C. Y. Turner

TREATING WITH THE INDIANS
FROM A PAINTING BY CHARLES YARDLEY TURNER

seemed more pleased than ever with this adopted son.

HE ESCAPES AND SAVES THE SETTLEMENT

Boone, of course, was only waiting his opportunity to escape. The Indians did not guard him closely, sometimes even permitting him to hunt. Boonesborough was 150 miles away. How could a man without food or rifle hope to travel that trackless waste? If he was not captured, he would starve.

But the Indians did not know Boone. One day he overheard them planning an attack on Boonesborough. That was quite enough. Watching his chance, he plunged into a thicket, and was gone.

Four days later the ghost of a man staggered into Boonesborough. It was Daniel Boone, given up as dead. It was Daniel Boone come back, in time to save the fort. The Indians had attacked, and all but overpowered the few defenders. They would attack again in superior numbers—five to one. But Daniel Boone had come back.

The Indians did indeed return—five Indians to one white. But Boone was there, so the odds did not matter; the Shawnees were driven off and finally dispersed.

Later in life Daniel Boone pushed West once more. When he died it was in Missouri—a hunter and trapper still at the age of 85. Kentucky and Missouri both cherish his name, but his figure is a national one. So his statue stands to-day in the rotunda of the Capitol at Washington—the figure of a hunter beset by two savages at once, and conquering both. It is a true incident, and one in keeping with the life of the great pioneer.

THE WIFE WHO TAUGHT HER HUSBAND TO BE PRESIDENT *

JAMES MADISON might never have been President if he hadn't married his wife. And she had not Mrs. Washington's strong character, ncr Mrs. Adams' fine mind. She was just beautiful, sweet and kind-hearted. Indeed, she was a sort of fairy queen, the loveliest person that can be put into a story.

About the time the Revolution was getting ready to begin, Dorothea Payne was born on a plantation in Virginia. Her father and mother were sober Quakers, but the merry baby wasn't a Quaker at all. Her dark blue eyes, curly brown hair, pretty dimples and bubbling laugh were as Irish as shamrocks. So everyone felt obliged to call her "Dolly."

By and by the family went to Philadelphia to live, lost their money, and Dolly's husband, Mr. Todd, died leaving her a widow with a little boy, at twenty-one. Such troubles! She and her mother were so poor they had to take boarders into their lovely quiet home. But they were ladies, and were often seen at Lady Washington's levees, where the beautiful widow Todd was much admired.

HOW "DOLLY" MET MR. MADISON

One morning Mr. James Madison, Senator from Virginia, saw her on the street. A wealthy bachelor, twice her age, very stiff and shy, "the great little Madison" had never been known to notice ladies. But, just like a story book, he lost his heart. Mrs. Washington heard about it, and sent for the heroine of the pretty romance.

"Dolly, I hear you are to make a great match, and marry Mr. Madison."

"If—if you please, ma'am." Demure Dolly dropped her prettiest curtsy.

"You sweet minx, the President and I are very much pleased. You must make people know Mr. Madison better—make him popular."

And so they were married, and lived happily for —oh, quite forty years. Dolly blossomed out like a queen rose, in the prettiest finery ever seen in America. Rich, petted, gay, she was not spoiled. She won all hearts by her gentle sweetness. She never forgot a face or a name, an interest or a trouble of other people. The poor were fed from her table. Shabby girls were dressed for parties from her wardrobe. And she loved to sit on a nursery floor and "play dolls" with little girls. Where she was everyone was at his best and happiest, and people flocked around her like bees around a honey pot. The heart of her elderly scholar of a husband was full of love and pride in her, and she drew him into social life, and won many friends for him by her kindness and tact. She didn't know so much as he did about books, but, oh, her wise little head and warm little heart knew all about people!

* From "Pictured Knowledge," published by the Compton-Johnson Company, Chicago; used by permission of the publishers.

In 1801 Mr. Jefferson was elected President. His wife was dead, and his daughters married

From a Thistle Print, copyright by Detroit Publishing Co.
DOLLY MADISON
FROM A PAINTING BY GILBERT STUART IN THE PENNSYLVANIA ACADEMY OF FINE ARTS

and busy with their young families. People said he had two reasons for wanting Mr. Madison to be his Secretary of State. One was, of course, that he considered him a fit man for the place. The other, it is said, was so that he could ask Mrs. Madison to be hostess when there was a state dinner or ball at the White House. Then Mr. Madison followed Mr. Jefferson in office. So "Dolly" Madison was first lady of the land for sixteen years, for the two terms Jefferson served and for the two terms Madison served. History says that she made those brilliant years "the golden age of American society."

Some of them were stormy years, too. She was mistress of the White House in 1814, when the British captured and burned the capital. Like the boy on the burning deck, Dolly stood at her post until her absent husband sent word for her to fly. Under cannon fire she saved papers, silver, and the Stuart portrait of Washington.

A SWEET MEMORY OF THE WHITE HOUSE

She lived to be very old, and became poor, but Congress provided for her, and when she appeared at a White House reception she was the belle of the evening at seventy.

There is a portrait of her in the President's mansion. Painted in the low-necked, short-sleeved gown of Napoleon's day, she looks much like the beautiful Empress Josephine. Her dark blue eyes smile down on the scenes where she reigned, and somehow she seems still to be there.

ANDREW JACKSON, SOLDIER AND SEVENTH PRESIDENT

BY IRVINGTON LEE

"HERE, you young scoundrel! What are you doing there? Whittling a stick, eh? I'll give you something to occupy your hands."

The speaker was a Captain of British dragoons; the scene, a log hut in the hills of North Carolina, in the closing days of the American Revolution. In the year before, things had looked black indeed for the colonies in the long, bitter struggle for independence. The British General, Lord Cornwallis, had defeated the colonial army under General Gates near Camden. In the Southern States further British activities followed. Here in the Carolinas the homes of the settlers were marked with blood and ruin.

The boy thus roughly addressed by the Captain of dragoons was a redheaded youngster of fourteen years. He was big for his age, with the hard muscles and tanned skin of one who had known hard toil from his early childhood. In the eyes of the dragoon he was just a country lout—fit only to do the dirty work around the camp. A prisoner of war, to be sure—for the boy had not yielded without a fight; and prisoners of war are not without certain rights. Yet his captor could only see him as the offspring of a peasant rabble who had dared to rebel against the majesty of King George. Scum of the earth, and traitors all, to whom it would be a weakness to show gentleness and mercy.

THE BOY DEFIES HIS CAPTOR

There were gallant officers in the British army—gallant officers and gentlemen who did not share this view. And there were people in England—many, many people—who did not approve of the war against the colonies, and who thought that their king had blundered. And as time passed, England came to see that this war had been stupid and unjust; that King George had never done a more foolish thing than to goad the Americans into taking up arms.

The boy, of course, could not know this. What he did know was that soldiers in red coats had come to conquer his country, and that the iron heel of an oppressor bore hard upon the land. He had seen his home destroyed; he had seen his mother and two brothers fall victims to the invaders. And when his own puny strength had proved no match for grown men, he had found himself a despised captive. He, a free-born American, with the fighting blood of Scotch and Irish ancestors in his veins. How could he endure the insults and humiliation heaped upon him?

"Come!" said his captor. "Get to work! Clean these boots, and see that you make a good job of it."

He flung his long riding boots at the boy, who had slowly risen and advanced a step, but made no motion to pick them up.

"Be quick, I say," repeated the dragoon. "What are you standing and staring at? Take off every bit of that red clay, and give them a good rubbing."

For a moment the boy stood looking at him, with clenched hands and flashing eyes. Then he spoke:

"Clean your boots!" he cried. "Do you take me for a slave? What right have you to ask me to be your servant? Do you think our own officers would treat a British prisoner like this? Clean them yourself!"

"SOMETHING TO REMEMBER"

Rage and astonishment overcame the Captain, and made him forget all he owed to his own dignity. Never before had anyone dared to disobey him. Now he found himself openly defied by a freckled-face youngster; in language that called for instant punishment. He would make an example of him.

"You impudent young hound!" he shouted. "I'll teach you something to remember as long as you live."

With that he drew his sword, and began beating the boy with the flat of the blade. But such was his excitement and wrath that he could not wholly control his weapon. The sword turned in his hand, and its edge, striking the captive on the wrist, cut through the flesh to the bone.

The sight of the blood brought the dragoon to his senses. Brute though he was, his education and associations as an officer had left some impress on his character. Suddenly he realized that he was doing a cowardly thing, and that in striking an unarmed prisoner he was disgracing his own uniform.

"I didn't mean to hurt you," he said roughly. "Learn to obey orders, and no harm will come to you. It was really your own fault."

Then, knowing he had done a foolish and a cruel thing, he strode away without another word.

But Andrew Jackson, future President of the United States, did not clean that British officer's boots.

A THREAT THAT BECAME A PROPHECY

"I'll teach you something to remember as long as you live."

When the British dragoon officer uttered this threat, following it up with a brutal assault on his boy prisoner, he little realized the true meaning of his words. Andrew Jackson, to be sure, never forgot them. The injury done him was burned into his brain. In all the years to come he did indeed remember; but the memory was of a nature far different from the impression his assailant had sought to make. The Captain had meant so to punish him that always he would know better than to defy the soldiers of the king; he would teach him to fear and respect a Redcoat all the days of his life. Yet already the power of that king was weakening; and many years later, when British troops again invaded these shores, young Andrew, become a General, was to lead his men to victory against them.

Had that British dragoon Captain been able to peer into the future, he would have stood aghast. This poor country boy whom he so despised was to win his way, step by step, till he came to rule the nation that was then struggling for its life. Andrew was an orphan. He was ignorant and penniless. He had no friends. In a country made desolate by war he was thrown upon his own resources. But he had health, strength, ambition. His mind was quick and vigorous. Above all, he had the strength of character and the spirit that made him persevere.

HIS RISE FROM POVERTY TO FAME

Somehow he overcame all obstacles in his path. Without schooling, he yet managed not only to make a living, but to educate himself in the law. He had crossed the mountains into Tennessee, where he worked at farming and at selling merchandise in a country store. But he had set out to be a lawyer, and a lawyer he became when but twenty years of age. Seven years from that day when he hurled defiance at the Captain of dragoons, Andrew Jackson became public prosecutor of the region we now call Tennessee. At thirty they elected him a Senator, then made him a Judge of the Supreme Court of his State. Whatever honor he sought, that honor was now accorded him.

When the war of 1812, with Great Britain, broke out, the thoughts of Andrew Jackson turned to fighting. Soon he was made a Major-General, first in the State militia and then in the Regular Army of the United States. When the Creek Indians took the war-path, General Jackson was sent to subdue them, and this he did with such a dash and vigor that the Indians never again gave much trouble to the Government.

Then came his crowning triumph at New Orleans—the final battle of the war of 1812.

HIS VICTORY OVER THE BRITISH

Louisiana in those days was a remote part of the United States. To people living in New England it seemed as far away as Alaska does now. All the neighboring region had belonged first to France, and then to Spain. Then it became the property of France again, and in 1803 France sold it to us. It was not till 1812 that the State was admitted into the Union.

It was this part of our country that the British selected for attack. On the sea the war had gone against them. But they had taken Washington, which they burned and pillaged, and now New Orleans seemed an easy prize. The city, built on flat land, with no defenses, was apparently at the mercy of a strong enemy bringing troops by sea through the Gulf of Mexico. It was a critical situation, and the President knew that only some leader of great skill and courage, in whom the people had confidence, could be relied upon to save the day. He chose Andrew Jackson.

Jackson lost no time. He acted with force and decision—making his own plans and permitting no one to interfere with them. When a city is besieged its defenders, though few in number, are able, behind the walls of a fort, to keep a superior foe at bay. But there was no fort. So General Jackson set about making breastworks. The great industry of Louisiana was cotton, and bales of cotton seemed just the thing with which to build defenses. Soon his men were working like beavers. Bale was piled upon bale, and when at last the British advanced to the attack they found the Americans prepared to give them a hot reception.

AMERICANS OUTNUMBERED

Even so, the odds were against the defenders. They faced an army of fifteen thousand men— seasoned soldiers who had fought in the campaigns against Napoleon. Opposing them, behind cotton bales and sugar hogsheads, was a nondescript army of barely six thousand. Every man who could bear arms was called upon to repel the invader. There were volunteer militia, hunters and frontiersmen, raw recruits who had never been under fire, sailors and farmers, along with some regular soldiers—the whole forming as strange a body of men as ever assembled to do battle. As for weapons, there were rifles, to be sure, in the hands of practiced marksmen. But some had only horse-pistols, others blunderbusses, or guns of an old pattern.

On came the British in perfect order. But they were met by a withering fire which broke their ranks and scattered them in confusion. Soon they rallied, encouraged by their officers, and again advanced to the attack, only to retreat once more. At each assault the Americans held their fire until the enemy were close upon them; at each repulse the British rallied and re-formed. There came a final, desperate charge—beaten back by a hail of bullets. This time the Redcoats did not rally, but turned and fled. General Jackson had saved New Orleans.

It was a brilliant victory. Never had the British suffered such a defeat. Their commander, Sir Edward Pakenham, was slain by an American sharpshooter. In all they lost 2,600 killed and wounded, while the Americans counted but eight men dead and thirteen wounded. This

JOHN C. CALHOUN

DANIEL WEBSTER

HENRY CLAY

LEWIS CASS

STEPHEN A. DOUGLAS

THOMAS H. BENTON

AMERICAN POLITICAL ORATORS

battle had been fought and won in something less than half an hour.

JACKSON ELECTED PRESIDENT

Andrew Jackson had already gained great military fame when he shattered the power of the Creek Indians, a year before, in the battle of Tallapoosa. The victory at New Orleans made him a popular hero, and this popularity was strengthened by his rise, through his own exertions, from an humble beginning. In the presidential election of 1824 he all but succeeded in defeating John Quincy Adams of Massachusetts; four years later, when Adams was again a candidate, Jackson was elected by a vote of more than two to one. In 1832 he received 219 electoral votes, and was again elected President, this time over Henry Clay, candidate of the National Republicans, for whom but 49 votes were cast.

Jackson was one of the most energetic and picturesque figures in American history. He was quick to make up his mind, and when a decision was reached he overcame all opposition. "Old Hickory," as he came to be known to his affectionate admirers, was more than once called upon as President to display the vigor and force of his iron character. In this brief sketch of his career, one such instance will suffice:

South Carolina did not like a tariff law framed by the National Congress, and threatened to secede from the Union if the law was enforced. President Jackson's answer to this was a proclamation commanding that State to obey the will of the Federal Government; and to enforce that command he sent a naval force under Farragut to Charleston harbor. Then Calhoun and his followers in South Carolina came to their senses. The "Nullifiers," as these hotheads were called, gave way to better counsels, and this great danger to the Union was averted.

Jackson named his own successor to the Presidential chair. Up to the very last his fiery character flamed out in word and action. "What would I have done to Calhoun and his friends?" he exclaimed, as he lay at the point of death. "What would I have done to them had they defied the Federal Government? I would have hung them, sir—hung them high as Haman!"

And nobody for a moment doubted him.

THE ADVENTURES OF LEWIS AND CLARK

BY IRVINGTON LEE

On a high plain, in the region of the Rocky Mountains, a herd of buffalo was grazing.

Where the buffalo roamed, there also roamed the Indian. Its meat he cut into thin strips, and dried in the sun. From its skin he made tents and clothing; from its sinews, bow-strings and thread; from its horns, drinking cups and spoons. Without the buffalo, the Indian would have perished.

Sometimes he made a sport of hunting the shaggy beast. Mounting his half-wild mustang, he would ride among the herd at break-neck speed, singling out his prey, and urging his horse alongside while he discharged his arrows. Or, again, he would set the dry grass on fire, head off the terrified herd as it sought to escape, and thus make his hunting much easier.

But the herd on this high plain in the Rockies fell victims in a stranger way.

Some distance off, in the direction the buffalo were headed, the plain ended abruptly in a steep cliff, with a river far below. Between this cliff and the herd, a solitary buffalo presently made its appearance. At least, it seemed to be a buffalo; and it looked so much like one, that the stupid herd was none the wiser. Actually, this creature was a Blackfoot Indian, who walked on all fours, with a buffalo skin covering his body, and buffalo horns rising from his head.

LURED TO THEIR DEATH

Then a band of Indians, without disguise, suddenly rode up in the rear of the herd, and began to yell. At this, the buffalo, badly frightened, galloped off toward the cliff. Faster and faster they galloped, toward the figure of the false Indian, who was now on the very edge of the precipice, to which he had lured the unsuspecting creatures. Then he vanished.

He had hidden himself safely in a ledge of the rocks; as he crouched there he could see the buffalo plunging down to their death. Many had galloped too far and too fast, and could not stop in time to save themselves.

When the Indians had taken their pick of the fattest animals, they left the rest in the river, and went their way. The strange sight was witnessed by a party of explorers—the first white men to penetrate this savage country. It was the Lewis and Clark expedition, sent out by President Jefferson to explore our new territory, Louisiana, and to find a way to the Pacific.

It was a romantic and a daring journey, filled with the perils of the unknown. If you look at a map of the United States made in 1803, you will see that its western boundary was the Mississippi River. Between this and the Rocky Mountains, from Texas on the south to the British possessions on the north, lay the vast region called Louisiana. Late in the seventeenth century, the French had not only pushed their way to the Ohio Valley, but had explored the Mississippi to its mouth, and established the city of New Orleans. Here they might have founded a new empire. But their war with England in America ended with the loss of Quebec in 1759, by which the British acquired Canada; and, four years later, France gave Louisiana to Spain. Then, in 1801, Spain returned it to France; and Napoleon planned to colonize it, but sold it to the United States instead.

It was President Jefferson who made the purchase, and his critics thought he had driven a poor bargain. Yet thirteen of our States have arisen from this territory, for which only $15,-000,000 was paid, and the West of to-day owes much of its greatness to his wisdom and foresight.

A LAND UNKNOWN

Beyond Louisiana, from the Rockies to the Pacific, lay a wilderness all unexplored. No one knew where the Missouri River rose. To reach the Pacific overland was a dream as yet unrealized. When Jefferson was minister to France, he encouraged John Ledyard, an American, in an attempt to enter the United States by way of the Pacific coast. This attempt failed; but in 1792 Captain Gray of Boston sailed around the Horn, and discovered the Columbia River in Oregon. As this was a large river, it now seemed possible that if explorers could make their way to the head of the Missouri, they might find the source of the Columbia, and thus travel by water to the Pacific Ocean.

It was, besides, desirable to explore our new possessions, to learn what riches they contained, and what were the Indian tribes. So the President persuaded Congress to provide the funds, and the expedition was soon organized.

Captain Meriwether Lewis and Captain William Clark, both Virginians, were chosen as the leaders of this adventurous party. Lewis, whose knowledge of science was increased by special studies made in preparation for the journey, had been a farmer and a soldier, and was private secretary to President Jefferson. Clark, who had also served in the army, was familiar with Indian ways, and was well qualified as military commander of the expedition.

There were only thirty men in the party. About half of these were soldiers who had volunteered; nine were backwoodsmen from Kentucky, who had grown up with rifles in their hands; two were Frenchmen, skilled in canoeing, known as voyageurs. The others included an experienced hunter, an interpreter who could speak several Indian languages, and a negro servant.

TO REACH THE PACIFIC

All these men were taking their lives in their hands. They were about to penetrate a wild, rough country, abounding in grizzly bears, and inhabited by tribes of wandering Indians who might easily dispute the progress of this little band. But if they could reach the Pacific, and blaze the way for the ox-teams of American settlers, they would find reward enough.

It took a long time to make ready. The boat supplied by the government was fifty-five feet long, with cabins fore and aft, a large square sail, and twenty-two oars. In this craft they floated down the Ohio, in the Summer of 1803; then rowed up the Mississippi till they reached St. Louis. Pitching their camp at a point some miles above that trading post, they spent the Winter laying in supplies, which included many ornaments and cloths of bright colors as presents with which to pacify the Indians. Then, in May, 1804, when the river was free from ice, they bent to the oars, and urged their boat against the swift and treacherous current of the Missouri. Rapids, sandbars and drifting trees made their progress slow; fifteen miles was an average day's journey.

One of the duties of Captain Lewis was to collect the strange legends and traditions related by the Indians, who had curious notions concerning their origin and early history. The Osages believed that the first Indian of their tribe was a snail, carried away by a flood, then warmed by the heat of the sun until he became a man. When a beaver questioned his right to hunt on the river banks, he settled the dispute by marrying the beaver's daughter; so, for a long time to come, the beaver was spared by Osage hunters, lest in slaying him they should take the life of a kinsman. According to the Mandans, their home was once beneath the earth's surface, in a kind of huge cave from which they made their escape by clambering up the roots of a grapevine.

IN WINTER QUARTERS

In July, the explorers passed the mouth of the Platte River, and made friends with the Indians of that region. Here, on a high bluff, a council was held, attended by the chiefs of the tribe, to whom Lewis explained the peaceful nature of the expedition. To-day this region is known to us as Iowa, and the city that grew up near the site of the meeting is called Council Bluffs.

For nearly six months the explorers had toiled their way up-stream, and had traveled about 1600 miles—a trip now made by railroad in less than 48 hours. Then, in October, the river began to freeze. It was time to make camp for the winter; so they settled down near what is now Bismarck, Dakota, and were frozen in for some five months. Their hunters were expert shots, and their huts kept out the cold, but it was rather tedious waiting. However, they had many visitors—Indians who happened by, and white men connected with the Hudson's Bay Company.

These they plied with questions concerning the country beyond; but their visitors knew little about it, excepting from vague reports brought them by trappers and Indians. How would they find their way through the tangle of mountains and rivers? When the stream they were following branched to the right and left, which branch should they take? Finally, how could they make themselves understood by the strange Indians speaking languages unknown to their interpreters?

AN INDIAN HEROINE

The answer came unexpectedly, in the person of an Indian woman, who was to prove their best guide and counselor. Sacajawea, "the Bird-woman," she was called in her native tongue. Born in the Rocky Mountains, she had been taken prisoner by a hostile tribe; then, carried eastward, she became the wife of Chaboneau, a local interpreter who had recently joined the party.

The story of the Bird-woman is a touching one. Burdened with a young child she could not leave behind, she showed herself the equal, in courage and endurance, of any man in the party. Some instinct, born of her savage blood, told her which path to take when the explorers stood perplexed. When meat was scarce she knew, as no man knew, just what could be done with bones. To a sick man who had done her a kindness she offered her last bit of bread. She was, in short, a heroine—somehow forgot when the time came for rewards. "Statues of her," predicted one admirer, "must yet be reared by grateful dwellers in lands she laid open for their happy homes. Western poets will liken her to Ariadne and Beatrice."

Setting out once more, in April, the explorers were now but half way up the Missouri. For four months, in this lonely land, they did not meet a single human being. When game was sighted, their rifles brought it down; but game there was none for many a weary day.

ON THE GREAT DIVIDE

In three weeks of perilous traveling, the party reached the Yellowstone; a month later they were cheered with a sight of the Rocky Mountains. From far away had come a noise as of distant thunder. It was the thunder of the Great Falls, where the river tumbled headlong in a cloud of mist: a thrilling sight that almost repaid them for a month's delay in getting around this obstacle.

Soon afterward, the great Missouri River had dwindled to a tiny trickle that a man could easily bestride. Five days more of climbing, and they were on the summit of the Great Divide, whence the springs that make the rivers flowed east to the Atlantic, and west to the Pacific Ocean. In a year and three months they had come three thousand miles, and had some narrow escapes.

In August, almost starved, they met some Indians. One of their chiefs approached, and the Bird-woman fell on his neck. It was her brother! Beside streams too swift for canoes, they toiled along—sometimes eating horses, sometimes dining on dogs; for there was no game at all. In October, they hollowed out logs with fire, set them afloat and embarked in them. They had found a branch of the Columbia; late in November the sound of breaking surf came to their ears. Now, at last, they had reached the Pacific Ocean.

CAPT. MERIWETHER LEWIS.   GENL. WILLIAM CLARK.

243

MARCUS WHITMAN'S RIDE

BY IRVINGTON LEE

"Hurrah for Oregon! The Yankees are too late! Hurrah for Oregon—the country is ours!"

Thus exclaiming, an excited young Englishman rose from his seat at the dinner table, and tossed his hat in the air.

The other guests of the Hudson's Bay Company, assembled in the dining room at Fort Walla Walla, caught his excitement. They, too, rose from their seats, and gathered in little groups to discuss the news.

To the British trading company and its supporters it was pleasing news indeed—news which seemed to indicate that the rich country called Oregon would soon become a colony of Great Britain. From Fort Colville, far up the Columbia, a messenger had arrived with the tidings that one hundred and forty colonists, British and Canadian, were hastening to settle on the farming lands of this disputed region. It meant that British subjects would outnumber the few Americans, and thus establish a claim to possession by the Crown.

But there was one guest present who took no part in the demonstration. Inwardly excited, he heard the news with a smile, seemed to accept the situation, and took his departure quietly. This was Marcus Whitman, an American missionary, who had come all the way from Boston, a few years before, and established a mission at Waiilatpui, among the Nez Percés Indians.

The first thing that Whitman did, on leaving the Fort, was to seek his friend, Amos Lovejoy, and acquaint him with what had happened.

"Lovejoy," he said, "you have recently come from the East, and you know as well as I do what this means. If something is not done, and done quickly, Oregon will be forever lost to the United States."

SHORT-SIGHTED STATESMEN

"But what *can* be done?" asked Lovejoy. "This is October. Before Congress adjourns in March, it will probably ratify the treaty settling the boundary line, and giving all this wonderful country to Great Britain, in exchange for the right to fish off the coast of Newfoundland. Think of that, Whitman! Was there ever anything so ridiculous? Is there not one statesman in Washington who can see beyond his nose?"

Apparently there was not. Even the great Daniel Webster—now, in 1842, our Secretary of State—had said on the floor of the Senate: "What do we want with this vast, worthless area, this region of savages and wild beasts, of shifting sands, of cactus and prairie-dogs? To what use could we ever hope to put these great deserts, or these endless mountain ranges, impenetrable, and covered to their base with eternal snow? What can we ever hope to do with the western coast—rock-bound, cheerless, and uninviting? I will never vote one cent from the public treasury to place it one inch nearer to Boston."

Yet this "vast, worthless area" is one of the richest and most fertile in the United States. It stretched from the Rocky Mountains to the Pacific, from Spanish California to Russian Alaska; it included what came to be British Columbia, as well as our own States of Oregon, Washington, Idaho, with parts of Montana and Wyoming.

The British Hudson's Bay Company well knew its worth. For its furs alone its value was past all calculation. The American John Jacob Astor had once been a rival in the field, with a trading station on the Columbia River; but in the war of 1812 his enterprise was absorbed by the Canadians, and thereafter the English traders held full sway.

It was then a country of Indians and trappers. Farming was discouraged by the British monopolists of furs; only a handful of American settlers had managed to straggle across the mountains, abandoning their wagons as they went, in their struggle with the terrors of the wilderness.

AN AMAZING HONEYMOON

What commerce and the pioneer farmer had failed to do was achieved by the zeal of the missionary. The Nez Percés of Oregon had shown an interest in the Christian religion; and Marcus Whitman, then a farmer in New York, responded to the call. With the authority of the American Board of Missions, he set out on one of the most remarkable trips ever made across the continent. He was the first man to cross the Rocky Mountains in a wagon; and with him went his young bride, sharing all the perils and hardships of this extraordinary journey.

Several times the wagon was all but wrecked.

It was overturned in a river, slid over a cliff, bounded and coasted down mountains. At Fort Hall, in Idaho, the Hudson's Bay Company's representative used every argument short of force to induce the plucky missionary to abandon it, and rely on horses alone. But Whitman would not be bullied, and refused to be discouraged by difficulties. He knew that if he stuck to his wagon, and took it across the mountains, he would be setting an example for settlers to follow. So, encouraged by his plucky wife, he persisted in his course; and, at last, what was left of his vehicle arrived in triumph and on two wheels in the promised land of Oregon.

A DARING IDEA

Whitman, it will be seen, was not a man to balk at dangers, or to hesitate in the face of what others called impossible. When he heard the news that the British colonists were coming, he was seized with a daring idea. Even now it might be too late. But some one must go to Washington at once; must see President Tyler, and tell him the true state of affairs. So when Lovejoy asked him, "What can be done?" he had thought out his plan and was ready with the answer.

"It's simple enough," he said. "I crossed the continent with a wagon. I can do it again on horseback. There is no other way."

There was, to be sure, no other way; yet this one way seemed madness. Lewis and Clark, the explorers, had spent eighteen months in traveling from St. Louis to the Pacific. Their party numbered thirty men; throughout the winter season, they did not travel at all. Yet Whitman proposed to mount a horse, carry his provisions on pack mules, and make a journey of four thousand miles in a matter of five months. The rivers would be frozen, the mountain passes blocked with snow; he must somehow find his way through a savage wilderness, pressing on with such haste that there would be no time for hunting. It seemed beyond the strength of any human being. But Whitman's mind was made up, and Lovejoy agreed to go with him.

It is greatly to the honor of his wife that she did not try to discourage him. He was going on a desperate errand from which he might not return—an errand offering none of the prizes which urge men to risk their lives. He was not in the service of his country; no one had ordered or asked him to do this thing. But she saw with his eyes the task he had set himself. "Go, and God be with you!" she said.

Even then, someone tried to stop him. "You are breaking the rules of the Mission Board," it was urged. "How can you leave your post without permission from Boston?"

Whitman turned on the objector. "You really mean that?" he exclaimed. "Very well, then. Let the Board dismiss me, if it takes that view of it. But when I became a missionary, I did not cease to be an American citizen. If anything I can do will save Oregon to the nation, I am willing to take the consequences."

OFF TO SAVE OREGON

It was October 3d when Whitman and Lovejoy set out, after warning their friends to keep it a secret from the Hudson's Bay Company. They took with them only their horses, three pack-mules, and a half-breed Indian guide. Riding in a southeasterly direction for eleven days, they came to Fort Hall, the southernmost station of the Canadian fur traders. Here, once more, Whitman met Captain Grant, whose arguments and half-veiled threats had discouraged so many American pioneers in their westward march across the mountains. Again he was ready with advice. "What! Cross the Rockies when the snow was twenty feet deep in the passes? Impossible! Only a crazy man would attempt it." Besides, the Blackfeet had gone on the warpath; if the snow did not turn the Americans back, the Indians surely would.

Whitman listened patiently till the Captain paused for breath. "This news about the Indians is a great help to us," he said. "You have probably saved our lives."

The Captain looked relieved; he had gained his point.

"That being the case," continued Whitman, with a twinkle in his eye, "we will bear to the south, instead, and shape our course in the general direction of the Great Salt Lake."

Then the Captain gave it up as hopeless, and the Americans resumed their journey. The plan was to strike for the Santa Fé trail, a famous route across the continent, which they could follow all the way to St. Louis, on the Mississippi. They would stop at Fort Uintah and Fort Uncompahgre, and find a guide who could take them on to Taos, in New Mexico.

SOME THRILLING ADVENTURES

Now the blasts of winter smote them. It was bitter cold, and the snow fell fast and thick. Attempting to cross a mountain pass, the storm drove them back. Sheltered in a ravine for ten days, they again pressed forward, only to be halted again by a second storm. Their guide lost his bearings, and would go no farther; their trail from the ravine was covered with drifts. It seemed that they must perish. In this desperate situation, Whitman knelt down in the snow, and prayed for help. Then a pack-mule, turned loose by the guide, began floundering through the drifts in the direction from which they had come. Following him, they soon reached camp.

Whitman was obliged to go back for another guide, leaving Lovejoy with the mules in the ravine. He returned in seven days; once more they pushed ahead, till they reached the banks of the Grand River. Ice lay along the shores; in mid-stream the current ran strong and deep.

"We can never cross," said the guide. "But we *must* cross," said Whitman.

Into the icy stream plunged horse and rider. Reaching the ice beyond, Whitman broke it with a pole he had cut for the purpose; then urged his horse ashore, where he soon had a fire blazing. Encouraged by his example, the others followed.

Their roundabout route to the south had added a thousand miles to the journey. Pretty soon their food gave out; so they ate a dog and a mule. Reaching a branch of the Arkansas, the only wood for a fire was on the opposite bank; and though the river was frozen from shore to shore, the ice was too thin to bear a standing man's weight. But Whitman threw himself flat on the ice, and, pushing his axe ahead, crept across in safety. No obstacle could stop this man.

HIS ERRAND NOT IN VAIN

Later, he rode on alone, to overtake a party bound from Bent's Fort for the Mississippi, and was lost in a mountainous country swarming with wolves. But at last he rode into St. Louis, where he learned he was not too late. Thence he traveled by stage coach, and on March 3 arrived in Washington, where he pleaded his cause so eloquently that the President was convinced. "Only give me time," said Whitman, "to lead a thousand settlers to Oregon."

This he did in the summer of the same year. Others followed; the claim of the United States was established, and in 1846 Great Britain signed the treaty which left Oregon in our possession. Whitman, the missionary, had not ridden in vain.

THE WESTERN PIONEER

BY LEVERETT S. LYON

Toward the close of a Spring day in the early seventies a "prairie schooner," canvas-covered and dusty, made its way slowly over the prairie of what is now a western State.

The wagon was drawn by a pair of tired but powerful horses. Led behind, trailed a jaded mustang. On the wagon seat was a large-framed, bronzed-faced man. He was thin, gaunt, and stoop-shouldered, but his deep chest and great hands indicated strength and endurance. His eyes were clear, his face bearded, and his brows drawn into the scowling squint that comes from living in the glaring sunlight.

For many days this man had been driving westward over the prairies. He was seeking a new home. He had left a wife and four small children in the settlements 200 miles behind and had gone into the open unsettled country to lay claim to land, build a house, and make certain that a living was to be found before he returned for his family.

As he rode his restless eyes were continually roving over the plains. Partly, he was on the lookout for danger, for the Indians had not yet entirely abandoned their claims to this territory; but even more carefully he was looking for the location that he could feel sure would yield him and his family a living.

Time and again, when he had camped on the bank of a river or in a sheltering grove, he had carefully studied the surrounding country, considering whether it was the sort of spot he was seeking. At times he had camped for several days on one location, half convinced that nothing could be gained by going farther. But always he had decided to move on; always he had decided that a spot could be found where a better living could be made or where a good living could be made more easily.

He came, however, upon a locality which at once pleased him. He brought his team to a willing stop and decided to camp for the night. His horses were watered at the river, at the bank of which he had paused, and were then tethered.

WESTWARD HO!

FROM THE PAINTING BY EMANUEL LEUTZE IN THE CAPITOL, WASHINGTON, D. C.

His simple refreshments over, he crawled under his wagon, rolled into a pair of heavy blankets, and was soon asleep.

NATURAL RESOURCES ARE IMPORTANT TO THE FRONTIERSMAN

The next morning the pioneer began to survey carefully the locality around him. He observed the land to be a slightly rolling prairie. The soil was black and, from the rank grass that covered it, appeared capable of producing a variety of crops. A river of fair size meandered across the plain. Along its banks cottonwood, oak, walnut, and other trees grew thickly at places; and where smaller streams joined the river the trees spread into dense groves.

The river and the smaller streams proved to be well stocked with fish, and frequent herds of buffalo and antelope could be seen on the prairie. Jack rabbits and prairie chickens now and again started out of the grass ahead of him, and in one of the groves he saw a pair of prairie wolves

skulking out of sight. The banks of the stream showed that mink and muskrat made their homes there, and several flocks of geese and wild ducks could be seen feeding in a marsh farther down the river.

The more carefully the frontiersman surveyed this locality, the more favorably was he impressed by its many desirable qualities. He saw that nature had provided here a storehouse from which he could draw a comfortable if not a luxurious living. In the rich black soil he saw the possibility of good crops of wheat, corn, and oats; while to secure hay for his horses he needed only to cut and cure the natural prairie grass. The trees of the groves and along the river offered him the natural resources for satisfying a variety of wants. The oak and walnut trees could be cut into logs from which a cabin of strength and warmth could be built. Their tough fibers would make a fort-like protection against the bullets of possible enemies. For other buildings, such as a stable for his horses and a shed for his wagon, the softer, more easily worked cottonwoods might do. He could easily get the raw materials for constructing furniture, for repairing his farm implements, or for making new ones if occasion required. The underbrush and dried limbs that had fallen would give him, with very little work, a plentiful supply of firewood.

The frontiersman was particularly pleased with the abundance of game. He knew well that his best efforts could not procure a crop of grain before early Autumn, and in the meantime the buffalo, the antelope, the prairie chicken, and the fish would furnish a plentiful supply of food for his table. The hides of some of these animals could also be used for clothing and as a covering for the floor of the cabin which he intended to build. The frontiersman was satisfied; he decided that he would end his pilgrimage and establish his new home in this place.

Temporarily this frontiersman could rely largely on the things which he brought with him on his journey. He had under the cover of his "prairie schooner" some tools and simple farm implements and a fair supply of seeds of various kinds. His bacon, sugar, and tea had not been entirely consumed. Some wearing apparel, bedding, a clumsy stove, and a few cooking utensils and dishes he had with him. While the weather was warm, his wagon would furnish him sufficient shelter. But these conditions could not be relied on permanently; the weather would turn cold and his provisions would run low. To make a permanent home here he must make this locality yield him a living.

THE SELF-SUFFICING PIONEER CANNOT SPECIALIZE

Within a few months the pioneer built himself into his new surroundings. Everywhere are evidences of the natural strength and skill which he used in making over the raw resources about him into things to meet his wants. In the side of a small hill he cut a clean perpendicular face. This flat surface was made to serve as one wall of a house, while the other three sides were made from logs. Between the logs of these walls were many wide cracks and small crevices not yet closed, though on the north side of the cabin they were effectively stopped with mud.

The roof of the new cabin was constructed of rafters of small logs overlaid with sod, in some of which the grass had not dried but grew as freshly as before it was taken from the prairie. The floor was rough and uneven, though the frontiersman made some attempt to smooth the surface. There is but one room and that, though

ample for the needs of this single pioneer, was not large in size. The clumsy stove furnished means of heating and cooking.

All about the room were evidences of new devices which the frontiersman made in an effort to satisfy his needs. These showed ingenuity, patience, skill, and strength, but indicated clearly that though the frontiersman is a jack-of-all-trades he was not a master of any of them. The workmanship of the cabin showed plainly that he was skillful with an axe but suggested equally clearly that the aid of a sawmill would have resulted in a much better structure. As a carpenter and woodworker, he could not claim to be more than a fair hand; and when ironwork was needed, he was handicapped both by a lack of materials and by a lack of skill. A pair of wolfskins carpeted the floor, and over the bed a half-tanned buffalo hide supplemented the blankets. The tanning process had not been by any means perfect, and the hair that came easily from the dried skins was scattered about the room and the bed.

Outside the cabin was the frontiersman's farm. A number of acres of ground had been plowed and a fair crop of corn was ripening. At farming he was at his best, as long practice before he left the settled country had given him a considerable degree of skill and knowledge in this work. Nevertheless, from the number of weeds that pervaded part of his cornfield, it was apparent that he was handicapped by a lack of implements or by the necessity of turning to other work when his corn needed attention.

In addition to the work in his cornfield, he had done the labor necessary to break the sod for a new field. In this he would sow during the Autumn a crop of winter wheat. He was not certain that his wheat seed would survive the Winter in this region, but he had no method of finding out other than by experiment.

The pioneer used good judgment in the distribution of the time that he had at his disposal. He succeeded in getting his cabin nearly enough completed to furnish a fair protection during the Winter, and at the same time he had not seriously neglected his farm.

HIS BRIDGE ILLUSTRATES THE IMPORTANCE OF CAPITAL GOODS

He realized that it sometimes pays to "make haste slowly." He constructed a bridge across a sharp ravine lying between his house and his fields. The bridge, crudely built of logs, required the work of several days, but several times each day it saved him the time that would have been consumed in driving his team to a place where they could cross safely. The bridge was but one illustration of several things he had done, the better to wring his living from nature. For example, he built a barn. He repaired several of the tools he brought with him, and he made a crude plow and a wooden harrow.

HIS ENVIRONMENT INFLUENCES HIS WANTS

Much as the conditions around the pioneer changed, they changed no more than the pioneer himself. He found that his wants expressed themselves in different ways. Although more hungry, more thirsty, and more tired from his arduous work than he had ever been before, he did not think of the satisfaction of these wants in the same terms that would have occurred to him when he was back in the settlements. When he was hungry, he was most likely to think how satisfying would be a large piece of roasted buffalo meat and a slice of corn bread of his own baking, made of his dwindling supply of meal.

Thirst expressed itself to him in a desire for nothing but the water that he habitually drank from the clearest stream in the neighborhood. When worn with work, it was for the comfort of his skin-covered bed that his body yearned. As the clothes that he brought with him became worn and cut by the rough work of hunting, carpentering, and farming, he had no thought of replacing them from the stocks of haberdashers. "Wearing quality" had for him become more and more important, and for this purpose the home-tanned skins of animals were well suited.

A cotton shirt still survived the wearing work of the farm, but his soft felt hat had been replaced by a squirrel skin cap of his own making, and in place of shoes he wore a pair of moccasins made from the hide of an antelope. What other people were wearing or what they might think of his clothes was of decreasing importance to him. The fashions of settled communities did not reach him; he was under the criticism and comment of no one, and in fact he gave the whole matter little thought. As the clothes that he brought with him wore out, or as his household utensils or farming implements were broken or gave way, he replaced them from the raw materials at hand in the way that best suited his needs.

NO SCHEDULES GOVERN HIS ACTIONS

In spite of the fact that the pioneer was fairly well established on the prairie farm, he seemed to be as crowded with work as he was in the early days of his first settlement. In fact, it seemed that tasks multiplied rather than diminished. At whatever hour he arose in the morning, his first task after his horses were fed and cared for was to prepare his breakfast. His hour of arising was, however, becoming very irregular. Sometimes he was up at sunrise and early at his work; at other times when especially exhausted from the preceding day or when heavy rain made work on the farm impossible, he slept far into the morning. If he was on a hunt which took him far over the prairie, he was not disturbed so far as regular hours are concerned if he did not get back until late in the light; or if a storm threatened when he was anxious to complete certain outside tasks, he would work as long as it was possible to see what he was doing. His time was his own. No one else was concerned with or disturbed by his irregularities, and he went about his daily duties more by the spirit than by the clock.

HE FINDS HE IS A GREGARIOUS ANIMAL

The pioneer was reasonably well fed, clothed, and sheltered. Those wants, changed somewhat in character by his environment, were met in at least a moderate fashion. Even concerning these wants, however, he did have periods when he wished a more varied diet. The bacon he brought with him lasted hardly a week after his arrival; his supply of sugar, flour, and tea was so low that he used them in miserly fashion. There remained the abundant game and wild berries of his environment, but more and more he thought of the sameness of his food.

But he had other wants which in his isolation he could not gratify. This fact was impressed upon him when for several days in succession he saw smoke signals of Indians. So far as he knows, the nearest soldiers were at the Government fort 100 miles farther west. If an attack should come, he must defend himself. He was no coward, but during several days he abandoned his work and watched. He had time and occasion during these days to think of the advantages of community life. He was impressed as never before with a great sense of his aloneness, his self-dependence, his isolation. He thought of the comfort that would come from having his family with him and the confidence and aid that he could find in neighbors. He realized well that neighbors bring new responsibilities and put restraints upon his absolute freedom. If neighbors come, they might question his right to the best areas for farming; they as well as he would make inroads on the supply of game. Tracts of timber would be preëmpted by others and he could no longer cut trees where he chose. He had come into the West to build his new home unhampered by the restraints that come from living in contact with other people, and he knew that if other settlers arrived he would find himself subjected to the will of other individuals and of the society that would grow up around him.

On the other hand, he saw that he would be safer in many ways if friends were around him. They would help protect him from the Indians. Very likely there would be a physician among these friends who could help him in case of accident or sickness. In addition to increased safety, he reflected, he would gain by having friends to help him in the heavier tasks. He remembered very clearly the toil involved in building his house by himself. And above all, now that he had time to think about it, he found that he was very lonely—that he wanted to see the faces and hear the voices of other people.

Even after all signs of impending trouble from the Indians disappeared and he was again about his work, he still turned these matters over in his mind. Finally, his thoughts resolved into the decision that he would not wait until Spring, as he had intended, before returning to the settlement for his family. He decided that as soon as his grain was harvested and under shelter he would undertake the journey to the settlement and bring his wife and children to their new home in the West. He decided, moreover, that he would encourage others to follow his trail the coming year. He would tell of the richness of the land, the supply of game, the salubrity of the climate, and of the comparative ease with which these could be turned into want-satisfying goods. He would point out that a group working together in the midst of such abundant resources should be able so to conduct things as to have a rich, full life. He would make every effort to bring people into the locality where he had lived alone and to convert his isolation into a community.

ABRAHAM LINCOLN, WHO SAVED THE UNION

BY IRVINGTON LEE

BLACK HAWK, chief of the Sacs Indians, had gone on the warpath. In our struggle with England in 1812 he had fought the Americans; and now, twenty years later, he laughed at treaties and promises, and crossed the Mississippi River into Illinois.

The people of Illinois were much excited by this invasion, and the Governor of the State at once called for volunteers. The call to arms was printed in the *Sangamon Journal,* and one of those who read it was a young grocery clerk named Abraham Lincoln.

Lincoln had never had any experience as a soldier. He had done much rough, hard work, and had put his hand to many sorts of jobs in his effort to make a living. But besides being tall and strong, there was something in his appearance that marked him as a leader of men; and so, to his great surprise, he was elected captain of his company.

He himself has told us that never did he obtain any success in life which gave him so much satisfaction. The truth is, he had undergone so many hardships and performed such humble tasks, that this seemed to him his first opportunity to show the stuff that was in him.

He did not seek military glory, but merely the chance to be of service to the State; and as things turned out, his modest ambition was gratified.

The men under his command gave him much trouble from the first. They were backwoodsmen, who had led free and independent lives, and had no notion of discipline and restraint. To obey orders without hesitation, and to perform the regular duties of a soldier, was a new experience to them, and they rebelled against it in many ways.

PROTECTS A DEFENSELESS INDIAN

Lincoln, however, rose to the occasion. No kinder-hearted man ever lived; none was slower to take offense or give way to anger. But he knew how to make himself obeyed and respected, and his company of raw militia soon came to see that their captain was not to be trifled with.

As it happened, there was no fighting, after all; and this made matters worse. The volunteers had gone forth in search of excitement. They asked nothing better than a fight with the Indians, and when this was denied them they sought some other outlet for their animal spirits. They had not been enlisted for any specified period, and were greatly discontented—demanding that they be allowed to return home.

It was in this state of mind that they greeted the appearance of an Indian who one day made his way into camp. He was an old Indian, not at all warlike, who carried in his hand some kind of a written message which he seemed anxious to deliver. But his peaceful looks and ways made no impression on the excitable volunteers. An Indian was an Indian, and he must have come there for no good purpose. Probably he was a spy, and as such should be treated without mercy.

"A spy, a spy!" some one called out to the others.

"A spy! Catch him! Kill him!"

Carried away by excitement, the soldiers became a mob. They surrounded the Indian, and with threatening words and gestures made it plain that they meant to murder him then and there.

At this moment Captain Lincoln appeared among them.

"What are you doing, boys?" he asked, quietly.

"He's a spy," growled the ringleader, "and we're going to shoot him."

"You mustn't do that, boys," said the Captain, without raising his voice.

Then the soldiers turned on their own commander, and threatened him, too.

At this the tall captain rolled up his sleeves; his voice grew stern, a new light shone in his eyes.

"If you want to fight so badly," he told them, "fight me. Come on, one at a time, and take it out of me, if you can. This Indian has come here for help; and he's going to get it, if I have to lick all Sangamon county."

The soldiers knew he meant it, and knew he was more than their match. So the Indian left the camp unharmed.

DEFEATS THE CHAMPION WRESTLER

Lincoln at twenty-three was six feet four, with hard muscles and powerful arms and hands. Fighting was not at all to his taste; but there were times when his gentle nature led others to believe he could be imposed upon, and at such times he used his great strength to good purpose.

Shortly before the Black Hawk campaign, he had been hired by a merchant named Offutt, who owned a grocery and "general store" in New Salem. Offutt soon discovered that his clerk and general assistant was not only remarkably honest and conscientious, but unusual in other ways. He talked well, and was always reading books in his spare time. Besides this, he could run, jump and wrestle with the best of them; and Offutt was so proud of the young man that he began to boast about him.

The other young men in New Salem soon grew jealous. In the small town of those days the champion wrestler of the community was looked upon as a hero. The champion of Clary's Grove, near by, was Jack Armstrong, and he decided that

ABRAHAM LINCOLN

FROM A PAINTING BY DOUGLAS VOLK

the first chance he had he would teach the grocer's clerk a lesson. Lincoln avoided him as long as possible; but one day Jack Armstrong attacked him, and the test of strength began. Pretty soon the champion found himself locked in a powerful embrace from which there was no escape. He had to own himself beaten by the grocer's clerk; and from that day Lincoln was no longer molested.

Lincoln's bodily strength was no doubt a great advantage. In the years to come he was no longer called upon to use it as a wrestler. But it made him better able to bear fatigue of mind, and to carry upon his broad shoulders the tremendous responsibilities that came to him as President.

KNOWN AS "HONEST ABE"

In New Salem at this time he had begun to get a reputation of another sort: a reputation for honesty. One evening, on casting up his accounts at the grocery, he found that he had charged a woman customer a few cents too much. It was late at night when he closed his shop, and she lived several miles away; but he did not go to bed till he had walked all the way to her house, to correct this trifling error.

Honest in act and purpose he always was. After leaving New Salem, he became a lawyer— a lawyer who would never be persuaded to charge as much as he could get. As one of his biographers has said, his duty to a client did not prevent him from seeing his duty to society as well; when some one brought him a bad case, he would decline to take it. "As a peacemaker," he once wrote, "the lawyer has a superior opportunity of being a good man. There will still be business enough. Never stir up litigation."

Noting the "vague popular belief" that lawyers are "necessarily dishonest," he gave this counsel: "Let no young man choosing the law for a calling for a moment yield to the popular belief. Resolve to be honest at all events; and if, in your own judgment, you cannot be an honest lawyer, resolve to be honest without being a lawyer. Choose some other occupation, rather than one in the choosing of which you do, in advance, consent to be a knave."

Thus it is easy to see how Lincoln early came to be known to his neighbors in Illinois as "Honest Abe."

HIS BOYHOOD DAYS

Fully to appreciate the rise of Lincoln from obscurity to greatness, we must go back to his boyhood days, and observe his persistent struggle against poverty and ignorance. Few men have overcome so much; few have been so patient, so determined.

He was born on February 12, 1809, in a log cabin in the backwoods of Kentucky. Thomas Lincoln, his father, was a carpenter who had not learned his trade very well; and, besides this, he was rather shiftless, and had formed the habit of moving from place to place, with a vague idea of bettering his condition. This, however, he never did, and his children grew up in great poverty. He had married a Virginia girl, Nancy

Hanks, and it was to her that Abraham owed the beginnings of his education. Unlike her husband, she could read and write, and was in other ways superior to him. In the one room of the little log cabin the greatest comfort was a huge fireplace, with a bearskin rug spread before it; and there the children would sit beside their mother, who read them Bible stories, and told them fairy tales.

When Abraham was about four years old, his father moved again—this time to a farm on Knob Creek, which he bought on credit, but never managed to pay for. Somewhat later, he put all his belongings on a kind of raft, or flatboat, and floated down the Ohio till he came to Indiana; and there, in Spencer county, he once more settled down on a farm.

Meanwhile he had built a rude shelter, with one side open to the weather, so that a fire could be made without a chimney. In this the Lincoln family lived for a whole year, making the best of things, as they were accustomed to do. There was no village near by, and no roads worth mentioning in what was then known as the Pigeon Creek settlement. When they needed cornmeal, little Abraham, now seven years old, would ride to the grist-mill, with a bag of corn thrown balanced across his horse. When they needed a doctor, it meant a ride of thirty miles.

Nor was it long before a doctor was badly needed. Mrs. Lincoln fell sick, and died. Others died, too, and Thomas Lincoln was called upon to make their coffins, which he fashioned from lumber with a whip-saw.

Three years later, he married again; and this proved a fortunate thing for the orphaned children. Abraham's stepmother was a kind, energetic woman. She brought to her new home a wagon-load of clothing and household goods; and for the first time in their lives Abraham and his sister Sarah had plenty of warm clothing and other comforts.

HOW HE TAUGHT HIMSELF

Best of all, his stepmother soon found out that Abraham had a quick mind and was eager to study, and she did everything in her power to encourage him. When he was ten, she sent him to the little log schoolhouse, where the window panes were greased paper, with a floor and benches made of split logs. Pen, ink and paper were scarce; there were few slates or pencils. Sometimes a spelling book was the only textbook in the school. Now and then, a traveling teacher would come to the settlement, and remain

LINCOLN AND HIS CABINET

FROM THE PAINTING BY F. B. CARPENTER

for perhaps a month. Nor was he likely to be much of a teacher. His knowledge was generally limited to an acquaintance with the "three R's"; if by any chance he knew a little Latin, he passed for a kind of a magician.

In a period of nine years, Lincoln attended three such schools, and was taught by five teachers; yet, all told, he received something less than twelve months of schooling.

He soon found out that if he was to get an education he must teach himself; and this he set about doing with a will. His stepmother tells us that he read every book he could lay his hands on; and when he came across a passage that struck him, he would write it down on boards, if he had no paper, and keep it there till he did get paper. Then he would rewrite it, look at it, repeat it.

As he had no slate or pencil, he would use a piece of charcoal and a wooden shovel. This shovel was a rude thing, made of a thin board and employed in lifting live coals from the hearth. In the long winter evenings, by the light of the fire, the boy would cover the shovel with sums in arithmetic; and when its surface would hold no more figures, he would shave it with a sharp knife, and begin afresh.

HOW HE BECAME A WRITER

It seems a kind of miracle that, with so many obstacles to knowledge, this self-taught boy lived to be one of the great masters of English speech —a statesman whose letters and addresses are treasured among the best examples of literature. Yet the explanation is a simple one. To one born with such a gift, the ability to write well rests chiefly upon three things: clear thinking, incessant toil, and a close acquaintance with the works of great authors. Now, Lincoln was in the first place a thinker; every one who knew him well has testified that he always gave much thought to whatever problem he had in hand. No matter what the subject, he did not rest till he had examined it from all sides, and made it his own. It was this application of mind that enabled him to succeed in the law, to win a foremost place among public speakers, and, finally, in one of the most trying times of our history, to grapple with and master the many hard problems of the Civil War.

His acquaintance with the best literature began in early boyhood. It was a time of few books; but these books were the classics, and he read them with the care that few persons nowadays give to such reading. It mattered little that the settlement had no newspapers or magazines. It was a poor family indeed that did not possess a Bible, and Abraham learned its parables, and drank in the beauty of its words, when he was still a child. Besides this, as a boy, he read Shakespeare, "Pilgrim's Progress" and "Robinson Crusoe"; and all these helped to form his thought, fire his imagination, and shape his style of expression.

THE GETTYSBURG ADDRESS

It is therefore not so surprising that at the dedication of a national cemetery on the battlefield of Gettysburg, this man who had once split rails for a living came to deliver a brief address that will live with the noblest utterances of all times. None other surpasses in eloquence and simple dignity its closing words:

"The world will little note nor long remember what we say here, but it can never forget what they did here. It is for us, the living, rather, to be dedicated here to the unfinished work which they who fought here have thus far so nobly advanced. It is rather for us to be here dedicated to the great task remaining before us—that from these honored dead we take increased devotion to that cause for which they gave the last full measure of devotion; that we here highly resolve that these dead shall not have died in vain; that this nation, under God, shall have a new birth of freedom; and that government of the people, by the people, for the people, shall not perish from the earth."

But the world *has* remembered what Lincoln said, and will long remember it. Not only in his public addresses and debates, but on many other occasions throughout his life, he had a way of saying things that people could not forget. In his early days in Indiana he was noted for his droll humor, his fondness for telling a good story, and his aptness in the use of anecdote to give point and flavor to his meaning. Later on, when he was President, oppressed by cares of state, he often relieved the strain of a trying situation by the employment of some happy phrase or the relation of some amusing tale. He greatly enjoyed the writings of the American humorist, Artemus Ward; and once, at an important Cabinet meeting, he startled the more sober members of his official family by pausing in the grave business before him, to read some passages from Ward's latest book.

LINCOLN'S TENDER HEART

Lincoln's tender-heartedness was expressed in many ways. He disliked to give pain to any

Copyright by Edward Simmons
From a Copley Print, copyright by Curtis & Cameron, Boston

RETURN OF THE BATTLE FLAGS

FROM A PAINTING BY EDWARD SIMMONS

living creature. Not only was he much affected by the suffering of animals, but even as a boy he would take no part in hunting the wild birds and beasts so plentiful in the woods. Once he spent a whole afternoon trying to rescue a hedgehog caught fast in the crevice of a rock; when he could not manage to pull it out, he walked a long way to a blacksmith's shop, borrowed a pole with an iron hook, and with this managed at last to set the little animal free.

Most of his companions took a pride in being able to shoot a squirrel through the head, but sport of this kind did not appeal to him. Only once did he give way to the hunter's instinct. A flock of wild turkeys came near the cabin, and Abraham, shooting through a crack in the wall, killed one of them. But after that he never pulled a trigger.

This tender-heartedness found another expression in the days of the Civil War. As President he had the right to pardon, and in the case of some young soldier who had gone to sleep on post, or been condemned to die for some like breach of discipline, he exercised the right so often that he displeased his own generals.

When Lincoln returned from the Black Hawk war he tried to get elected to the Illinois Legislature, but without success. He was now without means, and had no business, and at this time he seriously thought of becoming a blacksmith. However, he went into business instead with a man named Berry, who soon failed and left the town, leaving his young partner to pay the debts. Then he was made postmaster of New Salem, which brought him little money, but plenty of leisure for reading and study. In time he became a lawyer, served several years in the Legislature, and was elected to Congress.

ELECTED PRESIDENT

Lincoln had always opposed slavery. In 1854 this subject was hotly debated, and Lincoln won national fame in his public debates with Senator Stephen Douglas, known as the "Little Giant." In 1858, as Republican candidate for United States Senator, he uttered the memorable words: "'A house divided against itself cannot stand.'

I believe this government cannot endure permanently half slave and half free." Two years later the Republicans nominated him for President, winning the election over a divided Democratic party.

Lincoln as President at once proved himself strong where his predecessor, President Buchanan, had wavered and hesitated. Fort Sumter was fired upon and captured, and the Civil War began in earnest.

From this time forth, the story of Lincoln is the story of that war. He had treason and disloyalty to fight, warring factions to reconcile; more than any other man he bore the burden of the struggle. In 1862 he issued his Proclamation of Emancipation, freeing the slaves, and lived to see it adopted by Congress.

Even his critics now recognized in him one whose greatness of mind and soul had made it possible to save the nation from disruption, and when in April, 1865, he fell at the hand of an assassin, the people were stricken with grief. Only a few weeks before he had said in his second Inaugural Address:

"With malice toward none; with charity for all; with firmness in the right, as God gives us to see the right, let us strive on to finish the work we are in; to bind up the nation's wounds; to care for him who shall have borne the battle, and for his widow, and his orphan—to do all which may achieve and cherish a just and lasting peace among ourselves, and with all nations."

Such was his last public utterance—the Will of a great and tender-hearted Elder Brother to his people.

ROBERT E. LEE

BY JOSEPH LEWIS FRENCH

FIVE years after the Civil War ended Charles Sumner denounced Robert E. Lee in the Senate as a "traitor whom I leave to the pen of history." Yet to-day, fifty years after the great conflict has closed, the North as well as the South pays admiring tribute to the great memory of Robert E. Lee.

He came of a long line of distinguished Virginia ancestors reaching back to the early years of settlement, of old English stock. It was a race of gentlemen in whom the military tradition was prominent. His own father was a distinguished general in the War of the Revolution,

and as "Light-Horse Harry" Lee, so-called because he was a leader of cavalry, he will go down to history. His mother was Annie Carter, of an old Virginia family, and it has been remarked that "all the charm and inspiration of long descent in each line were blended in his person." His father was a Revolutionary hero and cultured gentleman "of the ancient southern day; his mother illustrated the purest ideal of womanly excellence developed in the early and unchecked period of our civilization." His father died when Robert was a lad of only eleven, and he early showed those splendid human qualities

LIEUT.-GENERAL ROBERT E. LEE, C. S. A.

which distinguished him all his life in his devotion to his mother.

Of the boyhood and youth in the stately Virginia home there is no close record. It was a free, healthful, happy life, in which much outdoor sport mingled, and which all tended to make a man, if the material was good. He was destined to a military career like his father, and at eighteen entered the West Point Military Academy. His four-year course was not only exemplary but brilliant. He graduated second in a class of forty-six, and during the whole four years he did not receive a single demerit. Two years afterward he married Mary Randolph Custis, the great-granddaughter of Martha Custis, the wife of George Washington, who brought him a fine estate in Arlington, Virginia.

He graduated from West Point as an engineer, and in 1834 he was appointed to the Chief Engineer's office in Washington as an assistant. Three years later he got his first wide knowledge of the country through being made superintendent of important improvements at St. Louis. He gradually rose in rank, and in 1842 was given charge of the defenses in New York harbor. On the outbreak of the Mexican War in 1846 he hailed the opportunity at last of actual duty in the field. Nothing chafes a soldier like inaction, and Lee had rare fighting blood in his veins. Here he distinguished himself at once. He took charge of the artillery before Vera Cruz, and the town surrendered in a few days. After every important battle in which he fought he was promoted. This happened at Cerro Gordo, at Churubusco, and at Chapultepec. At the end of the Mexican War he came back a man marked for advancement. At first he took charge of the important works then being built in the harbor of Baltimore.

A BIG MAN, DESTINED TO BECOME BIGGER

But it was felt that a larger field than constructing defenses when war with a foreign foe seemed a long way off must be found for him. He was a big man, destined to become bigger. So in 1852 when he was forty-five years old he was appointed to the post of superintendent at West Point. He remained here three years and improved the Military Academy greatly, not only in discipline but instruction. Still he longed for active service, and when a new cavalry regiment was formed, in 1855, to go to the far West he eagerly besought and was given the appointment of lieutenant-colonel. A few months later he was put in command of the regiment, on duty in

western Texas. He remained in the great New West, an almost undiscovered country in those days, for four years.

In 1859 he came home to visit his family, and during this visit the raid of John Brown and his followers occurred at Harper's Ferry near his home. Colonel Lee took charge of the troops

Courtesy of Ellington's Studio, Raleigh, N. C.

STATUE ERECTED TO THE WOMEN OF THE
CONFEDERACY IN RALEIGH, N. C.

and quelled the uprising promptly. Then he returned to Texas, where he was stationed at the head of his regiment of cavalry when the State seceded in 1861, and then he was recalled to Washington.

The great soldier who was to command the Armies of the Confederacy was at first entirely opposed to disunion. Still he was a Southerner, a Virginian, and his sympathies with the South were strong. The eyes of the Government at Washington were upon him as a man destined

JOHN C. BRECKENRIDGE

I. P. BENJAMIN

JEFFERSON DAVIS

ALEXANDER H. STEVENS

R. TOOMBS

CONFEDERATE STATESMEN AND LEADERS

259

to a great career, and a few days after he reached his home in Virginia he was called upon by a number of the Cabinet and offered on behalf of President Lincoln the chief command of the Army of the United States. He declined, because as he wrote later, "Though opposed to secession, and deprecating war, I could take no part in an invasion of the Southern States." A few days after he resigned his commission, and three days later was appointed by the newly organized Confederate Government at Richmond to the command of the forces in Virginia.

Within a month he had 30,000 men in the field ready to fight, and many other regiments forming. He threw himself wholly into the cause of the South from the hour he espoused it, and his great talents were employed to the utmost in getting the South ready for war. In the latter part of that year, 1861, he went to South Carolina, Georgia, and Florida to build coast-defenses and interior forts to protect the region which was to be the great base of food supply for the army.

After doing fine work, as well as inspiring strength and confidence by his strong character, he came back to Richmond in March, 1862, and was given chief command of all the military operations of the Confederacy. He early took the offensive against the great army of the North under General McClellan, and kept that commander in check till the whole people of the North began to lose faith in him.

LEE'S ARMIES HOLD McCLELLAN

The aim of McClellan was to reach Richmond, where the Confederates had established their capital, and by taking the city capture the government and end the war. The armies under Lee not only prevented this, but they won several important battles, such as that at Bull Run, and the North soon settled down to the fact that it must be a long war, nation-wide in its field of action. After proving to McClellan that he could more than hold his own, Lee took the offensive and almost reached the seat of the Federal Government, Washington. Washington and Richmond are only two hundred miles apart, and between these two cities a vast host battled stubbornly for four years, with little advantage to either side. The North, however, had the resources, and there could in the end be but one outcome.

Lee, early in the fall of 1862, invaded Maryland, and was striking for Pennsylvania when he was met and stopped by McClellan with a much larger army, which had been gathered for the emergency at Antietam. He was a master of the tactics of defensive warfare, and great skill prevented his forces from being destroyed in the retreat. On account of this defeat of Lee the Government at Washington thought it was time to try and take Richmond again. A great army advanced under General Burnside, but was met by General Lee at Fredericksburg and defeated with great loss.

For nearly six months the Federals rested, when they advanced again on General Lee with a force nearly double the size of his own under General Joseph Hooker. Again in a three days' battle at Chancellorsville (May 2-4) the superior military genius of General Lee, fighting with greatly inferior forces and supplies—most of his men had no uniforms and were nearly always hungry—triumphed in a complete victory.

Heartened by this great triumph, Lee, still dreaming of a complete conquest of the North, again started for Pennsylvania. June 3, 1863, he began to march with 80,000 men, and had crossed the border, when he was met by General Meade, who had succeeded Hooker. At first he repulsed Meade, but in the two days' fighting which followed around Gettysburg he gained no further advantage. Both sides lost heavily in this terrible conflict. General Lee took the offensive on both days with great bravery against a much larger army; on the third day his force was so shattered that it could not hold out. His ammunition nearly gone, Lee retreated, and got his army safely across the Potomac again.

During the following winter his brave army, which had always fought at great odds and with lack of food and supplies, suffered severely; quite as much, indeed, as the soldiers under Washington had, nearly a hundred years before, at Valley Forge. They had in truth little left but unflinching courage and a sublime faith in their commander. The North meanwhile gathered an overwhelming army, and placed General Grant, "the Man of Iron," in command.

He was to advance when Spring opened in a supreme effort to defeat Lee and crush the Confederacy. General Lee's army numbered only about one-half that of Grant, but Lee knew the country, which was a difficult one for the enemy, and he was fighting on the defensive. It was the last struggle of the Confederacy.

LEE'S LOSSES MUCH LESS THAN GRANT'S

For five weeks General Grant pushed his men forward and never stopped offensive warfare.

CONFEDERATE COMMANDERS

He sacrificed his troops ruthlessly, and at the end of the "Wilderness" campaign had lost 60,000 men. Lee lost only 14,000. The siege of Petersburg, the last stronghold protecting Virginia, was the final act in the terrible drama of the Rebellion.

It had lasted almost a year, and the fighting was incessant and at times terrible. The Federals erected defenses of their own, and had plentiful supplies. Toward the end the Confederates were almost wholly without food. On April 2, 1865, General Lee made up his mind to abandon Petersburg—which meant Richmond—and with his remnant of an army of 30,000 men try to work southward. The next day the Federals captured Richmond. Two days later, on arriving at his base of supplies, Lee found that by an irretrievable error they had been forwarded to Richmond, and were in the hands of his enemy. Surrender was the only opportunity to save his starving men, and on April 9, 1865, he handed his sword to General Grant at Appomattox Court House. As he bade his soldiers farewell, he said: "Remember that we are one country now. Do not bring up your children in hostility to the Government of the United States. Bring them up to be Americans."

His magnificent estate of Arlington had been confiscated by the Government at Washington, and is now used as a soldiers' home and cemetery; and he retired in very straitened circumstances to a quiet home in Richmond. In October of the same year, 1865, he was asked to take the presidency of a small college at Lexington, then called Washington College. Positions of greater emolument were open to him, but he chose to accept this one. He remained at the head of this institution, which prospered greatly under his guidance, till his death five years later. After his death the name was changed to Washington and Lee University in honor of his memory.

There is a great statue to General Lee at Richmond; and in the memorial church erected at Lexington there is a sarcophagus on which he lies at full length carved in stone; but his true monument is in the hearts of the Southern people, who will revere his name to the remotest generations.

The finest soldier in America in his day, he was offered the command of the great armies of the North. His heart was in the cause of his own people, and he chose the weaker side. And it is the unanimous verdict of history that he was the greatest commander of his century.

His enthusiastic biographer, Benjamin H. Hill, said of him: "He was a foe without hate; a friend without treachery; a soldier without cruelty; a victor without oppression; a private citizen without wrong; a neighbor without reproach; a Christian without hypocrisy, and a man without guile. He was Cæsar without his ambition; Frederick without his tyranny; Napoleon without his selfishness, and Washington without his reward. He was obedient to authority as a servant, and royal in authority as a true king. He was gentle as a woman in life; modest and pure as a virgin in thought; watchful as a Roman vestal in duty; submissive to law as Socrates, and grand in battle as Achilles."

U. S. GRANT, SOLDIER AND PRESIDENT

BY IRVINGTON LEE

It was Christmas time in a little Ohio town, in the year 1838, and young Hiram Grant was spending the holidays at home.

People in those days did not write or receive many letters. So one day, when the boy had called for the mail at the country post office, and was given a letter addressed to his father, with the post-mark, "Washington," he knew it must be something important, and made haste to take it to the house. Then, having delivered it, he turned to go—eager to rejoin his playmates, who were skating on a neighboring pond. But his father called him back.

"Wait a minute, Hiram," he said. "This letter is addressed to me, but it is really meant for you."

The boy turned in surprise. Who could be writing to him from Washington, the capital of the United States? His father must be joking.

"Yes," said Mr. Grant, with a smile, "this letter is really for you. It's a kind of Christmas present. And when you see what it is, you'll agree with me that you're the luckiest boy in Ohio."

Hiram took the letter, and read it, but it seemed to give him no great pleasure. Yet the writer

AMERICAN MILITARY AND NAVAL OFFICERS

was the Honorable Thomas Morris, United States Senator from Ohio, and he had written to say that the boy would soon receive an appointment to the Military Academy at West Point.

A MILITARY CAREER

That was a prize that falls to the lot of but few. Mr. Grant was a tanner. In the natural course of events, his son would complete his studies, and would then be set at work in the tannery to learn his father's business. But now a great career opened like magic before him. Instead of a dull trade, the life of an army officer, with all the romance that such a life might hold. Instead of the factory whistle, the stirring tones of the trumpet, and the call to boots and saddles. Offered such a choice, what boy would hesitate?

Yet Hiram, now sixteen years old, stood there staring at the letter in his hand, with no sign of excitement.

"Father," he said at last, "if you want me to go, I'll go. But I don't care to be a soldier."

Strange words, indeed, when we consider what this boy came to be. For Hiram was Hiram Ulysses Grant, or Ulysses Simpson Grant, as he was known in the years that followed: the U. S. Grant who led the Union armies to victory in our Civil War, and who was twice elected President of the United States.

It would seem that a father sometimes knows better than his son what that son is fitted for. In this case, Hiram Grant, being a dutiful son, with great respect for his father's opinion, decided at once to do as he was told. But this, of course, could not change his feelings. He himself has told us that he went to West Point unwillingly; that a military life had no charms for him, and that he had no idea of remaining always in the army, even if he were graduated.

HOW HIS NAME WAS CHANGED

At any rate, the notion of traveling pleased him. He packed his trunk, strapped it, then stood looking at it with an odd expression. On it were his initials, in big-letters: H. U. G.

"That will never do," said Hiram. "A fellow whose initials spell 'hug' would be laughed out of West Point. I'll just change them around a little."

So he made them read, U. H. G.; but that did not end the matter. His mother's maiden name was Simpson, and the Congressman who sent in his name to the Academy somehow got it into his head that the boy had been called after her.

The new cadet was entered on the books at West Point as Ulysses S. Grant, and as such he continued to be known for the rest of his days.

After all, the adopted initials made a good combination. He was now U. S. Grant, and in later years people referred to him with affection as "United States" or "Uncle Sam" Grant. Nor did this nickname seem an exaggeration; for on the shoulders of Grant rested the fate of the Union in its conflict with the South.

Some persons believe that the name was allowed to stand, as the Congressman sent it in to West Point, for the simple reason that Grant was not only modest, but remarkable for his silence as well. He was always a man of few words; but when he did speak, he spoke to the point, and some of his utterances will always live because of their brevity and force.

AT THE GATES OF MEXICO

By the time Grant was graduated from West Point, he had changed his mind about leaving the army. After service in Louisiana and Texas, we find him, in 1847, a lieutenant of infantry, fighting with our army in Mexico. General Scott had stormed the castle of Chapultepec; his forces were battering at the walls of the capital city itself. Should it fall, the war would be won. But the gates were stoutly held by the defenders, and the Americans could make but little headway.

Suddenly from the belfry of a church, just outside the city, came a puff of smoke and the report of a cannon. A shell from the cannon fell plump among the Mexicans guarding the San Cosme gate, and filled them with dismay. Again and again the cannon was discharged with deadly effect; at last the Mexicans fell back, and ran up a flag of truce.

The man who trained the cannon was Lieutenant Grant. He had taken in the situation, noted the favorable position of the church, and called for volunteers. The howitzer, as this kind of light cannon is called, was carried up into the belfry, trained on the gate, and speedily effected its purpose. It was Lieutenant Grant's own idea, and it brought him mention for bravery and promotion to the rank of captain.

Grant at this time was a quartermaster, and as such he was not required to do any actual fighting. But though he hated war, his good sense told him that when it came it could be ended only by vigorous measures. So then, as later, he fought with every means at his command, and knew no rest till his enemy sued for

GENERAL GRANT LEADING HIS TROOPS

peace. Then, when peace did come and new problems arose, he met them with the same determination. Thus, cholera attacked his men on the Isthmus of Panama, while bound for Oregon, and Grant by his energy and courage saved the situation as he had done in time of war.

HARD TIMES IN MISSOURI

In Oregon, his new station, a dreary time followed. The boy who went to West Point against his will had found the encampment, preceding his studies, a "very tiresome" experience. And now it seemed that, after all, he had been right. Army life in time of peace is a dull routine. He had served his country well in time of war. But now, as when a boy, military life "had no charms for him." Besides this, he had married, and the pay of a captain was small. So Captain Grant resigned.

Never again, he thought, would he be called upon to fight; he was done, once and for all, with the army. Yet he was thirty-two years of age, and he had no other profession. How could he make a living?

How, indeed? For six or more years to come, he often asked himself that question. He became a farmer near St. Louis, and as a farmer he failed. One does not easily take up farming at thirty-two; and, besides, his health was poor. The city itself did not promise much to a man without special training. But Grant had a wife and two children to support. So he tried real estate; then bill-collecting, and the other things to which men turn when they must somehow earn their bread. Finally, he left St. Louis, glad to get a clerkship, at seventy dollars a month, in an Illinois country store.

There he lived for a time, poor and obscure, with no way of bettering his condition. West Point had given him an education, but it was not an education that enabled him to earn money outside the army. It seemed as if he must pass all his days in poverty.

A SOLDIER ONCE MORE

Then came the Civil War. Fort Sumter was fired upon, and surrendered; President Lincoln called upon the States for 75,000 men, and proclaimed the blockade of the Southern coast. So Grant, with the blood of soldiers in his veins, responded to the call. He asked for an army appointment, believing that as the Government had educated him, he still owed it a duty in its time of need. This was denied him, so he set to work, drilling volunteers; and then at last they made him Colonel of the Twenty-first Illinois.

From the very first he showed himself a great soldier. Leaving his headquarters at Cairo, on the Mississippi, he marched into Kentucky and took possession of Paducah. To the south were two Confederate strongholds—Fort Donelson on the Cumberland River and Fort Henry on the Tennessee; and Grant, with his capture of Paducah, was in a favorable position to strike a hard blow. In this he was aided by Commodore Foote, who, with his gunboats, opened the Mississippi all the way to Vicksburg. Fort Henry fell before him, and then Fort Donelson.

"If I surrender," said the Confederate commander of Fort Donelson, "what terms will you give me?"

"No terms," answered Grant, "except an unconditional and immediate surrender can be accepted. I propose to move immediately upon your works."

So now Grant's initials, U. S., stood also for "Unconditional Surrender," and the people of the North were loud in his praise.

But the Confederates had not yet lost all of Tennessee. A little later, in the battle of Shiloh, they came near to defeating the Union army, and would have done so if Grant had not held out till General Buell was able to join him.

HE CAPTURES VICKSBURG

Early in 1863 came Grant's great victory at Vicksburg. Nearly all the Mississippi River had now been forced by Federal gunboats; but Vicksburg was so strongly fortified that it had resisted an attack by General Sherman, and no one believed that it could be taken. Grant himself had failed in his first attempt; but he would not admit that anything was impossible, so he tried—and failed again. At last, after a wonderful campaign, including much hard marching and several brilliant victories, he got so near to Vicksburg that he was able to lay siege to the city. Soon its inhabitants were starving, and Vicksburg could hold out no longer. Its commander surrendered, and Grant marched in. Then at once he gave orders—first, to feed the hungry Confederate soldiers who had fought against him; second, that no cheering be permitted when these men laid down their arms. "They have made a noble defense," he said, "and must not be humiliated."

So important was this victory that he was now made a Major-General, and became commander of all the armies west of the Allegheny Mountains. Then came the battle of Chattanooga—another victory for Grant. In March, 1864, he was put in command of all the Federal armies, and was made Lieutenant-General—a rank heretofore held only by Washington and Scott. Yet three years before, he had been only a clerk in a country store, and had seemed to have no future.

END OF THE WAR

Grant was now called upon to measure his strength against Lee, the great leader of the Confederates, and many bloody battles took place. The Confederates had suffered some serious defeats, and supplies of all kinds were scarce. Lee had fought a losing, but a brilliant fight; at last, at Appomattox he surrendered. The war was virtually over.

"Let us have peace," said Grant.

The Southern soldiers needed their horses with which to till the fields; they needed food and clothing. All these were supplied. Everything that Grant could do he did for them. No one was more grateful than he that the war had come to an end.

At the next election, the people made him President of the United States; four years later they elected him again. And though his calling was that of a soldier, he proved a faithful President, too. During his term of office, Great Britain paid our claims against her for permitting Confederate cruisers to sail from her ports to the Southern States. His policy toward the Indians was wise and tender-hearted, and did much to prevent uprisings, so often provoked by rascally Indian agents. By his firm stand against Congress, after the panic of 1873, he prevented what were already hard times from growing even harder.

To provide for his family, General Grant went into business in New York; but the business failed, owing to the dishonesty of others. Broken in health, and almost penniless, once more he stoutly set to work, writing the story of his life; and this he managed to complete, though suffering agony from a cancer of the tongue that finally destroyed him.

It was perhaps the bravest thing of all, in a life filled with brave deeds. To-day his body lies in a great tomb overlooking the Hudson; his name was among the first inscribed in our Hall of Fame.

A MAN LIKE A STONE WALL

BY BERTHA E. BUSH

"WHAT is your name?"

The teacher, quill pen in hand, was enrolling the pupils of the little field school. The group of big girls in the back seats fairly tittered as the answer came.

"Thomas Jonathan Jackson."

Just why they should think this a funny name is hard to tell. Perhaps it was because the boy who gave it was so awkward and lank and plainly ill at ease. He was more used to handling farm implements than books, but he studied his lessons with grim determination to get the most that he could out of them, and thus won their respect in spite of his awkward appearance.

He had been fatherless and motherless, dependent on the charity of relatives, some of them kind, some unkind, ever since he was three years old. How could he be expected to be elegant in dress and appearance and polished in manners? One thing was certain. He was good and earnest and kind and true and brave, brave as a lion. The girls who tittered at him that day came to be very proud that they had gone to school with him.

When he was sixteen, he learned that there was a vacancy in West Point and conceived the desire to apply for the position. The friend who learned of his desire told him of the high standard of scholarship required there, and asked young Thomas Jonathan whether he thought it was possible for him to prepare himself to enter.

"I am very ignorant, but I can make it up by study," answered the boy modestly. "I have the energy, and I think I have the intellect."

He succeeded in gaining admission, and he studied hard. He was slow, as was natural from the small amount of his previous training, but he never gave up trying. During the first year he was at the foot of his class. The next year his standing was better. The third year it was better still; and the last year it was so good that one of his companions declared that if only he

had four years longer to study he would graduate at the head of his class.

GOES TO THE MEXICAN WAR

The young cadet finished his course and went to the Mexican War. He wasn't handsome or dashing, but he was brave and faithful, and he fought with honor. In one battle the fire of the enemy was so terrible at a certain point that all the cannoneers fled. Only Jackson and one sergeant were left. Dismounting, young Jackson himself took up the sponge staff the hand of the gunner had dropped and, with the assistance of the sergeant, began to load and fire with the utmost coolness. The commander of the field thought it best to withdraw from the position, but Jackson remonstrated. He could hold the ground, he said, and if the general would send him fifty regulars, he would silence the enemies' batteries. The re-enforcements were given him. The enemies' batteries were silenced and the battle was won by the Americans.

Jackson always obeyed orders, and taught every student to obey them implicitly. After the Mexican War was over he taught in a military academy, and the boys thought he was too strict about this. They were gay young fellows, and he was shy and awkward yet, and they thought it fun to badger the stiff, silent young professor.

"That was a very hot place, wasn't it, Major?" asked one of them, referring to this occasion.

"Yes, very hot," was the reply.

"Why didn't you run?" asked the student.

With a smile, Jackson replied: "I was not ordered to do so. If I had been ordered to run I would have done so; but I was directed to hold my position, and I had no right to abandon it."

"Who is Thomas J. Jackson?" somebody asked, when it was suggested that he should be appointed a colonel in the newly-formed Confederate army.

* Used by permission of the F. A. Owen Publishing Company, Dansville, N. Y.

"I can tell you who he is," replied one of his friends. "If you put him in command of Norfolk, he will never leave it alive unless you order him to do so."

Every one soon knew that this was true. In his first battle he stood under a tree writing a dispatch. A cannon ball came whizzing along, struck the tree and tore it to fragments, scattering leaves and splinters all over him, but he never paused in his writing. Cannon balls nor anything else could not stop him in anything that he thought was his duty.

He inspired his men with the same spirit. Once when he was placing his division for battle, he said to the officer with whom he was riding:

"Captain, I want my brigade to feel that it can itself whip all the opposing army, and I believe it can do it."

PROMOTION MAKES NO DIFFERENCE

A little while after this, he was promoted from colonel to general. It made a difference in his rank, but no difference in his appearance or actions. He still wore the same shabby old gray coat; the old cap, faded by the sun until it was fairly yellow, was pulled far down over his eyes, and his men called him "Old Jack." But they had come to believe in him with all their hearts, and were ready to follow him anywhere and obey as he had obeyed in his under-soldier days.

It told in the battle of Bull Run. Discouraged soldiers were everywhere flying from the field. The main part of the army was in retreat. But Jackson and his men did not retreat. They stood in their place, and their standing saved the day.

"General, they are beating us back," cried the commander of the retreating corps.

"Then we will give them the bayonet," answered Jackson.

He knew that his men would die before they would be beaten back. The discouraged general galloped back to his broken lines and by heroic effort succeeded in reforming them.

"Look! There is Jackson standing like a stone wall. Rally on the Virginians!" he shouted, and his men looked and rallied and defeat was turned into victory.

It became a watchword. To say "Stonewall Jackson" was enough to inspire courage in the most disheartened. The name the tittering girls had laughed at was almost forgotten in the new title. It is not as Thomas Jonathan Jackson that the hero is remembered but always as General Stonewall Jackson.

He knew very well how serious were the conditions that he faced like a stone wall. "I fully expected that I and my men would be killed," he said, "but I felt that the occasion demanded the sacrifice."

He wouldn't admit that they could be defeated. When an officer rode up to him and exclaimed in great excitement, "General, I think the day is going against us," Jackson answered, "If you think so, sir, you had better not say anything about it."

When General Jackson wrote about this battle, he gave all the praise to his men and took none himself. He said that it was they and not he who deserved the title, and called them the "Stonewall Brigade." He wrote to a friend about them:

"You will find when my report shall be published, that the First Brigade was to our army what the Imperial Guard was to the first Napoleon; and that, through the blessing of God, it met the so far victorious enemy, and turned the fortunes of the day."

MEN GAVE HIM ALL THE PRAISE

But his men gave all the praise to him. They felt that it was he who had taught them to be brave and steady under any fire, and now that the value of his teaching was proved, they began to admire him immensely. Wherever he went they began to cheer. His division was prouder of belonging to the "Stonewall Brigade" than of anything else in the world. When he approached on his old sorrel horse, the word would flash up and down the line that "Old Jack was coming." Then such a shout as would go up. The very sky seemed to echo it back.

He was worth the favor of the sky, for always in his thoughts he looked up to Heaven. Every morning in his tent he read his Bible. He had a way of lifting his hand for an instant and looking up, in the midst of the most vigorous action, and the men who saw it said reverently that Old Jack was praying. Often they saw him do this, and saw his lips move when he stood over the body of a fallen soldier.

He was wonderfully skillful in the art of war, but his skill was won, like his increasingly high marks in West Point, by the most careful and persistent study and planning and estimating. Because he worked so very hard at it, he grew better all the time. Somebody says of him:

"His services became more and more valuable as his rank increased. He was better as brigadier than as colonel; better still as major-general; and as lieutenant-general was best of all."

The most remarkable thing he did was to get

his men where he wanted them so quickly. It was wonderful how he could have them fighting at one place and then, before the enemy had scarcely time to catch breath, striking a crushing blow at another place. So quickly did he pass from one position to another that once a dispatch was sent to him from headquarters addressed "General Jackson, Somewhere."

He would march all day and all night, go without food or water or shelter or blankets, anything to get his men in the most effective place in the shortest time. His soldiers did not complain for they knew that he was suffering as much as they were. They were ready to go anywhere and endure any hardship to carry out his plans. They made up this conundrum and said it over and over again with great delight:

"Why is Old Jack a better general than Moses?"

"Because it took Moses forty years to lead the Israelites through the wilderness, and Old Jack would have double-quicked them through it in three days."

And they loaded their guns as they double-quicked, and went without food and slept on the ground blanketless with the snow falling over them, and wore ragged shoes so full of holes that the rocks and brambles of the way tore their feet till they bled, and never complained. No hardship mattered to them if they could carry out Old Jack's plans.

NONE MADE MORE SKILLFUL PLANS

There never was a general who made more skillful plans than he. It was said that in the half year between May and December, 1862, Jackson's corps "made more forced marches and fought more battles against superior numbers and without a single defeat than can be claimed by any commander of modern or ancient warfare."

He died on the tenth of May, 1863. He had been shot at the battle of Chancellorsville, but, though his wounds were very severe, necessitating the amputation of his arm, it was not these that caused his death. For a week it was thought that he would get well, and he made plans for riding again at the head of his division. But he had caught a very severe cold before the battle. He had marched forward so rapidly that he had left his blankets behind him. A young aide, seeing this, gave him his own thick military cape to put over him. The night was cold, and Jackson waking, feared that the young man would suffer without it. So he rose and spread the cape over the sleeping soldier boy and lay down again shivering with the scantiest of coverings. The result was the severe cold that, combined with the weakness caused by his wounds, turned into pneumonia and brought about his death.

His last military order was given after he was wounded. A subordinate general reported to him that the lines were so much broken that he feared they would have to fall back. Stonewall Jackson lifted his head from the ground where he lay.

"You must hold your ground, General; you must hold your ground, sir," he cried.

As he was being carried away through the thick woods in the dark, one of the bearers of the litter stumbled over a grapevine and dropped the corner he held on the ground. Jackson struck on his wounded shoulder, causing terrible pain. But when the bearer asked anxiously whether he was much hurt he answered:

"No, my friend, don't trouble yourself about me." He was as brave about enduring pain as he had been going into battle.

"I am sure these wounds were given me for some good and wise purpose, and I would not part with them if I could," he said.

Almost his last conscious words when told that death was near were, "Very good, very good; it is all right."

Then his mind began to wander. He gave orders as if he had been on the battlefield—stirring orders for intense action. Then he smiled and said softly:

"Let us cross over the river and rest under the shade of the trees."

He has won everlasting rest and everlasting honor.

DEWEY, THE HERO OF MANILA

BY JOSEPH LEWIS FRENCH

Nations listen—nations wait,
At the portal of Time's gate,
For a hero!
Crowned of the century's years,
Rings the pæan in our ears—
Take your hero!

God of War and God of Sea,
Of all trophies deigned by Thee,
This the rarest, most complete,
This the crown, the Paraclete—
Hail our hero!

THE nation-wide sentiment which welcomed Admiral George Dewey back to America in the Spring of 1899 was well compressed in these stirring lines. No event since Grant's final triumph over the Confederacy had so profound an influence. In the case of Dewey, there was acclamation and rejoicing everywhere, north and south. He had not only achieved a remarkable victory in one of the most triumphant sea-fights known to history, but he had opened the East to us. He gave us for a moment the thrill of world-conquest — always the dream of every great nation. And not only had he conquered the Philippines, but he stayed till his conquest was assured. His diplomacy as well as his military genius were our shining possession. And thenceforward he lived among us till he died, the hero of the time.

The chief lesson of his life up to the hour of his great victory is, for the American boy, the great lesson of duty; duty never shirked, but always performed, whatever the service, with the most conscientious fidelity. This was the trait he inherited from a long line of New England ancestors.

He was born on the 26th of December, 1837, among the Green Mountains of Vermont, and he records in his autobiography that during his long stay in Manila Bay after the battle "certain angles of view in the irregular landscape of Luzon, from the deck of the flagship Olympia, often recalled the Green Mountains of my boyhood days. Indeed, I never look across a stretch of rolling country without a feeling of homesickness for Vermont. My ancestors were reared among the New England hills. They were of the old Pilgrim stock, whose character has so eminently impressed itself on that of the nation."

Of his parents he writes: "My mother I hardly remember, as she died when I was only five. To my father I owe primarily all that I have accom-

plished in the world. From him I inherited a vigorous constitution and an active temperament. He was a good deal more than a successful practicing physician. He was one of those natural leaders to whom men turn for unbiased advice. His ideas of right and wrong were very fixed, in keeping with his deep religious scruples."

Those ideas of right and wrong never deserted George Dewey. As a boy he was notable for animal spirits, and even a spirit of daring which prompted him to "stunts" that the other boys could not follow. He used to descend the steps of the courthouse in Montpelier, his home, blindfolded, and on one occasion he drove his father's horse and wagon over the swollen Winooski River, just for pluck. He lost the wagon, but was saved by climbing on the horse's back.

FROM A VERMONT ACADEMY TO ANNAPOLIS

His career began at the old Military Academy at Norwich, Vermont, which was founded by the first superintendent of West Point, Captain Alden Partridge. From there he went to the Naval Academy at Annapolis, whither his father accompanied him. On leaving him the old gentleman said: "George, I have done all I can for you. The rest you must do yourself."

"This advice," adds Dewey, "I have always tried to keep in mind."

The course at the Academy was more vigorous in those days than now, and of the sixty in Dewey's class only fifteen were graduated. It was a good rough school, too, and hazing and fistic fights were rife. But Dewey was born a gentleman, and he remained a gentleman through it all, though always quick to take his own part.

On graduating, in the Summer of 1858, he sailed on the steam frigate Wabash for an eighteen months' cruise, and got as far as Constantinople. Then he was sent on a cruise to Caribbean and Gulf ports, and there saw a good slice of the world before the war of the Rebellion called him into active conflict. In January, 1861, he got his commission as lieutenant, at twenty-three, and became a full-fledged naval officer.

He saw his first service in the Civil War on the "Mississippi," which was to help blockade the coast from Hampton to Key West and the boundaries of Mexico. When the Gulf Squadron under Farragut was formed in 1862 for the capture of New Orleans he joined it, and at once got into hot fighting. Farragut now became Dewey's ideal of a fighting commander, and remained so throughout his life. "Whenever I have been in a difficult situation I have often asked myself what Farragut would do." Valuable as the training at Annapolis was, it was poor schooling beside that of serving under Farragut in time of war.

When the squadron advanced on New Orleans, the "Mississippi" was leading the way just astern of the "Pensacola," with Dewey handling the ship from the hurricane-deck. "For a man of twenty-four," he says, "I was having my share of responsibility. I was also to have my baptism of fire. But I had little time to consider the experience. When it comes, you are utterly preoccupied with your work; you are doing what you have been taught is your duty to do as a trained unit on a man-of-war. Only after the danger is over is it time to reflect."

It was a baptism—of hell-fire. Not only had the dangerous forts of Jackson and St. Philip that guarded the city to be passed, but the river was full of fire-rafts and burning ships, and once the hull of the "Mississippi" met the ram "Manassas," that had already done terrible destruction in southern waters. But everywhere the fearful broadsides from Farragut's ships cleared the way up the river and New Orleans was soon won. This was the great achievement of the war thus far, and made Farragut the hero of the hour.

CO-OPERATES WITH ARMIES OF GRANT AND SHERMAN

Dewey remained on the "Mississippi," which was stationed off New Orleans as a guard-ship, for nearly a year. In March, 1863, the vessel was ordered up the river with the squadron to Port Hudson to co-operate with the armies of Grant and Sherman, which were pressing toward Vicksburg. Dewey had occupied much of his time before New Orleans in training his crew of three hundred men, and they were now at a high point of efficiency. In the engagement the "Mississippi" grounded, caught fire, and was abandoned, and officers and crew found safety on the "Richmond." In the fierce fight at Port Hudson only Farragut's ship, the "Hartford," got through. Dewey returned to New Orleans,

where for a short time he served as prize commissioner.

For a time thereafter he served under Farragut in his operations up and down the river, and in July, 1863, was transferred to the "Brooklyn," and ordered north to assist Rear Admiral Dahlgren in the blockade of Charleston. Here the "Brooklyn," being found out of repair, was ordered to New York and Dewey got his first holiday. When the "Brooklyn" was ready, Captain Alden wanted Dewey for his executive officer, but here again senior officers urged his youth against him, and owing to influence at Washington they prevailed. Dewey was no longer under Farragut, who knew his real worth. He was ordered to get the "Agawam," a third-rate vessel in Portsmouth harbor, ready for service. He went out on her as executive officer, and saw active and trying service on the James River during the Spring and Summer of 1864, supporting General Butler's attempt to take Richmond from that side.

Dewey's reputation as an executive officer was by this time established; and in September, 1864, Rear Admiral David D. Porter, who had succeeded to the command of the North Atlantic squadron, sent for him to take charge of the "Colorado," a big steam frigate, in the action against Fort Fisher. This was the final act in the terrific drama of the great Rebellion. The Mississippi River was now in the full possession of the North, and every port on the Gulf of Mexico was flying the national flag.

The Confederacy had but two ports left—Charleston and Wilmington. Of these, Wilmington was the most important, and at its entrance stood Fort Fisher, which they had made impregnable. It was to be silenced by the guns of the fleet, and then assaulted by troops under General Butler, brought by sea. The largest naval force of the war was assembled here. On the "Colorado," Dewey found himself in full charge of seven hundred men, and the crew was a tough one to handle. But Dewey tamed them, although he once had to use his revolver. The first attempt on Fort Fisher failed, but a second one three weeks later was successful.

Dewey was promoted to the "Kearsarge," the famous victor over the "Alabama," and was on her as executive officer when Lee surrendered. His rank at this time was that of lieutenant-commander.

A year after the war closed he was chosen by Admiral Goldsborough, in command of the European squadron, as his flag-lieutenant, thus getting his first foreign experience. After a short time he was given command of his old ship, the "Colorado," with which he remained abroad over two years. A week before she sailed for home Farragut came aboard at Cherbourg, France, and after going all over the ship turned to the captain of his own ship and said: "Pennock, I want the 'Franklin' to be just like this."

On arriving home Dewey was assigned to instruction duty at Annapolis, where he remained three happy years, having married at the beginning of his term Susan Boardman Goodwin, the daughter of ex-Governor Goodwin of New Hampshire. In the Spring of 1873 he was promoted to the rank of commander, and assigned to the "Narragansett," on board of which vessel he spent two years surveying the coast of Lower California and Mexico.

SEES WASHINGTON SOCIAL LIFE

In April, 1878, the future hero of Manila was made naval secretary of the Lighthouse Board, a post which he held four years, and during which he saw for the first time much of the social life of Washington. In October, 1882, he was ordered to the command of the "Juniata," to proceed to the China station, but by the time the vessel reached Malta he had developed an abscess of the liver which almost lost him his life. He was given sick leave, and finally recovered fully at Santa Barbara, California, in the Spring of 1884. On recovering, he was given command of the "Pensacola," on a cruise in European waters.

In the building of a new navy Dewey was destined to play an important part, and in July, 1889, he was made chief of the Bureau of Equipment. Here he put in four years of engrossing and vitally important work. In October, 1895, he became president of the Board of Inspection and Survey, a very important post, for this board was responsible for each new vessel as it was completed. The country had by this time become interested in the new navy. All the steel ships of the new navy passed under his mandate for the following two years, including the "Texas," "Maine," "Iowa," "Indiana" and "Massachusetts," and all the battleships which later vanquished the Spanish fleet at Santiago, except the "Oregon."

In May, 1896, he was promoted to the rank of Commodore, which entitled him to the command of a squadron. He was given, November, 1897, charge of the Asiatic Squadron through the far-sightedness and influence of Theodore Roosevelt, who was then Secretary of the Navy, and who insisted on his appointment. "I want you to go," Mr. Roosevelt declared. "You are the man who will be equal to the emergency if one arises." And so, indeed, history has proven.

Dewey had already scented a war with Spain, and his heart was set on having command of the Asiatic Squadron. On his appointment he discovered before leaving home that the quantity of ammunition in the squadron was not even a sufficient allowance for times of peace. Vigorously supported by Roosevelt, he succeeded finally in having an order issued that the "Concord," then fitting out in San Francisco, should carry out as much as she could hold. Seventy-five tons were needed to place the squadron on any kind of a war-footing, and all of this Dewey saw shipped from San Francisco by the "Concord" and the "Baltimore" before he sailed himself to take command. Even then Dewey found when he reached the Asiatic station that only sixty per cent of the magazines and shell-rooms could be supplied, and with this deficiency he was obliged, seven thousand miles from home, to go into action in Manila Bay. At this time he had fears of a prolonged action with the Spanish squadron. "However," writes Dewey, "even if we had had less ammunition, we should have gone into Manila Bay, for such were our orders, and such was the only thing to do."

No intimation of trouble with Spain reached Dewey until February 17th, at Hong Kong, two days after the destruction of the "Maine" in Havana harbor. February 25th came a sharp order, signed "Roosevelt," to keep the squadron close, and in the event of war proceed to offensive operations in the Philippines. Dewey's small fleet of four vessels was now re-enforced by the arrival of the "Boston," the "Concord," and the "Raleigh," and every preparation made for war.

THE BATTLE OF MANILA BAY

On the 30th of April the squadron entered the bay of Manila at night. Much to Dewey's surprise and chagrin, they met with no resistance whatever, excepting three shots from a shore battery. "Signal-lights, rockets, and beacons along the shore," writes Dewey, "gave us no concern whatever, now that we were sure of grappling with the enemy. With the coming of broad daylight we finally sighted the Spanish vessels formed in an irregular crescent in front of Cavite. The 'Olympia' headed toward them and in answer to her signal to close up, the distance between our ships was reduced to two hundred yards." Some of the Spanish vessels were under way, and others were moved so as to give their broadside batteries the best advantage. "Before me now was the object for which we had made our arduous preparations, and which indeed must ever be the supreme test of a

GEORGE DEWEY
FROM A PAINTING BY W. D. MURPHY

naval officer's career. I felt confident of the outcome, although I had no thought that victory would be won at so slight a cost to our own side."

At 5:15 the Cavite forts and the Spanish squadron opened fire. The American squadron sailed alternately back and forth over a course of two miles, remaining at a distance of about two thou-

sand yards from the enemy, and keeping up a hot fire all the time. The rapidity of this fire and its concentration, the ships being close together, was smothering, especially upon the two largest Spanish vessels, the "Reina Cristina" and "Castilla." The former and the "Don Juan" made brave and desperate attempts to charge the "Olympia," but were driven back by the concentrated fire of the American squadron. In this sortie the "Reina Cristina," Admiral Montojos' flagship, was almost destroyed. The "Castilla" fared little better. Shortly after seven o'clock the Admiral transferred his flag to the "Isla de Cuba." The "Don Juan de Austria" was by this time badly damaged, and on fire, the "Isla de Luzon" had three guns shot away, and the "Marques del Duero" was in a critical condition. The American crews which started on a cup of coffee at 4 A.M., were now given their breakfast. A consultation called on board the "Olympia" showed that a heavy flight of shells had passed over each ship, but that not a single man had been killed in the whole action. Only two officers and six men were wounded, and but slightly. The hull of the "Olympia" was struck five times, as was the "Baltimore." The "Boston" had four unimportant hits, and the "Petrel" was struck once. At 12:30 the "Petrel" signaled the fact of surrender, and the firing ceased. The battle of Manila was won, and a new star had been added to the American constellation.

For more than a year Dewey remained at Manila, where his cool, tactful diplomatic way of dealing with the many questions that arose in connection with his new conquest was vitally necessary. He came home to a country that rose as one man to receive him. Dewey arches, Dewey flags, and great blazing electric signs welcomed him everywhere. It was the greatest personal demonstration in American history since the visit of Lafayette. He was made Admiral for life, the rank being created especially for him, and he retired to Washington, where he was appointed President of the new General Board to prepare war plans, recommend the types and armament of vessels to be built yearly, and act as a clearing-house for all questions of naval policy. He was able to report at his office daily as an active officer till he was past seventy, and was a familiar and beloved figure on the streets of Washington up to the day of his death.

All his long, arduous life George Dewey had been more than equal to every responsibility thrust upon him, had never failed in any emergency, and when the occasion came he rose to the plane of a hero.

THEODORE ROOSEVELT *

BY HERMANN HAGEDORN, JR.

DEDICATION

HE WAS found faithful over a few things and he was made ruler over many; he cut his own trail clean and straight, and millions followed him toward the light ❧ He was frail; he made himself a tower of strength. He was timid; he made himself a lion of courage. He was a dreamer; he became one of the great doers of all time ❧ Men put their trust in him; women found a champion in him; kings stood in awe of him, but children made him their playmate ❧ He broke a nation's slumber with his cry, and it rose up. He touched the eyes of blind men with a flame that gave them vision. Souls became swords through him; swords became servants of God ❧ He was loyal to his country, and he exacted loyalty; he loved many lands, but he loved his own land best ❧ He was terrible in battle, but tender to the weak; joyous and tireless, being free from self-pity; clean with a cleanness that cleansed the air like a gale ❧ His courtesy knew no wealth, no class; his friendship, no creed or color or race. His courage stood every onslaught of savage beast and ruthless man, of loneliness, of victory, of defeat. His mind was eager, his heart was true, his body and spirit, defiant of obstacles, ready to meet what might come ❧ He fought injustice and tyranny; bore sorrow gallantly; loved all nature, bleak spaces and hardy companions, hazardous adventure and the zest of battle. Wherever he went he carried his own pack; and in the uttermost parts of the earth he kept his conscience for his guide.

I

THEODORE ROOSEVELT, twenty-sixth President of the United States, was born at 28 East 20th Street, New York City, on October 27, 1858. His father, Theodore Roosevelt, was a glass merchant, a figure in city affairs, a philanthropist widely respected and beloved; his mother, Martha Bulloch, was a woman of unusual beauty and charm, of cool good sense and passionate devotions. Both were aristocrats by lineage and the higher right of spiritual nobility. The Civil War, breaking upon them when Theodore the Younger was two

and a half years old, turned the sympathy of one to the North; that of the other, with equal ardor, to the South; but it did not cloud the affection they held for each other or the happiness of their home.

Theodore the Younger was, from his birth, a frail boy, who suffered much from asthma and other bodily ailments. For weeks on end he was forced to keep to his bed, and the rough-and-tumble of boyhood was during his early years altogether withheld from him. He learned to read while he was still in skirts, and before he was out of the nursery age books had become companions to him and comforters in pain. His sisters, his brother and their friends were his devoted followers, who found the stories he told them, hour after hour, altogether thrilling.

He went to school for a brief period at Professor McMullen's Academy, near Madison Square, but his health permitted him no regular schooling, and tutors and governesses gave him an uneven elementary education, which he extended and deepened by wide reading of heroic tales and natural history, of science and biography. When he was nine he was taken through Europe, but, to judge from the journal he kept, gained nothing from it except a small boy's spread-eagle homesickness for his own land. Rome, Paris, Vesuvius and the Trossachs were alike a bore to him. Another trip to Europe four years later opened his eyes. He had by that time become an ardent naturalist, and Egypt and the Continent were interesting for their birds, if not for their monuments. He spent a winter in a German family in Dresden, and returned to America with an understanding of foreign lands which served to give him a real appreciation of his own. Still handicapped by his physical frailness, he prepared himself for college.

Meanwhile, he had acquired certain ideals of life and conduct which exercised a deep influence on his character. He was a notable hero-worshiper, with his father as his greatest hero then as always, and behind him the company of the heroic dead, who had become familiar to him through books. He measured himself by them, found himself wanting both in courage and physical strength, and doggedly set to work to repair the defects. He took boxing lessons, and exer-

* This sketch was written originally for the Roosevelt Memorial Exhibition Committee of Columbia University.

THEODORE ROOSEVELT

cised, with a persistence that did not abate, in the gymnasium his father installed for him. The world of outdoors was a source of delight and adventure. His boy's love for birds and insects developed into the scientist's ardor for solid knowledge. When he went to college in the Autumn of 1876, it was with the determination to become a faunal naturalist.

His years at Harvard were years of growth

Courtesy of Women's Roosevelt Memorial Association
BIRTHPLACE OF ROOSEVELT
FROM A DRAWING

and joyous companionship. He studied hard, he read widely and deeply, he plunged into a dozen different undergraduate activities, from boxing and fencing and football to acting and writing and Sunday-school teaching and discussion of art at Professor Charles Eliot Norton's. He romped one day, he wrote history the next; he made many friends; he gained a few devoted followers who prophesied great things for him; meanwhile, he grew in body and mind.

He graduated in June, 1880. Shortly after, he married Alice Lee of Chestnut Hill, who had

been the radiant center of the group of boys and girls with whom he had "run" during his Harvard years. They went to Europe, where Theodore Roosevelt climbed the Matterhorn for no particular reason except that a pair of Englishmen with whom he had talked seemed to think that they were the only ones who had ever climbed it or ever would; and returned to America, more ardently American than ever, and settled in New York.

He had long given up his intention of becoming a naturalist, without, however, being able to decide what he would become. With no great enthusiasm for the law, he entered the Columbia Law School and, at the same time, the law office of his uncle, Robert Roosevelt. Meanwhile he completed a history of "The Naval War of 1812" which he had begun in college, looked about in the political world of his native city, and joined the Republican Club of the Twenty-first Assembly District.

He became a factor, if not a power, there at once, and on the initiative of a shrewd, keen-witted Irishman named "Joe" Murray, a local "boss," was nominated for the Assembly within a year, and elected.

In Albany he sprang almost at once into leadership. Before his first term was over he was a national figure, at the end of his third he was a force to be reckoned with in the Republican party, head of his State delegation to the National Convention, the hero of young men, the hope of all who were working for the triumph of the better elements in American politics. He gained his first fame through a fearless attack on a corrupt judge whom the leaders of his own party were seeking to shelter; but the real confidence of the public he won by solid and persistent work against odds for honest government and progressive legislation.

A personal catastrophe cut off completely and, it seemed forever, his political career. In February, 1884, his mother died suddenly. The same night his daughter Alice was born, and twelve hours later his wife died. He finished his term in the Assembly, did what he could to nominate the man of his choice at the Republican Convention in Chicago, failed, and hid himself, disheartened, on the ranch he had purchased the preceding Autumn on the banks of the Little Missouri River, in Dakota.

II

For the two years or more that followed, the gay world of New York City, and that other complex and tumultuous world of politics through which he had passed like a cyclone, saw Theodore Roosevelt only for hurried glimpses, if at all. He had altogether resigned whatever political ambitions he might have had. He wanted to write; and he did write an entertaining book of hunter's tales, a fresh and authoritative biography of Thomas H. Benton, another of Gouverneur Morris, a volume concerning ranch-life; but these were incidental. He had bought a great herd of cattle, he had called to his side from Maine a pair of old friends and stalwart backwoodsmen named "Bill" Sewall and Will Dow; with them he had built a house which he called Elkhorn; and he was now a ranchman whose life was bounded by the circle of cares and wholesome hardships and pleasures and perils that make up a ranchman's days. The bleak and savage country and the primitive conditions of life fascinated his imagination; the hardy men who were his companions gripped his affections and held them. The "women-folk" in Maine joined their husbands and took charge of Elkhorn, and for two years made a home where the days passed in a round of manly endeavor and simple-hearted fellowship that in the memory of all who were a part of it lingered as a kind of pastoral idyl.

Working on the round-up, riding for days on end after stray cattle, hunting over the bare prairies and up the ragged peaks, Theodore Roosevelt won at last the strength of body he had set out to gain fifteen years before. He won much else—an understanding of the common man and of the West, a deeper appreciation of the meaning of democracy, a revived interest in life. His career as a ranchman came to an end in the Autumn of 1886, when he went East to accept the Republican nomination for Mayor of New York.

He ran against Abram S. Hewitt, the Tammany nominee, and Henry George, the candidate of a short-lived United Labor party, and was disastrously defeated in spite of a lively campaign. He went to Europe, and in London married the friend of his childhood, Edith Kermit Carow.

He returned with his wife to America the following Spring and moved into the new house on Sagamore Hill which he had set about to build before his departure. There he gave himself to the writing of books, notably "The Winning of the West," a history of the frontier, which was to be his greatest book. A Republican victory in 1888, however, brought him again into public affairs. He was appointed a member of the U. S. Civil Service Commission in Washington, and for six years thereafter fought the battle of civil

service reform against the corrupt or foolish advocates of favoritism who still affirmed that "to the victor belong the spoils." It was a perilous position for a public man with political ambitions, for the work of the Civil Service Commission was unpopular with the leaders of both parties, and to administer it ably meant to antagonize the most powerful forces in Congress. Roosevelt carried the fight into the very Cabinet of the Republican President, and even while he drew the fire of the spoilsmen won the quick applause of men near and far who admired courage and skill in combat.

A reform victory in New York City in the Autumn of 1894 brought him, six months later, again to the city of his birth as President of the Police Board. The police department of the city was demoralized, favoritism and corruption were rampant, laws were unequally enforced, and vice and crime flourished openly to the scandal of respectable citizens, who were helpless, it seemed, to cope with the forces of disorder. Into these Augean stables Theodore Roosevelt courageously turned the flood of his turbulent energy and cleansing love of justice. He abolished at once the system of admission and promotion by pay or influence; he stood by his men when influential wrongdoers attempted to discredit them for doing their duty. Within six months he had put new spirit into the force and brought the law once more into repute. But in so doing he had stirred the anger of the politicians of both parties and of all the sinister forces which depended for their livelihood on vice and crime. His motives were misrepresented, his methods were ridiculed, until even the orderly elements, whose battle he was fighting, turned upon him. The newspapers attacked him savagely; even his colleagues on the Police Board thwarted him where they could.

"It is a grimy struggle, but a vital one," he wrote at the time in a letter to one of his sisters. "The battle for decent government must be won by just such interminable, grimy drudgery."

III

Into the tumult of his work on the Police Board came the rumors of impending war. Theodore Roosevelt believed with all his heart that Cuba should be freed from the intolerable yoke of Spain. He believed that only through the intervention of the United States could Cuba be thus freed. He had, ever since leaving college, preached national preparedness for war, demanding in particular the creation of an effective navy. When William McKinley, therefore, was elected

President in the Autumn of 1896, and offered
Roosevelt the position of Assistant Secretary of
the Navy, he accepted it with frank delight. He
became in the Navy Department what he had
been on the Civil Service Commission and the
Police Board, the moving spirit of the organization. His superior, Secretary Long, was by inclination a pacifist who looked with distrust and
some terror on Roosevelt's efforts to make the
navy into a vigorous fighting force. Roosevelt
utilized the brief periods when he was Acting
Secretary during his chief's absence to carry forward the policy which he deemed essential to the
national safety. It was by such almost surrepti-
tious action that Dewey was provided with the
coal and ships which ultimately enabled him to
destroy the Spanish fleet at Manila. When the
war came in April, 1898, he immediately resigned
his position, and offered his services to the President in raising the cavalry regiments which Congress authorized. General Alger, Secretary of
War, offered him the colonelcy of one of these
regiments. He refused, asking that the regiment
be given to his friend Leonard Wood, a veteran
of the Indian wars and at that time a surgeon
in the army, with himself as lieutenant-colonel.
The offer was accepted. Early in May the Rough
Riders, as they were nicknamed, began to gather
from all parts of the country, at San Antonio,
Texas. The training was brief but thorough.
Six weeks after the regiment was organized, it
stood trained and equipped on the firing line outside of Santiago de Cuba.

The Rough Riders came under fire for the first
time late in June, at Las Guasimas, where Roosevelt commanded first the center and later also the
left wing. He revealed himself there as a brave
soldier and an officer of calm judgment and
qualities of leadership altogether unusual.

The battle of San Juan Hill was fought a week
after the engagement at Las Guasimas. It was
a small but most sanguinary battle in which,
owing to the inefficiency and blundering of the
commanding general, the American casualties
were altogether out of proportion to the numbers
engaged. The day before the battle Colonel
Wood had been promoted to Brigadier General
and Roosevelt had been given command of the
regiment. All day, waiting for orders that did
not come, he lay with his men under the galling
fire of Spanish guns. One messenger after another whom he sent for orders was killed. At
last, late in the afternoon, the command came to
advance. He dashed forward, conspicuous on his
white horse, plunged through the line of regulars
who were obstructing his path, and led his men

through the tall grass up the long hill. To right
and left of him men fell, and the Mauser bullets
sang with the sound of ripping silk past his ears.
He remained untouched. At a barbed wire fence
he sprang off his horse and plunged on, his men
close at his heels. He gained the first crest,
pushing the Spaniards back; then another, and
a third. Inspired by his cool courage the American line advanced along the whole San Juan
range. At dusk the Spaniards were in full retreat
on the city.

Roosevelt returned home a popular hero. The
Republicans of New York State, facing defeat,
recognized that in Roosevelt lay their only hope.
He was nominated for Governor that Autumn,
and after a hot and close campaign was elected.

At Albany, Roosevelt revealed himself almost
at once as an able administrator, a clear-sighted
judge of men and a politician of tact, skill and
unswerving integrity. His own party machine
was distrustful of him as a reformer who had
said many hard things about party machines in
the past and who had handled neither the Democratic nor the Republican organization with
gloves during his battles as police commissioner.

More than once, the issues were sharply drawn,
and there was a clash that threatened to disrupt
the Republican party. But in every case Roosevelt's willingness to make concessions on in-
essentials and his evident determination to stand
firm as a rock on principles, averted what seemed
inevitable disaster.

Roosevelt had meanwhile become the acknowledged leader of the progressive elements in
American politics. His second annual message as
Governor, delivered in January, 1900, strikingly
revealed his comprehensive grasp of problems
confronting the nation. A movement to make
him candidate for Vice-President on the Republican ticket was started simultaneously among his
political enemies in the East, who wished to
shelve him, and his devoted followers in the West
who sought his promotion, and gained swift
headway even against his most frantic protests.
He looked upon the tranquil ineffectiveness of
the Vice-President's office with undisguised
horror. In the Convention in June his wishes
were overruled and he was forced to accept the
nomination. Having accepted, he put the full
force of his energy and enthusiasm into the campaign that followed, touring the country from
end to end. The Republican ticket was triumphantly elected and Roosevelt settled down in
Washington, with what grace he could command,
to four years of dull inaction which he prophesied
would leave him at their conclusion, at best, a

professor of history in a second-rate college, until the end of his days.

IV

An assassin's bullet, removing his chief from the field of action with sudden and terrible swiftness, brought Roosevelt unexpectedly into the very forefront of affairs. Six months after the second inauguration of President McKinley, Theodore Roosevelt became President of the United States. He retained the Cabinet of his predecessor and pledged himself to carry out his predecessor's policies. But it was inevitable that his strong personality should immediately impress itself on the whole administration. Friends and opponents alike recognized that a great new dynamic force was in control. His grasp of public questions, his wide range of interests, his understanding and love for all manner of men, his tireless energy, made him at once the center of public attention and the most widely popular of American executives since Andrew Jackson. He was a forceful and persuasive speaker, and again and again, when Congress blocked his measures, won the support of the people by direct appeals. He crossed and crisscrossed the continent, meeting the American people face to face and laying his causes before them for their judgment. He had the gift of making men of all sections feel that he was peculiarly an expression of their own dreams and aspirations. He was, in fact, at home in every part of the land, and through his Northern birth, his Southern ancestry, his residence in the West and his deep understanding of the Western point of view, was peculiarly a son of the whole country.

His conduct of domestic as well as foreign affairs was fearless and vigorous. He saw clearly that the question of most vital importance before the country was the control and strict regulation of the great corporations. In the famous Northern Securities' merger he presented a test case to the Supreme Court which ultimately opened the way for the prosecution of the other great corporations which had violated the Sherman Anti-trust Law. His fight against the conservative forces of both parties on this question, and kindred matters of railroad regulation, was intensely bitter and extended throughout his period of office.

His dealings with labor were equally far-sighted and firm. He favored combinations of labor as he favored combinations of capital, but stood as firmly against lawlessness on the part of laboring men as he stood against it on the part of capitalists.

"At last," said one of the "labor men" at luncheon one day, "there is a hearing for us fellows."

"Yes," cried the President emphatically. "The White House door, while I am here, shall swing open as easily for the labor man as for the capitalist, and no easier."

He was able to settle the anthracite coal strike in October, 1902, because he understood the points of view of both sides and was known by both as a just man of solid convictions whom threats could not swerve from his determined course.

His attitude in foreign affairs, as in domestic, was frank, clear-cut and firm, being based on the same principles which governed his personal relations with his fellowmen. He treated nations when they were bullies in the same direct manner he had used with certain "bad men" in Dakota. His vigorous handling of Germany, late in 1902, met a covert challenge of the Monroe Doctrine in a manner that left nothing to the Kaiser's imagination. His hint to England on the Alaska boundary question—"Arbitrate if you want to, but there is the map"—was equally unambiguous and fruitful of international good-will. He settled the century-old Panama question by swift and decisive action on the instant when such action was needed, and was digging the Canal before his opponents in Congress had recovered from their horror at his temerity. His reputation for integrity and candor, combined with an instant readiness to act, solved more than one knotty international problem before it reached a crisis, and gave him power, when the governments of Europe found themselves impotent and afraid to intervene in the Russo-Japanese conflict, to thrust his vigorous personality between the contestants and by a liberal "knocking of heads right and left," literally to force peace.

He found the government of the United States, when he took up the reins, in the position among world powers, of a new boy in school; he left it firmly established in the first rank, admired and feared, its favor eagerly sought after, its citizenship respected in the remotest corners of the globe. In domestic affairs his impress was no less remarkable. At a critical moment in the conflict between capital and labor he was able to exercise the mediating influence which averted the deep bitterness which that conflict had engendered in other nations, and to guide both parties away from the extremes whose final meeting place is revolution. He fought the battle of democracy against impending plutocracy; he insisted that the rights of the public to the natural resources of the country outweighed private rights, and fought men of all parties until his word prevailed and found expression in the conservation movement; above all, he kindled men and women, and especially young men, to an ardor for public service such as men had not known before in times of peace. He trumpeted the call of national and civic duty, and the conscience of the country awoke and responded.

V

Theodore Roosevelt left the Presidency in March, 1909, and a month later sailed for East Africa. There for a year he hunted big game— lion and elephant, rhinoceros, giraffe, ostrich and hippopotamus, meeting strange peoples and perilous adventures. He emerged from the jungle at Khartoum in April, 1910, to be greeted by a cheer of welcome that echoed around the world. His journey down the Nile and through Europe was a triumphal progress extraordinary in its evidence of admiration and wonder. He made formal addresses before half a dozen learned bodies, stirring up a hornets' nest in Cairo by his denunciation of a recent political assassination, another in Rome by refusing to allow his freedom of action to be circumscribed by the papal authorities, a third in London by criticizing England's government of Egypt. At Christiania he received the Nobel Prize, awarded to him the year previous for his efforts in bringing about the Peace of Portsmouth; in Berlin he reviewed, at the Kaiser's side, the crack troops of the Empire. Altogether, it was a memorable journey.

He returned to the United States to find the Party which he had left united and vigorous after its recent victory, disrupted by bitter factional strife, and slipping rapidly toward disaster. In the struggle between the progressive and the reactionary elements he could not stand to one side in dignified neutrality. He espoused the progressive cause, and in the campaign of 1910 fought with all the energy that was in him for the overthrow of boss-rule in New York State. He was decisively beaten after a contest that was bitter in the extreme. His enemies shouted that he was politically dead. He withdrew to Sagamore Hill and his editorial work on the staff of the *Outlook,* and, for the moment, let his foes rejoice.

But the struggle into which he had thrown, with such seeming recklessness, the stake of his great reputation, had been scarcely checked by the mid-term defeat. He was urged to be a candidate for President on the Republican ticket against President Taft, who was backed by the party machine and the so-called "stand-patters." He did not want to make the race, and it was against his own best judgment that he was persuaded at last to enter the contest. Once in, however, he fought with his whole being. One State after another, in the primary campaign, pledged its delegates to him. But the party machine was in the hands of his enemies, and in the convention held in Chicago in June they used it relentlessly to effect his defeat. The progressives, refusing to vote, marched out of the convention hall, leaving a disgruntled majority to carry through the program of the conservative leaders. A new Progressive party sprang into being overnight, and in August, amid scenes of the wildest enthusiasm, mingled with a devotion to a high cause absent hitherto from political conventions, nominated Theodore Roosevelt for President.

The ensuing campaign was fierce and rancorous. At the height of it Roosevelt was shot by a fanatic in Milwaukee as he was entering an automobile on his way to a mass-meeting he was about to address. He insisted on making his speech, went to the hospital, and after two weeks was again on his feet, campaigning. In the three-cornered election in November he polled over four million votes, but was defeated by Woodrow Wilson, the Democratic candidate. Once more his enemies rejoiced and said that he was "done for." He took his defeat with the same good grace and humor with which he had taken victory in the past, returned to his editorial work, wrote his Autobiography, and accepted the popular verdict that he was out of politics.

In the Autumn of 1913 he went to South America to address numerous learned bodies there and to make an exploring expedition into the jungles of Brazil, to which he had long looked forward. His journey from capital to capital in South America was a repetition of his triumphal progress through Europe. His plunge into the Brazilian wilderness, on the other hand, was infinitely more hazardous than the African trip. For months he and his expedition were completely out of touch with the outside world. He discovered a hitherto unknown river, vaguely indicated on existing maps as the River of Doubt, and at imminent risk of disaster explored the nine hundred miles of its course. The trip was indescribably arduous and full of peril; his life was constantly in danger in the treacherous rapids and along the fever-infested banks; savage Indians

ENTRANCE TO THE ROOSEVELT BIRD SANCTUARY AT OYSTER BAY, NEW YORK

The fountain was designed by Bessie Potter Vonnoh

This sanctuary is owned and maintained by the National Association of Audubon Societies as a memorial to Theodo.e Roosevelt

shot their poisonous arrows unseen out of the dark tangle. One after another his canoes were crushed in the rapids; one after another his men sickened. Finally he himself was laid low with fever, and for forty-eight hours was deadly ill. He pleaded with his son Kermit, who was with him, and with the Brazilian officers who had been assigned to his expedition by the government, to leave him behind and push on, in order that the whole expedition might not suffer the catastrophe which was always imminent of death by starvation. His companions refused to leave him. By a great effort of will he raised himself from his sick-bed and plunged on with them from rapids to rapids, until at last, when disaster seemed inevitable, a post on the river bank with the carved initials of some rubber trader indicated that they were on the outskirts of civilization once more. For weeks thereafter Roosevelt lay tossing with fever on the bottom of the canoe as they drifted down the placid reaches of the river. The Brazilian Government, in honor of his exploit, christened the river he had found the Rio Teodoro.

VI

He returned to his own country in May, 1914. Three months later the World War broke out. Roosevelt saw at once that America could not remain untouched by it. He pleaded for preparedness; he pleaded for an international tribunal backed by force to execute its decrees. His pleas were met with a tumult of abuse. He did not let it swerve him from his course. When the "Lusitania" was sunk, he pleaded for instant action—not a declaration of war, but a trade embargo against Germany and open ports for the ships of the Allies. At the outbreak of the brief and inglorious war with Mexico he offered to raise a division of troops. His offer was refused. Meanwhile his demand for national preparedness began to stir the country to a sense of the gravity of its position. Domestic issues faded into the background; the questions which had split the Republican party in 1912 were superseded by other questions at the moment more vital which served to reunite the opposing groups. In the national convention of the Progressive party he was nominated for President; in the Republican party the feeling was widespread that he should be the Republican candidate also. Justice Hughes

was named. Roosevelt forthwith refused the Progressive nomination and gave his support to the Republican candidate.

War with Germany came, as he had prophesied it must inevitably come if the United States were to keep a shred of self-respect. He offered again to raise a division of troops. Men from all over the country volunteered their services until 250,000 men had recorded their desire to go under his leadership to France. Congress passed a bill authorizing the creation of two divisions of volunteers. The President refused his consent. Roosevelt, forbidden to fight in the field, grimly and in bitter disappointment, accepted the decision and flung himself whole-heartedly into the work that lay at hand. During the months that followed no good cause called to him in vain. Here and there over the country he spoke for the Liberty Loan Campaigns, for the Red Cross and other relief agencies; and in the pages of the *Kansas City Star* and the *Metropolitan Magazine* fought week after week for speed in military preparation, for an honest facing of facts, for whole-hearted and unreserved participation in the war by the side of the Allies.

The fever he had contracted in Brazil returned now and again. For weeks he traveled and made public addresses in spite of it. In February, 1918, however, he became dangerously ill; was operated upon; recovered; returned to his full activity, and was again laid low. His illness scarcely abated his ceaseless activity, and in nowise weakened the terrifying force of his fighting spirit. In the Autumn he was again forced to take to the hospital. He returned to Sagamore Hill in time to spend Christmas with his family. The inflammatory rheumatism which had caused him much pain began to give way. He seemed on the road to recovery. He made plans for a hunt after devil-fish in the Spring.

From his sick-bed he fought his battle for realism and candor, and directed the policy of the Republican party, of which he was once more the recognized and undisputed leader. At midnight on January 5th he wrote a memorandum for the Chairman of the Republican National Committee. Four hours later, quietly in his sleep, with no other word, the man of many battles and much tumult slipped out of the company of living men.

He was buried on a hillside in Oyster Bay; but with new potency his spirit cried to the hearts of his countrymen.

A TRIBUTE TO THEODORE ROOSEVELT *

BY MAJOR-GENERAL LEONARD WOOD

AMERICA loved him and trusted him because he was, above everything else, an American. His broad vision, deep knowledge of the world's affairs, sound judgment, and courageous leadership were never more needed than in these days when it is necessary to stand together, shoulder to shoulder, for the Constitution and for the policies through which we have become great.

Born and reared under the best surroundings, well educated, widely read, with every opportunity to drift into the easy, careless life, his whole career from early youth was marked by a desire to do something worth while, to be of some service to the world. Frail in early youth, he made himself robust and strong. Handicapped by defective vision, he became an expert hunter, fearless explorer, a man who loved rough and dangerous places. He loved the simple, yet strenuous life. He worked hard and played hard. He was never inactive.

Married life was for him the ideal life. He was singularly devoted to home and family. His respect for women was profound. He appreciated their position and influence in the world as few men do. He was clean of speech, and his life was clean and moral. He abhorred, above all, suggestive speech, loose living, and immorality.

Travel, reading, study, and contact with men had given him a familiarity with men and affairs which is seldom found. He was a many-sided man; a human dynamo, driven by the forces of truth, humanity, and patriotism.

Like all men who do things, he made mistakes—mistakes which he was the first to recognize, once he saw them. His honesty, purpose, and purity of character were such that slander never touched him, and his real enemies were few. He had the old crusading spirit. He was always leading onward and upward, generally well in the advance. He feared nothing, unless it were duty undone. He was a profound student of history, and a devout Christian.

* Used by permission of General Wood.

He realized that progress comes generally through struggle, and seldom through ease and idleness.

He was the most inspiring, and consequently the most dominant, figure in our national life

Copyright by Walinger, Chicago

LEONARD WOOD

since Lincoln. The youth of the country turned to him; he was its ideal.

He was a many-sided man, but four-square to all the world—a wise statesman, naturalist, author, writer of history, scholar, soldier, builder of standards, a man with a clean soul and dauntless spirit, whose watchword was duty and whose life was one for the right, for country, and for God. Such was Theodore Roosevelt.

JOHN J. PERSHING

BY MARY LENA WILSON

Whenever I hear the name of the great Commander-in-Chief I think of the time I first saw him, marching at the head of the American troops in the parade in Paris on the fourteenth of July, 1919. "The most soldierly figure in the world" he has been called, and so he looked as he rode down the Avenue that day amidst the shouts and cheers of the hundreds of thousands of people who had gathered to witness the triumphal procession of the Allied Armies as they passed under the Arch of Triumph in celebration of their victory in the Great War.

Beside me, in the window from which I watched, stood a little, blond-haired boy of eleven. As the General passed directly by us and the applause of the crowds rose until it was a great roar of sound, a smile spread slowly over his face. That boy was Warren Pershing, the son of the Commander, and as I looked at him I wondered what his father had been like when he was that age.

When General Pershing was eleven years old he knew nothing of the grandeur and glory that his little son was seeing now. His home was a simple farmhouse near the village of Laclede, Missouri; and after school in the afternoons and on holidays he spent his time helping his father with the work. Times were rather hard with the Pershing family then, and all hands were needed.

But John Pershing had come of a family that knew hard work and privation. Over a century before his ancestors had come from Alsace to make their home in America. Like the true pioneers they were, they had pushed back from the seaboard and into the rough, uncultivated lands of the Middle West. Years of struggle and hardship had followed, but the Pershings had "fighting blood," and when John found that he had to work while many of his friends were playing, he didn't let that discourage him. He made up his mind that he was going to learn as much as he could, and some day he would make something of himself.

An education he was determined upon. There were too many other demands on the family budget to send boys away to school, so John made his own way. For two years he taught a negro school, and for two more a district school to earn the money to go to the Kirksville Normal School.

His first plan was to be a lawyer. Just when he was hesitating as to how he should carry out his idea, someone told him of a competitive examination being offered to the boys from his district to enter West Point. It seemed to him to be the solution to his problem. While this was not a law school, he knew that the course at the Academy would give him a good general education, which he felt was needed if he were to be a successful lawyer.

A great deal hung in the balance in the days that John Pershing was taking those competitive examinations. By only a few days was he within the age-limit set for entrance to the Academy. And it was by one point that he won the contest and was made a candidate.

At West Point young Pershing immediately won the admiration of both officers and men. Though he was not brilliant in his academic work, he studied hard, and was head of his battalion every one of the four years. The winning of his captain's brevets at the end of his third year, and his unanimous election to the presidency of the class of '86, he once said, were two of the proudest events of his life.

IS SENT DOWN TO NEW MEXICO

After his graduation, he was sent down to New Mexico to take part in the subjugation of the Apache Indians who were raising havoc. The young lieutenant had many adventures in this wild country, and always proved himself absolutely reliable and capable. Whatever service was demanded of him, he performed it to the very best of his ability.

After five years in Indian warfare, Pershing was called to the University of Nebraska to act as Instructor of Military Tactics. Once more in the atmosphere of school and college life, his old hankering for the law came back to him. He believed that there would "not be another gun fired for one hundred years," and since he had fulfilled his obligation to his country by his service in the Southwest, he decided to study law. But he did this while he was carrying on his regular duties as instructor.

It was not until the completion of eight years of service that he won his first promotion to the rank of first lieutenant. Some men might have become discouraged at such seemingly slow progress, but Pershing believed that service well rendered was what counted more than rank or glory, and he kept to whatever duties he was assigned with all the devotion and patience of his nature.

It was in the Spanish War that Pershing first had a chance to distinguish himself. At San Juan Hill and Santiago he led his company of negro cavalrymen against the enemy, and for his exceptional courage and coolness under fire and for his extraordinary faithfulness he was made a captain.

In appreciation of his gallantry in the war, he was given charge of subduing a band of Moros (Mohammedans) who were creating disturbances in the Philippines. He managed not only to conquer these fierce fighters, but to win their confidence and trust.

One very interesting story is told of his laying siege to a volcano-crater where the Moros had taken up their stand.

"You can never get them out of there," one of his fellow-officers had said.

"Yes, I will, if I have to take ten years to do it," he replied with his grim smile. He got them out, too, and in much less than ten years, and they were a very respectful and subdued company when they surrendered.

It was at this time that Pershing's achievements began to attract notice. Recommendations of his work were sent to Congress in 1903 by President Roosevelt. It so happened that on the day these recommendations were read, a very beautiful young visitor was attending. As she listened to the accounts of the bravery and ingenuity of this gallant captain, she turned to her father, Senator Warren, and said:

"I should like to meet that Captain."

THE MARRIAGE OF THE GENERAL

"Maybe you will," he answered, laughingly. Little did she think that before long not only would she meet him, but that, after a brief and romantic courtship, she would become his wife. In 1905 Captain Pershing and Frances Warren were married.

In 1906 President Roosevelt, who had long been a great admirer of the Captain's work, advanced him over eight hundred and sixty-two officers to the rank of Brigadier-General. Such an unusual promotion might have spoiled an ordinary man, but Pershing accepted it with the same spirit of dignity and lack of presumption that always characterized him.

Almost immediately after this the new General

was sent as military attaché to the Japanese Embassy. It looked as if he and his young wife were to enjoy a happy Winter together, but no sooner were they settled in Tokyo than orders came for him to report in Manchuria.

From Manchuria Pershing returned to the Philippines, where he was made Governor of the Islands. He served here until he was called to California just before the outbreak of trouble

JOHN J. PERSHING

with Mexico. In 1915 he was appointed head of the Mexican Expedition.

This was the opportunity to prove the results of his first hard years in ambush warfare with the Indian tribes. He was thoroughly familiar with the country, and he knew all the tricks of guerilla warfare.

But in the midst of his campaign terrible news came to the General. A telegram arrived at his headquarters saying that his wife and three little daughters had been burned to death in a fire which had broken out in the hotel where they were staying. Only the baby, Warren, was saved.

It was a tremendous test that the General had to meet that Summer, but he met it, as he had met whatever else he had had to face, with dignity and courage. In spite of his own personal suffering, he realized that he was a soldier whose duty it was to serve his country before all else. He went on with his campaign.

When, in April, 1917, the United States declared war against Germany, a great man was needed to take command of the American army. The English and French troops were worn out with their three years of hard fighting. On the fresh young American soldiers hung the balance of victory. John J. Pershing was the man appointed to lead them.

Through all the dark days that followed, when it seemed that the German forces must surely overwhelm the Allied armies before the American troops could be trained and brought to help, General Pershing never lost courage.

"We must win; we *will* win," he said. And anyone who has seen the firm set of his jaw and the determination in his blue eyes knows that when he makes a decision, he carries it through.

But it required patience and self-control to wait through the long months of 1917 while the German army pushed steadily on. Thousands of our boys went over to France every week, but still Foch, Commander-in-Chief of the Allied forces, did not call upon them.

At last, in the Spring of 1918, when the situation was getting desperate, General Pershing decided that the moment had come to act. He ordered his car and driver, and accompanied only by his aides, started to the Headquarters of the French army. For hours he rode through the mud and wet. On his arrival he went direct to the Generalissimo, and very simply offered him the services of the American Expeditionary Forces. Foch's acceptance marks the real entrance of America into active hostilities.

The thrilling story of Château Thierry, Belleau Wood, and the Argonne is familiar to every American boy and girl. But in giving due praise to the officers and men who fought in these battles we must always remember the Commander-in-Chief who was responsible for them, and whose wise decisions gave exactly the right sort of help to the sorely tried Allies at the moments when it was most needed.

"WE MUST WIN; WE WILL WIN"

Never once did his coolness and judgment fail him. His resolve, "We must win; we *will* win," was the spirit adopted by the whole army, and it was the spirit that enabled them to take their full share in the victories which brought about the armistice on November 11, 1918.

And now the General was riding in state under the great Triumphal Arch while the populace cheered and shouted. It was a long way he had traveled from the little farmhouse in Laclede to the head of the American Army in this greatest triumphal procession in the history of the world; a way that had been filled with hardships, struggles and sorrows. Yet always, in whatever situation he had had to meet, he had kept foremost the idea, "I must win; I *will* win."

He is a man of great faith—faith in ultimate success to the one who perseveres. And in that connection I am reminded of something he said to me when I had the pleasure of meeting and talking with him.

"You must never lose your ideals or become discouraged because success does not seem to come. Keep your faith in the big things and the best things, and don't let anyone laugh at you for being an idealist. Then *persevere! Persistence* will accomplish *anything*."

I can see him now as he spoke, and even the memory of his handsome, military figure riding so magnificently down the Paris boulevard fades away when I think of him as he was then—boyishly eager in his enthusiasm; intensely earnest, even in giving counsel to a young American girl who had volunteered for her country and who was far away from home. There is never any trace of self-consciousness of his position, nor sign of vanity or pretension. He is sincere and direct; and he listens to each one whom he meets with as much interest in the opinions he expresses as if each were a person of as much importance as himself. His simplicity is one of his greatest qualities.

And his smile! When the grimness of his expression, brought about by the years of struggle and strain, gives way, his geniality and good humor charm everyone. Yet with all his simplicity and friendliness, he has a dignity that commands respect; a dignity which comes not from pride in his achievements or in the honors that have been paid him, but a dignity of character.

Kings have given him gifts, governments have bestowed jeweled swords, universities have conferred degrees, and nations have acclaimed him as hero; but with it all he remains a simple American gentleman, the highest compliment that can be paid him. After the war was over, he remained in command of the army until in September, 1924, he reached the age of sixty-four, at which all American officers must give up their work. Then he retired followed by the regrets of the men whom he had led and by the good will and wishes of the whole nation.

WOODROW WILSON

BY HAPGOOD MOORE

THERE is one kind of story that is familiar in the accounts of America's great men. It is the story of the child born in a log cabin and who is (as we say) self-made. Another story, equally common in America but not so familiar, is the story of the child who is born into the home of poor but intelligent parents, with a good inheritance and an upbringing of refinement and culture.

This second story is the story of the boyhood of Woodrow Wilson. He was a minister's son. There is a well-known proverb about "minister's sons," which does not promise well for their success, but the last great Democratic President before Mr. Wilson was also a minister's son, and figures show that out of such godly homes, rich only in faith and hope and charity, come an unusual proportion of the nation's leaders.

December 28, 1856, was the day of Mr. Wilson's birth. His birthplace was a modest manse in Staunton, Virginia. After a year in a Southern college he entered Princeton, where he was a '79 man. There was a law-school training and a short period of practice. But "the law has become a trade, not a profession," was the young student's opinion, so he won his Ph.D. at Johns Hopkins, and entered upon his life-work as a student of government. It was a new vocation, but it led him straight and far.

We can hardly think of the courtly Chief Magistrate as professor in a girls' college, but he was one of the original faculty of Bryn Mawr, and then he went to Wesleyan, and back to his alma mater, where he remained, as teacher and president, for the next twenty years.

Three qualities have been remembered out of those early days in the life of this distinguished scholar. One was his humanity. He was a good ball-player and an enthusiastic "fan," a rare humorist, and an interesting teacher. "After twenty years of teaching," he said once, "I find that my students have forgotten my lectures and remembered my stories." His clear, animated way of presenting truth became of the greatest service when he was made the spokesman and interpreter of a mighty people. Once when he was spoken lightly of as "a schoolmaster in politics," he said in response: "Yes, a schoolmaster—one who tries to find out the whole truth and intends to tell it!"

FOR DEMOCRACY IN ALL THINGS

The second quality was his democracy. It showed in his administration of the university. It was he who introduced at Princeton the famous system of preceptors, trained advisers, half-way between professors and tutors, a bridge between the faculty and the students. It was he who fought the exclusive student clubs, seeking to retain the good-fellowship but endeavoring to open them to all. It was he who opposed building a palatial graduate school a quarter of a mile from the university, and who favored putting the money into men rather than buildings, and keeping these students close to the common life of the younger men. These activities in the end caused his resignation from the presidency of Princeton University, and paved the pathway to a bigger presidency.

The third quality was his self-reliance, the secret, so his friends believe, of his greatness; the cause, so say his enemies, of his failures. "He always played a lone hand."

After two years only as Governor of the State of New Jersey this man, so inexperienced in practical politics but already so eminent both in America and abroad as a foremost authority on political theory, heard the call of his leaderless party and became its successful candidate for the Presidency of the Republic.

Some day we shall have time to remember how clearly President Wilson outlined the program for Congress and how generously this program of what he termed "the new freedom" was written into the law of the land. But to-day our minds are more likely to dwell upon that series of events by which he became the first war President since Lincoln.

The story of the World War is written elsewhere in these pages. Just now it is enough to point out that the President made up his mind while the country was making up its mind. As Lowell said of Lincoln: "He kept step with the drum-beat of the nation." Most of us feel now that the declaration of war against Germany by the President was timed at the moment when it brought the nation together as one man, as it could not have come together had the declaration been issued earlier. During what was to us a short but tremendous conflict the people of the United States had frequent occasion to be grateful for the clear, the ringing, the eloquent messages in which the Schoolmaster-President was able to state for them and for the world the

Copyright by Harris & Ewing
WOODROW WILSON

ideals that led this peace-loving nation to arm itself and soon to turn the tide of the war of liberation to complete victory.

AT THE PEACE CONFERENCE

Of the issues that came before the Peace Conference it is too early now to speak. They are still clouded by the complexity of the entangled facts; they are still darkened by party feeling. It was the first time a President had ever left the American shores. It was the first time that one had endeavored to be both ambassador and spokesman for his people. Circumstances obliged him to speak for a nation while it was still bewildered. Into the circle of skilled and crafty diplomats Mr. Wilson entered, and sat at their council table practically alone. We may not, all

of us, be sure that what he sought was wholly desirable; we may not think he secured in the Peace Covenant what he sought, but nobody has ever denied that he knew what he was after. To him this was not an occasion for merely settling boundaries—it was the opportunity for establishing the foundations of a perpetual and universal peace. The country had many occasions to be proud of the intelligent, forceful and skillful presentation which Mr. Wilson made of his Fourteen Points, which the Allies and the enemy had accepted as the basis of a settlement. Woodrow Wilson was, by common consent, the foremost figure in the most notable gathering of leaders that ever assembled.

There are summits in a man's life so lofty that he can never attain them a second time. The time for coming down from the mountaintop had to arrive. To a country already disturbed by partisan strife the President returned, and vigorously and patiently, and even beyond the limit of his strength, explained the results of his great mission. For years to come these tremendous matters must continue to be debated, and await full settlement. The verdict of history upon the principles and work of our twenty-eighth President must tarry until some later day.

Baffled not only by illness, but by his own inability to share his mind with others, Mr. Wilson seemed, as time went on, a very lonely figure. Somebody said that he did not play to the grandstand. We ought to remember that this, however, is only one side of a many-sided man. His face was austere, and, as he himself confessed, homely. He used to enjoy quoting this limerick about himself:

"As a beauty I am not a star,
    There are others lovelier far.
        But my face, I don't mind it,
        For I am behind it—
    It is those who're in front get the jar."

The man who can laugh at himself like that, and who can rest himself after a trying day by reading detective stories, still has that human side which made him a popular teacher. He was taken ill in September, 1919, while on a trip during which he was speaking on behalf of the League of Nations. He had set his heart on having the nation enter the League, but he had already done too much. For months he lay helpless; but gradually recovered so far that he was able to drive with President Harding in the inaugural procession in 1920. His strength never returned, and he died February 3, 1924.

CHARLES THE GREAT, CALLED
CHARLEMAGNE

IN THIS story you shall first hear of the hatred Desiderius, King of Lombardy, nourished in his heart for Charlemagne, King of all the Franks, and the reason thereof; then it shall be told how Desiderius plotted against Charlemagne to compass his ruin by bringing division and strife into his realm; lastly shall be discovered to you something of the great power and might of that glorious Emperor, King Charlemagne, together with the story of his victory over Desiderius.

Had Desiderius known, as we know now, the great genius of King Charlemagne; had he known that the great Frank was to fight battle after battle, gain victory after victory, win country after country, until at last Italy, Saxony, Brittany, Bavaria, Spain, Greece, Hungary, besides other smaller powers, hailed him as conqueror, fighting his battles, obeying his laws—had Desiderius known all this, had he rightly understood the power that was in the man, would he have dared to meddle with Charlemagne, or, having dared, would he have dreamed of success, think you?

Nevertheless the dark Lombard had a subtle brain; his crafty schemes were not ill-laid, and his enmity might have caused trouble to any lesser man than Charlemagne. Charlemagne, you must know, had a brother whose name was Carloman. In the beginning Carloman reigned over one-half of Gaul, Charlemagne over the other. The kingdom of Gaul had been equally divided between them when their father, the brave King Pepin the Little, died. And in so sharing the realm they followed the custom of Gaul at that time.

Now these two brothers never agreed well together; although, mark you, this Carloman was to blame for more than half their quarrels. He was no match for his greater brother either in generosity or wit. However, peace was kept in some sort between them chiefly by the help of the wise Queen Bertrada, their mother. This often troubled and uneasy peace they kept until Carloman died, leaving a widow to weep for him with two, and maybe three, little children.

Thus the whole great kingdom of Gaul came to Charlemagne, and rightfully so. The people were not at all minded to choose a little child for their king even though he were a son of Carloman. In those troublous times they needed a man to rule them, a warrior to lead them, and with one consent they chose Charlemagne; and who shall say their choice was not just and good?

Carloman's widow, Giberga, thought differently, however. She coveted the throne for her little son. In the way of all mothers she longed to give him a great inheritance; so, knowing of the hatred Desiderius bore for Charlemagne, she fled to the Lombardy court with her children, pleading for shelter and safety. Let it be understood, however, that Giberga had no need to flee from her brother-in-law. Both she and her children were safe in his hands. He had no least thought of harming them

You will believe us when we tell you that Desiderius welcomed the distressed widow with much joy. He consoled her with many promises of aid. "You shall dwell in peace and safety here," he assured her, "until that time when I can help you win back your son's kingdom again. Charlemagne has already done injustice enough to make me ever eager to help those whom he has injured."

Now this Desiderius said because of the hate he bore Charlemagne, and indeed he had some cause for offense. Charlemagne had slighted him more than once in a way which the fiery Lombard was least likely to forgive; besides, there had been ill feeling between Lombardy and Gaul for some little time. Desiderius had waited long for a chance to pay back some of the ancient grudges he held against Charlemagne. Charlemagne, on the other hand, thought very little about them, and feared Desiderius not at all.

But now it seemed to the King of the Lombards as if his opportunity had come at last. Giberga's appeal for shelter and help had made him think of a new plan for revenge, and he set to work on it as quickly as might be.

If you think he instantly declared himself the champion of Carloman's son by making war upon Charlemagne straight away, you cannot have understood the wily nature of the man.

Desiderius aimed his first blow at Adrian, the Pope of Rome, Charlemagne's great friend. He sent messengers to Adrian, bidding him anoint Carloman's son king of his father's realm, at the same time threatening to make instant war upon the Church should the Pope refuse.

Mark you here the cunning of this! If Adrian, out of fear, should anoint the little Prince with holy oil, Desiderius hoped to win many brave knights to give up their allegiance to Charlemagne and fight for the son of Carloman. For to be anointed by holy oil and declared by the Pope of Rome to be the true heir of Carloman's kingdom would count for a great deal with these knights who had once served Carloman himself.

On the other hand, should Adrian refuse, Desiderius would have that excuse for making war upon Rome, and this he was longing to do. It would annoy Charlemagne and pay off some old grudges that he held against Adrian.

So then Desiderius felt that whether Adrian's answer was a "yea" or a "nay" he had the best of it. Adrian, as you must guess, refused point-blank. He who had already anointed and blessed the great Charlemagne, who had named him the friend and defender of the Church, was not going to bring trouble and division into Gaul, no matter what the Lombard threatened.

Upon this Desiderius marched forth with a great army, captured many of the cities belonging to the Church, and laid siege to Rome itself.

The Romans were terror-stricken. The fighting blood in them was still asleep, and they knew their beloved city was in no fit state to withstand assault. They rushed to Adrian begging him to surrender at once and do the Lombard's will.

"Talk no such coward's stuff to me," cried the old Pope stoutly. "Go, build up new gates and strong forts and prepare yourselves for battle. God will not forsake us when our cause is good. The Lombard's ways are evil; he cannot succeed."

"We cannot hold out for long," cried one.

"We can hold out just so long as we have faith in God and King Charlemagne," answered the undaunted Adrian. "God will never desert us, nor let us perish for his sake."

"King Charlemagne cannot know of our peril," cried another old councilor. "And if he knew, how could he help? He is in the far, far north conquering the fierce Saxons."

There was a silence. At last Pope Adrian cried, "We will send word to him of our plight, and meanwhile we will prepare to withstand the siege."

"He who takes the word will have to brave the dangers of the sea," said the old councilor, "and God knows what they are. Desiderius has guarded every pass through the mountains into Gaul."

At this all looked grave again, for in those days, when the ships were badly built and sailors scarce, a voyage by sea was no small undertaking.

One brave man, however, was found willing to thus hazard his life. He was a monk, and his name was Peter. He crossed to Marseilles, and after a long and adventurous journey through Gaul he came upon Charlemagne at last in the far north. The King and all his court were resting from the labors of war, for it was wintertime—the time of peace.

Peter, we may believe, never forgot his first sight of the hero-king seated at meat amidst the throng of wise and learned men whom he kept ever near him, for Charlemagne was not only a great warrior but a great scholar, a maker of laws, and a lover of learning. Peter knew him at once for the King, albeit he was clad more simply than many of his nobles. Surely it was an easy matter to distinguish him from the others. Was he not taller and stronger than them all? Was it not said that he was so hardy that he could hunt the wild boar single-handed and alone; so strong that he could fell a horse and its rider at one blow of his fist, or straighten four horseshoes joined together, or lift with his right hand a man in full war-dress?

If these things were known of him, how then should Peter have failed to know him? Besides, Charlemagne looked the great King that he was. His forehead was majestic, his nose like an eagle's beak. He had eyes like a lion, and were he angry no man dare look him in the face, so fiercely did those great eyes shine. Peter beheld them flash and burn fiercely for a second when the King looked up from the reading of Adrian's letter, and he took great comfort from their anger, knowing then that the Pope had not trusted his friend in vain.

CHARLEMAGNE
FROM AN OLD COPPER PRINT

But for a while it seemed as if King Charlemagne cared not overmuch about the matter; it seemed as if he were more anxious to conquer the Saxons than to make new war on Lombardy.

He sent, however, comfortable words of cheer and encouragement to Adrian, together with promises of speedy help. Also he despatched messengers to Desiderius, bidding him come to terms of peace. His first envoy was received with courtesy and respect by the Lombards, the second with scorn and contumely, and when the third arrived offering Desiderius gold if he would surrender the cities he had captured belonging to the Church, the dark King laughed aloud in triumph.

"The great Charlemagne is in no hurry to face me and my army," he boasted. "Doubtless he knows that every easy mountain path into Italy is guarded by my soldiers, while, as for the two that are open, he dared not bring his army through either of them. He would perish by the way, and he knows it. 'Twould be an impossible task."

"Nothing is impossible for Charlemagne," said Ogier the Dane, who knew Charlemagne, having served under him, then after offending him beyond pardon had fled to the court of Lombardy. "Nothing is impossible for Charlemagne," Ogier repeated warningly. But Desiderius laughed and returned a scornful message to the Franks.

Charlemagne by this time had moved southward and was holding a Champ-de-Mai. This was a gathering together of the people by the King to decide whether there should be peace or war.

Upon receiving the word of Desiderius, war was instantly declared; every Frank who could fight hurried to join the great army, bringing with him his weapons, horses, and what food he could carry. There was need for haste. Adrian, in spite of his brave resistance, could not hold out much longer. Desiderius, triumphing already, awaited another message from Charlemagne.

It came. It was brought by a frightened peasant from the hill country, riding in desperate haste. Desiderius heard with some dismay that Charlemagne had led a great army across the terrible, the impossible mountain pass, marching along ways where no man with an army behind him had marched since the time of Hannibal the Carthaginian.

Presently more tidings came. Charlemagne's uncle, the Duke Bernard, had led another great army over the other dangerous and unguarded pass. These two armies would, of course, join each other so soon as they were safely out of the hills. Desiderius in all haste marched his army northward, hoping to catch the enemy at a disadvantage while they were yet passing through the narrow defiles of the hills.

But he was too late, and the Lombard judged it more prudent to retire to Pavia, the capital of Lombardy.

In this he did wisely. Pavia was a strong city, well provisioned and almost invulnerable. Desiderius had little fear of its capture, yet for safety's sake he sent his son, and the widow Giberga with her children, to another of his strong cities. Then disdainful, sure of his power to withstand a long siege, Desiderius awaited his enemy.

Charlemagne did not tarry. When word came of his coming, Desiderius, together with Ogier the Dane, climbed a high tower, so better to catch the first glimpse of his approach. Presently in the distance, yet coming ever nearer, they saw a great army of soldiers who bore with them many formidable machines of war.

"Is Charlemagne among these soldiers?" asked Desiderius.

To which Ogier, who remembered the army of old, answered, "No, the King is not there."

Next came horde after horde of wild foreign soldiers, brought from every part of Charlemagne's vast domain.

"Surely Charlemagne walks triumphant among this great host," said Desiderius.

"No," answered Ogier, "he comes not yet."

On this Desiderius began to look dismayed. "How will he come, if not among his soldiers?" he asked.

"You will not mistake him when he does come," replied Ogier; "and may God have mercy upon us."

Even while he spoke there appeared a huge regiment of guards. "Verily, he must be among these!" cried Desiderius, and his voice trembled, but so slightly that you could not notice it.

"No," answered Ogier, "he comes not yet."

Lo, now they beheld an almost endless procession of bishops and priests and clerks of the Chapel Royal, and after them marched the great nobles and counts. At sight of these Desiderius grew pale.

"Behold the terrible King!" cried he.

"Not yet," answered Ogier. "When you see the grass in the meadows shake with fear, when you behold the rivers turn into iron and overflow and beat against the walls of the city with their iron waves, then you may believe that Charlemagne is here."

As he spoke, toward the region of the setting sun appeared a somber cloud which seemed verily to block out the light of the day with its terrible shadow. As it approached, a fearful sound was heard like the noise of thunder on a dark night. It was the clatter of armed men.

Then came Charlemagne riding upon his huge war-horse. He wore on his head an iron helmet; on his hands were iron gauntlets. His breast-plate and cuirass were of strong iron, and also his shield. He held an iron lance in his left hand, while always his right hand rested on his invincible sword. His horse had the strength and the color of iron.

All the soldiers who went before the monarch, all those who marched at his sides, all those who followed him, were clothed in iron armor. To Desiderius it was as if iron covered the plains and the roads; the very rays of the sun seemed tipped with it.

The folk, watching from the walls of the threatened city, beheld the sight with terror. "Alas! alas!" they cried, "we are lost!"

The sound of their crying rose to torment the ears of their King. "Behold Charlemagne," said Ogier at last, and he too looked pale. Desiderius bowed his head. He was dismayed; nevertheless he determined to hold out to the last.

The great army made its camp round about the city—making ready for a long stay. Charlemagne ordered them to build him a lovely chapel, so he might worship there undisturbed. He meant to show both his strength and his mercy. He would neither attack nor slaughter, nor would he leave Pavia until the city was his.

For many months he waited there, holding the siege. Nevertheless he sent parts of his army to rescue the cities Desiderius had taken. He even journeyed to Rome with all his train of bishops to pay a state visit to Adrian; and the Romans hailed him with great joy as their Emperor. Then the hero, after having given back to the Church all those cities which Desiderius had taken away from it, returned to his army still besieging Pavia.

And now was that city harder beset than ever. The citizens by this time were starving, and so strict a watch did Charlemagne keep that no living thing nor any morsel of food could pass the gates. Only the birds of the air were free to enter. Then the Pavians saw that they must perish with hunger if they resisted a day longer, so they surrendered. They gave up the keys of their city to Charlemagne; they gave up their King; then they waited, trusting in their conqueror's kindness of heart.

Charlemagne did not betray that trust. No citizen of Pavia was slaughtered or molested in any way. Desiderius was sent to a monastery, where he could do no more harm, and where he seems to have been not unhappy, while Charlemagne wore on his head the iron crown of the Kings of Lombardy.

As was his wont, he ruled his new subjects well and wisely, so that they loved him and were loyal to him as to one of their own race.

Now this is only one of a thousand tales that might be told in praise of the great Charlemagne who made of his conquests one vast empire, over which he ruled gloriously for many long years. He, too, and much more splendidly than Clovis, had made of Gaul a united and glorious kingdom. Yet after his death it became divided, shorn of half its possessions, and at last came to be known as the kingdom of the Franks—that is to say, France.

QUEEN ELIZABETH

BY DAWN POWELL GOUSHA

In the golden days of good Queen Bess! That is the way Englishmen of the sixteenth century referred to Queen Elizabeth's reign, and we of the twentieth century still look back lovingly on that jeweled chapter of English history. Buccaneering British sea-captains were scouring the globe for new lands and treasures, while at home young poets and playwrights were winning immortality with sonnets and dramas, and science was making rapid strides. Weaving all these various threads of progress into one pattern, is the vigorous personality of "Queen Bess," undoubtedly the greatest queen in English history.

Elizabeth was twenty-five when she ascended the throne, tall, pale, with aristocratic features and bearing. Her hands and eyes, of which she was very vain, were exceptionally handsome, and these, with the charm of manner which she inherited from her mother, Anne Boleyn, constituted her claim to beauty. She had been persecuted a great deal, before her accession to the throne, by her sister Mary I, whose death in 1558 had made Elizabeth queen, and even after her coronation she was constantly in danger of her life, for there were many who refused to recognize her right to the crown, believing that Mary Stuart, the Catholic Queen of the Scots was the true ruler of England. However, Elizabeth did not permit herself to become uneasy over the unsteadiness of her throne, but ruled with as high a hand as if there never were any question of rights, legitimacy, and such-like to trouble royal heads.

The people were soon assured that whether she was the rightful head of the kingdom or not, she certainly seemed to know what the public wanted and what it needed most, and she took steps at once to bring these things about. Lighter taxes and a no-war policy were two of the ideas to which Elizabeth held, and they represented pretty well what the public favored. The people, too, were sick of the whims of fickle rulers, Elizabeth's father, Henry VIII, being one of the best examples of this type. Elizabeth was fickle as to her personal favorites, but her policy toward the kingdom and her subjects was uniformly just. She never hesitated to lie to foreign ambassadors, whenever she felt there was occasion for it, but many historians believe this great fault in her character was partly made up for by her zeal for what she believed was England's good.

WAS STRONGLY PATRIOTIC

"Mere English" she boasted of being, and nothing could appeal more strongly to the vanity of the people. Her strong patriotic feeling induced her subjects to go to greater lengths than ever before to insure England's greatness on land and sea. English trade was being developed everywhere. In India, Ralph Fitch was paving the road for future British riches from that country, while in the tropical regions and West Indies Sir John Hawkins was finding untold wealth in African ivory, gold-dust and slave-trade. Martin Frobisher and John Davis were two other sea-adventurers, encouraged by Elizabeth's interest and the curiosity of the times regarding foreign parts, who explored the regions of the Northern Ocean in search of a passage to India. Chancellor had been braving the icebergs and glaciers of the frozen North before them, and had discovered the port of Archangel, Russia, and thereby opened up the way for trade with the Russian empire. Greatest and boldest of all sixteenth century navigators was Sir Francis Drake, whose dauntless vessels dogged the Spanish Main and the unprotected coast of South America, sparing none of the galleons which bore cargoes of precious metals and jewels to the King of Spain.

Philip II of Spain was naturally very angry at the manner in which the English seamen robbed him of his riches, and hated the daring Drake and his fellow-men who burned and ravaged his ships. Besides, Philip's vanity was much upset at the manner in which Queen Elizabeth had treated his attentions to her. When Mary had been executed Philip had written to the new Queen saying that although it would be a great sacrifice for him, he was willing to marry her, if she would uphold the Catholic religion. Philip had a very fair opinion of himself, and naturally expected the English queen to agree with him. But Elizabeth was a staunch Protestant, and being a clever woman would probably not have been interested in her too-confident suitor anyway. So she rejected him, and the hurt to his pride rankled in Philip's breast for some time afterward, while Elizabeth on her part heartily disliked the Spanish King. When he remonstrated about Drake's sea robberies, Elizabeth answered by making the fearless explorer a knight, and wearing in her hair the jewels which he had stolen. Philip heard of all this and planned the "Armada," which was to be the means of his revenge on that haughty and capricious person, Elizabeth of England.

Meantime the English court had never been so gay, so witty, so full of talented young men and beautiful women. Lord Leicester was one of the leading figures in the court because of his handsome face and because of the Queen's life-long partiality for him. She took no pains to conceal her fondness, fondling him publicly and calling him her "sweet Robin." Other cavaliers won her favor for the moment, or to a certain degree, but none could ever take Leicester's place in her esteem, although he was guilty of many crimes in his romantic career. Sir Walter Raleigh, who won her favor by flinging his costly new cloak across the mudpuddle which her Majesty was obliged to cross, was always popular in her court, and showed his loyalty toward her by his efforts to colonize America and thus spread the glory of Elizabeth and England to the New World.

One of the most gallant figures of the age was that of Sir Philip Sydney, whose character combined all that was best and most typical of the times. Spenser was planting the seed for a new age of poetry by his picture-poetry, the "Faerie Queene," Bacon was carrying on scientific and philosophical experiments, and looming above them all was the young playwright, William Shakespeare, whose comedies were making the

Queen laugh, and over whose tragedies all London wept.

NO THEATRICAL PROFITEERING THEN

"Blackfriars," now the site of the London *Times* office and Playhouse Yard, was one of the theaters where Shakespeare's plays were presented before the Queen and the play-loving public for "one penny at the gate, one at the entry to the scaffold, and a third for a quiet sitting." The Theater, opened to the public in the fall of 1576, and The Curtain, which gives the name to the present Curtain Road, were two other popular playhouses. Elizabeth loved to hear the witty dialogue and melodramatic acting which characterized the stage successes of that day, and encouraged all movements toward the erection of more theaters, and the creation of more plays.

In spite of her anxiety to have England develop her art, letters, and trade in peace, Elizabeth's contemporaries were constantly making advances which could be made causes for war if the Maiden Queen wanted to look at it in that way. Over in France, Mary, the beautiful Queen of Scots, and wife of the very young King of France, was adopting the English royal coat-of-arms, and proclaiming herself Queen of England as well as of the Scots and France. Mary was a devout Catholic, and because of her faith was able to get a large number of the Catholics in England to support her claim to their throne. The Pope, naturally, declared that Elizabeth was not the lawful child of Henry VIII, and therefore was not the lawful Queen of England. Mary was not the least backward in pressing her claims.

A very beautiful woman, Mary did not possess Elizabeth's ability to handle affairs of state, even though she was Elizabeth's superior in managing affairs of the heart. She left France reluctantly to return to Scotland and her queenly duties there. France was more suited to her pleasure-loving nature, and so her troubles began as soon as she set foot in the stern land of the Scots. The Dauphin's death had left her free, and now she married a worthless scamp, Lord Darnley, much to Queen Elizabeth's just disgust. For Darnley turned out to be a rogue, stabbing Mary's Italian secretary, David Rizzio, one evening when he was at dinner with the Scottish Queen. Soon afterward Darnley himself was murdered, and it was believed that Mary and her favorite nobleman, Lord Bothwell, were implicated in the tragedy.

Elizabeth was disgusted at the career of her rival to her throne, although her womanly sympathy was touched by Mary's continual trail of misfortunes. The latter was imprisoned for a year in Lochleven Castle, where she later escaped with her infant son James, and then flung herself on Elizabeth's protection by escaping to England. But Mary was too dangerous a person for Elizabeth to befriend with any feeling of assurance that her kindness would be well-spent. If Elizabeth should die, Mary would become Queen of England, and considering Mary's implication in Lord Darnley's death, she probably would not oppose a plot to kill someone else, whose death would be to her advantage. However, Elizabeth promised to help her if Mary could prove her innocence of the crime she was accused of. Mary refused to be tried by English judges, and so she was practically Elizabeth's prisoner for the next twenty years, moving about from one palace to another, and living in luxury, yet always under watch. On several occasions Walsingham, Elizabeth's famous Secretary of State, caught the ex-Scottish Queen in plots against Elizabeth, and of course these only served to lengthen her imprisonment.

INVOLVED IN FATAL PLOT

The plot of a young man called Babington, to which Mary had consented, was her ruination, for on its discovery she was recommended for execution by Parliament, and Elizabeth, after many days of anxious deliberation, was obliged to give way and sign the death-warrant. As long as she was in England, indeed as long as she lived, the beautiful Mary Stuart was a menace to Elizabeth's welfare and the Protestant supremacy in that land, so that no matter how one's sympathies may be aroused by the story of her tragedy, one is bound to see that her death was perhaps the only solution to the problem.

Mary's execution gave Philip II the much-longed for chance to launch his "Invincible Armada," a fleet of three hundred ships which he had been getting ready for some time with a view of conquering England. It was a great fleet, but Elizabeth's forty thousand seamen under such captains as Frobisher, Hawkins, and Drake—Lord Howard of Effingham was the commanding officer—were able with half as many vessels, to overwhelm them, and July, 1588, saw the defeat of the "Invincible Armada." The huge galleons were either burned or put to flight by the intrepid Englishmen, or dashed to pieces by the storms among the Orkneys, and Elizabeth's crown was firmer on her head than ever.

The last years of Elizabeth's eventful life were spent more peacefully. The Queen was a scholar, being versed in Greek, Latin, Italian and French, she wrote verses of some merit, and she spent much time with her books. She danced and rode, and took part in sports of many kinds, up to the very end of her reign, for it was her ability in these things as much as in anything else that made her popular with her people. The public loves to have its idols "good sports," and Elizabeth was one of the best.

She planned wisely for the poor of the country, and probably did more than any one ruler in making England's sun rise among the planets of nations. She died, the last of the Tudors, on March 24, 1603, and thus ended one of the most gloriously romantic chapters in English history— the day of Elizabeth.

SIR WALTER RALEIGH

BY MARY LENA WILSON

It is often by very trivial incidents that people rise to fame and fortune, and such was the case with Sir Walter Raleigh, one of England's greatest soldiers and explorers, and the first of her long line of "Empire builders."

He was just an unknown, handsome, young adventurer when he stood one day in the London street watching the progress of the great Queen Bess as she walked with her courtiers down the parkway. There had been an April shower earlier in the day, and just as Her Majesty came near the spot where Raleigh was standing she stopped: before her was a puddle of water which she could not cross without wetting her dainty slippers.

Quick as a flash, young Raleigh sprang forward. Tearing his handsome velvet cloak from his shoulders, he flung it in the path of the Queen, and thereby won the royal favor and a name for gallantry that has lasted more than three hundred years.

Within a year after this incident Walter Raleigh, adventurer, had become *Sir* Walter Raleigh, knight of the court of Elizabeth, the owner of vast estates and great riches, the idol of London, and the favorite of the Queen. Of course, Raleigh had not accomplished all this by his single act of throwing down his coat. He had shown himself as charming as he was gallant, and as brilliant as he was charming.

But though he had proven his qualities as a courtier, Raleigh had higher aims than being the darling of the court, the favorite of the tyrannical and capricious Queen. He had come of a sea-faring family, and down in his childhood's home in Devon he had dreamed great dreams of what he would do when he was old enough to go to sea. Those were the days when explorers and adventurers were doing big things for England and young Walter was eager to have a share in spreading the power and glory of his beloved country.

His first adventure after graduating from Oxford University was as a soldier of fortune in Europe, where he went to help the Protestants of the Netherlands in their struggle against the cruel King of Spain. It was on his return from the wars that he had his encounter with the Queen and was raised to royal favor.

Now he felt was his opportunity to carry out his early dreams. His half-brother, Sir Humphrey Gilbert, one of England's great sea-captains, was going on a voyage to Newfoundland, and he immediately begged his sovereign's permission to accompany him. To his great surprise and chagrin, Her Royal and very selfish Highness refused him his request. She did not wish this gay young courtier to risk the dangers of the unknown ocean.

It is well for England and for Raleigh that the Queen declined this favor. For on his return voyage, the brave Sir Humphrey was caught in a storm. With other boats at hand to rescue him, the doughty old sea captain stuck to his ship and went down to his death off the rock-bound coast of Newfoundland—still one more gallant fighter to give his life in the name of Old England.

HE SAILS FOR AMERICA

Raleigh's chance for conquest beyond the seas came two years later, in 1589, when the Queen fitted out an expedition to sail to America. With high hopes, Sir Walter set out, and at first his adventures met with success. He discovered a beautiful new land on the southeast coast of

North America which he called Virginia, in honor of his virgin Queen.

Raleigh's dream, as it has been the dream of all the Empire builders who followed after him, was to establish English colonies over all the world. To that end he sent out a company of men and women to build up a daughter state on the western continent.

But the men he sent had not his vision and his foresight. They settled on the island of Roanoke, just off the mainland, and almost the first thing they did was to antagonize the Indians. For petty acts of hostility on their part he burned all their crops. As a result, the whole settlement was on the verge of starvation when they were rescued in the Spring by an English sailing vessel.

Unwilling to give up with one attempt, Sir Walter sent out a second colony. For a whole year the little company struggled along, but they were men who loved adventure rather than hard work, and in the end they, too, gave up and came home.

It looked like a dismal failure, this attempt to plant the flag of England beyond the seas; but it was not. Raleigh's attempt paved the way for others which were successful, until to-day the British Empire is the largest and most powerful in the world.

Raleigh accomplished another thing, too. He discovered potatoes and tobacco, and brought them back to England where they were unknown. The story of Sir Walter's servant who came upon his master smoking a pipe is a very famous one. The poor fellow ran screaming from the room, calling out in horror, "The master is on fire! Smoke is coming from his mouth!"

Soon after the failure of Raleigh's second venture in America he lost the Queen's favor. And the reason was a lady—no lady of royal lineage, but one far younger and fairer than Elizabeth, whose lady-in-waiting she was. Sir Walter had no sooner seen this beautiful girl than he fell madly in love. So much so that he risked the Queen's displeasure and the end of his ambitions for her sake.

When Elizabeth heard that Sir Walter had asked one of her ladies-in-waiting to marry him she was enraged. She banished him from the court and sentenced him to the Tower. But at the end of six months her anger softened, and she released him from his imprisonment, gave him her royal permission to marry, but still forbade him the court.

This was where Sir Walter showed that charming and gracious though he was, his chief interests were in braver and more manly things than court life. He planned for a trip to the wonderful city of El Dorado, of which marvelous stories were being told. It was situated, so the reports said, in the land of Manoa, in South America, and it was a place of such wealth and splendor as had never been seen. Gold lay about in heaps, and beautiful jewels waited only to be mined.

Raleigh's plan was to find this wonderful city and claim it for the Queen and for England. Accordingly he set sail in 1595.

Once more he was doomed to failure. He landed safely, after a delayed voyage, at the mouth of the Orinoco, and sailed miles up the river, past lovely fertile valleys, and rich mountain country, but always the fairy city of El Dorado was just beyond his reach.

But his faith never wavered and he would have kept on had not the spring currents turned against him. His little boats could make no headway against the raging torrents, and he was pushed down stream despite all his efforts. He sailed for home, his belief in the wonderful city of gold and precious stones still unshaken.

Soon after his return Sir Walter had a chance to prove his devotion to his Queen and to win her entire forgiveness. The English fleet met the Spanish in a great naval battle at Cadiz, and the bravery and daring of Raleigh in command of the ship "Warsprite" brought him once more into royal favor. He was received in court again, and for the next few years was the favorite of the realm.

IS SENTENCED TO DEATH

But his prosperity was short lived. Elizabeth died in 1603 and her successor, James I, made trouble for poor Raleigh. There had been a great deal of opposition to his succession, and when one of the men who had plotted against him was detected, he freed himself by laying the blame on Sir Walter. Raleigh declared his innocence, but it was no use. He was convicted and sentenced to death for high treason. Only the pleadings of the Queen and young Prince saved his life and changed his sentence from death to imprisonment in the Tower.

Once more in the gloomy Tower it might be supposed that poor Sir Walter would have been completely discouraged. After all he had done, the hardships he had undergone and the dangers he had faced for the sake of his country, it seemed very unjust that his only reward should be imprisonment. But Sir Walter was a man of big thoughts. Instead of moodily thinking upon the injustices that had been heaped upon him he decided that he would still be of use to the country he loved so well.

Every day Sir Walter labored for hours on some experiments by which he hoped to benefit mankind. He finally succeeded in inventing a process for taking the salt out of water. He also wrote a "History of the World," which is a most interesting document, and must have been especially so to the people of his day, who had so little information on the subject.

All the while he kept thinking about the wonderful city of El Dorado, and scheming how he might make another attempt to discover it for England. At last, in 1617, he persuaded the King to let him make the attempt. Gathering together all the money that he had, and all the little that his devoted wife had, he made ready for his journey.

At this time, King James was trying to secure the friendship of Spain, whose colonies dotted the new continent, so he made Raleigh promise, under no circumstances, to get into any quarrel with Spanish colonists, or to encroach on their settlements. With everything he had at stake, with his very life as pledge that he would keep his promises to the King, Sir Walter set sail, accompanied by his young son.

The fates were surely against this daring sailor. First storms blew him off his course; one of his ships was sunk; he was becalmed for six weeks; and finally, on arriving at the mouth of the Orinoco, he was stricken with fever and was unable to leave his ship.

With true courage, he commanded his lieutenant to lead his men up the river. While he was lying weak with fever and wracked with anxiety, his stupid lieutenant was signing the death warrant to all his dearest hopes and ambitions. On arriving at the point at which Sir Walter had told him to disembark, he found a Spanish settlement. Contrary to all instructions he attacked, and in the fight which followed several Spaniards were killed and Raleigh's own son was lost.

When the expedition returned with word of their failure Raleigh was heart-broken. But despite his own deep grief he would have persisted in his venture, had not all his men refused to stand by him. So he turned his ships homeward, well knowing that disgrace and death awaited him at the end of his voyage.

On his arrival in England he immediately gave himself up, as he had promised to do in case of failure or of harm to Spanish settlers. Since he was under a former death sentence and could not be tried, his execution was ordered.

Raleigh went to his end bravely and nobly—as befitted a man who had all his life faced danger and death without flinching. Dressed in his finest clothes, he ascended the scaffold and made a farewell speech to the people. There was no bitterness or resentment in this speech. He did not even seem to think of what was awaiting him. He thought rather of the ideals for which he had given his whole life, and begged that those ideals would not be given up.

Though he himself had apparently failed, though death had been the reward for his loyal service, Raleigh's life was by no means a failure. No man who keeps his faith unbroken and his devotion unswerving is ever a failure. His last words to the people gathered about the scaffold were, "Cherish my dreams." And even to-day, three hundred years after, thousands of young Englishmen are cherishing those same dreams of England's colonial greatness, and giving their lives to the service of the ideas for which Sir Walter Raleigh fought so valiantly.

THE CROMWELL HOUSE AT STUNTNEY

WHEN CROMWELL WAS A BOY

BY ERNEST C. PEIXOTTO

WITH ILLUSTRATIONS BY THE AUTHOR

THE older readers of this volume will remember from their histories, the great figure of Oliver Cromwell, who did so much toward giving England her most prized liberties, and eventually became Lord Protector of the Commonwealth, and perhaps the greatest personage of his time. I feel certain that these readers will be interested to hear something of Cromwell's boyhood, and the places where he lived when a lad.

About seventy miles due north of London, on what used to be called the Great North Road—the main thoroughfare of England's east coast from the metropolis to Edinburgh—lies the good old town of Huntingdon. For centuries it has been a prosperous county-seat, and in its day possessed a castle fortified by William the Conqueror, and boasted no less than seventeen churches and monasteries. These latter, however, disappeared when Henry VIII. dissolved the religious orders in England—all except one which the King bestowed upon one of his trusty subjects, one Richard Cromwell, of whom the King was very fond.

Richard's son, called from his love of display the Golden Knight, inherited this monastery and on its site built a lordly mansion, Hinchinbrook Manor, still standing, as here pictured, in

HINCHINBROOK MANOR, WHERE CROMWELL'S UNCLE RECEIVED KING JAMES

all the glory of its towers, battlements and oriel windows above the valley of the River Ouse.

This Golden Knight had a younger brother, Robert Cromwell, who lived down in the town of Huntingdon in "Cromwell House," a spacious place with extensive lands.

Robert married a worthy dame, who, as one of the Stuntney Stewarts, joined to his estates

record of the birth of this "greatest and most typical Englishman of all time"—a sense of awe, however, that changes to amusement when one deciphers above the entry, written by some visitor: "England's plague for years." And this sentence, in turn, has been crossed out by some later traveler who evidently was loyal to Cromwell.

Oliver's birthplace, "Cromwell House," is to-

THE WEST TOWER OF ELY CATHEDRAL

the fine old brick farmhouse that appears in the drawing at the head of this article.

They were blessed with a large family, and in 1599, on the 25th of April, the fifth of their nine children was born, a boy named Oliver after his uncle.

At the top of the parish register page of All Saints Church at Huntingdon, is the record of this event, and it is with a certain sense of awe that one fingers the yellowing paper covered with faded Gothic letters, and reads the simple

day supplanted by a more modern structure, standing rather removed from the little town at the end of a twisting lane. As we peep through the iron gate, we feel sure that the general aspect is not so different from what it was some centuries ago: an ample, square house, with windows opening to the ground, through which the children could step out on the smooth English lawn shaded by oaks and fir-trees.

Here little Oliver grew up with his eight brothers and sisters.

The second day following his fourth birthday was a great day for Huntingdon, and a greater day still for the Cromwell family. Up on the hill at Hinchinbrook Manor, where Oliver's uncle lived, all was in a turmoil; the best linen was brought out; the pewter and silver polished to its brightest luster; cooks and scullions fumed in the kitchen; lackeys and maids scurried through corridor and hall, for there was to be a guest that night, and such a guest! —no less a personage than James VI. of Scotland on his triumphal progress from Edinburgh to London to succeed Queen Elizabeth, and to found the ill-fated house of Stuart as James I. of England. And when the august presence arrived, what a clatter in the courts as the heavy coach-wheels rolled over the paving stones! What a stamping of hoofs and neighing of steeds! What low obeisances, and what a sumptuous dinner—a table groaning under loads of silver and smoking viands!

Oliver's father, brother of the host, was much occupied we may be sure, as was his mother, too. So can we not picture our four-year-old boy, on his sturdy little legs, wandering about with his brothers and sisters under the guidance of a nursery-maid, his gray eyes wide, his mouth agape at all the goings-on? Can we not picture him staring at the young princes — at little Henry, Prince of Wales, who was to die scarce nine years later, and leave his brother Charles heir to the throne of England? Between Oliver and this same Charles, there was but a year's difference in age, and one cannot help wondering, in thinking of these two children face to face, if any thoughts but child-thoughts crowded Oliver's little brain; any inkling that one day he would wrest the crown of England from this same weak prince, and him-

self sit in the highest seat, be Lord Protector of the Commonwealth, the greatest man not only in England, but in all Europe! Next day King James went on, to sit upon his throne in Whitehall; and Oliver grew up, not—as some writers

THE OLD GRAMMAR-SCHOOL AT HUNTINGDON

would have us believe—in a country village, shut off from the active life of the day, but in a thriving town, only twelve hours' journey from the metropolis, and on the great highway between London and Edinburgh.

In the courtyard of the "George" (then much as it remains to-day) he might have seen the stages each day bring in their loads of people, and his father, who had been in Parliament, receive the news of the hour.

Soon the boy was put in the grammar-school under the tutelage of one Dr. Beard; and the teachings of this worthy master, a great friend of Richard Cromwell's, must have left an indelible imprint upon the lad's character. He seems to have conquered a lasting affection in his pupil's heart, for all through Cromwell's career, the two men remained in close touch.

The old grammar-school stands to-day, quite as it looked in Cromwell's time.

Toward the end of the last century it was discovered that the front of the building was only

When Oliver was fourteen there was another royal progress through the town; but this time attended with no banquets, no festivities, only with a mournful pomp. James had ordered the body of his mother, Mary, Queen of Scots, to be brought from Peterborough Cathedral down to London to its final resting-place in Westminster Abbey, and on its way it rested over night in All Saints Church. Surely Oliver was gaping in the crowd.

He was now growing up, and at home absorbed ideas and formed his character from the talks he overheard. Three of his uncles had been in Parliament, his father also; Dr. Beard was

THE RIVER OUSE AT ST. IVES

a shell, hiding a much more ancient structure. Under the direction of an able architect, the building was then restored to its old-time form. The expense of the work was borne by a distinguished playwright in memory of his son, who had been killed in a railway accident near by.

So now the quaint schoolhouse turns its battered Norman façade, its queer old gable and bell-cote toward All Saints churchyard.

As we sat in the whitewashed schoolroom, and wandered in the dormitory with its prim, snowy beds; or as, at luncheon, we shared the headmaster's table and watched the boys relishing their curdled plum tart; or as we sipped our tea by the tennis-court in the long afternoon shadows—that boyish figure with the great gray eyes, with the nose a bit to one side, with the broad square head and the manly figure, constantly hovered around us: strong, fond of his outdoor sport, and wilful, as they say he was.

He fits, too, into the landscapes by the Ouse— with its fishing, swimming, boating and visiting the country fairs.

thoroughly abreast of the times and they all discussed every phase of daily events, of the "despotism" of the King and the persecution of the Puritans.

Just two days before his seventeenth birthday, the lad went to Cambridge, a few miles away, and was enrolled a member of Sidney Sussex College.

Cromwell's college career was short-lived, cut off after the first year by the death of his father. The lad hurried home to the funeral of his parent, who was buried beside the Golden Knight.

Oliver at eighteen was now the head of his branch of the house, with a widowed mother and six sisters more or less dependent upon him, so it behooved him to fit himself as quickly as possible for a career. He accordingly went to London to gain a general knowledge of the law. His cares do not seem to have weighed too heavily upon him, for two years later he undertook new responsibilities by marrying, in Cripplegate church, Miss Elizabeth Bourchier.

Bride and groom went back to Huntingdon to live, as is supposed, with his mother. Then for nearly ten years history gives us no picture of him but it is easy to imagine him well occupied with his duties; with farming his lands; with yeomanry drills in which he took a vital interest, as his uncle and grandfather had before him.

In 1628 Cromwell was elected to Parliament. In his very first speech, he quoted his old schoolmaster, Dr. Beard.

But now Cromwell's great public career began.

He sold his portion of his father's estate to remove to St. Ives, and later to Ely, where he lived but a few steps from the grand old cathedral. The year 1638 found him father of nine children, five boys and four girls, and a very few years later, this "Lord of the Fens" was raising his famous Ironsides, and the great civil war of England between the Roundheads on one side and the Cavaliers on the other had begun.

CROMWELL

BY DAWN POWELL GOUSHA

WHAT would Queen Elizabeth have exclaimed if she could have known who was to have followed most closely in her footsteps in carrying on the glory of England! She would probably have made many a merry jest about that gray-eyed, somberly clad Puritan, called Oliver Cromwell, who did almost as much as she for the political growth of England, even though he did not inspire the development of culture, as the versatile Queen had done. Cromwell, in his turn, would probably have looked upon Elizabeth in her giddier moments as far too light a woman to ably guide the affairs of a nation. As a matter of fact, it is amazing how many ideals for England these two quite contrary-dispositioned persons held in common. They simply took different roads to the same goal.

Most people look upon Cromwell as a severe, thin-lipped, fanatically religious sort of person, too narrow-minded to have any sympathy at all for the ordinary harmless pleasures of mankind. It is true that during his time many innocent sports and pastimes were forbidden, and the spontaneous growth of art was made difficult by the Puritan régime, but Cromwell himself was not half as unlikable and inhuman as he is usually painted. He was devoted to music, and through his influence many works of art were saved from the too zealous and ruthless hands of his fellow Puritans. Drinking to excess was of course against his principles, but he was too much of an Englishman to altogether taboo the use of light wines and ale as sinful. He loved a good horse, and from boyhood was fond of the hunt and hawking, taking a healthy delight in all those out-door sports that tend to make a man broader in his views of life.

No one could say that this man of such high ideals for the moral and religious development of his nation did not have an appreciation of

a good piece of wit, too, for Cromwell loved a clever retort and a healthy jest. His own "human" qualities are too often overshadowed by the stern, unrelenting manners of his contemporaries, and Cromwell had enough of these manners himself to let them dominate the side of his nature that would have made him loved instead of feared by the people.

The thrifty little village of Huntingdon, just twelve miles from London, was the birthplace of the future leader of the Commonwealth, and here he spent his boyhood as one of the nine children in a typical family of English country gentlefolk. "Cromwell House," where Oliver was born April 25, 1599, is to-day supplanted by a house of later date, but the place has still many of the features that Cromwell knew in his boyhood days. At eighteen he was sent to Sidney Sussex College, but his father's death cut short his career there, and the young man went to London to study law, in order that he might be better able to take care of the family of which he now found himself the head. Here he married Elizabeth Bourchier, and brought her back with him to Huntingdon, where for ten years he lived as quietly and tranquilly as if he were destined for the career of a country squire instead of Lord Protector of England, actual ruler of three kingdoms. Indeed, there were moments later in his life when he looked back on those peaceful days and wondered if it would not have been better for him to have gone on in that quiet way.

APPEAL OF THE PASTORAL LIFE

"I would have been glad to have lived under my woodside, to have kept a flock of sheep," he once said, worn out by the strife with one of his Parliaments, "rather than undertake such a government as this."

The struggle between the Cavaliers, the followers of the royal party, and the "Roundheads," the Puritan and Parliamentary party, however, drew Oliver into the whirlpool of national affairs, and in 1642 we find him at the head of his own troop—the immortal Ironsides—in the war against Charles I which Parliament was waging. It was his organization of this brave troop that gives him the right to be called one of the greatest generals in English history, and the invincibility of these intrepid, God-fearing men showed the England of that day that men who have strong convictions of faith behind them make better soldiers sometimes than the gallant, swashbuckling cavaliers who fight simply for the glory of the battle. Cromwell's Ironsides were known as a body of splendidly trained, obedient, highly moral men, that brought victory wherever they went, and these were the men who gave victory to the Parliamentary side.

The Scots were willing to join the Parliamentarians against the Royalists, providing the English would establish Presbyterianism in England; and in the Solemn League and Covenant this was agreed to. In 1644 the Scottish leader, David Leslie, with Cromwell and his Ironsides met the Royalist army under the command of Prince Rupert at Marston Moor and overwhelmed them. Shortly afterward the Parliamentary army divided into two opposing factions, with the Presbyterians on one hand and the Independents on the other. Both were opposed to Charles I, but the Presbyterians offered to restore him his crown if he would support their form of worship and give Parliament control of the army for twenty years. His delay in deciding the issue caused the Scots to give him up to the Parliament to do with as they chose, in return for money enough to pay their war expenses. This made the Scots open to the charge later of having sold their King.

Independents, of whom Cromwell was the leader, were anxious for religious freedom, but Parliament, consisting mainly of Presbyterians, wished no form of religion to be observed but theirs. Whereupon, in order to bring matters to a speedy head, Cromwell's party took possession of the King, and entering the House of Commons in a body, obliged them to yield. Later Charles escaped from the Independents to the Isle of Wight, where he was again imprisoned. Here he made a treaty with the Scots to establish Presbyterianism and put down the Independents, so the Scots turned Royalist once again.

Cromwell and his party were incensed, and in a three-day engagement at Preston vanquished the Scots. The Presbyterian members of Parliament, who were meantime trying to come to favorable though dishonorable terms with the King, were summarily taken care of by Colonel Pride, who arrested over a hundred members in what was known as "Pride's Purge."

"There is nothing to be feared but our own sin and sloth," was one of Cromwell's characteristic sayings, and he believed that it was both sin and sloth to permit "Charles Stuart, that man of blood," to stir up more chaos among the English people. He determined that he should be brought to justice, and by preventing the faction of Parliament opposed to the Kings' execution from being present when the resolution was introduced he caused the trial of Charles to be brought about. The Parliament which passed the bill is known as the "Rump" Parliament. The trial ended, as it was intended it should end, in the execution of the King, whose majestic bearing at the end won nearly all England to his cause, and made the party that brought about his death the object of much hatred. "I go from a corruptible to an incorruptible crown, where no disturbance can take place," said Charles to Bishop Juxton, as he stood beside the block. He laid his head on the block, saying, "Remember"—the word around which Dumas weaves one of the romantic incidents of the relations of his Three Musketeers with the unhappy King. When the executioner held up the King's head, saying, "This is the head of a traitor," the groan of anguish which arose from the multitude showed the remorse of the people for what had been done, and not joy in beholding a "traitor's head."

PUTS DOWN IRISH REBELLION

Shortly afterward Cromwell was made Lord Lieutenant and Commander-in-Chief of Ireland, and he at once crossed the Channel with an army to put down the rebellion there. In Drogheda and Wexford he used very severe measures to quell the uprising, with the result that Ireland lost one-third of her population during the strife, and was made a land of paupers—small cause indeed for the invading general to call himself a victor.

"What a crowd came out to your lordship's triumph," someone remarked to him on his return to London and being acclaimed conqueror.

"Yes, but how many more there would be if it were to see me hanged," said Cromwell, with a sad smile.

Prince Charles had meantime been proclaimed King of Scotland, and Cromwell followed his Irish expedition with one into Scotland, where,

September 3, 1650, he put the Scots to flight at Dunbar. The Worcester victory followed this, on the anniversary of the Dunbar triumph, and Prince Charles fled to France, where he lived until the end of the Commonwealth in 1660, the date which marked the restoration of the Stuarts.

In 1653 Parliament decided to pass a bill that would prevent a general election to that body and would cause vacancies to be filled simply as they occurred. Cromwell, knowing the selfishness that prompted this move, reproached the members, and at their remonstrance, called in his musketeers and expelled the group by force. His own famous Parliament, of 140 members, chosen for their godliness, was then called. This was known as "Barebones' Parliament," because of the leader's name. Children then were often named according to some Biblical thought, and Barebones was called "Praise God Barebones," and his brother was "If-Christ-had-not-died-for-you-you-had-been-damned Barebones," the latter name usually being shortened to "Damned" Barebones. This group was so tactless and regardless of public wishes in its action that it was soon dissolved, and soon afterward Cromwell was installed as Protector by a new Parliament.

The five years of Cromwell's Protectorate were remarkable for the development of English trade, science, and religious thought. Letters were encouraged, and Milton, the Puritan bard, made known his greatness. The fleet of 160 vessels was keeping up England's prestige on sea, which Elizabeth's fearless seamen had built up. Admiral Blake was the great naval commander, and he won victory after victory from the Dutch admirals, Van Tromp and De Ruyter. He also helped to protect the English merchants in Spanish colonies from the Inquisition, and brought home treasure-ships of Spain. Cromwell was winning international fame as a general and statesman, and because he encouraged religious freedom was respected by his people. The Society of Friends, known as "Quakers," because they quaked with religious emotions, under the leadership of George Fox, was growing up in spite of public persecutions, and Cromwell disapproved of the popular prejudiced actions against them.

In spite of the justness of his reign—for it was really a reign, no matter if England was called a republic now instead of a monarchy—there were many things that the people resented. Theaters were closed and the pursuit of the beautiful in art and culture was warped and discouraged by the stern attitude of the political leaders. Cromwell was conscious of the public resentment toward him, and the idealizing of the executed King, for whose unhappy end he was held responsible. The Cavaliers were coming back into favor, and a book by one Colonel Titus encouraging the killing of Cromwell was circulated freely. One Parliament had offered the Lord Protector the title of King, but realizing well what taking the honor would mean, Cromwell refused. His last Parliament wrangled with him over the mode of government, and finally, worn out by his worries and the fear of assassination, Cromwell died on the anniversary of his successes at Dunbar and Worcester.

A great ruler and a great force for England's good, Cromwell was too self-willed to apply the tact and diplomacy to his dealings that would have made them seem less tyrannical. He knew what was best for the nation in a broad sense, but he failed to keep his hand on the "public pulse," which would have guided him in his methods, if not in the actions themselves.

LORD NELSON, ADMIRAL OF THE SEAS

BY IRVINGTON LEE

On a voyage of discovery toward the North Pole, two English vessels, the "Racehorse" and the "Carcass," were battling with the ice.

It was the month of July, and the weather seemed mild for those regions; but the ice had closed in upon them, and the two Greenland pilots on board showed signs of alarm.

The situation grew worse, as the sea was now solidly frozen. Great masses of ice, squeezed together in the drift, were piled so high that they towered far above the hulls of the ships. A thick fog came up. When it cleared, the sailors looked everywhere for a sign of open water; but the passage through which the ships had sailed from the westward was closed.

So they set to work, trying to cut a passage. But the ice was twelve feet thick in places, and though they sawed all day, with might and main, they were unable to move the vessels more than a few hundred yards.

Meanwhile the current bore the ice far to the northeast, and with the ice the ships were also borne along. Unless the wind shifted, there seemed little chance to save the vessels from destruction.

It was hard and dangerous work, even for strong men. Yet with this expedition was a boy of fourteen, who had begged to be taken along, and who, through the influence of his uncle, was at last allowed to go. His duties were those of a coxswain, and he was fully equal to the task; already he had piloted the longboat of His Majesty's warship "Triumph," and had learned to steer it safely among the rocks and sands.

ATTACKED BY WALRUSES

This new experience, in frozen seas, was highly relished by young Horatio Nelson. Whatever the danger, he did not flinch; Captain Phipps felt that he could trust him as he would trust a grown man. But, after all, he was a boy, and liked a little fun. It was rather a monotonous life, when one grew accustomed to it. If he could have his way, he would leave the ship, and try his hand at hunting polar bears.

Then, pretty soon, he had a taste of real adventure. The ice broke up in places, so that it was possible, with much labor, to force a rowboat through the floating cakes. The Captain decided that a boat should be sent to explore a passage, and try to find a way out for the ships. Young Nelson was put in command of it, and under his skillful direction it made good progress.

Meanwhile, a second boat had been sent out. Nelson could see it, slowly making its way through a stretch of open water. Suddenly a shot was fired by someone on board; then the boat tossed and pitched until it seemed that any moment it would be capsized with all its crew.

A startling thing had happened. One of the officers had fired at and wounded a big walrus, not realizing that its mates might be at hand, and would come to the rescue. But this very thing occurred. The wounded walrus dived, and soon reappeared in company with others. They are savage animals when aroused. Swarming around the boat, they all joined in an attack which the sailors, without proper weapons, resisted as best they could.

Nelson, the boy commander, was quick to act. His boat swung round, and headed for the scene of the struggle. Urging on his men, their backs bent to the task, and their muscular arms sent the little craft shooting through the ice.

"Keep her steady!" called the boy. "We'll soon be with you!"

What help he could lend when he reached them he did not know. But he was going to do his best, whatever came of it. Soon he was alongside the imperiled boat, and only just in time. A walrus had wrested an oar from a sailor. Trying to recover it, he tilted the craft to one side, and shipped so much water that it seemed about to upset.

But the walruses, frightened by the arrival of these new enemies, dived deep into the sea, and disappeared.

ADVENTURE WITH A BEAR

The boy's quickness had really saved the day; but he was disappointed. The walruses had fled without a fight; there was not much excitement in that.

"If I could just get a shot at a bear!" he said to himself. "That would be something worth while."

A few nights later, an alarm was sounded. Young Nelson and another boy were missing. As it was foggy weather, and pitch dark, there was nothing to do but wait. Then, along toward morning, the fog lifted; and there, in the distance, were the two boys, attacking a huge bear. They had stolen away in the fog, under Nelson's leadership, and gone on a midnight hunt.

"Come back!" The boys saw the signal; orders were orders, and must not be disobeyed. Yet Nelson hesitated. He had fired at the bear, across a chasm in the ice, and his ammunition was exhausted. "Never mind!" he cried. "Just give me another chance at him, with the butt-end of my musket."

Then the Captain himself fired, and the bear fled. The youthful hunters were obliged to make their way back to the ship, where a reprimand awaited them.

"What have you to say for yourself?" asked the Captain, sternly. "You were absent without permission, and came near being killed. What would your father think of you?"

"If you please, sir," answered Nelson, "I was thinking of my father. I wished to kill the bear so that I might carry the skin to him."

A STOUT HEART IN A WEAK BODY

It was because of a stout heart, a high spirit, and a strong sense of duty, that Horatio Nelson rose to be one of England's greatest admirals, and the victor in some of the bloodiest battles with France and Spain. Born in 1758, the son

FIELD-MARSHAL LORD RAGLAN

FIELD-MARSHAL LORD ROBERTS

GEN. SIR HENRY HAVELOCK

ADM. LORD NELSON

THE DUKE OF WELLINGTON

GEN. LORD KITCHENER

GEN. C. G. GORDON

BRITISH MILITARY AND NAVAL OFFICERS

of a country parson with a large family, the boy was so frail and weak that no one ever dreamed he was fitted for the sea. But the father had reason to know the strength of his son's character. So when Horatio, at twelve years of age, expressed a wish to go in the navy, his uncle, Captain Suckling, was persuaded to give him a chance. The Captain, however, who commanded the warship "Raisonnable," was not without his doubts. "What," he wrote, "has poor Horatio done, who is so weak, that he, above all the rest, should be sent to rough it out at sea? But let him come, and the first time we go into action a cannon-ball may knock off his head, and provide for him at once."

Yet at twenty-one "poor Horatio" had risen to be a captain in the Royal Navy.

One does not blame the Captain for his hesitation. Perhaps he had never even heard of one little incident in Horatio's childhood which served to show how brave a heart beat in the frail little body. One day, when a mere child, he had strayed into the country, looking for birds' nests, and when he had not returned to the house for supper, his grandmother was much alarmed. Searching for him, he was discovered, all alone, sitting cheerfully by a stream too deep for him to cross."

"I wonder," said his grandmother, when he was safe at home again, "why you are not half dead with hunger and fear."

"*Fear,* did you say, grandmamma?" asked the little boy. "What is fear? I never heard of it."

LOSES AN EYE AND AN ARM

Through all his life, fear was still a stranger to Nelson. He suffered ill health, and for a time was forced to retire. He took part in many battles, and was always in the thick of danger. It was, indeed, this habit of defying fear that made him reckless in the face of death, and caused him to be stricken down in the hour of his greatest victory.

For defeating the Spanish fleet at the battle of St. Vincent, Nelson was made a rear admiral. It was in 1797, France, with the aid of Spain, wished to crush England; so Admiral Sir John Jervis, to prevent the two fleets from combining their forces, attacked the Spaniards. Jervis won the battle with the aid of Nelson, who, as commodore, dashed into the enemy's ships, in disobedience of orders, and captured the flagship of the Spanish admiral.

He had already lost an eye, and in a battle that took place the same year he lost his right arm. These afflictions, however, in no way daunted his spirit. In the battle of the Nile he defeated the French fleet, anchored in Aboukir Bay, crushing part of it between two fires before the other French ships had time to come up. This action cut off Napoleon's army from France, and prevented his setting up a French Empire in the East.

Because of this great victory, Nelson was created Baron Nelson of the Nile. It was a bloody fight that raged far into the night, and Nelson was among the wounded. But he declined the services of a surgeon, saying, "I can wait my turn with the brave fellows." Then, hearing that the French admiral's ship was in flames, he rushed to the deck, ignoring his wound, and ordered boats to be launched, to save the French sailors, struggling in the sea.

HIS THOUGHTFULNESS FOR OTHERS

Always he showed this thoughtfulness for others whose lives were in peril. On his way to join Jervis in the battle of St. Vincent, his ship, the "Minerve," was pursued by the Spanish fleet, and almost overtaken. Just as it appeared that he must fight against these overwhelming odds, or run his frigate ashore, the cry came, "Man overboard!"

With the enemy's foremost ship about to engage him, a boat was lowered from the "Minerve," and succeeded in picking up the drowning sailor. But it could not catch up with the frigate; and on came the Spaniard, now ready to open fire.

Hardy, Nelson's lieutenant, was in the rescuing boat. Would Nelson leave it to its fate, or risk the loss of his ship? He did not hesitate a moment.

"Back the mizzen topsail!" he commanded. "I'll not desert Hardy."

The astonished Spaniards saw his ship slow down. The Englishmen, equally astonished, saw that the Spaniard held his fire. Then the pursuing ship gave up the chase. Why, no one could tell; but Nelson had gained his point, and his frigate bore him safe from pursuit.

It might be said that Nelson's blind eye won for England the battle of Copenhagen. Sir Hyde Parker, in command of the English fleet, had ordered Nelson to attack, and this he was doing in his usual vigorous manner, despite the strength of the enemy's ships and shore batteries. Then Parker, believing his fleet in danger, flew the signal to withdraw. At this, Nelson put his telescope to his blind eye. "I see no signal," he said.

Keeping his own signal for close action flying, he managed his ships with such skill that ere long the victory was his.

BATTLE OF TRAFALGAR

In 1805 came the climax of his great career, in the battle of Trafalgar. In this engagement the French and Spanish fleets suffered a crushing defeat that made England the mistress of the seas. It was then that Nelson flew from his flagship, "Victory," the famous signal: "England expects every man to do his duty."

Nelson, with his usual recklessness, wore on the breast of his admiral's frock-coat his four stars. These made him a conspicuous mark for riflemen, but he would not cover them up. "In honor I gained them," said he, "and in honor I will die with them."

Then, with the fight all but won, he fell upon his face, mortally wounded by a musket ball.

"They have done for me at last, Hardy," he said. "My backbone is shot through."

A few hours later he was dead. "Thank God, I have done my duty," were his last words.

TWELVE NATIONAL HEROES

JUDAS MACCABÆUS, "THE HAMMER"

"In eternity he walketh crowned in pomp,
As having conquered in a contest of stainless
struggles."

IN THE days when the Syrians were masters of Palestine, that country whose inhabitants have always loved to call it the Holy Land, an old priest named Mattathias with his five sons, who had been living in a small country village, rose up against the conquerors who had attempted to make them sacrifice to their foreign gods. This family stood in front of one of the false altars and slew the first of their countrymen who approached to be a traitor to his native land and its religion. They gathered to themselves a handful of faithful men, and by-and-by became strong enough in numbers to recapture some of the neighboring villages.

This brave father soon died, but his third son, Judas, took his place. Because of his tremendous forcefulness he was nicknamed Makkabi, or Maccabæus, which means "the Hammer." At Mizpah, with 6,000 men he defeated 70,000; at Bethzur, with 10,000, he defeated 65,000. He recaptured Jerusalem, the capital, and there set up again the national worship. He cleared away the shrubs that had been growing in the temple courts, built a new altar, and restored the sacred furniture.

After Judas was slain in battle at Elasa, the Jewish Thermopylæ, two brothers in turn succeeded him, and under the second the complete independence of the nation was regained.

The name Maccabæus came after a time to denote any man who had the spirit of Judas, who united in himself, so it was said, "the faith of Abraham, the zeal of Elijah, the stature of Saul, and the courage of David." A poet of his age said of him:

"He angered many kings, and made Jacob glad
    with his acts,
And his memorial is blessed forever."

Of such as he another Jewish poet sang:

"Therefore shall they receive the kingdom of
    splendor
And the diadem of beauty."

HOW ARNOLD VON WINKELRIED DIED FOR HIS COUNTRY

No people love liberty more dearly than those who dwell among the mountains or by the sea. There are two small nations in Europe that were once under the yoke of a foreign oppressor, and each of which found heroic leaders to win their freedom. One is a nation of mountaineers, and the other a sea-going folk.

The first of them is Switzerland, which once was subject to the Austrian archduke, who was sometimes emperor as well. Switzerland is divided into districts called cantons; and an officer appointed by the archduke used to rule them, and to rule very harshly.

Switzerland won its freedom at the battle of Sempach, where a great hero of the Swiss people gave his life for his country. A great host of Austrians came against the Swiss. They were clad in stout armor and had long spears and swords; but the Swiss were not protected by heavy mail. When the Swiss rushed upon their foes, they could not break through, but were thrust down and cut to pieces.

Then Arnold von Winkelried bade the Swiss draw together in the shape of a wedge or triangle, and follow him; and he ran upon the Austrians, stretching out his arms and gathering the enemies' spears in them till all the points, as far as he could reach, were drawn together and pierced his own body, so that he fell and died. But in this way he made a space where there were no spear-points, and there the wedge of Swiss drove in, and so fought hand to hand with the Austrians and put them utterly to rout. After that the Austrians saw that it would be no use to try to force their rule upon the Swiss.

HOW WILLIAM WALLACE AND ROBERT BRUCE DELIVERED SCOTLAND

After King Edward of England had taken away the old stone from Scone Abbey, that had been the Coronation Stone of all the Scottish kings, and crowned himself King of Scotland, there were sad days in the Highlands.

One day when a boy named William Wallace was coming home at evening from fishing, some English soldiers tried to take away his fish, but he used his fishing-rod upon them with such good effect that he put them to flight. After this he fled to the hills and soon was made an outlaw.

In time he gathered about himself a band of patriots, and one day with a small company he found himself face to face with 50,000 of Edward's soldiers at Stirling. Standing on rising ground, he waited until part of the confident enemy had crossed the stone bridge to attack him, and, when the army was divided, he descended upon them, drove them in panic and swept the greater part into the rushing stream.

He had one supreme triumph, then he was defeated, and carried away to London, where he was tortured and killed.

"What terms will you make?" asked the English general on the morning of Stirling. "The freedom of Scotland," answered Wallace. Even yet his name, said the poet Wordsworth, "is to be found like a wildflower, all over his dear country." In a short time, he fulfilled many days, and left to his native land imperishable renown—and freedom.

Robert Bruce, a Scottish nobleman, had been with King Edward when a boy at the English court. Everything in the way of personal interest tied him to the English allegiance. But his grandfather had been defrauded of the Scottish crown. Was it the splendid heroism of Wallace that enkindled his own romantic soul?

Crowned by his people at Scone as King of Scotland, Bruce proceeded to win back his kingdom. The final triumph was won at Bannockburn, in sight of Stirling. Here Bruce with 30,000 met England's 100,000. Here King Robert is pictured, in the stirring stanzas of Robert Burns, as addressing his liegemen:

"Scots, wha hae wi' Wallace bled,
Scots, wham Bruce has often led;
Welcome to your gory bed,
Or to victorie.

"Wha for Scotland's king and law
Freedom's sword will strongly draw,
Freeman stand, or freeman fa',
Let him follow me!"

The tide of battle turned, so it is said, when a horde of camp-followers came rushing upon the field on horseback, waving their tent-poles and shouting, causing the English to think that a reinforcing army had arrived.

When King Robert's reign was over, and it was time for him to die, the story is told that his last request to his best friend, Sir James Douglas, was that he should carry his heart, in a casket of gold, to the Holy Land, where he had longed himself to make pilgrimage, and bury it by the Holy Sepulchre of our Lord. But Douglas on his way to Palestine anchored in Spain, and there finding that King Alonzo was sore beset by the Moors, he thought it a sacred task to help him drive away the Infidels. In an action near Theba he was separated from his company and surrounded by the enemy. Then, rising upon his horse, he took from his neck the casket which contained the heart of Bruce and cast it before him, exclaiming with a loud voice as he fell dying: "Now pass onward as thou were wont, and Douglas will follow thee!"

"We laid our chief in Douglas Kirk,
The heart in fair Melrose;
And woeful men were we that day—
God grant their souls repose."

HOW SCANDERBEG HELD THE TURKS AT BAY

Another race of mountaineers found a heroic leader who won them freedom for a time. The Turks, who were followers of the religion of Mohammed, began to make conquest of lands in Europe a little more than five hundred years ago.

On the western side of what afterward became

the Turkish Empire is a mountainous land called Albania. Here the conquering Turks made their way, and forced the lords of the land to submit to them; and they carried away the young son of one great lord, and brought him up in the faith of Mohammed.

The young man, who was called George Castriot, fought in the Turkish armies, and became skilled in war. Yet he had no wish to serve the Turks, though he waited his own time, and when he was nearly forty years old he, with a band of Albanian followers, suddenly left the Turkish army and seized a fortress called Croya. Having done this, he declared himself a Christian, and called upon the Albanians to rise and wage war upon the Turks.

The Albanians drove out the Turks and took him for their leader, and because he showed himself so great a soldier men called him Scanderbeg, which means the Lord Alexander. The Turks sent mighty armies against him, and were very great warriors, yet he overthrew them in battle many times, though they might have four or five times as many men as he. For twenty-five years he held the Turks at bay, so that they feared his name greatly; but after he died, the Albanians, lacking a leader, and getting no aid from other nations, were overcome by the Turks, and lost the freedom which Scanderbeg had won for them.

ANDREAS HOFER, THE INNKEEPER, WHO FOUGHT NAPOLEON

Among the dominions of Austria is a land called the Tyrol, which borders upon Switzerland, and Napoleon caused the Austrian emperor to give the Tyrol to the King of Bavaria, who was always ready to do his bidding. But when the Austrians went to war again with Napoleon, the Tyrolese rose up under Andreas Hofer, who was an innkeeper, and drove the French and the Bavarians out of the Tyrol, though they themselves were only peasants. For a short time Hofer was made their ruler, as a loyal subject of the Austrian emperor, though he would not obey the Bavarian king and the emperor of the French.

But the French armies defeated the Austrian armies, and the Tyrolese could not openly resist the power of Napoleon unaided. And then, though the brave Hofer hid among the mountains, a traitor was found who showed the French where he was. He, being taken prisoner, was tried like William Wallace and Joan of Arc, and was condemned and shot as a rebel. Yet the stand that Hofer made helped to give heart to the other nations of Europe to rise against the rule of Napoleon, and so in due time Napoleon was overthrown, and the Tyrol was restored to its old freedom, for which Hofer had fought and died.

HOW WILLIAM THE SILENT WAS PUT TO DEATH BY A SPANISH PLOT

The sea-going people which won its liberty was the little state of Holland, where there are no mountains at all. In the days when Queen Elizabeth ruled in England, Holland and Belgium were ruled by King Philip of Spain, who tried to take away their freedom and to force them to give up the Protestant religion. He sent a merciless governor, the Duke of Alva, to Holland, with great armies, and the Protestants suffered great persecution. The Prince of Orange, called William the Silent, one of the nobles of Holland, formed a league to drive out the Spaniards; and though the Roman Catholic part of Holland would not join him, he led the Protestants so that they utterly refused obedience to Philip.

Yet, if the Dutchmen had been a little less sturdy, and William a little less resolute, they must have been crushed. They got some help from Queen Elizabeth, and a little from the French; but they owed far more to the skill and persistence of William than to anything else. Therefore Philip encouraged men, some of whom were merely scoundrels, though others were honest men who thought it right to kill by any means the man who fought so stoutly against the power of the Church of Rome, to murder William, and William, too, died for his country's freedom. After this the courage of the Dutchmen did not fail, but they went on fighting, and at last the power of Spain was broken, for there came open war between Spain and England, and England won. So the Spaniards gave up trying to subdue the Dutch and Holland became free.

Motley said of him: "As long as he lived he was the guiding star of a whole nation, and when he died the little children cried in the streets."

GARIBALDI, WHO MADE ITALY A NATION

You know that Italy to-day is one of the great nations of Europe, and one of the men who helped most to make her so was Garibaldi. When he was born, Italy was made up of several states, some of which were subject to Austria, while the northern part was ruled by the King of Naples, who was not an Italian.

Now, there were many people in Italy who wished to be free from foreign rulers, and there were some who dreamed that all Italy might become a free and united nation.

So, while Garibaldi was still a very young man, though he was already a skillful sailor, being a fisherman's son, he joined in a revolt against the rule of the Austrians. This, however, was easily crushed, so that he had to flee to South America. There he took part in the wars that were going on because the land was very unsettled, and he became famous as a leader whose men were always ready to follow him to the death.

But after a time he returned to Italy and joined in a fresh revolt, gathering men who were ready to fight because Garibaldi filled them with his own great love of their cause. Yet they were not strong enough to overthrow the Austrian rule, and again he had to go away. He came to the United States. Yet again he returned, and once more the men of north Italy rose. This time they were victorious, and before long all Italy became one nation. And this was in great part because Garibaldi filled those about him with his own courage and enthusiasm, even when their cause seemed hopeless.

LOUIS KOSSUTH, WHO FOUGHT FOR THE FREEDOM OF HUNGARY

Louis Kossuth set himself to win freedom for Hungary from the rule of Austria, at the time when the Italians were seeking their own liberty. He was not a soldier, but a writer and orator, and a statesman; but the Hungarians made him their leader. They were defeated at the time, and Kossuth had to flee from the country. Later, the Hungarians agreed to accept the emperor of Austria as their king if they could have certain rights of governing themselves; and this they owed, in the first place, to Kossuth. But Kossuth himself was not content with this. He would not own allegiance to Austria, and he died some years later, not in Hungary, but in Italy.

HOW SCHAMYL FOUGHT FOR HIS NATIVE LAND

All countries cherish the name of some patriotic man who has fought for the liberty of his native land. Just as Wales has its Llewellyn, Scotland its Wallace and its Bruce, Italy its Garibaldi, so the Caucasus has its Schamyl, who, for more than a quarter of a century struggled to keep the wild mountain land of his birth free from Russia's iron grip. He was weakly as a

child, but his physical strength was developed by outdoor games and sports, so that he grew up sturdy.

Schamyl was absolutely fearless, and such a youth of his word, that, when he found remonstrance had no result in curing his father's drunken habits, his oath to kill his parent if he again transgressed brought the father to his senses, and to the end of his life he abstained altogether from alcohol, knowing that Schamyl would carry out his threat.

When Schamyl was twenty-six years old, in 1824, he began his long fight against the Russian generals who were sent to subdue the land. He was a born leader, courageous in attack, skilled as a strategist, and clever in retreat. Many stories are told of his hairbreadth escapes from the Russians. Once his little band was surrounded by their enemies. If they could not fight their way through the bayonets of the Russians they must either starve or be cut to pieces, for they knew not the word "surrender." Schamyl, who was ever the foremost and the boldest in attack, galloped alone through the enemy's lines, and reached in safety his mountain fastnesses. He was the only one to escape with his life, and his pious Mohammedan countrymen believed the angel Gabriel specially protected him.

During another fight Schamyl killed three Russians, but was himself pierced through by a bayonet. Yet he slew his assailant, and got away as by a miracle. He was then chosen chieftain and ruler of the eastern Caucasus by his compatriots.

A mountain fortress long held by Schamyl was at last captured by the pick of the Russian troops, and again he was the only man to escape. It is said that he let himself down the steep rock by a rope to the river below, boarded a raft, and thus got away. Many generals were sent against Schamyl, but he eluded them all, and time after time rallied his countrymen to his standard. One general died through shame at being conquered by such a small band of mountaineers.

Russia's attention was for a time diverted by the Crimean War; but that over, new efforts were made to overcome Schamyl and his brave countrymen. The end was inevitable, for Russia's resources were enormous compared with Schamyl's. The latter took refuge in a little fortress on a hill in Daghestan, and there, when all except forty-seven of his men were killed, seeing that even if he did escape, there were no longer any patriots to rally, he submitted.

Schamyl was not a wild brigand, but a wealthy man of culture and high character, who ruled with justice and ability, was merciful to the Russian prisoners, and fought for love of his country during many long weary years.

DANIEL O'CONNELL,
THE GOLDEN-TONGUED IRISHMAN

In the year 1800, when all Ireland was stirred to prevent the proposed reunion with England, a young lawyer in Dublin made his first public speech, which caused such a sensation that he soon became the leader of his party. The task of organizing his fellow-citizens against the evils that came from the Union was a slow one, and many years later on one occasion when ten members were necessary to have a quorum the young orator had to rush downstairs and force a couple of priests whom he met by accident to come up to the meeting.

In those days Roman Catholics were excluded from sitting in Parliament, but in 1828 there was an outburst of enthusiasm for O'Connell, and he was elected. He did not attempt to take his seat, but he proceeded to organize what became literally a vast peaceful army to support the cause. The movement was so tremendous and so just that the English people recognized the wisdom of yielding, and even the doughty Duke of Wellington, who was then prime minister, bowed before the storm. So O'Connell came to Westminster.

Now, O'Connell made his life-work the Repeal of the Union. His magnetic voice awakened the harpstrings of Irish feeling, and he addressed a succession of enormous meetings, at one of which, on historic Tara Hill, it was stated that a quarter of a million people were present. The movement became so mighty that it swept to the brink of civil war, and then only O'Connell's magnificent self-restraint prevented the shedding of blood. O'Connell always fought in the open and stood for the settlement of this burning question by methods of reason.

He was imprisoned, but such was his popularity that his short stay in confinement was not burdensome. A writer of the time says that "he was addressed by bishops, complimented by Americans, bored by deputations, serenaded by bands, comforted by ladies, half smothered by roses." When he was released he had a frantic ovation.

But the old man was weakened in health, and the bright spirit that had sustained him in his triumphal pilgrimages no longer upstayed him. A younger element had arisen in his own party that counseled violence. His country was upon the brink of the terrible famine that became one of the world's worst catastrophes. He decided to leave his land and to die in Rome.

When he made his last appearance in Parliament even his enemies rose to greet him with respect and sympathy. His last words were a faltering but eloquent appeal for mercy to Ireland. He set sail for the Holy City, but died at Genoa on the way.

Not only was Daniel O'Connell the greatest, but he was the typical Irishman. It has been said that "every quality, every characteristic, good, bad, lovable or the reverse, was found in him." Not only did he know the Irish heart, but he had the force to be its leader. "His aims, hopes, enthusiasms were theirs, but the effective, controlling power was his alone. To the average Irishman of his day he stands as Mont Blanc might stand were it set down amongst the Magillicuddy Reeks. He had a great cause, and he availed himself greatly of it."

BOLIVAR, THE WASHINGTON OF
SOUTH AMERICA

Simon Bolivar, who had been born in Caracas, now the capital of Venezuela, and educated in Madrid, visited the United States in 1809, and, seeing the prosperity of that free country, determined to deliver his own land from foreign oppression.

Returning to his native land, he joined himself with the patriotic party and was sent by them to England, in the vain hope of securing English assistance. When he came back he enlisted in the army of freedom and at length captured Caracas, where he was given the title of "El Libertador," and made dictator.

He was defeated and driven to Jamaica, and at length to Hayti, where he established an independent government and freed the slaves, including those he himself owned.

He took an army over the Cordilleras and made himself master of New Grenada, which he renamed Colombia. In turn he conquered the realm of the old Incas, Peru. He was named president of Colombia and dictator of Peru. The southern provinces of Peru were renamed Bolivia in his honor, and the grateful people gave him a million dollars, with which he purchased the freedom of a thousand slaves.

After a time he was removed from the presidency of Peru, Venezuela separated herself from Colombia and he retired from the presidency of Colombia. He died at San Pedro, in Colombia, in 1830. His property was mainly devoted to the service of his country.

STATUE OF SIMON BOLIVAR AT CARACAS

After his death his unselfish character was better understood. His ashes were carried in pomp to Caracas, where a triumphal arch was built in his memory.

His example gave encouragement to the other South American countries to declare their independence and led to the removal of all Spanish domination in the southern continent.

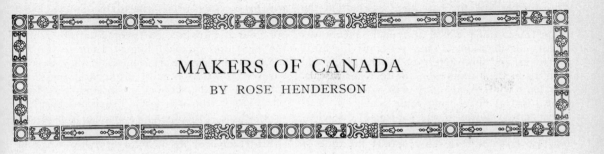

MAKERS OF CANADA
BY ROSE HENDERSON

STRANGE COLONIZATION VENTURES

"THEN I shall go to the prisons to find men," declared the Marquis de la Roche when he failed to secure enough volunteers for the French colony he had planned to found in Canada. To the prisons he went, and we have the strange spectacle of a body of convicts sailing away in 1598 with an ambitious noble to plant a settlement in the wilderness of the New World.

Across the stormy Atlantic came the lonely little ship, so small we are told that the convict passengers could reach over the sides and wash their hands in the waves. At length La Roche reached Sable Island, "the graveyard of the Atlantic," it has been called, because of the many ships which have met destruction on its long curved shore with treacherous shoals.

A low, sandy stretch of land lying between currents off the coast of Nova Scotia, "the graveyard" seemed a good place to land the untrustworthy settlers while La Roche was looking around for an appropriate site for his colony. There were no trees on the island, but plenty of long sand-grass and small shrubs.

"Here," said the Marquis to himself, "my prisoners can fish and hunt, and thus lay up a supply of food. There is no way of their escaping to wander after gold or adventure. Here they will be safe until my return."

And safe they were! Safer than La Roche had dreamed. For no sooner had he and his crew set sail than a storm swept down the gray waters and carried the helpless little ship, like a bobbing eggshell, back to the shores of France.

The convicts had been well satisfied on their island until they saw the ship swept away, leaving them alone in a strange land. Then they were indeed desolate. Even the jails they had left seemed preferable to this lonely waste in the midst of the thundering sea. There was plenty of fish, to be sure, and a stream of fresh water flowed through the sandy island. Wild ducks flew about the pools in the long grasses, wild berries ripened along the bleak pathways, and wild cattle wandered in droves, the descendants of herds brought by earlier visitors.

THE WRETCHED CRIMINALS QUARREL

You might have thought this much freedom would appeal to men who had been chained behind prison walls. But no! They were quite miserable in their solitude. A criminal, it seems, is seldom able to enjoy his own company, and the forty or more convicts were not a congenial group. They fought and killed each other in petty quarrels over their wild game. They roamed over the thirty miles of narrow island, and paced the barren shores watching for a sail.

The wind tossed the sand in ever-changing heaps, and the sea surged in darkening walls of wave and foam. Winter was creeping out of the north, and the desolate men stopped their quarrels to build huts of driftwood and to dig caves where they could take refuge from the fierce winds.

They continued to wander from tip to tip of the sandy island, and to search in vain for some means of escape. But they found only shifting sand hills, rank grasses, and rambling cranberry vines. The skies darkened with autumn storms. Rain fell, and then snow and sleet.

Many French boats were fishing off Newfoundland in the spring and summer months, but none of these came near enough to see the convicts' signals. Fishermen had learned to steer clear of the shoals of Sable Island. Sometimes the wretched colonists sighted a white sail on the horizon, only to watch it disappear beyond the moaning sea.

Some died of sickness, others were murdered by their maddened companions, and the graves grew thicker and the bare huts lonelier on the dreary little island.

The men killed cattle and made themselves clothing of the skins. They set traps for birds and foxes, and they stole each other's game, and lived up to their reputation for thieving rascals. The long winter monotony was especially irksome. But at last Spring came, and great seal-herds drifted down on the ice-pans. The colonists hunted these, collecting the furs for clothing, and also hoarding the skins against the time of escape.

SUMMER AND NEW HOPE

Summer again, with blue skies and green grass, was more endurable. And always there was the heart-sick hope of a sail. At last, after five years, the ship came. La Roche had been imprisoned by a powerful enemy, and had tried in vain to send for his deserted colonists. Only twelve remained out of the forty or more who had been abandoned. These were pitiful wrecks of men, with matted hair and beards, clad like savages in the shaggy skins of animals.

The villainous pilot who went to their rescue robbed them of their furs, but the king heard of this and sent for the convicts. They came before him in their wild attire, "like river gods of yore," according to an old chronicle. The king was sorry for their plight. He gave them their freedom, awarded each man a sum of money, and ordered their furs restored to them.

La Roche died soon after the return of his strange colonists, and thus ended one adventure in the history of Canadian colonization.

ANOTHER WILDERNESS VENTURE

In 1583, fifteen years before La Roche landed his convicts on Sable Island, Sir Humphrey Gilbert had set gayly forth with well-equipped ships and a large company of sailors, fishermen and mechanics, to plant a settlement in Newfoundland.

This settlement is called England's oldest colony. Sir Humphrey was a striking figure, in his rich lace and crimson velvet; and as an omen of good luck he carried a golden anchor presented to him by Queen Elizabeth. As was usually the case with these early colonies, much time was spent in explorations and in searching for gold and silver. The people did not realize the need for careful, diligent labor at raising crops and building warm houses, if they were to survive the harsh Winters in the wilderness.

On one of the trips of exploration Sir Humphrey's best ship was lost. Provisions began to grow scarce. And the long Canadian Winter was almost upon them.

Sir Humphrey decided to return to England. He gathered up some glittering rock which he believed to be gold, and had it loaded into his flagship, the "Squirrel." He set sail for England, riding away in the diminutive flagship of only ten tons' burden. A wild storm arose, and Sir Humphrey's men urged him to come on board the larger vessel. This he refused to do. He sat calmly in the stern of his tossing craft and uttered his famous response: "We are as near heaven at sea as on land."

During the night the "Squirrel" disappeared. The crews of the other ships watched in vain for its light to reappear. Sir Humphrey and his men were lost, though the rest of the boats reached England safely.

A COLONY AT TADOUSAC

In 1599, while the miserable convicts were spending their first year on Sable Island, a trader named Pontgrave and a naval officer, Chavin, formed a partnership to control the fur-trade of the St. Lawrence. In order to secure their trading privileges, they agreed to plant a colony.

They left sixteen men alone in the wilderness at Tadousac, with scanty provisions and poor protection from the severe Winter. When a French trading ship visited the "colony" in the Spring there was nothing left except empty huts. Most of the colonists had perished, and the rest had been given shelter by the Indians, and were scattered among the wigwams of friendly tribes.

Though these early attempts at colonization seem to us pitiful failures, they did open the way for later settlement by more thrifty and practical souls, who realized the dangers and difficulties before them. Later frontiersmen, such as the wily Radisson, combined the adventurous taste of these first visitors with a hardy skill in meeting the demands of life in a savage wilderness.

THE ADVENTURES OF JACQUES CARTIER

BY BECKLES WILLSON

NEARLY four centuries ago, in the spring of the year, the banks of the river Thames, in England, were lined from Windsor to Greenwich with a multitude of gayly dressed people. Artisans and their wives, tradesmen and apprentices, farmers in smock-frocks, gentlemen in doublets and hose, and ladies in farthingales, all came out to snatch a peep of a brave spectacle. From lip to lip ran the news that at last the royal barge in its crimson and gold trappings had set out from Windsor. Bluff "King Hal," as the people affectionately termed their monarch, King Henry VIII, and his new queen, Anne Boleyn, were that day making their first voyage together down the Thames to the royal palace at Greenwich.

Glance at this spectacle, for it will serve to fix the date of this story's opening firmly in your mind. The banks are reëchoing with loyal cheers, the state bargemen are plying their oars and the state trumpeters are sounding their trumpets, while beautiful Anne Boleyn smiles and nods merrily at the crowds who wave their silken kerchiefs in the sunshine. So this first water pageant of the season passes along.

On this selfsame day, April 20, 1534, when the English king was setting out on the river journey with his new queen, on the other side of the English Channel, at the little port of St. Malo, in Brittany, another and very different embarkation was taking place, and a very different voyage was begun.

The object of this enterprise was far indeed from pleasure, and its consequences were very important and far-reaching, not only to the king of France, but to King Henry's successors, and to the English people and the British Empire of our own day. Here, too, there was cheering and waving of caps and cries of "Vive le Roi!" (Long

LITTLE JACQUES LISTENS TO STORIES OF COLUMBUS, CABOT, AND OTHERS

CARTIER SAILS FOR THE NEW WORLD

live the king!) as the soldiers, sailors, and towns-folk on the dock at St. Malo bade lion-hearted Jacques Cartier godspeed on his adventurous voyage to the New World.

A YOUNG ADVENTURER

At this time, you must bear in mind, more than forty years had passed since Christopher Columbus had returned to Spain with tidings of his glorious discovery on the other side of the Atlantic. When Jacques Cartier, son of a Breton mariner, was born, all Europe was still ringing with the news. As the child grew up he heard tales of how often famous mariners had sailed boldly to the west and claimed for Spain, Portugal, and England the lands that might lead to India and serve as gateway to the Spice Islands of the East. Among these sailors were John Cabot and his son Sebastian, who, although themselves Venetians, sailed from the port of Bristol and flew the English flag. In 1498 the Cabots explored the whole coast of North America from Labrador to South Carolina, and they were the first Europeans actually to land in the country we to-day know as Canada. After the Cabots, who claimed all the northern lands for England, came, a quarter of a century later, a Florentine nav-

igator, Verrazano, who declared the entire region annexed to the French crown. And now, because of Verrazano's claim, King Francis of France was sending Jacques Cartier forth from St. Malo with two little ships and one hundred and twenty men to explore inland and set up the French flag and a French colony in a new France beyond the sea.

So this Frenchman, lean, rugged, and valiant, with his little band of compatriots, sailed away on that April day while Bluff King Hal of England was merrymaking on the Thames, well content with his little isle of England, giving no thought to empire or distant deeds of discovery and conquest among the savage nations of the earth.

A NOBLE GATEWAY

Straight toward the setting sun steered Cartier and his men. As they were not buffeted greatly by the waves, in twenty days' time, on May 10, they reached the straits leading to the gulf and river of St. Lawrence. How their hearts leaped when they sighted land! On their left they saw the great island of Newfoundland, and on the right Labrador's bleak shores stretched before them. "Surely," cried Cartier, "this is Cain's portion of the earth!" But their spirits rose when they sailed into the Gulf and came to rich forests of pine, maple, and ash, with abundance of blossom and wild berries on every hand. They had been afraid that the interior was as desolate as their first glimpse of Labrador. The few Indians on the banks gazed upon them with a wondering but friendly eye. The explorers were unprepared for the great heat which overtook them. By day the land was bathed in intense sunshine, and at night a gorgeous moon lit up the broad waters, while owls and bats wheeled in air heavily perfumed with wild shrubs and flowers.

To a bay in which he anchored Cartier gave the name Baie des Chaleurs, which means the Bay of Heat. Sailing on, he came to a promontory, which he christened Cape Gaspé. There he landed and set up a cross thirty feet high. On

CARTIER AT GASPE

its front was a shield with the arms of France. As you travel through eastern Canada to-day you will frequently come upon crosses by the wayside, where the country folk kneel and say their prayers. This at Gaspé was the first cross erected in New France. While the pious sailors were erecting it, Indians flocked near and surveyed the proceeding jealously, as if the white newcomers were about to charm away their land; but Cartier explained as best he could to their medicine men and distributed among them knives and trinkets, of which he had brought a goodly store.

Having quieted the suspicions of the Indians, Cartier lured two of the young redmen into his ship, that he might show them, on his return, to the king. Cartier had meant to continue his voyage much farther westward; but meeting with adverse winds, he abandoned this resolution, took counsel with his officers and pilots, and decided to set sail for France.

From the two natives whom he bore away

Jacques Cartier had learned of the existence of the great river St. Lawrence. As truly as Columbus he had discovered a new world. So much interest was awakened in France by Cartier's narrative of his voyage, that there was no difficulty about procuring the money for another expedition. The French court and people were filled with enthusiasm about Canada, and so they continued to be for more than two centuries.

CARTIER'S SECOND VOYAGE

When Jacques Cartier again took his departure from St. Malo, in May, 1535, he commanded three ships and one hundred and ten sailors. Some of the nobles and gentlemen of the proudest families in France went with him, eager for adventure. They thought, as marine adventurers often thought in those days, that this time surely they would find the gateway to the passage of Cathay (China) and win wealth untold. But they were not so lucky as at first; the winds were so bad that seven weeks elapsed before Cartier reached the Straits of Belle Isle. From this point the squadron steered for the Gulf of St. Lawrence, named by Cartier in honor of the saint upon whose day it was discovered. Keeping on, as his Indian interpreters (the two redmen he had taken to France) bade him do, he sailed up that stream which the Indians called "The Great River of Canada," now known as the St. Lawrence River.

Can you wonder that Cartier and his attendant nobles felt a thrill of excitement as the landscape no white man had ever seen before slowly unfolded itself to view? Opposite the great mouth of the mysterious Saguenay, redmen in birch-bark canoes came to greet them, and with these Cartier's two interpreters were able to exchange language. Their many months' residence in France had made the interpreters very different in appearance from their brother savages of Canada. They now wore slashed crimson doublets and brilliant striped hose, while the massive feathers in their heads caused the Canadian Indians to regard them as chiefs of great renown.

A DELIGHTFUL COUNTRY

Cartier led his ships on to what the natives called "The Kingdom of Canada," which stretched along the St. Lawrence as far as the island of Montreal, where the king of Hochelaga held his sway. To the fertile Isle of Orleans, which

Cartier reached on September 9, he gave the name of Isle of Bacchus, on account of the abundant grapevines growing upon it. From here the explorer could see on the north bank of the great river a towering promontory lit up by the morning sun. This was Cape Diamond, at whose base crouched the Indian village of Stadacona. Here Cartier anchored his little fleet, and the chief of the neighboring tribe, Donacona, came to greet him, with twelve canoes full of warriors. After a speech of welcome, the squaws (women) of the tribe danced and sang without ceasing, standing in water up to their knees.

Jacques Cartier was delighted with the country he had discovered, and lost no time in deciding to proceed up the river as far as Hochelaga. Donacona and the other chiefs, on hearing this, did their utmost to dissuade him by inventing stories about the dangers of the river. Seeing that these made little impression on the sturdy sailor, they had three Indians dressed as devils, "with faces painted as black as coal, with horns as long as the arm, and covered with the skins of black and white dogs." Cartier was told that these "devils" were the servants of the Indian god at Hochelaga, who warned the European strangers that "there was so much snow and ice, that all would die." Cartier only laughed at such tricks and told them that "their god was a mere fool, and that Jesus would preserve them from all danger if they would believe in Him." Wishing also to impress upon them his own great power, he ordered several

CARTIER TURNS THE TABLES ON THE INDIANS

AN INDIAN TOLD THEM HOW THEY COULD BE CURED

pieces of artillery to be discharged in the presence of the chief and his warriors; whereupon they became filled with astonishment and dread. Never before had they heard such terrible sounds. What were these strangers who could produce thunder at will? To reassure them, the "paleface" chief distributed trinkets, small crosses, beads, pieces of glass, and other trifles among them, and then he sailed on boldly up the river.

In a fortnight the town, consisting of about fifty large huts or cabins surrounded by wooden palisades, came into view. Twelve hundred souls belonging to a tribe of the Algonquins dwelt here in Hochelaga. The whole population assembled on the banks and gave the visitors friendly welcome. All that night the savages remained on the shore, making bonfires, dancing, and crying out "Aguaze!" which was their word for welcome and joy. The poor Indians took Cartier and his men for gods. Cartier distributed gifts among them and professed to heal their ailments.

MOUNT ROYAL

Near the town of Hochelaga was a mountain, to which the Indians conducted their visitors. From the summit this first band of Europeans in Canada gazed down at the wonderful view spread

before their eyes—glistening rivers, green meadows, and forest of maple brilliant in autumn scarlets and yellows. Naming this lofty eminence Mount Royal, Jacques Cartier and his companions returned to Stadacona. Having decided to spend the winter in Canada, they built a fort on the shore, but before the little colony could be more than half prepared, a fierce Canadian blizzard was upon them. Never had they known such cold and such tempests. From their lack of fresh food, scurvy rioted among them, and out of one hundred and ten men twenty-five died. When the disease was at its height an Indian told them that they could be cured by the juice of a spruce tree. Out of their fort they ran with axes, and so quickly did they drink the juice that in six days the whole of a great tree was consumed.

Thus was the little colony made well again. For a time they continued to fear lest the Indians should know how weak they were during that terrible winter; but no attack was made upon them, and in the spring Cartier made ready to return to France. This time Donacona and four other chiefs were seized by stratagem and taken on board ship. A cross thirty feet high, with the flag of France fastened to it, was set up on the shore, and in the middle of May the waters of the St. Lawrence began to bear them down to the

Gulf and the open Atlantic. Exactly one month later Cartier was being greeted by the cheers of the people of his native St. Malo.

Alas! Donacona and the other Indian braves whom the French had borne away never returned to Stadacona and their forest haunts. Before Cartier was ready to make another voyage to Canada, five years later, all had pined away and died. It was then that the Sieur de Roberval, a nobleman of Picardy, was appointed by King Francis of France as his lieutenant in the New World, with the high-sounding titles of Governor of Canada, Hochelaga, Saguenay, Newfoundland, Belle Isle, Carpunt, Labrador, the Great Bay, and Baccalaos, and Lord of Norembaga, a country that existed only in imagination. Roberval meant to have gone out with Cartier, but was detained until the following year.

CARTIER'S LATER EXPLORATIONS

On his third voyage Jacques Cartier again visited Hochelaga and tried to pass up the river beyond the village, but the dangerous rapids of Lachine made him pause. On the way back from another visit to France he met the Sieur de Roberval, who afterward built a fort on the St. Lawrence and explored the surrounding country. But Roberval accomplished nothing more, and famine at length reduced the survivors to a state of abject dependence upon the natives. In vain Roberval entreated the King to come to his rescue with supplies of colonists, food, and ammunition. Instead of granting this petition, King Francis despatched orders for his lieutenant to return to France. Roberval reluctantly obeyed, and thus the first attempt to establish a French colony on the banks of the St. Lawrence ended in failure.

Cartier was allowed by the King to bear always the title of "Captain." He undertook no more voyages into unknown lands, but died about 1577 in his own manor-house close to St. Malo. Years before, King Francis had been stricken by death, and thereupon his country was plunged in unhappy civil war. But in the midst of the long and deadly strife Canada was not wholly forgotten, and Frenchmen still spoke with pride of the valiant Cartier, whose adventurous courage had first unfurled their country's flag in the savage wilds of the western world.

MARGUERITE DE ROBERVAL*

BY W. S. HERRINGTON

THE story I am about to relate may be of no historical significance, but it furnishes an illustration of the courage and endurance of the women who first visited these shores.

It will be remembered that the third voyage of Cartier, in 1541, was made under Sieur de Roberval, whom Francis I appointed the first viceroy of Canada. He was a wealthy French noble of a most determined and cruel disposition. His niece, Marguerite de Roberval, was a member of his household. She was a bright young girl, full of the spirit of adventure of the age, and such a favorite with her uncle that he consented to her accompanying him upon the voyage. Like many another maiden in like circumstances, Marguerite had for some time, unknown to her uncle, been receiving the attention of a poor young cavalier whose love was not unrequited. He could not bear the thought of being separated from his sweetheart, so he managed to enlist as a volunteer with Roberval, and sailed in the same ship with him and his niece. In the course of the voyage the lovers' secret was discovered, and Roberval's affection for his niece gave way to a vengeance cruel and inhuman.

Off the coast of Newfoundland was an island called the Isle of Demons, supposed to be the abode of evil spirits. Turning a deaf ear to the supplications of the frightened girl, the cruel monster deposited her upon this lonely shore with no other companion to share her solitude than an old nurse. With scant provisions, four guns, and a limited supply of ammunition, he left her to her fate. Her lover was powerless to stay the hand of Roberval, and as the ship was getting under way again, strapping his gun and a quantity of ammunition to his back, he leaped into the sea and with sturdy strokes soon rejoined the heart-broken Marguerite.

In vain they hoped and prayed that their pitiable plight might move the stony heart of the governor. He never returned. Marguerite and her lover went

*From "Heroines of Canadian History," by U. S. Herrington. Published by William Briggs, Toronto. Used by permission of both author and publisher.

strength and courage to bear up under her heavy burden.

Only a few months before, she was the moving spirit in the castle of the "little king of Vimeu," as her uncle was called, and no luxury was denied her. She was his favorite and had often accompanied him upon his hunting expeditions, where fortunately she had become an expert with the arquebuse. His love had changed to hatred. The gayety of the court was now replaced by the dreadful solitude of this lonely isle. Want and privation, discomfort and fear now confronted her, and the three fresh mounds, bathed with her scalding tears, warned her that she, too, was likely very soon to join the only human beings who had shared her misery. Then there would be no tender hands to caress her in her last hours.

MARGUERITE IS LEFT TO HER FATE

through the form of marriage as best they could without the aid of a priest. Did ever a couple begin housekeeping under such trying circumstances? They built themselves a rude hut. The wild fowl and fish furnished their table, and from the skins of wild animals they provided themselves with clothing to resist the cold of the approaching winter.

In the following summer Marguerite became a mother and devoted most of her time to caring for her baby. Her husband had hoped that the cruel uncle would return to relieve their suffering, and the bitter disappointment he experienced crushed his spirit. Grieving over the suffering of his loving wife, he sickened and died. The baby did not long survive him, and the faithful nurse also succumbed. In the lonely forest this brave young woman knelt beside the graves she had made with her own hands and prayed for

THEY BUILD A RUDE HUT

She did not yield to these despairing thoughts, but determined to meet her fate with a bold front. For eighteen long and dreary months she wandered about the shores straining her eyes for a glimpse of a sail. Three or four times relief seemed at hand as a white speck appearing upon the horizon soon disclosed the dimensions of a ship, only to melt away again, leaving her more lonely than before.

The third winter was almost upon her when she again espied a welcome sail. How was she to lure the ship to this dreaded shore—the supposed home of mischief-making demons? Mustering all her strength for one final effort, she sacrificed her little store of fuel that she had painfully gathered from the forest and built a huge fire, in the hope that the smoke would attract the attention of the strangers. Nearer and nearer came the boat, a fisherman's barque. With frantic gestures she signaled for help. The fishermen drew near enough to descry a lonely figure, clad in skins of wild animals, wildly gesticulating as she ran along the shore. In doubt as to whether this was a human being or a dreaded spirit, they concluded to solve the mystery and land upon the island, and thus was Marguerite rescued from her perilous situation and shortly afterward was returned to France after an absence of nearly three years.

Do the annals of any history furnish a more pathetic or a more impressive tale than this? The courage that will lead battalions to the cannon's mouth might well waver when confronted with the terrors of the awful exile of this brave young girl. The strength that will carry hardened soldiers through a protracted battle would in most instances succumb to the long months of solitary suffering such as was endured by Marguerite de Roberval.

RESCUED

RADISSON, "THE CANADIAN ULYSSES"

"Do BE careful, Pierre, and promise that you will keep near the fort," urged Marguerite, the sister of Pierre Esprit Radisson, a French youth of about sixteen years of age, who was preparing for a hunt in the forest near Three Rivers. It was in 1653. The Iroquois were on the warpath. Only a short time before the Governor of Three Rivers and twelve leading citizens had been murdered a little distance from the gate of the fort.

But Pierre laughed merrily at his sister's fears. He was a tall, sturdy youth, as straight and lithe as a young Indian warrior.

"Ma petite sœur," he mocked. "Why did I come to America then? To sit behind walls, and leave the game for Indians to shoot? No! I can shoot as well as a greasy red-skin. Perhaps I shall bring you a Mohawk scalp. Yes?" He kissed his hand gayly to the anxious elder sister, and was off for the grassy-bordered lakes and the rough woodland trails.

It was near sundown when Pierre was returning. The sky glowed red and gold behind the brown maples. Wild ducks skimmed darkly above the gray swamp-lands. Pierre's game-bag was loaded. He tramped eagerly homeward, keeping a watchful eye on the darkening clumps of bushes. Something moved in the thick underbrush. Pierre slipped behind a tree-trunk, but was instantly surrounded by a band of Iroquois.

IN CAPTIVITY

He was taken to the Mohawk village and put through preliminary tortures. He was tied to a stake and his finger-nails torn out, and he watched the Indians gathering wood for his burning. But his insolent scorn of pain appealed to the red-men. Besides, he would make a fine warrior. He was released, and allowed to run the gauntlet. He ran and dodged so vigorously that not an arrow pierced him. The Mohawks cheered his skill and courage. He was given to a captive Huron woman for adoption, and treated as a member of the tribe.

Soon he attempted to escape with an Algonquin captive. He almost reached home, but was recaptured, and for two days subjected to tortures. Burned and mutilated, with his undaunted spirit he again stirred the Indians. Gifts which he made of wampum belts also helped his cause. He was released, and a second time allowed the freedom of the Mohawk lodges.

Again he stole away from his captors. All day he sped through the shadowy forests. Often he ran through streams to lose his trail from his pursuers. The months of training on Indian hunts proved valuable now. His muscles were like steel, his sense of danger as keen as that of a savage.

Night came, but still he ran, now stopping to drink from a bubbling spring, but always alert, like a hunted animal. Dawn came. He was dizzy with fatigue, and his moccasins were worn to shreds, but he staggered on. The second afternoon he reached the Dutch settlements on the Hudson. He hid for three days in Albany, with the Mohawks sniffing about in search of him. A priest gave him passage-money to Europe. He was passed down the river to New York and sailed in a Dutch boat to Holland.

RADISSON AGAIN FOILS THE INDIANS

The next May Radisson was back at Three Rivers. At the request of the Iroquois, a Jesuit mission had been opened on Lake Onondaga, but had been given up on account of the hostility of the Indians. The Iroquois now begged for missionaries, and a party of French and Hurons was setting out with some Iroquois to re-establish the abandoned post. Radisson, now a man in experience, though only eighteen years of age, volunteered to go along.

His knowledge of Indian ways and language made him a desirable scout. At first the Iroquois pretended to be greatly interested in Jesuit sermons. But as soon as they struck the wilderness they began to show signs of treachery. The French pretended to notice nothing, and pressed on toward the fort. Soon the converted Hurons were cold-bloodedly murdered. Only a few Indian women escaped. The French took refuge in the fort with their stock and provisions. Luckily it was large enough to accommodate everything.

The Iroquois warriors gathered in ever-increasing numbers outside the palisades. They threw aside all their pretended interest in religious teaching. With miles of savage winter forest between them and the white settlements, the French were helpless. They sent messages to Quebec, but these were captured by the Iroquois. The Indians waited, confident of their prey.

Week after week passed. Spring loosened the ice in the rivers, and the savages grew very watchful. Radisson, meanwhile, had not been idle. He had the French secretly building boats in the lofts of the fort. He came and went freely among the Indians, and presently he learned of a plot to murder half the colony and keep the rest as hostages to be exchanged for some Iroquois who were held at Quebec.

The French could delay no longer. Radisson spread word among the Indians that a great feast was soon to be given them by the inhabitants of the fort. And a great feast it was. Radisson knew the Mohawk ceremonial traditions. It was a rule that no food should be left uneaten which had been prepared for a religious feast, such as this was to be.

THE FEAST IS SPREAD

Corn-cakes, roast duck, roast pork, fish, venison—everything available was prepared for the occasion. Care was taken, also, to arrange the feast outside of the inner walls. Then the whole village was invited. Everybody came, even the watchful spies who had been lurking about to discover any attempt of the whites to escape from the fort.

Radisson played the merry host. The Indians danced and ate, and ate, and ate. In vain they begged to be excused. Radisson urged the sumptuous viands upon them, reminding them of their religious duty. Gorged and drunken, they at last fell asleep over the tables. And while the Indians were sleeping the French stole out of the rear gates, loaded their boats with provisions and ammunition and set forth down a little stream to the Oswego River, and from there to Lake Ontario.

To deceive the Indians, stuffed dummies had been placed on guard at the fort windows. A few dogs and chickens were left inside, and a pig was tied to the main gate, to tramp busily back and forth, like a watchful sentinel behind the walls.

Radisson's trick had worked. By April the French were safe at Quebec. The crowing chickens, a barking dog and a tramping pig kept up a semblance of life at the abandoned fort. It must have been a very disappointed Indian who first climbed up to peer over the deserted palisades.

WIDE WANDERINGS

When Radisson arrived at Three Rivers he found that his sister, Marguerite, had married an adventurous Frenchman named Chouart. The two men became fast friends. In June they set out westward with a party of French and In-dians, to slip through the hostile camps of the Iroquois.

After many thrilling experiences they explored Lake Huron, and went to Green Bay, Lake Michigan, as the guests of a party of Pottawatomies. All that Winter they wandered about, meeting tribes of Sioux and Crees and learning what they could of the country.

They visited the Mississippi and the adjoining territories. They declared Michigan to be "the delightfulest lake of the world—finer than Italy, as to climate, and more delightful the farther south one goes."

The next Winter was spent on Lake Superior and around the northern rivers. They heard from the Indians about a great "Bay of the North," and this they determined to visit. They said little about their plans. But after a year's rest at Three Rivers, they applied to the French Governor for a license to leave. They believed that not far beyond Lake Superior they would find the long-sought passage by sea to Japan and China.

The Governor's proposal that they take along two of his servants who would share in the profits of the venture did not appeal to Radisson and Chouart. They did not wish to be hampered with inexperienced men. So they escaped with a returning party of Northwest Indians, and were again free in the fascinating wilds.

After another year of exploration, Radisson and Chouart returned to Three Rivers. As the French Governor was very angry at their escape, and France would do nothing to aid them, the explorers offered their services to England, and brought about the formation of the Hudson's Bay Company, one of the most important factors in the life and settlement of Canada.

It is said that Radisson was never defeated in an undertaking, though he was always assuming the most daring risks. He was as fearless and as fickle as the Indians he tricked, and his resourcefulness and keen judgment made him a match for white men as well.

After a quarrel with the Hudson's Bay Company, he joined the French and established a French fort on the Bay. He returned to Europe, and again entered the service of England, and led an expedition which captured the fort he himself had founded.

Whether serving the French, English, or Indians, he was a cheerful soldier of fortune, who seemed always to draw a winning hand. His exploits opened new wilds for trading, and the narrative of his adventures is an interesting and valuable record of early exploration.

THE STORY OF MADELEINE DE VERCHÈRES
EDITED BY BLISS CARMAN

IN THE great struggle between France and England for the possession of the American Continent, the French were usually aided by the Algonquin tribes of Indians, and the English by the Iroquois tribes, the famous Five Nations. This stirring up of the Indians of course made the war very barbarous and life for the colonists very unsafe. The houses in the country were deserted, fields lay untilled, and people crowded to the towns for safety. Sometimes the people of a village would gather and all work together for greater protection. But while they worked, sentinels were kept on watch to give warning at the first sign of danger. Everywhere was lurking terror. No man was safe, no life was sure. The trader paddling downstream with his store of furs, the trapper returning from the woods, the farmer walking behind his plow, each knew that he held his life in his hands. "The enemy is upon us by land and sea," wrote Frontenac; "send us more men if you want the colony to be saved."

Many stories are told of brave deeds done at this time. One of the most famous is that of Madeleine de Verchères, a girl of fourteen, who held her father's fort against the Indians for a whole week.

It was autumn, and all the settlers at Verchères had gone to work in the fields some miles from the fort, leaving only two soldiers on guard. Besides them in the fort were a man of eighty and some women and children, among whom were Madeleine and her two brothers, one ten and the other twelve.

Everything seemed peaceful and quiet in the hazy afternoon. The crickets sang in the ripe grass; the air was still and warm; there was no sign of danger anywhere. But through the thick forest, which already glowed gold and red beneath the autumn sun, Indians were stealing on their

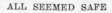

ALL SEEMED SAFE

327

"WHAT ARE YOU DOING WITH THAT MATCH?"

foes. Thinking that all was safe, Madeleine had gone down to the river that flowed not far from the fort. Suddenly through the still air was heard the sound of a gunshot. Hardly had the sound died away when to the girl's startled ears came a cry from the fort. "Run, Miss, run!" shouted the old man, "the Indians are upon us!"

Madeleine turned. There, not a pistol-shot away from her, was a band of forty-five or fifty Indians. On the instant she fled like a startled rabbit, her heart in her mouth, her light feet skimming the beaten path. But how long the way seemed! As she ran, she prayed.

The bullets of forty muskets sang in the air and whistled round her as she fled. It seemed as if she would never reach the fort! "To arms, to arms!" she shouted as she ran, hoping that some-one would come out to help her. No one came, but she was well ahead of her pursuers, and with a last burst of speed she reached the gate and sprang inside. With trembling hands and panting breast, she turned and closed and made fast the gate, then was almost overcome with joy at her escape. But that was only for a moment. She must waste no time. There was the fort with its other inmates to be guarded. She ran round the fort to see that all was made safe. Here and there logs had fallen out of the palisades, leaving

holes through which the enemy might get in. These she ordered to be replaced, herself helping to carry the logs. As soon as that was done she went to the guardroom where the gunpowder and shot were kept. Here she found the two soldiers hiding in terror. One had a lighted match in his hand.

"What are you going to do with that?" she asked quickly.

"I am going to set fire to the powder and blow us all up," he answered.

"You coward!" cried Madeleine. "Go!"

She was only a girl of fourteen, but she spoke so sternly that the soldier was ashamed. He blew out his match and left the room.

Madeleine now threw off her white muslin sun-bonnet, put on a steel cap in its place and, taking a gun in her hand, turned to her two brothers.

"Now, boys," she said, "let us fight to the death. Remember what father has taught you, that gentle-men must be ready to die for their God and their king."

The boys were only little fellows, but they were as brave as their sister, and taking their guns, they went to the loopholes and began to fire upon the Indians who were now close round the house. The women were much frightened in spite of Madeleine's brave example, and the little children were crying with fear. But this stout-hearted girl comforted them all as well as she could, telling the children that they must not cry, for if the Indians heard, they would learn how hopeless the state of the fort was and would attack more fiercely. So Madeleine encouraged the little band to help in the heroic defense of their stronghold.

All day long the fight lasted, and with the fall of night and darkness a terrible storm came on. The wind howled round the walls, and wailed dismally in the chinks and chimneys. It was a fearful night, and Madeleine, anxiously watching the movements of the Indians as well as she could in the half-light, became sure that they were making ready to attack the fort under cover of the darkness and the storm. She could just see their shadowy figures moving among the shadows of the woods, gliding silently from cover to cover, and always stealing nearer to their prey. It was a sight to try the nerves of the strongest man, but it did not break the courage of this dauntless little French girl. She was made of the finest spirit, and the blood of fearless adventurers and pioneers ran in her veins.

In that howling storm, on the edge of a lonely forest, beset by a band of cruel enemies, Madeleine gathered her little garrison and made a brief speech to them.

"God has saved us to-day from the hands of our enemies," she said. "But we must watch to-night lest we fall into their snares."

Then she gave her orders to each of the men, posting them as well as she could at the wall. So all night long the Indians heard the steady tread of sentinels on duty. Every hour from fort and blockhouse came the cry, "All's well!" The wily Indians, hearing that call ringing steadily above the storm, were completely deceived; and thinking that the fort was strongly garrisoned, they dared not attack.

Toward morning there was an alarm. The sentry nearest the gate suddenly called out:

"Lady, I hear something."

Hurrying to him, Madeleine peered anxiously through the loophole, straining her eyes to see. And there, against the whiteness of the new-fallen snow, black moving figures could be seen coming close round the house. For a few moments Madeleine watched in fresh dread. Then soft lowing and snuffing was heard, and the girl gave a sigh of relief. These were not Indians, but some of the cattle belonging to the fort that had found their way through the snow back to the gate. There were only a few of them, for the Indians had captured nearly all the herd.

"Open the gate and let them in," said someone.

"No, no," cried Madeleine, "you forget how cunning these Indians are! Very likely they are behind the cattle, wrapped in skins and ready to rush in the moment we are silly enough to open the gate."

"That is true," said the others.

Then after some talk it was decided to take the risk. For if they were long besieged they might be glad of the cattle to keep them from starving.

Calling her two brothers, Madeleine placed them one on each side of the gate, with their guns in their hands and their fingers on the triggers ready to fire. Then the gate was carefully opened. One by one the cattle came in, glad to be back in

MADELEINE CAREFULLY OPENED THE GATE

sheltered quarters, and the gate was again closed and barred in safety. And everybody drew a long breath of relief.

So the long night of anxiety wore on and ended at last. And as the sun rose and the darkness fled, the fears and terrors of the night fled too.

The sunlight glittered on the white, new snow; the sky was clear and blue; squirrels ran and chattered in the tall, dark spruce trees; and all the beautiful world looked smiling and safe; but the brave little garrison did not dare to go off guard, for no one knew how long the Indians might lurk hidden in the woods. So they took turns at keeping watch, and some did the necessary work of the besieged household, while others rested. So the short, bright day passed and another long night shut down on those brave defenders. It was starlight and cold, and the guards could see

"YOU ARE WELCOME"

their breath in the frosty air as they tramped steadily to and fro and cried their "All's well!" in the still night. Luckily their foes made no attempt to attack them, and so another night and a day passed, and another and another.

The brave little garrison still kept watch in the closed fort. And now and again they caught glimpses of the Indians prowling about in the woods. Hour by hour Madeleine marched round the posts, always smiling, always speaking cheer-ing words, however uneasy she might be at heart. For the first two days and nights she hardly slept, never laying down her gun nor taking off her clothes.

And so a week went by. On the seventh night Madeleine had gone into the guardroom to rest, for she was very weary. With her musket still in her arms, she sat down, laid her head upon the table for a moment—and went to sleep. How long she sat there she did not know. Suddenly she started wide awake in a panic. Listening, she heard the tramp of men around the house. Springing up, she seized her gun.

"Who goes there?" she called out into the darkness.

"French," came the reply; "it is La Monnerie come to help you."

Oh, how good his voice sounded! Running to the gate, Madeleine threw it open. But even now she did not forget to be careful. Posting a sentinel, she marched out to meet the Frenchmen, to the cheering of her little band.

"Sir, you are welcome," she said, giving La Monnerie, the leader, a military salute, "I surrender you my arms."

"Lady," replied the captain, bowing low before her, "they are in good hands."

With that she turned and led the way, and La Monnerie and his soldiers marched into the fort. Wonderingly he made a tour of the defenses and found all in good order, each "man" at his post. It was perhaps the strangest, bravest garrison he ever had seen. Among them were a man of eighty and a boy of ten; and this slim girl of fourteen was their leader!

"Sir," said Madeleine, a little wearily, but with a joyful pride, "relieve my men. We have not been off duty for eight days."

THE THERMOPYLÆ OF CANADA

BY WILFRED CAMPBELL

A NOTED historical spot on the Ottawa River is the Long Sault at the head of the famous rapids, where the heroic Daulac and his sixteen young followers, assisted by a few Huron Indians, withstood, it is said, fully twelve hundred Iroquois for the space of several days, and gave their lives in the end for the preservation of New France.

It seems that Canada had suffered for twenty years under the persistent attacks of the famous, cruel tribes of Indians called the Iroquois. The French population in the whole colony was less than three thousand souls, and they were saved from destruction only by the fact that their settlements were grouped around three fortified posts—Quebec, Three Rivers, and Montreal. To the Iroquois, Canada had become indispensable, and they determined, if they could, to destroy the French colony, their policy being a persistent attack on the outskirts of the different settlements. This became, in time, a perfect scourge to the French settlers, who saw no way of escape from this terrible condition. Outside the fortifications

there was no safety for a moment, and a universal terror seized the people.

When things were in this condition, Adam Daulac, or Dollard, appeared on the scene as a young officer of the garrison of Montreal. He formed a desperate plan. Shortly before, it had been discovered that twelve hundred Iroquois warriors were on the eve of descending on Montreal and Quebec, with the object of wiping out the whole colony.

Daulac's plan was a desperate one. He proposed to meet the Indians and waylay them on their descent of the river Ottawa, and fight them to the death. He asked for a party of volunteers. Sixteen of the young men of Montreal caught his spirit, determined to join him, and, gaining the governor's consent, made their wills, confessed, and received the sacrament, binding themselves by oath to fight to the death and receive no quarter. "As they knelt for the last time," says Parkman, "before the altar in the chapel of the Hôtel Dieu, that sturdy little population of pious Indian-fighters gazed on them with enthusiasm not unmixed with an envy which had in it nothing ignoble."

The spirit of this enterprise was purely that of the Middle Ages. Honor, adventure, and faith had to do with its motive and inspiration. Daulac was a knight of the New World. The names, ages, and occupations of the young men are still in the old register of the parish at Montreal. They were soldiers and artisans of various callings, but their spirit made them equal.

Leaving Montreal in their canoes, they at last entered the mouth of the Ottawa and slowly advanced up the stream. They soon passed the swift current at Carillon, and after much toil and travail reached the foot of the rapid called the Long Sault. Here they found an old ruined fort, of which they took possession, and were soon joined by a small band of Hurons and Algonquins, who, hearing of their intention, had followed them up the river to share in their victory or defeat.

Here, a few days later, they were besieged by an immense body of the Iroquois, and for five days, through hunger, thirst, and want of sleep, shut up in their narrow fort, they fought and prayed by turns. And here at last they died, but not until they had given the fierce savages such a dreadful lesson that they never forgot it.

MACKENZIE, THE GREAT EXPLORER

"The Indians say there is a great ocean beyond the mountains," observed Alexander Mackenzie to the commander of Fort Chippewyan. "If this is true, there lies our route to India."

It was the year 1789, and the little post on Lake Athabaska marked the western border of English occupation in Canada. The great Northwest was still an unknown wilderness, and men had not given up the search for a northwest passage to the riches of India, the route which Columbus and many others had set out to discover.

"It will be a long and dangerous voyage," remarked the officer of the fort.

"So much more to our credit if we make the discovery," urged the young explorer.

As an agent of the Northwest Fur Company, Mackenzie had shown his bravery and endurance. Though still in his early twenties he was recognized as a bold and resourceful leader.

It was a sunny June morning a few weeks later that Mackenzie set out with Indian guides and canoes and a few white companions. He proposed to follow the Slave River to its source, and to press on in search of the unknown ocean. An Indian guide, called "English Chief," was to direct the daring voyagers. The chief had his two wives with him who were to cook and help with the preparation of game.

The air was crisp, the water sparkled beneath the paddles, and ducks and cranes flew honking above the trail. It was not all easy sailing, but Mackenzie was a fit captain for such an expedition. Dangerous rapids in the Slave River compelled the explorers to travel miles overland, carrying their canoes and luggage around the falls. They fished and hunted along the way and stopped to make "pemmican," fish dried in the sun and ground to powder.

HUNTING WHALES AMONG THE ICEBERGS

On the islands of Great Slave Lake they found many kinds of delicious wild berries. But here, also, were fresh difficulties. Great cakes of ice drifted about in the lake even in this summer season, and the birch-bark canoes were in constant danger of being crushed. There were many things to try the skill and courage of the adventurous young leader. The Indians were often sulky and obstinate. They met strange tribes who told discouraging tales of the dangers and hardships ahead.

But they at last discovered the source of another stream, flowing north from Great Slave Lake, and Mackenzie pushed on up the river that now bears his name. Coal was found along the shores of the lake, and banks of it were burning, filling the air with a sulphurous smell. Further north, the Indians told of meeting the mysterious Russians from Alaska, and of Eskimos who fought with slings.

At last the intrepid explorer reached the mouth of the river and could look out upon the huge piles of ice in the Arctic Ocean. Eskimos were hunting whales among the huge icebergs. Mackenzie would have been glad to explore the new country further, but was afraid of delaying in this wild northland without more adequate provisions.

And it was well that he began the homeward journey at once. Traveling up-stream was slow and difficult. His Indians grew more troublesome and threatened to leave him. But by tact and cheerful persistence he managed to keep his party together and reached Fort Chippewyan early in September when the coming Winter made canoe travel exceedingly dangerous.

Mackenzie now spent a year in study in England so that he could give more scientific reports of the land he visited. He wanted to understand the significance of all he found. His next undertaking was to reach the Pacific, traveling westward on foot and by canoe.

His plan required patience as well as courage and endurance. By exploring Peace River from Slave Lake he found that it was possible to follow this stream into the Rocky Mountains. So he spent the Winter of 1793 on the banks of the river at a point as far west as he dared to press. As soon as Spring cleared the frozen streams he was ready for a start forward through the perilous mountain passes.

THEY FOLLOW ELK PATHS

Early in May he pushed up Peace River with his small party of French-Canadians and Indian guides. He describes the scenery as most beautiful, with green slopes, bold precipices, groves of poplars and thickets of wild shrubs in blossom. Elk and buffalo herded upon the grassy plains.

But as the ascent grew more rugged the party

was forced to travel on foot, carrying goods and canoe. Progress was slow, sometimes only a few miles a day. But the men pressed on through dense forests of pine, cypress, birch, poplar, and willow. They were able to follow paths which the herds of elk had made through the thick jungle of underbrush. They found whole acres of poplars cut down by the beavers.

As it grew warmer, the travelers were all but devoured by swarms of gnats and mosquitoes. Then they met tribes of hostile Indians. It took all of Mackenzie's skill and courage to win the friendship of these frightened natives.

He decided to camp for a while and see if he

ALEXANDER MACKENZIE

could not learn from the Indians about the best route to follow. He watched them make their canoes from spruce bark, instead of birch, and he studied their language and customs. They told him that a month's journey beyond the mountains there was "a great lake of stinking water." This was their description of the Pacific, the goal of the white chief's journeying.

Mackenzie was able to secure a guide from these Indians and pressed on to the west. This was the region in which were the southern sources of the great Mackenzie River which our explorer had traced northward four years before.

There were lofty mountain lakes and swiftly flowing streams. One of these streams which the Indians called "Bad River" came near mak-

ing an end of the luckless exploring party. The violent current dashed the canoe madly against the rocks. Mackenzie jumped into the water and was quickly followed by his men. They held on to the wrecked canoe as their one hope of safety. This kept them from being battered to death on the rocks and swept over the roaring falls.

MACKENZIE'S FOLLOWERS MUTINY

Most of the luggage was lost, and the rest had to be spread in the sun to dry. The Indians sat down and wept at the misfortune. But the French-Canadians were glad of the loss, as they thought it would discourage Mackenzie, and that he would turn back home. They were sick of the hardships of the trail, and wanted to give up the search for an ocean beyond the mountains.

The young leader had one friend, however, in his countryman, Alexander Mackay, whose Scotch pluck was as dauntless as Mackenzie's own. The explorer wisely refrained from arguing with his mutinous followers until they were dry and warm again, and had cooked and eaten a good dinner. Then he was able to persuade them to go ahead, with the canoe mended and the remaining goods re-packed.

The guide promised that they would soon reach a larger and less turbulent river. Flies and mosquitoes still tortured them, and they waded through swamps in which they were almost drowned. The new Indian guide now deserted them, and Mackenzie was obliged to direct the journey as best he could from what the Indians had told him. Floods of driftwood threatened their canoe with another disaster whenever they tried to embark on the swift mountain streams.

But at last they found themselves "on the bank of a navigable river on the western side of the first great range of mountains." Down this wide stream they paddled between snow-capped mountain ranges. Red deer grazed along the river, and the short rations were soon supplemented with plenty of venison.

Strange Indian tribes were again encountered, and not being able to speak their language, Mackenzie needed to be very careful not to give them offense. He made them presents of trinkets, and succeeded in making peace even when they approached with drawn bows. But he had to be prepared for war continually, in case his peace overtures should fail.

"I SHALL GO ON TO THE PACIFIC!"

The canoe was again full of holes from its rough voyaging among the rocks, and chilling rain and hail storms drenched the travelers. In the midst of these troubles his followers again grew mutinous. But Mackenzie faced the men fearlessly. "I know your plans to desert me," he declared. "But come what will, I am going on to the Pacific."

His courage probably shamed the mutineers. At any rate, they all went to work at building a new canoe. Perhaps they realized that a man who could command treacherous Indians and white men and fight his way cheerfully through such overwhelming odds was not an undesirable companion on a wilderness trail.

Whatever the reason, they stayed with Mackenzie, and they would surely have been badly off without his leadership. Presently the deserting guide returned with apologies. The party buried their belongings, so that they could be found on the return trip. They left their canoe with a shelter of boughs to protect it from the sun, and started on foot for the last long climb up the wooded mountains and on to the unknown sea.

Each man had his load of from seventy to ninety pounds, consisting of food, ammunition, and presents for the Indians. All of the white men also carried guns. Toiling up the steep slopes they would be soaked with perspiration and then drenched with chilling rains. They traveled thirteen miles the first day and were told by the natives that the coast was about a six days' journey west.

The Indians met with now were generally more friendly. They lived in fairly well-built wooden huts. They were tall, often gray-eyed, and dressed in leather. The men were unusually clean from being constantly in the water in their swimming and canoeing feats. When they found that the white travelers were hungry they fed them generously with roast salmon, berries, and salmon roe.

MACKENZIE MEETS THE INDIANS' ARROWS

Occasionally, however, the Indians ran away, or appeared very hostile. At one village the men armed themselves with arrows, spears, and axes, and stood waiting the signal for attack. Mackenzie walked up to them alone, and fearlessly shook hands with the first man he came to. This cool courage stirred the red-men. An old warrior came out of the crowd and threw his arms about Mackenzie. Another took off his beautiful robe of otter skin and put it over the shoulders of the brave young leader.

They took him to their homes, gave him their choicest food, and showed him every honor. So at last the little party reached the tossing waters of the blue Pacific. Mackenzie was the first white man to cross the continent north of Mexico.

On the face of a seaward-looking cliff the successful leader painted the following words: "Alexander Mackenzie, from Canada, by land, the twenty-second of July, one thousand seven hundred and ninety three." Then, yielding to the entreaties of his men, he led them safely back and reached Fort Chippewyan, August 24, 1793, after an absence of eleven months.

A trail had been blazed through the great northwest of Canada. The myth of an inland sea west of the Rockies was exploded; colonists and mounted police were soon following in the tracks of Mackenzie's party.

THE UNITED EMPIRE LOYALISTS

"I wonder what ships those are?" said a Canadian frontiersman as he looked out of his cabin doorway one morning and noticed loaded vessels landing their crowds of men, women and children on the shores of a northern lake. The man went down to speak to the immigrants, and discovered that they were United Empire Loyalists, exiles from the States, seeking new homes in the pine-forests of the north.

The people were a sad yet eager company. They carried their few household treasures as if they were precious mementoes of happy days that had long passed. There were fine gentlemen in velvet and laces and white silk stockings, and there were soldiers and farmers and city-bred clerks. Some of the women were dressed handsomely in silks and brocades, which were strangely out of place in the wilderness to which they had come.

Along the lakes and rivers, and across the border by rough forest or prairie roads, the Loyalists streamed into Canada. Some of them had left luxurious homes. Some of them had barely succeeded in paying for humble farm-houses. But all these possessions were now left behind. Many had helped to build roads, and bridges, and towns in a new land, only to find themselves now in another new land where fresh roads, and bridges, and towns must be built.

Canada owes much of her later prosperity to these bands of sturdy exiles who crossed over from the United States during or following the Revolutionary War. These were the people who wished to remain true to England, instead of joining the revolting colonists. They were severely persecuted by the zealous patriots, who could see no excuse for loyalty which differed from their own.

LOYALISTS PLUNDERED AND HANGED

After England's defeat and the establishment of American independence, the fate of the Loyalists was wretched in the extreme. England failed to provide for the protection of these Americans who had served her most faithfully. And though Washington and other wise and just leaders protested in their behalf, some of the Loyalists were hanged and others beaten and plundered. Their estates were confiscated, and they were exiled under penalty of death.

Thousands flocked into Canada and made homes for themselves on the lands which England at last provided. Two main divisions streamed across the border or along the coast in ships. One branch spread through the provinces of Nova Scotia, New Brunswick, and Prince Edward Island, and the other settled along the St. Lawrence and on the northern shores of the Great Lakes.

LOG HUTS AND CLAY CHIMNEYS

The British government issued land-grants, implements, and food, and agreed to provide rations for three years. Partial indemnity was paid for their losses in the war. Each family was given a plow and a cow. Many of the settlers were unaccustomed to pioneer life. But there was no choice now. They set to work industriously to make new homes in the wilderness.

They had to construct rude mills for grinding their Indian corn and wild rice. They felled trees for their log cabins, and built chimneys hastily of sticks and clay. Later better chimneys were made of stone or brick. In some places they suffered severely from cold and famine during the first winter. Deep vegetable cellars had to be dug to keep the precious garden vegetables from the penetrating frost.

Many homes were miles and miles from any neighbor. Towns and forts were far beyond stretches of savage wilderness. Their sheep were carried away by wolves and bears.

Little furniture had been saved or could be carried over the long forest trail. Rude beds were made of poles and bark, and men and women who had been used to luxuries were glad to find shelter in huts little better than Indian wigwams. Occasionally an old clock, or treasured chair or writing desk, added a touch of civilization to the crudeness of pioneer cabins.

But the Loyalists had scant time for grieving over their losses. Land must be cleared and planted, and supplies gathered for the long Winter. Some who had no knowledge of farming, or of the best methods of pioneering, were naturally not always successful in their first ventures. They had to learn by experience, often a costly teacher.

"THE HUNGRY YEAR"

In 1787, the year the government supplies ended, there was a general failure of crops in the lake region, and 1788 was known as the "Hungry Year." The people had to gather nuts and roots to keep from starving. Some ate poisonous plants which they dug up in the woods, and died from the illness which followed.

They had little ammunition, and spent much time and strength trying to kill game with poles or home-made traps. They fished clumsily with home-made hooks through holes cut in the ice. It was a gloomy, disheartening experience for the strongest. Some of the less hardy actually died of starvation before Spring came and plentiful harvests followed.

Housewives gathered eagerly the first buds of trees and cooked them with pigweed and other wild "greens." When the wheat-heads began to fill, the gaunt, hollow-eyed settlers devoured the young grain. With the growth of a good crop comfort crept back to the hunger-haunted homes.

The trials of the wilderness life taught them to co-operate; and they celebrated their returning prosperity joyously. Work became play when done by a band of jolly workers. There were "bees" or "frolics" when all hands joined to build a cabin, to clear a garden patch or to gather the harvest. "Husking bees" became merry occasions, with a hearty feast after the work was done. There were "sugarings off" in the spring woods on moonlight nights, with the sirup dripping into wooden troughs and the huge kettles boiling over red coals. The evening ended with a taffy-pull and perhaps a concert, before the young people went their homeward ways through the dim, fresh woods.

FROM VELVET TO HOMESPUN

The Loyalists began to know the joys of success after their hard struggles. The velvet coats and white silk stockings had disappeared. Men who had been used to ordering slaves or servants for every task had learned to swing their own axes, plow their fields, and wrest a living from the forest wilds.

Women spun and wove suitable garments for the rough toil. Many dressed in deerskin before other clothing could be provided. Soap and sugar as well as clothing were home-made. Burnt peas were used for coffee, and tea was made from the leaves of wild blackberries or other shrubs or herbs.

Wooden dishes and spoons were in general use. Venison and wild turkey were generally plentiful, after the "Hungry Year," and there was corn-bread, and flour for cakes and pastry. Wild berries and plums made excellent pies, with maple sugar for sweetening.

So these hardy pioneers have given to Canada a spirit of enterprise and devotion. In some places the refugees settled in towns and felt less the sting of frontier hardship. Schools and churches were built, and the Loyalists' love of independence had a large part in developing liberal, representative government.

FIGHTING FOR CANADA

National improvements were carried forward by the help of these new arrivals. The channel of the St. Lawrence was deepened and improved by those who settled near its shores. Where portages had been necessary, the passage was cleared for light ships. Gradually a system of canals was developed, and a great inland water-way opened.

Under General Brock's inspiring leadership the Loyalists showed their patriotism in the War of 1812. So many thronged to his call for defenders of Canada that arms could not be found to supply them all. Where a feeling of indifference or mere selfish greed had existed, the Loyalists brought convictions which they were ready to fight for. To them and to Brock's brave and sagacious planning and fighting Canada owed her success in the War of 1812. And in Canada's response to the need of England in the great World War there may be seen something of this same old Loyalist devotion.

SIR ISAAC BROCK, THE HERO OF QUEENSTOWN

Isaac Brock loved the wild sea and the dangerous cliffs of his boyhood home. No peak on the whole island was too rocky or steep for him to climb. He explored the hidden caves and the bare, jutting shelves where the seagulls nested. He laughed at the rough winds and the dashing clouds of spray.

Thus, while the Revolutionary War was being fought and the power of the English restricted to the northern section of the American continent, the English boy who was later to be called "the Savior of Canada" ran and played over the rocky island of Guernsey, near the coast of Britain.

Isaac was the eighth son in the Brock family, and he enjoyed many adventures with his "beloved brothers," as he called them. He grew up a handsome, athletic youth with winning manners and a kind and generous spirit which made him a favorite wherever he went.

He was very proud of the English flag, and when at the age of sixteen, he was made an ensign, he determined to study and advance as a soldier so that he would be ready to serve his country when she needed a loyal and efficient leader.

Cliff-climbing and athletic sports were all very well, but Isaac Brock realized that there were other things to be accomplished if he were to make a place for himself in the army. So, not minding the laughter of his companions, he set himself at his studies with the same dogged resolution with which he struggled up a lofty cliff. His heart was set on becoming a good soldier. And in this he succeeded.

After distinguished service in Jamaica and other English "frontiers," Brock went to Canada and was put in command of Fort George, the lonely post opposite Niagara. It has been noted that the English were not usually as successful as the French in making friends with the Indians. Brock was an exception to this rule. His genial and commanding personality won the allegiance of red-men as well as of French fur-traders and colonial aristocrats. Brock was a "good mixer." He joined the rough traders in their rollicking boat songs. He admired the strength and courage of a sturdy packman who could carry five hundred pounds on his back and jog merrily along over a rough portage in the midst of continual perils.

"THIS IS A MAN"

A strain of Viking blood in his own veins responded to the hardy life, and he longed to make

SIR ISAAC BROCK

these stalwart Canadians more loyal to the English King. He built roads in the wilderness, and reveled in the picturesque beauty of the great new land. He read Homer, studied history, and kept his soldiers under excellent control.

He hated the cruelty of brutal officers who put a man under the lash for the slightest offense. By tact and kindness he won the devotion of his regiment. His athletic training stood him in good stead in this wilderness life. He stood six-feet-two in his stockings, and his muscles were like iron. In the rich uniform of his country, he made an imposing officer.

"This is a man!" Tecumseh, the great Indian chief, is said to have remarked when he first

B. & G. F.—22

met the stalwart Englishman. The two were fast friends after this meeting.

In a wild trip across the lake in pursuit of deserters, Brock took his turn at the oars along with his men. He caught the deserters, too, though an English officer reproved the rashness of the journey. English officers, it seemed, were not in the habit of crossing the lake in open boats.

But Brock won the hearts of the Canadians. Fur-traders, soldiers, and farmers cheered at sight of his cocked hat and scarlet uniform. And the dashing young officer was equally popular in the clubs and ball-rooms of Montreal and Quebec. Thomas Moore, the Irish poet, was his guest at Fort George, and the two paddled down the St. Lawrence with the Canadian boatmen.

Brock's gentleness and modesty distinguished him as well as his energy and courage. Having ordered some mutineers to death, in accordance with the regulations of the army, Brock declared after their execution: "Since I have had the honor to wear the British uniform I have never felt grief like this."

BROCK PREPARES FOR WAR

There was no more trouble when Brock was put in command in place of a brutal officer who had really caused the uprising.

When, in 1806, Brock had gone to England, he heard rumors of a war with the United States. He realized the danger of Canada's long, unfortified frontier, and, without waiting until his leave was up, he returned to America to make ready for an attack. He was inadequately supplied with soldiers and supplies, but he made the most of the resources within his grasp.

The United Empire Loyalists who had come into Canada at the time of the Revolution flocked to his standard. He erected hospitals and fortifications, and drilled the raw recruits who came to his aid. He was made a Major-General, and President and Administrator of Upper Canada. With no hope of re-enforcements, and with an empty treasury, the situation looked desperate. Brock worked day and night to prepare for the threatened invasion.

He formed a brigade of the young volunteer farmers of York. He kept his alliance with Tecumseh and the other Indians he had been able to gather to his banners. Men plowed with their guns beside them, and drilled after working all day in the fields.

June 18, 1812, the United States declared war against England, with Canada as the point of attack. The Canadians rallied to the support of Brock, and he insisted that the Indians perpetrate no outrages. Their respect for his leadership kept them loyal to their pledge. It had been said in the United States that the taking of Canada would be a "mere matter of marching." Brock proposed to dispute this theory. With a handful of men he swept over the border and captured Detroit from the cowardly Hull. Many people in the United States were opposed to fighting Canada, and her soldiers often showed their lack of enthusiasm.

Brock planted batteries along the border, and thrilled the Canadians with his stirring addresses and his personal valor and resolution. England recognized his ability, but still sent him no more troops. Bells rang throughout the kingdom to celebrate his capture of Detroit. His brothers heard with pride the reports of Isaac's victory. In London, an extra order of the Knighthood of the Bath was conferred upon him.

AN ARMISTICE FOILS BROCK'S PLANS

An armistice signed at this point spoiled Brock's plans for further aggression and gave the United States time for new preparation. England was anxious to avoid war, and thought the United States would disavow the declaration. She was badly mistaken.

Brock was awakened at midnight by the sound of firing at Queenstown. He mounted his horse and rode till dawn, gathering his army, and himself leading the assault. Here again he opposed vastly superior forces, and many of his men had never seen service.

But his was a rare gift of leadership. Young and old rallied to the support of "the General," while the United States troops often fought half-heartedly. There were valiant leaders among the Americans at Queenstown, however. In his flashing British uniform at the head of his men,

Brock was an easy mark. He rode forward in the face of a scathing fire and fell mortally wounded.

"My fall must not be noticed, to stop the victory," he gasped. His men swept forward "to avenge the General." His death was one of the great tragedies of war. During his funeral the guns of Fort George were answered by the American batteries of Fort Niagara, salute for salute, and the Stars and Stripes floated at half-mast as a tribute to the valorous foeman.

Though successful at first, the Americans were later driven from their position and forced to surrender. Brock's enthusiasm and courage made him a national hero. His work of inspiring and unifying Canada was not lost, though his death deprived the colonists of magnificent leadership. He had awakened a sense of loyalty and idealism in the rough frontiersmen, had strengthened Canada for the winning of this war and for the difficulties which came with the settlement of the great Northwest. His work led naturally to the splendid service of the Mounted Police, and aided the labors of such faithful teachers as the zealous Father Lacombe.

The motley character of Brock's army attested his personal magnetism and faith in the cause. French, Loyalists, English regulars, Indians, traders—outnumbered but not out-generaled, they followed their adored chief, and caught the fire of his high-spirited devotion.

In St. Paul's Cathedral, London, you may find a monument to the memory of this champion of Canadian freedom. The carved scene shows the stricken general in the arms of a British soldier, and an Indian looks down sadly on the face of the fallen leader. A lofty monument marks the field where he fell at Queenstown, and it has long been a custom for Canadian schoolboys to go through military drill in regimental form on the anniversary of Brock's heroic death at the Battle of Queenstown Heights.

A BLACK-ROBE VOYAGEUR

"Who knows? Some day our little Indian may be a priest and work for Indians," said the old curé. For years he had taught Albert Lacombe, the ambitious Canadian farmer boy who was now anxious to go to college.

"Mon petit sauvage" (my little Indian) was a favorite nickname which the curé had for this dreaming, dark-eyed youth. A strain of Indian blood ran in the boy's veins. His mother was a

descendant of a beautiful young French woman who married an Ojibway chief. Perhaps this remote ancestor was responsible for Albert's love of roving and his interest in the Matis, or half-breeds.

At any rate, the curé's kindness made college possible. The old priest provided the money himself, and persuaded Albert's father to let the son have an education and go to teach Indians if he liked. The boy had worked faithfully on the frontier farm, plowing, feeding hogs, picking up stones. Meantime, he had his dreams of books and far places.

At Quebec he enjoyed college life, and he liked to meet the pleasant, kindly priests who taught and worked in the town. But their lives did not attract him. "No, that is not for me. I would not live a quiet life like that for the world," he would say to himself. "I must go out and work."

The wild camps of the Indians called him. There, he believed, was his mission.

Ordained as priest in June, 1849, the young father returned to Montreal to learn of the death of his beloved patron. He remembered the old curé's words as the two had walked together only the evening before.

"Mon cher Albert, I shall pray to-morrow that you will always be a good priest." This prayer of the curé's was to be realized. Up and down the far prairies, and along the forest ways, Father Lacombe came to be known and loved as the "Black-robe Voyageur," and the "Man of Good Heart."

He began his work with a taste of the pioneer hardships which he was to endure for over sixty years of service. He was assigned to the mission of Pembina, on the Red River. On the muddy trail to the post his party was attacked by Indians and robbed of most of its provisions.

THE BUFFALO HUNT

But the young priest was not dismayed. He loved the wild beauty of woods and prairies, and the bold spirits of the roaming hunters. Buffaloes still herded on the plains in unnumbered thousands. At the time of the hunt the mission became a village of Indian tents.

Father Lacombe was made chaplain of a great hunting expedition. He gathered the bands about him in the open and taught them hymns translated into Indian. A half-breed hunter was chosen chief. There was early mass, and the party moved out over the prairie like a vast primitive pageant. There were about a thousand wagons and over a thousand men, women, and children, together with horses, oxen and dogs.

Scouts rode ahead and signaled the advance of the herd. Then the hunters plunged against the brown line of galloping animals. It was a fierce combat between men and beasts. At any moment a hunter might be hurled from his horse and trampled under the stamping hoofs.

In twenty minutes the great herd was routed, and about eight hundred buffaloes lay dead or wounded. The next day a wooden cross was planted in the mountains. Says a historian describing this period:

"From the first, the missionaries had learned to look upon the time of the buffalo hunt as most favorable for teaching Christian doctrine to the Indians. They were then most comfortable and correspondingly amiable, and in the long evenings and longer days, when they sat sunning themselves while the women prepared the meat of the last kill, the Indian warrior smoked his pipe and listened with pleasure to the old story of the redemption."

So began the long service of Father Lacombe, "the praying-man, the man of good heart." As chaplain, physician, counselor, peacemaker, he won the love of his untamed flock.

HEALING THE SICK

"They were a beautiful race, then—those children of the prairies," he declared. Mass was held in the Father's tepee. Wood-smoke scented the altar linen, and travel frayed the robe of the nomadic priest.

At Fort Edmonton, on the Saskatchewan, a still larger field awaited. As a physician to the Blackfeet during a scarlet-fever scourge the tireless Father won the hearts of these fiery tribes. With almost no resources the little missions grew. Devoted Indians built houses and chapels. Cornfields were planted, corn mills constructed, and schools for the children followed the humble churches.

It was Father Lacombe's habit to found a settlement, leave it to the care of some younger priest, and push on to the wilds with his Red Cross flag, his medicines and his plow. He foresaw the time when the buffalo herd would fail, and he wanted to prepare his people for the dark days of change. Food, clothing, tepees, weapons — everything the Indian needed was largely provided by the buffalo. A new way of life must be learned.

Taken desperately ill, the priest awaited death cheerfully. "I will die happy among my neophytes," he declared. "I will minister to them as long as I have strength."

But with health restored, he wrote joyfully: "Hurrah for the prairies! I am in my element. I feel like a king here, a new Moses in this new Land of Israel."

While in camp with the Blackfeet he was awakened by the bullets of a band of Crees. The priest was alert and fearless. He rushed out with his Red Cross flag, shouting to the warriors.

But they could not hear or recognize him in the tumult of the attack. A bullet struck his forehead, and a Blackfoot cried out, "Dogs, you have killed your Black-robe!"

Then the Crees ceased firing and withdrew. The wound proved slight, and Father Lacombe reappeared at Edmonton on Christmas Eve, to the great joy of the Crees.

On a trip over the plains to collect funds for his missions, the priest and some Indian friends were almost starved. They had only soup made from moccasins and old skins which had been used for bags.

"Up to that time," he confessed, "in my sermons and instructions to the Indians I had proclaimed that those who did not want to work should not eat. But now, after such an experience I have changed my ideas, and I have taken the resolution to share my last mouthful with anyone who is hungry."

SMALLPOX RAVAGES THE BLACKFEET

Poverty, hunger, thirst, cold and disease, all were a part of the priest's lot. Smallpox swept a camp of 2,700 Crees in 400 tepees. Father Lacombe took care of the sick and dug graves for the dead. His simple heroism in the face of the plague moved the warriors more than any sermons or prayers. After this the Black-robe was always welcome.

General Sir William Butler wrote: "No other man but Father Lacombe could pass from one hostile camp to another—suspected nowhere, welcomed everywhere, carrying as it were the 'truce of God' with him wherever he went."

As time went on, matters grew worse for the Indian, and Father Lacombe grieved over the destitute Blackfeet. Says his biographer, Miss Hughes:

"He had known them in their pride, kings of the open plains in their barbaric power, brave, proud, honorable and hospitable; dwellers in frail skin lodges, yet lords of all the outer world. Now he heard of them as miserable dependents upon the charity of mounted police and missionaries."

Whiskey-peddlers brought vice and destruction in their wake. But the tireless Father toiled on, bronzed and eagle-eyed as one of his Indian charges. He was made permanent chaplain for the workmen who were building the Canadian Pacific Railway, and he exerted a splendid influence over the rough camps of men, which included many types and nationalities. His work was praised by the president of the company and by contractors who employed the men.

Father Lacombe's willingness to understand and make allowances for the temper of his Indians is seen in his "picture-catechism," planned to catch the attention of the imaginative redmen. It represented a history of mankind, from the Creation to the missionary activities of the church. It was printed by the thousands, and used in the work of the Catholic missionaries all over the world.

On a visit to Europe the priest was welcomed by the Pope and by the great statesmen of England, who recognized what he was doing for Canada. He sought aid for the French-Canadians, but was more successful in England than in France. But he longed for his wild prairies. In England he says:

"I am writing from a nobleman's palace, but it is not as precious as my poetic tent in the wilderness, where I wrote on my knees my sermons in Cree and Blackfeet."

In an address in England, Sir John Macdonald declared: "The finest moral police force in the world is found in the priesthood of French Canada." No more heroic figure could be found among this loyal band than that of Father Lacombe, the black-robe voyageur, the brother of every man of whatever color or creed. You feel his influence still in the life of the great Northwest.

BROTHER TO THE INDIANS

He was happy to return to end his days among the western camps. And he must have been thrilled by the tribute paid him by Chief Crowfoot, who by his magnificent personality stirred an English audience at a reception in Ottawa. Said this Indian: "This man is our brother; not only our Father, as the white people call him, but our brother. He is one of our people. When we weep, he is sad with us; when we laugh, he laughs with us. We love him. He is our brother."

The Indians did well to realize his worth. He brought them ideals of peace, and justice, and brotherly helpfulness. He was able to do much toward the difficult adjustment of Indian and white settler, and his line of missions was a tangible evidence of the splendid dreams which stirred his soul. It is pleasant to know that such men as Father Lacombe were successful in showing the Indians the highest qualities of the white race, and to erase in a measure the memory of early wrongs which the red-man had been made to suffer.

THE STORY OF LAURA SECORD

EDITED BY BLISS CARMAN

In the early years of the nineteenth century the great Napoleon was fighting England. He was fighting her on many a bloody battlefield; and he was fighting her in other ways, doing his best to ruin British trade and shipping. He forbade any country to trade with Great Britain, and his ships watched the seas, ready to attack any vessel carrying goods to British ports.

King George's ministers replied by forbidding any nation to trade with France, and threatened to seize all ships carrying goods to French ports. Here was a state of things likely to ruin the trade of many lands. The United States did a great deal of trading with France, and the Americans were very angry with King George and his government for the Orders in Council, as the decree was called. They quite forgot that Napoleon had begun the quarrel by forbidding people to trade with Britain.

Great Britain, being an island, has always needed a large navy to watch her shores. At this time it was difficult to find enough sailors to man her ships, and sometimes, too, the sailors would run away. So the British claimed the right to search all ships belonging to neutral countries (that is, all countries taking neither one side nor the other in the quarrel), in order to find runaway sailors. Countries at war have always had this right, but it made the Americans angry, and on June 18, 1812, they declared war against England once more.

The Americans of course did not sail across the sea to fight Great Britain there. They had no thought of that. But they would have been glad to possess another and much nearer land. They marched over into Canada, and carried the war into that country. The Canadians had really nothing to do with the quarrel, and the Americans thought that Canada would not wish to fight for England, because a large part of Canada was settled by French people and had only lately been conquered by England. They were much mistaken. The French of Quebec had been allowed complete self-government under British rule—had been allowed to keep all their national customs, beliefs, and habits—and they remained loyal to England.

If you look on the map, you will see that all across the continent of North America the United States and Canada lie side by side. The line where one country touches another is called a frontier. Canada had seventeen thousand miles of coast and frontier to defend, and not six thousand men to do it with. And Great Britain, fighting in Europe against Napoleon, had few soldiers to spare.

But the people of Canada, both French and English, gathered to defend their homes. Many Indians, too, well pleased with British rule, joined them, and the Americans found they had no easy task in front of them.

A British officer named Fitzgibbon had been sent to hold a post called Beaver Dams, about twelve miles from Niagara. He had only sixty men, half of whom were Indians. The post was important, and the Americans made up their minds to seize it. With great secrecy they made their preparations to take the place by surprise, for a few miles off, at a place called Twelve Mile

JAMES SECORD OVERHEARD THEIR PLANS

Creek, lay another force of two hundred men. The Americans hoped to surprise Fitzgibbon so that he should have no time to get help.

But the secret leaked out. A Canadian named James Secord, who was lying ill, overheard their arouse the suspicion of the sentinels. So she made no sign of haste. There was nothing to show that she was beginning a journey. In order to deceive people more easily, she set out slowly driving a cow before her, as if she were taking

SHE SET OUT DRIVING A COW BEFORE HER

talk and learned their plans. He had fought with Brock at Queenstown Heights, where he had been badly wounded, and he was still unable to move.

With five hundred men, fifty horses, and two cannons, the Americans were marching upon the handful of men at Beaver Dams. Secord knew this, but could do nothing. To the helpless sick man the knowledge was torture. Only twenty miles away his fellow-countrymen were awaiting certain death, and there was no means of warning them! There was no man he could send, for all the country was watched by American sentinels. Even if any man had been willing to risk his life, Secord knew of none he could trust. But there was one person that he could trust—his wife. To her he whispered the thought that tormented him.

"They must all die," he said, "for lack of a word of warning!"

"But that shall not be," said Laura Secord; "I will go."

So as the sun rose on a still June morning, Laura Secord started on her long and dangerous walk. And she had to be very careful not to it home to be milked. So she passed the American sentinels in safety. Slowly down the country road she passed, with excitement in her heart, you may be sure, but not a trace of it in her look or manner.

The birds were singing in the dawn, the air was sweet with the scent of wild flowers, and as that brave woman walked, her dress brushed the dew from the grass. But she had no eyes nor ears for the beauty of the day. With beating heart she strolled along. And at last the edge of the forest was reached. Under the shadow of the great trees passed the woman and the cow. Soon they were deep in the forest, shut from all eyes. Then there was no more need of pretense. Leaving her cow to find its way home as best it might, Laura ran through the cool, still woods upon her heroic errand. The way was rough, but she did not hesitate. On and on she went, panting, breathless, now stopping a moment to rest, now hurrying on again, startled by a rustle in the bushes, trembling at the call of some wild animal, but always pressing forward to the end of her journey.

FOR TWO HOURS THE FIGHT AGAINST AN UNSEEN FOE LASTED

She was not made of the stuff that turns aside for difficulties.

A walk of twenty miles along a level, well-made road may not seem a great task for a strong woman used to life in the country. But to go twenty miles through a pathless wilderness, up hill and down, over rocky streams, through swamp and bog, haunted every moment by danger of discovery, is a task that needs all the strength and courage of a brave woman.

Hour after hour Laura walked and ran and scrambled onward. The sun rose high and beat down in the hot woods; the brambles caught and tore her clothes; the stones bruised her feet. Still she pushed on. At last the sun began to sink; twilight came, and the moon rose, before she neared the end of her journey. Just as she thought her labor was over, Indians rushed out upon her from behind some trees and barred her path. For a moment it seemed that all her toil and courage had been of no use, and that a death of torture was to be her fate. Then with relief she saw that the Indians were friendly, and in a few minutes she was led before Fitzgibbon.

Quickly Laura's story was told, and as the soldier listened he bowed in respect before the brave woman. Then with glowing words of thanks and praise ringing in her ears, she was led away to a nearby farmhouse to rest.

Fitzgibbon made his plans quickly. First he sent a messenger hurrying toward Twelve Mile Creek to ask for help. Then he ordered his Indians to scatter through the woods and watch for the approach of the enemy.

The night passed quietly, but as day dawned, the gleam of steel was seen and the tramp of men was heard. As the Americans came on, the Indians, yelling horribly, fired upon them from all sides. They made so much noise and fired with such deadly aim, keeping out of sight all the time, that the Americans believed there were hundreds against them. For two hours this fight against an unseen foe lasted. Then the Americans began to waver. Their leader was uncertain what to do. Believing himself surrounded, he hesitated whether to go on or to go back. At this moment Fitzgibbon, at the head of his thirty redcoats, appeared bearing a flag of truce. The firing ceased, and after a few minutes' parley the American commander surrendered.

Fitzgibbon had hardly expected to succeed so easily. Now he scarcely knew what to do with the prisoners he had made. How could thirty soldiers and a few savages guard five hundred? But soon, by good fortune, two hundred men arrived from Twelve Mile Creek, and his difficulties were at an end.

Canada did not forget Laura Secord and her brave deed. Nor did Britain forget her. Years later, when the Prince of Wales, afterward King Edward VII, visited Canada, he found time in the midst of many balls, parties, and official engagements, to go to see an old woman, and hear from her own lips how, when she was young, she had carried a message through woods and wilderness to save her country from defeat.

SIR JOHN A. MACDONALD, THE FIRST PREMIER OF THE DOMINION OF CANADA

BY W. J. HEALY

In 1837, the year in which Abraham Lincoln hung out his shingle as a lawyer in Springfield, Illinois, young John Alexander Macdonald did likewise in the Canadian town of Kingston, on Lake Ontario. Like Lincoln, he had to defend himself more than once with his fists. The times were rough. Many years later, when he was an old man, he used to tell the story of his first case. He and the lawyer opposing him went at each other vigorously with words at first, and then with blows. They clinched and fought in open court. The judge ordered the court crier to separate them. The court crier was an old man, who was a great admirer of Macdonald. In obedience to the judge's order, he circled round the two fighting lawyers, shouting as loud as he could "Order in the court! Order in the court!" But coming close to Macdonald he said in a low voice, "Hit him again, John!" Often in later life Macdonald, who as a political leader had the devoted loyalty of his followers, used to say that in a hard-fought contest he seemed to hear an encouraging voice saying, "Hit him again, John!"

It was in that same year of 1837 that the rebellion broke out in Upper Canada (as the present Province of Ontario was then called), which resulted in the establishment of democratic self-government. Young Macdonald shouldered his flintlock musket on the side of law and order. In the year following occurred the brief invasion of Canada by a party of armed men from the State of New York, who crossed the St. Lawrence River at Ogdensburg and captured a windmill near Prescott on the Canadian side, which they held for eight days, when they were dislodged and captured. Their leader was Von Shoultz, a Pole by birth, who was tried by court-martial, condemned, and hanged. Macdonald did all that was possible in defense of the unfortunate Von Shoultz; and his connection with that case did a great deal to establish his reputation as a lawyer.

Life in those early years was a hard struggle for him. He had had to begin as a boy of fifteen to earn his own living and help support his family. His father, Hugh Macdonald, had been a merchant in Scotland, and failing at that had started a factory for making bandanna handkerchiefs. The factory failed, too; and in 1820 the family sailed from Glasgow to seek a new home across the Atlantic in Canada. Hugh Macdonald tried farming for a time, after which he tried storekeeping; but he prospered at neither. Nor was he successful at his next, and final, venture as a miller. His eldest son, John Alexander, thus found heavy responsibilities placed upon his shoulders at an early age. He told the story once in his later life that at the time of a general visitation of sickness in Kingston, when many died, he came home from school one day to find the door of the house locked. He had to climb in at the kitchen window. The whole family were ill in bed, and for several days he had to attend to them. Among his duties at that time was the baking of the family's supply of bread; not knowing how to go about doing it, he carried his sister downstairs on his back and placed her on a couch before the kitchen fire, and under her supervision kneaded the dough.

An earlier memory of his dated back to his seventh year, when he and his brother James, two years younger, were left in the care of an old soldier named Kennedy, while their father and mother and sister went to visit a neighboring family. Kennedy took the two little boys to a tavern, and compelled them to drink some gin with him. Continuing his own drinking, he became violent; and John, taking James by the hand, started home. The drunken man followed them with loud threatenings of what he would do to them if they did not come back and stay with him. The younger boy tripped and fell, and as he lay on the ground, Kennedy struck him with a heavy stick. The child, already made ill by the liquor and terrified by Kennedy's behavior, collapsed, and soon afterward died in convulsions.

His father died the year before John Alexander began to practice law. His mother it was who, to use his own words, "kept the family together." From her he inherited his energy and strength of will. He loved her with constant and affectionate devotion; she did not die until he was a man of forty-seven and had already made a great success of his life. The life-span of John Alexander Macdonald covered a space of Canadian history in which the struggle for the establishment of government by the people was fought and won, and the establishment of the principles of democracy was followed by developments which led to the formation of the federal union of the Dominion of Canada. Macdonald became the leading figure in the work of bringing about this union, which began in 1867 with only four Provinces, and at the time of his death, in 1891, numbered seven Provinces linked together by a transcontinental railway.

From 1867 until his death he was at the head of the Dominion Government as Premier, except for the years between 1873 and 1878, when he and the political party led by him was out of power on account of the manner in which certain wealthy men who were interested in getting contracts for building the transcontinental railway, which has just been mentioned, furnished large sums of money to be used in helping the political party led by Macdonald to win in the elections. Not that he himself was ever accused of taking a dollar for himself dishonestly. One great lesson of his life is that he pulled himself successfully out of those dark days, and gained completely the confidence of the Canadian people again. He was triumphantly restored to power in 1878; and during all the remaining years of his life he was the captain of the Canadian ship of state.

It was on the formation of the Dominion that he was given the title of "Sir" to wear in front of his name. Even Wilfrid Laurier, who became Premier of Canada in 1896, and who had previously declared that he was "a democrat to the hilt," had not found it possible to avoid escaping the title of "Sir" which was conferred on him when he visited London in 1897 for the Jubilee celebration of Queen Victoria's completion of the sixtieth year of her reign. The feeling of the Canadian people against this went on growing until in 1917, the year before the end of the World War, the Parliament of Canada passed a resolution suggesting to England that no more titles be granted to Canadians.

When John Alexander Macdonald became a

"Sir," some of his admirers announced that he was descended from the Macdonalds, Lords of the Isles in Scotland, whose line goes back to legendary times. One of them, Alexander, who had been at war with King James I of Scotland, was

SIR JOHN A. MACDONALD, FIRST PREMIER OF CANADA

invited by that monarch, with a great show of friendliness, to meet him at Inverness, where he was treacherously seized by the King's soldiers, and on Easter Sunday in 1429, in the royal chapel at Holyrood, he had to appear clothed only in his shirt and drawers, and on his knees, holding a naked sword by the point, implore the King's forgiveness. One close friend of the Canadian statesman said: "That chieftain has a descendant and namesake who would never have walked into the trap of the Scottish King!" Certainly no belief was more strongly held in Canada than that nobody could outwit "Sir John," as he was known from coast to coast, though older people continued to call him by his former appellation, "John A."

He had a wonderful influence over his fellow-countrymen. His followers served him with unfailing devotion. Among the things believed of him was that he rarely if ever forgot anybody with whom he had once spoken, but could always greet him by name. One great source of his power and popularity was his kindliness and humor. Innumerable stories about his good nature and his wit became current throughout all the Provinces of Canada. He was not merely popular, he was beloved, because with all his great abilities, people felt that he was sincerely one who loved his fellowmen and did not hold himself above them.

It was said by one of his political opponents that fortune always favored "John A." The truth of the matter was that he was unfailingly bold and resourceful in taking advantage of every opportunity. After his party was defeated in the elections of 1873 he did not lose heart, but set to work immediately to prepare for the next elections, which came in 1878. In the years between 1873 and 1878 there came hard times in Canada. There was scarcity of employment and wages were low, the farmers were getting low prices for their products, the manufacturers were not prospering, and the general discontent throughout the country made the party that was in power unpopular. "John A." and his friends held meetings throughout the country, and announced a tariff policy, which they named the National Policy; they promised to introduce that policy, if they were returned to power, and predicted confidently that it would bring back good times to the country. In the elections of 1878 "John A." and his party, the Conservatives, were triumphantly returned to power. They proceeded without delay to introduce their promised tariff policy of protection.

About the end of the year 1879 came the beginning of an era of prosperity in Canada. The good times were said by the supporters of Macdonald and his National Policy to be due to him and that policy. The opposite political party said that there had been a period of world-wide hard times, which had now come to its end, and that Canada was sharing in the return of good times to every country. In any case, the Canadian people were satisfied, and Macdonald and his colleagues in the new Dominion Government received the full benefit of the general satisfaction. The building of the Canadian Pacific Railway across Canada to the Pacific Ocean was proceeded with vigorously, and was completed in 1885. Sir John Macdonald had several other political campaigns to fight, but he was successful in every one of them, and continued to be at the head of the Canadian Government until his death in June, 1891.

He had a genius for managing men and for political leadership. Around no other name in Canadian history gathers so much of story and legend. The great majority loved him and trusted him. He had a humor which the people understood. For example, there was a Colonel Playfair, who bothered Sir John about the construction of a colonization road of which he desired to be appointed superintendent. Finally, failing to get what he wanted, he went to Ottawa and sent an urgent message to Sir John to come out of the Cabinet chamber. When Sir John saw him, he grasped him by both hands and exclaimed, "Well, Colonel Playfair, is that you? I am delighted to see you! We have been discussing a military matter which we cannot decide. Now you, with your military experience, will be able to solve the question. How many grains of gunpowder would have to be put under a bull's tail to blow his horns off?" And with that Sir John disappeared again through the door into the Cabinet chamber, and left the Colonel gasping. Later on Sir John appointed the Colonel to the position he desired.

One of the rules by which Sir John A. Macdonald guided his life was that a man should cherish no resentments. "It is a fatal mistake," he said, "for a public man to be led by his hates." He cherished his friends; but he never let dislike of an opponent prevent him from doing justice to an opponent's good qualities. His strongest characteristic was his love of Canada and his desire to serve Canada. His daily thought might well be expressed in the words of Daniel Webster: "Let our object be our country, our whole country, and nothing but our country." Above all others of the statesmen who are remembered in Canadian history as the Fathers of Confederation he was the greatest. In the supreme art of managing and governing men he was gifted as few men in any land have been gifted; he would have been a leader in any land. When he entered public life as a young man, Canada consisted of what are now the Provinces of Ontario and Quebec. There are still old people in Nova Scotia and the other Eastern Provinces of the Canada of today who when they say Canada mean what the word meant when they were young. The three Atlantic Provinces, namely, Nova Scotia, New Brunswick, and Prince Edward Island, are still spoken of by all Canadians as the Maritime Provinces, though Canada has also a vast maritime Province on the Pacific coast, namely, British Columbia. John Alexander Macdonald took the leading part in the work of linking up the scattered Provinces and Territories which lay across the map in disunion into the federal union of the Dominion of Canada, which consists now of nine Provinces spanning the continent, with Manitoba as the keystone of the arch.

He said in one of his greatest speeches: "I have fought the battle of Confederation, the battle of Union, the battle of the Dominion of Canada. It is no vain boast for me to say that there does not exist in Canada a man who has given more of his time, more of his heart, more of his wealth, or more of his intellect and power, such as they may be, for the good of this Dominion of Canada." On the day following his death, Sir Wilfrid Laurier, who some years later became Premier of Canada himself, said in the House of Commons at Ottawa: "His loss overwhelms us, as if, indeed, one of the institutions of the land had given way." The sorrow which was manifested from coast to coast throughout all the Provinces of the Dominion when he died gave convincing proof of how large a place he filled in the hearts and minds of his fellow-countrymen. Like his great successor in the premiership of the Dominion, he could say with truth at the close of his life that he had labored faithfully to make Canada a united country. He was in his seventy-seventh year when he died at Ottawa on June 6, 1891.

JOSEPH HOWE OF NOVA SCOTIA

BY W. J. HEALY

WHEN Joseph Howe was a boy his father taught him to box and to swim and to be good at games as well as at his books. One Sunday morning when he was in his fifth year his father took him after church down to the waterfront to see a large new ship which had just come into Halifax harbor from the West Indies. There were no steamships until Joseph Howe was a grown-up man; when he was a boy there were only sailing ships, and he used to watch them setting sail from Halifax for the West Indies with cargoes of fish and coal and lumber, and arriving back with cargoes of sugar and rum and molasses. On that Sunday morning his father, holding him by the hand as they walked down to the wharf, saw two men fighting. He called out to them to stop, and asked what they were fighting about. They paid no attention to him, but continued to roll on the ground and strike each other when they could.

"Here, hold my Bible and stick, Joe!" said Joseph Howe's father, who was a man of great strength. Taking hold of each of the two fighting men by the neck, he swung them round, half raised them from the ground, and then with a lunge from one shoulder, followed by a lunge from the other, he sent them sprawling in different directions. "Let this be a lesson to you," he said to the two men, taking back his Bible and walking-stick from the youthful Joe, "to behave yourselves on Sunday."

Joseph Howe was born in Halifax in 1804. At the age of thirteen he went to work in his father's printing office, and continued his education while learning his trade. The youngest hand in a printing office, being usually smudged with ink, was always called "the printer's devil." Young Joe Howe, being called as a witness in a trial, the lawyer who was questioning him said, "So you're the devil?" "Yes, sir, in the office, but not in the Courthouse!" he replied, with a look and gesture that threw the name back at his questioner, and caused laughter against the lawyer. He was a quick-witted boy, fond of fun and sports of all kinds, and was a great favorite; he played as hard as he worked. Thus he grew from a boy to a young man, mastering his trade, making himself an athlete, and at the same time enriching his mind.

As a young man it was his usual practice on summer nights before he went to bed to go for a swim in the Northwest Arm, the beautiful inlet of the Atlantic which extends from Halifax harbor for several miles behind the city. Howe's home during his whole life was the house in which he was born, on a hillside near the beach of the Arm, which is there not more than a quarter of a mile wide. An orchard of apple and cherry trees surrounded the house. One night as he was having his swim, he was seized with cramp. He knew that the thing to do when such a mishap befalls you in the water is to kick vigorously and throw yourself on your back and float; but a cramp seems to make a swimmer unable to do these things. Young Howe felt that he was about to drown in the darkness, alone; but, suddenly, his eye being turned toward his home on the hillside, he saw the candle being placed by his mother on the window-sill for him. The thought of his father and mother and of all that home meant to him, and of the grief of his father and mother if he were drowned, made him give so fiercely vigorous a kick that it drove the cramp out of his leg. He was able to swim to shore, where he sank down exhausted, and had to rest before he could go home. Often in the struggles of his later life, the thought of what he had been taught at home and of the noble purposes he was fighting for saved him and made him win out, just as that candle placed on the window-sill by his mother saved him from drowning by inspiring him to an effort into which he threw all his power of mind and body.

That experience did not make him give up swimming at night. He kept up that practice for many years, as he also kept up his cruises in his sailboat, his fishing and lobster-spearing, and his skating in the winter. He was only in his twenty-fourth year when he managed to make himself proprietor of a small weekly newspaper, and began his journeyings on horseback through all the districts of Nova Scotia, getting the people to subscribe for his paper and writing interestingly and humorously about his travels. His reports were printed in the paper week after week. He made himself at home in every nook and corner of his native Province. Everywhere he went he was liked. Before long he came to be known from end to end of Nova Scotia, and to be spoken of as "Joe Howe," the name by which he was popularly known not only in Nova Scotia but in the other Canadian Provinces until the end of his life.

His journeying on horseback throughout Nova Scotia and his visiting the people in their homes won for him their confidence, which grew into loyalty to him as their leader. Gradually he began criticizing and attacking the evils of the existing system in Nova Scotia, by which, as he wrote in his newspaper, "the hard earnings of the people were taken in taxes and lavished upon an aristocracy." The ruling families at first regarded him and his newspaper with scorn. Then, as they felt the growing strength of his attacks upon their power and privileges, they became angry. Young men of the aristocratic families talked of horsewhipping him and driving him from the country. On one occasion one of those young bloods, inflamed by drink, mounted his horse, sword in hand, and swore loudly he would kill Howe. He rode upon the wooden sidewalk in front of Howe's printing office and began to smash the windows, calling on Howe to come out. Howe was setting type at the time. He hastened out, pulled the young man from his horse, took his sword from him and threw him on his back in the street. The young man's friends took him away, shrieking in drunken rage against Howe. But he took care never to cross Howe's path again.

The government of Nova Scotia was then in the hands of a few families of wealth and social distinction, who considered themselves as of finer clay than the common herd of humanity, to which Joseph Howe and the great mass of the people of Nova Scotia belonged. Their manners and ways of life were modeled on those of the highest aristocratic circles on the other side of the Atlantic, of which some of those families were members. One of the grandees sent out from England to govern Nova Scotia was Lord Falkland, a young nobleman singularly handsome and singularly lacking in sense. The fact that his wife was a relative of King William IV increased the haughtiness which was his chief characteristic. Howe in carrying on the campaign for the establishment of government by the people, of the people, for the people, covered Lord Falkland with so much ridicule that he resigned the governorship and returned to England; King William consoled him for his unpleasant experience in Nova Scotia by having him appointed governor of Bombay. Before he sailed away from Halifax, Lord Falkland had his carriage-horses shot, lest after his departure they might be bought by any of "the common people" and be used by them, after having had the honor and glory (as he considered it) of drawing himself and Lady Falkland in their state carriage.

In the course of his campaign, which extended over a number of years before it was finally successful, Howe printed in his newspaper, *The Nova Scotian*, an article accusing the magistrates in Halifax of carelessness, inefficiency, and corruption. They prosecuted him for criminal libel, counting upon being able to put him in prison and so silence him. He sought legal advice, but every lawyer told him it was a hopeless case. He devoted a week to studying law books and preparing his defense; and defended himself in court without the help of any lawyer. His address to the jury was so eloquent and powerful that they brought in a verdict in his favor, amid the great rejoicings of the people of Halifax. After that he was elected to the Legislature, and became the recognized leader of the fight for popular self-government. In the end the fight was won. The irresponsible power of the governor and his executive council was done away with, and the Legislature, elected by the people, was made the really governing body.

Not long after his election to the Legislature, Howe was challenged to a duel by the son of Chief Justice Haliburton on account of certain things he had said about the Chief Justice in a speech. He had on several previous occasions been challenged, but took no notice of the challenges. Now he felt that he had to fight a duel, or be branded as a coward. The meeting took place at dawn on a spring morning. Haliburton fired first, and narrowly missed hitting Howe, who then discharged his pistol in the air. Howe went home to breakfast, and was so silent at that meal that Mrs. Howe said, "One would think you had been at a funeral!" Then for the first time he told her of the duel. On the day before he had written two letters for publication in case he should be killed. In the letter for his wife, after telling her the provision he had made for her and the children, he wrote: "There shall be no blood on my hand. Yours till death."

In the letter addressed to the people of Nova Scotia he wrote, after declaring that several attempts had already been made to make him pay the penalty of life for fighting the people's fight: "Knowing that even a shadow of an imputation upon my moral courage would incapacitate me for serving my country with vigor and success hereafter, I feel that I must hazard my life, rather than blight all prospects of being useful. If I fall, cherish the principles I have taught, forgive my errors, protect my children." Very soon afterward he was challenged by Sir Rupert George, another member of the ruling caste. Howe replied in a letter in which he said: "Having never had any personal quarrel with Sir Rupert George, I should certainly not fire at him, if I went out; and I have no great fancy for being shot at whenever public officials whose abilities I may happen to contrast with their emoluments think fit to consider political arguments and general illustrations 'insolent and offensive.'" Howe had no more need of paying attention to challenges. He had given

JOSEPH HOWE

proof that he possessed the courage of his convictions.

Before he was forty years old Howe had succeeded in bringing about a complete change in the system of government of Nova Scotia. Having won the battle for self-government, he turned next to the problems of transportation. He was the first man in British North America to have the vision of the possibilities of railway expansion; and he lived to see much of his vision realized. In 1851 he said in a speech in Halifax, before the first stretch of Canadian railway was in existence: "I believe that many in this hall will live to hear the whistle of the steam engine in the passes of the Rocky Mountains, and to make the journey from Halifax to the Pacific in five or six days." These words were uttered sixteen years before the Canadian Provinces united to form the Dominion, and thirty-four years before the steel of the first Canadian transcontinental railway was laid through the passes of the Rocky Mountains.

Howe, in addition to being responsible for the construction of the first stretch of railway on Canadian soil, also led the way in securing the establishment of the first steamship service between Great Britain and Canada by his friend, Samuel Cunard, of Halifax. Still earlier in his career he had been a leader in the work of laying the foundations in Nova Scotia of the first Canadian public school system. His whole life was devoted to work for the welfare and progress of his native land and for the betterment of its conditions of life. He said truly in one of his speeches: "You seat eight or nine men on red cushions in gilded chairs, with nothing to do but pocket their salaries, and call that a government! To such a pageant I have no desire to belong. Those who aspire to govern others should be afraid neither of the saddle by day nor of the lamp by night. In advance of the general intelligence they should lead the way to improvement and prosperity. I would rather assume the staff of Moses and struggle with the perils of the wilderness and the waywardness of the multitude, than be a golden calf elevated in gorgeous inactivity, the object of a worship which debased."

No State or Province has ever been loved more strongly by a favorite son than Joseph Howe loved Nova Scotia. In one of his speeches in England he said: "You boast of the fertility and beauty of England. Why, there's one valley in Nova Scotia where you can ride for fifty miles under apple blossoms. Talk of the value of land, I know an acre of rocks near Halifax worth more than an acre in London. Scores of hardy fishermen catch their breakfast there in five minutes, all the year round, and no tillage is needed to make the production equally good for a thousand years to come." He said once to an audience of Nova Scotian schoolboys: "Boys, brag of your country! When I'm abroad I brag of everything that Nova Scotia is, or has, or can produce. And when they beat me at everything else, I turn on them and say, 'How high does your tide rise?'" One boast can always be made by Nova Scotians; nowhere else in the world do the tides rise as high as in the Bay of Fundy.

No other Canadian public man has excelled Joseph Howe in breadth of view, in eloquence, or in the power of the pen. None other among the makers of Canada better deserves to be an outstanding figure in the national memory of the Canadian people. Not only was he a statesman of vision and creative power and true love of country; he was a warm-hearted man, full of love of humanity. He was genuine and sincere to the core of his being.

It was fitting that Joseph Howe should die in the honorable position of occupant of Government House in Halifax, the position held long before by Lord Falkland, and that he should die, as he did, on his feet, a month after attaining that post of highest dignity in his native Province. His death was on June 1, 1873. A column of Nova Scotia granite marks his grave near Halifax, within sound of the murmuring pines and the salt sea water he knew and loved as a boy. His statue in bronze stands near the building of the Legislative Assembly, which so often rang to his eloquence. His name will live in the memory of his countrymen.

SIR WILFRID LAURIER
BY W. J. HEALY

THOUSANDS of French-Canadians work during the winters in the lumber woods. In the summer of 1911 one of these loggers who had been two years in the far northern regions of Quebec came down home to his native parish near Tadousac. When his family were telling him about the notable things that had happened while he was in the lumber woods, they mentioned that King Edward VII had died the year before, and George V was now King in London. He said: "Dat George you spik about, who get de King job, say, he mus' sure have some beeg pull wit' Laurier—hey?" Sir Wilfrid Laurier, who had been Premier of Canada since 1896, was thus thought by the simple-minded "habitants" of his native Province to be a potentate with far-reaching power in the world at large. Throughout all the Provinces of Canada he was immensely popular.

He was the first native of the French-Canadian Province of Quebec to become Premier of the Dominion. Most of the French-Canadian families go back for more than two hundred years on Quebec soil. The father of the future Premier was Carolus Laurier, a farmer near the village of St. Lin. His family had settled in Quebec in 1666, six generations before. In addition to being a farmer, he carried on the business of land surveyor. He was a man of an inventive turn of mind. Dissatisfied with the old method of threshing wheat and oats and barley with a flail, he devised and constructed the first attempt at a threshing machine in Canada. It was not a striking success, but it attracted a great deal of attention. Another invention for which he took out a patent looked like a clock; he fastened it on the dashboard of his buggy, and it registered the number of miles he traveled when he was going about the country as a land surveyor. It was a forerunner of the instrument which is now seen in every automobile.

Carolus Laurier was a man of strong character and ability. He realized early that his son Wilfrid was a boy of great natural gifts; and he determined that Wilfrid should have the best education it was within his means to provide. The boy spoke French as his mother-tongue, like all French-Canadians. His father realized the importance of his having an equally good command of the English language, and with that end in view sent him to live for several years in the Quebec village of New Glasgow, the center of a Scotch-Canadian settlement. In later years, when Sir Wilfrid was an honored visitor both in England and in France, his oratory in French was no less admired in France than his oratory in English was admired in England.

Wilfrid Laurier's mother died when he was six years old. He was not strong in his boyhood, and his father was greatly distressed about his health; but as he grew to manhood he became stronger. By wise care of his health and by exercise he made himself an exceptionally vigorous and long-lived man. From his earliest youth he gave signs of his liking for public affairs. Even as a boy he liked to attend political meetings and listen to the speeches. He studied law in Montreal, and it is recorded that in a speech he made to his fellow-students in 1864, when he was twenty-two years of age, he said he "would gladly devote his whole life to serve Canada and bring about true friendly understanding and concord between all the different elements of the Canadian people." In 1871 he was elected to the Quebec Legislature, in which he served until in 1877 he was elected to the Parliament of the Dominion of Canada, of which he was a member continuously during the remaining forty-two years of his life. In 1887, when he was forty-six years old, he was chosen the leader of the Liberal party then

out of office. In 1896 his party defeated the Conservative party in the Dominion elections, and he became Premier of Canada. The country was then suffering from hard times.

Soon after the Laurier administration began, prosperity returned to Canada. New settlers poured into the vast prairies of the Western Provinces in tens and scores of thousands from the United States and from Europe. The Laurier administration revised the tariff and introduced certain preferential duties in favor of manufac-

SIR WILFRID LAURIER
The first French-Canadian to become Premier of Canada

tured goods coming from Great Britain; and later on negotiated a reciprocity arrangement with the United States, which, however, failed to be ratified by the votes of the Canadian electors in an election in which the issue was confused with others. One of the first things to which he gave attention after he became Premier was the completion of the Canadian canal system. The construction of new lines of railway all across the continent was gone on with vigorously, Canada's ocean ports and harbors and navigable rivers were improved, a Railway Commission, like that in the United States, was created, a Labor Department instituted, postal rates were reduced, and free rural mail delivery introduced, a Canadian mint was established, trade treaties with various countries were negotiated, and in many other ways the welfare and progress of the country were furthered.

In London and in Paris he did important work in helping to lay the foundation for the alliance between Great Britain and France which proved its strength in the World War. President Loubet of the French Republic, who signed that agreement as the French head of state, declared afterward that Sir Wilfrid Laurier had "implanted in his mind and confirmed the belief that France and Great Britain should be united by strong bonds of friendship and alliance." Sir Wilfrid also played an important part in advocating the policy of giving the South African Union self-government, a policy which prevailed. Self-government had been established in Canada, in Australia, and in New Zealand long before. Laurier was all his life a leader in the development of self-government, and was one of the earliest as he was one of the most eloquent exponents of the conception of the Empire as "a sisterhood of self-governing nations."

When he was knighted in London in 1897 and became Sir Wilfrid Laurier, instead of plain Mr. Wilfrid Laurier, the news came as a surprise to his followers in Canada, because he had in previous years most emphatically declared himself opposed to all such titles. Upon the facts coming to light, it appeared that he had been placed in a position in which he could not very well refuse the knighthood. The occasion of his visit to London in 1897 as Canada's chief representative was the Diamond Jubilee of Queen Victoria, in celebration of the completion of the sixtieth year of her reign. The aged Queen made him sit at her right hand at the state dinner in Windsor Castle. When Mr. Laurier took his place at the table, he found a card before him, on which the Queen had written: "The Right Honorable Sir Wilfrid Laurier." There was no way out for him but to accept the title from the great and good Queen. Titled, or untitled, he was himself; no title could confer upon him any honor equal to that which he already possessed, by his own high character and achievement. The Canadian people understood that Wilfrid Laurier accepted the title of "Sir" in front of his name because, in the circumstances, he could not do otherwise. Twenty years later, in 1917, when the Parliament of Canada passed its declaration against any further titles in Canada, Sir Wilfrid Laurier said (Queen Victoria being then dead) that he would gladly see a bonfire made of all such titles, and would throw his upon the bonfire, too. He was a true democrat to the end of his life.

Richard Harding Davis, in his description in *Harper's Magazine* of the scenes in and around Westminster Abbey at the time of the Diamond Jubilee of Queen Victoria, wrote that the two individuals who, after the venerable, white-haired Queen herself, most aroused the enthusiasm of the hundreds of thousands of people who thronged the streets of London, were the aged Field Marshal, General Lord Roberts, whose military career contained so many instances of heroism, and Sir Wilfrid Laurier. Sir Wilfrid was a tall and strikingly handsome man, who looked what he was, the born leader of men. Honors were showered upon him in England and in France. But he never lost his head, and never forgot that he was, in his own proud words, "a democrat to the hilt." Pomp and display did not appeal to him. Genuine and sincere himself, he had a clear-sighted perception of the same qualities in others. He had no use for flatterers or pretenders.

The man in all history whom he admired most was Abraham Lincoln. In his early manhood he began to collect books about Lincoln; it was his ambition to possess every book of any real value about Lincoln, and when he died a section of his library consisted wholly of such books. When he went to Washington for the first time he spent his first day in that city in visiting the places consecrated by association with Lincoln. His likeness to Lincoln in rising above strife and turmoil was often commented on. He never failed to stand steadfastly by his principles and convictions; but at the same time he never failed to speak and act with broadmindedness and toleration.

This spirit was manifested in his last speech in London, in which, turning to a number of young men who were present, he said: "As for you who stand to-day on the threshold of life, I shall remind you that many problems rise before you, problems of race division, problems of creed differences, problems of economic conflict, problems of national duty and national aspiration. Let me tell you that for the solution of these problems you have a safe guide, an unfailing light, if you remember that faith is better than doubt, and love is better than hate. Banish doubt and hate from your life. Let your souls be ever open to the strong promptings of faith and the gentle influence of brotherly love. Be adamant against the haughty; be gentle and kind to the weak. Let your aim and your purpose, in good report or in ill, in victory or in defeat, be so to live, so to strive, so to serve as to do your part to raise the standard of life." Speaking in 1913 to a large assembly of students in Toronto, he said: "My young friends, go out into the world to service. Make the highest thought of service your inspiration. Problems there are—big problems. To-morrow and the day after to-morrow it will be your turn to grapple with them. Serve God and your country. Be firm in the right, as God gives you to see the right. You may not always succeed. Progress is often punctuated with reverses. You may meet reverse—but the following day stand up again and renew the conflict for truth, and justice will triumph in the end."

His whole career was guided by the principles to which he gave expression in a speech to the Acadians of Nova Scotia, to whom he said: "Thank Providence that we live in a country of absolute freedom and liberty. Let us always bear in mind our duties, for duty is always inherent in right. Our fathers had to labor to secure these rights. Now let us fulfill our part. Three years ago, when visiting England, I visited one of the marvels of Gothic architecture which the hand of genius, guided by an unerring faith, had made a harmonious whole, in which granite, marble, oak and other materials were blended. That cathedral is an image of the nation I hope to see Canada become. As long as I live, as long as I have the power to labor in the service of my country, I shall always repel the idea of changing the nature of its different elements. I want the marble to remain marble; I want the granite to remain the granite; I want the oak to remain the oak; I want the sturdy Scotchman to remain the Scotchman; I want the brainy Englishman to remain the Englishman; I want the warm-hearted Irishman to remain the Irishman; I want to take all the elements in the Canadian people and build a nation that will be foremost among the nations of the world."

He was nearly half a century in active politics. His first recorded speech is a pledge to devote himself to the cause of conciliation, harmony, and concord among the different elements of the Canadian people. He was before all else a patriot. His devotion to Canada was his strongest feeling.

During his Premiership, from 1896 to 1911, Canada had its greatest period of expansion. Speaking at the beginning of the twentieth century, he stirred every Canadian heart by claiming the new century for Canada. "The nineteenth century," he said, "has been a century that has been remarkable for the marvelous development of the United States. During the whole period of that cycle of time the United States has been the great center of attraction for all the world. But a new star has arisen upon the horizon, a star not in the orbit of the American constellation, but a star standing by itself resplendent in the western sky, and it is toward that star that every immigrant, every traveler, every man who leaves the land of his ancestors to come and seek a home for himself, turns his gaze." Fittingly the London *Morning Post* said of him on his sixty-sixth birthday: "No other statesman could have accomplished so much in the space of a lifetime as the great French-Canadian who combines an imaginative eloquence unsurpassed in British history with the charm and courtesy of a cultivated Frenchman."

When Sir Wilfrid Laurier died on February 17, 1920, in his seventy-eighth year, there were no warmer tributes paid to his memory than by the leading journals of the United States. "Among Canadian statesmen of our day," said the *New York Tribune,* "Sir Wilfrid Laurier ranked first. The Canada of the present is in a large measure his work. His horizon was spacious." The New York *Sun* said: "The fifteen years in which he served as Premier saw the greatest growth of the Dominion in railroads, trade, and agriculture, of any period in its marvelous history." Said the New York *World:* "His name is one of the greatest in the history of the sister republic"—thereby making note of Canada's advance as a self-governing nation, and while not a republic, a sister democracy. And the *New York Times* said: "No other Colonial statesman so impressed the English. This French-Canadian, this first French-Canadian Premier, this bilingual orator, this personage of suavity, dignity, and distinction, has not left his like behind. Resourceful, subtle, a master of debate, the unmatched leader of the Liberals, he seemed to belong to the generation of Disraeli and Palmerston and Gladstone."

Speaking within a few weeks after the invasion of Belgium which began the World War in 1914, at a great mass meeting held in Toronto under the auspices of the American Aid Society, an organization of American residents of that city, Sir Wilfrid Laurier said: "All vestiges of political differences have vanished. This war must be fought to a finish, and Canada will help, to its last man and its last dollar. Arms must not be laid down until the principle fought for is vindicated, and the day has come when right takes the place of might. There can be no peace in the world until it knows that it is to be governed by truth, liberty, and justice." Later on, in regard to conscription, he found himself at variance with the majority of the Canadian people. But there was never any question of the steadfast sincerity of his patriotism.

Not many days before he died he said: "I am content to leave my record to the judgment of men's thoughts and to future generations of Canadians." The demonstration of feeling throughout Canada, from ocean to ocean, when he died, proved that those words were justified. Sir Wilfrid Laurier was the seventh Premier of Canada, and the only one whose tomb is in Ottawa, the capital of the Dominion.

THE ROYAL NORTHWEST MOUNTED POLICE

"As LITTLE gold lace, fuss and feathers as possible," was the instruction for the planning of uniforms for the Royal Northwest Mounted Police when this famous frontier patrol was first organized. The men were required to be good riders and expert marksmen, able to read and write both French and English.

Scarlet, to impress the Indians, was considered a practical feature of the police garb. "We all know that the soldiers of our Great Mother wear red coats and are our friends," one old chief is said to have observed, when discussing the probable character of some soldiers who wore dark-colored uniforms.

So red coats were decreed for the Northwest Mounted. Friendship of the Indians was a thing greatly to be desired by all lovers of peace in Canada. It was certainly a welcome aid to some six hundred troops whose task was to establish law and order throughout the thousands of square miles from the Red River to the Rocky Mountains and north to the frozen Arctic.

This was the country first penetrated by Pierre Radisson and his camping pal, over a hundred years before the police took possession. Peopled by scattered Indians, half-breeds, and adventurers from all corners of the globe, it was a region remote from the restraining hand of the law. So the mounted police rode into the west carrying the law with them. And they wore scarlet jackets, and in Winter, fur caps and coats and moose-hide moccasins.

In 1873, when Father Lacombe's little missions were feeling the grip of new disasters for the Indian, the police force began its efficient service. Whiskey and the encroachment of white settlers, together with the scarcity of buffaloes, were hastening the tragic downfall of the red-men. In the lawless raids of greedy adventurers abuse of the Indian was common.

Treaties lived up to by all concerned, fair terms and justice without bloodshed, was the aim of the British Government in policing these western wilds. It was a sane and sensible idea. And the work of the mounted police is a matter of legitimate pride to Canada.

CHANGES ARE REPORTED

With good horses and practical equipment, the men patrolled the great plains, for a long time the favorite haunts of infamous desperadoes. They were vigorous, resourceful leaders—pioneers as well as soldiers. Soon a vast change was noted.

Colonel MacLeod was "happy to report" that the whiskey trade had been completely stopped in a whole section where drunken riots had been the rule. By being scrupulously honest with the Indians, the police won their confidence. Said Chief Crowfoot: "If the police had not come to the country where would we be now? Bad men and whiskey were killing us so fast that very few of us indeed would have been left to-day. The police have protected us, as the feathers of the bird protect it from the frosts of Winter. I wish them all good, and trust that our hearts will increase in goodness from this time forward."

"Before you came, the Indian crept along," said one old chief. "Now he is not afraid to walk erect."

Indian wars in the United States led to a great influx of tribes across the border and complicated the work of the police. Duties were heavy and irregular. A man never knew how many hundred miles he might have to ride after an outlaw. Scores of incidents reveal the endurance and faithful devotion of these fearless, hardy troopers.

Three men ride 120 miles through a blinding snowstorm to capture a horse-thief. They find their man in a camp of eighty half-breeds who are all ready to fight. But the cool courage of the policemen and the traditional magic of the red jackets prove equal to the occasion. Three to eighty, they triumph and ride back with their prisoner in safety.

LOST IN A BLIZZARD

"Lost. Horse dead. Am trying to push on. Have done my best." This was the note taken from the pocket of one of these riders of the plains who was found dead in the snow after a blizzard. It suggests the traditions of these soldiers.

Many died in forest fires, in river-floods or shipwrecks on the stormy lakes, or were murdered by hostile Indians. The heroism and service of the faithful troopers has been suggested by Kipling in such ringing lines as these:

RANGERS' CABIN AT SUMMIT LAKE

"Follow after—we are waiting by the trails
  that we have lost,
For the sound of many footsteps, for the tread
  of a host.
Follow after—follow after, for the harvest
  is sown;
By the bones about the wayside ye shall come
  to your own."

The building of the Canadian-Pacific called
for additional police. The discipline of the remote railroad camps, with thousands of workmen
of all nationalities, was no easy job. And the
Indians often got mixed up in the trouble.

The story of Pie-a-Pot is typical. This Cree
chief decided to block the way of the railroad
builders. Two mounted police were notified, and
rode out to the village where Pie-a-Pot sat
stolidly before his tepee. The chief insolently
refused to listen to the sergeant's order of evacuation. Indian men rode about shooting off their
guns and telling what they would do to white
men who got to interfering. Other land had
been given them, in this instance. They were
asked only to move aside for the railroad.

But they were obstinate. The women sat
around making faces and calling names. The
police sergeant told the chief he would give him
fifteen minutes to make up his mind. But Pie-a-
Pot's mind was made up. The policeman took
out his watch. The quarter ticked away, and the
chief sat still.

Then the sergeant left his horse, walked up
to the tepee and began kicking down the poles.
The women scrambled about with loud screams,
but the sergeant went on, knocking down other
tent-poles, and the Indians quietly picked up
their belongings and moved on.

CARING FOR THE INSANE

Cool courage in a mob of strikers who outnumbered the police ten times over brought
obedience among rioting white men. In the
north the police traveled by dog-sleds, or floated
in Eskimo "kayaks," skin boats with a hole in
the cover just large enough for a man's body.
These were paddled through the icy waters and
down foaming rapids.

In gasolene launches they patroled the lakes
and protected fisheries. The variety of duties
which fell to these patrols was often great, especially in the more remote Provinces. The tasks
included: patrols, rescue work, care of the asylums and penitentiaries, court bailiffs, health-
supervision, mining-recorders, inspectors, timber-
agents, royalty-collectors, customs-house agents,
magistrates, coroners, mail-carriers, postmasters.

A Yukon wilderness drives many a lonely
camper mad. The police are responsible for his
safe conduct to an asylum. One sergeant with a
dog-team carried a raving Indian 500 miles
through the white desolation of winter plains and
forests.

Another similar trip was made with an insane
missionary. This policeman was three weeks on
the lone and terrible journey. Storm-bound for
forty-eight hours, he tied himself and his patient
to a tree and put up the sled as a wind-shield.
At night he built huge fires to keep away packs
of timber-wolves who were sniffing along his
trail. The patient refused to eat, and had to be

fed by force. He tried to escape whenever he had a chance, and once gave his keeper a long chase and a hard struggle to get him back on the sled.

With never a thought of giving up, the officer kept on. The missionary's life was saved, and he recovered his sanity after receiving treatment. But the long strain proved too much for the sergeant. He started back on the return journey, but lost his mind and was taken in charge at one of the stations he visited. He went to an asylum, and was afterward pronounced cured and returned to the service. But he never seemed quite himself again after the blighting experience of the terrible trip through the wilderness.

So the work of these men has thrilled Canada, and has kept her frontier decent and law-abiding. There is no Roll of Honor for this important service. Heroism is taken for granted. Fighting a prairie fire, quelling an Indian riot, taking care of a sick man, or dying in a blizzard is all a part of the job. Courage, resourcefulness, honesty, devotion, faith and the milk of human kindness are needed for such duties.

The numbers of the patrol were greatly reduced during the war with Germany. And the dashing Canadian regiments carried into the battlefields of France some of the same sort of fighting spirit which has distinguished the mounted police. It is a spirit that has attracted the admiration of the world, as well as the gratitude and pride of the British Empire.

GENERAL INDEX

IN the following pages is an INDEX. Just what is an Index? The dictionary tells us that anything that points out, or shows, something else is an index. The guide-post we find where two roads meet is an index, because it tells us whither the roads lead. An index to a book, or to a set of books, is a guide to the things mentioned therein, and shows where each is to be found.

The very first necessity in using a book-index is to know the alphabet—not just know an A when you see it, but know that A is the first letter of the accepted order in which the letters of the alphabet are arranged. It is upon this arrangement of letters that dictionaries, encyclopedias, and indexes depend for their usefulness in helping us find our way. Thus, when you want to find out what the BOOKSHELF tells you about *Schools*, you open this INDEX and turn the pages until you come to the letter S; if you are thoroughly familiar with the order of the alphabet, you will not waste time among the first few pages, but will quickly pass to about three-quarters of the way to the end. After finding S you will run your eye down the entries there, quickly passing over all those beginning with Sa, and going more slowly when you reach those beginning with Sc. Now you watch the third letter of each word until you come to Sch; then the eye follows the fourth letters until Scho is reached; then you follow the fifth letters until o is again reached, and you have words beginning Schoo.

You now understand the principle on which an index is made. All words beginning with the same letter are grouped together; then these groups are divided into others depending upon the second letter of the word; then these divisions are subdivided into still smaller groups, depending upon the third letter of the word; and so it goes on until there are no letters alike in the same column, and the word drops into its individual place.

When the same word begins two or more entries, we must continue our subdividing through the second word, and in some cases through the third, fourth, and fifth words, and sometimes even further.

There are a few special points about this INDEX which the user should remember.

First: The black-faced figures indicate the volume, and the light-faced indicate the page; thus "**6**, 25" means that the reader should look on page 25 of volume six. Second: Sometimes only the light-faced figure, indicating the page, appears; then the reader refers back in the same paragraph to the nearest black-faced figure for the volume number. Third: Entries printed in large-and-small capitals are the names of authors, editors, composers, or artists. This enables you to tell at once whether the item referred to is by, or about, the person indexed. Thus, "WASHINGTON, GEORGE: Privations at Valley Forge, **9**, 202" indicates that in volume nine, on page 202 you will find a statement by him: while the entry just below, "Washington, George, (1732-1799) American General, patriot and statesman, first president of the United States, Boyhood of, **9**, 22," indicates that in volume nine you will find something about him. Fourth: In the entry last quoted are two numbers inclosed in parentheses (1732-1799). These are the years of Washington's birth and death. Fifth: Not in all entries about persons is it possible to give two dates, or to give them accurately. One date and a long dash, as "John Joseph Pershing (1860———)," indicates that the person is living. The letters "*ca.*" before a date is an abbreviation of the Latin word "circa," meaning "about." Thus, "Carver, John (*ca.* 1575-1621)," indicates that no record has been found giving the exact year of the birth of John Carver, but we know from other evidence that it was about 1575. Sixth: There are no useless entries in this INDEX. You will not find under "London" any reference to Benjamin Franklin's visits there, because the mere fact that he did go to that city does not tell you anything about London. Neither under "Franklin" will you find a great many references. The first one says "story of"; this could have been subdivided into twenty or more entries, but they would each and all have referred to the article about him which begins on page 204 of volume nine.

This INDEX will guide you to information on many subjects which would probably be entirely overlooked by you without its assistance.

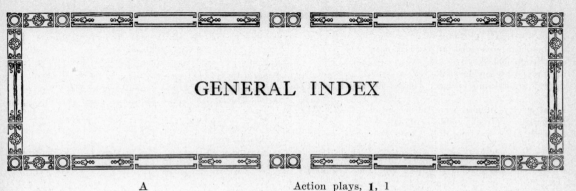

GENERAL INDEX

B

I

Mc & MAC

M

T

X, Y, Z

INDEX TO ARTISTS

KEY TO PRONUNCIATION

ā as in āle

â " " senâte
â " " câre
ă " " ăm
ă " " ăccount
ä " " ärm
à " " àsk
a " " sofa

ē " " ēve
ê " " êvent
ĕ " " ĕnd
ĕ " " recĕnt

ē as in makēr

ī " " īce
ĭ " " ĭll

ō " " ōld
ô " " ôbey
ô " " ôrb
ŏ " " ŏdd
ŏ " " sŏft
ŏ " " cŏnnect

ū " " ūse

û as in ûnite

û " " ûrn
ŭ " " ŭp
ŭ " " circŭs
ü " " menü

ōō " " fōōd
ŏŏ " " fŏŏt
ou as in out
oi " " oil
ŋ " " iŋk
κ = ch in the German ich
N = N in boN (French)

INDEX TO ARTISTS